# LISTS AND RETURNS

OF

# CONNECTICUT MEN

IN THE

# REVOLUTION.

1775-1783.

HARTFORD
CONNECTICUT HISTORICAL SOCIETY
1909

## Notice

In many older books, foxing (or discoloration) occurs and, in some instances, print lightens with wear and age. Reprinted books, such as this, often duplicate these flaws, notwithstanding efforts to reduce or eliminate them. The pages of this reprint have been digitally enhanced and, where possible, the flaws eliminated in order to provide clarity of content and a pleasant reading experience.

*Lists and Returns of Connecticut Men in the Revolution, 1775-1783*

Originally published
Hartford, Connecticut
1909

Reprinted by:

Janaway Publishing, Inc.
732 Kelsey Ct.
Santa Maria, California 93454
(805) 925-1038
www.janawaygenealogy.com

2014

ISBN: 978-1-59641-338-2

*Made in the United States of America*

# CONTENTS.

|  | PAGE. |
|---|---|
| INTRODUCTION, . . . . . . . . . . | ix |
| CONTINENTAL REGIMENTS, 1775, . . . . . . | 1 |
| ROLLS AND RETURNS, 1776, . . . . . . . . | 17 |
| CONNECTICUT LINE, 1777-1781, . . . . . . | 21 |
| CONNECTICUT LINE, 1781-1783, . . . . . . | 260 |
| CONNECTICUT LINE, 1783, . . . . . . . . | 327 |
| CONNECTICUT LINE, . . . . . . . . . | 345 |
| MILITIA REGIMENTS, . . . . . . . . . | 361 |
| NAVAL RECORD, . . . . . . . . . . | 365 |
| MISCELLANEOUS. . . . . . . . . . . | 369 |
| INDEX. . . . . . . . . . . | 371 |

# INTRODUCTION.

This Society published in 1901, as the eighth of its series of Collections, a volume of "Rolls and Lists of Connecticut Men in the Revolution, 1775-1783." As explained in its introduction, the material in that volume supplemented what had already been published in 1889 in the officially issued "Record of Service of Connecticut Men in the War of the Revolution, 1775-1783."

The material herewith issued as the twelfth volume of Collections, with the title Lists and Returns of Connecticut Men in the Revolution, 1775-1783, is intended to supplement what has already been published in the two volumes mentioned above.

The major part of this volume, as its title might indicate, is composed of officially written lists and returns of soldiers who were serving in the Continental regiments of the "Connecticut Line." There are also some rolls of companies in service which had not previously been printed, particularly in 1782 and 1783. Comparatively few new names of soldiers or additional records of service are printed in this volume. Its chief value will be found to consist in the addition in the case of a great majority of the soldiers, of the name of the town from which the soldier came. This will supply much sought for information, and in many cases will doubtless serve to identify the soldier.

Many of the statements made in the introduction to the volume of Rolls and Lists apply equally well to this volume. A part of the copy was made by Mr. Thomas, and all of the cards for the index were written by Miss Gay. All comparison of index cards and reading of proof of both text and index has been done by the editor. Much the same method has been used in indexing as in the former volume. All surnames have been indexed exactly as they appear in the text; but in the case of Christian names, where both a correct and an incorrect spelling of the same name appeared, both are indexed under the correct spelling.

The sources from which the material in this volume has been printed are, with the addition of volume 39 of the Revolutionary War series in the State Library, practically the same as those used in the previous volume of "Rolls and Lists" and enumerated in the introduction to that volume.

A word of explanation seems advisable regarding the rolls of Col. Samuel B. Webb's regiment for 1782 and 1783. which are found in volume 39 of the Revolutionary War series, and are here printed on pages 303-344. These rolls were formerly in the Comptroller's office and have but recently been transferred to the State Library, where they have been arranged and bound. They are not original rolls of the period which they represent, but are comparatively modern copies, perhaps made about 1843. The source from which they were copied is not now known. The majority of them are written in a free running hand which leaves not a few of the letters in the names poorly formed and doubtful, while many of the names are closely written, owing to the copyist's anxiety to crowd them into the limited space on a certain uniform size of paper. Apparently the copyist was sometimes careless in his writing and set down letters which could not by any possibility be construed as forming a name. Monthly muster rolls of the staff and of the different companies in this regiment for some or all of the months of February, March, May. June, July, September, October 1782. December 1782-January 1783. and February 1783, are preserved in these copies. In this volume only the earliest roll in each year of each of these companies has been printed. The later monthly rolls have been compared with this, and differences, except occasional unimportant variations of spelling, are noted on the printed page. Thus it appears that the name of the same person is found on one roll as Chester Upham and on another as Christopher Upham (page 307), or on one roll as Amos Gustin and on another as Amos Griffin (page 310). Whether or not these differences appeared on the original rolls is a matter for conjecture. In numerous instances a name after having appeared on several successive monthly rolls is dropped from

INTRODUCTION. xi

succeeding rolls without any mention being made of the man's discharge, desertion, or transfer to another company (such as John Gimson, page 311). Such disappearances are noted on the printed page, as well as the occasional appearance of names on later which are not found on earlier rolls (such as David Clark, page 312). By printing the earliest roll and thus noting the differences found on later rolls the wearisome repetition which would have occurred in printing practically the same roll a half dozen times has been avoided.

Much of this volume is made up of official lists which had themselves been copied and compiled from other lists, made up probably by the town's authorities in the absence of the persons named in the lists. In making such a compilation the opportunity for error is great, and not a few of the names as they appear in the lists and are here printed are evident errors. In some instances the true name is very evident, although badly misspelled; but in others not even by the trial of a phonic pronunciation can the real name be guessed.

In printing these documents it has been impossible to avoid some duplication of names and services, but it has been thought better to allow occasional duplication than to run any risk of omission.

ALBERT C. BATES,
*Chairman of the Publication Committee,*
*and Editor of this Volume.*

THE SOCIETY'S LIBRARY, DECEMBER 16, 1908.

# CONTINENTAL REGIMENTS, 1775.

### RETURNS OF MEN IN SERVICE.

[*See Record of Connecticut Men in the Revolution, pages 34-94.*]

[Each of these Returns, sent in to the State authorities from the different towns, is signed by the Selectmen of the town from which it is sent and gives the names of persons resident in that town who had been employed in the Continental service in 1775, and who under a law passed in December of that year were exempted from the payment of certain taxes to the State. Some of the Returns give the number only and not the names of those who had been in service.]

[*State Library, Revolution 6, 1-131.*]

## BOLTON

Richard Skinner
Zenas Skinner
Ebenezer Wright
Benjª Griswold
Joseph Carver
Simeon Griswold
William Richardson

Ruben Searls
Edward Paine
Jeremiah Chapman
Zadock How
Roswel Paine
Jedediah Lenord
Asa Lenord

## BRANFORD

Benjamin Bartholomew
Mason Hobart
Levi Baldwin
Caleb Frisbie
Ralph Hoadly
Gideon Bartholomew
Titus Frisbie
Zaccheus Maltbie
John Palmer Junʳ
Barnebas Palmer
Timothy Barker
Benjamin Butler
Aaron Baldwin
Ephraim Rogers

Artemas Johnson
Jacob Rogers
Walter Butler
Stephen Wade
John Negus
Alling Smith
Ephraim Chidsey
Roswell Chidsey
Andrew Burr
Samuel Whedon
John Mallery
Reuben Johnson
Samuel Hoadly, Junʳ
William Baldwin

Andrew Morris
Philemon Rogers
James Barker Jun'
Hooker Frisbie
Simeon Linsly
Joseph Whedon
John Whitne Jun'
Joseph Jones
Robert Stewart
William McQueen
Oliver Lanfere Jun'
John White
Asher Sheldon, Jun'
John Guy
Joseph Russell
Joseph Willford
Josiah Fowler Jun'
Benjamin Henshaw
Jonathan Byintun
Benjamin Norton
Solomon Talmage
John Bunnel
Abraham Bunnel
Wooster Harrison
Asahel Harrison
Levi Rose
Abraham Cook
Mark Mazuzen
Joel Howd
Levi Rogers Jun'
Rufus Rogers
Ebenezer Foot
John Lodewick Abberhart
Ebenezer Byintun
Jairus Harrison
Matthew Butler
Jacob Page
Luther Page

## DERBY

Adam Vorse
Benjamin Tomlinson
Charles Whittelse
David Tomlinson
William Tucker
David Canfield
Ebenezer Hitchkook
Enos Jones Prindle
Eben' Turill Witemore
Amos Fooks
Jonathan Brown
Georshom Bearsley
Gideon Tomlinson
Abijah Beard
Hezekiah Woodin
Jonathan Lyman
Elezer Durand
Jabez Pritchard
John Smith
Isaac Durand
Samuel Hull
Samuel Durand
Edward Basset
Joseph Lum
Isaac Tomlinson
Oliver Chatfield
Ritchard Haters
Abraham Basset
William Tomlinson
William Clark
William Woshbon
William Woodin
Reuben Canfield
Caleb Chatfield
Gideon Cande
Bowers Woshbon

## DURHAM

John Jones
Joseph Smith
Phin' Parmele
Jacob Clark
Sexton Squier
Asa Brown
Aaron Camp
Gideon Chittenden
Zebulon Lewis Clark
Amos Fowler
Amos Davis
Dan'' Bishop
John Meeker
David Ward
Eben' Squier
Eph'" Clark
Joseph Snow
John Stocking
Benj" Sutlief
Benj" Tainter
Jon" Wells
Charles Parmele
Hez'' Parmele
Phin' Picket
Sam'' Savage
Sam'' Seaward
Abr'" Shelley
Abiathar Fowler

CONTINENTAL REGIMENTS, 1775. 3

Eben' Hall
Nathan Hall
Husted Hinman
Benj$^n$ Hogins

W$^m$ Johnson
Jon$^n$ Loveland
Sam$^{ll}$ Lucas
Jared Whedon

## EAST HADDAM

Warren Ackley
Gideon Brainard
Jonah Brainard
Henery Cone
Elisha Adams Fowler
Timothy Hosmer
Hezekiah Mack
Joseph Rolo
Elias Lay
Aron Lyon
William Harvey
John Harvey
John Attwood
Timothy Fuller
Zechariah Gates
Jonah Gates
Luther Barney
Simeon Spencer
John Peck
Gabriel Ely
Samuel Smith
Isaac Taylor
Nathaniel Beebe
Matthew Smith 3$^d$
Bethuel Fuller
Phenihas Cone
Roberson Williams
Ethan Pratt
David Fox Jr

Israel Cone
Jonah Cone Jr
Duren Whittlesey
Nathan Harvey
Ezra Harvey
Silas Ackley
Elihu Huntley
Joshua Fox
Noah Huntly
Nathan Beebe
Daniel Gates 3$^d$
Noadiah Emmons
Jonathan Kneeland
Joseph Knolton
Daniel Shepperson
Jesse Willey
David Spencer
Samuel Chapman
Levi Crosby
William Beckwith
Samuel Post
Amaziah Spencer
Robert Harvey
Elihu Minor
Oliver Cone
Barzileel Ackley
Timothy Fuller 2$^{nd}$
Ezra Beckwith
Zachariah Rolow

## FAIRFIELD

Joseph Squire
W$^m$ Jenings
Andrew Thorp
Ebe$^r$ Knap
John Parret Jn$^r$
James McKay
John Persons
David Burr 3$^d$
Judson Sturges
Thomas Elwood
Hill Stirges
W$^m$ Carter
Levey Mallery
David Anibell
Lyman (?) Jenings
David Stirges Ju$^r$
Nath$^{ll}$ Taylor
Nehemiah Phypeney (?)

John Knap
John Perrey
Jonath$^n$ Spears
Nath$^{ll}$ Spears
Nehemiah Fowler
John Williams Jn$^r$
Isaac Jervis
Nathan Thorp
John Fuller
Sam$^{ll}$ Squire 2$^d$
Hez: Goold
Peter Morehouse
Aaron Hubbell
Ezekel Canfield
Ichabod Canfield
W$^m$ Remong
Steph$^n$ Guyar
Gideon Holibord

REVOLUTION LISTS AND RETURNS.

Andrew Bennitt
Dan[ll] Bennitt
Hez: Bennitt
John Sherwood
Joseph Batterson
W[m] Batterson
John Batterson
George Batterson Jn[r]
Russel Disbrow
Simon Disbrow
Gabrel Allen
Abrahm Wincop
Joshua Baker
Andrew Baker
Edmon Ogden
Nath[ll] Johnson
John Johnson
Joseph Elwood
Nath[ll] Godfrey Jn[r]
Ezra Wood
Sam[ll] King
Joshua Couch
George Moser
James Coal
Thomas Couch
Moses Stirges
Peter Winton
James Redfield
Gershom Banks
Joseph Bradley
John Blakman
Joseph Thorp
Jehial Sherwood
Thomas Goodsel
Joseph Frost
Thad[s] Stapels
John Staples
Dan[ll] Roberson
Amos Williams
John Mills
James Goodsel
Chancey Downs
Dan[ll] Ketchem
Josiah Jenings
Cresterfey Godfrey
Edman Ogden
Eliphalet Gray
Frances Hutinock
Hezekiah Bears
Joel Gilbord
John Squire
Joseph Dickson

Joseph Whitlock
Joseph Green Jn[r]
Enoch Towner
Silas Hanes
Joal Jenings
Sam[ll] Bradley
Gershom Hubbell
John Gilbord
Justice Bradley
David Bradley
Elisha Bradley
Beter Stocker
Stephen Straten
Dan[ll] Squire
Nehemiah Thorp
Fayweather Brothwell
Wolcutt Bennitt
Wheeler Cable
Thomas Duffey
Soloman Green
Liman Gray
W[m] Hubbell
Jos: Hubbell Jn[r]
Benj[m] Hall
Zach Sherwood
W[m] Hawley
Nathan P[t] Jackson
Eliphalet Jenings
Richard Lacey
Isaac Odell
Eben[r] Meaker
David Morehouse
Ezra Morehouse
Isaac Stephen
Eurial Morehouse
Isaac Hubbell
John Beardslee
Justice Jenings
Jeremiah Johnson
Nehemiah Cable
Onesimas Bradley
Asa Bradley
Fenias Squire
Shubal Goraham
Stephen Holibod
Dan[ll] Blackman
Dan[ll] Silliman
James Jambers
Reuben Chapman
Moses Dimon
Seth Webb
Elijah Cable

## GUILFORD

James Bishop
Son of Wait Monger
Indented Indian servant of
  Simeon Chittenden
Son of Gideon Hoppen

Nath[ll] Allis Ju[r]
Tho[s] Bevin
Jedidiah Cruttenden
Salmon Cruttenden
Gilbert Cruttenden

## CONTINENTAL REGIMENTS, 1775.

Zachariah Doud
Ruben Doud
Tim⁰ Field
Chris'ʳ Foster
Sam¹¹ Hoit
Pember Josselin
Jonᵃ Murray
Wait Munger
Jn⁰ Parsons
Noah Scrantom
Abᵐ Scrantom
Tim⁰ Wilcox Juʳ
Charles Norton
Eber Hall
Joseph Rowlason
Jared Scrantom
Sam¹ Acaly
John Hill
Moses Hill
Josiah Fowler Junʳ
William Fowler
Dan¹¹ Chittenden Junʳ
Neriah Bishop
Simeon Chittenden Junʳ
John Ball
Benjamin Norton
Josiah Fowler
Luke Field
Amos Tole
Nathan Meigs
Son of Josiah Fowler
Timothy Field
Joel Dudly
Jn⁰ Scovell Jr
Dan¹¹ Scovell
Willᵐ Willasey

George Ferrol
Jared Chittenden
Dan¹ Murray
Joseph Parmele Jr
Ezra Griswold
Reuben Shelley Juʳ
Jonathan Handy
Philemon Hall
Zebulon Benton
Thalmeno Bishop
Isaac Chalker
Roswell Woodward
David Hull
John Johnson Juʳ
David Morse
Two sons of Willᵐ Parmele
Son of Peter Vaill
Son of Jairus Handy
Johnson Bishop
Zebulon Cruttenden
Thomas Dudley
Thomas Griswold
Jn⁰ Harris
Mark Hotchkiss
Moses Doud
Jn⁰ Doud
Barnabas McKeine
Levi Lee
Son of Westall Scovill
Dan¹¹ Stone Jʳ
Isaac Stow
Son of Seth Stone
David Dudley 8ᵈ
Ebenʳ Bragg
Timothy Scranton

### HADDAM

John Smith
John Arnold and Son
Robert Clark
James Young
Abner Tibbald
Richard Wakely
James Cone
Jacob Baily Junʳ
Abraham Tyler
William Smith
Elisha Spencer
Reuben Smith
Daniel Ray
Gideon Baily Juʳ
Jonathan Bordman
Samuel Brooks
William Baily
Asaph Young
John Baily Juʳ
Joseph Clark

Ephraim Sawyer
Cornelius Higgins Jʳ
Bezaliel Shailer
Arnold Hazelton
Eleazer Bate
John Russel
Timothy Baily
Gideon Baily
Aaron Thomas
William Porter
Giles Cone
Gideon Goff
Josiah Arnold
Elias Cone
Timothy Towner
Joseph Smith
Aaron Brainerd
Charles Hazelton Juʳ
Augustus Lewis
Amos Baily

# REVOLUTION LISTS AND RETURNS.

Abraham Brooks Ju<sup>r</sup>
David Brainerd
Joseph Dickerson
Jonathan Clark
Joseph Lungrel Rowley
Joel Hubbard
Jacob Baily & Son
Reuben Bates

Samuel Cone
Samuel Marsh
Sylvenus Clark
Seth Arnold
Thomas Brainerd
Reuben Brainerd
Jabez Baily

[It is not actually stated that these men from Haddam were in service in 1775, but it is to be presumed that they were from the fact of their taxes being abated and the list being placed with lists of persons from other towns who did serve.]

## HARTLAND

Euriah Church
Charles Phelps
Elisha Giddings
Joshua Giddings
Asa Andrews
Abel Moses
Phinehas Parkins
Jason Parkins
Samuel Phelps
Daniel Bill
Daniel Benjamon
Daniel Bushnel
Titus Alling
Nathaniel Alling

Jonathan Wilder
Timothy Tiffaney
Thomas Sill
Ezekel Beach
Ashbell Beech
Obed Crosby
Ephraim fox
James Hungerford
Josiah Meeker
Preeda Stephens
Childs Taylor
Timothy Couch
William Williams

## HARWINTON

Abnur Willson
Jese Poter or Jesse Potter
Oliver Phelps
Hezekiah Phelps
Daniel Cook
Ashbel Poter or Portter
Solomon Buller or Butler
Hezekiah Leach
Abraham Catlin
Sam<sup>ll</sup> Weson or Weston
James Olcut Jr
    or James Olcut
Benja<sup>m</sup> Barbur
Sam<sup>ll</sup> Lambart
Jabez Frisbey
Elijah Loomiss
Enos Scoot or Enes Scot
Alyn Haydon
Eli Catlin

Isaiah Butler J<sup>r</sup>
Christopher Jonson
Timothy Barbur
Simian Barbur
    or Simon Barbor
Zimry Skinnor
White Griswould
Sam<sup>ll</sup> Phelps J<sup>r</sup>
George Loomiss
Joseph C Hawley or Holley
George Jones
Sam<sup>ll</sup> Wesson Jr
    or Sam<sup>ll</sup> Weston Jur
Sam<sup>ll</sup> Jonson
Jonathan Cook
Asa Griswould
Lavinas Holt
Amus Gilbert

## MIDDLETOWN

Ebenezer Blake
Paul Bunn
W<sup>m</sup> Butler
Othniel Clark

Barachiah Fairbanks
Joseph Farnsworth
Rich<sup>d</sup> Hamlin
Samuel Johnson

## CONTINENTAL REGIMENTS, 1775.

Charles Knowles
*Col° Return J. Meigs
W<sup>m</sup> Mitchell
Tim° Starr Jun<sup>r</sup>
Elijah Tuells
*Samuel Tuells
Joseph Willis Jun<sup>r</sup>
Charles Whiting
Ely Butler
James Dewey
James Johnson
Simeon Savage
Stephen Sage
Elnathan Thrasher
Aaron White Jun<sup>r</sup>
Peet. Galpen
Selah Hubbard
Ithuriel Hulburd
Timothy Hubbard
Elijah Loveland
Abijah Peck Jun<sup>r</sup>
Jesse Peck
Elisha Peck
Roger Riley
Elisha Savage
Dan<sup>l</sup> Willcocks
Daniel Cornwell
Elisha Cornwell
Frederick Winthrop
Christo<sup>r</sup> Whitebread
Josiah Atkins
Nehem<sup>h</sup> Barns
Freelove Blake
Edward Crowell
Solomon Crowell

Edmund Fairchild
Wid° Babbits Son
Benj<sup>a</sup> Babbit
Ebenezer Field
David Hull
James Johnson 2<sup>d</sup>
Elihu Lyman
John Roberts Jun<sup>r</sup>
Amos Wetmore
Henry Bonfoy
Ashbell Cornell
Butler Gilbert
Joseph Harris
Joseph Lung
Comfort Marks
Dan<sup>l</sup> Sizer
Abraham Sage
Ichabod Swaddle
Sol° Hubbard
Dean Hubbard
Jn° Hubbard
Caleb Johnson Jr.
Lemuel Lee
George Seaton
Joseph Driggs Jun<sup>r</sup>
Jesse Gilbert
Hez<sup>a</sup> Goff Jun<sup>r</sup>
Hez<sup>a</sup> Hubbard Jun<sup>r</sup>
W<sup>m</sup> Lucas
Nath<sup>l</sup> Miller
Sam<sup>l</sup> Markham
Edward Powers
Charles Plum
Simeon Roberts
Joseph Starrs Son

### NEW FAIRFIELD

Samuel Nichols
Phineas Bardsly
Bille Trowbrdge
Talmage Hall
John Lacy
Jonas Brath (?)
Daniel Trowbridge
Stephen Gregory
Joseph Barss
Elish Hibbard
John Hendrick
John Mourhouse
John Mitchel
Neil Clerk
Abel Cosher (?)
John Hulbard
Ezra Hubbel

Elijah Crane
Joseph Osburn
Timothy Taylor
Abel Sherwood
David Wakman
Moses Knap
Amon Bebee
Joseph Dubury (?)
William Phelps
Amos Hubbel
John Osborn
Barzilla Brown
Benjamin Bennet Ju<sup>r</sup>
Joel Botchford
Abraham Nichols
William Towner
Benjamin Giddings

---
*His tax was abated for the service of two persons.

Calib Pitt
Stephen Jurden
Seth Lacy

John Perkhust
John Hambleton

## NEW HAVEN

Elias Townsend
Evlyne Pierpont
Caleb Ball
Nathaniel Bishop
Mases Potter
Sam[l] Squire
James Richards
Will[m] Alling
Robert Simpson
John Jocelin
Joseph Moulthrop
Sam[l] Perkins
Sam[l] Peck
Joseph Collings
Henry Sanford
Jacob Barns (?)
Hugh(?) Clark
Eldad Hotchkiss

Walter Wilmot
John Andrews
Martin Clark
Thomas Gardiner
John Miles
Eliakim Sperry
Sam[ll] Smith
Benj[a] Smith
Eliphalet Barns
Yale Todd
Eben[r] Allin
Fredrick Harding
Son of Freeman Huse, now (1777) prisoner in Great Britain
Son of Asa Smith died in the Continental Service.

## NEWTOWN

Jo[s] Smith
Jabez Botsford
Henry Fairman
Clement Botsford
Nath[l] Little
George Peck
W[m] Allen
Abel Baldwin
John Botsford
Jo[s] Booth
Isael Burritt
W[m] Barnett
Levi Bostwic
Isaac Bloodgood
Amos Benedict

Mat[t] Clark
Francis Drake
Jesse Fairchild
Enoch Hubbel
James Fairchild Jun[r]
Stephen Hawley Jun[r]
George Murry
Peter Prindle
Abijah Prindle
Aaron M[c]Gregory
James Bennitt
Jonathan Hurd
Andrew Northrop
Philo Beardsle

## NORWALK

Addams Joshua
Betts Thomas J[r]
Betts James
Bassey Peleg
Bassey Silas
Bouton Eleazor
Benedict John J[r]
Benjamin James
Brown Nathan
Benedict Thomas J[r]
Betts Thomas
Brown Daniel
Betts Rheuben
Baker James

Brown Jonathan
Clenton Joseph
Cole Alvin
Chard Joseph
Chard Samuel
Chase Jared
Deforest David
Elles J. Bard
Fox Jonathan
Grummon Nehemiah
Gilbert Gershom
Gilbert Thadeus
Griffith William
Gates Samuel

CONTINENTAL REGIMENTS, 1775.

Gregory Elias
Gregory Ezra
Hendrick Nathan
Hyat Abraham
Hyat Alvin
Hoyt Thomas
Hanford Theop$^s$ 3$^d$
Hanford Theop$^s$ J$^r$
Hanford Stephen
Hoyt Nathan J$^r$
Hoyt Joseph J$^r$
Hoyt Justice
Hubble Thadeus
Hendreck David
Hulburt Stephen
Hanford Eleazor
Jones Thomas
Johnson John
Keeler Samuel 3$^d$
Kellogg Jona$^t$
Keeler Isaac
Keeler Lockwood
Lockwood David
Lockwood James
Morehouse Michael
Mead Mathew
Mallery Giles
Mead Elias
Marvin Ozias
Morehouse Thomas
Meeker Stephen
Nash Eben$^r$ Ju$^r$

Olmsted Silas J$^r$
Raymond W$^m$
Richards John
Raymond Jona$^t$
Reed Nathan
Reed Abraham
Reed Hezekiah
Rockwell Joseph
Raymond Benj$^n$
Scribner Elias
Smith Daniel
Seymour William
Sherrod Mathew
Selleck Jacob
S$^t$ John Nehemiah
S$^t$ John Nehemiah J$^r$
Starling Thadeus
Scribner Zacheus
Sloan Allexander
Scofield Peter
Scribner Abraham
Selleck James
Tuttle Levi
Taylor Levi
Taylor Elijah
Tuttle Peter
Wright J. Allyn
Whitlock Oliver
Whitlock Nathan
Wyat Henry
Gregory Isaac

## PRESTON

Co$^l$ John Tyler
Co$^l$ Sam$^ll$ Mott
Cap$^t$ Edward Mott
Cap$^t$ Nathan Peters
Cap$^t$ Jeremiah Halsey
Lieu$^t$ Nathaniel Gove
William Whitney
Jedediah Whitney
Silas Brewster
Nath$^ll$ Larabe
Josiah Witter
Phineas Freeman
Sam$^ll$ M$^c$Daniels
Elijah Park
Giles Tracy
Benj$^n$ Freeman
Cyrus Ames
Levi Tracy
Matthias Ames
Jonas Satterlee
Dick Fitch
Thomas Meech
Amasa Standish
Jesper Black

Solomon Story
Peter Ellis
Eli Hill
Tho$^s$ Averill
Gager Freeman
Prentis Avery
Manasseh Prentice
Walter Fanning
Dan$^l$ Smith
Joseph Stanton
Joshua Meech
Charles Miles
Jason Rude
Moses Park
Ezekiel Tracy
Willi$^m$ Butler
Joseph Swan
Dan$^ll$ Freeman
Nathan Freeman
Elisha York
Dan$^l$ Yerrington
Sanford Hrreck
Isaac Herreck
Preserved Brumbly

Bethuel Brumbly
Dan<sup>l</sup> Bellus
Tho<sup>s</sup> Bellus
Mathew Coy
Ephraim Coy
Mathew Ray
Abel Bennit
Elijah Stanten
Jacob Averill
John Benjamin
Rozel Benjamin
Tho<sup>s</sup> Aldridge
Peleg Sweet
Thaddeus Downer
Uriah Beman
Simeon Rouse
Asa Kinne
Jacob Kinne
John Poolman
Sam<sup>l</sup> Wheler
Peleg Billings
Joseph Billings
Jacob Burton
Robart Halley
Joseph Northrop
John Peterson

Elijah Phillops
Henry Walton
Nathan Walton
Allen Geer
Jonathan Averill
Sam<sup>l</sup> Huntington
Steven Gates
John Wheler
Moses Smith
Leuis Huit
Peres Tracy
Joshua Woodward
Asa Burnam
Elijah Johnson
David Green
Asa Story
Jonas Boardman
Roger Coit
Farewell Coit
Elish Belcher
Nathan Belcher
Lem<sup>l</sup> Geer
John Gates
David Green
Rouse Bly

## SIMSBURY

Elisha Cornish Ju<sup>r</sup>
Timothy Humphry
Wiliam Andrus
Azriah Willcox
Solomon Buel
Elijah Barber
Eli Tuller
Levi Piney
Aron Piney
Asahel Strickland
John Willson
Ebenezer Brown
Oliver Case
Stephen Terry
Benjamin Slarter
John Roundey
Richard Andrus
Daniel Merrill
Daniel Barber
Jacob Tuller
Roderick Adams
Jonathan Montecu
Oliver Adams
Samuel Barnard
Joseph Grimes J<sup>r</sup>
Joel Humphry
John Alderman
Elijah Nobel
James Eno
Roger Willcox

Abel Adams
Stephen Langatha
Amoziah Barber
Shubal Moses
John Fletcher
Elisha Harington
Moses Liley
Jesse Russel
Thomas Phereton
Stephen Harington
Jonathan Humph J<sup>r</sup>
Joseph Tuller
Eseck Allen
Luthar Lawrence
Theophilus Hump<sup>r</sup>
Elijah Tuller
Timothy Woodbridg
Martin Case
Jacob Davis J<sup>r</sup>
Permenio Adams
Benjamin Bodwel
Thomas Phelps J<sup>r</sup>
Theophilus Woodbrig
Jared Ingram
John Pettibone
William Andruss
Daniel Johnson
Benjamin Holcom
Levi Dibol
Noadiah Holcomb

Levi Frisby
Ebenezer Lamson
Eli Holcomb
Jacob Hays
Seth Hays
Seth Holcomb
Azriah Holaday
Amos Holaday
Timothy Cossit
Micah Case
Daniel Buttolph
Samuel Dewolf
Zebinah Burr
Luke Hays
Nath<sup>ll</sup> Griffen
Elijah Evens
Asahel Hays
Oliver Hays
Elishama Holcomb
Israel Mesenger
David Mesenger
Thomas Totton
Wiliam Hays 3<sup>rd</sup>
John Valance
John Drake Ju<sup>r</sup>
Richard Gay Ju<sup>r</sup>
Reuben Clark
John Hill 2<sup>d</sup>
Thomas Winchel J<sup>r</sup>
Edmun Murfey
Rufus Mason
Judah Phelps
Phinehas Wolworth
Joseph Burrill
Joseph Hinkston
Reuben Wollworth
Jehial Winchel
Simeon Winter
Abner Warner
Ebenezer Mereman
Arunah Moore
Theophilus Hide

Israel Warner
Daniel Warner
Benjamin Adams
Jonathon Morgan
William Case
Abraham Case J<sup>r</sup>
Benjamin Dyar
George Humphry
Oliver Humphry
David Hill
Solomon Humphry J<sup>r</sup>
Gideon Mills
John Pooler
Pliney Case
James Andrus
Seth Willcox
Joseph Willcox
Daniel Barber
Eliphilit Curtis
Samuel Millar
Othaniel Gillet
Nathaniel Johnson
Solomon Curtis
Job Barber
Ephraim Mills
William Tailor
John Matson
Aron Mesenger
Ruben Mesenger
David Clerk
James Ward
Thomas Wright
Henry Edwards
Jacob Pettibone
Daniel Barber
Nathaniel Piney
Hezekiah Andrus
Michael Willson
Jonathon Couch
Elijah Holcomb
Moses Holcomb

## SOMERS

Abraham Coy
Peter Piney
John Russel
William Elmer
Roburt Pease 2<sup>d</sup>
Matthew Bewel
Daniel Kibbe
David Ritchardson
Amisa Buck
James Kibbe 2<sup>d</sup>
Jesse Ritchardson
Jacob Brown
Bildad Kibbe

Joseph Root
Abner Pease
Moses Pelton
Reuben Sikes
Elijah Sexton
William Parsons
Joseph Sexton
Eliacom Wardwell
Ritchard Pease
Edward Laurance
Samuel Right
Daniel Burchard
David Pease

REVOLUTION LISTS AND RETURNS.

John Orcutt
Amasa Allin
Jacob Orcutt
John Fairman

Levi Hamblin
Stephen Jones
Alexand Brown

## TOLLAND

Comfort Carpenter
Hemon Bocor
Elijah Chapmon
Luke Washbon
Joel Stimson
Elias Newton
Samuel Steel
James Steel
John Abbot
Elijah Bradley
Jonathan Burros
Josiah Benton
Jonathan Benton
Samuel Benton
Azariah Benton
Asa Baldwin
John Carlton
Darius Carlton
Richard Carlton
Ebenezer Cook
Edward Dimock
Isaac Fallows
Christopher Francis
Simeon Griswold

Ebenezer Grant
John Huntington
Abner Hatch
Dan Hatch
Andrew Minor
Andrew Minor Jun[r]
Rufus Price
Joshua Parks
Fyrus Preston
Ammi Poalk
Perez Steel
Elisha Stibbins
Isaiah Sparks
Simon Stimson
Nehemiah Sabins
Stephen Failor
Jabez West
Eliab Lad
Willobe Lowil
Ira West
Elijah Johnson
Samuel Price
Elijah Price

## VOLUNTOWN

Serg[t] Perez Briggs
" John Wylie
" Moses Wylie
" David Dorrance
Corp. Daniel Hopkins
" Jonathan Millet
" Joseph Bowdish
" William Kasson
" Joseph Gordon
Comfort Titus
William Hopkins
Amos Babcock
John Braughton
Joseph Randall
Simeon Stevens
Benoni Kinne
Elijah Hodge
James Swift
Charles Swift
William Clerk J[r]
James Wylie J[r]
William Smith
Ichabod Shaw
William Stewart

Benjamin Rhoades
Elijah Fayr
Joseph Kennedy
Robert Campbell
Noble Campbell
Allen Stephenson
Nathan Dennison
James Kiegwin
Thomas Kiegwin
Amos Kiegwin
Nathan Coy
Robert Jameson J[r]
George Gordon J[r]
Job Bennet
Joseph Sweet
William Gray
William Bennet
John Bennet
Sampson Williams
Negro Ceaser
Mark Croswell
John Lowden
David Campbell
Anthony Eames J[r]

## CONTINENTAL REGIMENTS, 1775.

Mark Eames Ju$^r$
Isaac Eames
Jonathan Chilson
Benjamin Burden

Gideon Tower
Alexander Williams
Elisha Eagleston
Andrew Jillson

## WALLINGFORD

A list of the Mens Names that Was out With me in the Year 1775.

Ephraham Chamberlin
Joseph Shailor
Daniel Hall
John Mansfield
Moses Hall 2$^d$
Aaron Hull
Samuel Orsburn
Titus Hall
Aaron Persons
Samuel Collins
Ephraim Merriams
John Anthony
Thadeous Averet
Amos Austin
Benjamin Austin
Jared Benham
John Butlar
Titus Brockitt
Ira Bartholomew
Abel Barns
Samuel Benham
Elisha Cowls
Joel Cowls
Elisha Curtis
James Corbit
Benj$^m$ Chittenden
Israel Daton
Thomas Dudley
Amos Davis
James Frances
Giles Griswell
John Griswould
Rufas Hall
Sam$^{ll}$ Hough
Caleb Hull
Sam$^l$ Hall
Enos Hall
Charles Hall
Asa Hall
Simeon Hopson
Raphel Hulbart
Jonah Hill
Phenihas Hough
Israel Hall
Moses Hall 3$^d$

Sam$^{ll}$ Johnson
Aaron Ives
Thomas Janes
Levi Ives
Dan Johnson
Sam$^l$ Johnson 2$^d$
Epaphras Nott
Phenihas Lyman
John Meriam
Joel Mattoon
Sam$^l$ Mattoon
Ichabod Merriman
Barnibas Moss
Enos Mix
Sam$^l$ Miles
Benj$^m$ Preston
Edmond Parker
Benj$^m$ Parker
John Perce
Elisha Perker
Phenihas Peck
Gidion Roys
Joseph Roys
Jonathan Slead
Miles Sperry
John Slead
Daniel Smith
Seth Smith
Abel Thorp
Elihu Thompson
Charles Tuttle
Jesse Vorse
Joseph Ward
Joseph Wolcott
Moses Warner
Ebenezar Warner
Nash Yale
Joseph Yale
Jonathan Yale
Elihu Lewis
Daniel M Mullin
Thadeous Carter
Timothy Hart
Gedeon Bristol
Isaac Shepard

A true list of the Mens Names that Went out of Wallingford With me in 1775 which Belong$^d$ to this town

Certified pr Isaac Cook Jun$^r$   Wallingford Sep$^t$ 2$^d$ 1777

Wallingford December 1st 1777

These May Cartifie that the Following Persons Ware in the Service with Me att Boston in the Year 1775

Timothy Moltrop
Linus Hopson
Pren (?) Hopson
Sam<sup>ll</sup> Hopson Jur
Ambrose Avered
Cornelus Koberling (?)
Giles Cook
Arch Allin
John Frances
John Booth
Amos Frances
Samuel Culver Ju<sup>r</sup>
Thomas Mix Ju<sup>r</sup>
Street Yale
Amasa Yale
Daniel Sled (?)
Titus Hart
Archabel McNale
Abram Hall
Joel Hall
Isaac Doolittle
Enos Page
Ruben Bristol
Ichabod [ ? ]
Sam<sup>ll</sup> Bunnil
W<sup>m</sup> Munrow
Rubin Tyler
Josiah Mix

Certified pr Me Street Hall

## WINDSOR

Job Allyn
Jonathan Loomis
Increase Mather
Roger Rowel
Jacob Judd
George Wolcott
John Roberts
Elnathan Filley
Elijah Marshall
Phenihas Drake 3<sup>d</sup>
Isaac Pinney Jun<sup>r</sup>
William Phelps 3<sup>d</sup>
Lanslott Phelps
Elijah Griswold
Martin Holcomb Jun<sup>r</sup>
Solomon Clark Jun<sup>r</sup>
James Wilson
Israel Warner
Edward Barnard Jn<sup>r</sup>
Zacheus Phelps
John May
Luke Thrall
Oliver Winchell
Theophilus Hide
Ashbel Stiles
Thomas Haydon
Martin Denslow
Samuel Wing
Ezekiel Thrall
Oliver Clark
Sam<sup>ll</sup> Gibbs
David Gibbs
Eleazer Gaylord
William Davice
Alpheus Munsell
Lemuel Welch
William Parsons
Elias Brown
Cornelius Russell
Daniel Eley
Samuel Munrow
Aaron Lyon
Nath<sup>l</sup> Stanley
Shubel Barber
Jesse Thrall
Roger Mills
Ruben Loomis
Thomas Allyn Jun<sup>r</sup>
William Manley
Moses Cook
David Filley
Jonathan Bidwell
Moses Drake
Simeon Grayham
"Two Heads"
Stephen Fosbury
John Fosbury
Joseph Fitch
Jonah Gillet Jun<sup>r</sup>
Jonathan Gillet
Ezekiel Case
John Rowell Jun<sup>r</sup>
Isaac Skinner
Th<sup>o</sup>ma<sup>s</sup> Gillet
Abiel Wilson
Aaron Webster

# ALARM SERVICE, 1775.

## CAPT. BORDMAN'S COMPANY

Wee y° Subcribers Beloning to Cap¹ Bordmans Company Beeing Cald out att two alarams to Defend y° See Ports to Wit on y° 7 Day of August 1775 y° 2 on y° first Day of Sep<sup>tr</sup> in y° year 1776 Wee Do hereby acknowledge that Wee and Each of Vs have Recd our Wages as it Was allowed Pr y° Pay table May y° 6 1777

Roger Billing
Nathan Stanton
Abel Stanton
William Hartshorn
Thomas Rix
Thomas Bellows
John Cogswell
Nathan Cogswell
Benajah Cook
John Cook Ju<sup>r</sup>
Remengton Seers
Israel Herrick
Ezra Benjamin
Gideon Ray
John Ray
Elisha Guile
Amos Hutchinson
Nathan Burton
Isaac Burton
Pearly Brown
Abial Benjamin Ju<sup>r</sup>
Elijah Lester
James Hatch
James Rix
Theophilus Rix
David Bordman

Christ° Smith
Alex<sup>r</sup> Stewart
Daniel Rix
Eleazar Prentice
Peleg Sweet
Hezekiah Boardman
Sam<sup>ll</sup> Bliss
Christo. Babcock
Ebenezer Herrick
Jedediah Ensworth
Henry Burton
Joseph Wilbur
Thomas Wilbur
Banjmin Asten
Jese Banjmin
Elias Brown
Barton Cooke
David Benjamin
Preserved Brumbly
Isaac W. Stanton
John Cleaveland
Spencer Kinne
Ezra Kinne
Amos Hutchson
Joseph Starkweather

[The above names are all autographs.]

Captain Joseph Bordman and his Company was from Northern Preston now the town of Griswold [Added in a modern handwriting.]

[*State Library.*]

# ROLLS AND RETURNS, 1776.

## CAPT. WELLES' COMPANY

[*See Record of Connecticut Men in the Revolution, page 896.*]

Apprisement of the Soldiers guns under Com^d of Cap^t Sam^l Welles

Cap^t Sam^l Welles
Abraham Tallcott
George Tallcott
Rich^d Smith
Jesse Churchel
Josiah Lumis
Josiah Stevens
Serj^t Benj^a Stevens
Benj^a Howard
Frances Nichalson
Barnabas Fuller
Thomas Brooks
Ashbil Webster
Steven Couch
Peter Stevens
David Hubbard
John Morley
Jon^th Loveland
David Nigh fifer
Edward Potter
Elijah Covel
Jon^th Covel

Joseph Bidwell
Jon^th Gains
Leu^t Tho^s Hollister
Serj^t Aaron Hubbard
Elijah Hubbard
Josiah Brooks
Sam^l Daniels
Joseph Churchel
Eliz^r Hubbard
Ebez^r Benton
Sam^l Hills Jun^r
W^m Densmore
Timothy Stevens
Aaron Hollister
Josiah Hollister
Timothy Wood
John How
Elemuel Tubbs
Hez^h Wickham
Nathan Nichalson
Tho^s Morley
Elez^r Goodale

Glastonbury 18th 1776

[*State Library, Revolution 6, 173.*]

## CAPT. PEASE'S COMPANY

[*See Record of Connecticut Men in the Revolution, page 439*]

A Muster roll of Cap¹ Abial Peess Company

Capt Abial Peese
Lieu John Pomry
Lieu Israel Converse
Ens. Abner Wood
Serj Issacher Jones
Serj Samuel Hall
Serj Samuel Edson
Serj John Warner
Corp Stephen Jones
Corp Benajah Kent
Corp Sam¹¹ Warner
Drum Erastus Peese
Fifer Sylvanus Peese
Uriah Austin
Reuben Bradly
Samuel Blogget
Josiah Bradly
David Brace
John Comes
Oliver Chapin
Serel Chafe
Reuben Cooly
Daniel Chapens
John Carpenter
Uriah Clough
Jonathan Cross
Philander Denslow
John Dimmick
Simeon Dimmuck
Samuel Davis
Lemuel Davis
Nathan Edson
Josiah Edson
Joseph Edson
Benjamin Edson
Samuel Eaton
John Ferinan (?)
Natⁿ Fuller
Elijah Fay
John Goudy
Samuel Goudy
William Goudy
Josiah Gibbs
William Green
Joshua Hudson
John Hamlin
Levi Hamlin
Moses Horton
Nat¹ Hide
Israel How
Abner Hathway
Elcizer Jones
Ephraim Jonson
Abel Kent
Philip Langdon
Juston Lombord
James McCluer
Joel Noble
Timothy Noble
Shadrach Norton
Joseph Pearman
Nathaniel Pomroy
Russel Prat
Abner Pease
Peter Pecse
Sanˡˡ Peese
Joel Pecse
Augustus Peese
Jonathan Parks
Sanford Richardson
Jesse Richardson
Abijah Remington
Elijah Robins
Ezra Saxton
James Spenser
Joseph Saxton
Isaac Shepherd
Jonathan Shead
Eliphalet Spenser
Ebenezer Thresher
Amos Torry
James Ward
John Ward
Simeon Webster
Nathan Webster
Ebenezer Walker'
Samuel Warms (? Warner)
Levi Woolworth

[Indorsed] A Muster Roll of Cap¹ Abial Peas's Company at New London in the year 1776

[*State Library.*]

## CAPT. BARNS' COMPANY.

A Pay Role for a Number of Capt Barns Company in the State of Connecticut who marched to New York from Waterbury in August Last and Home again. [Other documents show the date to be 1776.]

| Names | When arivd | When returd home |
|---|---|---|
| Lieu$^t$ Lazarus Ives | Aug$^t$ 18 | Sep$^t$ 14 |
| Serg$^t$ Aaron Fenn | " | " |
| Corp Benjamin Barns | " | " |
| Cephas Ford | " | 19 |
| Paul Griggs | " | " |
| Elnathan Ives | " | " |

[*State Library, Revolution 10, 181.*]

## CANTERBURY RETURN

[*See Record of Connecticut Men in the Revolution, page 412.*]

Arms & Accoutraments bo$^t$ hired, or impress$^d$ by the Select Men of Canterbury & delivered to Soldiers of that Town for Camp$^n$ 1776

| to whom d$^d$ | of whose Company |
|---|---|
| Tracy Cleveland | Capt Bacons |
| Warren Williams | " |
| Dan$^l$ Kendal | " |
| Solem$^n$ Cleveland | " |
| John Curtis | " |
| Asa Burges | " |
| Rich$^d$ Parsons | " |
| David Addams | " |
| Abner Addams | " |
| Nehem$^a$ Parrish | " |
| Jacob Staples | " |
| Elkanah Smith | " |
| Silas Gates | " |
| Philip Withy | " |
| Nath$^l$ Carver | " |
| Pender Jennison | " |
| David Smith | " |
| Elijah Spencer | " |
| Rufus Downing | " |
| John Gro (?) | " |
| Nath$^n$ Williams | " |
| Tm$^o$ Hall | |
| W$^m$ Shaw | Capt Elderkin |
| Eph$^m$ Goram | " |
| Curtis Cleveland | Capt Cutlers |
| Dan$^l$ Cushman | Capt Sharps |
| Tho$^s$ Cotten | " |
| Eben$^r$ Kingsly | " |
| Rufus Baker | " |
| Ja$^s$ Bennet | " |
| Oliv$^r$ Perkins | " |

[*State Library, Revolution 6, 166.*]

# CONNECTICUT LINE, 1777-1781.

[*See Record of Connecticut Men in the Revolution, pages 125-238.*]

## SUPPLIES, 1777-1779.

An Alphlabitical Account of the Names of those who have Reciv⁴ Supplies from Towns, there Value at the Stated Price of 1776, & the Value of the Money Lodg⁴ by the Soldjer, together with the Name of y⁰ Town to which they belong.

[In December 1776 the Assembly passed an act fixing and stating the price of sundry articles of provision and other commodities. The following August another act was passed permitting soldiers to deposit a certain proportion of their wages with the selectmen or a committee of the town in which they resided who were authorized to expend the sum so deposited in the purchase "at the stated price" of provisions and supplies for the support of the family of the soldier making such deposit.]

|   | Names |   | Town |
|---|---|---|---|
|   | Allen | Daniel Cap\* | Ashford |
| 6 |   | David | Derbey |
| 2 |   | Eben\* | Fairfield |
| 6 |   | Thomas | " |
| 2 |   | Moses | " |
|   |   | Jonathan | Newhaven |
| 4 |   | Samuel | Suffield |
| 5 |   | Amos | Sharon |
| 1 |   | Ashur | Mansfield |
| 4 |   | Adams | David Jun\* | Canterbury |
| 4 |   | David Doct\* | " |
| D |   | Samuel | " |
|   |   | John | Farmington |
| A |   | Jonathan | Greenich |
| 4 |   | William Lieu\* | Hartford |
| 7 |   | Asael | Norfolk |
| 1 |   | Andrus | Thomas | East Haddam |
|   |   | William | East Windsor |
| 3 |   | Theodore | Farmington |
| 3 |   | Obediah | " |
| 9 |   | James | Groten |
| 9 |   | Ezra | Newhartford |
| 3 |   | Asa | Weatherfield |
| 1 | Ackly | Thomas | East Haddam |
| 0 | Andeson | William | East Windsor |
| 1 |   | Thomas | Lime |

|   | Names | Town |
|---|---|---|
|   | Abbe Thomas Cap[t] | Enfield |
| 3 | Eleazer | Hartford |
| 1 | Jeduthan | " |
| 1 | John | Mansfield |
| 3 | Albert Thomas G. Serj[t] | Farmington |
|   | Avory Thomas Lieu[t] | Groten |
| 1 | Simeon Ens[n] | " |
| 1 | Annew Andrew | " |
| 1 | Arnold Jehiel | Haddam |
| 3 | Augustus Cesar | Hartford |
| 5 | Angur George | Middletown |
| A | Aken James Serj[t] | Newhaven |
| A | Alley William | " |
| 7 | Aspenwall Aaron | Norfolk |
| 7 | Caleb | " |
| 1 | Auldredg W[m] | Preston |
| 3 | Austen Richard | Suffield |
|   | Antoney John | Wallingford |
| 4 | Brandon Charles | Ashford |
|   | Barker Sam[ll] Cap[t] | Branford |
| 7 | Barber Nath[ll] | Torrington |
| 6 | Bunnel Abraham | Branford |
| 6 | Bagdon Cezar | " |
|   | Bacon Abner Cap[t] | Canterbury |
| 6 | William | Midletown |
| 4 | Nehemiah | Pomphret |
| 5 | Henery | Voluntown |
| 3 | Bowers Benajah Corp[l] | Chatham |
| 3 | Ephraim | " |
| 3 | Benj[a] | " |
| 9 | Butler Peter | " |
| 6 | Walter | Greenich |
| 3 | John | Labenon |
| 3 | Steaphen | Saybrook |
|   | Biggelow Eli | Colchester |
| 4 | Bill Jonathan | " |
|   | Beriah Cap[t] | Norwich |
|   | Blancherd Robbin | Colchester |
| 8 | Jacobe | Stamford |
| 8 | Brigham Paul | Coventry |
| 7 | Bishop David | Danbury |
| 7 | Thalmenus | Guilford |
| A | Nathan[ll] | Newhaven |
|   | Nathan[ll] Leiu[t] | Norwich |
|   | Baldwine Silas | Derbey |
| 7 | Calib Leiu[t] | Killingsworth |
|   | Henery | Saybrook |
| 3 | Booth Henry | Enfield |
| 5 | Burr Daniel | Fairfield |
| 8 | Buckley Seth | " |
| 9 | Edward Cap[t] | Weathersfield |
| 5 | Bradley Eliphalet | Fairfield |
| 2 | Nathan | " |
| 5 | Philip B. Col[o] | Ridgfield |
| 6 | Daniel | Wallingford |
| A | Oliver | Newhaven |
| 2 | Beers Hezekiah | Fairfield |
|   | Brown Jonathan Cap[t] | Farmington |

CONNECTICUT LINE, 1777–1781.       23

|   | Names | Town |
|---|---|---|
| 0 | Brown W<sup>m</sup> | Midletown |
| 7 | Charles Corp<sup>l</sup> | Newfairfield |
| 8 | Henery | Newhaven |
| 8 | Jacobe | Summers |
|   | Charles | Stonington |
| 1 | Joshua | " |
|   | Oliver | " |
| 5 | Eben<sup>r</sup> | Tolland |
| 9 | Edward | Weathersfield |
| 0 | Josiah Leiu<sup>t</sup> | E Windsor |
| 5 | Judah D<sup>o</sup> | " |
| 8 | Barns Daniel Cap<sup>t</sup> | Farmington |
| 9 | Thomas | Midletown |
|   | James Lieu<sup>t</sup> | Newfairfield |
| A | Solomon Serj<sup>t</sup> | Newhaven |
| 6 | Moses | Wallingford |
|   | David | " |
| 8 | Daniel | Waterbury |
| D | Brunson Roger | Farmington |
| 5 | Asa | " |
| 8 | Bates John | " |
| 6 | Eleazer | Haddam |
| 6 | Amos | " |
| 6 | Dan<sup>ll</sup> | " |
| 8 | David | Stanford |
| 6 | Bonfoy Benunuel | Haddam |
|   | Brainord Encrease | " |
| 6 | Boardman Jonathan | " |
| 0 | Moses | Middletown |
| 6 | A. Sam<sup>ll</sup> | " |
| 8 | Barnard John Cap<sup>t</sup> | Hartford |
| 9 | Brewer Daniel Serj<sup>t</sup> | " |
| 8 | Bevens Eben<sup>r</sup> | " |
|   | Buckland Steaphen Cap<sup>t</sup> | " |
| D | Bull Eppiphras Cap<sup>t</sup> | " |
| 9 | Bushnal Daniel | Hartland |
| 4 | Baxter Aaron | Hebron |
| 3 | Francis | E Windsor |
| 7 | Barnum Liu<sup>t</sup> | Kent |
| 7 | Steaphen Ser<sup>t</sup> | " |
| 7 | Amos Corp<sup>l</sup> | " |
|   | Burnum Asa | Litchfield |
|   | Joseph | Lyme |
|   | Asa | Preston |
| 7 | Barlow John | Kent |
| 1 | Betts James | Labenon |
| 8 | Badcock John | " |
| 1 | Ball Humphry | " |
| 1 | Blackman Jonathan | " |
|   | Elijah Cap<sup>t</sup> | Middletown |
| 4 | Beckwith Phineas | Lyme |
| 1 | Ickeabud | Newlondon |
| 4 | Bogue Ickabd | Lime |
|   | Blake Eben<sup>r</sup> | Middletown |
| 6 | Bull John L<sup>t</sup> | Guilford |
| 7 | Billens Steaphen L<sup>t</sup> | Groten |
| 1 | James | Stonington |

|   | Names | Town |
|---|---|---|
| 6 | Benton Edward Serj$^t$ | Guilford |
|   | Bailey Gideon L$^t$ | Haddam |
| 6 | Jacobe | " |
|   | Robert | " |
| 1 | Brightman Henrey | Groten |
| 3 | Bristol Jonathan | Milford |
| 5 | John | Windsor |
| 6 | Benjamin | Wallingford |
| 6 | Bens Thomas | Milford |
| 4 | Bend John | Norwich |
| 7 | Bottom John | Litchfield, |
| 8 | Bouten David | Stamford |
| 2 | Bissel John | E Windsor |
|   | Beeman Jonathan | " |
|   | Friend | Washington |
| [ ] | Baker Bartholemew | Redding |
| 6 | Edward | Newhaven |
| [ ] | Beebe Boanerges | Newlondon |
| 6 | Joel | Milford |
| 1 | Ammon | Norwich |
| 2 | James Cap$^t$ | Stratford |
| 1 | Bolles James | Newlondon |
|   | Brind Edward | Haddam |
| 6 | Belden John | Milford |
|   | Burk John | " |
| 0 | Basset Joshua | Mansfield |
| 2 | William | Waterbury |
| 2 | Barrows Jacobe | Mansfield |
| 1 | Bugbe John | " |
| 1 | Bennet Joshua | " |
| 1 | Benj$^n$ | Norwich |
|   | Berdsley Phineas Cap$^t$ | Newfairfield |
| 2 | Brocket Hezekiah | Newhaven |
| 6 | Blakslee Zealous | " |
| 6 | Britton Samuel | " |
| 7 | Bostwick Eben$^r$ | Newmilford |
|   | Buns Isaiah Sr(?) Washington | " |
| 7 | Buns Isaiah Jr(?) Newmilford | Washington |
|   | Bewel David | Newmilford |
| 2 | Buck Josiah | " |
| 7 | Botsford Joel | Newtown |
| 4 | Briant John | Norwich |
| 0 | Brewster Hezekiah | " |
| 5 | Bigsbe Elias | Reading |
| 1 | Brumly W$^m$ | Stonington |
| A | Benjamins John | Stratford |
|   | Burrus Josiah | " |
| 6 | Blodget Artimas | Salisbury |
| 9 | Blinn Abraham | Weathersfield |
| 9 | Justus | " |
|   | Burnap Benj$^n$ | Windham |
| 7 | Bingham John | " |
|   | Abishai | " |
| 2 | Bartholomew John | Woodstock |
| 2 | Bruce Eli | " |
|   | Brown Nathan | Norwalk |
| 8 | Bouton John | Norwalk |

## CONNECTICUT LINE, 1777–1781.

| | Names | Town |
|---|---|---|
| 8 | Bedient Mordica | Norwalk |
| 8 | Beers Jesse | " |
| 8 | Comstock Sam¹¹ Cap¹ | Norwalk |
| 8 | Cheney Eben' Corp¹ | Ashford |
| 7 | Richard | Kent |
| 7 | Culver Aaron | Canaan |
| 8 | Timothy | Farmington |
| 4 | David | Hebron |
| | Daniel | N. London |
| 7 | Chambers Will" | Canaan |
| 4 | Cleaveland John Serg¹ | Canterbury |
| | Timothy Leiu¹ | " |
| 2 | Moses Leiut | " |
| 7 | Josiah | Sharon |
| 2 | John | Stanford |
| 1 | Jonas | Colchester |
| 4 | Cady Abijah | Canterbury |
| | Darius | Stonington |
| 1 | Carter Reuben | Canterbury |
| 8 | Aaron | Chatham |
| 4 | Edward | Colchester |
| | James | Lebanon |
| 4 | Coburn Samuel | Canterbury |
| D | Cushman Daniel | " |
| | Cole Marcus Leiut | Chatham |
| | John Leiut | Farmington |
| 9 | Samuel | Hartford |
| 7 | John | Waterbury |
| | Clapp Nathan | Coventry |
| 5 | Chapman Collens | Danbury |
| 4 | Joseph Leiu¹ | Norwich |
| 6 | Dan[ ] Serj¹ | Saybrook |
| | John | " |
| 6 | Cook Thomas | Durham |
| 4 | Case | Norwich |
| 8 | Joel | Waterbury |
| 1 | Clark Samuel | E Haddam |
| 8 | Lyman | Farmingtown |
| 1 | Samuel | Haddam |
| 0 | Aaron | " |
| 8 | Abraham Serj¹ | Hartford |
| 8 | John | Labenon |
| 5 | Othniel Leiu¹ | Midletown |
| 9 | Joel | Newhaven |
| A | David Serj¹ | " |
| 6 | Marten | " |
| 4 | Jacobe | Norwich |
| 4 | James | Weathersfield |
| 8 | Richard | Waterbury |
| | Asael Ens" | Woodstock |
| 9 | William | Newlondon |
| | Churchel Elijah | E Windsor |
| 2 | Chandler Joseph | Enfield |
| 5 | Coggin David | Fairfield |
| 2 | Cable W" | " |
| | Curtice Amos | Farmington |
| 3 | Daniel | Hartford |

|   | Names | Town |
|---|---|---|
| 7 | Curtice George | Kent |
| 8 | Steaphen | Waterbury |
| 8 | Camp Isaac | Farmingtown |
| 8 | Samuel | Waterbury |
| 8 | Sam[ll] Jun[r] | " |
|   | Phineas | Woodbury |
| 3 | Canada David | Glastenbury |
| 3 | Crary Richard | " |
|   | Conlee John | " |
| 7 | Convers Thomas Cap[t] | Goshun |
|   | Chase Walter | Haddam |
| 8 | Case Richard | Hartford |
| 0 | Church Samuel | Haddam |
|   | Eben[r] | Woodbury |
| 6 | Cone Elisha | Haddam |
| 5 | Ozias | Middletown |
|   | Joseph | " |
| 5 | Daniel | " |
| 3 | Combs William Serj[t] | Hart[d] & Weathf[d] |
| 9 | Corney Maleciah | Hartford |
| 9 | Cadwell Matthew S[t] | " |
| 1 | Simeon | Stoningtown |
|   | Coleman Noah Doct. | Labenon |
| 1 | Colefox W[m] Ens[n] | Newlondon |
|   | Chappel Joshua | " |
| 1 | W[m] 3[d] Corp[l] | " |
|   | Comfort | " |
| 9 | Ameziah | Labenon |
|   | Curtice | Salisbury |
| 1 | Corwin Selah | Lime |
|   | Jonathan | Norwich |
|   | Selah | Norwich |
| 9 | Crittenden Gideon | Middletown |
| 5 | Cahales Cornelius alias Frost Sam[ll] | Milford |
| 4 | Conant Sam[ll] | Mansfield |
| 3 | Calib | " |
| A | Coshall Thomas | Newhaven |
| 7 | Canfield Elijah | Newmilford |
| 1 | Comestock Gid[n] | Norwich |
|   | John | Saybrook |
| 8 | Car James alias Miller | Norwich |
| 4 | Cleff Lem[ll] Cap[t] | Plainfield |
| 5 | Cooley Nathan | Redding |
| 5 | Ruben | Somers |
| 3 | Comestock Sam[ll] | Seybrook |
| 5 | Cummes W[m] | Ridgfield |
|   | Cottrel Nathan | Stonington |
| 5 | Cynamon Thom[s] | " |
|   | Collins W[m] Lock | Stratford |
| 6 | Clanghorn Eleaz[r] Leu[t] | Salisbury |
| 9 | Crane Curtice | Weathersfield |
| 5 | Coy Sam[ll] | Windsor |
| 8 | Calkens Israel | Waterbury |
| 7 | Chamberlin Eph[m] | Wallingford |
| 1 | Chadwick John | Lime |

## CONNECTICUT LINE, 1777-1781.

| | Names | Town |
|---|---|---|
| 8 | Cole Alben | Norwalk |
| 2 | Davinson W<sup>m</sup> | Ashford |
| | Robert | Greenwich |
| 6 | Isaac | Milford |
| 6 | John | Washington |
| 4 | Dawner Ezra | Bolton |
| 2 | Caleb | E Windsor |
| 2 | Duggins James | Canterbury |
| | Downing Steaph<sup>n</sup> | " |
| | Christopher | Norwich |
| 8 | Doubleday Joseph | Coventry |
| A | Dixon George | Danbury |
| | Durfe Thomas | Fairfield |
| | Disborough Justus | " |
| 8 | (?) Joshua | " |
| 2 | Dimon Moses | " |
| 2 | John | Woodbury |
| 8 | Dutton Oliver Serj<sup>t</sup> | Farmington |
| | Titus Serj<sup>t</sup> | Waterbury |
| 8 | Dunham Cornelus | Farmington |
| | Dealing Sam<sup>ll</sup> | Glastenbury |
| A | Davis Isaac | Greenwich |
| 9 | Daniel | Groten |
| 8 | Jonathan | Waterbury |
| | Steaphen | " |
| 7 | Daton Richard | Groten |
| | Israel | Newhaven |
| 6 | Davis James | " |
| 9 | Eben<sup>r</sup> | Weathersfield |
| 6 | Dowd Moses | Guilford |
| 7 | Demming Wall | Goshun |
| | David Leiu<sup>t</sup> | Hartford |
| 1 | Darrow Christoph<sup>r</sup> | Hartford |
| 4 | Delibar James | " |
| 9 | Day Westbrook | " |
| | Die Dan<sup>ll</sup> | Kent |
| | Dodg Daniel | Lyme |
| | Nathan | Colchcster |
| 1 | DeWolf Steaphen | Lime |
| 1 | Edward | " |
| | Dewey James | Midletown |
| 1 | Dextor John Corp<sup>l</sup> | Mansfield |
| 6 | Doyle Hugh | Newhaven |
| | Dickermon Joseph | " |
| 7 | Dunwill William | N Milford |
| 7 | Dailey James | " |
| | Drinkwater W<sup>m</sup> | " |
| 4 | Durke John Col<sup>o</sup> | Norwich |
| | Benj<sup>n</sup> Leiu<sup>t</sup> | Windham |
| | Jeremiah | " |
| | Dudley Zebulon L<sup>t</sup> | Saybrook |
| 1 | Davel John | Stonington |
| 1 | Dennison Amos | Voluntown |
| 5 | Denslow Marten | Windsor |
| 2 | Dimmok Joseph | Willington |
| 8 | Dunbar Amos } | |
| | alias Joel Brunson } | Waterbury |
| | Miles | " |

|   | Names | Town |
|---|---|---|
| 0 | Danzy W<sup>m</sup> | Newlondon |
| 1 | Daniels Ezekiel | " |
|   | Douglass Solomon | " |
| 1 |     Richard Lieu<sup>t</sup> | " |
| 5 | Deforest Sam<sup>l</sup> Ens<sup>n</sup> | Norwalk |
|   | Eams Everet | Danbury |
| 8 | Earl W<sup>m</sup> | Enfield |
| 2 | Evans Abiathar | Hartford |
|   |     Sam<sup>ll</sup> Jun<sup>r</sup> | " |
| 8 |     Henery | " |
|   | Edgcomb Ezra | Newhartford |
|   | Evan Isaac | Preston |
| 8 | Elmer Calib | Harrington |
| 5 |     Daniel | Sharon |
| 2 |     W<sup>m</sup> | Somers |
| 3 | Ells Edward Cap<sup>t</sup> | Midletown |
| 1 | Ellis John   Chaplan | Norwich |
| 6 | Eagleston David | Newhaven |
| 5 | Eaton Solomon | Tolland |
| 8 | Easton Eliphalet | Woodbury |
| 4 | Edwards Nath<sup>ll</sup> | Waterbury |
|   | Elderken Vine Cap<sup>t</sup> | Windham |
| 2 | Fountaine Enos | Stamford |
| 6 | Foot Eben<sup>r</sup> | Branford |
| 6 |     Ezra | Derbey |
| 7 |     Eben<sup>r</sup> | Harrington |
| A |     Isaac Serj<sup>t</sup> | Newhaven |
| 8 |     Elijah | Newtown |
| 8 | Freeman Elisha | Canaan |
|   |     Jack | Colchester |
| 6 |     Frank | Derbey |
|   |     Sampson | Glastenbury |
| 3 | Sifax alias Mosely | " |
| 0 |     Edward | Groten |
| 7 |     Guy | " |
| 0 |     Micael | " |
|   | Freeman Providence | Newlondon |
| 8 | Fitch Rufus | Canterbury |
| 6 |     Joseph Trumbull | Salisbury |
| 6 | Fits Gerald Henery | " |
|   | Fox John | Colchester |
| 8 |     Elisha | Farmington |
| 9 |     Asa | Glastenbury |
|   |     Jacobe Leiu<sup>t</sup> | Norwich |
| 1 |     Joshua | E Haddam |
| 6 | Farmer Th<sup>o</sup> Ens<sup>n</sup> | Derbey |
| 2 | Fuller John | Fairfield |
| 5. | Fegoe Peter | " |
| 4 | Fargoe W<sup>m</sup> | Newlondon |
|   | Fowler Nehemiah | Fairfield |
|   |     Caleb Corp<sup>l</sup> | Guilford |
|   | French Samuel | Fairfield |
| A | Fletcher Joseph | Greenwich |
| 0 | Fanning Elisha | Groten |
| 4 |     Charles Leiu<sup>t</sup> | Norwich |
| 8 | Frisbey Benj<sup>n</sup> | Torrington |
| 7 | Franklin Samuel | Killingsworth |

CONNECTICUT LINE, 1777-1781.    29

| | Names | Town |
|---|---|---|
| 9 | Flowers Elijah | Newhartford |
| 4 | Foster Zephaniah | Lebanon |
| 3 | John | Midletown |
| 7 | Benj[a] | Sharon |
| 5 | Fisher Cristoper | Midletown |
| 7 | Isaac | Sharon |
| 6 | Frances James | Midletown |
| 6 | John | Wallingford |
| 2 | Franklen Jehial | Woodbury |
| 5 | Frost Sam[ll] | |
| | alias Cornelu Cahales | Milford |
| 1 | Fenton Jonathan | Mansfield |
| 2 | Solomon Leiu[t] | " |
| | John | Willington |
| 6 | Ford Daniel | Newhaven |
| 1 | Fellows Joseph Ens[n] | Stongton |
| 1 | Nath[ll] | " |
| 5 | Forgarson Dan[ll] | Salisbury |
| 8 | Fattendon John | Waterbury |
| 8 | Fulford John Serj. | " |
| | Farnum Ruben | Windham |
| | Filets Francis | Woodbury |
| 9 | Fay Gershome | Winchester |
| 9 | Tim[o] | " |
| 9 | W[m] | " |
| 9 | Filley Remembrance | " |
| 5 | Fenn Dan[ll] | Washington |
| 1 | David | Colchester |
| 1 | Farnsworth Nath[ll] | " |
| 6 | Garret John | Branford |
| | John | Newhartf[d] |
| 1 | Goff Sam[ll] | |
| | alias Rich[d] Faiman ? | Chatham |
| 8 | Geer Elihue | Enfield |
| hired | Giddens Richard | Chatham |
| 1 | Gladding W[m] | Haddam |
| 1 | Gray James | Newlondon |
| 7 | Elijah | Groten |
| 1 | Goodfaith David | Newlondon |
| 4 | Gardiner David | Newlondon |
| 1 | Sherman | Norwich |
| | De Tubs | " |
| 9 | Gilbert Joseph | Newhartford |
| 9 | Theodore | " |
| 7 | Obediah | Stratford |
| 7 | Green Sam[ll] | Canaan |
| 8 | Josiah | Fairfield |
| | William Cap[t] | Hartford |
| | Robart | Voluntown |
| 8 | John Corp[l] | Woodstock |
| | Gates Nath[ll] Leiu[t] | Canterbury |
| 3 | Graham Joseph | Chatham |
| 6 | { Grimes Silus } | Saybrook |
| | {  Cyrus  } | " |
| 3 | Gutrich Levey | Chatham |
| 7 | David | Sharon |
| | Ephraim | Weathersf[d] |
| 8 | Graves Peter | Colchester |

|   | Names | Town |
|---|---|---|
|   | Graves Simeon | Waterbury |
| 5 | W<sup>m</sup> | Midletown |
|   | Grant Azeriah | E Windsor |
| 6 | James | Saybrook |
| 8 | Griswold Joseph | Infield |
| 8 | White | Harwington |
| D | Glover John | Fairfield |
| 2 | Goodsill Eppiphras | " |
| 7 | Grover Phineas L<sup>t</sup> | Glastenbury |
| 8 | Amasa | Killingly |
| 2 | Jacobe | Stratford |
| 5 | Goold John | Goshun |
| 8 | Gridley Seth | Harwington |
| 1 | Gross Samuel | Lebanon |
| 6 | Gilston Jacobe | Midletown |
| 5 | Gillson Eleazer | Sharon |
| A | Gibson Sam<sup>ll</sup> | Newhaven |
| 4 | Goodale Jacobe | Pomphret |
| D | Guyant Luke | Preston |
| 8 | Granger Samuel | Suffield |
|   | Phineas | " |
| 0 | Gibs Josiah | Summer |
| 3 | Sam<sup>ll</sup> Leiu<sup>t</sup> | Windsor |
| 1 | Griffen James | Stoningtown |
| 9 | Giffin Simon Serj<sup>t</sup> | Weathersfield |
|   | Gorum Sam<sup>ll</sup> | Stratford |
| 0 | Gaylord Benj<sup>n</sup> | Waterbury |
|   |   | & Torington |
| 1 | Hardy Nathaniel | Ashford |
|   | Hall William | " |
| 8 | Israel | Enfield |
| 5 | Stephen | Fairfield |
| 7 | Stephen Cap<sup>t</sup> | Guilford |
| 7 | Philemon L<sup>t</sup> | " |
| 7 | David | Danbury |
|   | Samuel Corp. | Killingworth |
| 7 | Talmadge Ens<sup>n</sup> | N. Fairfield |
| 6 | Rufus | Wallingford |
|   | Nathaniel | Waterbury |
|   | William | N. London |
| 0 | Howe Zadock L<sup>t</sup> | Bolten |
| 9 | Joshua | N. Haven |
|   | Hubbard Elihue | Chatham |
| 8 | John Ens<sup>n</sup> | Branford |
| 3 | Hezek. L<sup>t</sup> | Middletown |
| 0 | Roswell | " |
| 6 | Harrison Jairus Sg<sup>t</sup> | Branford |
|   | William Corp<sup>l</sup> | Lebanon |
|   | Hoadley Sam<sup>l</sup> | Branford |
| 8 | Higby Elihu | Canaan |
| 7 | Holembok John L<sup>t</sup> | Branford |
|   | Hale Aaron L<sup>t</sup> | Chatham |
| 1 | Higgins Heman | " |
| 3 | Jesse | " |
|   | Cornelius | Haddam |
| 6 | Humphry E. Cap<sup>t</sup> | Derbe |
| 6 | Elijah Cap<sup>t</sup> | Woodbury |

CONNECTICUT LINE, 1777–1781. 31

|   | Names | Town |
|---|---|---|
|   | Hotchkiss Levi L⁺ | Derbe |
| 3 | Zadock Cap⁺ | Farmington |
| 7 | Ira | Guilford |
| 6 | Hawkins Zadock | Derbe |
| 6 | Hinman Hustead Cor. | Durham |
| 1 | Holmes Eliphat Cap⁺ | E. Haddam |
| A | Nathaniel | Greenwich |
| 8 | David Doct⁺ | Woodstock |
|   | Harvey Ithamar Cap⁺ | E Haddam |
| 1 | Ezra | " |
| 5 | William | Saybrook |
|   | Hagar Simeon Serj⁺ | Enfield |
| A | Hubbel, William L⁺ | Fairfield |
| A | Isaac L⁺ | " |
| 7 | Hutonet Francis | Fairfield |
| 7 | Hilton Atkinson | " |
| 6 | Hosmer Tim° Doct⁺ | Farmington |
| 3 | Hart Jonathan Adj⁺ | " |
| 7 | Benjamin | Wallingford |
| 8 | Hayden David | " |
|   | Thomas L⁺ | Windsor |
| 4 | Hill Daniel | Glassenbury |
| 7 | Eben⁺ Cap⁺ | Kent |
| 4 | Hill Phillip | Lebanon |
| 4 | John 2ᵈ | Symsbury |
| 8 | Holden John | Glassenbury |
| A | Hays Abraham | Greenwᶜʰ |
|   | Titus | Hartland |
| A | Harriot Israel | Greenwich |
| 1 | Harrinton Isaac | Groten |
| 3 | Elisha | Symsb |
|   | Hannabal Joseph | Groton |
|   | Joseph | Stonington |
| 0 | Holley Joseph | Groton & Preston |
| 8 | Hally Abraham | Stanford |
|   | Hawley C. Joseph | N. Milford |
| 7 | Handy Samuel Serj⁺ | Guilford |
| 8 | Heath Peleg L⁺ | Hartford |
| 8 | Hadlock Reuben | " |
| 9 | Hooker William | " |
| 6 | John | Milford |
| 8 | Hodge Asael Cap⁺ | Harwinton |
| 6 | David | Milford |
| 7 | Holdridge Hezekiah Col. | Hebron |
|   | Hyde Rufus | Lime |
| 4 | James Ensᵃ | Norwich |
| 1 | Horron John | Lyme |
| 1 | Hayns, Jonathan | " |
| 1 | Hudson Eleazer | " |
|   | John | Stonington |
| 5 | Henshaw Willᵐ L⁺ | Middlet. |
| 6 | Hull David | " |
| 6 | Giles Serj⁺ | Salisbury |
| 7 | Samuel | N. Haven |
| 8 | Oliver | Saybrook |
|   | James | Waterbury |
|   | Stephen | Woodbury |

|   | Names | Town |
|---|---|---|
| 8 | Harris John | Middletown |
| 1 | John | Mansfield |
| 8 | Champlin | Colchester |
| 6 | Hine Titus | Milford |
| 1 | Huse Bodwell | N. Haven |
| 6 | Howel Nicolas | " |
|   | Harden Frederick | " |
|   | Hunt Richard | " |
| 7 | Hamlin Joel | Norfolk |
| 5 | Hopkins Henry | Redding |
| 4 | Harmon John Cap[t] | Suffield |
| 7 | Herrick Libeus | Stonington |
| 4 | Hazard Jeffry | . " |
|   | Hiscox Thomas | " |
|   | Hawks Hannah p Son | " |
| 2 | Hallop Joseph | Stratford |
| 2 | Hinkley Ichabod Cap[t] | Tolland |
| 2 | Heacock Samuel Serj[t] | Stanford |
|   | William Jun[r] | Waterbury |
| 8 | Elisha | " |
|   | David | Woodbury |
|   | Hastings John | Wallinford |
| 8 | Hait Joseph Col | Stanford |
|   | Houghton James | Union |
| 2 | Hoyt Philemon Serj[t] | Willington |
| 6 | Samuel | Wallingford |
| 0 | Peter | N. London |
|   | Hendry Daniel | " |
|   | Hatch Hemon Corp | Willington |
|   | Hitchcock Lemuel L[t] | " |
| 8 | Thomas | " |
|   | Hambden William | Woodstock |
| 9 | Howard George | Farmington |
| 1 | Halloway William | N. London |
|   | Jones Joseph | Branford |
| 1 | Daniel | Lebanon |
| 3 | Thomas | Pomph. |
| 9 | Aaron | Saybr. |
| 3 | Eleazer | Somers |
| 6 | Jasper | Stratford |
| 5 | Isaiah | " |
|   | Thomas | Wallingf[d] |
|   | Henry | N. London |
| hired | Jennings Elnathan | Chatham |
| 4 | Johnson James | " |
| 6 | Will[m] | Durham |
| 9 | Nathaniel | Fairfield |
| [ ] | John | Farmington |
| 8 | William | Greenwich |
| 6 | Isaac | Guilford |
| 5 | Jonathan Col. | Middlet. |
| 3 | David | " |
| 6 | Abrah[m] Corp. | N. Haven |
| 1 | Benjamin | Plainfield |
| 8 | Nathaniel | Stanford |
|   | Robert | Sharon |
| 2 | Elihu | Tolland |
| 6 | John | Wallingf[d] |

CONNECTICUT LINE, 1777-1781.

| | Names | Town |
|---|---|---|
| | Judd Daniel Serj[t] | Colchester |
| 3 | William Cap[t] | Farmington |
| 8 | Stephen | Waterbury |
| 2 | Bruster | " |
| | Jackson P. Nathan L[t] | Fairfield |
| 1 | Thomas | Preston |
| 8 | Jesup Nathaniel | Greenw. |
| 9 | Jarrels Tho[s] Serj[t] | Hartford |
| 1 | Jolly William | N. fairfield |
| 5 | Jackknife Robert | Stonington |
| 1 | Ingram Mary p Son | " |
| 8 | Judgson Joseph | Woodbury |
| | Jordan John | Washington |
| 6 | Jocelin John | N. Haven |
| | Jacobs M. | Norwich |
| 7 | Knap Timothy | Goshen |
| 5 | James | N. Fairfield |
| 2 | Usel | Stamford |
| 5 | James | " |
| 8 | Keeney Benj[a] | Hartford |
| 6 | Kimbal Abrah. | Middletown |
| | Kinning Thomas | N. Fairf[d] |
| 4 | King George | N. Haven |
| 9 | Orry | Stratf[d] |
| 8 | Kimberly L[t] | N. Town |
| | Kirtland Cap[t] | Saybrook |
| | Karril John | Symsb |
| 5 | Kelsey Noah | Sharon |
| 9 | Kilby Christopher | Weathersf[d] |
| 8 | Lyon Henry | Ashford |
| 2 | Samuel | Fairfield |
| 8 | Abiel | Pomphret |
| 0 | Asa Q. M. | Woodstock |
| 1 | Thomas | N. London |
| | Lane William | " |
| | Lee Levi | " |
| | Elisha Cap[t] | Lime |
| 1 | Ezra L[t] | " |
| 8 | Abner | Woodbury |
| 8 | Lester Andrew | Cant. |
| 7 | Luke Phineas | Cornwell |
| 5 | Ludeman John | Danbury |
| 4 | Lord John | " |
| 6 | Jabez | N. Haven |
| 6 | William | Saybrook |
| 9 | Jeremiah Serj[t] | " |
| | Loomis Moses | E. Windsor |
| 9 | Israel | Hartford |
| 2 | Lockwood Stephen | Fairfield |
| A | Moses | Greenwich |
| | Sam[l] Cap[t] | " |
| 2 | Timothy | Stamford |
| 5 | Eliph. Serj[t] | " |
| 4 | Moses Serj[t] | Weathersfield |
| 9 | Lamb Joseph | Glassenb. |
| 9 | Loveland Thomas | " |
| 8 | Elisha | " |
| | Levi | " |

3

|   | Names | Town |
|---|---|---|
| 7 | Layre Jacob | Goshen |
|   | Lukus Samuel | Hartford |
| 7 | Leet Allen | Killingw. |
| 7 | Lambskins Benjⁿ | Kent |
| 1 | Lay Richard | Lyme |
| 6 | Asa Leiut. | Saybrook |
| 8 | Lung Joseph | Middletown |
| 7 | Lacey F. Fairchild | N. Fairfield |
| 5 | Josiah Capᵗ | Newtown |
| 6 | Levingsworth Eli Majʳ | N. Haven |
|   | Lines John | " |
| 1 | Leeds Thomas | Stonington |
| 1 | Lewis Valentine | " |
|   | Ebenezar | Wallingfor |
|   | Samuel Serjᵗ | Waterbury |
| 8 | Lunsbury Peter | Stamford |
|   | Larrebee Willet | Salisbury |
| 2 | Luce Jonathan | Tolland |
| 3 | Lilly Ebenezer | Union |
| 5 | Lamberten Obed | Windsor |
| 5 | Lawrence Amos | " |
|   | Littlefield Ebenʳ | Windham |
| A | Leverick Gabriel | Fairfield |
| 2 | Lockwood Gersham | Norwalk |
|   | Miner Silvester | N. London |
|   | James | " |
| 1 | Elihu | E. Haddam |
|   | Andrew | Tolland |
| 1 | Munro John | N. London |
| 1 | Manwaring George | " |
| 0 | Mallerson Benjⁿ | " |
|   | Mac Fall William | N. London |
| 9 | Merrils Cypron | N. Hartford |
| 9 | Aaron | " |
| 8 | Asher | Hebron |
|   | Cyprian | Farming. |
|   | Marcy Thomas | Ashford |
|   | Miller Daniel | Chatham |
| 3 | Daniel | " |
| 5 | John | Glassenb. |
| 3 | Charles Lᵗ | Hartford |
| 1 | Nathan | Lyme |
| 3 | Nathaniel | Weathersfᵈ |
| 4 | Markham Joseph | Chatham |
|   | MᶜCorn William | " |
| 1 | Matthews James | Danbury |
| 8 | William | Midletown |
| 7 | Robert | Newhaven |
| 1 | Mitchel Samuel | E Haddam |
| 2 | John Serjᵗ | Fairfield |
|   | George | Norwich |
| 1 | Murfe Thomas | E Haddam |
| 1 | Mott Samuel | E Haddam |
| 9 | Adam | Winchester |
| 6 | Mobs Piercey | E Haddam |
| 5 | Morehouse David | Fairfield |
| 7 | Meeker Steaphen | " |
| 2 | Daniel | " |

CONNECTICUT LINE, 1777-1781.   35

|   | Names | Town |
|---|---|---|
|   | Meeker Steaphen | Reading |
| 2 | Mills Joseph | Fairfield |
| D | Samuel Leiu$^t$ | Simsbury |
| 2 | Murry Abraham | Derbey |
|   | Noah Serj$^t$ | Kent |
| 6 | Moses Jonas | Derbey |
| 2 | Mix John | Farmington |
| A | Tim$^o$ Leiu$^t$ | Newhaven |
| 4 | Thomas Jun$^r$ | Wallingford |
| 8 | Momosuck Daniel | Farmington |
|   | M$^c$Dowel Alexand$^r$ En. | Glastenbury |
| 9 | M$^c$Lane Matthew | Groten |
|   | M$^c$ Donald John | " |
| 4 | M$^c$ Danield James | Preston |
| 7 | Miles Isaac Serj$^t$ | Goshun |
| A | John Leiu$^t$ | Newhaven |
| 7 | Charles Leiu$^t$ | Preston |
|   | Mattocks Sam$^{ll}$ | Hartford |
| 8 | Mahar James | " |
| 8 | Mize William | " |
|   | MacOrlander Leiu$^t$ | Hebron |
| 6 | M$^c$ Lane Jacobe | Salisbury |
| 4 | M$^c$ Gregor John Cap$^t$ | Plainfield |
| 1 | M$^c$ Censey James |   |
|   | alias George | Stonington |
| 2 | M$^c$ Anotter John | Stamford |
|   | Mauenborough Jedadiah | Hebron |
| 8 | Marble Thomas | " |
| 5 | Marshal Elisha | Harrington |
|   | More John Jun$^r$ | Kent |
| 8 | W$^m$ Jun$^r$ | Union |
| 5 | Mason John | Litchfield |
|   | Munger Daniel | " |
| 6 | Billey | Salisbury |
| 6 | Mather Elias Leiu$^t$ | Lyme |
|   | Maccoy Allexander | " |
| 6 | Meigs Return Col$^o$ | Midletown |
|   | Marks Comfort | " |
| 6 | Mansfield Jos$^h$ Cap$^t$ | Newhaven |
| 6 | Dan | " |
| 6 | John Leiu$^t$ | Wallingford |
|   | Munson W$^m$ Cap$^t$ | Newhaven |
| 6 | Levy Lieu$^t$ | Wallingford |
| 6 | Moultrup Joseph | Newhaven |
| 6 | Steaphen | Newhaven |
| 6 | Mallery Amos Corp$^l$ | " |
| A | Melone Daniel | " |
| 6 | Marten Lewis | " |
| 4 | George | Windham |
|   | Moss John | Newhaven |
| 6 | Daniel | " |
| 1 | Manning W$^m$ | Norwich |
| 2 | Phineas | Stafford |
|   | W$^m$ Cap$^t$ | Woodstock |
| 4 | Marsh Peter | Plainfield |
| 5 | Abner | Killingley |
| 1 | Meach Joshua | Preston |

| | Names | Town |
|---|---|---|
| 2 | Millington Sam[ll] | Stafford |
| 9 | Migat Zebulon | Weathersfield |
| 4 | Munn Isaiah | Colchester |
| 5 | Mead Jasper L[t] | Norwalk |
|   | Nash Eben[r] | Norwalk |
| 6 | Norten Benj[n] Ens[n] | Branford |
| A |   Jedadiah | Chatham |
| 7 |   Rufus Corp[l] | Guilford |
| 7 |   Elon | " |
| 5 |   Joseph | Goshun |
| 0 | Newton Isaac | E Windsor |
| 2 |   Elias | Tolland |
| 8 |   Ezekiel | Washington |
|   | Nickerson Urana | Greenwich |
| 6 | Niger Phillip | Guilford |
| 6 | Newel Robert | Saybrook |
| 7 | Nichols Sam[ll] | Newfairfield |
|   | Negro Briston | Saybrook |
|   |   Cuff | Colchester |
| 4 | Nelson Daniel | Suffield |
| 6 | Nugent John | Stonington |
| 8 | Nichols Sam[ll] | Norwalk |
| 6 | Otis Joseph | Branford |
| A | Oryon alias Rian Jerem | Danbury |
| 6 | Okeain Jeremiah | Derbey |
| 5 | Osburn Stratten | Fairfield |
|   | Oswold Col[o] | Farmington |
| 8 | Olmstead James Ens[n] | Hartford |
|   | Oharra Tim[o] | Newhaven |
| 7 | Orvis Eleazer | Norfolk |
|   | Olin W[m] | Norwich |
| 6 | Owen Eliphalet | Salsbury |
|   | Owen Alvin |   |
|   |   alias David Thrall | Windsor |
| 2 | Orcut Calib Serj[t] | Willington |
| 8 | Olds Aaron | Woodbury |
| 6 |   Oliver | Washington |
| 6 | Post Abner | Saybrook |
| 2 | Pool Daniel | Ashford |
| 6 | Potter Steaphen Cap[t] | Branford |
| 3 |   Lemuel Corp[l] | Farmington |
|   |   Israel Leiu[t] | Newhaven |
| 6 |   Moses | " |
| 4 | Pelton George | Chatham |
| 0 |   Eben[r] | Groten |
|   |   David | " |
| 2 |   Benj[n] | Guilford |
| 3 | Parks Daniel | Chatham |
|   | Price Levy | Cornwell |
|   |   Rufus Leiu[t] | Tollan |
|   | Picket Thomas | Danbury |
| 6 | Prichard James | Derbey |
| 8 |   George Jun[r] | Waterbury |
| A | Prindle J Enos | Derbey |
| 8 |   Abijah | Newtown |
| 2 | Porter Hezekiah | E Windsor |
| 9 |   Amos | Haddam |

## CONNECTICUT LINE, 1777–1781.

|   | Names | Town |
|---|---|---|
| 3 | Porter Eleazer | Hebron |
| 3 | Nathan | Mansfield |
| 5 | Daniel | Windsor |
| 2 | Pierce Daniel | E Windsor |
| 2 | Parsons David Cap* | Enfield |
| 2 | Jonathan | " |
| A | Theodocious | Greewich |
|   | Perkens Daniel Jun* | Enfield |
| 5 | Patching Elijah Corp* | Fairfield |
| 1 | Purcivael Paul Q M | Farmingtown |
| 6 | Powers James | " |
| 0 | Thomas | Midletown |
| 8 | Nathan | Woodstock |
|   | Pees Peter Serj* | Glastenbury |
| 1 | Pomp Samuel | Groten |
| 1 | Jacobe alias David | " |
|   | Peck Zebelon | Goshun |
| 2 | Silas | Lime |
|   | Silas Jun* | " |
| 0 | Ariel | Midletown |
|   | Darius Leiut | Norwich |
| A | Charles Serj* Aro | Wallingsford |
| 3 | Pomeroy Ralf Leiu* | Hartford |
|   | Benj* Doct* | Hebron |
| 7 | Phelps Charles | Hartland |
|   | Pieffer Lazarus | Hebron |
|   | Perry Silvanus | Killingsly |
| 7 | Elisha | Ridgfield |
|   | Eben* Serj* | Windham |
| 4 | Palmer Elijah | Lebanon |
| 5 | Benj* | Litchfield |
| 1 | W Jonathan Leu* | Stonington |
| 5 | Plant Timothy | Litchfield |
|   | Prentice Jonas Cap* | Newhaven |
|   | Parmele Jeremiah Cap* | Newhaven |
| A | Parker Edmond | " |
| 9 | Samuel | Stratford |
| 5 | John | " |
| 6 | Elisha | Wallingsford |
| 3 | Benj* | " |
|   | Eliab | Waterbury |
| 6 | Isaac | " |
| 7 | Peet Lemuel | Newmilford |
|   | Polly Alpheus | Lebanon |
| 7 | Plumb Ameriah | Norfolk |
| 1 | Peter | Norwich |
| 4 | Perigo W* | " |
| 0 | Pollard W* | " |
| 8 | Isaac | Woodbury |
| 1 | Pratt Ethan | Saybrook |
| 0 | Russel | Somers |
| 2 | Pearman Joseph | Suffield |
| 4 | Peters Peter | Stoningtown |
| 6 | Phillups Thomas | Stratford |
| 5 | Parkinson Dene | Stamford |
| 5 | Pellet Enos | Sharon |
| 2 | Preston Tiras | Tolland |
| 8 | Amasa | Waterbury |

## REVOLUTION LISTS AND RETURNS.

|   | Names | Town |
|---|---|---|
|   | Patterson Andrew | Tolland |
| 5 | Pinney Aaron | Windsor |
| 5 | Prior Abner Cap$^t$ | " |
| 7 | Page Tim° | Wallingsford |
|   | Parde Jonathan | Waterbury |
|   | Pendleton Daniel | " |
| 8 | Parrish Eliphas | Windham |
| 1 | Quindley Thomas | Newlondon |
| 4 | Quash Catoe | Colchester |
| 4 | Quy Libeus alias Negro | Norwich |
| 4 | Robertson James | Newlondon |
| 9 |   Ephraim | Coventry |
|   |   John | Midletown |
|   |   Jared Leiu$^t$ | Newhaven |
|   |   Samuel Q M | " |
| 6 |   Thomas | " |
| 4 |   Elias Leiu$^t$ | Windham |
|   |   Simeon Jun$^r$ | " |
| 1 |   Sam$^{ll}$ | " |
| 1 | Richards Steaphen | Newlondon |
| 1 |   W$^m$ Cap$^t$ | " |
| 4 | Rogers Peter | " |
| 1 |   Asael | E Haddam |
| A |   James | Greenwich |
| 1 |   Lemuel | Lime |
| 1 |   Joseph | " |
| 9 | Roberts Elisha | Newhartford |
| 3 |   Nathan | Colchester |
| 7 |   Benj$^a$ | Newfairfield |
|   |   Abial | Waterbury |
| 8 |   Joel | " |
| 8 | Ranne Jabesh | Chatham |
| 3 |   Steaphen | " |
| 4 | Rowley Jesse | Colchester |
|   | Roswell Jeremiah | Danbury |
|   | Rigs Laban | Derbey |
| 6 |   James | " |
| 2 | Raymond W$^m$ | Fairfield |
| 2 |   David | " |
|   |   Sam$^{ll}$ | Reading |
|   | Rows Amos | Farmington |
| 1 | Rouse Simeon alias Oliver | Preston |
| 7 |   Jabez Serj$^t$ | Windham |
| 8 | Rundle John | Greenich |
| 3 | Randol Elijah | Windham |
| A | Ritch Edward | Greenich |
| 9 | Risley Steaphen | Hartford |
| 7 | Reed Benj$^a$ | Hartland |
| 1 |   Enoch Cap$^t$ | Lime |
| 1 |   Nathan | Mansfield |
|   |   Ruben | Norwich |
| 4 |   Oliver | Pomphret |
| A | Rumbelo Thomas | Killingworth |
| 6 | Rosseter Sam$^{ll}$ | Litchfield |
|   | Roach John | Lime |
| 5 | Remmington Steaphen | Ridgfield |
| 4 | Rising James | Suffield |

CONNECTICUT LINE, 1777-1781.

| | Names | Town |
|---|---|---|
| 8 | Russel Giles Col° | Stonington |
| 8 | Wᵐ Junʳ | Stratford |
| 9 | Ashur | Weathersfield |
| 5 | Rust Jonathan | Sharon |
| 5 | Robbers Joseph | Voluntown |
| 9 | Riley John Leiuᵗ | Weathersfield |
| | Root Nathan Leiuᵗ | Willington |
| 8 | Rice Nehemiah Capᵗ | Waterbury |
| | David | Willington |
| 7 | Ripley Charles Serjᵗ | Windham |
| 2 | Rood Simeon | Woodbury |
| A | Ryon Jeremiah alias Green (?) Junʳ | Redding & Danbury |
| | Steaphens Aaron | Newhartford |
| | Peter Junʳ | Canterbury |
| | Roswell | Farmington |
| 3 | Tim° | Glastenbury |
| | Aaron Capᵗ | Killingsworth |
| 2 | Peter | " |
| 6 | Wᵐ | Newhaven |
| 6 | Elijah | Saybrook |
| | Seymour Elias discharged | Newhartford |
| | Shipman John | Saybrook |
| | Samuel Leuᵗ | " |
| 2 | James Serjᵗ | " |
| | Stannard Jasper | " |
| 5 | Samuel | Litchfield |
| 3 | Smith Peter | Ashford |
| 3 | Abijah | " |
| 6 | Jordan | Branford |
| 4 | Ezra Leuᵗ | Chatham |
| D | Asaph | Farmington |
| 3 | David | " |
| 0 | John Leiuᵗ | Haddam |
| | George Ensⁿ | Hartford |
| 5 | Henery | Litchfield |
| 4 | Enoch | Lime |
| 6 | Wᵐ Leiuᵗ | Milford |
| 3 | John Junʳ | Mansfield |
| 6 | Ambrus | Newhaven |
| 5 | Henery | Pomphret |
| | Job Leiuᵗ | Ridgfield |
| 1 | Daniel | Stoningtown |
| 8 | Isaac | Stamford |
| 5 | Isaac Junʳ | " |
| 7 | Daniel | Wallingford |
| 7 | John | Waterbury |
| 8 | Levy | " |
| | Samuel | " |
| 8 | David Major | " |
| | James | Windham |
| 2 | Daniel Corpᵗ | Woodstock |
| 2 | Spaldin Ephraim | Ashford |
| | Shaw William | Canterbury |
| 4 | Jonathan | " |
| | Benjⁿ | " |
| 4 | Richard | Stoningtown |
| 5 | Schallem Abraham Serjᵗ | Chatham |
| 0 | Stocken Marshal | " |

|   | Names | Town |
|---|---|---|
| 1 | Stark Tim⁰ | Colchester |
| 1 | Samuel | " |
|   | Steaphen | " |
|   | Steaphen | Hebron |
|   | Simons Isaac | Infield |
| 9 | Eli | Colebrook |
| 8 | Simmons Samuel | Cornwall |
|   | James | Stonington |
| 7 | Swift Heman Colʳ | Cornwall |
|   | Robert | Groten |
| 6 | Strong Eliakim Serjᵗ | Durham |
| 7 | John Serjᵗ | Guliford |
| 1 | Barnabas | Lebanon |
| 5 | David Leiuᵗ | Sharon |
| 6 | Phineas | Salisbury |
| 6 | Seward Samuel | Durham |
|   | Daniel | Milford |
|   | Wᵐ | " |
| 6 | Nathan | Waterbury |
| 6 | Squire Saxton D M | Durham |
| 6 | Abiathur | " |
|   | S. Samuel | Farmingtown |
| 6 | Daniel | Newhaven |
| A | Stent. Samuel | " |
|   | Spencer David Leiuᵗ | E Haddam |
|   | Obediah | Hartford |
| 1 | Ichabud Leiuᵗ | Lime |
|   | Salley James | E Haddam |
| 2 | Sturges Moses Leiuᵗ | Fairfield |
| 8 | Steel Josiah | Farmingtown |
|   | Smithers William | Glastenbury |
| 7 | Simbo Prince | " |
| 0 | Staunten Amos Capᵗ | Groten |
| 4 | Suntsemun Aaron | " |
|   | Speers John | " |
|   | Starts alias States | " |
| 6 | Sharper Tuis | " |
|   | Sharp Joseph | Milford |
| 4 | Benjamin | Pomphret |
| 0 | Sterry Silas | Groten & Preston |
| 1 | Solomon Amos | Groten |
|   | Shortman William | " |
| 4 | Sholes Nathan | " |
| 5 | Sealey John | Goshun |
| 8 | Segwick Samuel | Hartford |
| 8 | Scot Elijah | Harwington |
| 2 | Shelley alias Kellᵞ John | Litchfield |
| 1 | Lemuel | Stoningtown |
| 8 | Ebenʳ Serjᵗ | Stratford |
| 5 | Stone Josiah alias Joseph | Litchfield |
|   | David | Wallingford |
| 1 | Sill David Colᵒ | Lime |
| 1 | Selden Ezra Capᵗ | " |
| 4 | Saunders John | " |
| 7 | Wᵐ Serjᵗ | Newfairfield |
| 6 | Sawyer Asa | Lime |
| 0 | Sullard Jacobe | " |

CONNECTICUT LINE, 1777-1781.                      41

| | Names | Town |
|---|---|---|
| 4 | Sumner John Col° | Midletown |
| 0 | Savage Abijah Cap⁺ | " |
| 6 | Starr David Leiu⁺ | " |
| 1 | Josiah Col° | Newmilford |
| 6 | Sizer Jonathan | Midletown |
| 6 | Steward John | Milford |
| 8 | Sanford Sam¹¹ Cap⁺ | " |
| 6 | Thomas | Newhaven |
| 7 | James | Newlondon |
|   | Ezekiel | Waterbury |
| 1 | Shumway John Cap⁺ | Mansfield |
|   | Sherman Wᵐ Cap⁺ | Newhaven |
| 6 |   John Leiu⁺ | " |
|   | Sperry Chauncey | " |
| 6 | Sugden Abraham | " |
| 6 | Stockwell Abel | " |
| A | Simpson Robert | " |
| 6 | Shepard John | " |
| 7 | Stilwell Steaphen | Newmilford |
| 7 | Sturdevant Nathan | Norfolk |
|   | Sydleman John | Norwich |
|   | Spicer Samuel | " |
| 1 | Stilman Robert | " |
|   | Starkweather Asa | " |
| 4 | Stoddard Joshua | Plainfield |
| 3 |   Enoch | Weathersfield |
| 8 |   Nathan Cap⁺ | Woodbury |
| 8 |   Ely | " |
| 4 | Shadden John | Pomphret |
|   | Stoel Elisha | " |
|   | Seers Obediah | Preston |
| 5 | Sherwood Nehemiah | Reading |
| 2 | Speers Elijah | Suffield |
| 4 | Sowas Richard | Stoningtown |
|   | Searl Constant | " |
|   | Suncheman Nath¹¹ | " |
| A | Sunderland John | Stratford |
|   | Scofield Selah | Stanford |
| 5 | S⁺ John James | " |
| 2 | Sabens Nehemiah | Tolland |
| 3 | Summit Prince | Voluntown |
|   | Sprague James Leiu⁺ | Union |
| 6 | Shaler Joseph Leiu⁺ | Wallingford |
| 8 | Southmaid | Waterbury |
|   | Scovel Steaphen | " |
| 9 |   Steaphen | Winchester |
| D | Shelden Elisha Col° | Sharon |
| 5 | Scribner Asa | Norwalk |
|   | Thomas Abselom | Newlondon |
| 5 |   Steaphen | Chatham |
| 3 |   Patrick | Hartford |
| A |   John | Newhaven |
| 6 |   Samuel | " |
|   |   James | " |
| 6 |   Ephraim | " |
| 5 | Taylor John | Newhartford |
| 5 |   Baruck | Fairfield |

| | Names | Town |
|---|---|---|
| 8 | Taylor Ephraim | Hebron |
| 3 |     Thomas | Union |
| 8 |     Simeon | Woodbury |
| 6 | Towner Jacobe | Branford |
| 2 | Tickens Tiras | Canterbury |
| 4 | Tarble W$^m$ | Colchester |
| 7 | Tanner Tryal Leiu$^t$ | Cornwall |
| 8 | Thomson Nathaniel Serj$^t$ | Coventry |
| A |     Isaiah Leiu$^t$ | Farmington |
| 6 |     David Serj$^t$ | Guilford |
| D |     Appiphras | Saybrook |
|  | Tomlinson David Ens$^n$ | Derbey |
| 9 | Treat John | Glastenbury |
| 3 | Tryon Ezra | " |
| A | Townd John | Greenich |
| 6 | Teal Sam$^{ll}$ | Guilford |
| 5 | Tuttle Levey | Litchfield |
| 8 |     Ezekiel | Waterbury |
|  |     Tim$^o$ | Waterbury |
| 8 |     Jabez | " |
|  |     Tim$^o$ Ens$^n$ | " |
|  |     Hezekiah |  |
|  |     Peter | Norwalk |
| 7 | Trowbridge John Serj$^t$ | Newfairfield |
| 6 |     John Leiu$^t$ | Newhaven |
| 5 |     Eben$^r$ | Newmilford |
| A | Troop John Leiu$^t$ | Newhaven |
| 4 |     Benj$^n$ Maj$^r$ | Norwich |
| 6 | Tolls Elnathan | Newhaven |
| 3 | Tounsend Solomon | " |
| A | Todd Yale | " |
| 7 | Tubs Nathan | Norfalk |
|  | Tracey Hezekiah Leiu$^t$ | Norwich |
| 1 |     W$^m$ Ens$^n$ | " |
| 4 |     Moses | " |
| 1 | Tyler Nathan | Preston |
| 6 | Tooley Andrew | Saybrook |
| 6 | Tupper W$^m$ Corp$^l$ | Salisbury |
| 5 | Thrall David alias Alven Owen | Windsor |
| 8 | Thayr Asa | Waterbury |
| 8 | Terril Joel | " |
|  | Trowbridg Sam$^{ll}$ | Norwalk |
| 8 | Taylor Elijah | " |
| 3 | Verry Jonathan | Chatham |
| 8 | Vaun Daniel | Lebanon |
| 6 | Verguson John | Newhaven |
| 8 | Upson Ezekiel | Waterbury |
| 4 | Wright Elisha | Newlondon |
| 3 |     John | Chatham |
| 8 |     Simeon | Hebron |
|  |     Isaiah | " |
| 5 |     James | Litchfield |
|  |     Ezekiel | Norwich |
|  | Weekes Joseph | Newlondon |
| 1 | Wiley Edward | " |
| 1 | Willey Jonathan | E Haddam |
| 4 | Wales Eben$^r$ Leiu$^t$ | Ashford |

| | Names | Town |
|---|---|---|
| 3 | Waters Wᵐ | Ashford |
| A | Wᵐ | Greenwich |
| 3 | Warren John | Bolten |
| 8 | Abraham | Farmingtown |
| 6 | White John Ensⁿ | Branford |
| 6 | Joseph | Derbey |
| 6 | Samuel | Newhaven |
| 6 | Oliver | Saybrook |
| 8 | Wood Jacobe | Chatham |
| 3 | Lemuel | Enfield |
| 6 | Elisha | Newhaven |
| 2 | Thomas | Somers |
| 3 | Whitney Daniel S M | Colchester |
| | Henery P M | Derbey |
| 4 | Williams John | Colchester |
| 1 | Thomas | E Hadam |
| A | Richard | Fairfield |
| 0 | Henery Leiuᵗ | Groten |
| 0 | Uriah Serjᵗ | Groten |
| 9 | Danˡˡ Serjt | Weathersfield |
| 8 | Obed | Waterbury |
| | Wix Uriah | Cornwall |
| 4 | Wack Frederick | Colchester |
| 6 | Warner Ebenʳ Serjᵗ | Derbey |
| 3 | Robert Capᵗ | Midletown |
| 6 | Worster Henery | Derbey |
| | Thomas Capᵗ | Newhaven |
| 2 | Washburn Benjᵃ | Derbey |
| 8 | Samuel | Stratford |
| 6 | Watrus Richard | Derbey |
| 6 | Wakeley Jonathan | " |
| 1 | Watken Ephraim | Easthadam |
| 1 | Wheeler Joshua | " |
| 6 | Thomas | Guilford |
| 5 | David | Stonington |
| 0 | Wallace Abʳᵐ | Eastwindsor |
| 0 | Wadsworth J B Doctʳ | " |
| 5 | Roger Leuᵗ | Hartford |
| 2 | Ware Danˡˡ Serjᵗ | Enfield |
| 2 | Webb Hezekiah | Fairfield |
| | Jonathan | Norwich |
| A | Gideon | Wallingford |
| 4 | Nathˡˡ Capᵗ | Windham |
| D. | Wainwright Samˡˡ | Farmington |
| 7 | Thomas | Sharon |
| | Willcox James | Farmington |
| | James | Harwington |
| 8 | Welten Benjᵃ | Farmington |
| | Steaphen Junʳ | Waterbury |
| | Webster Joshua Serjᵗ | Glastenbury |
| A | Wessels Herculus | Greenwich |
| A | Wilson David | " |
| 1 | George | Lime |
| 6 | John | Newhaven |
| A | Warrin Henery Leiuᵗ | Greenwich |
| A | Whiting Samˡˡ Leiuᵗ | " |
| 3 | Whitmore Lemuel Sᵗ | " |

| | Names | Town |
|---|---|---|
| 7 | Wyard Thomas | Goshun |
| 3 | Wyllys Sam[ll] Col[o] | Hartford |
| 4 | Eben[r] | Midletown |
| 6 | Joseph | " |
| 5 | Wattles Roswell Serj[t] | Hartford |
| | Way Hammon | " |
| 3 | Walters Thomas | " |
| | Walter W[m] | |
| D | Silas | Newhaven |
| 1 | Woodworth Jedadiah | Norwich |
| 4 | Benj[n] | Lebanon |
| | Ward William | " |
| 1 | Waid John | Lime |
| | Marten | " |
| 7 | Wilder Aaron | Newfair[d] |
| D | Wilds Jonathan | Newhaven |
| 7 | Wilkeson Iccabud | Newmilford |
| 9 | Jesse | Winchester |
| | Whitley W[m] | Newmilford |
| 7 | Watson Tetus Cap[t] | Norfolk |
| 1 | Waterman Eben[r] Jun[r] | Norwich |
| | Wedge Joshua | " |
| 9 | Warden Isaac | Saybrook |
| 1 | Walter | Stoningtown |
| 7 | Waterhouse Steaphen | Saybrook |
| 2 | Widger John | " |
| 3 | Woodbridg Theoph[l] | Simsbury |
| 5 | Woodward Oliver | " |
| | Woodward Oliver | Windsor |
| 8 | Walker Nathan[ll] | Stafford |
| A | Robert Cap[t] | Stratford |
| 8 | Elisha | Woodbury |
| | Nathan alias Zacheriah | " |
| 2 | Wallbridg Ames Maj[r] | Stafford |
| 1 | West John | Stoningtown |
| | Joseph | Windham |
| 2 | Wardwell Jacobe | Stamford |
| 8 | W[m] | " |
| 2 | Weed Benj[n] | " |
| 5 | Thadeus Leiu[t] | " |
| | Western Benj[n] Ens[n] | Weathersfield |
| 9 | Wells Joshua | " |
| 5 | Wedg Josoph | Windsor |
| 5 | Wing Samuel | " |
| | Waldow Albigence | Windham |
| 8 | Welch Luke | Woodbury |
| | Micael | Washington |
| | Moses Wairing | Norwalk |
| | Wilcox Elias | " |
| 8 | Williams John | " |
| 1 | Yerrington Jesse | Groten |
| 7 | Yale Waitotite | Sharon |
| | Nash | Wallingford |
| | Yates W[m] | Salisbury |
| | Zander Gad | Newhaven |

The Characters annexed to the Names of the Men in carrying the Supplies into the Acc[ts] to denote what Reg[t] they belong to viz:

| | | |
|---|---|---|
| 1[st] Regt . . . 1 | Col[o] Webb's . | 9 |
| 2 Do . . . 2 | Col[o] Shirburn's . | 0 |
| 3[d] Do . . . 3 | L[t] Dragoons . | D |
| 4[th] Do . . . 4 | Artillery . . | A |
| 5[th] Do . . . 5 | | |
| 6[th] Do . . . 6 | | |
| 7[th] Do . . . 7 | | |
| 8[th] Do . . . 8 | | |

[Indorsed] Alphabet of Family Supplies in 1777, 8 & 9.
Alphabetical List of Persons in the Connecticut Line who rec[d] Family Supp[s] before 1780

[*State Library, Revolution* 30, 1.]

## RETURNS OF MEN IN SERVICE, 1777-1779.

[The Archives relating to the Revolution volume 30, numbers 51-147, consist of returns from the various towns, giving particularly the names of soldiers serving in the Continental Line from these towns whose families had received supplies from the town during the years 1777, 1778, 1779. Many of the returns give, in addition to those whose families had received supplies, the names of other soldiers serving from the respective towns during those years. The names of those whose families had received supplies are carefully checked with a cross, and such names comprise the "Alphabetical List" which forms the first document in the same volume of the Archives, and is printed in this volume beginning on page 21. The names of such soldiers as are not thus checked are here given under their respective towns.]

### ASHFORD

Names of Officers and Soldiers Single

Daniel Eldrige Lei[t]
Benj[a] Dimmuck Se[r]
Samuel Allen
Lemuel Allen
David Peck
Dyer Brown
Ephraim Aery In the Light Dragoons
Jason Crofford
Joseph Ingly
Jonathan Crane
Comfort Tyler
Jedediah Smith
Abijah Brooks J[r] Dead
Eleaser Russell
John Lane
Eleaser Smith
Asa Davison Dead
Elias Dimmuck
Elias Robinson
Jonathan Bullock
Paul Davison
Joseph Snell

John Watkins
Stephen Eaton
Robert Patterson
James Hale
Josiah Bicknall
William Southworth
Joseph Southworth
James Eaton
Eleasor Owen
Robart Hale
Caleb Hendee Ju[r] In his Excellency Gen[ll] Washingtons Gard
Joseph Hunter
Joshua Knowlton
James Grant
Chester Rogers
Amos Dowsett
Lawrence Dowsett
Tytus Prescoot Negro Dead
Tone Smith Negro
Aaron Keyes Negro

### CANAAN

Col. Swifts Reg[t]
Simon Tubbs
Isac Smith
Samson Hunt
John Curtis
Richard Bishop
Joseph Cowles

Col. Chandlers or Rusels Reg[t]
Serj. Joshua Whitney
Thomas Stevens
William Mix
Serj. Elias Lee
Stephen Stevens
Warren Grizwold Deceased
Abner Miller
Bille Laurance
David Preston

## COLCHESTER

Gideon Chapman
Asahel Newton Jun'
Ezekiel Daniels
John Smith
Gideon Fox
Amos Fox
John Hall
Cuff Wells
Dolphin Kellogg
Esau Kellogg
Joshua Frank
Hendrick Townsend
Asher Carter
James Dodge
Nehemiah Daniels
Joshua Isham
Jeremiah Stanton

Jesse Brown
Ephraim Deathic(?) Ju
John Roberts
Robert Douglas
Frederic Bowman
Nathan Scovel Jun'
Joseph Thompson
William Jones
Samuel Loomis Ju'
Thomas Pilgrim
James Morgan Jun'
William Gardner
Charles Brown
Ebenezer Billings
Israel Johnson
Joseph Whood (?)
Elijah Taylor

## CORNWALL

Abraham Grimes
Peres Bonney
Joshua Hartshorn
Silas Dibble
} Those were Detached the 26th July 1778 to serve till the 15th of Jan<sup>y</sup> 1780

## DANBURY

[The following men received bounty.]

Ezra Ketcham
David Hall
Thad' Starr
John Barnum
Noah Barnum
Will<sup>m</sup> M°Lean
Noah Taylor
Natha<sup>ll</sup> Robinson
Roben Negro
Variah Negro

James Guthery
Jesse Peck
Joshua Taylor
Will<sup>m</sup> Griffeth
Jonath<sup>n</sup> Dickeman
Benja<sup>n</sup> Sillick
Will<sup>m</sup> Porter
Ebenezer Barnum
John Curtis
Collins Chapman

## DERBY

Reuben Blake
David Chapman
David Hull

Daniel Nichols
Charles Perkins

The Above five Men are now serving in the Continental Army have not Received any bounty from the Town

[The following men received bounty.]

Joseph Smith
Eleazer Durand
Gawham (? Garsham) Bardsley
John Dow

William Whitney
John Allen
Thomas Cook
Joseph Fairchild

Philo Lewis (?)
William Smith
James Luch
George Waterous
Levi Chatfield
Benjamin Black
Abner Riggs
Walter Wooster
Philow Wooding
Amos Fox

Thomas Phillips
Bether Nicols
John Hatchet
Edward Warren
Andrew Waterous
Moses Reggs
Daniel Brown
Jeremiah Woodin
Joseph Tomlinson
Ebenezer Durand

## EAST WINDSOR

Soldiers in the Continental army now in service E: Windsor

### North Society Sould''

Francis Baxter
Alex' Tomson
Erastus Booth
Elnath⁰ Fitch
John Hadlock
John Pierce

John Bissel
Israel Orsborn
Aaron Fargo
Moses Elsworth
Zepheniah Baits
Abel M⁰Intire

### Elenton Soulders

L⁺ Josiah Brown
Doct' B Wadsworth
Serj⁺ Warham Foster
Russel Prat
Will^m Anderson
Zedekiah Peek
Sam^ll Taylor
Dan^ll Pierce
Elihu Bissel
Stephen Bartlet
W^m Brown
Jude Brown
Levi Charter
John Indian

Abram Wallis
Chancy Foster
John Taylor Jun'
W^m Wallis
Hez Elsworth
Abner Slade
David Clark
Ezra Leonard
Benoni Hills
John Newel ffilr (?)
Zebulon Burroos
Joseph Kingsberry
Eliphalet Lord
Benj^a Hubbard Ind^n

### East Windsor 1st Parish Soldiers

L⁺ Erast. Wolcutt Pris'
Abiel Allin
Tomo Chapin
John Gaylord
W^m Jones
Leonard Munro
Mark Filly
Sam^ll Hadlock
Thom^s Raymond
Jonath Fowler

Christopher Horton
Elijah Churchil
Israel Strong
Step^n Dorman
Hez Porter
Leonard Rogers
Abel Negro
Gurdon Munsil
Porter Negro

[The families of Bissel, Beaman, Andrss, Grant and Wadsworth appear to have received supplies, although the names are not checked in the list.]

## ENFIELD

Serj$^t$ Jabez Parsons
Benj$^a$ Butler
Tho$^s$ Root Jun$^r$
Othniel Allen
Eben$^r$ Pease 3$^d$
Simeon Pease
Benj$^m$ Henington
John Ward
Tho$^s$ Hale Jun$^r$
Hiram Hall
Amasa Allen
David Bullen Ju$^r$
David Phelps Jun$^r$
Eben$^r$ Aames

Isaac Markham
Tho$^s$ Justus Davis
John Graham
William Thomson
Nathan [iel ?] Ros [e ?]
John Delaney
Benj$^m$ Baxter
Joel M$^c$ griggry
Benj$^a$ Bugbee
James Erl
Levi Terry
Isaac French
Jared Simons
James Russel

## FARMINGTON

Ezekial Curtis Eight Months Man
Sol$^n$ Welton Eight Months Man

Hezekiah Stanley
William Davice
Serj$^t$ Luke Wadsworth
Thomas Green
Ebenezer Lee
Samuel Adams
Hartwell Barns
Samuel Coe
Zeb$^a$ Woodruff
Josiah Lensley
Steph$^a$ Brunson
Thomas Collet
John Corner
Timothy Wells
Elisha Wells
James Tayler
Wise Barns
Hosea Gridley
Asa Brunson Ju$^r$
William Lee
Elijah Porter
Paul Welman
Serj$^t$ Joel Smith
Phinehas Judd
Cornelius Dunham Ju$^r$
Mark Mildrum
Jason Hitchcock
Sam$^l$ Hitchcock
Elisha Heart
Tim$^o$ Heart
Steph$^a$ Hotchkiss
Roger Lewis
David Jasroms
Levi Frisby
David Enos
Benoni Brunson

Tim$^o$ Bibbins
Isaac Byington
James Foster
James Mitchel
Joseph Patterson
Semion Persons
Asher Heacox
David Heyden Jun$^r$
James Cole
Ebn$^r$ Hills
W$^m$ Smiley
James Tryon
Israel Winchel
John Smith
James Couch
Amos Barns
Mark Newell
Bliss Heart
Prince Negro
Joshua Smith
Steph$^a$ Chapman
Isaac Hall Negro
Sol$^a$ Tuttle
Sol$^a$ Buck
Sam$^l$ Ingham
Corp$^l$ Ichabod Hawley
Normon Newell
Jese Mathews
Hubbard Mathews
Pharoah Gomer
Dan$^l$ Allyn Negro
Moses Merriman
Eben$^r$ Darren
W$^m$ Woodruff
Levi Hatchcock
Reubin Cole

4

Elisha Linkton
Aaron Mores
Eliakim White
Gad Negro
Dick Negro
John Andrus
Josiah Cole
Kitt Moore
Joel Welton
Elix' Dorchester
Elijah Royce
Elisha Webster
Robert Cook
George S¹ George
Abel Scipeo
Ira Winchel
Luther Adkins
Lemuel Potter
Nathan Gellett
Roswell Webster
Sam¹ Comstick
W⁼ Mathews
Ichabod Bailey
Reuben Heart
Reuben Peck

Tom Negro
Charles Woodruff
Elisha Bailey
Liverpole Wadsworth Negro
Elijah Heart
Nathan Savage
John Wintworth Strong
Jacob Teal
Jonth⁸ Lankton Negro
Jonth⁸ Brigham
Joseph Teal
Barabas Clark
Jeremiah Gillett
Prince Denison
Peter Keehole
W⁼ Robbards
Salmon (?) Root
Levi Hamlin
Isaac Fisk
Riverius Newell
Constant Robbards
Thomas Twist
Mingo
Paul Williams
Simion Adams

## GOSHEN

Stephen Mix
Simeon Hall Deceased

York Negro Deceased
John Willoughby Deserted

## GROTON

Serg¹ Eben' Morgan
Serg¹ Daniel Nikerson
Serg¹ Joseph Bently
Joseph Cornish
Jesse Starr
John Pemberton
Moses Stoddard
Sam¹ Backer
Cuff Negrow
Abel Wassonks
Isaac Rogers
Joseph Meson
Joseph Queekets
George Buckmaster
Elisha Avery
George Avery J'
Wheler Shouls
Amos Latham
John Burnham
W⁼ Paul
Asa Baley
John Pomp
Cato Robison
Abraham Pharoah

Serg¹ Robert Allyn
Serg¹ Tho⁸ Malison
Bildad Edward
Andrew Wiger
Robert Williams
Tho⁸ Williams
Andrew Backer
Daniel Wiger
W⁼ Davis
Jonathan Ruff
John Dabol 3ᵈ
Andrew Forseth
Diariah Elderkin
John Williams
Solomon Williams
Nath⁸ Williams
Nath⁸ Smith
Ezekiel Billing
Sim⁸ Comstock
Gilbert Edgcom
Roswil Parish
Natha¹ Noys
Chris' Chester
Joseph Willey

CONNECTICUT LINE, 1777-1781. 51

Wᵐ Devenport
Nathˡ Solomon
Jack Negro
Israel Brown
Robert Stanton
Rufus Holdredge
Jacob Williams
Joseph Williams
David Fanning
Nathan Fanning
Thoˢ Gallup
Prentice Gallup
Elisha Stoddard
Lemuel Chester
Ralph Williams
Jonathan Mongo
Asa Lamb
Joseph Colver
Thoˢ Fanning

Nathan Stoddard
Nathanel Bellows
Gershom Brown
Fraderic Park
Aaron Sholes
James Park
Constant Avery
Benjⁿ Petice
James Pelton
Danel Stoddard
Danel Holway
Cyrus Killam
Fraderick Stoddard
Ebenʳ Pollerd
James Pattison
Miner Allyn
Fraderick Fanning
John Brown

## GUILFORD

George Ranney
Amos Hall
Abraham Woodard
Nathan Megs
Ebinezer Hoadley
Thomas Hall
Benjamin Waterous
James Wand
Ebinezer Cook
Jared Chittenden
Bela Scovel
Chandler Renton
Benjamin Kirkham
William Kirkham
Ambrous Norton
William Stone
Gad Negro
Jonathan Nonesuch
Nathˡˡ Smith
Thomas Sanford
Jonothan Parker
William Bayley
Jehial Doud
Jonathan Arnall

Solomon Doud
Cuff Negro
David Adhins
Moses Hill
William Chittenden
William Rowleson
Timothy Stephens
Samuel Akerly
Samuel Teal
Zebulon Benton
Xyper Tyley
Torrey Scrantom
Benjamin Crampton
Timothy Scrantom
Joel Bishop
Elnathan Seward
Calvin Crampton
Josiah Adkins
Joseph Terrey
William Beadle
Jonothan Wilcox
Isaac Hotchkiss
Nathˡˡ Smith
Pompy Negro

## HADDAM

A List of Soldiers Belonging the Town of Haddam in the Continental Army that had no families to be Supplyed

Serᵗ John Baily
Serᵗ Jeremy Baily
Cesor Chapman
Shumer Wilcox Dead
William Porter dead
William Baily

Timothy Smith Deserted
James Smith deserted
Timothy Brainerd deserted
David Thomas deserted
James Brooks
Joseph Porter

Wells Smith
Abner Porter Discharged
Aaron Porter dead
Ashbil Bradly
John Nickols
Cudjo Negro
Ebenezer Wilcox dead
London Sawyer
Nathᡃ Cook
Jesse Cone
Stephen Burr
Hezʰ Clark

Henry Smith
Lemuel Pratt
Christopher Baily
Timothy Baily
Gurdon Baily
Noadiah Cone
Serᵗ Lowdon Baily
Daniel Crane
Oliver Cone Deserted
Jerathmeul Bonfoy Deserted
Seth Spencer
Wᵐ Clark

## HARTFORD

Battalion Men that have received nothing but Bounty

Peter Philips
Stephen Fox
Elijah Porter
Moses Porter
Jonathan Arnold
John Vibart
Eliphalet Hills
David Wood
Samuel Easton
Levy Risley
Seth Kellogg
John Whiting Jʳ
William Whiting
Jonathan Shepard
Isaac Merrill
Benjᵃ Flowers
John Turner
James Chadwick
Joseph Day
John Adams
John Watson Jʳ
David McLean
James Parks
Grove Kellogg

Thomas Spencer
Hezekiah Goodwin
Asa Seymour
Thomas Wells
Timothy Andruss
Abdiel Flowers
Wᵐ Whistler
Zadock Sealey
Robert Culbert
Richᵈ Jackson
Daniel Miller
Benjᵃ Jobb
Wᵐ Henry
Wᵐ Tryon.
Benjᵃ Webster
Robert Stiles Junʳ
Davis Johnson
Simeon Hosmer
Asa Bunce
William Hinsdale
James Barnard
Horrace Kellogg
Theodore Chamberlain

## KILLINGWORTH

Lieuᵗ Joseph Willcox
Serjᵗ George Griswold
Serjᵗ Caleb Turner
Serjᵗ William Linn
Serjᵗ Nathaniel Crane
Corpˡ Philip Redfield
Drumʳ Barnabus Wellman
Drumʳ James Parmele
Fifer Benjamin Wright
Benjamin Tooly
Asa Buel
Reuben Chittenden
James Chittenden
Zenas Griswold

Jesse Jones
John Kelcey
Samˡˡ Nettleton
Elias Redfield
Daniel Willcox
John Crane
Paul Wellman
John Wellman
Oliver Kelcey
Hubbel Steevens
Benjamin Pelton
William Gaylor
William White
Abel Hull

CONNECTICUT LINE, 1777–1781.

John Chittenden
John Lewes
Edward Griffin
John Chatfield
William Wellman
Oliver Teal
Constant Parmele
Reuben Wright

Joseph Hull
Daniel Dwolf
Giles Willcox
Joshua Kelcey
George Hull
Joseph Teal
Richard Jackson
Joel Crane

The following is an account of those that are Dead & Discharged

Serj⁏ Orel Turner Died April y⁰ 8 1777
Hollum Nettelton Died May y⁰ 10 1777
John Hall Died August y⁰ 23 1777
Eber Chittenden Died January y⁰ 26 1778
Joh William Died March 1778
Silvanus Merry Died March y⁰ 24 1778
Stephen Blachly Died April y⁰ 8 1778
Jensourah Evarts Died January y⁰ 9 1778
Zepheniah Clark Died Septem⁏ 1777
William Nettelton Died January y⁰ 7 1778
William Tooly Ded
John Tooly Dead
Daniel Carter Dead
Tites Teal Dead
Abraham Steevens Discharg⁰
Samuel Steevens Discharg⁰
Eliakim Steevens Discharg⁰
Simon Steevens Deserted

## LITCHFIELD

Ephraim Bates L D.              Jn⁰ Shether Capt. L D.

Alphabetical List of Soldiers who have already or probably may hereafter receive the said annual Pay of 20/ p⁏ Month Viz.

[That amount was voted by the town April 15, 1777, to each soldier who should inlist to make up the towns quota of 92. The families of those checked (x) received supplies.]

Giles Alcock
Cash Africa
John Bottom
Enos Barns 2
Enos Barns 3ᵈ
Ambrose Barns
James Columbus
Abial Canfield
Simon Crosby
John Cowl
Eldad Camp
Dyar Cleaveland
Abel Culver
Isaac Clough
Putnam Catlin
Reuben Craw
Joseph Collyer
Rufus Fancher
John Farnam

Aaron Fox
Sylvanus Graves
Isaac Grant
George Hamilton
Amos Herick
Tucker Hart
Abel Hitchcock
Medad Hotchkiss
John Johnson
Samuel Kilborn
Abraham Kilborn
David Kilborn
Peter Kelcy
x John Kelly
Jared Knapp
John Larow
x John Mason
Ashbel Mason
Eli Mix

Nicholas Manjent
x Daniel Munger
x Benjamin Palmer
　Paul Price
x Timothy Plant
　Isaac Parker
x Samuel Rossetter
　John Royal
　Thomas Roberts
　Simeon Ross
x Josiah Stone
　Jonathan Smith
　John Smith
x Henry Smith
　David Seelye
　John Seelye
　Seeley
　John Simpson
x Samuel Stannard
　Enoch Sperry
　David Strickland
　John Sweet
x Levi Tuttle

Benjamin Taylor
Samuel Todd
John Vaughn
Samuel Vaughan
Samuel Waugh
Thaddeus Waugh
Samuel Woodcock
James Wright
Philemon Wilcocks
Ebed Meleck
Jack Negro
George Dixon
Reuben Smith
Thomas Owen
Isaac Trowbridge
Benjamin Bissell
William Sales
Anthony M°Daniel
John Breck
Asa Laraby
Willet Laraby
Peter Hawley
Adam Stevenson

## MANSFIELD

[All of the following named persons received a grant of additional pay from the town. There are no check marks against those of whom it is noted that their families received supplies, to indicate that the names have been carried into the other list.]

John Dextor
Charles Wood
Joshua Bennet
Aaron Royce
Elijah Royce
Luther Chaimberlane
Benj⁵ Lylley
Nathan Reed
John Turnor
John Bugbe
Steaphen Dunham
Josiah Conant Jun⁵
Jonathan Fenton
John Smith
John Eldredg
Asael Dunham
Lummim Case
Darius Dextor deceased
James Dextor
Roger Freeman
Luther Eaton
John Baker
John Hartshorn Jun⁵
Jacobe Barrows
Iccabud Hovey
Benajah Geer
John Abbe
Nath¹¹ Cary Jun⁵

John Marten
Ashur Allen
Phineas Allen
Diarca Allen
Samuel Conant deceased
Calib Conant
Elijah Baldwine
W⁵ Dodg
Willord Church
Jonathan Nichols Jun⁵
Ezra Phelps
Benj⁵ Bugbe
Amariah Crane
W⁵ Storrs
Jeremiah Gillit
Bigsbe Rogers
Nathan Porter
John Balch Jun⁵
Eben⁵ Snow Jun⁵
Jonathan Snow
Joshua Basset
Joshua Davis
James Strong
Daniel B. Perkens
Daniel Bosworth
Josiah Burt
John Harris

CONNECTICUT LINE. 1777-1781.

Supplies for the Families of the Soldiers belonging to the Town of Mansfield

Joshua Basset
Sam[ll] Conant
John Harris
Calib Conant
Nathan Porter
John Smith Jun[r]
Jonathan Fenton
Jacobe Barrows

Cap[t] John Shumway
Ashur Allen
Lieu[t] Solomon Fenton
Nathan Reed
John Bugbe
Joshua Bennet
John Abbe
John Dextor

## NEW MILFORD

The following is the Names of those men who are intitled to the Bounty granted by New Milford agreeable to the Inclosed Vote Viz.

[The bounty voted was £12 for the first year and £6 each year for the second and third year's service.]

Oliver Bostwick
William Whitely
Charles M[c]Donald
Liffe Sanford
William Drinkwater
Ralph Smith
Ebenezer Drinkwater
Ichabod Wilkinson
Ebenezer Bostwick
Mathew Wildman
William Dunwell
Joseph Clarke
Elijah Canfield
Abijah Moger
Garshom Nichols
Isaiah Bunce
Shubal Phillips
Eli Nichols
Lemuel Peet
Ebenezer Keeler
Chileab Palmer
David Cole

Samuel Phillips
Jeruel Phillips
Abraham Barns
Mingo Treat  27

David Merwin
William Foot
Goodman Noble
Theophilus Comstock
Eleazar Hendrick
John Knap
Daniel Rogers
Liverius Hawley  8

David Beach
David Bostwick
Stephen Wheeler
Ebenezer Trowbridge  4

James Bennit
Joseph C. Hawley

NB. The first mentioned 27 men Inlisted in Cap[t] Elizur Warners Company in Col[o] Swifts Regiment, and the nex 8 Inlisted in Cap[t] Halls Comp[y] in the same Reg[t]. And the next four Inlisted under Cap[t] Eli Catlin in Col[o] Bradleys Reg[t] — but what Comp[y] the other two belong to is not Ascertained.

## NEW HARTFORD

A Return of Supplies Made the Officers and Soldiers In the Continental army belonging To the Town of New Hartford

Elijah Flower Serj[t]
Joseph Gilbert  "
Theodore Gilbert Private
Ezra Andruss

Aaron Steevens
Elias Seymour
Elisha Robbarts
Cyperon Merrill

Aaron Merrill
John Taylor

Ezra Edgcomb
John Garrit

[None of the above names have check marks showing that they have been carried into another list.]

## POMFRET

Major Thomas Grosvenor
Capt Stephen Brown dead
Ensª Silas Holt
Elias Jones
Ebenezer Gilbert
Benjamin Bufinton
Sam[ll] Glass
Rowland Cotton
John Bryant
Abiel Varnum
Will[m] Cleaveland
Jonathan Hill
Joseph Griffin J[r]
Obadiah Brown
Abner Chapman
Dick A Negro Man
Jacob Hovey
Beezer Owen
Jesse Earls
James Paine Fitch
Amasa Copeland
Joseph Gunner
Simeon Camp
John Lilly
Sam[ll] Cady
General Putnams Negro Man
Jonas Newport
Oliver Goodell
Will[m] Wanslow
Will[m] Cart
John Cheney Deserted
Andrew Morrison

Lem[ll] Fling
Will[m] Earls
John Whealer
Billings Sabin
Sam[ll] Cleaveland
James Jones
Will[m] Lashbrooks
Lewis A Negro Man
Will[m] Ervin
Thos Hill
Ezra Goodell
John Wampee
Elijah Cheney Deserted
Silas Covel
Ezekil Loomis
Sam[ll] Millington
Jahazaniah How
Jos Holms
John Barker
Joseph Ross
Sam[ll] Bugbee
Abner French
Elias Robertson
Zenas Harthaway
Cyrus Cartwright
Ebenezer Grow
James Grant
Nethaniel Stowell
Cesar A Negro Man
Jonathan Crain
Caleb Conant
Jonathan Bullock

## PLAINFIELD

Reuben Bryant
Amos Bennet
Jonathan Whipple

Nathaniel Sabins
Jacob Heard

## RIDGEFIELD

Cap[t] S[t] John
Lieut Keeler
Levi Keeler
Jeremiah Keeler
Elijah Weed
Barack Nickerson
Eliphaz Nickerson
Elisha Lincoln

Thomas Keeler
John Condrick
Ezekiel Whitney
Lewis Jacklin
Solomon Ren
Abraham Resegue
Daniel Benedict
Nehemiah Olmsted

CONNECTICUT LINE, 1777-1781. 57

Jeremiah Osburn
Gilburt Brush
Thomas Hutcherson
Thomas Warson
Sylvarnus Sealey
Hezekiah Hawley

John Hitchcock
Micajah Weeks
James Stanton
Benjamin Bennit
Stephen Meeker

## SALISBURY

L' Noah Lee

L' James Coon

## SHARON

Stephen Wells
Amos Allin
Jonas Knap
William Stewart
James Loughlin
Timothy Brockway
Nathaniel Tyler
James Knap
Jonathan Tobias
Ezekel Whitney
Zelophehead Williamson
 (? Withamson)
William Low
Derias Gray
David Row
Samuel Gray
Josiah Strong

Abner Colkin
Cornelius Hamlin
Jabez Lewis
Joseph Strong
Daniel Elmer Jun
Henery Stephens
Nathaniel Richard
James Tobias
Derias Calkin
Jude Bill
Adonijah Pangborn
Amasa Warner
Phinehas Benjaman
Ephelit Smith
Azerial Acley
Henery Mackintire
Joseph Tucker

## STAFFORD

Maj' Ames Walbridge
L' Silas Blogget
Josiah Edson
Nathan Edson
Joseph Wheston
Joseph Edson
Joseph Green
Porter Walbridge
Joshua Wheler
Tim° Wheler
Zadock Wheler
Hezekiah Wheler
Tim° Luce
Isaac Pinny
Nehemiah Washbon
Benjⁿ Washbon
Solomon Tupper
Robert Thomson
Joshua Walbridge
Stephⁿ Whileaker (?)
Obediah Walker
Phillup Kibbe
Benj. Buller

Asa Buller
Elijah Russele
Nathan Kent
Ben Jon Orcutt
Sam¹ Worner
Stephⁿ Moulton
Thoms Worner
Alva West
Joseph Cross
Chester Morse
Reuben Putman
Jacob Green Ju'
Simⁿ Webster
Nathan Washbon
Isaac Cushmon
Israel Butler
Benj Rennals
William Brown
Tim° Herington
Zach Green
Nath¹¹ Cushmon Ju'
David Green
Nathan¹ Foster

## STRATFORD

Josiah French
Benjamin Brayzer
London Good Luck p⁴ to
   Jn° Willcockson
Joseph Usurp Negro to
   David Willcockson
John Gilbert
John McKensey
Abel Cuff
Richard Handy
Gideon Seley
Miles Dixon
Lemuel Seley
George Leman
William Beden
Elisha Pulford
Daniel Hawley's Negro
John Willcockson Junr
John Bennitt
Jeremiah Blackman
Stiles Curtiss's Negro Amos
John Edwards's " Ceaser
Toney — Negro
Heber Smith
Pompy Moss
Nathaniel Beach
David Sillick
Abijah Perrey
John Blackman
David Jackson
John Turney's Negro
David Duclos
Abijah Beardslee
Andrew Porter
John Benjamin Mitchel
Samuel Blackman
Samuel Whitney
Jehiel French
Robert Welch
John Bassitt
Elihu Blackman
Nathan Thompson
Daniel Jones
Samuel Pulford
John Waklee
Jeremiah Ryan
Daniel Sherwood
Stephen Hall
Robert Simmons
John Titus
Caleb Chatfield
Timothy Blackman
Daniel Barlow
Amos Saunders
Alexander Fairchield
Lewis Anjevine

John Beers Junr
Charles Burritt
Timothy Chapman
Abraham Hawley
Nathaniel Booth
Gersham Turney (? Tumey)
John Crawford
John Downes
James Downes
William Daskam
David Eves
Nathan Hawley Junr
David Hurd
Benjamin Beach
Peter Lewis a free Negro
Isaac Brown
Joseph
Gideon Seeley
John Munrow
Robert Freeman, Negro
Benjamin Hilton
Benjamin Waklee
James Hide
John Beardslee Junr
Jesse Dickinson
John Peet
Jesse Smith
Eli Nichols
Samuel Waklee
David Barlow Junr
Samuel Henman
Ephriam Seeley
Richard Hawley
James Wayland Junr
Daniel Munrow Junr
Samuel Maning
Silus Glassgow
Jesse Primas
Thomas Ivers for his Negro
   Jack
Joel Beers
Joseph Loaring
Prosper Wetmore
Joseph Waklee
Timothy Gauney
Richard Damenery
Nathan Turell
Benjamin Benjamin
David Wells
Bryan Montecue
David Willcoxson, for Josiah
Joseph Cleark
John Chops p⁴ Ezra Hawley
Ned Sherwood p⁴ Levi Jackson
John Beach p⁴ for his Negro

Grant Johnson
Isaac Dickerson
Joseph Hubbert
Ephraim Mollato

Silus Nickols paid him for his Servant
Samuel Richmond

## TOLLAND

Serg<sup>t</sup> Ebanez<sup>r</sup> Stebins
Ammi Paulk
Martin Davis
Will<sup>m</sup> Huntington
Will<sup>m</sup> Johnson
Isaac Squire
Abel Crandel
John Proc<sup>t</sup> Burrus

William Sole
Shubal Dimock
Edy Hatch
Simon Stimson
George Hubbard
Joseph Sparks
Amos Harris
David Pierse

## TORRINGTON

Sam<sup>ll</sup> Keley Ju<sup>r</sup>
Cleark Roberts
Ambros Fyler
Ebenezer Scovil
Ebenezer Leach
Isaac Day
John Towee
John Camp
Coonrod Weaver
Seth Stannard
Daniel Farmen
Bennajah Abrow

Timothy Fay
Samuell Jones
Remembrance Filley
Amos Jarols
John Whrite
Ithurel Flowers
Aaron Merells
Daniel Beneduk
A Negro Man
Gemalial Omsted
George Nottingham
Rivaous Newell

## UNION

Sergn<sup>t</sup> Nehemiah Cage (? Case)
John Laflin
George Dillaba
James Walker
Samuel Peirce
John Wright
Joseph Snell

James Laflin
Nehemiah Pecker
Benjamin Bullen
John Smith
Luthar Loomis
Joshua Ephraim
Eleazer Pagan (?)

## WALLINGFORD

Almond Munson
Amasa Tharp
Amos Tharp
Sam<sup>l</sup> S. B. Hotchkiss
Orange Munson
Lent Munson
Charles London
Jn<sup>o</sup> Hulbert
Elihu Cook
Johnson Cook
Warren Cook
Enos Mix
Andrew Andrews
Jesse Vose

Sam<sup>l</sup> Wright
Jn<sup>o</sup> Sled
Selah Stedman
Joseph Clark
George Cook
Sam<sup>l</sup> Blakslee
Benaiah Hall
Ja<sup>s</sup> Brown
Israel Dodge
Hull Shepherd
Toney Negro
Roswel Beach
Joel Cook
Will<sup>m</sup> Cook

60 REVOLUTION LISTS AND RETURNS.

Sam¹ Perkins
Jesse Peck
James Tibbel
Daniel Cady
Will™ Parker
Reuben Moss
Amos Mix
Sam¹ Spencer
Isaiah Moss
Lieut. Giles Curtis
Thos Dudly
Timothy Parker
Jn° Parker
Hiel Peck
Joseph Wolcott Jr
Charles Heydon
Asa Beach
James Miles
Israel Johnson
Sam¹ Parsons
Wait Yale
Amos Parker
Anthony Goodsill
Abram Parker
Charles Merriman
Eliakim Johnson
Lieut. Lem¹ Hitchcock
Ebenez' Lewis
Tho⁸ Hitchcock
Tim⁷ Parker, Serg.
David Stone
Jn° Anthony, discharged
Enoch Merriman
Benj. Ford
Benj. Raxford
Elisha Hall
Seth Smith
Joab Sanderson
Eph™ Meriam
Edm⁴ Merriam
Jotham Hall
Jonathⁿ Ford
Levi Robinson
John Pierce
Jotham Rice
James Coburn
Joseph Coburn
Asaph Merriam
Sam¹ Collins
Moses Hall 3⁴
Lem¹ Willcox
Barnabas Mitchel
Elisha Bishop

Samson Smith Negro
Boston Negro
Chatham Freedom Negro
Lemmon Cumber Negro
Andrus Moor
Ruel Affrica Negro
William Buntin
Benj. Johnson
Dan¹ Johnson Hall
Aaron Hall
Timothy Hart
Abel Tharp
Timothy Page
Titus Hart
Luke Kerns
Sam¹ Spellman
Thaddeus Todd
Sam¹ Jones
Luther Johnson
Medad Potter
Benoni Moss
Elisha Parker Jr.
Will™ Prout
Peter Sibbels
Benj. Hendric
Tho⁸ Davis
Ebenezer Brockitt
Adam Molatto
Dick Freedom Negro
Asa Bellamy
Abel Clark
Amos Andrews
Joel Willmott
Elmer Russel
Charles Kimberly
Levi Hitchcock
Levi Bunnel
Job Tyrrel
Prince Negro
Ambrose Hine
Titus Atwater
Job Negro
Chauncey Lewis
Peter Negro
Sharp Negro
Nath¹ Tyler
Levi Tyler
Eldad Porter
Will™ Grant
Abel Lewis
Divan Clark
Jn° Perkins

## WINCHESTER

William Leach
Steaven Hurlburt
Jese Wilkenson

Adam Moot
Timothy Fay
Wiliam Fay

CONNECTICUT LINE, 1777-1781. 61

Seth Stanard
Remembrance Filley
David Hudson
Pebody Stanard
Steaven Scovils

Gershom Fay
Levi Welkenson
Jonathan Preston
Prince Neagro

## WOODBURY

Sam¹ Lamfear
Jethro Tona
Galloway Peter
James Parks
Moses Hawkins
Wᵐ Stanclift
James Negro
Samuel Cofrin
Elisha Hubbert
Aaron Curtiss
Frederick Barnee
John Slauter
Henry Wakely
Shem Doel
Gideon Bristol Junʳ
David Hecock
John Bulford
John Hubbart
Moses Strickland
Lewis Hurd
Daniel Potter
Sheldon Potter
Timothy Hinman
Joseph Stiles
Cummy Simons
James Sharp
Simeon Barns
Abel Wakely
John Thompson
William Bondy
Aseph Hurlbut
James Abenathy
George Fields
Ephraim Selcy
John Clarke
Pomp London
John Turrel
Benjᵃ Avery
Jonathan Twist
James Brown
Ira Way
Matthew Read
Tint Gillis
Elisha Perry
Zuar Bradley
John Herrick
Jnᵒ Davenport
Robert Smith
Michael Robin
Anthony Stoddard
Gideon Hurd Junʳ

Abiel Linsley
Jehiel Bradley
Benjᵃ Wheeler
George Hows
Julian Easton
Titus Negrow
Joseph White
Aner Adee
Joseph Walker Junʳ
Solomon Reynolds Junʳ
Benjᵃ Hinman 3ᵈ
Aquila Sturgiss
Peter Johnson
Hezekiah Keeler
Enoch Thomas
Phineas Palmer
Daniel Stephens
David Reynolds
Justus Reynolds
David Dixon
Amos Clerk
Samuel Jackson
Jared Dixon
Stephen Ranney
James Hucker
Daniel Tucker
Alexander Mills
Joseph Blakesley
Hinman Wooster
Sam¹ Lee
Charles Sheldon
David Robinson
Wᵐ Beamont
Moses Church
Jonathan Munger
Robin Negrow
George Bannister
[            ] Hurlbut (?)
Barnabas Blenney
Peter Kellis
Elijah Pixlie
Jnᵒ Laflin
John Nails
Samuel Wilson
Freeman Judd
Benjᵃ Buel
Eliphalet Downs
Tom Gage
Isaac Bloom
Thomas Mitchel

# TOWN BOUNTIES ETC., 1777-1779.

[The Archives relating to the Revolution 80, numbers 8-50, consist of returns from the various towns, giving particularly the names of soldiers serving in the Connecticut Line, who received "Town Bounties etc. before 1780," from the towns for which they served. The returns are dated about April 1, 1779, and include from the beginning of the year 1777.]

## BOLTON

Leut Zadock How
Ezra Downer
John Worner
Sam<sup>ll</sup> Lilington
Enoch Carter
Sam<sup>ll</sup> Loomis
Solomon Chappel
Isaac Jones
Ezra Chapen
Zepheniah Thayer
Hiel Chapen
Roger Loomis

Levit Millard
Joseph Spencer Dec<sup>t</sup>
Ebe<sup>r</sup> Dart
Na<sup>th</sup> Taylor
Elijah Howard
Josiah Bordman
Joshua Flint
Andrew Loomis
Jerijah Thayer
Donnety
Moredock M<sup>c</sup>Lane Dec<sup>t</sup>
Asa Lanord Deserted

## CANAAN

Col<sup>o</sup> Rusels Regiment
  Serjent Joshua Whitney now Ens<sup>a</sup>
  Serj<sup>t</sup>  Elias Lee
  Serj<sup>t</sup>  Aaron Brownel
  Bille Lawrance Drum Maj<sup>r</sup>
  David Preston
  Samuel Peirce
  William Mix
  Elisha Freman
  John Watson
  Andrew Lester
  Thomas Stevens
  Abner Miller
  Stephen Stevens

Of Col<sup>o</sup>  Meiggs Reg<sup>t</sup>
  Ozias Baker
  Himan Coole

Of Capt Bucklands Matrosses
  Neil M<sup>c</sup>Neil

Col<sup>o</sup> Swifts Reg<sup>t</sup>
  Leu<sup>t</sup>  John Holombeck
  Serj<sup>t</sup>  William Fellows

Isaac Smith
William Chambers
Samuel Green
Simon Tubbs
Isaac Higby
Seth Curtis
Peter Serdam
Samuel Hunt
Serj<sup>t</sup> Rusel Hunt
Nathaniel Douglass
Aaron Culver
Benjamin Scovel
Richard Bishop
Timothy Woodford
John Curtis
Eben<sup>r</sup> Church
John pervett

David Preston
Joseph Cowles
John Curtis
Richard Bishop
Samson R Hunt
Nathaniel Douglass
Timothy Woodford

Aaron Culver
Aaron Brownel
Elish Freman
Andrew Lester
Thomas Stevens

William Mix
Elias Lee
Stephen Stevens
Abner Miller
Bille Lawrance

## CANTERBURY

Andrew Hebbard
Ser[t] Joen Cleveland
Sam[ll] Coburn
Thomas Harris
Jacob Cleveland
  Isaac Basset
Daniel Edwards
James Litchfield
Daniel Durfee
Sam[ll] Glass
Reuben Lilliee
John Lillie
Abiel Farnam
Jerule (? Jerub) Mott
Sam[l] Thomson
Dan[l] Fitch
Sam[l] Stoddard
Israel Dodge
David Adams
Abijah Cady
Tius Tykins Indian
Frederick Curtiss
John Jeffards
Cap[t] Abner Bacon
Leiut. Tim[o] Cleveland
Doct. David Adams
Serj[t] Eben[r] Felch
Thomas Austin hired Jon[t] Bill
James Johnson
John Ames Samson indians man*
John Ames
James Dixon
Jeriel Dodge
William Shaw
Elijah Munroe
Nathaniel Edwards
Jedidiah Brown
Nathan Lester
Elias Shaw
Aaron Faulkner

James Duggin
Josiah Burnham
Benj[a] Shaw
Rufus Fitch
Roger Green
James Morse
Francis Perkins
Robert Herrick
Reuben Carter
Peter Stevens
Ser[t] Nathaniel Gates
Nathan Stevens
Walcott Justin
Leiu[t] Moses Cleveland

Light horse men { Sam[l] Adams / Dan[l] Cushman / Tho[s] Cushman / Elisha Litchfield

The following are Men died in the Service hired for three years & during the war viz
James Wharf
Silas Gates
Amos Brewster
Josiah Munroe
Joseph Bond
Jona[t] Shaw
James Clark
John Shaw
Nehemiah Munroe
John Cleveland Jr
Stephen Farnam
Prince Lillie
Lee Woodward
Jeremiah Reed
Clark Herrington
Ezekiel Herrington
Jedidiah Adams
Bartlet Bingham

## CHATHAM

L[t]    Ezra Smith
L[t]    Marcus Cole
L[t]    Aaron Hale
Serg[t] Benj[n] Bowers
Serg[t] Ab[m] Schallenx

Serg[t] Levi Goodrich
Serg[t] Nath[ll] Montgomery
Serg[t] Elnath[n] Geanings
Serg[t] Abner Cole
Serg[t] Rich[d] Giddins

*John Ames partly erased and Samson indians man added in another handwriting

CONNECTICUT LINE, 1777-1781.       65

Serg' James Johnson J' dead
Corp'' Benaj'' Bowers
Corp'' John Paine
Corp'' Ebur Stocking
Corp'' Nath'' Cook
Corp'' Jos'' Markham
Corp'' Othniel Brainard
Corp'' W'' Stocking
Lemuel Goodrich
Bethuel Goodrich
Jonathan Verry
Jonath' Stocking
Peter Butler
W'' Cook
Reuben Schallenx
Elihu Mott Dec'd
W'' M'Corne
Seth Knowles
W'' Grey
Giles Knowles
Jos'' Andrews
Jos'' Graham
Ephraim Bowers
Jn° Graham
Josiah Davies
Stephen Ranney
Jacob Wood
Jacob Wood J'
David West J'
Joshua Morgan Dec'd
Marshal Stocking
Stephen Thomas
Elijah Whiting
Dan'' Robarts
Joel Doolittle
Jabez Ranney
Ephraim Brigs
George Brown Dead
Thomas Brown
Daniel Pelton
John Gill
Tho' Fitz Simons
Charles Martin

James Shields
John Wright
Heman Higgins dead
Jesse Higgins dead
Jesse Higgins Jr dead
Benj' Benjamin dead
Nath' Powers
Tho' Rich
Joseph Rich
Peter Sharman
George Pelton
William Exton
Followdan Damewood
Joel Green
John Goodrich
Sam'' Rich
Nath'' Rich
Dan'' Parks
Sam'' Goff J'
John Parks
Ezra Smith Jun' dead
Abel Abel
Tim° Chipman
Sylv' Smith
Thomas Sorow
John Strong
Dan'' Millar
Elihu Hubbard
Lem'' Rich
Joseph Chace
Aaron Carter
Benj' Troubridge
Ichabod Lucas
Zebadiah Briggs
Sam'' Freeman
Thomas Hodge
Robert Stiles
Sam'' Goff
Beriah Stiles
Joshua Goff
Martin Stiles
Hewet Aloord
Rhoderice White

## COLEBROOK

Eli Simonds
Joseph Simons

Samu'' Philleps
Abial Canfield

## COVENTRY

Cap' Paul Brigham
Serj' Eleazer Loomis
Serj' Nathaniel Thompson
Corp' James Barnabee
Robert Lane
John Savory
Conant Sawyer

Ephraim Robertson
Joseph Doubleday
Asael House
Samuel Burden
Joseph Badcock
Joseph Doubleday Jun'
Noah Chappell

5

Benjamin Grover
Nathaniel Rose Desarted
John Brown
Aaron Stimson of Toland
Elias Newton of Toland
Elisha Stebbins of Toland
Nathan Walker of Staford
Richard Davenport
Jonathan Delano of Toland
Philip Lewis of New London
Nathaniel Harris
Jules Burns
Isaac Kellogg
Daniel Edwards

Richard Carlton of Toland
Serj't Amos Avery
Justus Brewster
John Bill
Roger Welch
William Bourns
John Parker
Nathan Parker
Job Leson
Jesse Leson
Evens of Hartford
Cristian name unknown
Jerijah Shair of Bolton

## DURHAM

L't Charles Burrit
Se'r Eliakim Strong
Se'r Benjamin Sutliff
Co'r Hust : Henmin
Co'r Sam'll Lucas
Du'r Saxton Squire
Du'r Phinehas Squire
Du'r Reuben Brown
Du'r David Brown
Du'r John Bishop
Fif'r Sam'll Brown
Fif'r Nathaniel Brown
Eliakim Hull
Timothy Dunn
Warrop Murry
William Lucas
Simeon Mallery
Phinehas Miggs
Seth Strong

Sam'll Seaward
Enos Crane
John Meaker
Nathan Keelsoy
William Carr Ju'r
Bryan Rosseter
Skiler (?) Goddard
Gideon Chrittendon
Thomas Cook
Abiather Squir
Amos Davis
William Johnson
John Handcox
Sharp Negro
Cato Negro
Des't (?) Robart Kneel
Des't (?) Gashom Brown
De'd (?) Cyrus Newton
De'd (?) Joseph Hickcox

## ENFIELD

Cap't David Parsons
Cap't Tho's Abbe
Serj't Jabez Parsons
Serjt Dan'll Ware
Serjt Simeon Hager
Joseph Chandler
Henry Booth
Joseph Griswold
Jonathan Parsons
Isaac Simons
Irael Hall
Benj'n Butler
Tho's Root Jun'r
Othniel Allen
Ebenezer Peese 3'd
Simeon Pease
Benj'n Herrington
John Ward

Tho's Hale Jun'r
Hiram Hall
Amasa Allen
David Bullen Jun'r
David Phelps Jun'r
Ebinezer Ames
Isaac Markham
Tho's Justus Davis
John Graham
William Thomson
Nathaniel Rose
John Delaney
Benj'n Baxter
Joel M'egriggay
Benj'n Bugbee
Lemuel Wood
Jams Erl
John Phips

CONNECTICUT LINE, 1777-1781.

Dan[ll] Perkins Jun[r]
Ichabad Meacham Jun[r]
   Matrosses
Jonathan Terry Jun[r] Listed
   and Since Dead
Levi Terry
Isaac French
William Erl
Jared Simons

Eben[r] Perkins
   Hired by two Men
James Russel
Richard Fairman
Stephen Butler
Asa Hall
William Prier
Tho[s] Athington

## FAIRFIELD

*Maj[r] Albert Chapman
*Cap[t] Josiah Lacey
*Leu[t] Isaac Hubbel
*Leu[t] William Hubbel
*Leu[t] N. Peet Jackson
*Leu[t] James Chapman
 Leu[t] Daniel Bradley
*Jos[h] Disborow   Serg[t]
*Moses Sturgis     "
*Stephen Hall     "
*Richard Williams "
*Atkisson Hillton "
*Tho[s] Allen
*Ebn[r] Allen
*Stephen Lockwood
*Nath[ll] Johnson
*Moses Allen
*William Raymong
*David Raymong
*Joseph Mills
*Justice Disborow
Benjamin Allen
Eliphalet Allen
William Johnson
John Johnson
Gershom Jeacocks
Isaac Elwood
Nathan Elwood
Joshuah Jeacocks
Henry Disborough
Abraham Sturgis
Nath[ll] Sturgis
Ezra Wood
Joseph Batterson
James Batterson Jun[r]
Jonathan Poor
Simon Disberow
Stephen Batterson
John Couch
Abraham Couch
Gideon Hulbert
Nathan Taylor
Francis Hebbern
*Daniel Bennit

*John Mitchel Corp[l]
Joseph Mosier
*Eppaphras Goodsel
*Eliphalet Bradley
Nathan Bradley
Aaron Sturgis
Hez[h] Webb
Peter Stocker
Aaron Whaley
Ezekiel Thorp
Aaron Thorp
John Beaher (?)
Nathan Winton
Isbon Hubbell
John M[c]Mullin
*Jonathan Spears
John Gilbert
Daniel Barlow
William Jackson
Francis Hibbert
Tho[s] Stephens
*Francis Hutonot
Hez[h] Whaley
Wakeman Hull
Augustus Sturgis
*John Fuller
*Daniel Burr
*Nehemiah Fowler
William Gold
Edward Field
Nathan Squire
John Lerone
Philip Frenchman
Lewis Grisson
Josiah Armstrong
Peter Fegro
*David Morehouse
*Elijah Patchin Corp[l]
*Tho[s] Durfee Corp[l]
Isaac Odell Serg[t]
*David Coggins
Burr Gilbert
Ebn[r] Meaker
Joseph Read Indian

---
*These are designated as Married Men

Simon Cheapeak I[nd]
Zackriah Sherwood
Paschall Southwell
Isaac Hubbel
Isaac Smith
*Barrack Taylor
Wolcot Patchin
Simeas (?) Shervin
Benj[n] Stigley (? Higley)
John Hallett
Jo[s] Prindel
James Hesket
*Seth Bulkley
David Jackson
Stephen Evens
John Hubbard
Stephen Clerk
John Downia
John Coggins
Benj[a] Bennit
Peter Negro

Amos Marshell
David Barlow
Jonathan Edwards
Michael Bowing
Eliphalet Gray
Josiah Green
David Wallace
Isbon Jennings
Hezekiah Meeker
John Cook
Patrick Linch
Richard Clark

Teams Men
Nathan Bulkley Jun[r]
Joseph Lyon Jun[r]
Sam[l] Staples Jun[r]
Seth Webb
John Jennings Jun[r]
Ephraim Beers
Alexander Weeks

## GROTON

Cap[t] Amos Stanton
L[t] Henry Williams
L[t] Stephen Billing
L[t] Simeon Avery
Searg[t] Limuel Whitman
Searg[t] Uriah Williams
Searg[t] Eben[r] Morgan
Searg[t] Daniel Nikerson
Elijah Gray
Robert Swift
Jesse Yerington
Sam[l] Pomp
Robert Davis
Andrew Annew
John M[c] Donel
John Spears
Jonas Sunseman
Tuis Sharper
Henery Britman
James Andrus
Daniel Davis
Ebenezer Pelton
Amos Solomon
Silas Stery
Joseph Holley
James Simon
Nathan Sholes
David Pelton
Joseph Bentley
Jesse Starr
John Pemberton
Richard Daton

Moses Stodard
Abel Wassonk
Isaac Roger
Joseph Meason
Joseph Quacheets
Elisha Avery
George Avery J[r]
Wheler Shoules
Amos Latham
John Burnam
W[m] Paul
Asa Beley
Cato Roberson
Robert Allyn
Tho[s] Malison
Bildad Eadwards
Andrew Wigar
Robert Williams
Tho[s] Williams
Andrew Baker
Daniel Wiger
W[m] Davis
Jonathan Ruff
John Dabol
Andrew Foreseth
Diarka Elderkin
John Williams
Solomon Williams
Nathan Williams
Nathan Smith
Ezekiel Billing
Simeon Comstok

---
*These are designated as Married Men

CONNECTICUT LINE, 1777-1781.

Gilbert Edgcom
Roswell Parish
Joseph States
Nath[l] Noyse
Chris[r] Chester
Joseph Willey
Jack Negro
Elisha Fanning
Robert Stanton
Rufus Holdredge
Jacob William
Joseph Williams
David Fanning
Nathan Fanning
Prentice Gallup
Elisha Stodard
Lemuel Chester
Ralph Williams
David Chapman
Asa Lamb

Tho[s] Fanning
Nathan[l] Bellows
John Brown
Gershum Brown
Fradrick Park
Aron Shoules
James Park
Constant Avery
Benj[a] Pettice
Daniel Stodard
James Pelton
Daniel Holway
Cyrus Kiltam
Fradrick Stodard
Eben[r] Pollard
James Patterson
Miner Allyn
Fradrick Fanning
Cato Negro

## GOSHEN

Capt Thomas Converse
Liut William Starr
Zebul Peck
John Gould
Timothy Knap
James Brown
Jacob Lair
Serg[t] Jonathan Demming
Serg[t] Isaac Miles
David Hurlbut
Jonathan Wheaton
Joel Galord
Wait Demming
Obil Beach
Nathaniel Sizer
Abel Basset
Robert Morris
Javis Boney
Matthew Buckley

Simeon Hall
David Langly
John White
Joseph Norton
Caleb Miles
Justice Squire
Elisha Mix
Ebenezer Lewis
David Holms
Asa Brooks
Stephen Mix
Linas Moss
John Willoughby
John Sealy
George Tankard
Jack Negro
George Gardner
Thomas Wyard
How

## HADDAM

Leiut Gideon Baily
L[t] John Smith
L[t] Cornelius Higgins
Serj[t] Loudon Baily
" Jeromy Baily
" Jesse Cone
" Jehiel Arnold
" Hezekiah Clark
" John Baily
Corp[l] Jacob Baily
" James Smith
Ashbel Bradley
Timothy Baily

Gurdon Baily
Robert Baily
Aaron Clark
Joseph Porter
Stephen Burr
Lemuel Pratt
Wells Smith
William Gladen
Elisha Cone
Oliver Cone
Samuel Church
Jerathmel Bonfoy
Benanuel Bonfoy

Noadiah Cone
David Thomas
Seth Spencer
John Nichols
Nathniel Cook
Timothy Smith
Daniel Crane
Henry Smith
William Clark
William Baily
Cudjo Negro

London Sawyer
Cesar Chapman
Amos Bates
Daniel Bates
Eleazer Bates
Christopher Baily
James Brooks
Jonathan Bordman
Amos Porter
Walter Chase
Timothy Brainerd

## HARTFORD

Samuel Wyllys Col[a]
Christopher Darrow Maj[r]
Stephen Buckland Cap[t] Art[y]
William Green Cap[t]
Samuel Mattocks Cap[t]
John Barnard Cap[t]
Ralph Pomeroy Pay Master
William Adams  "
Roger Wadsworth Lieu[t]
David Deming Lieu[t] Artl[y]
Charles Miller Lieu[t]
Peleg Heath  "
George Smith Ensign
James Olmsted  "
Daniel Brewer Serg[t]
William Combs  "
Mathew Cadwell  "
Thomas Jarrell  "
Roswell Wattles  "
William Mize
Daniel Curtis
Reuben Hadlock
Patrick Thomas
Obediah Spencer
Thomas Waters
James Mahar
Ebenezer Beevins
Samuel Sedgwick
Caesar Augustus
Abraham Clark
Israel Loomis
Stephen Risley
Ablather Evans
James Delibar
Samuel Evans Jun[r]
Samuel Lucas
Richard Case
Benjamin Keeny
Eleazer Abby
Malachi Corney
Hammon Way
John Adams
John Watson Jun[r]
David McLean

James Parks
Grove Kellogg
Thomas Spencer
Hezekiah Goodwin
Asa Seymour
Thomas Wells
Timothy Andruss
Abdiel Flowers
William Whistler
Zadock Sealy
Robert Culbert
Richard Jackson
Daniel Miller
Benjamin Job
William Henry
William Tryon
Benjamin Webster
William Hinsdale
Davice Johnson
Simeon Hosmer
Asa Bunce
James Barnard
Theodore Chamberlain
John Foster
John Bath
Samuel Hancy
Horrace Kellogg
John Turner
William Hooker
Joseph Day
James Chadwick
Peter Phillips
Seth Kellogg
John Whiting Jun[r]
William Whiting
Jonathan Shepard
Isaac Merrills
Benjamin Flowers
Samuel Easton
Jonathan Arnold
Eliphalet Hills
John Vibert
Stephen Fox
Moses Porter

CONNECTICUT LINE, 1777-1781.

Elijah Porter
Samuel Roberts Jun'
David Wood
Levi Risley

Asa Burnhams family not belonging to the Town but being there were supplied.

## HARTLAND

Enlisted out of the State
Major Theodore Woodbridge
Bartholomew Barrett
Cyrus Dubbs
Moses Wooster
Benjamin Darling
John Call
John Wheeler
John Harrison
Samuel Hall

Ruben Hall
Ser' Benjamin Giddinge
Cor' Obed Crosby

fifer Joseph Gilbert
Benjamin Reed
Charles Phelps
Benonia Evans
David Rood
Edward Cowdry
Harris Fox
Daniel Bushnell
Titus Hays
Ebenezer Hall        Deceased
Jonathan Butler      Deceased
Richard Clemons      Deceased
Samuel Wier          Deceased

## HARWINTON

Caleb Elmore
Seth Gridley
Samuel Hinsdel
Elisha Hinsdel
James Wilcox
Joseph Halsted
Timothy Stedmon

Elijah Scott
Ethel Scott
Roswel Catlin
Tho' Green
Ozem Cook
Joseph C. Hawley
Lieu' Asahel Hodge

## KILLINGLY

Jabez Kingsbury
Thomas Barns
Mathew Moffit
John Meason
John Meason J'
Ward Walton
Daniel McDaniel
Cato Hunt
Serj' Pennel Child
Charles Lebret
Joseph Robins
Joseph Sheffield
Abner Marsh
John Keith
Tom Black
Will'm Jones
Archelaus Town
Jason Harris
Lemuel Barns
Amasa Grover
Comfort Redway
Benj'm Bobinson

Silas Rickard
Crummil Luther
Squir Knight
Oliver Jinks
Cornelus Havens
James Runalds
Jacob Runald
Will'm Arven
Benj'm Cady y' 3'd
John Pike
Simeon Lenord
Jack Green a negro man
David Runalds
Will'm Blanchard
Zibee Roberts
Jabez Leach
Jacob Bixby
Nath'll Turner
Parker Adams
Sam'll Hall
Philip Keach
Perley Herren

Jeremiah Wilkey
Will<sup>m</sup> Adams
Isaac Barrows
Josiah Barrows
John Russel
Solomon Johnson
Gidion Martain
Silas Rickard

Sam<sup>ll</sup> Runalds
Squier Whitmon
Jacob Warren
Nicholas Shippy
Daniel Sweet
Joseph Starkweather
Lieut Silverus Perrey

## KILLINGWORTH

Cap<sup>t</sup> Aaron Steevens
Lieu<sup>t</sup> Caleb Baldwin
Lieu<sup>t</sup> Joseph Willcox
Serj<sup>t</sup> George Griswold
Serj<sup>t</sup> Caleb Turner
Serj<sup>t</sup> William Linn
Serj<sup>t</sup> Nathaniel Crane
Corp<sup>l</sup> Sam<sup>ll</sup> Hull
Corp<sup>l</sup> Philip Redfield
Drum<sup>r</sup> Barnabas Wellman
Drum<sup>r</sup> James Parmele
Fifer Benjamin Wright
Joel Crane
Elifelet Clorck
Peter Steevens
Benjamin Tooley
Asa Buel
Reuben Chittenden
James Chittenden
Zenas Griswold
Jesse Joans
John Kelcey
Sam<sup>ll</sup> Nettelton
Elias Redfield
Daniel Willcox
Sam<sup>ll</sup> Franklin
John Crane

Paul Wellman
John Wellman
Oliver Kelsey
Eliakim Steevens
Hubble Steevens
Benjamin Pelton
Thomas Rumbelow
Allen Leet
William Gaylor
William White
Abel Hull
John Chittenden
John Lewes
Edward Griffin
John Chatfield
William Wellman
Oliver Teal
Constant Parmele
Reuben Wright
Joseph Hull
Daniel Dwolf
Giles Willcox
Joshua Kelcey
George Hull
Joseph Teal
Richard Jackson
Simon Steevens

## MANSFIELD

Capt John Shumway
Ens<sup>n</sup> Solomon Fenton
Jonathan Snow
James Step
Calib Conant
John Marten Jun<sup>r</sup>
Bigsbey Rodgers
Diarca Allen
Amarah (?) Crane
Jeremiah Gellit Jun<sup>r</sup>
Joshua Basset
Benjamin Bugbe
John Bugbe
Joshua Bennet
Asher Allen
John Dextor
Aaron Royce

Elijah Royce
Charles Wood
Steaphen Dunham
Nathan Reed
Benj<sup>a</sup> Lilley
Nathan<sup>ll</sup> Hardey
John Smith Jun<sup>r</sup>
Jonathan Fenton
Josiah Conant Jun<sup>r</sup>
John Hartshorn
Phineas Allen
Assel Dunham
James Dextor
Luther Eaton
John Eldredg
Elijah Baldwine
Jonathan Nichols

CONNECTICUT LINE, 1777-1781. 73

William Dodg
Willard Church
Nath^ll Cary Jun^r
John Abbe
John Balch Jur
Nathan Porter
Benajah Geer
John Baker
Ichabud Hovey
Rodger Freeman
Lumey Case
Jacobe Barrows

Daniel Bosworth
Sam^ll Herrington
Eben^r Snow
Josiah Burt
Daniel B. Perkens
Isaac Park   Groton
Ralph Williams D°
Clement Minor   Tollan
Newport Molattow D°
John Saunders   Mansfield
Joshua Bassett Jun^r D°

## MILFORD

Samuel Bryan Marshall
Serj^t Peter Hepburn
Isaac Davidson
Abel Hitchcock
Jared Hitchcock
Isaac Northrop
John Heath
Amos Mallery
Joel Bebee
William Goldsmith
Elisha Thares
John Naugason
Titus Hine
David Hodge
Benjamin Pritchard
Justus Woods
David Mallery
Samuel Stow
James Goldsmith
Amos Clark
John Peters
Congo Zado
Elijah Bryan
Samuel Green
Thomas Binns
Samson Church
Job Woodruff
John Hooker
Peter Negro
Jube Negro
Daniel Soward
John Peck Jun^r
Phinehas Johnson
Tim° Johnson
Anguis M^cFee
Toney Prudden
Jeffery James

Sharper Rogers
Elnathan Tolls
Timothy Beard
John Gellitt
James Pene
Samuel Eells Jun^r
Joseph Plumb Mertin
William Rusell
Elackander Burk
Samuel Dickerson
Joseph Sharp
Hezekiah Brackitt
John Morris
Pomp Cyrus
Anthony Fransway
William Ovitt
Elisha Lewis
Stephen Marchant
Jonathan Bristoll
Joseph Goldsmith
Benjamin Burn
Jeffery Rogers
John Stewart
William Soward
Gabril Leverick
John Jackson
George Clark
Elijah Clark
Joel Sperry
John Belden
Peter Bristoll
Samuel Frost
James Cebra
John M^cRenneck
Cap^t Charles Pond
Cap^t Samuel Sanford
Lieu^t William Smith

## NEW MILFORD

Col° Josiah Starr
Lemuel Peet
William Dunwell

Ebenezer Bostwick
James Daily
Abijah Moger

Isaiah Bunce
Wil<sup>m</sup> Drinkwater
Abram Barns
Ichabod Wilkenson

Elijah Canfield
Stephen Stilwell
Joseph C Hawley

## NORFOLK

Titus Watson Cap<sup>t</sup>
John Trobrig Cor<sup>l</sup>
Moses Turner "
Elijah Knap "
Aaron Aspinwell
Asael Addams
Calob Aspinwell
Joel Hamblin
Nathan Tubbs
Levi Norton
Reuben Stevins
Sam<sup>ll</sup> Orvis
Amiriah Plumb
Calob Sturdifunt

John Walter
Einathan Seward
Abr<sup>m</sup> Knap
Reufus Trall
Jeames Benidict
Hiland Hall
Bates Tufner
Silas Cowles
Edward Fuller
Charles Walter
W<sup>m</sup> Turner
Jonas Hubbard
Lem<sup>ll</sup> Sperry

## NORWICH

Jedidiah Huntington
    Brigadier General
John Durkee Colonel
Ebenezer Huntington Major
Benjamin Throop Major
Ebenezer Perkins Captain
Beriah Bill      "
Rufus Abell
James Lord      Lieutenant
Nathaniel Bishop    "
Darius Peck      "
John Durkee Jun<sup>r</sup>    "
Andrew Griswold    "
Silas Goodale      "
Jacob Fox      "
Hezekiah Tracy      "
Charles Fanning      "
Joseph Chapman      "
James Hyde 3<sup>rd</sup>    Ensign
Reuben Pride      "
Diah Hartshorn      "
William Tracy      "
John Ellis      Chaplain
Philip Turner    Surgeon
Nathaniel Gardner Surgeon's
    Mate
John Fanning    Surgeon's
    Mate
Jedidiah Waterman Jun<sup>r</sup>
David Pelton
Eleazer Pond
John Bond
Uriah Polley
Prince a free Negro

Alexander M<sup>c</sup>Coy
Aaron Bailey
Barzil Bowdril
John Vandewson
William Bacon
Allen Pratt
John Whiting
Andrew Simons
Jedidiah Richards
Abner Pitcher
Elias Moores
Solomon Goodrich
James Greer
Dyar Manning
Roger Manning
David Gardner
Elijah Pike
Phill a Negro
Charles Avery 3<sup>d</sup>
Peter Granger
Israel Webster
Miles Avery
Morris Jones
Titus Teal
Luke Brown
John Howell
Joseph Waterman
Oliver Arnold Jun<sup>r</sup>
William Branch
Ebenezer Snow Jun<sup>r</sup>
David Hunn
Cato Grover
Jedidiah Hyde Jun<sup>r</sup>
Phinehas Durkee

## CONNECTICUT LINE, 1777-1781.

Oliver Rogers
Joseph Lathrop
Ephraim Whitaker
Case Cook
Stephen Lee
Christopher Palmer
John Patten
Asa Eams
William Manning Jur
John Frederick Ancraman
Francis Green
John Briant
James Carr alias Miller
Edward Moore
Cuffee Wells
Aaron Baxter
Thomas Powers
John Simpson
Oliver Teal
Absalom Thomas
Bristo Augustus
Daniel Thomas
Sherman Gardner
Peter Plumb
Elijah Vergison
Isaiah Wright
Jabez Kingsberry
John Mirach Whitney
Thomas Gardner
Abimeleck Uncas
Rufus Hartshorn Junr
William Hallowell
William Pollard
Joshua Williams
Elkanah Meech
Gideon Comstock
Reuben Read
Jason Corning
John Gaylord
Thomas Mix Junr
Samuel Roath Junr
John Jacob Sidleman
Frederick Avery
Thomas Patten
Asher Spicer
Robert Stillman
William Holdridge Junr
Roger Fitch
Timothy Raymond
Samuel Clark
Benjamin Bennet
Benjamin Mott
Francis Donity
Jabez Post
Stephen Calkin
John Reynolds
John Hyde Durkee
Joseph Mesum

Kedar a free Negro
Micha a free Negro
Moses Tracy
Nathaniel Hill
Samuel Spicer
Toby Pendall a free Negro
Lebbeus a free Negro
Hezekiah Brewster
Adon Ames
Elijah Thomas
William Densey
Ned a Negro Man
Solomon Lothrop
John Wompee an Indian
Ephraim Wheeler
Charles Adams
Andrew Harrington
Asa Rothbourn
Joseph Branch
Benjamin Craft
John Bishop Junr
Selah Corwin
Jonathan Corwin
Ephraim Durfey
Daniel Bennett
Amos Brewster
George King
Newport a free Negro
John Wight
Ceaser Stewart a free Negro
Daniel Hawley
Jeremiah Capron
Ebenezer Perrigo
Elijah Knight
James Kingsley
William Perrigo Junr
Israel Dodge
James Morse
Abner French Junr
Daniel Fitch
Francis George
Thomas Malcom
John Allen
Ebenezer Waterman Junr
Samuel Ladd Junr
Everet Eams
John Pond
William Moore
Richard Lyman
John Martin
Samuel Goold
Richard Penhallow
Amos Green
John a Negro
John Thompson
Ebo. Raimond a Negro
Solomon Huntley
Backus Fox a free Negro

Edward Simons
Ebenezer Broughton
Araunah Hackley
Abner Hurlbut
Abner Waters
Ebenezer Armstrong
Oliver Story
John Packard
Benoni Congdol
Luther Waterman
John Brown
Jacob Clark
Hunt Simons an Indian
Samuel Huntington
Abraham Brown
Lathrop Davis
Hiram Huntington
William Harriss
Levi Deains
Thomas Meach
Joseph Fox
William Hinson Jun'
Darius Woodworth
Andrew Harriss
Joshua Reynolds
Noah Peas
Peregrine Gardner
Rozwel Crocker
Eleazer Groto a Mulato
Robert Bartlet
Jeremiah Osgood
Russel Chapel
Ammon Beebee
Alpheus Polley
Simon Choichoi an Indian
John Swaddle
Asa Fitch
Jesse Forsyth
Joseph Robbins
Jabez Choat
Samuel Geer
William Davis
Thomas Trapp 3rd
Cooper Polegreen
Edward Ewen Jun'
Benjamin Brooks
Jonathan Snow
William Fargo
Frederick Fanning
John Gleason
Samuel Bolles
Joseph Freeman
Jonathan Colefox
William Taylor
Joseph Randall
Eli Widger
Nathan Shoals
William Harrison
Jacob Rand
Cornelius Griffin
Peter Rogers
Simeon Reynolds
Levi Wentworth
Samuel Lathrop
Roger Avery
Isaac Cocheits
Christopher Downing
George Mitchel
Daniel Tracy
Joseph Truman

## PLAINFIELD

Maj' Wills Cleft
Cap' John M°Griegier
Cap' Lieu' Lem[11] Cleft
Serg' Asa Jones
" W" Waterman
Joshua Stoddard
Reuben Briant
Amos Bennet
Phinehas Hulet
Sip Watson Negro
Jonathan Whipple
Benjamin Johnson
Ned Negro
Stephen Bennet
John Satterlee
Sam[11] Stafford
Nath[11] Sabins
Jacob Hurd
Lott Chase
Sam[11] Deates Negro
Frederick Waldo
Peter Marsh
Abel Franklin
Cudgo Negro
Josiah Rogers
W" Meach

## POMFRET

Jacob Goodell
Nehemiah Bacon
John Shadden
Abiel Lyon
Benj[a] Sharp
Oliver Reed
Thomas Jones
Elisha Stowell

Henry Smith
Jaazaniah How
Joseph Holmes
John Barker
Joseph Ross
Samuel Bugbee
Abner French
Elias Robison
Zenas Hathway
Cyrus Cortwhrite
Ebenezer Grow
James Grant
Nathⁱⁱ Stowell
Cezar Negro Man
Jonathan Craine
Caleb Conant
Jonathan Bullock
John Duggins
Elias Jones
Ebenʳ Gilbert
John Cambell
Benjᵃ Buffington
Samˡˡ Glass
Rawland Cotton
John Briant
Abial Farnam
William Cleavland
Jonathan Hill
Joseph Griffin
Obadiah Brown
Abner Chapman
Ebenezer Cheney
Dick a Negro Man
Jacob Hovey
Eleazer Owens

Nehemiah Buckin
Jesse Earles
James Pain Fitch (Dead)
Amasa Coussland
Joseph Gunner
Simeon Camp
John Lilley
Samuel Cady
Genˡˡ Putnams Negro Man
Jonas Newport
Alvin Goodell
William Winslow
William Cart
John Cheney
Andrew Morrisson
Lemuel Fling
William Earl
Thomas Jones
John Wheeler
Billinds Sabin
Samuel Cleavland
James Jones
William Lashbrooks
Lewis a Negro Man
Henry Smith
Oliver Reed (Dead)
Elisha Stowell (Dsmissᵈ)
William Arvin
Thomas Hill
Ezra Goodell
John Wampee
Elijah Cheney
Silas Covel
Ezekiel Lomiss
Samuel Millinton

## PRESTON

Lᵗ Charles Miel
Silas Storry
William Aldrish
Thomas Jackson
James McDanields
Simeon Rouse
Nathan Tyler
Luke (? Duke) Guyant
Obediah Seers
Serjᵗ Asa Burnham
Joseph Holly
Joshua Meech
Isaac Evens
Andrew McLorey
William Prince Negᵒ
Ezra Ames
Lemuel Herrick
Daniel Thomas
John Johnson
John Dugan

Christopher Avery
Abraham Patinger
Elisha Baldwin
Ephᵐ Coye
Josphᵇ Billing
Nathan Ayres
Jesse Benjamins
Seth Frink
Elisha Frink
Joab Burton
Serjᵗ Isaac Coit
Serjᵗ Daniel Coit
John Boardmun
Wᵐ Little
Jonᵗʰ Brown
John Austen
Luther Gates
Merit Rockwell
Thomas Frink
Theophilas Frink

Jos[h] Gideons
Joshua Bunday
Henry Burnside
Stephen Downer
John Potter
Serj[t] Ephrain Morgan
Asa Bowdish
Jos[h] Prentice
Zebulon Ames
Carpender Ellis
Reuben Park
Azariah Lorthup
Ephram Withy
Joseph Woodard
David Parke
Sam[l] Vallet
James M[c]Clain

John Stringer
Robert Bruce
Stephen Danield
John Paul
Elias Meason
Nathaniel Whitechurch
James Frink Jun[r]
Josiah Wood
Gideon Lynde
John Chambers
Nathaniel Holt
Thomas Hallet
Nathan Elies
John Ayer
Joseph Rowse
Constant Avery
Thomas Bundy

## RIDGEFIELD

Col[o] Bradley
Lieu[t] Kafin
Cap[t] S[t] John
Lieu[t] Smith
Stephen Rementon
Levi Keeler
Jeremiah Keeler
Elipha Perry
Elijah Weed
Barack Nickerson
Eliphaz Nickerson
Elisha Lincoln
Thomas Keeler
Williams Cummus
John Condreck
Ezekiel Whitney

Lewis Jacklin
Solomin Ren (?)
Abraham Russego
Darius Benedict
Nehemiah Olmsted
Jeremiah Osborn
Gilbert Brush
Thomas Hutchenson
Thomas Wason
Sylvanus Sealy
Benjamin Bennett
Hezekiah Hawley
John Hitchcock
Mousiah (?) Weeks
James Stanton
Stephen Meaker

## SALISBURY

Lieu[t] Elezer Claghorn
Serg[t] Giles Hull
Corp[l] John M[c]Lean
Corp[l] Daniel Evarts
Corp[l] William Tupper
fifer Jacob M[c]Lean
Champeon Ackley
Artemus Bloget
Hildrick Barrot
James Bradley
Ozias Baker
Curtice Chappel
Jacob Coon
Thomas Chipman
Isaac Cool
Daniel Cammell
Nathanael Emmeson
Henery Fits Jerell
Daniel Forgerson

Joseph Trumble Fitch
Bezellel Farnum
Samuel Fisk
Benjamin Graves
Amasa Grinall
George Griswould
Samuel Griswould
Henery Hull
Daniel Hull
Moses Hull
Jonathan Hull
John Havens
John Hawley
Willard Larrebee
Thomas Lewis
Billy Munger
William Mattherson
Simeon Meigs
Eliphelet Owen

CONNECTICUT LINE, 1777-1781.

Phinias Strong
Benjamin Schophel
Peter Serdam
Gamalel Terry
Asa Owen
Martain Tubbs
Abraham Welden

Isaac Wellden
William White
Solomon Whitney
John Wield
William Yates
Job Towsley
Dan¹ (?) Bostwick

## SAYBROOK

| | | |
|---|---|---|
| John Hart | Cap¹ | Ethan Pratt Jun' |
| Asa Lay | Lieu¹ | Sam¹ Doty Jun' |
| Benoni Shipman | " | Gideon Buckingham Ju' |
| Henry Hill | " | John Nichols |
| Jeremiah Lord | Sarj¹ | Philip Daras |
| James Shipman | " | John Widger |
| Sam¹ Clark Jun' | " | Stephen Waterhouse |
| Elias Pratt | " | Sam¹ Hansan |
| Wᵐ Lord | " | Stephen Ludlow |
| Wᵐ Chapman | " | Oliver White |
| Wᵐ Doty | " | Stephen Butler |
| Dann Chapman | " | Cyrus Grimes |
| Morris Jones | " | Robert Newell Jun' |
| Stephen Ingham | " | Wᵐ Cooper |
| James Foster | Corpʲ | Aaron Jones |
| Benjⁿ Mack | do | Jonathan Butler |
| Sam¹ Williard | do | Zebedee Brown |
| Sam¹ Beamont Jun' | do | Gift Negro |
| Wᵐ Bartholomew | do | Amos Lord |
| Hezekiah Buckingham Jr (?) | do | Soldiers Hir'd by Two Men |
| Robert Newell | Private | Oliver Hull |
| Jediah Gladding | | James Post |
| Jesse Chalker | | George Spencer |
| Joseph Hand | | Constant Chapman |
| Prince Doan | | Thomas Quiba |
| Jediah Chapman Jun' | | Ebenezer Stevens |
| Jediah Denison | | Cornilus Wright |
| Isaac Warding | | James Grant |
| Andrew Tooly | | Wᵐ Harvy |
| Wᵐ Stephens | | Elijah Stevens |
| Zepheniah Bowers | | Simeon Luis |
| Isaac Caby | | Andrew Lewis |
| James Springard | | Benjⁿ Sherman |
| Limbo Negro | | Taber Smith |
| Pabady (?) Pratt | | Ethan Pratt |
| Adam Crammer | | Sam¹ Comstock J' |
| Jesper Pratt | | Martin Dibble |
| John Widger Jun' | | Pearce White |
| Asa Pratt Jun' | | |

## SHARON

Lieu¹ David Strong
NathanielWhipel
Daniel Elmer
Josiah Cleaveland
Jonathan Russ
Robert Jonson
Ebenezer Gilson

Amos Allin
Wait Yale
Thomas Wanerite
Enos Pettet
David Goodrich
Isaac Fisher
Stephen Wells

Jones Knap
William Stewart
James Laughlin
Timothy Brockway
James Knap
Noah Kelsey
Jonathan Tobias
Ezekel Whitney
Zelphehead Williamson
William Low
Derias Gray
Derias Colkin
James Tobias
Jabez Lewis
Samuel Gray
Cornelius Hamlin
Josiah Strong
Abner Calkin
Jude Bill
Nathaniel Richards

Joseph Strong
Daniel Elmer Jun
Henery Stephens
Amasa Warner
Phin: Benjamens
Eliphelit Smith
Ariel Acley
Henery Mackintire
Joseph Tucker
Adonijah Pangborn
Lemuel Sherod
Ben Foster
John Goodrich
Eliphalit Everit
Daniel Avery
Isaac Pierce
Isaac Persons
Jonathan Tobias
Nathaniel Tyler
Negor by Name

## SOMERS

The Regiment and Company of Maj$^r$ Walbridges Comp$^a$ Col Shermans Regiment.
  Serj$^t$ W$^m$ Elmer
  Thomas Wood
  Jacob Ward Jun$^r$
  Joel Pease
  William Maning
  Nathan Jones
  Dan$^{ll}$ Bewel
  W$^m$ Quirk
  Amos Lane an Indian supposed to be Deserted.

Cap$^t$ Blackmans Company.
Col Sherlburns Reg$^t$
  Russel Pratt
  James Spencer
  John Hitchcock
  Levi Hamblin
  John Hamblin
  Josiah Gibbs

Isaac Shepard
Philip Langdon
Alex$^r$ Baxter
John Ferman
Dan$^{ll}$ Rice

Cap$^t$ Wrights Comp$^a$
Col. Bradleys Reg$^t$
  John Orcott
  Ruben Coley
  Peter Pease

Cap$^t$ Abeys Comp$^a$
Col. Willys Reg$^t$
  Jacob Brown
  John Cleveland
  Ichiel Gibbs
  James Taylor listed with Leut Chapman Toland, Supposed to be Deserted
  Eleazer Jones Deceast

## SIMSBURY

Voluntarily Inlisted for three years or during the war
Lieu$^t$ Theophilus Woodbridge
  Lieu$^t$ James Andrus
  Stephen Langathe
  John Humphry
  Ezekiel Messenger
  John Hill 2$^d$
  Roland Linsey

Josiah Linsey
Israel Humphry
Hezekiah Phelps Ju$^r$
Samuel Church
Elisha Harrington
John Thorril
Benjamin Hays
Asa Hays
James Slaughter
Jacob Davis

CONNECTICUT LINE, 1777–1781.

James Kirtland now
          Discharged
William Talor
David Clark now Ded
Joseph Weed now Ded
Consider Holcomb Ju<sup>r</sup>
Hired for three years or during
the war
  Elisha Case
  David Egelstone
  Oliver woodword
  Thomas Phelps
  Benjamin Bodwill
  Josiah Higley
  John Farron
  Francies Olmsted
  Ebenezer Drake
  Uriah Pees now Ded
  Thomas Burn
  Zackery Prince now Ded
        Rec<sup>d</sup> his freedom

Luke Guiant
Philister Pinney
David Eno Ju<sup>r</sup>
W<sup>m</sup> Clark
John Davis
George Hills
James Nocak
London Wallace (?)
Ashbel Olmsted
Samuel Spray
Jaben Bennet
William Clark
Samuel Spencer
James Gallet
Samuel Wampey
Calob Curtis
Elijah Clark
Gilbert Whitney
Benjamin Brewer now Ded
Jacob Holloday
A Negro name not known

## STAFFORD

Maj<sup>r</sup> Amos Walbridge
Serj<sup>t</sup> Sam<sup>ll</sup> Worner
  " Josiah Edson
  " Isaac Pinny
  " Jos<sup>h</sup> Green
Corp<sup>l</sup> Jos<sup>h</sup> Whiston
  " Jos<sup>h</sup> Walbridge
Nathan Washbon Drum<sup>r</sup>
Fife Porter Wolbridge
Steph<sup>n</sup> Moulton Bond musick
Asa Thompson
Phin. Manning
Nathan Edson
Robert Thompson
Benj<sup>n</sup> Washbon
Ebenez<sup>r</sup> Snell
Joshua Wheler
Zadock Wheler
Hezekiah Wheler

Joseph Cross
Benj Reynalds
Steph<sup>n</sup> Whiteaker
Tim<sup>o</sup> Herrington
Sam<sup>ll</sup> Millington 3<sup>d</sup>
Nanh<sup>ll</sup> Cushmon
Asa Butler
Israel Butler
Simeon Webster 3<sup>d</sup>
Reuben Putman
Isaac Cushmon
Benj<sup>n</sup> Orcutt
David Green Ju<sup>r</sup>
Benj<sup>n</sup> Butler
Philip Kibbe
Nath<sup>ll</sup> Walker
Timothy Wheler Dest.
Nath<sup>ll</sup> Foster Dest.

## TOLLAND

Cap<sup>t</sup> Ich<sup>d</sup> Hinckley
L<sup>t</sup> Rufus Price
L<sup>t</sup> Elijah Chapman
Doc<sup>r</sup> Jeremiah West
Serj<sup>t</sup> Eben<sup>r</sup> Stebens
Nehemiah Saben
Jonathan Delano
Jonathan Luce
Elihu Johnson
Tirus Preston
Andrew Peterson
Elias Newton
Martin Davice
W<sup>m</sup> Huntington

W<sup>m</sup> Johnson
Solomon Eaton
Ebenezer Brown
Isaac Squire
Abel Crandal
J. Procter Burrows
W<sup>m</sup> Sowl
Shoball Dimmick
Edy Hatch
Simon Stimson
Clement Miner
Rausel Miner
Jacob Haskal
John Crandal

George Hubbard
Elijah Benton
Joseph Sparks
Richard Carlton

Amos Harris
Ame Paulk
David Paine

## UNION

In the Year 1777 Inlisted without any Hire
  Leiu$^t$ James Sprague
  Serg$^t$ Nehemiah Coye (?)
  John Laflen Jun$^r$
  George Dillabur
  Samuel Peirce
Hired for three years & have families
  Thomas Taylor
  James Houghton
  Ebenezer Lillie
  William Moor Jun$^r$

Hired for three years & have no families
  James Walker
  Benjamin Bullin
  John Smith
  Luthar Loomis
  Joshua Ephraim
  Eleazer Payon (?)
Hired to Inlist in y$^e$ year 1778 for three years
  James Laflen
  John Wright
  Joseph Snell
  Abraham Laflin
  Nehemiah Packer

## VOLUNTOWN

3$^{rd}$ Comp$^y$ allarm List
|   | Reg$^t$ Listed into |
|---|---|
| Peter Morras | Col Huntington |
| Robert Green | " |
| Henry Bacon | " |
| Henry Carpentor | " |
| Moses Culver | " |

6 Comp$^y$ alarm List
| Lem$^{ll}$ Shelle | " |
|---|---|

3 Comp$^y$ Militia
| Rob$^t$ Campbell | Col Durkee |
|---|---|
| Nathan Coy | Col Prentice |
| Zoath Tucker | " |
| Peleg Shaw | " |
| Joseph Robens | " |
| Joseph Shely | Col Sherbum |
| Rich$^d$ Soles | " |
| Joseph Peters | Col Wyllys |
| Mark Crosswell | Col Prentice |
| Prince Summut | Col Wyllys |
| Ceser Negro | " |

6 Comp$^y$ Militia
| John Gray | Col Huntington |
|---|---|
| Alex$^r$ Williams | " |
| Jaduthan Heard | " |
| W$^m$ Adams | Col Durkee |
| Squir Wright | Col Huntington |
| W$^m$ Gray | " |
| David Cady | " |
| W$^m$ Knight | " |

7 Comp$^y$ Militia
| Amos Denisen | " |
|---|---|
| Phenis Ellis | " |
| W$^m$ Pierce | " |
| David Coy | " |
| W$^m$ Beazel | " |
| Emanuel Redrik | Col Durkee |
| Christ$^o$ Brown | Col Sherburn |
| Heney Hall | Col Huntington |

## WALLINGFORD

Cap$^t$ Eph$^m$ Chamberlain
L$^t$ Levi Munson
" Joseph Shailor
" John Mansfield
" Lem$^l$ Hitchcock
Charles Peck Serj. Artill.
Jehiel Peck Serj. Art$^y$
Jesse Peck
Titus Hart
Aaron Hall

Abel Tharp
Tho$^s$ Mix
Enos Mix
John Francis
Andrew Andrews Serj$^t$
Edmond Fields
Jesse Vose
Sam$^l$ Wright
John Sled
Selah Stedman

CONNECTICUT LINE, 1777–1781.      83

Joseph Clark
Johnson Cook
Warren Cook
George Cook
Timothy Hart Serj<sup>t</sup>
Benj<sup>a</sup> Hart
Sam<sup>l</sup> Blakslee
Benajah Hall
James Brown
Perigree Dodge
    alias Israel Dodge
Hull Shepherd
L<sup>t</sup> Giles Curtis
Joel Cook
Will<sup>m</sup> Cook
Toney Negro
Tho<sup>s</sup> Janes
Roswel Beach
Elisha Parker
Jotham Rice
Moses Barns
Tho<sup>s</sup> Dudly
John Parker
Timothy Parker
Joseph Wolcott Jun<sup>r</sup>
Charles Heydon
James Prout
Asa Beach
James Miles
Dan<sup>l</sup> Smith
Benj<sup>a</sup> Johnson
Irael Johnson
Wait Yale
Amos Parker
Anthony Goodsill
Abram Parker
Elisha Parker
Eliakim Johnson
Charles Merriman
Dan<sup>l</sup> Cady
Dan<sup>l</sup> Bradly
Dan<sup>l</sup> Johnson Hall
Will<sup>m</sup> Parker
Reuben Moss
Thaddeus Todd
David Hall
Elisha Hall
Asaph Merriam
Edm<sup>d</sup> Merriam
Nash Yale
Lem<sup>l</sup> Willcox
Joseph Coburn
Ja<sup>s</sup> Coburn
Rufus Hall
Jonathan Ford
Levi Robinson
Benj. Ford
Jatham Hall
Benj. Rexford Ju<sup>r</sup>
Moses Hall

John Anthony
Seth Smith
Barnabas Mitchel
Elisha Bishop
Lemon Cumber Negro
Boston Negro
Chatham Freeman Negro
Samson Negro
Gideon Webb
Abel Clark
Joel Willmot
Elmor Russel
Reuben Moss
John Johnson
Prince Hotchkiss Negro
Ambrose Hine
Job Hull negro
Chauncy Lewis
Nathan<sup>l</sup> Tyler
Eldad Porter
Sam<sup>l</sup> Jones
Medad Potter
Benoni Moss
Asa Bellamy
Aaron Clark
Amos Andrews
Ichabod Hitchcock
Levi Hitchcock
Benj. Bristol
Amos Mix
Sam<sup>l</sup> Spencer
Isaiah Moss
Almond Munson
Amasa Tharp
Amos Tharp
Sam<sup>l</sup> S. B. Hotchkiss
Orange Munson
Lent Munson
Charles London
John Hurlbert
Elihu Cook
Will<sup>m</sup> Prout
Abij: Ives
Dick Freedom Negro
Eben<sup>r</sup> Lewis
Sam<sup>l</sup> Perkins
John Hasting
John Pierce Serjt.
Enoch Merriman Serjt.
Sam<sup>l</sup> Collins
Eph<sup>m</sup> Merriam
Will<sup>m</sup> Grant
Sharp Yale Negro
Abel Lewis
Dimond or Divan Clark
Peter Sibbels
David Barns
Dan<sup>l</sup> Hummerston
Benj. Parker

## WATERBURY

[The families of each of these soldiers received supplies in 1778 or 1779.]

Asa Thair
Sam[ll] Camp
Isreal Calkins
Richard Clark
Jonah Mallery
Stephen Welton Jun[r]
W[m] Hickcox Jun[r]
John Cole
Eliab Parker
John Smith
Serg[t] Ezekiel Tuttle
Joel Cook
Serg[t] Sam[ll] Lewis
Sam[ll] Camp Jun[r]
Cop[l] Nemiah Royce
Stephen Curtis
Amos Dunbar
Obed Williams
William Southmayd
Ezekiel Sanford
Simeon Graves
Ens[n] Timothy Tuttle
Jonathan Parde

Dan[ll] Barns
Serj[t] Ezekiel Upson
George Prichard Jun[r]
Abial Robbards
Lue Smith
Joel Robbards
Jabez Tuttle
Stephen Judd
John Tattendon
Stephen Scovill
Sergt John Fulford
Sergt Titus Dutton
Sam[ll] Smith
Leiut Nath[ll] Edwards
W[m] Bassit
Jonathan Davis
Bruster Judd
Timothy Andrews
Elisha Hickcox
Nath[ll] Hall
Major David Smith
Isaac Parker
Stephen Davis
Stephen Curtis 3[d]
Hezekiah Tuttle
Dan[ll] Pendleton

## WINCHESTER

George Hudson
Pabdy Stanard
Jonathan Preston
Prince Neagro
John Fay
Seth Stanard
William Leach
Steave Hurlburt

Levi Wilkenson
Steaven Scovils
Adam Mott
Remembrance Filley
Jesse Wilkenso
Garshom Fay
William Fay
Timothy Fay

## WILLINGTON

Serj[t] Caleb Orcutt
Serj[t] David Hinckley
Serj[t] Richard Lord
Corp[l] Haman Hatch
Solomon Fenton
John Scriptor
Nath[a] Carpenter
Allen Carpenter
Corp[l] Adonijah Fenton
James Johnson
John Hinckley Drumer
Asa Stoel

John Scott
Fradrick Pearl
Jabez Flint
Joseph Cushman
William Blanchard
Gideon Noble fifer
David Johnson
Cop[l] Eliphelit Cushman
William Stiles
Joseph Dimick
David Rice

## WINDHAM

Belonging to the 2[d] Society
Lieut Benj[a] Durke
John Burnam

Nathan Burnam
Benjamin Burnap
James Burnap

CONNECTICUT LINE, 1777-1781. 85

Calvin Burnap
John Frame
John Fuller
Abner French
Thomas Farnam
Abial Farnam
James Hale
Nathan Hovey
Philemon Holt
Nath¹ Martin
Meecham Jerem⁵
Meecham Jona⁽ʰ⁾
Martin George
Parry Eben'
Eliphaz Parrish
Jsaiah Rogers Dead
Ruben Farnam
Jonathⁿ Flint
Jacob Hovey or Roger Smith
Elijah Randall
James Smith or Sharper
     Negro
Elias Bingham
Belonging to the first Society
Ebenezer Gray Lᵗ Colº
Nathˡˡ Webb Capᵗ
Amos Woodward
Levi Hibbard
John Bingham Sergᵗ
Timº Hibbard
Asa Hibbard Sergᵗ
David Young Drumer
Eleaz' Robinson
Dyar Hibbard
Uriah Hibbard
Seth Larribe
Caleb Fitch
Elijah Backus
Ezek¹ Dunham
Garshom Dunham
Joseph Read
Mason Abbe
Jonah Palmer
Walter Chaise
Ephᵐ Terry
Ebeⁿ Hibbard
Elijʰ Linkon
Adriel Simons
Salomⁿ Tracy Sergᵗ
Elijʰ Spafford Sergᵗ
Benjⁿ Ripley
Joseph Johnson
Benaijⁿ Geers
John Holly

Joseph West Fief Majʳ
Comfort Foster
Abisha Bingham
Samˡˡ Robinson
Samˡˡ Murdock
Samˡˡ Spencer Artificer
Josiah Read
Jnº Huntington
Jnº Spencer Sergᵗ Light
      Horse
Abner Backus
Jabez Rouse Sergᵗ
Charles Ripley Sergᵗ
Andʷ Warner Corpˡ
Jnº Holliss
Richᵈ Howard
Wᵐ Placey ⎫
Jnº Leathercoat ⎬ Indians
Joseph Robbins ⎪
Joseph Meason ⎭
Silas Frink
Samˡˡ Brown
Joseph Holcom of Windsor
Belonging to the third and fourth
  Societys
Albigenor Waldo Surgion
Samˡˡ Cogswell 1ˢᵗ Lieut
Elias Robinson Ensign
Josiah Burnham Sergᵗ
Alfred Hurlbutt Sergᵗ
Thoˢ Hurlburtt Corpˡ
Nathan Morgan Fiefer
Fradrick Whiting Sergᵗ
Levi Deans
Edwᵈ Coburn
Peter Scovill
Joseph Ginning Juʳ
Zopher Robinson
Nathˡˡ Bennit
Thoˢ F. Gerrald
Asa Walden
Francis Pirkins
Benjⁿ Cary Juʳ
Jabez Pottage an Indian
Abel Robinson
Hezʰ Cary
James L. Flint
Turner Lille
Abner French
Elipaz Kingsley
   Lieut of yᵉ artificers
Levi Cary
Oliver Cary

## WINDSOR

Danˡˡ Bissell Junʳ
Obed Lamberton Jʳ
David Thrall

Joel Denslow Dead
David Gibbs
David Barber Jʳ

Joseph Saymour
Shubel Berber Dead
Ezekiel Clark J'
Joseph Barnard
Simeon Moore J'
Cor¹¹ Russell
Thomas Parsons
Ezra Beckwith
Oliver Woodward
Isaac Thrall
Tim° Hoskins
Palashel Wakefield
Amos Lawrance
Eb¹' Woolworth
Elias Brown
Stephen Loomis J'
Martin Denslow
Sam¹¹ Wing Dead
David Daniels
Aaron Pinney Dead
Dan¹¹ Porter
Barzil Henry
Isaac Phelps Dead
Joseph Wing Dead
Allyn Pryor
Robert Westland J'
Zeb. Hoskins
George Loomis
Phin Griswold
Neil M°Lean J'
Tim° Phelps
Sherman Rowland
Mathew Holcomb Dead

Edward Negro Dead
Cap' Abner Prior
L' Seth Phelps
L' Sam¹¹ Gibbs
Ezekil Case J'
Sam¹¹ Marshall
Joseph Egelston
Levi Charter
Elihu Mills
Elias Crow
Nath¹¹ Egelston J'
Isaac Egelston
Sam¹¹ Brown J'
Abel Gillet J'
Abel Cook Dead
Ephriah Loatwall
Isaac Chandler
Joseph Westland
Timothy Egelston
Will Munrow
Alvin Hurlbut
Sam¹¹ Coy Dead
Shubel Cook
Richard Cook
W^m Cook
John Brister
John Winchel
John Daset
Norman Fyler
Elihu Mather
Nath Mather
Jon^th Bidwell J'

## WOODSTOCK

Serj' Jn° Bartholomew
Corp¹ Dan¹ Smith
  do  Theo' Luther
Lemuel Allen
W^m Jepson
W^m Press
John Briant
David Lawrence
Denis Spencer
Asa Winton
Elihu Hebbard
Timothy Hebbard
Fifer Aaron Hebbard
Fifer Jn° Brock
Tho' Spencer
Jo' Pagan
Nathan Powers
Dan¹ Evans
Jn° Vinton

Abrm White
Nath¹ Robins
Cato Negro
Jason Crawferd
Fredrick Green
Simeon Camp
Peter Saunders
Eli Bruce
Robert Chandler
Dan¹ Bowen
Paul Haradan
Q. M. Asa Lyon
Aas Hibbard
Richard Guile
Amasa Frissel
now { Amos Bunnal
Dead { Corp¹ Jn° Greene
{ James Guile
{ Phelix Negro

## COLCHESTER

[The heading of another part of this document seems to show that it covers service in the Continental Army "up to the first day of Jan'y 1780.] These following are the Names of Soldiers Belonging to the Town of Colchester Who are some of them hired by two men and part of them We Suppose are entitled to 5/ p month from the Towns but have not as Yet Recev'd any

| | |
|---|---|
| John Burns | Amasa Brown |
| John Frederick | Lewis Ackley |
| Elisha Pomp | William Isham |
| Abijah Pratt | Joshua Goff |
| Jonª Isham | Aaron Holmes |
| Nicholas Ackley | Aaron Chamberlin |
| Naomi Beebe | Ebenezer Isham |
| Dennis Gardner | Ephraim Judd |
| Labbeus Loomis | William Burnham |
| Robert Ransom | Arkelaus Free |
| Abner Chapman | Elisha Brown |
| William Baker | Isaac Brown |
| Peregreen Dodge | Samuel Kneeland |
| Roswel Chappel | Joel Fox |
| Edward Rathbun | |
| Jacob Rathburn | [*Comptrollers Office*] |

## WALLINGFORD

[The following names of Continental soldiers from Wallingford are found in another list among others already printed in this volume.]
[These received £5 bounty each.]

| | |
|---|---|
| Daniel Thade | Moses Marus |
| John Stead | Jesse Thorp (?) |
| Timothy Thorp | Saml Holt |
| Elijah Parker | |

[These did not receive bounty]
Benj Kendrich Decd          John Hastens

Edmon Field of this town has drawn a bounty from Waterbury.

[*George M. Curtis, Meriden.*]

## PRISONERS.

The following is a list of the officers belonging to the State of Connecticut that were liveing and in Captivity on Longisland the 2nd of May 1777

Colo. Hobbey Greenwich
Colo. Heart Farmington
Maj. Wells Colchester
Capt. Bennedick Danbury
Capt. Bissel East Hartford
Capt. Percefeild Chatham
Capt. Trobridge N. Haven
Capt. Keeler Norwalk
Capt. Parit Milford
Capt. Couch Walingford
Capt. Smith Colchester
Capt. Beebe Litchfield
Capt. Wells Glasenbury
Lieut. Clark Danbury
Lieut. Trobridge Danbury
Lieut. Gove Preston
Lieut. Fanning Norwich
Lieut. Fitch Norwich
Lieut. Blacklidge Stratford
Lieut. Brainard East Haddam
Lieut. Eells Norwalk
Lieut. Grant Litchfield
Lieut. Gillit Hartford
Lieut. Brewster Preston
Lieut. Tanner Cornwall
Lieut. Orcut Willington
Lieut. Cleaveland Norwich
Lieut. Edwards Waterbury
Lieut. Cooke Torrington
Ens. Forsdich New London
Ens. Hall Derby
Ens. Bradford Plainfield
Ens. Taylor N. Fairfield
Ens. Burnham Danbury
Ens. Lyman Middletown
Ens. Bradford Haddam
Ens. Knowlton Ashford
Storrs Quartermaster Mansfield
Smith Wagonmaster

[*State Library, Revolution 11, 139*]

CONNECTICUT LINE, 1777-1781.            89

## RETURN FROM 4TH BRIGADE OF MILITIA.

A Return of the Soldiers that have inlisted and been draughted or detached from the 4th Brigade of Militia in the State of Connecticut commanded by Brigadier General Silliman to serve in the Continental Army commanded by his Excellency General Washington. May 1, 1778.

| Soldiers Names | Towns they belong to | Company | Regiment | Time they inlisted for | Detached to serve till |
|---|---|---|---|---|---|
| Stephen Meaker | Rodding | | | | |
| Elias Bigsby | " | | | | |
| Nathan Coley | " | | | | |
| Ephraim Bectley | " | | | | |
| John Rumsey | " | | | | |
| Eph<sup>m</sup> Wheeler | " | | | | |
| Eben<sup>r</sup> Patchen | " | | | | |
| Dan<sup>ll</sup> Monroe | " | | | | |
| Abijah Burret | " | | | | |
| Bartholomew Baker | " | | | | |
| Jeremiah Byne | " | | | | |
| Sam<sup>ll</sup> Raymond | " | | | for 8 years | 1 Jan<sup>y</sup> next |
| Peter Drew | " | | " | " | " |
| Nath<sup>l</sup> Morgan | " | | " | " | " |
| Nathan Lyon | " | | " | " | " |
| Moses Knap | " | | " | " | " |
| Lazarus Beach | " | | " | " | " |
| James Sanford | " | | " | " | " |
| Dan<sup>ll</sup> Hill | " | | " | " | " |
| David Hill | " | | " | " | " |
| Israel Rowland | " | | " | " | " |
| James Adams | " | | " | " | " |
| Enos Lee | " | | " | " | " |
| James Green | " | Cap<sup>t</sup> G. Morehouse | " | dureing y<sup>e</sup> Warr | |
| Nathan Rumsey | " | " | " | " | |

## REVOLUTION LISTS AND RETURNS.

| Soldiers Names | Towns they belong to | Company | Regiment | Time they inlisted for dureing y<sup>e</sup> Warr | Detached to serve till |
|---|---|---|---|---|---|
| Nehemiah Sherwood | Redding | Cap<sup>t</sup> G. Morehouse | " | " | |
| Eben<sup>r</sup> Williams | " | " | " | " | |
| Henry Hopkins | " | " | " | " | |
| Gershom Fairchild | " | " | " | " | |
| Jabez Williams | " | " | " | " | |
| Ned Negroe | " | " | " | " | |
| Jack Negroe | " | " | " | " | |
| Nath<sup>ll</sup> Booth | Stratford | Cap<sup>t</sup> Brinsmaid and Nichols | Col<sup>o</sup> Whiteing | " | |
| Joseph Hubbard | " | " | " | " | |
| John Crawfoot | " | " | " | " | |
| John Downs | " | " | " | " | |
| James Downs | " | " | " | " | |
| Abell Peet | " | " | " | " | |
| Reuben Beach | " | " | " | " | |
| John Jones | " | " | " | " | |
| Gideon Seely | " | " | " | " | |
| Daniel Jones | " | " | " | " | |
| Daniel Averies | " | " | " | " | |
| William Dascomb | " | " | " | " | |
| Nathan Hawley | " | " | " | " | |
| Nath<sup>ll</sup> Beach | " | " | " | " | |
| Ephraim Seely | " | " | " | " | |
| John Gilbert | " | " | " | " | |
| Eben<sup>r</sup> Shelly | " | " | " | " | |
| Joel Mosier | " | " | " | " | |
| Gideon Hawley | " | " | " | " | |
| Joseph Wakeley | " | " | " | " | |
| Dan<sup>l</sup> Sherwood | " | " | " | " | |
| Nero Negro | " | " | " | " | |
| Caesar Negro | " | " | " | " | |
| Tony Negro | " | " | " | " | |
| Peter Lewis | " | " | " | " | |
| Sam<sup>ll</sup> Hinman | " | " | " | " | |

## CONNECTICUT LINE, 1777–1781.

| Name | Town | Captain | Colonel | Term |
|---|---|---|---|---|
| Jacob Grover | " | " | " | " |
| John Riggs | " | " | " | " |
| Abrahm Hawley | " | " | " | " |
| Samll Manning | " | " | " | " |
| John Sunderland | " | " | " | " |
| John Downing | " | " | " | " |
| Robert Freman | " | " | " | " |
| Pinkerman Clark | " | " | " | " |
| Jack Freeman | " | Capt J. Benjamen | " | For 8 years |
| Ebenezer Shelly | " | " | " | During Warr |
| Samll Osborn | " | " | " | " |
| Alexr Fairchild | " | " | " | " |
| Samll Richmad | " | " | " | " |
| Amos Saunders | " | " | " | " |
| Prosper Wetmore | " | " | " | " |
| Caleb Chatfield | Derby | not known | Colo Thompson | " |
| John Munroe | Stratford | Capt P. Curtiss | Colo Whiteing | 1 Jany next |
| Samll Lewis Junr | " | " | " | " |
| Israel Hawley | " | " | " | " |
| Jesse Dickerman | " | " | " | " |
| Isaac Dickerman | " | " | " | " |
| Samll Parker | " | Capt S. Beardsly | " | For 8 years |
| Ephm Quosh, Molatt | " | " | " | Dureing ye Warr |
| Lively Negro | " | " | " | " |
| Pomp Negro | " | " | " | " |
| Josman Negro | " | " | " | " |
| Joseph Negro | " | " | " | " |
| David Hard | " | " | " | " |
| Ebenr Smith | " | Capt J. Birdsly | " | " |
| Timothy Chatman | " | " | " | " |
| James Hide | " | " | " | " |
| Benja Wakeley | " | " | " | " |
| Shubael Freeman | " | " | " | " |
| John Williamson | " | " | " | " |
| Gideon Leavensworth | " | " | " | " |

| Soldiers Names | Towns they belong to | Company | Regiment Col° Whiteing | Time they inlisted for During ye Warr | Detached to serve till |
|---|---|---|---|---|---|
| Wallaston Hawley | Stratford | Capt J. Birdsly | | | |
| William L. Jedon | " | " | | | 1 Janry next |
| Benjn Shelton | " | " | | | |
| John Nobles | " | Capt Burroughs | | | |
| Abraham Noble | Fairfield | " | | | |
| John Chaps | " | " | | | |
| Barack Taylor | " | " | | | |
| Burr Gilbert | " | " | | | |
| Ebenezer Meaker | " | " | | | |
| Thomas Durfee | " | " | | | |
| Seth Buckley | " | " | | | |
| Robert Simmons | Stratford | Capt S. Judson | | | |
| John Bennett | " | " | | | |
| John Feers | " | " | | | |
| Daniel Munroe | " | " | | | |
| David Minot | " | " | | | |
| Silas Glasgow Negro | " | " | | | |
| James Beers | " | " | | | 1 Janry next |
| Isaac Hubbell | " | " | | | " |
| John Eopkins | Suratoga in N. York State | hired into Capt Booth's Compy Capt J. Booth | | For 8 years Dureing ye Warr | |
| John Easset | Stratford | Capt Eb. Coe | | | |
| Benjamin Dean | " | " | | | |
| Jesse Frimus | " | " | | | |
| Amos Temp | " | " | | | |
| Samuel Pulford | " | " | | | |
| Lewis Anjevine | " | " | | | |
| Ephraim Seely | " | " | | | |
| Briant Montegue | " | " | | | |
| Eli Lewis | " | " | | | |
| John Benjamen Junr | " | " | | | 1 Janry next |
| Jesse Smith | " | " | | | |
| David Barlow | " | " | | | |
| Isaac Brown | " | " | | | |

## CONNECTICUT LINE, 1777-1781.

| Name | Place | Captain | Colonel | Term | Date |
|---|---|---|---|---|---|
| Orry King | " | " | " | " | " |
| Josiah Barrow | " | " | " | " | " |
| Joel Beers | " | " | " | " | " |
| John Beardsley | " | " | " | " | " |
| Samuel Whitney | " | " | " | " | " |
| John Peet | " | " | " | " | " |
| Jasper Jones | " | " | " | " | " |
| Justus Seely | " | " | " | " | " |
| Nath¹¹ Beebee | " | " | " | " | " |
| Daniel Mosier | Stanford | not known | Col Mead | For 8 years | |
| David Selleck | Stratford | Ensign Nichols | Col⁰ Whiteing | Dureing y⁰ Warr | |
| Stephen Hall | " | " | " | " | |
| Eli Nichols | " | " | " | " | |
| Henry Bayley | " | " | " | " | |
| Abell Mallet | " | " | " | " | |
| Sam¹¹ Parker | " | " | " | " | |
| Truman French | " | " | " | " | |
| Abrah= Fabrique | " | " | " | " | |
| Benj= Bennitt 3ᵈ | " | " | " | " | |
| Tim⁰ Blackman | " | " | " | " | |
| Daniel Barlow | " | " | " | For 3 Years | 1ˢᵗ Janʳʸ next |
| David Watkins | " | " | " | " | " |
| Abijah Beardsley | " | " | " | " | " |
| Sam¹¹ Curtiss | " | " | " | " | " |
| Asa Winton | " | Cap¹ Leavensw^th | " | During y⁰ Warr | |
| Jn⁰ Benjamen Mitchel | " | " | " | " | |
| Abijah Perry | " | " | " | " | |
| George Leaming | " | " | " | " | |
| Toney Freeman | " | " | " | " | |
| Peter Lewis | " | " | " | " | |
| Joseph Lawin | " | Cap¹ Tomlinson | " | " | 1ˢᵗ Janʳʸ next |
| George Hall | " | " | " | " | " |
| David Blackman | " | " | " | " | |
| Jeremiah Blackman | " | " | " | | |
| Sam¹¹ Blackman | " | " | " | | |

## REVOLUTION LISTS AND RETURNS.

| Soldiers Names | Towns they belong to | Company | Regiment | Time they Inlisted for During ye Warr | Detached to serve till |
|---|---|---|---|---|---|
| Miles Dickson | Stratford | Capt Tomlinson | Colo Whiteing | " | |
| Richard Hawley | " | " | " | " | |
| Samll Riggs Mills | " | " | " | " | |
| Elisha Pulford | " | " | " | " | |
| Lemuel Seeley | " | " | " | " | |
| Nathan Thompson | " | " | " | " | |
| Samll Washborn | " | " | " | " | |
| Isaiah Wilcockson | " | " | " | " | |
| Robert Welch | " | " | " | " | |
| James Wayland | " | " | " | " | |
| James Hide | " | " | " | " | |
| Nehemiah Gearham | " | Capt Sterling | " | " | |
| Charles Burrit | " | " | " | " | |
| Samll Lewis Brooks | " | " | " | " | |
| Josiah French | " | " | " | " | |
| Richard Handy | " | " | " | " | |
| John McKenzie | " | " | " | " | |
| Samll Wakely Junr | " | " | " | " | |
| David Wells Junr | " | " | " | " | |
| Timothy Gaunecy | not known | " | " | " | |
| Isaac Hubbell | Fairfield | " | " | " | |
| Zachariah Sherwood | " | " | " | " | |
| David Jackson | " | " | " | " | |
| David Morehouse | " | " | " | " | |
| Isaac Odell | " | " | " | " | |
| Elijah Patchen | " | " | " | " | |
| Burr Gilbert | " | " | " | " | |
| Transient Persons hired by Jeremiah Rines | Sratford | not known | not known | " | |
| Ephm Porter | " | " | " | " | |
| James Hamhidon | " | " | " | " | |
| Thomas Jacklin | " | " | " | " | |
| John Williams | " | " | " | " | |
| Richard Danbury | " | " | " | " | |

| | | | | |
|---|---|---|---|---|
| John White | " | " | " | " |
| Ephraim Rose | " | " | " | " |
| William Braizier | " | " | " | " |
| John Titus | " | " | " | " |
| David Day | " | " | " | " |
| John Davenport | " | " | " | " |
| John Jones | " | " | " | " |
| William Lock | " | " | " | " |
| John Wright | " | " | " | " |
| Jonath" Goodwell | " | " | " | " |
| Ashel Tirrel | " | " | " | " |
| Andrew Porter | Fairfield | Cap' Barham | " | " |
| Daniel Burr | " | " | " | " |
| Richard Williams | " | " | " | " |
| Andrew Porter | " | " | " | " |
| Lewis Garrison | " | " | " | " |
| Joseph Armstrong | " | " | " | " |
| Phillip Frenchman | " | " | " | " |
| Peter Rowfiner | " | " | " | " |
| Seth Bulkley | " | " | " | " |
| Joseph Lorian | " | Cap' Thorp | " | " |
| Wakeman Hull | " | " | " | " |
| Augustus Sturgis | " | " | " | " |
| Stratton Osborn | " | " | " | " |
| John Fuller | " | " | " | " |
| Gilbert Dudley | " | " | " | " |
| Richard Williams | " | " | " | " |
| Nathan Squire | " | " | " | " |
| Peter Stalker | " | " | " | " |
| Daniel Bennitt | Norwalk | not known | Col° Mead | " |
| Abrah" Raymond | Fairfield | Cap' G. Burr | Col° Whiteing | " |
| John Mitchel | " | " | " | " |
| Epaphras Goodsell | " | " | " | " |
| Moses Sturgis | " | " | " | " |
| Daniel Meaker | " | " | " | " |

| Soldiers Names | Towns they belong to | Company | Regiment | Time they Inlisted for | Detached to serve till |
|---|---|---|---|---|---|
| Ezra Williams | Fairfield | Cap" G. Barr | Col° Whiteing | During y" Warr |  |
| Jonathan Poor | " | " | " | " |  |
| James Cole | " | Cap" Nash and Wakeman | " | For 8 years |  |
| Stephen Lockwood | " | " | " | " |  |
| Eben' Allen Jun' | " | " | " | " |  |
| Alexand' Wicks | " | " | " | " |  |
| Joseph Batterson | " | " | " | " |  |
| James Batterson Jun' | " | " | " | " |  |
| Stephen Batterson | " | " | " | " |  |
| W" Raymond | " | " | " | " |  |
| Joseph Mills | " | " | " | " |  |
| Nath" Sturgis | " | " | " | " |  |
| Isaac Elwood | " | " | " | " |  |
| Abr" Sturgis | " | " | " | " |  |
| Joshua Jecocks | " | " | " | " |  |
| Ezra Wood | " | " | " | " |  |
| Joshua Disbrow | " | " | " | " |  |
| Issac Disbrow | " | " | " | " |  |
| Henry Disbrow | " | " | " | " |  |
| Simon Disbrow | " | " | " | " |  |
| Gideon Hurlburt | " | " | " | " |  |
| John Couch | " | " | " | " |  |
| John Johnson | " | " | " | " |  |
| William Johnson | " | " | " | " |  |
| Justin Disbrow | " | " | " | " |  |
| Abrah" Couch | " | " | " | " |  |
| John Crossman | " | " | " | " |  |
| Ephraim Beers | " | " | " | " |  |
| Gershom Jecox | " | " | " | " |  |
| Moses Dimon | " | Cap' Wheeler | " | Dureing y" Warr |  |
| William Cable | " | " | " | " |  |
| Tony Lyon a Molatt | " | Cap' Silliman | " | " |  |
| Nehemiah Turner | " | " | " | " |  |
| Dan' Wingfield | " | " | " | " |  |

|  | | | | |
|---|---|---|---|---|
| John Fuller | " | " | | |
| William Gold | " | " | | |
| Peter Stalker | " | " | | |
| Samuel Chapman | " | " | | |
| Richard Williams | " | " | | |
| John Baker | " | " | | |
| John Lyon | " | " | | |
| Stephen Lyon | " | " | | |
| Asa Turney | " | " | | |
| Josiah Armstrong | " | " | | |
| Enos Jones Prindle | " | " | | |
| Dan'l Meaker | " | " | | |
| Paschal Churchet | " | " | | |
| Thomas Allen | " | " | | |
| Samuel French | Stratford | " | Cap' N. Seely | |
| Amos Freeman | " | " | " | |
| Nathan Tirrell | " | " | " | |
| John Jones | " | " | " | |
| Enos Wheeler | Fairfield | " | " | |
| Eben' Beech | " | " | " | |
| Eleazer Hall | " | " | " | 1 Jan'y next |
| John Gilbert | " | " | Cap' Bennitt | " |
| Dan'l Jackson | " | " | " | " |
| Isband Hubbell | " | " | " | " |
| Ebenezer Gilbert | Stratford | " | " | " |
| Jedediah Hall | " | " | " | |
| John Blackman | " | " | " | |
| Nath'l Treadwell | Fairfield | " | Cap' Lyon | 1st Jan'y next |
| William Jackson | " | " | " | " |
| Sam'l Lyon | " | " | " | " |
| Daniel Vance | " | " | " | 1st Jan'y next |
| Thomas Treadwell | " | " | " | " |
| Hezekiah Fanton | " | " | " | " |
| Josiah Cable | | | | |
| John Stalker | | | | |

| Soldiers Names | Towns they belong to | Company | Regiment | Time they inlisted for Dureing the War or 3 years | Detached to serve till 1st Jan'y next |
|---|---|---|---|---|---|
| Gold Dimon | Fairfield | Cap't Lyon | Col° Whiteing | | " |
| Eliphalet Bradley | " | Cap't Hill | " | | " |
| Natham Bradley | " | " | " | " | |
| Daniel Raymond | " | " | " | " | |
| Sam'll Turney Jun'r | " | " | " | " | |
| Nathan Winton | " | " | " | " | |
| Aaron Wayley | " | " | " | " | |
| Hezekiah Webb | " | " | " | " | |
| Joseph Moster | " | " | " | " | |
| Ezekiel Thorp | " | " | " | " | |
| Aaron Thorp | " | " | " | " | |
| Francis Swords | " | " | " | " | |
| Peter Stalker | " | " | " | " | |
| Hezekiah Wayley | " | Cap't Godfrey | " | " | |
| Nath'll Johnson | " | " | " | " | |
| Michael Bowen | " | " | " | " | |
| Josiah Green | " | " | " | " | |
| John Teen | " | " | " | " | |
| Elip'h Gray | " | " | " | " | |
| Bradley Dean | " | Cap't Dean | " | " | |
| Thiah Beers | " | " | " | " | |
| Dan'll Canfield | " | " | " | " | |
| Sam'll Green | " | " | " | " | |
| Benjamen Allen | " | " | " | " | |
| Atkinson Hilton | " | " | " | " | |
| Francis Hutternock | " | " | " | " | |
| Joseph Ogden | " | " | " | " | |
| Stephen Hurlburt | " | " | " | " | |
| Stephen Dickeman | " | " | " | " | |
| Joel Gilbert | " | " | " | " | |
| Stephen Lockwood | Ridgefield | not known | Col° Beardsley | " | |
| Ezekiel Hawley hired | | | | | |

CONNECTICUT LINE, 1777-1781.

| | | | | |
|---|---|---|---|---|
| Jonathan Edwards | { Massachusetts Bay State Woodbury } | not known Cap' A. Mallary | not known Col° Moseley | During y° Warr |
| Stephen Hull | " | " | " | " |
| Eliphalet Easton | " | " | " | " |
| Sam'l Wilson | " | " | " | " |
| Elisha Walker | " | " | " | " |
| Phinehas Camp | " | " | " | " |
| Tite Negro | | | | |
| Isaac Pollard | Waterbury | not known | not known | |
| Freman Judd | Woodbury | Cap' Mallary | Col° Mosely | |
| Jabez Bacon | " | " | " | " |
| Eben' Talman | " | " | " | " |
| Daniel Bedson (?) | " | " | " | " |
| Eli Stoddard | " | Cap' T. Judson | " | " |
| Zachariah Walker | " | " | " | " |
| Chapman Judson | " | " | " | " |
| Abel Linsley Jun' | " | " | " | " |
| John Slaughter | " | " | " | " |
| Abell Mix | " | " | " | " |
| Adam Crammer | " | " | " | " |
| Phinehas Demming | " | Cap' N. Hine | " | " |
| Delucena Bacchus | " | " | " | " |
| Simeon Tylor | " | " | " | " |
| John Davenport | " | " | " | " |
| John Herrick | " | " | " | " |
| Zuor Bradley | " | " | " | " |
| Jonathan Twist | " | " | " | " |
| Aner Adye | " | " | " | " |
| Julian Easton | " | " | " | " |
| Benj" Avery | " | " | " | " |
| Benj" Wheeler Jun' | " | " | " | " |
| John Tirrell | " | " | " | " |
| James Brown | " | " | " | " |
| Gideon Hurd Jun' | " | " | " | " |
| Anthony Stoddard | " | " | " | " |

1st Jan'y next
"
"

1 Jan'y next
"
"

| Soldiers Names | Towns they belong to | Company | Regiment | Time they inlisted for During yᵉ Warr | Detached to serve till |
|---|---|---|---|---|---|
| Jehiel Bradley | Woodbury | Capᵗ N. Hine | Colᵒ Mosely | | 1ˢᵗ Janʸ next |
| Truman Crissey | " | " | " | | " |
| Iri Way | " | " | " | | " |
| Michael Molatto | " | " | " | | " |
| Timᵒ Gibbs | Newtown | not known | Colᵒ Beardsley | | |
| Matthew Read | " | " | " | | |
| John Burns | Woodbury | Capᵗ N. Hine | Colᵒ Mosely | " | |
| Zachariah Prentice | " | " | " | " | |
| Timᵒ Tomlinson | " | " | " | " | |
| Elijah Sherman | " | " | " | " | |
| Nicholas Masters | " | " | " | " | |
| Chapman Judson Junʳ | " | Capᵗ E. Smith | " | | |
| Reuben Hotchkiss | " | " | " | | |
| Zachariah Beers | " | " | " | | |
| Norman Easton | " | " | " | | |
| John Drummonds | " | " | " | | |
| Simeon Barns | " | " | " | | |
| Zadock Hawkins | " | " | " | | 1ˢᵗ Janʸ next |
| Zadock Hawkins Junʳ | " | " | " | | " |
| Jonas Hinman | " | " | " | " | |
| Joel Hinman | " | " | " | " | |
| Enos Hinman | " | " | " | " | |
| Israel Curtiss Junʳ | " | " | " | " | |
| Charles Strong | " | Capᵗ D. Hinman | " | " | |
| Elisha Hobart | " | " | " | " | |
| John Hobart | " | " | " | " | |
| David Hicock | " | " | " | | |
| Gideon Bristol Junʳ | " | " | " | | |
| John Bulford | " | " | " | | 1ˢᵗ Janʸ next |
| Moses Strickling | " | " | " | | " |
| Davis Demmonds | " | " | " | | " |
| Thomas James | " | " | " | | |
| Edmund Washband | " | " | " | " | |
| Stephen Stillwell | New Milford | Capᵗ B. Bostwick | " | | |

CONNECTICUT LINE, 1777-1781.   101

| | | | | |
|---|---|---|---|---|
| Dan'l Dye | " | " | " | " |
| John Fish | " | " | " | " |
| Sam'l Phillips | " | " | " | " |
| A man whose Name is unknown | " | " | " | " |
| James Dally | " | " | " | " |
| Nath'l Durkee | " | " | " | " |
| James Bennitt | " | " | " | " |
| Oliver Bostwick | " | " | " | " |
| Josiah Buck | " | " | " | " |
| Joseph Clark | " | " | " | " |
| Christopher Cockran | " | " | " | " |
| W'm Drinkwater | " | " | " | " |
| Theoph's Comstalk | " | " | " | " |
| A Person hired by some of the Comp'y his Name forgot | " | " | " | " |
| Eben'r Drinkwater | New Milford | Cap't B. Stone | " | " |
| James Weeks | " | " | " | " |
| Lemuel Peet | " | " | " | " |
| John Frothingham | " | " | " | " |
| W'm Foot | " | " | " | " |
| Matthew Wildman | " | " | " | " |
| W'm Danwell | " | " | " | " |
| David Cole | " | " | " | " |
| Truman Wooster | " | " | " | " |
| Azariah Canfield | " | " | " | " |
| Chileab Palmer | " | " | " | " |
| Elijah Canfield | " | " | " | " |
| Francis Eustace | " | " | " | " |
| James Wilson | " | " | " | " |
| Robert Nichols | " | " | " | " |
| Perry a transint Person | | | | |
| Prince Gratis | | " | " | " |
| Robert Smith | | " | " | " |
| Israel Phillips | | " | " | " |
| Shubael Phillips | | " | " | " |

| Soldiers Names | Towns they belong to | Company | Regiment | Time they inlisted for | Detached to serve till |
|---|---|---|---|---|---|
| James Abernerthy | New Milford | Cap¹ A. Hurburt | Col⁰ Mosely | During y⁹ Warr | 1 Jan⁹y next |
| Luke Welch | " | " | " | " | " |
| Shem Negro | " | " | " | " | " |
| W⁽ᵐ⁾ Bryant | " | " | " | " | " |
| David Blakeley | " | " | " | " | |
| Phinehas Baker | " | " | " | | |
| John Gold | Woodbury | " | " | | |
| David Mallary | " | " | " | | |
| Jonathan Blakeley | " | " | " | | |
| Gideon Hurlburt Jr. | " | " | " | | |
| Robert Hurlburt | " | " | " | | |
| Thomas Calihan | " | " | " | | |
| John Hunt Jun⁽ʳ⁾ | " | " | " | | |
| James Hawley | " | " | " | | |
| Simeon Hunt | " | " | " | | |
| Matthew Royce | " | " | " | | |
| Joseph Tonance | " | Cap¹ D. Leavensw⁽ᵗʰ⁾ | " | During y⁹ Warr | |
| Francis Field | " | " | " | " | |
| George Field | " | " | " | | |
| Abell Wakely | " | " | " | | |
| John Thompson | " | " | " | | |
| W⁽ᵐ⁾ Bunday | " | " | " | | |
| Joseph Westcott | " | " | " | | |
| David Rumsey | " | " | " | | |
| John Booth | " | Cap¹ N. Chapman | " | | 1ˢᵗ Jan⁽ʸ⁾ next |
| Aseph Hurlbutt | " | " | " | | " |
| Tho⁽ˢ⁾ Squire 3⁽ᵈ⁾ | " | " | " | | " |
| Tho⁽ˢ⁾ Weller | " | " | " | | " |
| Dan Stephens | " | " | " | | " |
| Stephen Reany | " | " | " | | |
| Hinman Wooster | " | " | " | | |
| Joseph Judson | " | " | " | | |
| Charles Sheldon | " | " | " | | |
| W⁽ᵐ⁾ Bennedict | " | " | " | | |

Ebenr Church
George Howe
Justus Reynolds
Amos Clark
Alexr Mills
Robin Negroe
David Dixon
Samll Lee
James Hooker
Jared Dixon
Samll Jackson
Aaron Olds
David Reynolds
David Robinson
Joseph Blackley
Phinehas Palmer
Danll Tucker
Moses Churchill
Hezekiah Keeler
Friend Beeman
Enoch Thomas
Jonathan Munger
Stephen Barnum — Kent
Samll Bates
Primus Hubbell
Cuff Comstalk
Cult Freeman
Thomas Warrups
Peter Warwehew
Danll Sucknuck
John Ashly
John Smith
Elijah Chapman
Benjn Bolt
Wm Bradshaw

Capt E. Hawley

Capt Mills

| Soldiers Names | Towns they belong to | Company | Regiment Col° Mosely | Time they inlisted for | Detached to serve till |
|---|---|---|---|---|---|
| Elip⁴ Simpson | Kent | Cap¹ Mills | | During y⁰ Warr | |
| Sam¹¹ Chamberlain | " | Cap¹ A. Fuller | " | " | |
| Jesse Merwin | " | " | " | " | |
| Amos Barnum | " | " | " | " | |
| Joseph Dixon | " | " | " | " | |
| Sam¹¹ Hubbell | " | " | " | " | |
| Zenus Barnum | " | " | " | " | |
| Dorias Sperry | " | " | " | " | |
| Prentice Fitch | " | " | " | " | |
| Sam¹¹ Fairchild | " | " | " | " | |
| John Main | " | " | " | " | |
| Dan¹¹ Dye | " | " | " | " | |
| Joseph Hurd | Woodbury | Cap¹ S. Hurlburt | " | " | |
| Ezekiel Newton | " | " | " | " | |
| Robert Burton | " | " | " | " | |
| Noah Hurlburt | " | " | " | " | |
| Tom Indian | " | " | " | " | 1ˢᵗ Jan'y next |
| Job Molatto | " | " | " | " | " |
| Roger Blaisdell | " | " | " | " | " |
| James Hawley | " | " | " | " | " |
| John Woodruff | " | " | " | " | " |
| Peruda Isbell | " | " | " | " | |
| John Weeks | " | " | " | " | |
| Joel Titus | " | " | " | " | |
| John Sears | " | Cap¹ J. Farrand | " | " | |
| William Ingraham | " | " | " | " | |
| Isaac Lyon | " | " | " | " | |
| Enos Prindle | " | " | " | " | |
| Asa Durkee | " | " | " | " | |
| Peter Negro | " | " | " | " | |
| Dan¹¹ Fenn | " | " | " | " | |
| Gamaliel Parker | " | " | " | " | |
| Oliver Olds, not joined | " | " | " | " | 1ˢᵗ Jan'y next |
| Eleazer Ingraham | " | " | " | " | |

## CONNECTICUT LINE, 1777-1781.

|  | | | | |
|---|---|---|---|---|
| Darius Fisher | " | | | |
| John Jordan | " | | | |
| Thad⁴ Hicock Jun⁴ | " | | | |
| Calvin Hurd | " | | | |
| William Reynold | " | | | |
| Abijah Moger | New Milford | Cap¹ P. Yates | " | |
| David Beech Jun⁴ | " | " | " | |
| James Beers | " | " | " | |
| David Sherman | " | " | " | |
| Edward Fuller | State of Vermont | " | " | |
| Benajah Leonard | " | " | " | |
| Wᵐ Blanchard | " | " | " | |
| David Rowe | " | " | " | |
| Danˡˡ Yarington | " | " | " | During yᵉ Warr or 8 years |
| Edward Grates | " | " | " | " |
| John Frothingham | " | " | " | " |
| Mingo Treet | " | " | " | " |
| Goodman Noble | New Milford | Cap¹ N Hine | " | " |
| Jehabad Wilkinson | " | " | " | " |
| Ebenʳ Bostwick | " | " | " | " |
| Gershom Nichols | " | " | " | " |
| Stephen Wheeler | " | " | " | " |
| David Merwin | " | " | " | " |
| Ebenʳ Trowbridge | " | " | " | " |
| Liffie Sanford | " | " | " | " |
| Wᵐ Whitely | " | " | " | " |
| Eli Nichols | " | " | " | " |
| Ralph Smith | " | " | " | " |
| Danˡˡ Rogers | " | " | " | " |
| John Knap | " | " | " | " |
| David Bostwick | " | " | " | " |
| Solomon Bostwick | " | " | " | " |
| George Rush | " | " | " | " |
| Alexʳ Dulford | " | " | " | " |

| Soldiers Names | Towns they belong to | Company | Regiment Col⁰ Mosely | Time they inlisted for During y⁰ Warr or 8 years | Detached to serve till |
|---|---|---|---|---|---|
| Abiaha Dudley | New Milford | Cap¹ N. Hine | " | | |
| Othniel Sax | " | " | " | | |
| Asa Sprague | Kent | " | " | | |
| John Warren | " | " | " | | |
| Patrick Downs | " | Cap¹ J. Sackett | " | " | |
| Fredrick Temple | " | " | " | " | |
| Thomas Fenn | " | " | " | " | |
| Peleg Holmes | " | " | " | " | 1st Jan'y next |
| Sam¹¹ Hawes | " | " | " | " | " |
| Joel Whitlock | " | " | " | | |
| John Thomas | " | Cap¹ J. Carter | " | " | |
| John Finney | " | " | " | " | |
| Eben' Focher | " | " | " | " | |
| Eben' Hill | " | " | " | " | |
| Lemuel Beeman | " | " | " | " | |
| Elisha Beeman | " | " | " | " | |
| Nathan Wheeler | " | " | " | " | |
| Matthias Beeman | " | " | " | " | |
| George Curtiss | " | " | " | " | |
| John Beeny | " | " | " | " | |
| John Brown | " | " | " | " | |
| John Graham | " | " | " | " | |
| Isaiah Bunce | New Milford | Cap¹ E. Couch | " | " | |
| Edward Finkins | " | " | " | " | |
| A man hired by Jos. Bostwick & and Son, Name forgot | " | " | " | " | |
| Noah Murray | Kent | " | " | " | |
| Joel Murray | " | " | " | | 1st Jan'y next |
| A man, Name unknown hired p Joel Murray & Benj" Adams | " | " | " | | |
| Abraham Barns | New Milford | Cap¹ W. Cogswell | " | " | |
| Tho' Davenport | " | " | " | " | |
| Bernard Davenport | " | " | " | " | |
| Eleazer Hendrick | " | " | " | " | |

CONNECTICUT LINE, 1777-1781.

| Name | Town | Captain | Term |
|---|---|---|---|
| Sam'l Smith | | | " |
| Henry Williams | | | " |
| Elisha Mix | | | " |
| Jesse Gratis | Kent | | " |
| James Taylor | | | " |
| David Dains | | | " |
| Asa Starkweather | | | " |
| Michael Welsh | | | " |
| Sam'l Beeman | | | " |
| Tho' Woodward | | | " |
| Edward Goodyear | | | " |
| Asiah Roberts | | | " |
| Sam'l Richards | | | " |
| John Barlow | | | " |
| Galloway Negro | Woodbury | Cap' B. Treat | 1 Jan'y next |
| Tony Negro | " | " | " |
| Jem Negro | " | " | " |
| Justus Peirce | " | " | " |
| David Dunning | " | " | " |
| Zadock Henries | " | " | " |
| Macock Ward | " | " | " |
| Joseph Squire | " | Cap' J. Sanford's | " |
| Simeon Rood | " | " | " |
| Lewis Hurd | " | " | " |
| Dan'l Potter | " | " | " |
| Solomon Reynolds | " | " | " |
| Sheldon Potter | " | " | " |
| Aaron Curtiss | " | " | " |
| Tim° Hinman | " | Cap' E. Hinman | " |
| Joseph Stiles | " | " | " |
| Aquilla Sturgis | " | " | " |
| James Negro | " | " | " |
| Cummy Negro | " | " | " |
| Jehiel Franklin | " | " | " |
| W'm Stanclift | " | " | " |

| Soldiers Names | Towns they belong to | Company | Regiment | Time they Inlisted for During yr War or 3 years | Detached to serve till |
|---|---|---|---|---|---|
| James Parks | Woodbury | Capt E. Hinman | Colo Mosely | | |
| Simeon Rood Junr | " | " | " | | |
| Moses Hawkins | " | " | " | | |
| Samll Lamphere | " | " | " | | |
| Ezra Weed | Norwalk | Capt Scovil | Colo Mead | for 3 years dureing yr War | |
| Nathaniel Nash | " | " | " | " | |
| James June | " | " | " | " | |
| Nathll Pardy | " | " | " | " | |
| Simeon Bouten | " | " | " | " | |
| William Waterbury | " | " | " | " | |
| David Keeler | " | " | " | " | |
| Asahel Green | " | " | " | " | |
| Richard Everet | " | " | " | " | |
| Abijah Arnold | " | " | " | " | |
| Stephen Hait | " | " | " | " | |
| Timo Hathorly Hanford | " | " | " | " | |
| Ebenezer Benedict | " | " | " | " | |
| Matthew Marvin | " | " | " | " | |
| Nathan Brown | Norwalk | Capt Eli Reed | " | for 3 years dureing yr War | |
| Abrahm Raymond | " | " | " | " | |
| Moses Waring | " | " | " | " | |
| John Williams | " | " | " | " | |
| Abrahm Hawley | Stanford | " | " | " | 1 Janry next |
| Bill Smith | " | " | " | " | |
| Dan Provost | " | " | " | " | |
| Bethel Hickock | " | " | " | " | |
| Jonathan Scovil | " | " | " | " | |
| Silvanus Scovil | " | " | " | " | |
| Ezra Bates | " | " | " | " | |
| Denny Parkenton | Stanford | Capt Scovil | " | " | |
| David Bouten | " | " | " | " | |
| Charles Stewart | " | " | " | " | |
| John Cleveland | " | " | " | " | |
| Joshua Stone | " | " | " | " | |

CONNECTICUT LINE, 1777-1781.        109

| | | | | | |
|---|---|---|---|---|---|
| Stephen Davenport | " | Cap' E. Lockwood | " | " | |
| Hezekiah Rogers | Norwalk | " | " | " | |
| William Jackson | " | " | " | " | |
| Dover St John | " | " | " | " | |
| Nehemiah Hait | " | " | " | 1st Jan'y next | 1st Jan'y next |
| Stephen Scribner | " | " | " | " | " |
| Sam'l Ketchum | " | " | " | " | " |
| Nathan Jervis | " | Cap' O. Marvin | " | During y' Warr | |
| Stephen Meaker | " | " | " | " | |
| Nathan Taylor | " | " | " | " | |
| Gershom Lockwood | " | " | " | " | |
| Ozias Hanford | " | " | " | " | |
| Jesse Beers | " | " | " | " | |
| Peter Tuttle | " | " | " | " | |
| Josiah Taylor | " | " | " | for 3 years | |
| Noah Taylor | " | " | " | " | |
| Hezekiah Hawley | " | " | " | " | |
| John Teen | " | " | " | " | |
| Aaron Sturgis | " | " | " | " | |
| Moses Scribner | " | " | " | " | |
| Uriah Mead | " | Cap' Clap Raymond | " | During y' Warr | |
| Abin Cole | " | " | " | " | |
| Bartholomew Parsons | " | " | " | " | |
| John Bouten | " | " | " | " | |
| Nathaniel Sterling | " | " | " | " | |
| Jonathan Sesar | " | " | " | " | |
| Theophilus Mead | " | " | " | " | |
| Uriah Keeler | " | " | " | " | |
| Josiah Green | " | " | " | " | |
| Seth Hubbell | " | " | " | " | |
| Nathan Jackson Jun' | " | " | " | " | |
| W'm Jenkins | " | " | " | " | |
| Mordecai Bedient | " | " | " | " | |
| Calvin Jenkins | " | " | " | " | |
| Moses Scott | " | " | " | " | |

| Soldiers Names | Towns they belong to | Company | Regiment | Time they inlisted for | Detached to serve till |
|---|---|---|---|---|---|
| Isaac Olmstead | Norwalk | Cap' Clap Raymond | Col° Mead | During y° Warr | |
| David Parsons | " | " | " | " | |
| Osborn Parsons | " | " | " | " | |
| John Rockwell Jun' | " | " | " | " | |
| Aser Patchen Jun' | " | " | " | " | |
| Sam¹¹ Trowbridge | " | " | " | " | |
| Isaiah Whitney | " | " | " | " | |
| Gregory Thomas | " | " | " | " | |
| Sam¹¹ Green | " | | " | " | |
| Aaron Cumstalk | " | Cap' N. Gilbert | " | " | |
| James Whelpley | " | " | " | " | |
| Henry Keeler | " | " | " | " | |
| Jeremiah Mead | " | " | " | " | |
| Sam¹¹ Mead | " | " | " | " | |
| Sam¹¹ Holmes | " | " | " | " | |
| Justin S' John | " | " | " | " | |
| John Johnson | " | " | " | " | |
| Nath¹¹ Hendrick | " | " | " | " | |
| Jonathan Nichols | " | " | " | for 8 years | |
| Pelatiah Lyon | " | " | " | " | |
| David Whitlock | " | " | " | " | |
| Zaccheus Scribner | " | " | " | " | |
| Moses Jackson | " | " | " | during y° Warr | |
| Nathan Jackson | " | " | " | " | |
| Gershom Gilbert | " | " | " | " | |
| Thad° Gilbert | " | " | " | for 8 years | |
| Jasper Mead | " | " | " | during y° Warr | |
| Sam¹¹ Deforest | " | " | " | " | |
| Matt. Gregory | " | " | " | " | |
| Sam¹¹ Gates | " | " | " | " | |
| Asa Scribner | " | " | " | " | |
| Elijah Taylor | " | " | " | " | |
| Aaron Keeler | " | " | " | " | |
| Moses Gilbert | " | " | " | " | |

CONNECTICUT LINE, 1777-1781.    111

| | | | | | | |
|---|---|---|---|---|---|---|
| John Williams | | .. | Cap' J. Gregory | .. | | 1st Jan'y next |
| Azor Patchen | | .. | | .. | | |
| Sam'l Nichols | | .. | | .. | | |
| Isaiah Betts | | .. | | .. | | |
| Sam'l Hyatt | | .. | | .. | | |
| David Westcott Jun' | | .. | | .. | | |
| John Harrison | | .. | | .. | | |
| Thomas Woodbridge | | .. | | .. | | |
| Jesse St John | | .. | | .. | | |
| Aaron St John | | .. | | .. | | |
| Aaron Keeler | | .. | | .. | | |
| Abijah Olmstead | | .. | | .. | | |
| Levi Clinton | | .. | | .. | | |
| Henry Selleck | | .. | | .. | | |
| Simon Wood | | .. | | .. | | |
| Matthew Gregory Jun' | | .. | | .. | | |
| Aaron Raymond | | .. | Cap' U. Raymond | 8 years | | |
| Joseph Bouten Jun' | | .. | | .. | | |
| Dan'l Brown | | .. | | .. | | |
| William Garner | | .. | | .. | | |
| Stephen Frost | | .. | | .. | | |
| Zebulon Jackson | | .. | | .. | | |
| James White | | .. | | .. | | |
| Thomas Rowland | | .. | | .. | | |
| Stephen Wood | | .. | | .. | | |
| Stephen Kellog | | .. | | .. | | |
| Daniel Hait | | .. | Cap' El. Raymond | | | 1st Jan'y next |
| James Seymour | Stanford | .. | | .. | | .. |
| Eli Tuttle | " | .. | | .. | | .. |
| W'm Reed Jun' | | .. | Cap' J'o Richards | .. | | |
| Jacob Selleck | | .. | | .. | | |
| John Bissell | | .. | | .. | | |
| Enoch Kellog | | .. | | .. | | |
| John Paylar | | .. | Cap' Morehouse | | | 1st Jan'y next |
| Barnabas Marvin | Norwalk | ., | | | | |

## REVOLUTION LISTS AND RETURNS.

| Soldiers Names | Towns they belong to | Company | Regiment | Time they inlisted for | Detached to serve till |
|---|---|---|---|---|---|
| John Fillean | Norwalk | Cap* Morehouse | Col° Mead | | 1st Jan'y next |
| Elias Wilcox | " | " | " | | |
| Ned Negro | " | " | " | | 1st Jan'y next |
| Eliakim Wareing | " | " | " | | |
| Casar Negro | Stanford | " | " | | |
| Transient Persons for | Norwalk | " | " | | |
| John Sear | " | Cap* J. Raymond | " | | |
| Eben* Nash Jun* | " | " | " | | |
| W*m* Spurr | " | " | " | | |
| Isaac Smith | " | " | " | | |
| Robert Hunter | " | " | " | | |
| Peter Merritt | " | " | " | dureing y* Warr or 3 years | |
| W*m* Gorddin | " | " | " | " | |
| W*m* Canady | " | " | " | " | |
| James Hamilton | " | " | " | " | |
| Sam*ll* Dickenson | " | " | " | " | |
| W*m* Hill | " | " | " | " | |
| Joseph Thompson | " | " | " | " | |
| Stephen Wood | Stanford | Cap* S. Hait | " | " | |
| David Pope | " | " | " | " | |
| John Margaro | " | " | " | " | |
| Benjamin Stoves | " | " | " | " | |
| Benjamen Byington | " | " | " | " | |
| Thomas Woodertory | " | " | " | " | |
| Nathan White | " | " | " | " | |
| Andrew Edmonds | " | " | " | " | |
| Eb*en*r Armstrong | " | " | " | " | |
| Eph*m* Waistcoat | " | " | " | " | |
| Stedly Eumun | " | " | " | " | |
| W*m* Scott | " | " | " | " | |
| Joseph Thompson | " | " | " | " | |
| Thomas Mitchel | " | " | " | " | |
| Thomas Wood | " | " | " | " | |

## CONNECTICUT LINE, 1777-1781. 113

| | | | |
|---|---|---|---|
| John Dickson | " | Cap¹ J. Bell " | " |
| Benjamin Weed | " | " | " |
| John McNumlly | " | " | " |
| Sam¹¹ Hait | " | " | " |
| 20 Stephen Brown | " | " | " |
| Jonas Weed | " | " | " |
| Francis Bell | " | " | " |
| John Weed | " | " | " |
| Dan¹¹ Shay | " | " | " |
| Isaac Smith | " | " | " |
| Negro Man | " | " | " |
| William Canady | " | " | " |
| John Bishop | " | " | " |
| Benjamen Allen | " | " | " |
| Stephen Wood | " | " | " |
| George Shaver | " | " | " |
| Charles Powers | " | " | " |
| John Thompson | " | " | " |
| Joseph Ingly | " | " | " |
| James Phloman (?) | " | " | " |
| Eben¹ Hait | " | Cap¹ J. Lockwood | " |
| Andrew Doghardy | " | " | " |
| William Heldrig | " | " | " |
| Thomas Lewis | " | " | " |
| John McDonald | " | " | " |
| Deliverance Conkling | " | " | " |
| Newton Crawford | " | " | " |
| James H. Wright | " | " | " |
| Thomas Mitchel | " | " | " |
| Thomas Wood | " | " | " |
| Bruster Bidd | " | " | " |
| Seth Winchel | " | " | " |
| Sam¹¹ Welchard | " | " | " |
| Michael Kingsbury | " | " | " |
| Sam¹¹ Clark | " | " | " |

| Soldiers Names. | Towns they beong to | Company | Regiment | Time they inlisted for | Detached to serve till |
|---|---|---|---|---|---|
| David Wallis | Stanford | Capt J. Lockwood | Colo Mead | During ye Warr | |
| Joseph Cheshire | " | " | " | " | |
| John Mather | " | " | " | " | |
| Joseph Boyinton | " | " | " | " | |
| John Ashley | " | " | " | " | |
| Benjamen Tarbox | " | " | " | " | |
| Two transient Persons Names unknown | " | " | " | " | |
| Samuel Hickox | " | Capt S. Knap | " | " | |
| Samll Wheeton | " | " | " | " | |
| Enos Fountain | " | " | " | " | |
| David Webb | " | " | " | " | |
| Seely Scovil | " | " | " | " | |
| Jacob Wardwell | " | " | " | " | |
| Samuel Bush | " | " | " | " | |
| Ushal Knapp | " | " | " | " | |
| Stephen Davenport | " | " | " | " | |
| Charles Selleck | " | " | " | " | |
| Timo Lockwood | " | " | " | " | |
| Josiah Smith | " | " | " | " | |
| Silas Scovil | " | " | " | " | |
| Jacob Blanchard | " | " | " | " | |
| George Mills | " | " | " | " | |
| William Wardwell | " | " | " | " | |
| Peter Lounsbury | " | " | " | " | |
| Borden Knap | " | " | " | " | |
| Thomas Newman | " | " | " | " | |
| Nathl Johnson | " | " | " | " | |
| Isaiah Smith | " | " | " | " | |
| Peter Smith | " | " | " | " | |
| Clement Loyd | " | " | " | " | |
| Austin Smith | " | " | " | " | |
| Isaiah Jones | " | " | " | " | |
| John Smith | " | " | " | " | |

| | | | | |
|---|---|---|---|---|
| Justin Whitney | " | " | " | " |
| James Waterbury | " | " | " | " |
| David Maltby | " | " | " | " |
| Nathan Knapp | " | " | " | " |
| Moses Webb | " | " | " | " |
| James Knap | " | " | " | " |
| Isaac Brown | " | " | " | " |
| James St John | " | " | " | " |
| George Finchley | " | Cap<sup>t</sup> Ch<sup>s</sup> Smith | " | 3 Years |
| Eliph<sup>t</sup> Lockwood | " | " | " | " |
| Ezra Green | " | " | " | " |
| Sam<sup>ll</sup> Wareing | " | " | " | Dureing y<sup>e</sup> Warr |
| Caleb Smith | " | " | " | for 8 Years |
| Stephen June | " | " | " | " |
| Jonathan Edwards | " | " | " | " |
| John Smith | " | " | " | " |
| Joel Hait | " | " | " | " |
| Samuel Finch | " | " | " | " |
| Eben<sup>r</sup> Webb | " | " | " | for 3 Years |
| Eben<sup>r</sup> Wareing | " | " | " | " |
| Joseph Cowdry | " | Cap<sup>t</sup> David Wood's | " | Dureing y<sup>e</sup> Warr |
| David Austin | " | Cap<sup>t</sup> Ch<sup>s</sup> Smith | " | for 8 Years |
| Benjamen Reynolds | Greenwich | " | " | " |
| Isaac Palmer | " | Cap<sup>t</sup> Ed. Brown | " | " |
| William Jemison | " | " | " | " |
| Joseph Fletcher | " | " | " | " |
| William Waters | " | " | " | " |
| Mead Marshall | " | " | " | " |
| Edward Ritch | " | " | " | " |
| Sam<sup>ll</sup> Close | " | " | " | " |
| William Town | " | Cap<sup>t</sup> B. Green | " | Dureing y<sup>e</sup> Warr |
| Isaac Davis | " | " | " | " |
| John De Pew | " | " | " | " |
| Henry De Pew | " | " | " | " |
| Abraham De Pew | " | " | " | " |

| Soldiers Names | Towns they belong to | Company | Regiment | Time they inlisted for | Detached to serve till |
|---|---|---|---|---|---|
| Francis De Pew | Greenwich | Cap.ᵗ G. Peck | Col.º Mead | for 8 years | |
| Ezekiel Daton | " | " | " | " | |
| Joshua Taylor Jun.ʳ | " | " | " | " | |
| Tho.ˢ Wheaton | " | " | " | " | |
| George Edgett | " | " | " | " | |
| Nath.ˡˡ Holmes | " | " | " | " | |
| David Wilson | " | " | " | " | |
| John Reed Jun.ʳ | " | " | " | " | |
| Abrah.ᵐ Sherwood | " | Cap.ᵗ J. Anderson | " | for 8 Years | |
| Moses Lockwood | " | " | " | " | |
| Jonathan Whelpley | " | Cap.ᵗ G. Peck | " | " | |
| Charles Knap | " | " | " | " | |
| Peter Betts | " | " | " | " | |
| David Lockwood | " | " | " | " | |
| Jonathan Adams Jr | " | " | " | " | |
| Jeremiah Finch | " | " | " | " | |
| Sam.ˡˡ Finch | " | " | " | " | |
| Joseph Lockwood Jr | " | " | " | " | |
| Jared Lockwood | " | " | " | " | |
| Sam.ˡˡ Knap | " | " | " | " | |
| John Reed | " | " | " | " | |
| Timothy Lockwood Jr | " | " | " | " | |
| John Burley | " | " | " | " | |
| Sam.ˡˡ Mead | " | " | " | 1.ˢᵗ Jan.ʳʸ next | |
| Jacob Blancher | " | " | " | " | |
| Joseph Judson | " | " | " | " | |
| Ebenezer Whelpley | " | " | " | " | |
| Dan.ˡˡ Johnson | " | " | " | " | |
| Elphalet Tilding | " | " | " | " | |
| Alexander Mills | " | " | " | " | |
| Jeremiah Rundell | " | " | " | " | |
| Amos Lockwood | " | " | " | " | |
| Moses Peck | " | " | " | " | |
| Israel Reynolds | " | " | " | " | |

|  | | | |
|---|---|---|---|
| William Marshall | Cap' Odle Clase | ... | for 8 Years |
| Nath'l Brown | | ... | " |
| Nehemiah Wilson | | ... | " |
| Garret Hait | | ... | " |
| Joseph Traverse | | ... | " |
| Stephen Hall | | ... | " |
| Benjamin Rose | | ... | during y'' Warr |
| Samuel Johnson | | ... | for 8 years |
| John Reed | | ... | " |
| Israel Harret | | ... | " |
| James Vessels | | ... | " |
| Hercules Vessels | | ... | " |
| John Rundal | | ... | " |
| Will'm Johnson | | ... | " |
| John Brown | | ... | dureing Warr |
| William Seamaf | | ... | " |
| Richard Williams | | ... | " |
| John Town | Cap' J. Hobby | ... | for 8 years |
| Abraham Hayse | | ... | " |
| Gilbert Wilson | | ... | " |
| William Crudock | | ... | " |
| Iran Nickerson | | ... | " |
| John Mackrady | | ... | " |
| John Smith | | ... | " |
| Josiah Wood | Cap' D. Wood | ... | " |
| Nath'l Jessup | | ... | " |
| Joshua Barker | | ... | " |
| Silas Howe | | ... | " |
| Frederick Pole | Cap' J. How | ... | " |
| Abr'm Ferris | | ... | " |
| Theodotius Parsons | | ... | " |
| Jesse Parsons | | ... | " |
| Silvenus Conkling | | ... | " |
| Elijah Mead | | ... | " |
| Jonathan Mead | | ... | " |

| Soldiers Names | Towns they belong to | Company | Regiment | Time they inlisted for |
|---|---|---|---|---|
| Jesse Whitney | Greenwich | Cap¹ J. How | Col° Mead | for 3 years |
| John Taylor | " | " | " | " |
| John Belaheaserlies | " | " | " | Dureing Warr |
| Joseph Marshall | " | " | " | " |
| Samuel Banks | " | " | " | " |
| Transient Persons hired for David Slater | | | | |
| Transient Persons hired for George Nottingham | Greenwich | | | |
| Jesse Purdy | " | | | dureing Warr |
| James Rogers | " | | | " |
| Neal McCowen | " | | | " |
| Wᵐ Brown | " | | | " |
| Jnº Wienkleman | " | | | " |
| James Richardson | " | | | " |
| Danˡˡ Selleck | Danbury | not returned | Col° Beardsly | " |
| John Barnum | " | " | " | " |
| Jack Negro | " | " | " | " |
| Thomas Names | " | " | " | " |
| Aeral Ackley transient P. for | | " | " | " |
| James Blakely | Ridgfield | " | " | " |
| Joseph Jackson | Danbury | " | " | " |
| William Porter | " | " | " | " |
| Wᵐ Griffin | | " | " | " |
| Wᵐ Mc Lean | | " | " | " |
| Samˡˡ Barnum | | " | " | " |
| Noah Barnum | | " | " | " |
| Frederick Dikeman | | " | " | " |
| Uriah Clark's Negro | | " | " | " |
| William Taylor's Dº | | " | " | " |
| James Matthews transient P. for | | " | " | " |
| Robert Bowman | | " | " | " |
| Andʷ Simons | | " | " | " |
| Caleb Maxfield | | " | " | " |

## CONNECTICUT LINE, 1777–1781.

| Name | Town | | | |
|---|---|---|---|---|
| Ezra Ketchum | " | " | " | " |
| Stephen Barber | " | " | " | " |
| Aaron Knap | " | " | " | " |
| William Hokhins | " | " | " | " |
| John Curtiss | " | " | " | " |
| Nathll Robertson | " | " | " | " |
| Jonathan Dikeman | " | " | " | " |
| David Hall | " | " | " | " |
| Jonath Williams } Transient Person | N. London | " | not returned | " |
| Miner Allen | Sharon | " | " | " |
| Daniel Elmer | Ridgefield | Not returned | Col° Beardsly | Dureing ye Warr |
| Josiah Whitney | Danbury | " | " | " |
| Isaac Collen | " | " | " | " |
| Thaddeus Starr | " | " | " | " |
| Joseph Moss White | " | " | " | " |
| Nehemiah Dibble | " | " | " | " |
| Isaac Reed | " | " | " | " |
| Danll Dikeman | " | " | " | " |
| Danll Dibble | " | " | " | " |
| Christopher Glover | " | " | " | " |
| Comfort Benedict | " | " | " | " |
| Wm Stone | " | " | " | " |
| Levi Starr | " | " | " | " |
| Levi Peck | " | " | " | " |
| James Stevens | " | " | " | " |
| Peter Starr | " | " | " | " |
| Benja Cozier | " | " | " | " |
| Wm Patch | " | " | " | " |
| Isaac Barnum | Newtown | " | " | " |
| Joseph Hepburn | " | " | " | 3 Years |
| Israel Burrit | " | " | " | " |
| George Murray | " | " | " | 1st Jan'y next |
| Thomas Brooks | " | " | " | During ye Warr |
| Samuel Brooks | " | " | " | " |

| Soldiers Names | Towns they belong to | Company | Regiment | Time they inlisted for | Detached to serve till |
|---|---|---|---|---|---|
| | | Not returned | Col⁰ Beardsly | 8 Years | |
| Charles McDonald | New Milford | | | | |
| Eben' Keeler | " | " | " | | |
| Liverus Hawley | " | " | " | | |
| Joseph Hawley | " | " | " | | |
| Othniel Sax | " | " | " | | |
| David Bishop | Danbury | " | " | dureing yᵉ Warr | |
| Danˡˡ Osborn | Ridgefield | " | " | { Dureing yᵉ Warr or 8 Years } | |
| Elisha Gilbert | " | " | " | | |
| Ebenezer Jacklin | " | " | " | | |
| Thomas Sagar | " | " | " | | |
| James Patrick | " | " | " | | |
| Abrᵐ Russigue | " | " | " | | |
| Stephen Remington | " | " | " | | |
| Nehemiah Olmstead | " | " | " | | |
| Jeremiah Olmstead | " | " | " | | |
| Joseph Jackson 2ᵈ | " | " | " | | |
| Jeremiah Dean | " | " | " | | |
| Darius Benedict | " | " | " | | |
| Levi Keeler | " | " | " | | |
| Jeremiah Keeler | " | " | " | | |
| Bartholomew Baker | " | " | " | | |
| Silvenus Seely | " | " | " | | |
| Benjⁿ Bennett | " | " | " | | |
| Hezekiah Hawley | " | " | " | | |
| Elisha Perry | " | " | " | | |
| Thoˢ Keeler | " | " | " | | |
| Elijah Weed | " | " | " | | |
| Barack Nickerson | " | " | " | | |
| Gilbert Brush | " | " | " | | |
| Danˡˡ Canfield | " | " | " | | |
| Lewis Jacklin | " | " | " | | |
| John Street | " | " | " | | |
| Thoˢ Whitney | " | " | " | | |

## CONNECTICUT LINE, 1777-1781.

|  | | | | |
|---|---|---|---|---|
| Ezekiel Whitney | " | " | " | " |
| Eliaphas Nickerson | " | " | " | " |
| Joseph Smith | " | " | " | " |
| Elisha Lincoln | " | " | " | " |
| Solomon Ben | " | " | " | " |
| Reuben Craw | " | " | " | " |
| Haman Craw | " | " | " | " |
| Dan'l Riggs | " | " | " | " |
| Stephen Stillman | " | | " | |
| Transient Persons inlisted for | | | | |
| Joseph Sears | " | Dureing Warr | " | |
| Peter Kellis | " | " | " | |
| John Roberts | " | " | " | |
| John Hitchcock | " | " | " | |
| Micajah Weeks | " | " | " | |
| Thos Warson | " | " | " | |
| Wm Mitchel | " | " | " | |
| James Burns | " | " | " | |
| Wm Newton | " | " | " | |
| John Hayes | " | " | " | |
| John Butler | " | " | " | |
| Benjn Dawns | " | " | " | |
| Thos Wasson | " | " | " | |
| Joseph Shaw | " | " | " | |
| Henry Williams | " | " | " | |
| Wm Fleet | " | " | " | |
| Charles White | " | " | " | |
| Solomon Brown | " | " | " | |
| Thos Hutchinson | " | " | " | |
| Fortune White a Negro | Danbury | " | not returned | 1st Jany next |
| Benjn Knap | " | " | " | " |
| David Knap | " | " | " | " |
| John Knap Junr | " | " | " | " |
| Caleb Starr | " | " | " | " |

| Soldiers Names | Towns they belong to | Company | Regiment | Time they inlisted for Dureing ye Warr or 3 Years | Detached to serve till |
|---|---|---|---|---|---|
| Talmage Hawley | New Fairfield | " | " | " | |
| Charles Brown | " | " | " | " | |
| Elijah Beardsley | " | " | " | " | |
| Jno Fairchild Lacy | " | " | " | " | |
| Jno Hambleton | " | " | " | " | |
| Reuben Stevens | | " | " | " | |
| Elipt Simpson | State of N. York | " | " | " | |
| Jonah Jones | " | " | " | " | |
| Aaron Wilder | " | " | " | " | |
| Benja Roberts | " | " | " | " | |
| James Wyllys transient P. for | N. Fairfield | " | " | " | |
| Wm Bostwick | " | " | " | " | |
| Saml1 Stratton | " | " | " | " | |
| Jno Roberson | " | " | " | " | |
| Eleazer Waller | New Fairfield | " | " | " | |
| Thos Kenning | " | " | " | " | |
| Wm Saunders | " | " | " | " | |
| Matthew Fowler | " | " | " | " | |
| Sam11 Nichols | " | " | " | " | |
| Ithiel Barns | " | " | " | " | |
| Eleazer Waller | " | " | " | " | |
| Francis Ferguson | " | " | " | " | |
| John Brown | " | " | " | " | |
| John Ryan | " | " | " | " | |
| Joseph Hodges | " | " | " | " | |
| Ezra Prindle | " | " | " | " | |
| Ebenr Perkins | N. Hampshire | " | " | " | |
| A Negro hired by Jonah Giddings | N. Fairfield | " | " | dureing ye Warr | |
| Toby Boston | " | " | " | " | |
| William Jolly | " | " | " | " | |
| John Cooper | " | " | " | " | |

| | | | |
|---|---|---|---|
| Joel Botsford | Newtown | " | Dureing War or 8 Years |
| W<sup>m</sup> Barnet | " | " | " |
| John Williams transient Person for N.T. | | " | " |
| James Sanford | Newtown | " | " |
| Eben<sup>r</sup> Barnum | Danbury | " | " |
| Abell Booth | Newtown | " | " |
| Silas Barlow | Danbury | " | " |
| Ichabod B. Palmer | New Milford | " | 1<sup>st</sup> Jan<sup>ry</sup> next |
| Abr<sup>m</sup> Wheeler | | " | " |
| Joseph Hatch | Newtown | " | " |
| Abrah<sup>m</sup> Baldwin | " | " | Dureing y<sup>e</sup> Warr |
| Sam<sup>ll</sup> Fairweather | " | " | " |
| Saul Murry | " | " | " |
| Nathan Hubbell | " | " | " |
| Isaac Baldwin | " | " | " |
| John Kimberly | " | " | " |
| And<sup>w</sup> Blackman | " | " | " |
| W<sup>m</sup> Crawford | Danbury | " | " |
| Robert Nailor | " | " | " |
| John Curtiss | " | " | " |
| James Guthra | " | " | " |
| Prince Cromwell | " | " | " |
| David Coy transient P for | | " | " |
| Amos Seely | " | " | " |
| John Fitcher | " | " | " |
| Patrick Brian | " | " | " |
| John Ludeman | " | " | " |
| John Finnigham | " | " | " |
| Mingo Jiles | " | " | " |
| Isaac Collen | " | " | Dureing Warr or 8 Years |
| Robin Starr Negro | " | " | " |
| Thaddeus Starr | " | " | " |
| David Bishop | " | " | " |

| Soldiers Names | Towns they belong to | Company | Regiment | Time they inlisted for | Detached to serve till |
|---|---|---|---|---|---|
| Joshua Taylor | Danbury | | | Dureing Warr or 3 Years | |
| Jesse Peck | " | " | " | " | |
| Jabez Williams | " | " | " | " | |
| Collins Chapman | " | " | " | " | |
| Isaac Goarham | Redding | " | Col⁰ Whiteing | " | 1ˢᵗ Janʳʸ next |
| Robert Welch | Stratford | " | " | " | " |
| James Davis | Sharon | " | not returned | " | " |
| Samˡˡ Dibble | Danbury | " | Col⁰ Beardsly | " | " |
| Asahel Benedict | " | " | " | " | " |
| Ebenʳ Judd | " | " | " | " | " |
| Eleazer Bennedict | " | " | " | " | " |
| Zelotes Roberson | " | " | " | " | " |
| Clauson Hawley | " | " | " | " | " |
| Reuben Judd | " | " | " | " | " |
| Benjⁿ Williams | " | " | " | " | " |
| Samˡˡ Crowfoot | " | " | " | " | |
| Robert Anderson Junʳ | " | " | " | " | |
| Comfort Barnum | " | " | " | " | |
| Abell Baldwin | Newtown | " | " | Dureing yᵉ Warr or 3 Years | |
| Abijah Prindle | " | " | " | " | |
| Zalmon Prindle | " | " | " | " | |
| Matthew Clark | " | " | " | " | |
| Sampson Negro | " | " | " | " | |
| Jack Negro | " | " | " | " | |
| Toby Negro | " | " | " | " | |
| Elijah Foot | " | " | " | " | |
| Nathan Little | | " | " | " | |

The foregoing is a true and exact Return of the Soldiers inlisted and draughted from the 4th Brigade of Militia in the State of Connecticut for Continental Service according to the several Regimental Returns that have been made to me. The Term of Service is in many Instances left uncertain and I could not ascertain it because the Regimental Returns were uncertain, specifying it to be 3 Years or dureing the Warr. I am informed and believe that the Men in Many Companies that are engaged in the Carting Service and in the Companies of Artificers make a Part of the Soldiers returned in this Return; which I suppose to be wrong and where I found a Man's Name entered in any of the Returns as being entered in either of those Branches of the Service I have neglected to enter his Name in this Return. After all there are many others that belong to those Departments that are included us I am well but not Officially informed; Nor do I think that this Matter can be placed in its proper Light so as to know certainly how Many of them do & how many do not belong to the Battalions raised by this State, unless the General Assembly shall think proper to adopt some particular Method of Examination to ascertain it.

I am indebted to the Authority & Select Men of Newtown for the Materials wherewith to make a Considerable Part of the Return that respects Newtown Soldiers. There are in that Town Three or Four Companies that have no Officers: they have heretofore chosen their Officers, but of Persons so unfriendly that I am informed it has not been thought proper to give them Commissions; And there is at present no Probability that any Officers would be chosen by those Companies, that it would be thought proper to give a Commission to; as there are so many unfriendly Voters in those Companies, that are under Age and not obliged to take the Oath of Fidelity to qualify them to vote that (as I am informed) they will carry a Vote as they please: hence it comes to pass that we can have little or no Help from those Companies. I hope some Method will be adopted to give them such Officers as the Publick can have Confidence in, and then we may expect them to yield their Proportion toward filling up the Army and not before.

I find several Instances in the foregoing Return where the same Man is returned as a Soldier inlisted in Three or Four Companies in the same Town: and and to which of them he belongs I am not able to determine and so am obliged to let the same Man stand three or Four Times returned, because I don't know to which Company he belongs. And even if I had the Power to put this Matter right these Returns have come in so late that I have had no Time for it.

Fairfield May 8th 1778

G. SELLECK SILLMAN Brigr Genl[1]

The whole Number of Soldiers belonging to the Several Towns in the Brigade Selected from all the Returns and placed to their respective Regiments in the Brigade, etc.

| Regiments | Towns in Each Regim<sup>t</sup> and other Places out of the Brigade returned | Number of Soldiers inlisted and detached from each Town &c. | Number of Soldiers inlisted from each Regiment |
|---|---|---|---|
| Col<sup>o</sup> Whiteings | Redding | 33 | |
| Do | Stratford | 169 | |
| Do | Fairfield | 126 | |
| Do | Derby | 1 | |
| | Suratoga | 1 | |
| | Massachussets | 1 | |
| Total | | 331 | 331 |
| Col<sup>o</sup> Moseley | Woodbury | 165 | |
| Do | New Milford | 75 | |
| Do | Kent | 58 | |
| Do | Waterbury | 1 | |
| | State of Vermont | 8 | |
| Total | | 307 | 307 |
| Col<sup>o</sup> Mead's | Norwalk | 137 | |
| Do | Stanford | 123 | |
| Do | Greenwich | 96 | |
| Total | | 356 | 356 |
| Col<sup>o</sup> Beardsley's | Danbury | 82 | |
| | Newtown | 30 | |
| | Ridgefield | 57 | |
| | New Fairfield | 31 | |
| | N. Milford in this Reg<sup>t</sup> | 7 | |
| | N. London | 1 | |
| | Sharon | 2 | |
| Total | | 210 | 210 |
| | | | 1204 |

The Above is the exact Amount of the Soldiers contained in the Return wrote on the first Thirty-two Pages of this Return.
May 8<sup>th</sup> 1778

G. S. SILLIMAN Brig<sup>r</sup> Gen<sup>l</sup>

N. B. Since the Several Regimental Returns came in Asa Sherwood of Fairfield is inlisted into the Army during the Warr.

## RETURNS FROM MILITIA, 1778.

### FIFTH REGIMENT.

A Return of the Names of those Men who are Inlisted into the Continental Service from the 5th Regiment of Militia in the 5th Brigade in the State of Connecticut, The Towns to which they Belong & Comp<sup>y</sup> Distinguishing the Names of those now in Continental Service as allso the Names of those Inlisted or Detached pursuant to Orders of January Last.

#### Windham

| | Inlisted or Detach<sup>d</sup> |
|---|---|
| Cap<sup>t</sup> N. Wales Comp<sup>y</sup> | |
| Charles Ripley | now in Service |
| Jabez Rous | " |
| Andrew Warner | " |
| John Hobs | " |
| Richard Howard | " |
| W<sup>m</sup> Placey } Indians | " |
| John Leathercoat } | " |
| Joseph Robens | " |
| Joseph Masa | " |
| Silus Frink | " |
| Sam<sup>ll</sup> Brown | " |
| Cap<sup>t</sup> Tinkers Comp<sup>y</sup> | |
| John Bingham | now in Service |
| Asa Hibbard | " |
| Amos Woodward | " |
| Levy Bingham | " |
| Tim<sup>o</sup> Hibberd | " |
| David Young | " |
| Eleaz<sup>r</sup> Robinson | " |
| Dier Hibberd | " |
| Seth Larrobe | " |
| Calib Fitch | " |
| Elijah Baccus | " |
| Ezekiel Dunham | " |
| Gershom Dunham | " |
| Joseph Reed | " |
| Mason Abbe | " |
| Walter Chase | " |
| Jonah Palmer | " |
| Ephraim Terry | " |
| Eben<sup>r</sup> Hibberd | " |
| Elijah Linkon | " |
| Adriel Simons | " |
| Solomon Tracey | " |
| Elijah Spafford | " |
| Frances Shellis | " |
| Benj<sup>n</sup> Ripley | " |

|  |  |
|---|---|
|  | Inlisted or Detach[d] |
| Joseph Johnson | now in service |
| Benajah Geer | " |
| John Hayley | " |
| Joseph West | " |
| Comfort Foster | " |
| Sam[ll] Robenson | " |
| Sam[ll] Murdock | " |
| John Huntington | " |
| Vriah Hibberd | " |
| Cap[t] Maltier Binghams |  |
| Steaphen Calif | in C[l] Service |
| Samuel Stubbs | " |
| Alven Ames | " |
| Asa Ames | " |
| Benj[n] Lamb | now in Service |
| Jonathan Meacham | " |
| Simeon Robenson | 1[t] Jan[y] 1779 |
| Reuben Welsh Detach[d] | 1[t] Jan[y] 1779 |
| Cap[t] Perkens Comp[y] |  |
| Elus Vpton | Inlisted 1[t] January 1779 |
| Cap[t] Sam[ll] Bingham |  |
| Elius Robenson | now in Service |
| Josiah Burnham | " |
| Thomas Hurlbut | " |
| Samuel Brown | " |
| Abner French | " |
| Turnor Lilley | Inlisted 1[t] Jan[y] 1779 |
| Aaron Overton | " |
| Simeon Bunde | " |
| Daniel Doughtey | " |
| Luke Flint | " |
| Hez Hibberd | Drafted 1[t] Jan[y] 1779 |
| Cap[t] Jonathan Rudd |  |
| Nathan Morgen | now in Service |
| Levy Dean | " |
| Edward Coburn | " |
| Peter Scovel | " |
| Joseph Jennings Jun[r] | " |
| Zopher Robenson | " |
| Nathaniel Bennet | " |
| Th[o] Fitsjareld | " |
| Asa Walden | " |
| Frances Perkens | " |
| Benj[n] Cary Jun[r] | " |
| Abel Robenson | " |
| Jabez Potage | " |
| Ephraim Robenson | Inlisted to y[e] 1[t] Jan[y] 1779 |
| Elius Upton | " |
| Simeon Robenson Jun[r] | " |
| Cap[t] Eben[r] Mosely |  |
| Philemon Holt | now in Service |
| Eliphaz Parrish | " |
| James Burnet | " |
| Elijah Benton | " |
| Nathan Hovey | " |
| Jacob Hovey | " |
| Abner French | " |

CONNECTICUT LINE, 1777–1781.  129

|  | Inlisted or Detach⁴ now in Service |
|---|---|
| Ruben Farnam | now in Service |
| Ebenʳ Perry | " |
| James Smith | " |
| Abner Ashley | Detachᵗ 1ᵗ Janʸ 1779 |
| Capᵗ Wᵐ Howard | |

---

### Mansfield

|  |  |
|---|---|
| Capᵗ Nathˡˡ Hall | Inlisted or Detach⁴ |
| Eleazer Conant | In Continental Service |
| Jonathan Snow | " |
| Caleb Conant | " |
| John Martin Junʳ | " |
| Joshua Basset | " |
| Joshua Davis | " |
| Asher Allen | " |
| James Strong | " |
| Jonathan Davis | Detachᵗ until yᵉ 1ᵗ January 1779 |
| Wᵐ Campbel | " |
| Henery Balch | " |
| Samuel Sergeant | " |
| Joel Starkweather Junʳ | " |
| Capt Eleazʳ Huntington | |
| Phineas Allen | In Continental Service |
| Diarke Allen | " |
| Samuel Conant | " |
| Elijah Baldwine | " |
| John Harris | " |
| Wᵐ Dodg | " |
| Ezra Phelps | " |
| Jonathan Nichols Junʳ | " |
| Amariah Crane | " |
| John Abbe | " |
| Jeremiah Gillet | " |
| Willard Church | " |
| Wᵐ Fitch Storrs | " |
| Bixbie Rodgers | " |
| Benjⁿ Rugbe | " |
| Nathan Porter | " |
| Gideon Arnold | Detach⁴ until 1ˢᵗ January 1779 |
| Matthew Warnor | " |
| Aarad Simons | " |
| Isaac Hall | " |
| Capᵗ Isaac Barrows | |
| Samˡˡ Herrinton | In Continental Service |
| Ebenʳ Snow Junʳ | " |
| Daniel B. Perkens | " |
| Josiah Burt | " |
| John Balch | " |
| Nathˡˡ Cary Junʳ | " |
| Joshᵃ Basset Junʳ | " |

Groton Isaac Park

Andrew Hall }
Peter Davinson } Drafted for yᵉ 1ˢᵗ January 1779
Samˡˡ Nichols }

|  |  |
|---|---|
| Cap[t] Whitmore | Inlisted or Detach[d] |
| Josiah Conant Jun[r] | In Con[l] Service |
| Jonathan Fenton | " |
| John Smith | " |
| John Saunders | " |
| John Harde | " |
| Isaac Cheets | " |
| Tolland Clement Minor | " |
| Jacobe Bosworth | " |
| John Wampe | " |
| Seth Chaimberlen | Detach[d] until Jan[y] 1779 |
| Moses Webster | " |
| James Kidder | " |
| Cap[t] Am[s] Williams | |
| John Dextor | In Continental Service |
| Joshua Bennet | " |
| John Bugbe | " |
| Aaron Royce | " |
| Elijah Royce | " |
| Benj[a] Lille | " |
| Nathan Reed | " |
| John Turnor | " |
| Charles Wood | " |
| Luther Chaimberlen | " |
| Groton Ralph Williams | |
| Cap[t] Sam[ll] Thomson | |
| Benajah Geer | In Contin[l] Service |
| Jon[o] Baker | " |
| Ichabod Hovey | " |
| Rodger Freeman | " |
| Jon[o] Eldredg | " |
| Leumy Case | " |
| Luther Eaton | " |
| Jacobe Bosworth | " |
| Darius Dextor | " |
| James Dextor | " |
| Jacobe Barrows | " |
| Dan[ll] Bosworth | " |
| Asael Dunham | " |
| Robert Fox | " |
| John Hartshorn | " |

### Ashford

|  |  |
|---|---|
| Cap[t] Benj[a] Clark | Inlisted or Detach[d] |
| Nath[ll] Harde | In Con[l] Service |
| Chester Rodgers | " |
| Amos Dowset | " |
| Lem[ll] Dowset | " |
| Philemon Holt | " |
| Eben[r] Brown | " |
| Lem[ll] Allen | " |
| James Grant | " |
| John Watkens | " |
| Th[o] Morey | " |
| Robert Paterson | " |
| Aaron Kyes | " |
| Cyrus Chafe | " |
| John Abbot Jun[r] | Drafted 1[st] Jan[y] 1779 |

| | |
|---|---|
| Cap<sup>t</sup> Caleb Hinde | Inlisted or Detach<sup>d</sup> |
| Robert Hale | In Continental Service |
| James Hale | " |
| Josiah Bicknal | " |
| James Eaton | " |
| Eleaz<sup>r</sup> Owen | " |
| Jas. Southworth | " |
| Steap<sup>n</sup> Eaton | " |
| W<sup>m</sup> Wators | " |
| W<sup>m</sup> Hall | " |
| Caleb Hende | |
| Joseph Hunter | |
| W<sup>m</sup> Southworth | |
| Joshua Fenton | |
| Cap<sup>t</sup> Squier Hill | |
| Abijah Smith | In Cont<sup>l</sup> Service |
| Samuel Mosely | " |
| Jonathan Crane | " |
| Benj<sup>n</sup> Dimmock | " |
| Dan<sup>ll</sup> Poole | " |
| Jedadiah Smith | " |
| Abijah Brooks Jun<sup>r</sup> | " |
| Robert Lewis | " |
| Negro Tone | " |
| Daniel Smith | Inlisted for y<sup>e</sup> 1<sup>st</sup> Jan<sup>y</sup> 1779 |
| Comfort Tyler | " |
| Joab Enoe | Detached for Jan<sup>y</sup> 1779 |
| Cap<sup>t</sup> Sim<sup>n</sup> Smith | |
| Asa Davison | In Con<sup>tl</sup> Service |
| Elias Dimmock | " |
| Elias Robenson | " |
| Eph<sup>m</sup> Spalden | " |
| W<sup>m</sup> Davison | " |
| Jon<sup>a</sup> Bullock | " |
| Charles Kimboe | for 2 years |
| Sam<sup>ll</sup> Rob (?) | Detach<sup>d</sup> to Jan<sup>y</sup> 1779 |
| Clark Robinson | Detach<sup>d</sup> to Jan<sup>y</sup> 1779 |
| Elius Chapman | " |
| Cap<sup>t</sup> Benj<sup>n</sup> Sumner | |
| Eben<sup>r</sup> Cheney | In Continental Service |
| Peter Smith | " |
| Charles Brandon | " |
| Sam<sup>ll</sup> Allen | " |
| Henery Lyon | " |
| Eleaz<sup>r</sup> Russel | " |
| Eleaz<sup>r</sup> Smith | " |
| John Lane | " |
| Titus Negro | " |
| Benj<sup>n</sup> Coals Jun<sup>r</sup> | Drafted for 1<sup>st</sup> Jan<sup>y</sup> 1779 |
| Cyrus Powers | " |
| Cap<sup>t</sup> John Sumner | |
| Samuel Allen | In Continental Service |
| Joseph Engle | " |
| Eph<sup>m</sup> Avery | " |
| David Peck | " |
| Obediah Brown | " |
| Aaron Bosworth | Drafted to y<sup>e</sup> 1<sup>st</sup> Jan<sup>y</sup> 1779 |
| Sam<sup>ll</sup> Bolls | " |
| Elius Anderwood | " |
| Jonathan Howard | " |

Coventry

|  |  |  |
|---|---|---|
| | Cap¹ John Arnold | Inlisted or Detch⁴ |
| | Ebenʳ Perkens | In Continental Service |
| | Joseph Atkens | " |
| | Joseph Doubleday | " |
| | Richard Deavenport Junʳ | " |
| | Mark Negro | " |
| | Jonathan House | " |
| | Habackock Turnor | " |
| Tolland { | Jonathan Dileno | " |
| | Richard Carlton | " |
| Labenon { | Nathˡˡ Harris | " |
| | Isaac Kellog | " |
| | Cap¹ Jerᵉ Ripley | |
| | Asael House | In Conˡˡ Service |
| | Samˡˡ Burden | " |
| | Daniel Edwards | " |
| | Joseph Badcock | " |
| | Joseph Doubleday Junʳ | " |
| | Noah Chapple | " |
| | Benjᵃ Grover | " |
| | John Brown | " |
| | Nathˡˡ Rose | " |
| Stafford | Nathˡˡ Walker | " |
| Tolland | Aaron Stemson | In Conˡ Service |
| | Elius Newton | " |
| | Elish. Stebbens | " |
| Coventry | Elias Janes | Drafted until yᵉ 1ˡ Janʸ 1779 |
| | Cap¹ Wᵐ Wilson | |
| | Nathˡˡ Thomson | In Contˡ Service |
| | Amos Avory Junʳ | " |
| | John Bill | " |
| | Solomon Dean Junʳ | " |
| | John Parker Junʳ | " |
| | Samˡˡ Evens | " |
| | Wᵐ Burns | " |
| | Samˡˡ Allen | " |
| | Nathan Parker | " |
| | Julius Burns | " |
| | Rodger Welsh | " |
| | Benjᵃ Buell Junʳ | " |
| | Andʷ Kingsbury | " |
| | Noah Porter Junʳ | Detachᵈ until Jany 1779 |
| | Noah Grant | " |
| | Hez. Richardson | " |
| | Oliver Ladd | " |
| | Jonᵃ Johnston | " |
| | Ezekiel Wentworth | " |
| | Elijah Wright Junʳ | " |
| | Cap¹ Amaᵃᵃ Rust | |
| | Robert Lane | In Continenˡ Service |
| | Abrahᵐ Brown | " |
| | Justus Brewster | " |
| | Samˡˡ Allen | " |
| | Danˡˡ Rockwell | " |
| | Elisha Adams | Detachᵈ until Janʸ 1779 |
| | John Ladd | " |
| | Josiah Porter | " |

CONNECTICUT LINE, 1777–1781. 133

         Inlisted or Detach⁴
Noah Carpenter   Detach⁴ until Jan⁷ 1779
Elijah Carpenter    "
Nath¹¹ Eells      "
John Thomson     "

To Brigad' Gen¹¹ J. Douglas Esq' of the 5ᵗʰ Brigade of Militia in the State of Connecticut. The within is a Return of those in the 5ᵗʰ Regiment in Said Brigade who are now in the Continental Service, Except Remov⁴ by Death or Discharge. Also the Names of those Inlisted or Detach⁴ to Serve in the Continental Service until the first of January next, together with the names of the Towns to which they belong, made agreeable to the Returns from the Respective Campanies in Said Regiment, Those men who are Retund as belonging to Towns out of this Regiment were Hired Prinsipally by the Town of Coventry with Money Rais⁴ by the Inhabitants of Said Coventry, They having the hiest Asurance that Said Towns had furnished there Quota of Men before the Men were hired, as apears by the Returns. In Compliance With the Orders from the Honᵇˡᵉ the Gen¹¹ Assembly of this State of Jan⁷ Last. From your Honʳˢ most Obed⁴
           Humble
         Serv' Exp Storrs Col°
Mansfield y° 10ᵗʰ March
      Anno Dom¹ 1778
         [*Connecticut Historical Society*]

## ELEVENTH REGIMENT

A Return of that Part of y° 11ᵗʰ Rig' in Woodstock in State of Connecticut

  Cap' Frissell Company
   for the war
 Asael Clark ⎫ Woodstock
 Cato Negro ⎭ Ashford
  for three years ⎫
 Abijah Bugbee ⎪
 Ely Bruce   ⎬ Woodstock
 Richard Gile  ⎭
  Inlisted untill January
 Comfort Tuytor Transient Parson
 James Dodg Woodstock
 John Morse hired ⎫ Benjⁿ Ballen of union 3 years
 John Goodale ju' ⎪
 Hewlett Martain ⎬ Detached
 John Hewlett  ⎪
 Esre Chamberlin ⎭
 Daniel Perry hir'd ⎭ John Right of union 2 y°
  Cap' Bowen Company
   for 3 years
 David Holmes  Woodstock
 Willᵐ Manning  Woodstock
 Briant Brown   Woodstock
 Willᵐ Gibson   Woodstock
 Paul Hernden   Tran' Person
 Lemuel Allin   Ashford
 John Green    Woodstock
 Nath¹¹ Robbins  Tran' Person

David Lawrence ⎫
Willm Martin     ⎬ Detached
Joshua Lauton   ⎭
  Capt Paine Compy
    for 3 years
John Bartholomew ⎫
Willm Press      ⎪
Dennis Spenser   ⎬ Woodstock
Robart Chandler  ⎪
Daniel Brown     ⎭
James Chafee Jur ⎫
Richard Bolls    ⎪
Philip Brown     ⎬ Detacht
Richard Shapley  ⎪
Jonas Haughton   ⎭
Bille Manning Inlisted Jany
  Capt Stephen Lyons Compy
    for 3 years
Theophilus Luther ⎫
John Vinton       ⎪
John Brock        ⎪
Amos Burnal       ⎪
Daniel Evans      ⎬ of Woodstock
Abraham White     ⎪
Elihu Hebbard     ⎪
Aaron Hebbard     ⎪
Asa Lyon          ⎪
Asa Winter        ⎭
  Capt Stones Compy
    for 3 years
Timothy Hebbard ⎫
Thos Spenser    ⎪
Nathan Powers   ⎬ of Woodstock
David Negrow    ⎪
Josiah Pagan    ⎭
John Lyon Detacht until the First of Jany
  Part of Capt Lyon Cy
Daniel Smith    ⎫ Draughted
Asa Hebbard     ⎬ Woodstock
Abijah Williams ⎭
  Capt Morris Company
    for 3 years
James Gould     ⎫
Jason Crawford  ⎪
Simeon Camp     ⎬ Woodstock
Poter Sanders   ⎪
Fradrick Green  ⎪
John Felen      ⎭
John Bowen         ⎫
Joseph Haward      ⎪
John Wilson        ⎪
Joseph Bartholomew ⎬ Detached
Jethnel Perrin     ⎪
Asa Morris         ⎪
Stephen Abbot      ⎪
Micah Barlow       ⎭

          Killingly March the 10th 1778
                    Willm Danielson Coll

CONNECTICUT LINE, 1777–1781.     135

A Return of that Part of y* 11ᵗʰ Reg* in Killingly in State of Connecticut

Cap* Larneds Company
for y* War
John Kath
  for 3 years
Elisha Mayo
Abnar Marsh
Archabel Town
Lemuel Barrows } All of Killingly
Tom Negrow
Will⁼ Jones
  Detached
Jonathan Lee
Joseph Alton

Cap* Convers Company
for 3 years
Solomon Johnson
Gideon Martin
Isaac Barrows
Josiah Barrows
Sam¹¹ Runnels
John Russel
Silas Richards } All of Killingly
  Drughted
David Harscall
Nath¹¹ Mils ju*
Chostor Convers
Thoˢ Eliot
Will⁼ Whitemore
Simeon Stone

Cap* Chandler
Charles Lebret
Penuel Child } for 3 years
Joseph Robins
Isaac Atwood
Nath¹¹ Bundy
Jacob White } Detachd until y* 1ˢᵗ of January
Jacob Daly
  All of Killingly

Cap* Dikes Company
for the War
Cato Negroo
  Detached
James Roads } All of Killingly
Thoˢ Wever
Enos Smith
Penual Cady

Cap* J. Cady Company
for y* War
Benjamin Cady
Jesse Robart
Joseph Walker
for 3 years
Amasa Grover
John Pike
John Lawrance } All of Killingly
James Reynolds
Jacob Reynolds
Will⁼ Arvin
Comfort Redaway
Benjᵃ Robison
Crumel Luther

Cap⁺ D. Cady's Comp⁷
Thoˢ Barrows ⎫
Mathew Moffitt ⎪
John Jones ⎬ for 3 years
Ravid Runnels ⎪
Thoˢ Taylor ju⁺ ⎭
John Anderson ⎫
Oliver Kingsbury ⎪ Detached to Sarve
John Kee ⎬ untill Janery
Nath¹¹ Kee ⎪
Elezar Fairman ⎭
John Bush Inlisted till Jen⁷.
   All of Killingly
  Cap⁺ Warrins Comp⁷
Daniel Sweet ⎫
Jacob Warrin ⎪
Joseph Starkwether ⎪ for 3 Years
Elijah Russel ⎬ of Killingly
Richard Hopkins ⎪
Nicholas Shippee ⎪
Simeon Russel ⎭
Tibbee Robarts Transiant Person
Squier Knight Plainfield
Jonas Baker ⎫
Will⁼ Walton ju⁺ ⎪ Detached to Sarve
Thoˢ Wood ⎬ untill Jenuary
Nath¹¹ Lovegoy ⎪
Ephriam Warren ⎭
  Cap⁺ Hawkins
  for 3 years
Ward Walton a tran⁺ Person
Will⁼ Durfy ⎫
Henry Carpenter ⎬ Detach⁴
Will⁼ Straight ⎭
  Cap⁺ Eaton
Jabez Kingsbury ⎫ for 3 years
John Robards ⎬ Killingly
John Meegan (?) ⎭
Elijah Goar Detached
  Part of Cap⁺ Stones Comp⁷
Josiah Child ⎫ for 3 years
Joseph Sheffield ⎬ Killingly
Benjᵃ Fairbanks Detached
John Gilbart Groton
Inlisted until January
Michel Crosby ⎫
John Bond ⎪
Joseph Carrel ⎬ Transiant Parsons
Caleb Eady ⎪ Not in any Com⁷
Zenus Hathaway ⎪
Will⁼ Blanchard ⎭
  Cap⁺ Greens Company
──Turner a Transiant Parson
Will⁼ Adams ⎫
Jeremiah Wilkie ⎪
Jacob Bixby ⎪ for 3 years
Parker Adams ⎬
Perley Herrin ⎬ all of Killingly
Cornelus Havens ⎪
Jason Harriss ⎪
Philip Keach ⎪
Sam¹¹ Hall ⎭

Jonathan Porter }
Lemuel Knap
Ebenezar Plumer
Henry Stone
Jonathan Aldrige  } Detached
Aaron Alger
Will<sup>m</sup> Stockwell
Nath<sup>ll</sup> Carrill }
  Part of the Granadear Comp<sup>y</sup>
Barnew Tortolott
Comfort Woodart } Detached
Jose Joslen
Salvenus Perrey
Simeon Leonard    for 3 years
Jabez Leach
Jack Negrow } all of Killingly
Jonathan Jenkes
David Runnels
Joseph Jinkes
Jacob Leavens } Detached
Abijah Fleng
              Killingly March y<sup>e</sup> 10<sup>th</sup> 1778
                      Will<sup>m</sup> Danielson Co<sup>ll</sup>

A Return that Part of y<sup>e</sup> 11<sup>th</sup> Reg<sup>t</sup> which belongs to Pomfrett in State of Connecticut
In Continental Sarvis for three years or During the War

    Capt. J. Williams

| | |
|---|---|
| Joseph Ross | Pomfrett |
| Salos Covel | " |
| Tho<sup>s</sup> Hill | " |
| Oliver Read | " |
| Ezra Goodale | " |
| John Wamper | N. London |
| Elijah Cheney | Pomf<sup>t</sup> |
| Jaazaniah How | " |
| Joseph Holmes | " |
| Tho<sup>s</sup> Jones | |
| Sam<sup>ll</sup> Millington | Stafford |
| Ezekiel Lomis | Lebanon |
| Abiel Farnam | Windham |
| Henry Smith | Pomf<sup>t</sup> |
| Joseph Griffin | " |

    Cap<sup>t</sup> Welds Company

| | |
|---|---|
| Elias Jones | Pomf<sup>t</sup> |
| [   ] Sabin | " |
| James Jones | " |
| Rowland Collon | " |
| Joseph Griffin | " |
| John Cheney | " |
| Joseph Ross | " |
| Jonathan Hill | " |
| Joseph Hunter | " |
| John Morrisson | " |
| Matthew Jackson | " |
| William Clevland | " |
| Ebenezer Gilbert | " |
| Will<sup>m</sup> Earl | " |
| Will<sup>m</sup> Lashbrooks | Pomf<sup>t</sup> for the war |
| Benj<sup>a</sup> Buffinton | Tran<sup>t</sup> Parson |
| John Briant | Norwich |

Jonath<sup>n</sup> Bullock — Tran<sup>t</sup> Parson
John Campbell — Pomf<sup>t</sup>
  Cap<sup>t</sup> S. Williams Company
Jacob Goodale for 3 years — Pomfrett
Dick Negro — "
James Indian for the War — "
Nehemiah Bacon for 3 years — Pomfrett
Detach<sup>d</sup> until 1<sup>st</sup> January
Charles Putnam } for 3 years
Amasa Deaolph }
Luis Negrow 3 years
  Cap<sup>t</sup> Crafts Company
Silas Holt of — Pomf<sup>t</sup>
Elisha Stowel — "
Abiel Lyon — "
John Shadden — "
Eben<sup>r</sup> Owen — "
Elias Robinson — Ashford
John Fuller — Windham
Sam<sup>ll</sup> Bugbee — Tran<sup>t</sup> Parson
Negro Name unknown
Jacob Havey — Windham
Caleb Conant — Mansfield
Will<sup>m</sup> Tarnham — Windham
James Eaton — Ashford
Tho<sup>s</sup> Grosvenor — Pomfrett
Stephen Brown — "
Ebenezer Force — "
  Cap<sup>t</sup> Ingalss Company
Lemuel Fling — Pomfrett
Benjamin Sharpe — "
Cyrus [     ] — "
Ebenezer Groo — "
Nath<sup>ll</sup> Stoel — "
John Lille — Cantabury
Ceaser Negro — Pomf<sup>t</sup>
  During the War
Zenas Harthaway — Pomf<sup>t</sup>
James Grant — "
  for 3 years
James Duggin ⎫
Sam<sup>ll</sup> Cady ⎪
Amasa Copland ⎪
Alvin Goodale ⎬ of Pomf<sup>t</sup>
Jesse Earl ⎪
Cap<sup>t</sup> Adams ⎪
Septimer Gardner ⎪
John Wheler ⎭
  Part of Granadear Comp<sup>y</sup>
Obediah Brown — Trantion Parson
Ebenezar Cheney — Ashford
Abnar Chapman — Colchester
Abnar French — Canterbury
  for three years

Killingly March y<sup>e</sup> 10<sup>th</sup> 1778<br>Will<sup>m</sup> Danielson Co<sup>ll</sup>

A return of the Non Comisond officers and Soldiers that Belonged to the 5<sup>th</sup> Brigade in the State of Connecticutt who are Now Engaged in the Continental Armey March y<sup>e</sup> 20<sup>th</sup> 1777

[*Connecticut Historical Society.*]

CONTINENTAL REGIMENTS, 1775. 139

## TWELFTH REGIMENT

A Return of the Men Raised for the Continental Army By The Town of Lebanon as P<sup>r</sup> Returns

| Name | Town | Term | Notes |
|---|---|---|---|
| Jonathan Bill | Lebanon | for 3 years | |
| John Clark Jun<sup>r</sup> | " | " | |
| Ameziah Chappel | | | |
| Thomas Doyle | Transient Person | " | Hired in Lebanon |
| James Denison Fish | Lebanon | " | |
| Rowswold Minor | " | " | |
| Charles Quameny | " | " | |
| John Crandol | " | " | |
| Michael Barry | " | " | |
| Jediah Woodworth | " | " | |
| William Williams Jun<sup>r</sup> | " | " | |
| Joseph Laws | " | " | |
| Daniel Vaughan Jun<sup>r</sup> | " | " | |
| Lemuel Case | " | " | |
| Samuel Groos | " | " | |
| Jonah Case | " | " | |
| Rowland Swift Jun<sup>r</sup> | " | " | |
| John Allen | " | " | |
| John Bray | " | " | |
| Cash Negro Man | " | " | |
| Abraham Merefield | " | " | |
| John Groos | " | " | |
| Charles Wright | " | " | |
| Jonathan Richardson | " | " | |
| Walter Harris | | | |
| Samuel Robbenson | Windham | " | Hired by Lebanon |
| Elijah Bill | Lebanon | " | |
| Benjamin Luis | N. London | " | |
| Zepheniah Foster | Lebanon | " | |
| Phillip Hills | " | " | |
| Alpheus Polly | " | " | |
| Benjamin Butler | " | " | |
| Thomas Watles | " | " | Not Joined |
| Jabez Metcalf | " | " | |
| Amherst Bartlet | " | " | |
| Jared Hinckley Jun<sup>r</sup> | " | " | |
| James Mckartey | " | " | |
| Rawswold Richardson | " | " | |
| Moses Clarke Jun<sup>r</sup> | " | " | |
| Joshua Carpenter | " | " | |
| Joshua Franck a Melato | " | " | |
| Joseph Clark | " | " | |
| Benjamin Woodworth | " | " | |
| Ed. Webster | " | " | |
| Lemuel Washborn | " | " | |
| Jonathan Edgerton | " | " | |
| Richard Lyman 2<sup>d</sup> | " | " | |
| Stephen Hall | " | " | |
| Richard Lyman 3<sup>d</sup> | " | " | |
| Dan Metcalf | " | " | |
| Ignatious Waterman | " | " | |
| Jabesh Palmer Jun<sup>r</sup> | " | " | Hereby Enlisted |
| Thomas Mershal | " | " | |

| | | |
|---|---|---|
| David Bruce | Lebanon | for 8 years |
| Gideon Geer | " | " |
| Fitch Lanphear | " | " |
| Ezrael Caswell | " | " |
| Zera Page | " | " |
| John Felows | Tollon | " |
| Ammi Doubledee | Lebanon | " |
| Jonathan Moredock | " | " |
| Ariel Moredock | " | " |
| Ephraim Terry 3d | " | " |
| James Newcomb Junr | " | " |
| Olliver Bemont | " | " |
| Isaiah Tiffeny 3d | " | " |
| Asa Richardson | " | " |
| John Vaughan Junr | " | " |
| Jesse Torry | " | " |
| Jonah Groos | " | " |
| Horton Lee | " | " |
| Barnebas Strong | " | " |
| James Bettis Junr | " | " |
| Ollever Hyde | " | " |
| Abner Doubledee | " | " |
| Lothrop Davis | " | " |
| William Ward | " | " |
| Nathll Holebrook Junr | " | " |
| James Barnibee | " | " |
| Flaviel Clark | " | " |
| John Rithbie | Transient Person | " Hired by Lebanon |
| John Barnes | " | " Hired by Lebanon |
| Vmphrey Ball | Lebanon | " |
| Nathll Harris | " | " |
| Ezekiel Loomis | " | " |
| Phinehas Sprague | " | " |
| John Pineo | " | " |
| Timothy Woodworth | " | " |
| John Huntington | Windham | " Hired by Lebanon |
| Seth Doubledee | Lebanon | " |
| Elijah Palmer | " | " |
| William Bentley | " | During the War |
| Isaac Bartlet | " | for 8 years |
| Daniel Jones | " | " |
| Daniel Ingraham Junr | " | " |
| Shubel Otis | " | " |
| Thomas Earl | " | " |
| Allen Prat | " | " |
| John Butler | " | " |
| Bruister Chappel | " | " |
| Uriah Polly | " | " |
| Simeon Puffer | " | " |
| Rawswold Bourn | " | " |
| Noah Robbords | " | " |
| Hoseah Burge | " | " |
| Amos West | " | " |
| Elisha Luther | " | " |
| Samuel Helmes | " | " |
| John Babcock | " | " |
| Samuel Mordock | " | " |
| Joseph Martin | " | " |
| Daniel Puffer | " | " |

CONTINENTAL REGIMENTS, 1775.          141

Isaac Kellogg              Lebanon       for 8 years
Judah West                    "              "
Ezekiel Lyman Jun'            "              "
Dan Lyman                     "              "
Israel Webster                "              "
Ezrah Dorner (? Downer)       "              "
John Humphrey                 "              "
  Detached Men in Lebanon to Serve in Continental Army until Janry
Next are —
  In Capt. Sam<sup>ll</sup> Dunham's Compy —
Phinehas Post
Samuel Bruister
  In Capt. Elias Bliss' Company        In Lebanon 119 Enlisted
Edward Hawkins                                    7 Detached
Jonah Swetland                                   ———
Joseph Buckingham                                126
Nath<sup>ll</sup> Fitch
  In Capt. Andrew Waterman's Company
Walter Mackaul

  A Return of the Men In Hebron In The 12<sup>th</sup> Regiment In the State of
Connecticut that have joined and Detached To join the Continental Army
Thomas Marble              Hebron       for 3 years
Aaron Baxter                  "              "
Cesar Negro man               "              "
Lazrus Puffer                 "              "
James Gallet                  "              "
Stephen Stark                 "              "
Ephraim Taylor                "              "    New Enlisted
Brister Negro man             "              "
Joel Fox                      "              "
Samuel Rude                   "              "
William Hills                 "              "
William Danielson       Transient Person     "    Hired by Hebron
John Winship               Hebron            "
Ephraim Bemus                 "              "
Cesar Negro man               "              "
Joseph Indian Man             "              "
Dan Blackman                  "              "
Eleazer Newcomb               "              "
Aaron Bingham                 "              "
Joseph Larnord                "              "
William Peters                "              "
Eleazer Porter                "              "
Isaiah Wright                 "              "
Abner Mack                    "              "
Solomon Guttrege              "              "
James Prat                    "              "
Henry Goslin                  "              "
Jared Phelps                  "              "
Elexander Porter              "              "
Beriah Skinner                "              "
Joel Mack                     "              "
Homer Phelps                  "              "
Peter Negro man               "              "
John Phelps                   "              "
Elijah Hutchinson             "         During the War
Joseph Belcher                "              "

| | | | |
|---|---|---|---|
| Hezekiah Marks | Hebron | During the War for 8 years | |
| Reuben Merrils | " | " | |
| Ashur Merrils Jun'r | " | " | |
| Joshua Bill | " | " | |
| Elius Wires | " | " | |
| Samuel Mack | " | " | |
| Gill Belcher | " | " | |
| Ely Phelps | " | " | |
| Robert Cox | " | During the War for 8 years | |
| Osten Brown | " | " | |
| Eleazer Brown | " | " | |
| John Colver | " | " | |
| Israel Gillet Jun'r | " | " | |
| Benjamin Mackinborough | " | " | |
| Israel Stark | " | " | |
| Thomas Skinner | " | " | |
| Jedadiah Mackinborough | " | " | |
| Simeon Wright | " | " | |
| Abijah Gardner | " | " | |
| Daniel Watrous | " | " | |
| Wiman Parker | " | " | |
| Joseph Chapman | " | " | Newly Enlisted |
| Ashur Merils | " | " | |
| David Colver | " | " | |
| Garner Gilbert | " | " | |
| Daniel Polly | " | " | |

The Men Detached In Hebron to Serve in Continental Army untill Janry Next as p'r Returns is

    In Capt Stephen Barber's Company
        Samuel Right
        Neziah Gilbert
    In Capt Simeon Edgerton's Company
        Samuel Raymond
    In Capt Thomas Terril's Company
        Joseph Larnord
    In Capt Joshua Phelp's Company
        Stephen Stiles Jun'r    62 Enlisted
    In Capt Skinner's Company    14 Detached
        Zadock Man
        Joseph Wain Case    76
    In Capt David Tarbox Company    In Hebron
        Benjamin Archer Jun'r
    In Capt Samuel Gilbert's Company
        Asa Hutchinson
        Ebenezer Hutchinson
        Amos Hall
        John Merrill
    In Capt David Miller's Company
        Eleazer Root
        Jeremiah Boles

The Whole of The Detached Men In Hebron to Serve In The Continental Army is 14

A true Return of the men Enlisted and Detached to join the Continental Army in Lebanon and Hebron in the 12th Regiment in the State of Connecticut According to Returns. Errors Excepted

        Jeremiah Mason Colo
          March 10th A.D. 1778
            [*Connecticut Historical Society.*]

## EIGHTEENTH REGIMENT.

A Return of Men Detatch⁴ from the 18th Regiment of Malitia in yᵉ State of Connecᵗ Commanded by Jonᵃ Humphry Esqʳ Colˡ to Join the Continental Army until Janʸ Next     May 1778

| Names of Men Detached | Names of Men hired Inlisted or Excused by Phisician | Town hired, Inlisted or Detached men belong to | Time Engaged for | Compᵃ Inlisted into | |
|---|---|---|---|---|---|
| Timᵒ Phelps | Excused by yᵉ Doctʳ | | | | |
| Daniel Barber | S⁴ to have March⁴ to Join Simsbury | | | | |
| Joel Eno | hir⁴ Sariah Fox | East Hartford | 1 Janʳʸ 1778 | | |
| Eliph Mitchel | hir⁴ Josiah Higley | of Simsbury | Do | | |
| Elisha Griswold | Excus⁴ by Phisician | | | | |
| Abijah Roe | | | | | Taken by Recruiting officer |
| Einathan Strong | hir⁴ London Wallas Juʳ | of Simsbury | 1 Janʳʸ | Capᵗ Wᵐ Judd | |
| Wᵐ Rothbone | | of Simsbury | | | Absconded |
| Jonah Rice | hir⁴ Hezʳ Phelps 3⁴ | of Simsbury | 1 Janry | Capᵗ Wᵐ Judd | |
| Asa Priest | hir⁴ Keny | of East Hartford | During War | Capᵗ Abbot | |
| Alex⁴ Marshel | hir⁴ Elezʳ Abby | of Do | Do | Do | |
| Jared Merril | hir⁴ Issaac Loveland | of Glassenbury | Do | Capᵗ Barnard | |
| Reubin Case | hir⁴ | | Do | | |
| Ichabod Gilbert | hir⁴ London Free Body | | 1 Janʳʸ | Capᵗ Judd | |
| Stephen Perring | hir⁴ Dan Dibol | | Do | Do | |
| John Wright | Inlisted | | Do | Do | |
| Wᵐ Shepherd Jʳ | Excus⁴ dy Phisician | | | | |
| Joel Holcomb | | | Do | Do | |
| Matthʷ Griffin | | | | | absconded |
| Benjᵃ Reed | hir⁴ Joseph Sharp | | 1ˢᵗ Janʳʸ | Do | |
| Ebenezʳ Holcomb | | | Do | Do | |
| Joab Gillet | hir⁴ Rufus Case | | Do | Do | |
| Aaron Dibol | | | | | |
| Aaron Cook | | | | | |
| Amasa Case Juʳ | hir⁴ James Keny | of Hartford | 3 years | Capᵗ Bar⁴ | |
| Luke Moor | sick Present | Simsbury | | | |
| Edw⁴ Thomson Juʳ | | Do | | | absconded |

| Names of Men Detached | Names of Men hired Inlisted or Excused by Phisicion | Town the hired, Inlisted or Detached men belong to | Time Engaged for | Comp⁴ Inlisted into | Absconded |
|---|---|---|---|---|---|
| Reubin Phelps | | Do | 1ˢᵗ Janʳʸ | | |
| Eppaᵇ Alderman | hirᵈ Garahum Fay | Winchester | 1ˢᵗ Janʳʸ | | |
| Ozias Moor | hired | Simsbury | 1 Janʳʸ | Capᵗ Judd | absconded |
| Reubin Tuller | Inlisted | Do | Do | Do | |
| James Beach | Inlisted | Do | During yᵉ War | Capᵗ Walbridge | |
| Asa Case | hirᵈ James Noacoke | Do | 8 years | | |
| John Barber Jʳ | hirᵈ Felix Curtis | Do | 1ˢᵗ Janʳʸ | Capᵗ W. Judd | |
| Amos Willcocks Juʳ | hirᵈ Gilbert Whiting | Do | | | |
| Edwᵈ Prouty | Excused by Phisian | Do | | | |
| Ephᵐ Sanden | | Simsbury | | | |
| Ozias Higley | hirᵈ Zenos Hays | Simsbury | 1ˢᵗ Janʳʸ | Capᵗ W Judd | absconded |
| Nichᵒ Gosard | hirᵈ John Gosard | Do | 1ˢᵗ Janʳʸ | Do | |
| John Griffen | Inlisted | Do | Do | Do | |
| Micah Haʸs | hirᵈ Benjᵃ Hays | Do | Do | Do | |
| Jacob Hays | hirᵈ Jacob Hallady | Do | 3 years | | |
| Nᵃᵗʰ Gillet | hirᵈ Joseph DᵉWolf | Do | 1ˢᵗ Janʳʸ | Capᵗ W Judd | |
| Benjᵃ Holcomb | hirᵈ Wᵐ Thorn | Do | 1ˢᵗ Janʳʸ | Do | |
| Noadiah Kendol | hirᵈ Ebenʳ Gosard | Do | Do | Do | |
| Reuben Hurlburt | hirᵈ Roᵇ Case (?) | Do | | | |
| Joshua Holcomb Juʳ | | Do | | | Absconded |
| Silas Phelps | | Do | | | Absconded |
| Elisha Eno | hirᵈ Israel Humphrey | Do | 1ˢᵗ Janʳʸ | Capᵗ W Judd | abscondet |
| Ichabod Strickland | | Do | | | absconded |
| Abner Griffen | | Do | | | |
| Isaac Eno | hirᵈ Malachi Corning | Hartland | During yᵉ War | Capᵗ W Judd | |
| John Moses | hirᵈ Jonᵃ Mountigue | Simsbury | 1ˢᵗ of Janʳʸ | | Absconded |
| Abel Loomis | hirᵈ Reubin Cadwell | Hartland | During rᵉ War | | Absconded |
| Jonᵃ Adams Juʳ | | Simsbury | | | |
| Jesse Negro | | | | | |
| Daniel Gains | hirᵈ Amos Holcomb | Do | 1ˢᵗ January | Capᵗ Judd | absconded |
| Joshua Austin | | Do | | | |
| Ezra Holcomb Jʳ | | Do | | | |

CONNECTICUT LINE, 1777-1781.   145

| | | | | |
|---|---|---|---|---|
| David Phelps | | Simsbury | 1 Jan'y | Cap' W Judd |
| Daniel Stiles | | Do | Do | Do |
| Isaac Penfield | Inlisted | Hartland | Do | Do |
| Jabez Gideons | hired Samuel Church | Do | Do | Do |
| Aaron Warner | Excus'd by Phisisian | Do | | |
| Stephen Richardson | Do | Barkhamsted | | |
| Jonas Weed | | Do | | |
| Samuel Eno | | Do | | |
| Amos Case | hired | | During War | |
| John Backon | hir'd Jon⁴ Andrus | Simsbury | 1ˢᵗ January | Cap' Champion |
| Noah Holcomb | hir'd Jacob Davis 3ᵈ | Do | Do | Do |
| Joel Buttolph | hir'd Gideon Perkins | Hartland | Do | Do |
| Thomas Coble | hired | Farmington | During y' War | Cap' W Judd |
| Consider Holcomb Jur | Inlisted | Simsbury | 1ˢᵗ January | Do |
| Elijah Holcomb | Do | Do | Do | |

10

The Within & Above is a True Return of the Men Detached & Inlisted out of the 18ᵗʰ Reg' of Malitia in the State of Connec'
as Recruits to fill up the Continental Army According to the Best of Our Knowledge

[*Connecticut Historical Society*]

## TWENTY FIRST REGIMENT

A Return of the Solders Now in the Continental Army; those Detach'd to Serve till the First Day of January Next or Inlisted for Said Term from and belonging to the Towns of Canterbury Plainfield and Voluntown and belonging to the 21th Regiment of militia in the State of Connecticut.

Men's Names Belonging to Canterbury — their Quota 76

Cap$^t$ Sherebiah Butts's Comp$^y$

Rufus Fitch  
Roger Green  
Jacob Mott  
Sam$^{ll}$ Thomson  
Sam$^{ll}$ Stoderd  
Jeremiah Read  
Clark Herington  
Ezekiel Herington  
Robert Herrick } Inlisted for 3 years or During the War  
Jed$^d$ Adams  
David Adams  
Ruben Carter  
Bartlet Bingham  
Isaac Evens  
Jed$^d$ Green  
Daniel Fitch  
Westly Perkins  
Wescut Perkins } Listed Feb 7 1778 for 3 years  
Nathan Steavens

Cap$^t$ Benj$^n$ Bacon's Company

Tho$^s$ Herris  
John Shaw  
Jacob Cleavland  
Nehemiah Monrow  
Elijah Monrow  
Isaac Basset  
John Cleavland Ju$^r$  
Jedediah Brown } Inlisted for 3 years or During the War  
Nathan Lester  
Nath$^{ll}$ Edwards  
Elias Shaw  
Aaron Falkner  
John Tefford  
Rdugen (?) an Irish Man

Cap$^t$ W$^m$ Hebbards Company

Elijah Burnam  
Fredrick Curtice  
Daniel Durfey  
Stephen Farnam  
Sam$^{ll}$ Glass  
Ruben Little } Inlisted for 3 years or During y$^e$ War  
Prince Little  
John Little  
Lee Woodard  
Benj$^a$ Shaw

Cap$^t$ John Johnson's Company

Thomas Astin  
James Whorfe  
Silas Gates  
Ebenez$^r$ Felch } Inlisted for three years or During the War.  
Abijah Cady  
James Johnson  
James Morse

CONNECTICUT LINE, 1777-1781.

Tias Ticker listed Feb 7 1778 for 8 years
Abel Williams } Inlisted till y⁰ 1ˢᵗ
Amon Stanton } Janʸ next

Capᵗ Jo⁰ Ransfords Company

Amos Bruster
Isiah Monrow
Joseph Bond
Andʷ Hebbard } Inlisted for 3 years or During yᵉ War
Jonᵗʰ Shaw
James Clark
John Eames
James Dixson Listed till first Janʳʸ next
John Green   Detachᵈ    Do

Capᵗ Aaron Fullers Company

Jeriel Dody
Wᵐ Shaw
John Cleavland } for 3 years or During yᵉ War
Samˡ Cobom
Abiel Farnam

Men's Names Belonging to Plainfield — their Quota 46

Lieuᵗ Joshua Bottom's Company

Asa Jones
John Saterly
Jacob Heard
Samˡˡ Staford
Boaz Tyler
Isaac Heard } Inlisted for 3 years or During the War
Nathˡ Sabens
James Dick
Wᵐ Benson
Joshua Simmon
John French
Stephen Spaulding } Detachᵈ till 1ˢᵗ Janʸ next
Rozel Aply

Capᵗ Joshua Dunlap's Company

William Waterman
Joshua Stoderd
William Knight
Ruben Bryant
Amos Bennet
Phinehas Hulet
David Wheler } Inlisted for 3 years or During the War
Epheram Dunlap
Manual Jones
Slip Watson
Lot Chase
Jonᵗʰ Whipple
John Clark
John Manly Listed till 1ˢᵗ Janʸ
Elijah Cook Detachᵈ

Capᵗ Branch[ ] Compʸ

William Meach
John Jack
Jonᵗʰ Chipmon
Amos Clain } for 3 years or During yᵉ War
Ned a Negro
Daniel Donvon
Elias Woodard Detachᵈ

Cap<sup>t</sup> Waterman's
Benj<sup>a</sup> Johnson
Andrew Spaulding
Stephen Bennet
Abel Franklin
Cuggo a Negro
Josiah Rogers
Gideon Wells Detach<sup>d</sup>
Henry Backon } inlisted till
John Tho<sup>s</sup> Trantom } 1<sup>st</sup> Jan<sup>y</sup>
Roger Avery of Norwich   Do
Edward Tylar of Pomfret  Do
Jesse Williams Groton

### Men's Names Belonging to Voluntown—their Quota 48

Cap<sup>t</sup> Moses Campbells Comp<sup>y</sup>
Robert Campbell
Nathan Coy
Zoath Tucker
Joseph Robbens
Peleg Shaw       } Inlisted for 3 years or During the War
Mark Croswell
Prince Summit
Joseph Peters
Seaser a Negro
William Crary Detach<sup>d</sup>
Jon<sup>th</sup> Gates   Detach<sup>d</sup>
Wheler Gallup Detach<sup>d</sup> but has pecured one Richard Sholes to Inlist into the Continental Army for 3 years under one Henry Williams L<sup>t</sup>

Cap<sup>t</sup> John Dixsons Comp<sup>y</sup>
William Gray
Robert Heard
John Gray
Jeduthen Heard
Alex<sup>dr</sup> Williams } Inlisted for 3 years or During ye War
W<sup>m</sup> Adams Ju<sup>r</sup>
Squir Knight
James Patrick
David Day
Robert Thomson
Ichabod Peevy
Amos Gore        } Detach<sup>d</sup>
James Dixon

Cap<sup>t</sup> Sam<sup>ll</sup> Robbens Comp<sup>y</sup>
William Pierce
David Coy
Amos Deneson    } Inlisted for 3 years or During y<sup>e</sup> War
Phinehas Allas
Abraham Herrington
Christopher Colegrove
Bennony Kinne
Moses Robens Ju<sup>r</sup>   } Detach<sup>d</sup>
Emmanuel Redrick
Phenies Lewis
Nath<sup>ll</sup> Petyes Inlisted till 1<sup>st</sup> Jan<sup>y</sup> next
Isaac Newton Detached but has procured one Christopher Brown to inlist into y<sup>e</sup> Continental Army for 3 years with H<sup>y</sup> Williams L<sup>t</sup>

Cap⁺ Robert Dixsons Compʸ
Moses Culver ⎫
Peter Morras ⎪
Henry Carpenter ⎬ Inlisted for 3 years or During yᵉ War
Robert Green ⎪
Henry Bacon ⎭
Jacob Patrick Detachᵈ
  Cap⁺ Ezra Cary Compʸ
James Kinne ⎫
Jonᵗʰ Hillard ⎬ Detachᵈ
Gideon Palmer ⎭
  Gideon Ray Detachᵈ but has procured one Christopher Billing to inlist in Room as pʳ Certificate
  Benjamin Gallup Detachᵈ but has procured one Lemuel Shelly in his Room as p Certificate,

Voluntown March 10ᵗʰ A D 1778

  The above is a true List of the Names of the Solders now in the Continantal Army and that are now Detachᵈ or Inlisted to Serve in the Continental Army agreeable to the Return from the Several Captains in the above Sᵈ towns belonging to the 21ˢᵗ Regᵗ of Militia in the State of Connecticut ( Excpt. Cap⁺ Smith's Company from which I have Recᵈ no Return nor from Cap⁺ Timothy Backus )

Certifᵈ P<br>James Gordon Lᵗ Col.<br>[ Connecticut Historical Society.]

## RETURNS FROM MILITIA, 1779.

### SECOND REGIMENT.

A Return of the Non Commissioned officers and Privates in Listed in the Connecticut Line of Infantry in the Continental Army for the 10th Company in the 2d Regiment of Milisha in this State

| Names of those Inlisted for three years or during the war | Regiments into Which they are Inlisted | Inhabitants of what town or Transient persons | Town Accounted for |
|---|---|---|---|
| Justus Wood | Meggs | New haven | New haven |
| Martin Clark | " | " | " |
| David Dorman | " | " | " |
| Samuel St Squir | Lamb | " | " |
| Abel Hitchcox | Meggs | Milford | Milford |
| Jared Hitchcox | " | " | " |
| Isaac Northrop | " | " | " |
| George Clark Jr | | " | " |
| Elijah Clark | | " | " |
| Samuel Champen | Lamb | Transient | New haven |
| Walter Booth | B Webbs | New haven | " |
| John Alling | " | " | " |
| Isaac Ford | " | " | " |
| Ephraim Thomas | R Meggs | " | " |
| Samuel Woods | " | " | " |
| John Vergurson | " | " | " |
| John [ ] | " | Transient | " |
| James Gainer | " | New haven | " |
| Elijah Osborn | Chanler | " | " |
| Thaddeus Thompson | Lambs | " | " |
| Brister Mix | Meggs | Transient | " |
| Richard Gore | " | New haven | " |
| Jesse Benjamin | Durkees | Preston | |
| Joseph Bonds | " | Canterbury | |
| Dan Chapman | Meggs | Transient | |
| John Johnson | " | Wallingford | |
| David Lounbuary | B Webbs | New haven | New haven |
| Joshua Meech | Huntingtons | Preston | |

A true Return Test
Samuel Osborn
officer of said Co.

Dated at New Haven
the 7th Day of May A. D. 1779      [*State Library, Hebard papers, 36.*]

A Return of the Non Commissioned Officers & Soilders, Inlisted in the Continental Army, in the Connecticut Line of Infantry; as Returned by the Captains of the Several Companies in the 2d Regt of Militia in this State; belonging to Towns in this State, not Included in said Regt
Branford May 24th 1779

| Soldiers Names | Regt Inlisted in | Inhabitants what Town | Town Acct for |
|---|---|---|---|
| Samll Lumis | Col. Wyllys | Colchester | N. Haven |
| John Mason | Col. Durgy | Killingworth | " |
| Amos Bruster | " | Canterbury | " |

CONNECTICUT LINE, 1777-1781   151

| Soldiers Names | Reg't Inlisted in | Inhabitants what Town | Town Acc't for |
|---|---|---|---|
| Nathan Gillet | Col. Douglass | Farmingtown | N. Haven |
| Benj'a Wright | Col. Swift | Killingworth | " |
| Sam'll Dickerson | Col. Webb | Norwalk | Milford |
| John McCannack | " | Fairfield | " |
| Jarib Mott | Col. Durgy | Canterbury | N. Haven |
| Abijah Bardsley | Unknown | Stratford | Derby |
| Charls Bradly | Col. Bradly | Sharon | " |

The Soldiers Above Named is the Whole (Some few Transiant Persons Excepted) that is Returned in the 2'd Reg't not belonging to the Towns Included in Said Reg't. Certifyed P Edward Russell Col.

Since the within Return was Compleeted I have Rec'd A Return from Cap't Horseey of Seven Men in Service, & belonging to and Counting for Derby. Names as follow't

James Prichard                  Ebenez'r Warner
Ebenez'r Durand                 Henry Wooster
Daniel Nichols                  Thom's Philips
Philo Lewis                       P E Russell Col

[*State Library, Hebard papers*, 35.]


A Return of the Non-Commissioned Officers & Privates inlisted in the Connecticut Line of Infantry, in the Continental Army for the Militia Company in the 2'd Regiment of Militia in this State.

| Names of those Inlisted for three years or During the War | Regiments into which they are inlisted |
|---|---|
| Jonathan Brown | Col'o Meggs y'e 6'th |
| Daniel Brown | " |
| Richard Watres | " |
| Andrew Watres | " |
| [ ] Leach | " |
| William Whitney | " |
| William Smith | " |
| Joseph Smith | " |
| Jeremiah O Cain | " |
| Abraham Murry | 2'd Battalion |
| Gersham Beardsce | Col'o Meggs y'e 6'th Batt'a |
| William Woshbon | Col'o Bradley |
| John Halchet | Col'a Meggs y'e 6'th |
| George Watress | Col'a Meggs y'e 6'th |
| David Chapman | " |

Derby May 8'th 1779             Cap't Joseph Holbrook return

[Each man was an inhabitant of, and was accounted for the town of Derby.]

[*Connecticut Historical Society.*]

## SEVENTH REGIMENT.

A Return of the Non commisoned Officers and Privates inlisted in the Connecticut line of Infantry in the Continental Armey for the 8th Company in the 7th Regiment of Militia in this State

| Names of those inlisted for three years or during the war | Regiments into which they are inlisted | Inhabitants of what town or transient persons |
|---|---|---|
| Jasper Pratt | Col Willys | Saybrook |
| Taber Smith | unknown | " |
| John Widger | Col Charls Webb | " |
| John Widger Jur | Col Swift | " |
| John Tucker | Col S. Webb | " |
| Asa Pratt Junr | Col Megs | " |
| Reuben Buckingham | unknown | " |
| Ethen Pratt Junr | Col Prentice | " |
| Samuel Doty Junr | " | " |
| Hezekiah Buckingham | " | " |
| Gideon Buckingham 2d | Col Megs | " |
| Wm Turner | Col Prentice | " |
| John Nickels | Col Megs | " |
| Martin Dibble | Col S. Webb | " |
| Stephen Waterhouse | Col Swift | " |
| Oliver Graham | Col Worner | " |
| John King | Col Megs | Transient |

[All are accounted for the town of Saybrook]
Dated at Saybrook the 10 Day of May A D 1779
Dan Platts Commanding officer
of Said Company

[*State Library, Hebard Papers*, 39.]

A Return of the Non Commissioned Officers and Privates Inlisted in the Connecticut Line of Infantry, in the Continental Army for the 17th Militia Company in the 2d Regiment of Militia in this State

| Names of those Inlisted for three years or during the war | Regiment into which they are inlisted | Inhabitants of what town or Transient person |
|---|---|---|
| William Cook | Col Lambs | New Haven |
| Danieal Ford | Col Megs | " |
| Noah Jonson | " | " |
| Richd Mansfield | " | " |
| Saml Robinson | Col Hastens | " |
| Moses Potter | Col Megs | " |
| Abraham Cooper | | |
| Charles Mansfield | Col Megs | " |
| Joseph Jonson | | |
| Samuel Fraser | Col Megs | " |
| John Hicks | " | |
| Francis Clarage | | |
| John O Briant | Col Megs | Transient |
| Ezekel Taphan | " | " |
| Joseph Dickerman | " | New Haven |
| Willm Wate | " | " |
| Timothy Potter | " | " |
| Eli Denslow | Col Russel | " |

[Each man was accounted for the town of New Haven.]
Dated at New Haven the 8th Day of May 1779
John Gilbert Commanding Officer of
said Company

[*State Library, Hebard Papers*, 41.]

CONNECTICUT LINE, 1777-1781.      153

A Return of the Non-Comisioned Ofisers and Privite Inlisted in the Conneticut Line of Infantry in Continental Army for the first Company alarm list Seventh Regement of militia in this State Saybrook may 10 1779

| Names of those inlisted for three years or During the War | Reg<sup>t</sup> into which they Inlisted |
|---|---|
| Zebada Brown | Sam<sup>ll</sup> B Webbs |
| Peter Floro | Return meaggs |
| Gift Freeman | Return maiggs |
| Jeremiah Lord | Sam B Webbs |
| William Lord | Return meggs |
| James Foster | Sam<sup>ll</sup> B Webbs |
| Isaac Wardin | Sam<sup>ll</sup> B Webbs |
| Olover White | Return Meggs |
| Robart Newell | Return meggs |
| Sam<sup>ll</sup> Hanson | Sam<sup>ll</sup> B Webbs |
| Jedidiah Gladin | Return meggs |
| Prosper Booth | Charles Webbs |
| Stephen Ludlow | Charles Webbs |
| Joseph Hand | Sam<sup>ll</sup> B Webbs |

[Each person was accounted for the town of Saybrook, and excepting James Foster a Transent Person each was an inhabitant of that town.]

Certified Elisha Chapman Cap 1 alarm Comp 7 Reg<sup>t</sup>
[*Connecticut Historical Society.*]

## SIXTEENTH REGIMENT.

A Return of the Noncomision officers and Souldiers inlisted into the Connecticut Line of the Continental army belonging to the 16<sup>th</sup> Regiment of militia as Returned by the Commanding officers of the Companies on y<sup>e</sup> 10<sup>th</sup> Day of May 1779

Names of those inlisted what town & Company

Capt<sup>n</sup> Comfort Hoyts Company Danbury
Benj<sup>n</sup> Seymor Sellick
John Barnum
Benj<sup>n</sup> Numes
[   ]ben Lord
Amos Negro
James Long
Joseph Jackson

W<sup>m</sup> MacLean
Sam<sup>ll</sup> Barnum
Noah Barnum
Fradrick Diteman
W<sup>m</sup> Negro

Capt Daniel Hecock Danbury
Sargt Joshua Taylor
Jesse Peck
Collaris Chapman

Captn James Clarks Company Danbury
Andrus Simmons
James Mathews
Jack Negro
John Ludiman
W<sup>m</sup> Griffith
David Row
Josiah Whitney
John Davidson
Uriah Negro
Uriah Acley
George Doolittle
W<sup>m</sup> Porter

Isaac Gorham
Benj<sup>n</sup> Waters
Minor Allen
Cato Login
Robart Welch
Edward Godard
Jonas Gates
[   ] Flint

Captn Eph<sup>rm</sup> Barnums Danbury
Isaac Collar
Thad<sup>us</sup> Starr
John McGlaffin

Names of those inlisted what town & Company

Joseph Perker
Robin Starr
Tobe Boston
James Davis
Jeremiah Russel

Captn Richard Shute Danbury
Minor Allen
John Nails
Aaron Knap
Ezra Ketchum
David Hall
Nath[ll] Robinson
Caleb Maksfield
Dan[ll] Elmer
John Curtis
Jon[ll] Diteman
John Williams
David Cay
W[m] Hopkins

Captn Richard Barnum's Danbury
Robart Nalor
James Gutheric
Mingo Giles
Fortin (? Foster) White
Prince Cornell
John Finnington
Amos Seelye
Patrick Rian
Joseph Plum
Steph[n] Rial
John Flisher
John Larabee

Captn Joseph Smith Newtown
James Sanford
George Clapham
Joel Botsford
Nathan Lummis
David Bishop
Stephn Benjamin
Mathew Marvin
Tho[s] Barnum
W[m] Barnet
W[m] Ryne

Captn Richard Smith Newtown
David Byshup
Tho[s] Brooks
Sam[ll] Brook
George Murry
Israel Burret

Joseph Hauley
Lyberias Hauley
James Waklee
Charles McDonald
Othniel Salks
Ebenz[r] Keeler

Capt Abel Botsford Newtown
Mathew Clark
Joseph Hatch
Nathan Hubbell
Isaac Baldwin
Sam[ll] Fareweather
Isaul (?) Murry
Andrew Blackman
W[m] Crawford
Hezekiah Meaker
Jacob Persons
Brester Judson

Captn Elijah Botsford Newtown
John Kimberlee
Zalmon Prindle
Wait Lewis
Lemuel Hubbell
Josiah Turrill
Smith Turrill

Captn George Turrills Newtown
Benjm Grgory

Captn John Botsford Newtown
Elijah Foot
Nath[ll] Little
Abijah Prindle
Peter Fairchild
Tobe Bennitt
Jack Botsford
Levi Wolfe
John Umphrey

Capt Benj[m] Sumers Newtown
Abel Baldwin Junr

Captn Peter Penfield Newfairfield
Sergt Talmage Hull
Benj[m] Robards
Corpl Charles Brown
John F Lacey
Ruben Stevens
Elijah Beardsley
Jonah Jonas

Names of those inlisted what town & Company

Captn Steph<sup>n</sup> Pardee New-fairfield
Sergt John Trowbridge
Tho<sup>s</sup> Cannan
W<sup>m</sup> Briant
Eliezer Wallen
John Hamilton
Aaron Wilder

Captn Dan Towner New fairfield
W<sup>m</sup> Jolly
Steph<sup>n</sup> Stilwell
David Corbin
Edward Dunham

[*State Library, Hebard Papers, 10.*]

## TWENTY-FIRST REGIMENT.

A Return of the Non Commissioned Officers and [ ] Connecticut [ ] Infantry in the Continental Army for the 21st Regiment of Militia in this State

| Names of those Inlisted for three years or During the war | Regiments into which they are Inlisted | Inhabitants of What Town or Transient person | Town accounted for | Company Accounted for |
|---|---|---|---|---|
| **2d Compy Alarm list** | | | | |
| Ebenezor Felch | Col Durkee | Canterbury | Canterbury | Capt Johnson |
| Silas Gates | " | " | " | " |
| James Whorf | " | " | " | " |
| Thomas Austin | " | " | " | " |
| Abijah Cady | Col Webb | Transt person | | |
| Tias Tiken Indian | 2d Battallion | | | |
| Francy Clergio | Col Durkee | Canterbury | | |
| Samson Indian | Col Webb | | | |
| Nathan Stevens | | | | Capt Butt |
| **5th Compy Alarm** | | | | |
| Andrew Hibbard | Col Durkee | Canterbury | Canterbury | Capt Raynsford |
| Jonth Shaw | " | " | " | " |
| John Ames | " | " | " | " |
| Joseph } h Munraw | | | | |
| } ond | | | | |
| James Clark | | | | |
| Peter Stevens Jr | Col Meigs | Transt person | | |
| Nathan Smith | Col Durkee | | | |
| **2nd Compy Militia** | | | | |
| Rufus Fitch | Col Wyllys | Canterbury | Canterbury | Capt Butt |
| Roger Green | Col Huntington | " | " | " |
| Jarub Mott | Col Durkee | " | " | " |
| Samll Thompson | " | " | " | " |
| Samll Stoddard | Col Wyllys | " | " | " |
| Jereh Read | Col Durkee | " | " | " |
| Clark Herrington | " | " | " | " |
| Ezekiel Herrington | " | " | " | " |
| Robert Herrick | " | " | " | " |

CONNECTICUT LINE, 1777-1781.   157

| | | | |
|---|---|---|---|
| Jedediah Adams | " | " | " |
| David Adams | " | " | " |
| Reuben Carter | Col Hunting | " | " |
| Bartlet Bingham | Col Durkee | " | " |
| Isaac Evens | " | " | " |
| Jedediah Green | " | " | " |
| Daniel Fitch | Col Wyllys | " | " |
| Francis Perkins | Col Durkee | " | " |
| Walcut Justin | " | " | " |
| Nathan Stevens | " | " | " |
| | Col Melgs | | |
| [ ] Cle[ ]nd | Col Durkee | | Cap' B. Bacon |
| Nehem Munro (?) | " | " | " |
| John Jeffords Indian | " | " | " |
| Isaac Basset | Col Webb | " | " |
| John Cleveland | Col Durkee | " | " |
| James Duggan | " | " | " |
| Jedediah Brown | Col C. Webb | " | " |
| Elias Shaw | | " | " |
| Nath'l Edwards | | " | " |
| Elijah Munrow | | " | " |
| Aaron Faulkner | | " | " |
| Nathan Leeter | | " | " |
| Sam' Adams Light Dragoon | | | |
| 8th Company Militia | | | |
| Josiah Burnham | Col Wyllys | Canterbury | Cap' Hibbard |
| Benj' Shaw | Col Durkee | " | " |
| Frederick Curtis Jr | " | " | " |
| Daniel Durfey | " | " | " |
| Reuben Lilley | " | " | " |
| Abial Farnam | | " | " |
| John Lilley | Col Wyllys | Canterbury | " |
| Sam'l Glass | | [ ] | " |
| Stephen Farnam | Col Webb | | " |

## REVOLUTION LISTS AND RETURNS.

| Names of those inlisted for three years or during the war | Regiments into which they are inlisted | Inhabitants of what Town or Transient person | Town accounted for | Company accounted for |
|---|---|---|---|---|
| Lee Woodward | Col Durkee | Canterbury | Canterbury | Cap¹ Hibbard |
| Prince Lilley | " | " | " | " |
| 7ᵗʰ Comp⁽ʸ⁾ Alarm list | | | | |
| John Cleveland | Col Durkee | Canterbury | Canterbury | Cap¹ Fuller |
| Wᵐ Shaw | Col Meigs | " | " | " |
| Samˡˡ Coburn | Col Durkee | " | " | " |
| James Paine Fitch | " | Pomfret | Pomfret | " |
| Jerial Dody | | | Canterbury | |
| Israel Dodge | | Canterbury | | |
| 10ᵗʰ Comp⁽ʸ⁾ of Militia | | | | |
| Samˡˡ Cleveland | Col Wyllys | Pomfret | Pomfret | Cap¹ I Tylar |
| Nathˡˡ Edwards | Col Durkee | Canterbury | Canterbury | " |
| James Litchfield | " | " | " | " |
| James Duggan | " | " | " | " |
| John Jeffords Indian | " | Trans⁺ person | " | " |
| Can[  ] Comp⁽ʸ⁾ Alarm list  Jy 18ᵗʰ May 1779 | | | Obediah Johnson Col. | |
| Daniel Donwon | Col Huntington | Transient person | Plainfield | Cap¹ Branch |
| Jonaᵗʰ Chapman | Col Sherburn | Groton | Plainfield | " |
| Frederick Waldo | Col Sherburn | Transient person | | " |
| Amos Clain | Col Sherburn | Plainfield | | " |
| John Jack | Col Wyllys | | | " |
| Wᵐ Meach | Col Huntington | Tranˢ person | | " |
| Ned Negro | Col Sherburn | | | " |
| John McLarlene | Col Durkee | | | " |
| 4ᵗʰ Comp⁽ʸ⁾ Do | | | | |
| Benjᵃ Johnson | Col Durkee | Plainfield | Plainfield | Cap¹ Waterman |
| Stephen Bennet | " | " | " | " |
| Josiah Negro | " | | | " |
| Cuggo Rogers | | N. London | | " |
| Jesse Williams | Col Sherburn | Groton | | " |
| Andrew Spalding | Col Durkee | Plainfield | | " |
| Abel Franklin | " | Transˢ person | | " |

CONNECTICUT LINE, 1777–1781.

| Name | Officer | Location | Company/Notes |
|---|---|---|---|
| Sam'll Dexter Negro | " | Plainfield | " |
| Peter Marsh | " | Trans't person | " |
| 1st Comp'y Militia | | | |
| Asa Jones | Col Durkee | Plainfield | Cap't Bottom |
| [Satterlee / Sabins] | " | " | " |
| Jacob Heerd | " | " | " |
| Sam'll Stafford | " | " | " |
| James Dick | Col Wyllys | " | " |
| Boaz Tylar | " | Trans't person | " |
| Isaac Heerd | " | Trans't person | " |
| W'm Renson | Col Sherburn | Groton | |
| Joshua Cinnamon | " | Preston | |
| John Baker | " | Groton | |
| Nath'll Holt | Col Prentice | Trans't person | |
| Amos Chapman | " | " | |
| Sipeo Negro | Col Durkee | Plainfield | Capt Dunlap |
| 4th Comp'y Militia | | | |
| W'm Waterman | Col Huntington | " | " |
| Amos Bennet | " | | |
| Reuben Briant | " | | |
| Joshua Stoddard | " | Trans't person | |
| W'm Knight | " | Plainfield | |
| Sip Watson | " | Voluntown | |
| Cuy Shepard | " | Norwich | |
| Mark Loswell | Major Porter | Trans't person | |
| Heze'b Kingsley | Col Durkee | Plainfield | |
| John Clark | " | | |
| Phinehas Mulet | " | | |
| Jon'th Whfpp[ ] | " | Trans't person | |
| Lot Chase | " | | |
| Abel Franklin | " | | |
| Peter Marsh | | Plainfield Return | Canterbury 18th May 1779 — Obadiah Johnson Col. |

## REVOLUTION LISTS AND RETURNS.

| Names of those inlisted for three years or during the war | Regiment into which they are inlisted | Inhabitants of What Town or Transient person | Town accounted for | Company Accounted for |
|---|---|---|---|---|
| 3rd Compy Alarm list | | | | |
| Peter Morris | Col Huntington | Transt person | Voluntown | Capt R. Dixon |
| Robert Green | " | Coventry | " | " |
| Henry Bacon | " | Voluntown | " | " |
| Henry Carpenter | " | Transt person | " | " |
| Moses Culver | | | | |
| 6th Compy Do | | | | |
| Lemuel Shelle | Col Huntington | Indian | Voluntown | Capt Wm Edmonds |
| 3rd Compy Militia | | | | |
| Robert Campbell | Col Durkee | Voluntown | Voluntown | Capt Campbel |
| Nathan Coy | Col Prentice | " | " | " |
| Zoath Tucker | " | " | " | " |
| Peleg Shaw | " | " | " | " |
| Joseph Robbins | Col Sherburn | Groton | " | " |
| Joseph Halley | " | " | " | " |
| Richard Shols | | | | |
| Joseph Patters | Col Wyllys | Voluntown | " | " |
| Mark Croswell | Col Prentice | " | " | " |
| Prince Summits | Col Wyllys | " | " | " |
| [     ] Negro | " | " | " | " |
| 6th Compy Militia | | | | |
| John Gray | Col Huntington | Voluntown | Voluntown | |
| Alexr Williams | " | " | " | |
| Jeduthun Hurd | Col Durkee | " | " | |
| William Adams | Col Huntington | " | " | |
| Squire Knight | | | | |
| William Gray | | | | |
| David Day | In Regt of Artificers | | | |
| 7th Compy Militia | | | | |
| Amos Dennison | Col Huntington | Voluntown | Voluntown | Capt S. Robbins |
| Phineas Ellis | " | " | " | " |
| Wm Pierce | Col Wyllys | " | " | " |
| David Coye | Col Melgs | " | " | |

| | | | | | |
|---|---|---|---|---|---|
| Wᵐ Bearzal | Col Huntington | " * | | " | |
| Emmun-Rederax | Col Durkee | " | | " | |
| Christ° Brown | Col Sherburn | " | | " | |
| | Voluntown Returns | Canterbury 13ᵗʰ May 1779 | Obadiah Johnson Col | | |

| Names of the men | regᵗ Inlisted into | Inhabᵗˢ of wᵗ town | Town accounted for | Company accounted for |
|---|---|---|---|---|
| 8ᵗʰ Compʸ of Alarm list | | | | |
| Jabez Kingsbury | | Killingly | Killingly | Capᵗ J Eaton |
| John Meazon Indian | | " | " | " |
| John Meazon Jr Do | | | | |
| 9ᵗʰ Compʸ of Militia | | | | |
| Thomas Barrus | Col Durkee | Killingly | Killingly | Capᵗ D Cady |
| Matthew Moffitt | " | " | " | " |
| The above Companys Belong to Killingly. | | | | |

[*Connecticut Historical Society.*]

11

## UNKNOWN REGIMENT.

Col. N. Beardslee's Return May 1779

Captn W<sup>m</sup> G Hubbell New fairfield
W<sup>m</sup> Sanders
Mathew Fowler
Sam<sup>ll</sup> Nichols
Abraham Nichols
Ethel Barns
Joel Botsford
Edward Dunham
Francis Foster
John Brown
Charles Farguson
W<sup>m</sup> Scott
Miles Wolman
David Corbin
Tobe Negro
Ned Negro
Jona an indian
Eliphalit Simson
Ezra Prindle
W<sup>m</sup> Jole

Captn Jonah Foster Ridgefield
Joseph Sears
John Robarts
Joseph Smith
Gibbart Brush
Elisha Lincoln
Ruben Cran
Amon Cran
John Condruy
Lewis Jacklin
Dan<sup>ll</sup> Rigs
Elisha Perry

Captn David Olmstid Ridgefield
Steph Remington
Neh<sup>h</sup> Olmstid
Jeremiah Olmsted
Joseph Jackson
Jeremiah Dean
Derias Benedic
Levi Keeler
Bartholomew Baker
Jeremiah Keeler
Selvinis Seelye
Benj<sup>a</sup> Bennit
Hezekiah Hawley
Jeremiah Osburn
John Hitchcock
Tho<sup>s</sup> Wason
James Barnes
John Hays
Benjn Downs

Joseph Shaw
W<sup>m</sup> Platt
Charles White
Solomon Brown
Tho<sup>s</sup> Hutchinson
Lucus Brown
James Stanton

Captn Knoles Sears Ridgefield
Sarg<sup>t</sup> John Street
Tho<sup>s</sup> Whitney
Ezekiel Whitney
Micajah Weeks
Eliphas Nicoson
Solomon Ren
Dan<sup>ll</sup> Canfield
W<sup>m</sup> Mitchel
W<sup>m</sup> Newton
John Butler
Baruch Nicoson
Elijah Weed
[    ] Keeler
[    ] Dodge

Captn Isaac Hine Ridgefield
Nehemiah Sherwood
Mical Frank
Dan<sup>ll</sup> Osburn
Sarg<sup>t</sup> Elisha Gibbard
Ebenz<sup>r</sup> Jacklin
Tho<sup>s</sup> Seagor
Abraham Russigu
W<sup>m</sup> Cummins
John Hitchcock
Micajah Weeks
Tho<sup>s</sup> Wason
W<sup>m</sup> Mitchel
James Barns
W<sup>m</sup> Newton
John Hays
John Butler
Peter Kelue
Henry Williams

inlisted Since the 19<sup>th</sup> of April 1779
Town of Newtown

Captn Elijah Botsfords Company
Wait Lewis
Lemuel Hubbell
Josiah Turrill
Smith Tuttle

Captn Jabez Botsfords Company Newtown
Levi Wolf

The Town of Newtown Dificent 25 men
Certified P<sup>r</sup> Nehemiah Beardsly Col

[*State Library, Hebard Papers,* 57.]

## SUPPLIES, 1780.

An Alphabetical List of the Names of the Officers and Soldiers in the Connec' Line who have rec'd Family Supplies from the several Towns for 1780.

| | Names | Towns to which they belong |
|---|---|---|
| 4 | Adams W<sup>m</sup> Lieut. | Hartford |
| x | Abbe Jeduthan | " |
| 3 | Eleazer | " |
| 3 | Augustus Zezar | " |
| x | Andrus Thomas | E. Haddam |
| x | Ackly Thomas | " |
| | Arnold Jehiel | Haddam |
| 5 | Angar George | Mdletown |
| 3 | Andrus Asa Serj. | Weathersfield |
| | Austin Richard | Suffield |
| 4 | Allen Samuel | " |
| 5 | Anderson William | E. Windsor |
| O | Andrus Thomas | Simsbury |
| O | Andrus W<sup>m</sup> | " |
| A | Alley W<sup>m</sup> | New Haven |
| H | Alling Jonathan | " |
| A | Akin James Serj. | " |
| 3 | Alvord G. Th<sup>o</sup> Serj. | Farmington |
| 3 | Adrus Theodore | " |
| 6 | Atkins Josiah Jun | Waterbury |
| x | Thomas Anderson Lieut. | Lyme |
| * | Akely Samuel | Guilford deserted |
| 2 | Allen Moses | Fairfield |
| 2 | Allen Eben<sup>r</sup> | " |
| x | Aldrich W<sup>m</sup> | Preston |
| x | Avery Simeon Lieut. | Groton |
| x | Anew Andrew | " |
| 9 | Andrus James | " |
| 9 | Andrus Ezra | New Hartford |
| x | Allen Asher | Mansfield |
| x | Abbe John | " |
| 4 | Adams David Surg. | Canterbury |
| 4 | David | " |
| D | Sam<sup>ll</sup> | " |
| 7 | Andrus Tim<sup>o</sup> | Watertown |
| 6 | Blodget Artimas C<sup>ler</sup> | Salsbury |
| 2 | Barrows Jacobe Corp. | Mansfield |
| x | Bugbe John | " |
| x | Basset Joshua | " |
| 7 | Brown Charles | Newfairfield |
| 7 | Bunce Isaiah | Washington |
| 2 | Basset W<sup>m</sup> | Watertown |
| 2 | Buck Josiah | Newmilford |
| 7 | Bostwick Eben<sup>r</sup> | " |
| 7 | Bewil David | " |
| * | Bissel Benj<sup>a</sup> | Litchfield Deserted |
| 8 | Brigham Paul Cap<sup>t</sup> | Coventry |
| x | Ball Umphry | Lebanon |
| D | Bull Eppiphras Maj. | Hartford |
| | Buckland Steaphen Capt. | " |

## REVOLUTION LISTS AND RETURNS.

|   | Names | Towns to which they belong |
|---|---|---|
| 8 | Barnard John Capt. | Hartford |
| 9 | Brewer Daniel | " |
| 3 | Beevins Eben' | " |
| 3 | Brown Jacobe | Summers |
| 3 | Brown Eben' | Tolland |
| 3 | Booth Henery | Enfield |
| 6 | Blanchard Robbins | Colchester |
| 6 | Bates Amos | Haddam |
| 6 | Bonfoey Benanual | " |
| 6 | Boardman Jonathan | " |
| 6 | Bates Daniel | " |
| 6 | Bates Eleazer | " |
| 6 | Bailey Robart | " |
| 6 | Bacon W$^m$ | Mdletown |
| 9 | Brown W$^m$ | " |
| 6 | Boardman Sam$^{ll}$ A | " |
| 9 | Barns Thomas | " |
| 9 | Boardman Moses | " |
| 5 | Brisler John | Windsor |
| x | Brown Elias | " |
| 9 | Brown Edward | Weathersfield |
| 9 | Blin Justus | " |
| 9 |    Abraham | " |
| 9 | Bulkley Edward Capt. | " |
| 3 | Bowers Ephraim | Chatham |
| 9 | Butler Peter | " |
| 3 | Bowers Benjamin Serj. | " |
| 3 | Bowers Benaiah | " |
| 8 | Brown Josiah Lieut. | E. Windsor |
| 8 | Baxter Francis | " |
| 8 | Barns Daniel Capt. | Southington |
| 7 | Baldwine Calib Capt. | Killingsworth |
|   | Brunson Rodger | Farmington |
| 6 | Baker Edward Serj. | New Haven |
| A | Barns Solomon Serj. | " |
| A | Burroughs Samuel | " |
| A | Bishop Nath$^{ll}$ | " |
| 3 | Brown Henery Serj. | " |
| 6 | Blakesly Zealus | " |
| 6 | Bracket Hez. | " |
| 6 | Blakesley Jared | " |
| 4 | Beckwith Phineas Serj. | Lyme |
| 6 | Bunnell Abr$^m$ | Branford |
| 6 | Bagdon Cezar | " |
| 6 | Belding John | Milford |
| 3 | Bristol Jonathan | " |
| 6 | Bebe Joe | " |
| H | Burk John | " |
| 6 | Bradley Daniel | Wallingford |
| Inv$^d$ | Barns Moses | " |
| 6 | Bristol Benjamin | Cheshire |
| 6 | Barns David | " |
| 6 | Ball John Lieut. | Guilford |
| 6 | Benton Edward S$^t$ | " |
| 7 | Bishop Almeno | " |
| 5 | Baker Bartholomew | Reading |
| 3 | Belding Moses | " |

## CONNECTICUT LINE, 1777-1781.

| | Names | Towns to which they belong | |
|---|---|---|---|
| 7 | Barnum Sam<sup>ll</sup> Lieut. | Kent | |
| 7 | Barnum Steaphen S<sup>t</sup> | " | |
| 7 | ⎯⎯ Amos Corp. | " | |
| 7 | Barlow John | " | |
| 2 | Bradley Nathan | Fairfield | |
| | ⎯⎯ Eliphalet | " | not in y<sup>e</sup> Ab. |
| 8 | Bulkley Seth | " | |
| 8 | Bates David | Stamford | |
| 5 | Barns Ambrose | Norwalk | |
| 7 | Bedient Mordica | " | |
| 8 | Bouton John | " | |
| A | Benjamin John Lieut. | Stratford | |
| 8m | Bebe James Capt | " | |
| 5 | Bradley B Philip Col. | Ridgfield | |
| x | Bebe Ammon | Norwich | |
| x | Bennet Benj<sup>a</sup> | " | |
| 9 | Brewster Hez. | " | |
| 4 | Briant John | " | |
| | Blakesly Jeremiah | Danbury | |
| 7 | Bishop David | " | |
| 7 | Bingham John Serj. | Windham | |
| W | Bingham Abishai S<sup>t</sup> | " | |
| | Burnap Benj<sup>a</sup> | " | |
| 4 | Bacon Nehem<sup>a</sup> | Pomphret | |
| 7 | Bill Judah | Sharon | |
| 7 | Billings Steaphen Capt. | Groton | |
| x | Brightman Henery | " | |
| 4 | Benjamins Jesse | Preston | |
| 5 | Chapman Collens | Danbury | |
| 7 | Cleaveland Josiah | Sharon | |
| 4 | Chapman Joseph Lieut. | Norwich | |
| 4 | Cook Case | " | |
| 4 | Clark Jacobe | " | |
| | Comstock Gideon | " | |
| 5 | Cummins W<sup>m</sup> | Ridgfield | |
| | Collins L. W<sup>m</sup> | Stratford | |
| 8 | Comstock Sam<sup>ll</sup> Capt. | Norwalk | |
| * | Cole Alben | " | |
| | Comestock Samuel | Saybrook | |
| 9 | Crane Curtis | Weathersfield | |
| 3 | Cones W<sup>m</sup> Serj. | " | |
| 5 | Chapman Albert Maj. | Fairfield | |
| 7 | Chapman James Lieut. | " | |
| 5 | Coggins David | " | |
| 7 | Curtis George | Kent | |
| | Cheney Richard | " | Died Oct 1779 |
| 5 | Cooly Nathan | Readding | |
| 7 | Chaimberlanc Ephraim Capt. | Wallingford | |
| x | Clark Samuel | E. Haddam | |
| 6 | Claghorn Eleazer Capt. | Salisbury | |
| W | Chipman John Capt. | " | |
| W | Coon James Lieut. | " | |
| 7 | Church Eben<sup>r</sup> | Woodbury | |
| 7 | Convers Th<sup>o</sup> Capt. | Goshen | |
| 8 | Clark Ab<sup>m</sup> | Hartford | |
| 8 | Case Richard | " | |
| 9 | Comey Mallehi alias Allen | " | |

|   | Names | Towns to which they belong |
|---|---|---|
| 9 | Cadwell Matth<sup>w</sup> | Hartford |
| 9 | Cowls Sam<sup>ll</sup> | " |
| 8 | Curtis Daniel | " |
| 8 | Clark John | Lebanon |
| 5 | Cooley Ruben | Somers |
| 3 | Cheney Eben<sup>r</sup> | Ashford |
| W | Clap Nathan | Coventry |
| 4 | Cleft Lem<sup>ll</sup> Capt | Plainfield |
| 7 | Canfield Elijah | New Milford |
| 8 | Camp Samuel | Wattertown |
| 3 | Crary Richard | Glastenbury |
| 2 | Chandler Joseph | Infield { Enter<sup>d</sup> to Medad Pomroy his Substitute |
| D | Churchill Elijah | " |
| 4 | Edward Carter | Colchester |
| 6 | Cone Elisha | Haddam |
| 8 | Sam<sup>ll</sup> Church | " |
| 8 | Clark Aaron | " |
| 5 | Clark Othniel Lieut. | Middletown |
|   | Cone Joseph | "   Discharged 79 |
| 5 | Ozias | " |
| 5 | Daniel | " |
| 9 | Crittendon Gid<sup>o</sup> | " |
|   | Carril John | Smsbury |
| 3 | Culver Tim<sup>o</sup> | Southington |
| 3 | Carter Aaron | Chatham |
| O | Cary George | " |
| 4 | Cleaveland John Ens. | Canterbury |
| x | Carter Ruben | " |
| D | Cushman Dan<sup>ll</sup> | " |
| x | Chatfield John | Killingworth |
| 8 | Camp Samuel | Waterbury |
|   | Clark Lyman | Farmington |
| A | Curtis Dan<sup>ll</sup> Jun<sup>r</sup> | " |
| 8 | Camp Isaac | " |
| D | Churchill Elijah | E. Windsor |
| 6 | Cook Thomas alias Miles | Durham |
| 6 | Clark Martin | New Haven |
| A | Coshall Th<sup>o</sup> | " |
| O | Clarriage Francis | " |
|   | Clark Joel | " |
| x | Carwin Selah | Lyme |
| 5 | Cornelius Cohale al<sup>s</sup> Sam<sup>ll</sup> Foot | Milford |
| 8 | Cæsar Bristol | Newtown |
| 6 | Davidson Isaac | Milford |
| O | Daniels Sam<sup>ll</sup> | " |
| 3 | Dunham Cornelius | Farmington |
| 6 | Dunn Tim<sup>o</sup> | Durham |
| 2 | Duggin James | Canterbury |
| X | De Woolf Steaphen | Lyme |
| 2 | Davison W<sup>m</sup> | Ashford |
| 7 | Dunwell W<sup>m</sup> | New Milford |
| 7 | Dailey James (Sapper) | " |
| O | Dutton Titus Lieut. | Watertown |
| 8 | Davis Jonathan | " |
| 8 | Dunbar Miles | " |
| 5 | Denslow Marten S<sup>t</sup> | Windsor |

CONNECTICUT LINE, 1777–1781.

|   | Names | Towns to which they belong |
|---|---|---|
| 7 | Demmon Wait | Goshen |
| x | Darrow Christoph' Maj. | Hartford |
| 2 | Demmon John | Woodbury |
| 6 | Doud Moses | Guilford |
| x | Dextor John Serj. | Mansfield |
|   | Downing John | Fairfield |
| 6 | Disborow Justin | " |
|   | Joshua Ser' | " |
| 8 | Durfe Thomas | " |
| 9 | Davis Eben' | Weathersfield |
| 8 | Donatis Francis | Preston |
| 6 | Doyle Hugh | New Haven |
| O | Dayton Israel | " |
| 6 | Davis James | " |
|   | Dickerman Joseph Discharged | " |
| 4 | Durke John Col. | Norwich |
|   | Durke Jeremiah | Windham |
| D | Dorman Gershom | Sharon |
|   | Dickinson George | Danbury |
| 5 | De Forest Sam'l Lieut | Norwalk |
| 7 | Dalton Richard Corp. | Groton |
|   | Davison Robert | " |
| 9 | Davis Daniel | " |
| 5 | Eaton Solomon | Tolland |
| 5 | Elmore Dan'l | Sharon |
| * | Evis Daniel | Stratford Desert. |
| 6 | Eagleston David | New Haven |
| x | Ellis John Chapln | Norwich |
| 8 | Easton Eliphalet | Woodbury |
| 8 | Elmon Calib | Harwington |
| 2 | Evans Abiather | Hartford |
| 8 | Henery | " |
|   | Edwards Nath'l Lieut. | Watertown |
| 6 | Ely Elisha Capt. | Lyme |
| 3 | Eells Ed'd Capt. | Middletown |
| 6 | Foot Ezra | Darby |
| 6 | Farmer Th° Lieut. | " |
| 5 | Foot Sam'l alias Cohale Cornels | Milford |
| 6 | Eben' | Branford |
| * | Francis James | Middletown |
| 5 | Fisher Crestop' | " |
| 8 | Foster John | " |
| 7 | Franklin Sam'l | Killingsworth |
| 6 | Fowler Calib Corp. | Guilford |
| 2 | Fenton Solomon Lieut. | Mansfield |
| x | Jonathan | " |
|   | Fitch Nehem* | Lebanon |
| 4 | Fuller John | Chatham |
| 6 | Ford Daniel | New Haven |
|   | Marten | " |
| A | Fryar Charles | " |
| A | Foot Isaac | " |
| 9 | Flowers Elijah S' | New Hartford |
| 8 | Fox Elisha | Farmington |
| * | Fuller John | Fairfield Deserted |
| x | Farnsworth Nathan | Colchester |
| 8 | Fulford John | Watertown |

|   | Names | Towns to which they belong |
|---|---|---|
|   | Flag Jonathan | Hartford |
| 7 | Foster Benj[a] | Sharon |
| 7 | Fisher Isaac | " |
| 6 | Fitch Joseph Trumb[ll] | Salisbury |
| 7 | Freeman Sampson | Glastenbury |
| 9 | Fox Asa | " |
| 6 | Fields Edmund | Wallingford |
| 6 | Francis John | " |
| O | Fox Eben[r] | " Ches[r] |
| 9 | Fay Gershom alias Moses | Winchester |
| 9 | W[m] | " |
| 9 | Tim[o] | " |
| 9 | Filley Remembrance | " |
| 9 | Fanning Elisha | Groton |
| 8 | Freeman Edward | " |
| 8 | Micael | " |
| 8 | Fields Francis | Woodbury |
| 2 | Franklin Jehiel | " |
| * | Forgo Peter | Fairfield |
| 4 | Fanning Charles Lieut. | Norwich |
| 7 | Grover Phineas Capt. | Glastenbury |
| 8 | Gibbs Josiah | Sommers |
| 8 | Gridly Seth | Harwington |
| 7 | Goodrich David | Sharon |
| 5 | Gelson Eleazer | " |
| D | Glover John | Fairfield |
| 8 | Graves Peter | Colchester |
| 8 | Griswold Joseph | Enfield |
| 8 | Grainger Sam[ll] | Suffield |
| 2 | Phineas | " |
| 9 | Gilbert Joseph Serj. | New Hartford |
| 9 | Theodore | " |
|   | Gillet Adna | " |
|   | Gibson Sam[ll] | New Haven |
| 4 | Grant James | Saybrook |
| 6 | Graham Cyrus | " |
| 7 | Gilbert Obediah | Stratford |
|   | Gould John | Goshun |
| 3 | Gibbs Sam[ll] Lieut. | Windsor |
| D | Giants Luke | Preston |
| x | Goff Sam[ll] | Chatham |
| 8 | Graham Joseph | " |
| 8 | Goodrich Levi Serj. | " |
| [?] | Gladding W[m] | Haddam |
| 9 | Giffin Simon S[t] | Weathersfield |
|   | Gillit Zacheriah S[t] | Southington |
| x | Gardiner Sherman S[t] | Norwich |
| [?] | David | " |
| 5 | Graves W[m] (Sapper) | Medletown |
| 6 | Gilson Jacobe | " |
| 6 | Garrit John | Branford |
| 6 | Gooldsmith W[m] | Milford |
| O | Green Joseph | " |
| 6 | Hinman Houghton | Durham |
| 3 | Harris alias Harrison Champlin | Colchester |
|   | Hull Giles | Salisbury |
| 8 | Hecox E | Watertown |

CONNECTICUT LINE, 1777–1781.       169

| | Names | Towns to which they belong |
|---|---|---|
| 7 | Hill Eben' Capt | Kent |
|   | Hager Simeon | Enfield |
| 3 | Hall Israel | " |
| A | Hubbel Isaac Capt.Lt. | Fairfield |
| A | William Lieut. | " |
| 5 | Hall Steaphen S' | " |
| 7 | Hutenot Francis | " |
| 7 | Hilton Atkenson | " |
| 8 | Higgins W<sup>m</sup> | Lyme |
| 7 | Hall David | Danbury |
| * | Howard Richard | Windham deserted |
| 8 | Hodg Assel Capt. | Harwington |
| 7 | Hamblin Joel | Norfolk |
| 2 | Hinckley Iccabud Capt. | Tolland |
| 4 | Hills Daniel | Glastenbury |
| 3 | Holden John | " |
| 3 | Heath Peleg L. Lieut. | Hartford |
| 8 | Hadlock Ruben | " |
| O | Hopson Linus | Wallingford |
| O | Hall Titus | " |
| 7 | Hart Benj<sup>a</sup> | " |
| 6 | Hall Rufus | " |
| x | Holmes Eliph' Capt | E. Haddam |
| x | Harvey Ezra Corp. | " |
| 5 | Harvey W<sup>m</sup> | Saybrook |
| 8 | Hull Oliver | " |
| A | Harris Henery | Stratford |
| 2 | Harrop or Harlop Joseph | " |
| 2 | Hawley Nathan | " |
| 8 | Hubbel Seth | Norwalk |
| 8 | How Zadock | Bolton |
| x | Harde Nath<sup>ll</sup> | Ashford |
| 3 | Hall Robert | " |
| x | Hide R. W<sup>m</sup> | Lyme |
| 4 | Hide James Ens. | Norwich |
|   | Higgins Cornetuis Lieut. | Haddam |
| 9 | Hollis Joseph | Preston |
| 7 | Holdridg Hez. Col. | Hebron |
| 3 | Hubbard Hez. Lieut. | Middletown |
| 3 | Harris John | " |
| 5 | Henshaw W<sup>m</sup> Lieut. | " |
| 8 | Hubbard Roswell | " |
| 8 | Hull David | " |
| 6 | Howell Nicholas | New Haven |
| 9 | Hull Sam<sup>ll</sup> | " |
| O | Harden Fredrick | " |
|   | Huse Boardwell | " |
| 9 | Howe Joshua | " |
| 6 | Hosmore Tim<sup>o</sup> Doct. | Farmington |
| 8 | Heyden David | " |
|   | Howard George | " |
| 3 | Hart Jonathan Lieut. | " |
|   | Hotchkiss Zadock | " |
| 7 | Hall Stephen Capt. | Guilford |
| 7 | Philemon Lieut. | " |
| 7 | Handey Sam<sup>ll</sup> S' | " |
| 7 | Hotchkiss Ira | " |

| | Names | Towns to which they belong |
|---|---|---|
| 4 | Hill John | Simsbury |
| * | Harrinton Elisha | " |
| 5 | Hall Sam'l Corp | Killingworth |
| 8 | Hobart John Lieut. | Branford |
| 6 | Hoodley Sam'l | " |
| 6 | Harrison Jarus | " |
| 6 | Hooker John | Milford |
| 6 | Hodg David | " |
| 6 | Hine Titus | " |
| 2 | Hiccock Sam'l Lieut. | Stamford |
| 2 | Hait Joseph Col. | " |
| 8 | Holley Abraham | " |
| 6 | Humphry Elijah Capt. | Darbey |
| x | Hanes Jonathan | Stamford |
| 5 | Jones Isaiah | " |
| | Johnson Robert | Sharon |
| 6 |     Abraham Corp. | New Haven |
| 6 | Joslin John | " |
| 8 | Judson Joseph | Woodbury |
| H | Jones Joseph | Branford |
| x | Jackson Th° | Preston |
| 2 | Johnson Elihue | Tolland |
| 6 | Johson Isaac | Guilford |
| x | Jones Daniel | Lebanon |
| 5 | Johnson Jonathan Col. | Midletown |
| H | Jones Th° | Wallingford |
| O |     Charles | " |
| 6 | Johnson John | Cheshire |
| 9 | Jeralls Th° | Hartford |
| 6 | Jones Jasber | Stratford |
| * | Judd Brewster | Watertown |
| 9 | Jones Aaron | Saybrook |
| 6 | Johnson W<sup>m</sup> | Durham |
| 8 | Judd Steaphen | Waterbury |
| 3 | Judd W<sup>m</sup> Capt. | Farmingtown |
| * | King Orrey Deserted | Stratford |
| 7 | Knap Tim° | Goshen |
| O | King Hez | Wallingford |
| 3 | Keney Benj<sup>a</sup> | Hartford |
| 6 | Kimball T. Abraham | Midletown |
| 9 | Kilbey Christopher | Weathersfield |
| 5 | Kelsey Noah | Sharon |
| 2 | Kelley John | Litchfield |
| | King George | New Haven |
| 8 | Kimberly E Lieut. | Newtown |
| x | Lee Ezra Lieut. | Lyme |
| x | Lay Richard | " |
| 9 | Loomis Israel | Hartford |
| | Lyon Ezra | Ashford |
| 7 | Lambkins Benj<sup>a</sup> | Kent |
| 5 | Lawrance Amos S<sup>t</sup> | Windsor |
| 5 | Lamberton Obed | " |
| 3 | Lung Joseph | Midletown |
| 2 | Luce Jonathan | Tolland |
| 9 | Loveland Thomas | Glastenbury |
| 3 |     Elisha | " |
| 7 | Leet Allen | Killingworth |

CONNECTICUT LINE, 1777-1781.   171

|   | Names | Towns to which they belong |
|---|---|---|
| 4 | Lockwood Moses | Weathersfield |
| 8 | Lee Abner | Woodbury |
| 6 | Leavenworth Eli Maj. | New Haven |
| 6 | Lord Jabez | " |
|   | Lines John | " |
| 7 | Lake Phineas | Cornwall |
| 5 | Lacy Josiah Capt. | Fairfield |
| A | Leverick Gabriel S$^t$ | " |
| 8 | Lilley John | Canterbury |
| 3 |   Eben$^r$ | Union |
| 9 | Lord Jeremiah S$^t$ | Saybrook |
| 6 | Lay Asa | " |
| H | Lee Noah Capt | Salisbury |
| 5 | Ludiman John | Danbury |
| 2 | Lewis Peter | Stratford |
| 3 | Marble Th$^o$ | Hebron |
| 8 | Mack Abner | " |
| D | Minor Elisha | Woodbury |
| 7 | Miels Charles Capt. | Preston |
| 4 | M$^c$Daniels Jams | " |
| O | Matthews John S$^t$ | New Fairfield |
| D | Mills Sam$^{ll}$ L$^t$ | Simsbury |
| 2 | Mecker Stephen | Redding |
| 5 | Mason John | Litchfield |
| Inv. | Munger Daniel | " |
| 3 | Moore W$^m$ | Union |
| 8 | Mallery Jonah | Watebury |
| x | Macks Jeremiah | Danbury |
| x | Minor Elihue | E. Haddam |
| D | Morrison W$^m$ | Weathersfield |
| 3 | Miller Nath$^{ll}$ | " |
| 9 | Maggot Zebulon | " |
| 4 | Mix Thomas Jur | Wallingford |
| 6 | Munson Levi | " |
| 6 | Mansfield John | " |
| O | Matthews Eliada | Chester |
| 4 | Martin George | Windham |
| 2 | Mix John Lieut. | Farmington |
| 3 | Monossuk Daniel | " |
|   | M$^c$Daniel John | Groton |
| * | Miller Daniel | Chatham Deserted |
| 4 | Markham Joseph | " |
| 5 | Meed Jeremiah | Norwalk |
| 5 |   Jasper L$^t$ | " |
| 9 | Merrils Cyprian | New Haven |
| 9 |   Aaron | " |
| 6 | Mather Elias Ens. | Lyme |
| 8 | Miller Charles L$^t$ | Hartford |
|   | Meeker Daniel | " |
| 8 | Mize W$^m$ | " |
| 8 | Mahar James | " |
| 6 | Meigs J Return Col. | Midletown |
| 3 | Mosely Sifax | Glastenbury |
| 5 | Morehouse David | Fairfield |
| 2 | M$^c$Nutters John | Stanford |
| 2 | Manning W$^m$ | Norwich |
| 4 | M$^c$ Gregor John | Plainfield |

|   | Names | Towns to which they belong |
|---|---|---|
| 4 | Marsh Peter Corp. | Plainfield |
| 2 | Murrey Abraham | Darbey |
| A | Mix Steaphen | Goshen |
| 4 | Munson W<sup>m</sup> Capt. | New Haven |
| A | Miles John Capt | " |
| 6 | Mansfield Joseph Capt. | " |
| A | Mix Tim° L<sup>t</sup> | " |
| 7 | Matthews Robert (Sapper) | " |
| 6 | Mallery Amos S<sup>t</sup> | " |
| 6 | Malthrop Joseph | " |
| 6 | Mansfield Dan. | " |
| 6 | Malthrop Steaphen | " |
| x | Murphy Thomas | E. Haddam |
| x | Mitchel Sam[11] | " |
| 6 | Northrup Isaac | Milford |
| 9 | Norton Sam[11] | Hartford |
| 5 |     Joseph | Goshun |
| A | Newel James | Farmington |
| A | Norton Jedadiah | Chatham |
| 6 |     Benj<sup>a</sup> Ens. | Branford |
| 7 | Norton Rufus | Guilford |
| 7 |     Elon | " |
| 6 | Niger Phillip | " |
| 8 | Nichols Samuel | Norwalk |
| 5 | Nickerson Barret | Ridgfield |
|   | Nash Eben<sup>r</sup> | Norwalk |
| 8 | Nutton Ezekiel | Washington |
| 6 | Newel Robart | Saybrook |
| 5 | Owen Alvin | Windsor |
| 6 | Oulds Oliver | Washington |
| 6 | Owen Eliphalet | Salisbury |
| Sm. | Osburn Nath[11] | Stratford |
| 2 | Orcutt Calib S<sup>t</sup> | Willington |
| 6 | Oatis Joseph | Branford |
| 5 | Olmstead Isaac | Norwalk |
| 8 | Olmstead James L<sup>t</sup> | Hartford |
| A | Parker Edmund | New Haven |
| 4 | Perrigo W<sup>m</sup> | Norwich |
| 6 | Potter Moses | New Haven |
| D |     Amos | " |
| 4 | Powers Thomas | " |
| A | Prindle Y. Enos | Darbey |
| 5 | Petit Enos | Sharon |
| 9 | Porter Amos | Haddam |
| 3 | Parker Benj<sup>a</sup> | Wallingford |
| 6 |     Elisha | " |
| A | Peck Charles | Cheshire |
|   | Peckit Th° | Danbury   Susquehannah Comp |
| 2 | Peirce Dan[11] | E Windsor |
| x | Patterson James | Norwich |
|   | Patchin Elijah | Fairfield |
| 8 | Prichard George | Waterbury |
| 8 | Powers Thomas | Midletown |
| 8 | Peek Ariel | " |
| 3 | Pomeroy Ralph | Hartford |
| x | Parseval Paul Q<sup>m</sup> | Farmington } in list of |
| 3 | Potter Lem[11] | "           } Errors |

CONNECTICUT LINE, 1777-1781. 173

| | Names | Towns to which they belong |
|---|---|---|
| 6 | Powers James | Farmington |
| = | Pratt Isaac | " Six months man |
| | Palmer Benjᵃ | Litchfield |
| 3 | Parks Daniel | Chatham |
| 6 | Potter Steaphen Capt. | Branford |
| | Powers James | Southington |
| 8 | Pratt Russel | Somers |
| 3 | Porter Nathan | Mansfield |
| x | Pompey Samˡˡ | Groten |
| | Polly Alpheus | Lebanon |
| 7 | Perry Elisha | Ridgfield |
| x | Plumb Peter | No[    ]h |
| 2 | Parenan Joseph | Suffield |
| 2 | Preston Tirus | Tolland |
| 6 | Pratt Ethan | Saybrook |
| | Pool Daniel | Ashford |
| 9 | Parker Samˡˡ | Stratford |
| 6 | Phillips Thomas | " |
| O | Painter Gamaliel Capt. | Salisbury |
| O | Pendleton Danˡˡ Capt. | Watertown |
| 6 | Parker Isaac | " |
| 8 | Preston A | " |
| | Porter Daniel | Windsor |
| x | Prior Abner Maj. | " |
| 7 | Peet Lemˡˡ | New Milford |
| A | Purdey Jesse | " |
| 2 | Parsons Jonathan | Enfield |
| 2 | David Capt. | " |
| 3 | Perry Silvanus Lᵗ | Killingly |
| 8 | Prindle Abijah | Newtown |
| 4 | Quashe Cato | Colchester |
| 4 | Qui Lebbeus | Norwich |
| 4 | Rowley Jesse | Colchester |
| O | Reynolds John | Hartford |
| 9 | Risley Steaphen | " |
| 6 | Rosetor Samˡˡ | Litchfield |
| 9 | Roberts Elisha | New Hartford |
| Sm | Ramong Samˡˡ | Reading Sapper & Miner |
| A | Rian Jerry | " |
| 7 | Roberts Benjᵃ | New Fairfield |
| 3 | Ranney Steaphen | Chatham |
| 8 | Jabez | " |
| x | Reed Nathan | Mansfield |
| 9 | Roberson Ephᵐ | Coventry |
| | Rose Samˡˡ | " |
| | Remmington Steaphᵃ | Ridgfield |
| A | Rombelow Thomas | Killingworth |
| 7 | Rust Eppiphras | Cornwall |
| 4 | Riseing James | Suffield |
| 8 | Russell Wᵐ | Stratford |
| 8 | Rice Nehemiah Capt. | Watertown |
| x | Reed Enoch Capt. | Lyme |
| 9 | Roberts David | Midletown |
| 4 | Reynolds John | Norwich |
| 9 | Russel Ashur | Weathersfield |
| 9 | Ryley John Lieut. | " |
| 6 | Rozel Jeremiah | Danbury |

| | Names | Towns to which they belong |
|---|---|---|
| O | Rexford Benj<sup>n</sup> | Wallingford |
| 6 | Benj<sup>n</sup> Jun<sup>r</sup> | " |
| 5 | Rust Jonathan | Sharon |
| 7 | Rouse Jabez S<sup>t</sup> | Windham |
| 4 | Robinson Elias Ens. | " |
| | Simson Ju<sup>r</sup> | " |
| 3 | Randol Elijah | " |
| H | Robinson Sam<sup>ll</sup> Lieut. | New Haven |
| 2 | Rayming David | Fairfield |
| 8 | Robards Joel | Waterbury |
| 7 | Sanford James | Newtown see Danbury |
| 6 | Sherman John Lieut. | New Haven |
| 6 | Sanford Th<sup>o</sup> S<sup>t</sup> | " |
| 6 | Smith Ambrus | " |
| 6 | Sugden Abraham | " |
| 6 | Stockwell Abel | " |
| A | Sherman Edmund S<sup>t</sup> | " |
| 6 | Shephard John | " |
| 2 | Steaphens W<sup>m</sup> | " |
| 5 | Strong David L<sup>t</sup> | Sharon |
| 8 | Smith John L<sup>t</sup> | Haddam |
| 3 | Smith John | " |
| 4 | Joshua | " |
| 7 | Daniel | Wallingford |
| 7 | Sanford James | Danbury see Newtown |
| * | Stodard Enoch | Wethersfield deserted |
| 6 | Seward Nathan | Waterbury |
| 8 | Smith Lue | " |
| A | Simons Robert | Fairfield |
| 5 | Smith Isaac | Stamford |
| 6 | Starr David Capt. | Midletown |
| O | Sizer W<sup>m</sup> Capt. | " |
| O | Savage Stephen | " |
| 6 | Sizer Jonathan | " see David Hungerford |
| 4 | Sumner John Col. | " |
| S | Savage Abijah Capt. | " |
| x | Sill David L C | Lyme |
| x | Selden Ezra Capt. | " |
| x | Spencer Ichabud | " |
| 4 | Saunders John | " |
| * | Sullard Jacobe | " |
| 6 | Sawyer Asa | " |
| | Smith Enoch | " |
| 8 | Sanford Sam<sup>ll</sup> Capt. | Milford |
| 6 | Smith W<sup>m</sup> L<sup>t</sup> | " |
| 6 | Steward John | " |
| 8 | Smith David Maj. | Watertown |
| * | John | " 7th Deserted |
| 2 | Spear Elijah | Suffield |
| 8 | Shilley Eben<sup>r</sup> Serg. | Stratford |
| A | Sunderland John | " |
| 7 | Swift Heman Col. | Cornwall |
| 7 | Steaphens Aaron Capt | Killingworth |
| 2 | Steaphens Peter | " |
| | Smith Jobe L<sup>t</sup> | Ridgfield |
| x | Shumway John Capt. | Mansfield |
| x | Smith John | " |

CONNECTICUT LINE, 1777–1781.    175

|   | Names | Towns to which they belong |
|---|---|---|
| 4 | Smith Ezra L$^t$ | Chatham |
| [ ] | Stockin Marshall | " |
| 5 | Schullens Abr$^m$ S$^t$ | " |
| x | Starr Josiah C Col. | New Milford |
|   | Stilwell Steaphen | " |
| D | Sheldon Elisha Col. | Salisbury |
| 6 | Strong Phineas | " |
| O | Swetland As[    ] S$^t$ | " |
| * | Smith Abijah | Ashford deserted |
| 6 | Steaphens Elijah | Saybrook |
| 2 | Sabins Nehemiah Corp. | Tolland |
| 9 | Scovil Steaphen | Winchester |
| 4 | Shaw Benjamin | Canterbury |
| 6 | Steaphens Peter alias Asa | |
| 6 | Squire Abiathur alias Ashar | Durham |
| 6 | Squire Saxton | " |
| 6 | Seaward Samuel | " |
| 6 | Strong Eliakim | " |
| 3 | Steaphens Tim$^o$ | Glastenbury |
| 7 | Simbo Prince | " |
| 7 | Strong John L$^t$ | Guilford |
|   | Stannord Elijah | " |
| 6 | Swift Robert | Groten |
| 6 | Sharper Tuis | " |
| 8 | Sterry Silas | " |
| 3 | Shortman W$^m$ | " |
| 8 | Stanton Amos Capt. | " |
| A | Squire Sam$^{ll}$ Serj. | Southington |
| 6 | Smith Jordan | Branford |
| 5 | Scribner Asa | Norwalk |
| 8 | Stodard Eli | Woodbury |
| 5 | Stannord Sam$^{ll}$ | "    & Litchfield |
| 5 | Smith Henery | Litchfield |
| x | Sears Obediah | Preston |
|   | Stark Sam$^{ll}$ | Colchester |
|   | Tim$^o$ | " |
| O | Spencer John L$^t$ | Hartford |
| 9 | Stone Th$^o$ | " |
| 3 | Smith David | Farmington |
| D |    Asaph | " |
| 3 | Steel Josiah | " |
| 9 | Steaphens Aaron | New Haven |
| 5 | Sherwood Nehem$^a$ | Reading |
| 7 | Saunders W$^m$ | New Fairfield |
| 6 | Shalor Joseph L$^t$ | Wallingford |
| 6 | Sowers W$^m$ | Milford |
| 5 | S$^t$ John John Capt. | Norwalk |
| 9 | Simons Eli | Colebrook |
| A | Thomson Isaiah L$^t$ | Farmington |
| 5 | Taylor John | New Hartford |
| 7 | Trowbridg John S$^t$ | New Fairfield |
| 6 | Towner Jacobe | Branford |
| 8 | Taylor Elijah Ens. | Norwalk |
| [ ] | Tarble W$^m$ Invalid | Colchester |
| 6 | Taylor Simeon | Woodbury |
| 6 | Thomson David S$^t$ | Guilford |
| 6 | Teal Samuel | " |

| | Names | Towns to which they belong |
|---|---|---|
| [ ] | Tryon Isaac | Glastenbury |
| [ ] | Tiken Tias | Canterbury |
| [ ] | Thomson Epaphr[ ] | Saybrook |
| [ ] | Tooly Andrew | " |
| 6 | Tupper W<sup>m</sup> S<sup>t</sup> | Salisbury |
| 5 | Trowbridge Eben<sup>r</sup> | New Milford |
| 5 | Thomas Steaphen | Chatham |
| 7 | Tubbs Nathan | Norfolk |
| 3 | Taylor Ephraim | Hebron |
| 8 | Thompson Nath<sup>ll</sup> | Coventry |
| D | Tucker Jarvis | Milford |
| 3 | Taylor Thomas | Union |
| 4 | Throop Benj<sup>n</sup> Maj. | Norwich |
| 4 | Tracey Moses | " |
| x | W<sup>m</sup> Ens. | " |
| * | Taylor Barrick | Fairfield |
| 8 | Thayer Asa | Waterbury |
| 8 | Tattendon John | " |
| A | Throop John L<sup>t</sup> | New Haven |
| 6 | Trowbridg John L<sup>t</sup> | " |
| A | Todd Yale | " |
| 6 | Thomas Ephraim | " |
| A | Thomas John | " |
| 6 | Tolles Elnathan | " |
| 6 | Thomas Samuel | " |
| 6 | Verguson John | " |
| 8 | Upson Ezekiel | Waterbury |
| 8 | Vaughn Daniel | Lebanon |
| 3 | Verry Jonathan | Chatham |
| 3 | Wright John | |
| 4 | Woodsworth Benj<sup>n</sup> | Lebanon |
| x | Jedadiah | " |
| x | Willcox Philemon | Waterbury |
| 6 | Willson John | New Haven |
| 6 | Wood Elisha | " |
| D | Wilds Jonathan | " |
| 6 | White Sam<sup>ll</sup> | " |
| O | Walter W<sup>m</sup> | " |
| 4 | Webb Nath<sup>ll</sup> Capt | Windham |
| 7 | Wainwright Th<sup>o</sup> | Sharon |
| 6 | White Joseph | Darbey |
| O | Wilcox Jarius Capt. | Wallingford |
| A | Webb Gideon | Cheshire |
| S | Wallis Abr<sup>m</sup> | E Windsor |
| S | Wadsworth B. Joseph Doc<sup>r</sup> | " |
| 9 | Williams Daniel S<sup>t</sup> | Wethersfield |
| 9 | Wells Joshua | " |
| x | Williams Thomas | E. Haddam |
| x | Willey Jonathan | " |
| x | Wadkins Ephraim | " |
| 2 | Wheeler Joshua | " |
| A | Williams Rich<sup>d</sup> | Fairfield |
| x | Waterman Eben<sup>r</sup> | Norwich |
| 6 | W[ ] | Midletown |
| 3 | Wa[ ]nor Robert Capt. | |
| 5 | Weed Th[ ] Capt | Stamford |
| 2 | Wardwell Jacobe | " |

CONNECTICUT LINE, 1777-1781.

| | Names | Towns to which they belong |
|---|---|---|
| A | Willson David | Stamford |
| 8 | Waterbury W<sup>m</sup> | " |
| x | Wade John | Lyme |
| x | Willson George | " |
| x | Wade Martin | " |
| 8 | Williams Obediah | Watertown |
| 8 | Washburn Sam<sup>ll</sup> | Stratford |
| 7 | Wier Thomas | Goshen |
| 5 | Woodward Oliver | Simsbury |
| 8 | Woodbridg Theoph<sup>s</sup> L<sup>t</sup> | " |
| D | Wood Thomas | Sommers |
| | Worden Isaac | Stonington |
| 2 | Ware Daniel | Enfield |
| 3 | Welton Benj<sup>a</sup> | Farmington |
| 8 | Willcox James | " |
| D | Wainwright Sam<sup>ll</sup> | " |
| 8 | Warren Ab<sup>m</sup> | " |
| = | Welton Solomon | "    Six months man |
| D | Ward John | New Hartford |
| 7 | Wilder Aaron | New Fairfield |
| 6 | White John L<sup>t</sup> | Branford |
| 8 | Williams John | Norwalk |
| A | Wilcox Elias | " |
| A | White Eliakim | Southington |
| 6 | Wadsworth Theodore Do<sup>r</sup> | " |
| 8 | Williams Hencry L<sup>t</sup> | Groton |
| 3 | Whitman Lem<sup>l</sup> S<sup>t</sup> | " |
| 8 | Williams Uriah S<sup>t</sup> | " |
| 6 | Wheeler Thomas | Guilford |
| 3 | Warren John S<sup>t</sup> | Glastenbury |
| 9 | Wilkenson Jesse | Winchester |
| 9 | Wording Isaac | Saybrook |
| 6 | White Oliver | " |
| 7 | Waterhouse Steap<sup>a</sup> | " |
| 4 | Wales Eben<sup>r</sup> L<sup>t</sup> | Ashford |
| 3 | Waters W<sup>m</sup> | " |
| 7 | Whitley W<sup>m</sup> | New Milford |
| 8 | Wyllys Sam<sup>ll</sup> Col. | Hartford |
| 9 | Wood Jonathan | " |
| 3 | Waters Th<sup>o</sup> | " |
| 4 | Wack W Fredrich | Colchester |
| 3 | Whitney Dan<sup>ll</sup> | " |
| 8 | Welch Luke | Woodbury |
| * | Wright James | Litchfield |
| X | Willcox Philemon | " |
| 6 | Yates William | Salisbury |
| | Yarrington Jesse | Groton |
| 6 | Yale Nash | Wallingford |
| 7 | Yale Wait | Sharon |

Appendix

| | | |
|---|---|---|
| 7 | Aspenwall Calib | Norfolk |
| 7 | Aspenwall Aaron | " |
| 7 | Adams Asael | " |

x denotes 1<sup>st</sup> Reg<sup>t</sup>
2 " 2<sup>d</sup> "

3 denotes 3ᵈ Regᵗ
4    "    4ᵗʰ  "
5    "    5ᵗʰ  "
6    "    6ᵗʰ  "
7    "    7   "
8    "    8   "
9    "    Colº Webs Regᵗ
D.   "    2ᵈ Lᵗ Dragoons
A.   "    Artilery
O.   "    Artificers
W.   "    Colº Warners
H.   "    Colº Hazens
L.   "    Coloº Livingstons
S    "    Sherburns
*    "    Deserted
=    "    Short Recruit or 6ᵐº m[ ]
Sm.  "    Sapper & Miner

[*State Library, Revolution* 30.⁴⁵.]

# FIRST REGIMENT — COL. STARR.

## FIRST COMPANY — COL. STARR.

Pay Roll of the Short levies Col. Starr's Comp'y 1st C't Reg't

| Names | Comm't of service | Expiration of service | Towns |
|---|---|---|---|
| Isaac Lyman Serg't | Aug. 1 | Sep. 15 | Lebanon |
| Oliver Kent | July 1 | Oct. 25 | Suffield |
| Asa Mason | " | " | Ashford |
| Zach'b Chapman | " | Nov. 20 | E'st Hadam |
| Will'm Middleton | 22 | Dec. 3 | Groton |
| Zebulon Fervin | 1 | " | Suffield |
| Jonah Rising | " | " | " |
| Peleg Watson | " | " | Windsor |
| John Lay | " | " | Lyme |
| Lawrence Dowsit | June 26 | 5 | Ashford |
| Nath'll Fenton | July 1 | " | Mansfield |
| Azariah Hillard | 15 | " | Stonington |
| Joshua Reynolds | 20 | 4 | Norwich |
| Moses Fitts | 1 | 5 | Ashford |
| Ethen Rogers | 15 | " | Branford |
| W'm Royce | 1 | 4 | Ashford |
| David Carpenter | " | 9 | " |
| Ethen Barker | " | " | Suffield |
| Silas Dewey | " | " | " |
| James Lathrop | Aug. 1 | " | Lebanon |
| John Holmes | July 1 | " | Stafford |
| And'w Colegrove | 5 | " | Voluntown |
| Samuel Pitts | 1 | 18 | Ashford |
| Archib'd Greenfield | 15 | " | Lyme |
| Amos Dowsit | 1 | " | Ashford |
| Phil'a Andrews | " | " | E'st Hadam |
| George Coit | " | " | Preston |
| Will'm Campbill | " | 25 | Suffield |

Dec'r 29th 1780         J. Tiffany, Ens'n

[*State Library, Revolution 17, 48.*]

## SECOND COMPANY — LIEUT.-COL. SILL

Pay-roll for the new Levies in Lieu't Col'o Sill's Comp'y 1st Connec't Reg, 1780

| Names | Comm't of Service | Expiration of Service | Towns to which they Belong |
|---|---|---|---|
| Ebenezer Conant | July 15 | Dec. 4 | Hartford |
| Eleazer Barrows | June 26 | 31 | Mansfield |
| Ethan Barrows | July 1 | 18 | " |
| Robert Brown | 15 | 4 | Stonnington |
| Jonathan Bassit | June 26 | 18 | Mansfield |
| Amos Conant | " | 4 | " |
| David Lawson | Aug. 8 | 18 | Union |

| Names | Comm't of Service | Expiration of Service | Towns to which they Belong |
|---|---|---|---|
| Nathan Conant | July | Dec. 8 | Mansfield |
| Walter Carey | June 26 | 4 | " |
| Nathan Cottrill | July 1 | 8 | Stonington |
| Cato Cuffe | 15 | 9 | " |
| John Elsworth | " | 13 | Torrington |
| John Gifford | 1 | 4 | Norwich |
| Guy Lester | " | 9 | Lyme |
| Timothy Miner | " | " | " |
| Charles Miner | " | 4 | " |
| Edward Otis | " | 31 | " |
| Daniel Preston | " | 13 | Mansfield |
| Tuish Sharper | 15 | 8 | Groton |
| Morris Woodbourn | " | 9 | Stonnington |
| John Wilson | 9 | 14 | Hartford |
| John Wilson Jun' | " | 9 | " |
| Stephen Thompson | 6 | 4 | Union |

Joseph Clark Ensign

[*State Library, Revolution 17, 44.*]

## FIFTH COMPANY.

Pay Roll of the Short Levies 5th Company 1st Connecticut Reg't Dec'r 1780

| Names | Commencement of Service | Expiration of Service | Towns they belong to |
|---|---|---|---|
| Asa Williams | July 15 | Dec. 5 | Hartford |
| George Woodbridge | " | " | " |
| Sam'l Deliber | " | " | " |
| George Abby | " | " | " |
| Joseph Kent | 1 | " | Stafford |
| Solomon Tupper | 20 | " | " |
| Timothy Dimmick | " | " | " |
| Daniel D. Wolf | 1 | " | Enfield |
| John Hellermegy | " | " | " |
| Joseph Stewart | " | " | East Haddam |
| Thomas Larroby | " | " | N London |
| Elihu Huntley | 15 | " | Lyme |
| Theophilus Rathbon | " | " | " |
| Joseph Emerson | " | " | " |
| Charles Wood | 20 | 18 | Stafford |
| Jabez Cary | " | 9 | Mansfield |
| Jacob Hills | 1 | " | Enfield |
| Gurdon Rogers | " | " | East Haddam |
| Elisha Lyman | 15 | 11 | Lebanon |
| Elisha Peck | " | 13 | Lyme |
| Asa Wilson | 1 | 9 | Enfield |
| Tho' Keney | 15 | 21 | Hartford |

Tho' Anderson Leut

[*State Library, Revolution 17, 19.*]

## CAPT. DOUGLASS' COMPANY.

Pay Roll of the New Levy' in Cap' Douglass Company 1ˢᵗ Connecticut Reg' 26ᵗʰ Dec' 1780

| Names | Commen' of Service | Expiration of Service | Towns |
|---|---|---|---|
| Jonaᵗʰ Metcalf | July 1 | Oct. 26 | Lebanon |
| Guy Chapel | 15 | Dec. 9 | N London |
| Jedᵗʰ Cady | 1 | " | Mansfield |
| Abner Cady | " | 4 | |
| Stephen Eaton | " | " | |
| Stephen Ellis | " | " | Norwich |
| Ephraim Frost | " | " | Mansfield |
| Nathˡˡ Fitch | " | " | |
| Wᵐ Fagins | " | " | Groton |
| Joseph Herrick | " | " | |
| Cuff Hurlburt | 18 | " | Groton |
| Caleb Johnson | " | 9 | N London |
| Asael Kingley | 1 | " | |
| Elnathan Keys | " | Nov. 15 | |
| Josiah Lockwood | 5 | Dec. 4 | |
| Zadock Lee | 1 | " | Lebanon |
| Nathˡˡ Little | " | " | |
| Samˡˡ Mobbs | " | 13 | East Haddam |
| Timʸ M'Intosh | " | " | Lyme |
| Abner Peck | 15 | 4 | Huntington |
| Henry Smith | 5 | 9 | Hadam |
| Asael Southwell | " | " | |
| Zackeus Spencer | 1 | 4 | Labanon |
| Jnº West | " | 13 | |
| Badwell Watkins | " | 4 | |
| Shoram Stanton | 15 | Oct. 26 | Groton |

Ezra Lee Lieuᵗ

[*State Library. Revolution* 17, 30.]

## CAPT. SELDEN'S COMPANY.

Pay Roll of the New Levies Captain Seldens Company 1ˢᵗ Connecticutt Regiment Dec' 1780

| Names | Commen' of Service 1780 | Expiration of Service | Towns they belong to |
|---|---|---|---|
| Oliver Brown | July 1 | Nov. 21 | Stonington Deserted Nov 21 |
| Nathan Bebee | June 27 | Oct. 27 | East Haddam Deserted Oct. 24 |
| James Chandler | " | Dec. 4 | Ashford |
| Benedict Church | " | 6 | Voluntown |
| Elijah Cone | 18 | 18 | East Haddam |
| Edward Coney | 15 | 3 | Norwich |
| Samuel Garret | 1 | 15 | Stonington |
| Paul Harris | Aug. 1 | 9 | Canterbury |
| Robert Jackson | July 1 | 21 | Voluntown |
| Zephaniah Mitchel 2ᵈ | 15 | 6 | Colchester |
| Philip Meachum | 1 | 9 | Suffield |
| Stephen Mosher | " | " | Lyme |
| Elisha Royce | 27 | " | Ashford |
| Elisha Rogers | " | 4 | " |

| Names | Comment of Service 1780 | Expiration of Service | Towns they belong to |
|---|---|---|---|
| Joseph Scott | July 1 | Dec. 4 | Willington |
| Benjamin Smith | 15 | 15 | Voluntown |
| Ezra Sibley | 1 | 9 | Willington |
| Simeon Snow | June 27 | 4 | Ashford |
| Asahel Woodworth | July 1 | 3 | Norwich |
| Stephen Butler | Sep. 22 | 15 | Ashford |
| Zephaniah Mitchel | July 15 | Aug. 17 | Colchester |
| | E Selden Cap[t] | | |

[*State Library, Revolution 17, 25.*]

## CAPT. DORRANCE'S COMPANY.

Pay Roll of the New Levies Captain Dorances Comp[y] 1[st] Connec[t] Reg[t] Dec[r] 1780

| Names | Commencement of Service | Expiration of Service | Towns they belong to |
|---|---|---|---|
| Joseph Kinney | July 1 | Dec. 4 | Preston |
| Ameziah Corwin | " | " | Lyme |
| Sam[l] Daniels | " | " | " |
| Levi Hitchcock | " | " | Darby |
| Sam[l] Utley | " | 9 | Woodstock |
| Elisha Wilcox | " | " | " |
| Pell Collins | " | " | Stonington |
| Abraham Wade | " | " | Lyme |
| Jabez Frink | " | " | Stonington |
| Stephen Jackson | " | " | Woodstock |
| George Jackson | " | " | " |
| Sam[l] Davis | " | " | Stafford |
| Darius Woodworth | " | 10 | Norwich |
| Roswell Lamphier | " | " | " |
| Luther Skinner | " | " | Woodstock |
| Eliab Edson | " | 11 | |
| Jonah Cushman | " | 13 | Woodstock |
| Joseph Ransom | " | " | Lyme |
| Ichabod Allen | " | 15 | Stonington |
| John Gould | " | " | |
| Simon Newcomb | " | 16 | Lebanon |
| Richard Crosby | " | 4 | Mansfield |

High Lands 22[d] Dec[r] 1780

David Dorrance Cap[t]

[*State Library, Revolution, 17, 18.*]

## CAPT. RICHARD'S COMPANY.

Pay Roll for the New Levies in Cap[t] W[m] Richards[s] Comp[y] 1[st] Conn[t] Reg[t] 1780

| Names | Comment of Service | Expiration Service | Towns they belong to | |
|---|---|---|---|---|
| Thomas Attwood | July 1 | Nov. 4 | Mansfield | |
| Nath[ll] Ames | 13 | Dec. 12 | Preston | |
| Jn[o] Abbee | 7 | Nov. 14 | Windham | gave certificate 17 Feby 1835 |
| Ephraim Brown | 15 | Nov. 4 | Stoning Town | |

CONNECTICUT LINE, 1777–1781. 183

| Names | Commen't of Service | Expiration Service | Towns they belong to |
|---|---|---|---|
| David Bennet | July 1 | Oct. 26 | Stoning Town |
| Jabez Breed | " | Dec. 11 | " |
| Jn° Center | " | 9 | Norwich |
| W⁼ Daniels | " | 4 | East Haddam |
| Benjⁿ Diggins | 15 | 9 | Stoning Town |
| Richᵈ Dye | " | 4 | " |
| Joel Davis | " | 9 | Mansfield |
| W⁼ Eaton | 1 | 8 | " |
| W⁼ Glading | 2 | " | Haddam |
| Cesar Griswold | 1 | " | Lyme |
| James Mitchel | " | 9 | East Haddam |
| Abraim Niles | Sep. 1 | 4 | Stoning Town |
| Jn° Scott | " | 18 | Killingly |
| Joseph Cook Stubs | July 15 | 9 | Stoningtown |
| Arnold Worden | 1 | " | " |
| Roger Woodworth | " | 8 | Lebanon |
| Stephen Wilcox | " | 4 | Stoning Town |

Ezra Lee Lieuᵗ

[*State Library, Revolution 17, 10.*]

## CAPT. SHUMWAY'S COMPANY.

Pay Roll of the New Levies Captain Shumways Company 1ˢᵗ Connecticut Regiment, Decʳ 1780.

| Names | Commenc't of Service 1780 | Expiration of Service 1780 | Towns they belong to |
|---|---|---|---|
| Caleb Handee Serg'ᵗ | June 27 | Dec. 14 | Ashford |
| William Southward Corpˡ | " | 4 | " |
| Peter Ayers | July 13 | " | Norwich |
| David Brooks | 11 | " | Wollingsford |
| Thomas Barrett | 16 | 13 | Woodstock |
| Joshua Baker | Aug. 27 | 11 | Ashford |
| John Bugbee | 1 | 13 | Mansfield |
| Samuel Chaffee | July 5 | 4 | Woodstock |
| Comfort Carpentor | 1 | 9 | Mansfield |
| Plina Camberlin | 5 | 16 | Woodstock |
| Oliver Chapman | " | 4 | " |
| Timothy Clark | 1 | 9 | Lebanon |
| Benjⁿ Daboll | 15 | 16 | Groton |
| Jeduthan Dimmick | 1 | 9 | Mansfield |
| Varny Fellows | " | 11 | " |
| Solomon Dimmick | Oct. 1 | 13 | " |
| Phillip Dimmick | Aug. 21 | 4 | " |
| Benjⁿ Green | July 15 | 9 | Preston |
| Gardner | 11 | 16 | |
| Jeremiah Hedges | 1 | 11 | Mansfield |
| Joseph Lamb | 13 | " | Willington |
| Benjⁿ Pirce | 1 | 9 | Mansfield |
| William Press | 5 | 4 | Woodstock |
| Thomas Rock | 15 | 16 | Groton |
| Joseph Scarborough | Aug. 21 | 9 | Ashford |
| Samuel Smith | July 15 | 4 | Norwich |
| Abel Sanders | 5 | " | Woodstock |
| Benjⁿ Tucker | " | 9 | " |
| Jesse Waldo | 1 | 4 | Mansfield |

Simⁿ Avery Lieuᵗ

[*State Library, Revolution 17, 45*]

## CAPT. REED'S COMPANY.

Pay Roll for the New Levies in Cap[t] E Reeds Comp[y] 1[st] Connecticut Reg[t] 1780

| Names | Comm[t] of Service | Expiration of Service | Towns to which they belong |
|---|---|---|---|
| Timothy Aldrich | July 1 | Dec. 4 | Preston |
| John Baker | " | 9 | Mansfield |
| Maturen Hopkin | 15 | 4 | Woodstock |
| Robert Hammond | " | 16 | Mansfield } gave a certificate Nov[r] 11, 1816 |
| Nathaniel Hewit | 5 | 4 | Stonington |
| Robert Hewit | 20 | 9 | " |
| Edmond Halley | 10 | 4 | " |
| Jonas Kenny | " | " | Preston |
| Thomas Leeds | 18 | " | Stonington |
| Thomas Morrow | 10 | " | Norwich |
| Christopher Miner | June 29 | " | Lyme |
| John Mielkin | July 13 | 13 | Preston |
| Elijah Porter | 15 | " | Mansfield |
| Amos Royce | 1 | 4 | " |
| Gideon Rogers | 8 | 9 | Lyme |
| James Reives | 9 | 18 | " |
| Augustus Stores | 10 | 9 | Mansfield |
| Gilbert Shaw | " | 4 | Ashford |
| Obadiah Sears | " | 9 | Preston |
| Amos Thomson | " | 4 | Mansfield |
| Jared Tozer | " | " | Simsbury |
| Charles Hunt | Aug. 15 | " | Lebanon |
| Manchester Halley | " | " | Preston |
| Phillip Prince | Sep. 1 | 13 | Stonington |

Enoch Reed Cap[t]

[*State Library, Revolution 17, 50.*]

CONNECTICUT LINE, 1778-1781.

## SECOND REGIMENT — COL. BUTLER.

### FIRST COMPANY — COL. BUTLER.

Pay Roll of The Levies in the 1st Company 2 Connecticut Regiment Commanded By Zebulon Butler Col°

| Mens Names | Commencement of Time | | To what time Paid | | Towns To which they Belong |
|---|---|---|---|---|---|
| Nathan¹ More | Aug. | 1 | Dec. | 8 | Windsor |
| Zeanas Burnan | " | | | 18 | Hartford |
| Asbel Warren | " | | | 9 | Windsor |
| Isaac Bellows | " | | | 18 | Hartford |
| Charles Kinball | July | 1 | | 8 | Ashford |
| Fradrick Tubbs | " | | | 18 | Newtown |
| Daniel Judd | " | | | 12 | Farmington |
| Jonathan Merrils | " | | | 9 | " |
| Joseph Munro | " | | | 18 | Danbury |
| Adoniram Benton | " | | | " | Goshen |
| Eli Bliss | " | | | 12 | Suffield |
| Joshua Symons | " | | | 3 | Tolland |
| Absalom Mooney | | 25 | Oct. | 1 | Ridgfield |
| Joseph Pease | | 1 | Dec. | 8 | Enfield |
| Thoˢ Hollister | " | | | 9 | Farmington |
| Samˡ Read | " | | | " | Tolland |
| Joseph Allyn | " | | | " | Danbury |
| Salvanus Booth | " | | | " | Farmington |
| Amos Clark | " | | | " | " |
| Samˡ Craft | | 18 | | 8 | Norwich |
| Willᵐ Stevens | | 16 | | 18 | New Haven |
| James Scariot | | 25 | | " | Hebron (?) |
| John Mooney | | 1 | | " | Ridgfield |
| Jack Gregory | | 25 | | 9 | Stratford |
| Manoah Crowel | Aug. | 1 | | " | Tolland |
| Joël Perkins | July | 1 | | 18 | |
| John Welman | | 25 | | 8 | Farmington |
| Hezekiah Porter | Oct. | 1 | | 9 | Windsor |

J. Hinckley Capᵗ Comdᵗ

[Indorsed] Pay Roll of the Short Levies in Col° Butlers Company 2 Connect Regᵗ 1780

[*State Library, Revolution 17, 3.*]

## SECOND COMPANY—LIEUT.-COL. HAIT.

Pay Roll of The Short Levies in L' Col° Haits Company 2ᵈ Connecti' Reg' Commanded By Zebulon Butler Col°

| Mens Names | Commencement of Service 1780 | To what time Paid | Towns To Which They Belong |
|---|---|---|---|
| Abiel Wolcutt  Fifer | July 15 | Dec. 9 | Windsor |
| Jonathan Amedown | 1 | " | Willington |
| Sam' Brocker | " | 13 | Simsbury |
| Abijah Phelps | " | 8 | " |
| Richard Andrews | " | 13 | " |
| Lemuil Wiard | " | 8 | Farmingtown |
| Archabel Cook | " | 9 | " |
| Lott Humphrys | " | " | Simsbury |
| Tho' Wadsworth | " | 18 | Windsor |
| James Duggen | " | Nov. 15 | Hartford |
| Mathew Peck | " | Dec. 8 | Farmington |
| Jonathan Barber | " | " | Simsbury |
| Eliph' House | Aug. 1 | " | Farmington |
| Clement Minor | 15 | " | Tolland |
| Daniel Mack | July 1 | " | Farmington |
| Wᵐ Anderson | 15 | " | Willington |
| John Wate | " | " | Norwich |
| Joshua Button | " | 8 | " |
| Wᵐ Mill Ross | " | " | Willington |
| Josiah Button | " | " | Farmington |
| Peter DeWolf | " | " | Symsbury |
| Joseph Tuller | " | 9 | " |
| Noah Miller | " | " | Farmington |
| John Booth | " | 13 | " |
| Nathan' Andrews | " | " | " |
| John Turrel | " | " | " |
| Joseph Videto | " | " | N Milford |
| Oliver Lomis | 20 | " | Windsor |
| David Burnam | Aug. 15 | " | Farmington |
| Eli Skinner | Sep. 1 | " | |
| Justis Weed | " | 9 | Stamford |
| Solomon Lusk | " | 13 | |
| Simeon Rennels | " | 8 | Woodbury |

J. Hinckley Cap' Comd'

[*State Library, Revolution 17, 29.*]

## THIRD COMPANY—MAJ. WALBRIDGE.

Pay Roll of The Levies in Major Walbridges Company 2 Connec' Reg' Commanded By Zebulon Butler Col°

| Mens Names | Commencement of Time 1780 | To What Time Paid | Towns To which They Belong |
|---|---|---|---|
| Daniel Brewer | July 1 | Dec. 6 | Hartford |
| Abel Bester | " | " | Stafford |
| Edward Burges | 12 | " | Enfield |
| David Booth | 1 | " | |
| Phinˢ Brownson | " | " | Farmington |
| Austin Bishopp | " | 13 | Danbury |
| Reuben Bradly | " | 6 | Stafford |
| Zadock Benton | " | 9 | " |
| Sam' Dunham | " | " | |

CONNECTICUT LINE, 1777-1781. 187

| Mens Names | Commencement of Time 1780 | To What Time Paid | Towns To which They Belong |
|---|---|---|---|
| Daniel Eaten | July 1 | Dec. 6 | Windsor |
| Levi Eno | " | 9 | Simsbury |
| James Fisk | " | 6 | |
| Abel Goodrich | " | 9 | Danbury |
| Phil⁸ Holt | " | 22 | Willington |
| Reuben Hill | " | 6 | Simsbury |
| Appleton Holster | Sep. 1 | " | |
| Theodore King | July 1 | " | Windsor |
| Noah Munro | " | 13 | Danbury |
| Sam¹ Parks | 20 | " | Tolland |
| Isaac Pratt | 1 | " | Farmington |
| James Powers | Sep. 1 | 6 | |
| Daniel Roberts | July 1 | " | Hartford |
| Isaac Rice | " | " | Meridan |
| Timothy Rositer | " | 9 | Harwington |
| Nathan¹ Tamage | " | " | Southington |
| Adrian Wadkins | 18 | 6 | Stafford |
| Wᵐ Fuller | 1 | 13 | |
| Eastus Hatch | " | 6 | New Haven |
| John Ford | " | " | Somers |
| Elias Baskam | " | " | Windsor |

J. Hinckley Capᵗ Comdᵗ

[*State Library, Revolution 17, 26.*]

## CAPT. BETTS' COMPANY.

Pay Roll of The Short Levies in Capᵗ Betts Company 2 Connecticut Regiment Commanded By Zebulon Butler Colᵒ

| Mens Names | Commencement Of Time | To What Time Paid | Towns They Belong To |
|---|---|---|---|
| Jesse Dickison Fifer | June 26 | Dec. 9 | Stratford |
| Oliver Boge | July 5 | " | Farmington |
| Levi Woodford | " | " | " |
| Calvin Judd | " | " | " |
| Amos Andrews | " | " | |
| Ephraim Monson | " | " | " |
| David Lee | " | 13 | " |
| Joseph Dutton | " | 9 | " |
| Eleazer Payne | " | " | Windsor |
| Isaac Gillit | Sep. 7 | " | |
| Thoˢ Hadlock | July 5 | 13 | " |
| David Fuller | " | 9 | Willington |
| John Hill | " | " | " |
| Jonathan Benton | " | 13 | Coventry |
| Jnᵒ Drinkwater | " | 6 | N Milford |
| Job Terrel | " | 9 | " |
| Aling Catling | " | 6 | Harwington |
| Reuben Grant | " | 9 | N London |
| Jonathan Quivey | " | 6 | " |
| Robert Coe | " | 13 | Farmington |
| James Roberds | " | 9 | " |
| Joseph Cook | " | " | Harwington (?) |
| Willial Barnard | " | " | Tolland |
| Stephen Rossiter | " | " | " |
| James Gleason | Aug. 1 | 13 | " |

J. Hinckley Capᵗ Comdᵗ

[Indorsed] Pay Roll of the Short Levies in Capᵗ Betts Company 2 Connecᵗ Regᵗ 1780.

[*State Library, Revolution 17, 4.*]

## CAPT. ALDIN'S COMPANY.

Pay Roll of The Short Levies in Cap$^t$ Aldins Company 2$^d$ Conn$^t$ Reg$^t$ Commanded By Zebulon Butler Col$^o$

| Mens Names | Commencement of Time | To what time Paid | Towns To which they Belong |
|---|---|---|---|
| Sam$^l$ Robards | July 1 | Dec. 18 | Winchester |
| John Balcom | " | " | New Hartford |
| Tim$^y$ Alderman | " | 9 | Simsbury |
| Eber Higley | " | " | " |
| Ozias Hawley | " | " | " |
| Enos Holcum | " | " | |
| Moses Wright | " | " | Danbury |
| Oliver Grant | " | " | Windsor |
| Amasa Rockwell | " | 18 | " |
| Oliver Grant 2$^{nd}$ | " | " | Danbury |
| Josiah Hall | 20 | 8 | Somers |
| David Lotroop | 1 | 18 | Windsor |
| Solomon Savage | 18 | " | Middletown |
| Asa Ripnear | " | " | |
| Jonathan Rice | 22 | 9 | Tolland |
| James Niles | 20 | " | Willington |
| Joseph Hale | 22 | " | Farmington |
| Freeman James | " | 4 | Willington |
| Theop$^s$ Hunt | " | " | New Milford |
| Ebenezer Smith | " | 18 | Fairfield |
| Eph$^m$ Bidwell | 26 | " | Windsor |
| Amos James | Aug. 1 | 4 | Willington |
| Anthony Kibby (?) | July 20 | Oct. 18 | Somers |
| Joseph Elmore | 26 | Dec. 18 | Windsor |
| David Linn | Aug. 1 | " | Killingworth |
| Israel Tuller | " | 9 | Simsbury |
| Timothy Anderson | " | 16 | Windsor |
| Lemuel Walter | Sep. 1 | 9 | Winchester |
| Mathew Reynolds | July 12 | Sep. 6 | Woodbury |

J. Hinckley Cap$^t$ Comd$^t$

[Indorsed] Pay Roll of the Short Levies in Cap$^t$ Aldins Company 2 Conn$^t$ Reg$^t$ 1780

[*State Library, Revolution 17, 8.*]

## CAPT. TEN EYCK'S COMPANY.

Pay Roll of The Short Levies in Cap$^t$ Ten Eycks Light Infantry Company 2 Conn$^t$ Reg$^t$ Commanded By Zebulon Butler Col$^o$

| Mens Names | Commencement of Time 1780 | To what time Paid | Towns To which they Belong |
|---|---|---|---|
| Ede Hatch D$^m$ | July 1 | Dec. 9 | Toland |
| Eber Olford | " | 4 | Simsbury |
| Sam$^l$ Chase | " | " | Toland |
| Zacheus Gillit | " | " | Farmington |
| Hezk$^h$ Huntington | " | 9 | Toland |
| Sam$^l$ Hitchcock | " | " | Farmington |
| Ambras Hitchcock | " | " | " |
| Ezek$^l$ Holcumb | " | " | Simsbury |
| Enoch Haze | " | " | " |
| Erastus Hills | " | " | Windsor |
| Elijah Hill | " | " | Simsbury |

CONNECTICUT LINE, 1777-1781.        189

| Mens Names | Commencement of Time 1780 | To what time Paid | Towns To which they Belong |
|---|---|---|---|
| Geo. Blackburn | July 1 | Dec. 9 | Hartford |
| Jos" Newbury | " | " | Windsor |
| Eben' Snell | " | " | Stafford |
| W" Rockwell | " | " | Windsor |
| Martin Dickins | " | " | |
| Joel Slayter | " | " | Simsbury |
| Chancy Atkins | " | " | Farmington |
| Simeon Barns | " | " | " |
| Joel Holcomb | " | 31 | Simsbury |
| Dan¹ Pardy | " | 18 | Farmington |
| Ezek¹ Beeman | " | " | Kent |
| Asa Brownson | " | " | Farmington |
| George Buck | " | " | Hartford |
| Daniel Andrus | " | " | Danbury |
| Jed" Blanchard | " | " | Simsbury |

J. Hinckley Cap' Comd'

[*State Library, Revolution 17, 18.*]

## CAPT. PARSONS' COMPANY.

Pay Roll of The Short Levies in Cap' Parsons Company 2 Connecticut Regiment Commanded By Zebulon Butler Col°

| Mens Names | Commencement of Time | To what time paid | Towns they Belong to |
|---|---|---|---|
| Jonathan Allyn | July 1 | Dec. 4 | Hartford |
| Theophilus Allyn | " | 9 | |
| Ellihu Allyn | " | 18 | Danbury |
| Richard Abby | " | 9 | Enfield |
| Phinias Blodget | 23 | 18 | Windsor |
| Sam¹ Billings | 1 | 3 | Somers |
| Peter Bugbee | 20 | " | Enfield |
| Jonathan Bement | 26 | 18 | Windsor |
| Ambras Cowdy | 1 | 9 | Hartland |
| Oliver Coe | " | 17 | Winchester |
| Peletiah Daniels | " | 9 | Hartland |
| David Dunham | 20 | " | Canaan |
| Nathan Fox | 1 | 3 | Simsbury |
| Levi French | " | 9 | Enfield |
| Uriah Gates | " | 18 | Hartford |
| Hills Gowdy | Aug. 1 | 9 | Enfield |
| Sam¹ Gowdy | July 10 | " | " |
| Thamar Granger | 1 | " | Simsbury |
| Sam¹ Halkins | 29 | " | Enfield |
| Sam¹ Mott | 1 | 31 | Barkhanstead |
| Sam¹ M'Gregory | " | Nov. 13 | Enfield |
| Mathew Mansfield | Sep. 1 | Dec. 18 | Fairfield |
| Abner Pearce | July 1 | 18 | Enfield |
| Aaron Pearce | 10 | 9 | " |
| Edward Pearce | " | " | " |
| Sam¹ Spencer | 23 | 6 | Somers |
| Gideon S' John | " | 17 | Canaan |

J. Hinckley Cap' Comd'

[Indorsed] Pay Roll of the Short Levies in Cap' Parsons Company 2 Connect' Reg' 1780

[*State Library, Revolution 17, 27.*]

## CAPT. WOLCUTT'S COMPANY.

Pay Roll of Cap¹ Wolcutts Company 2 Connecticut Reg¹ Commanded By Zebulon Buller Col°

| Mens Names | Commencement of Time | To what time Paid | Towns to which They Belongs |
|---|---|---|---|
| Ezra Austin | July 17 | Dec. 9 | Wallingford |
| Justice Bissel | 19 | " | Windsor |
| Daniel Braymon | June 27 | 6 | " |
| Seth Canada | 24 | " | Farmington |
| Enoch Crowel | July 12 | 18 | Enfield |
| Lemuil Church | " | " | Killingly |
| Rufus Crain | 19 | 9 | Windsor |
| Benjª Elsworth | June 29 | 13 | Danbury |
| John Gaylor | 24 | " | Farmington |
| Jered Smith | " | " | Wallingsford |
| David Grant | July 21 | 9 | Windsor |
| Walter Holms | June 29 | " | Stafford |
| Lemuel Higby | July 17 | 18 | Wallingsford |
| Abner Johnson | June 29 | 9 | Toland |
| Asaph Merrium | July 17 | 18 | Wallingford |
| Erastus Merriam | " | 6 | " |
| Wyllin McKey | " | 18 | " |
| Elisha Peck | June 24 | " | Southington |
| Seth Penfield | " | 6 | Farmington |
| Timothy Porter | July 12 | 9 | Windsor |
| George Potwain | June 29 | Nov. 7 | " |
| Noah Pearce | July 19 | Dec. 9 | " |
| George Shipman | 12 | 6 | Lyme |
| Peter Wolcutt | June 29 | 13 | Windsor |
| Simeon Rice | July 17 | " | Willington |

[Indorsed] 1780    J. Hinckley Cap¹ Comd¹

[*State Library, Revolution 17, 34.*]

## CAPT. HINCKLEY'S COMPANY.

Pay Roll of The Short Levies in Cap¹ Hinckleys Company 2 Connecticut Reg¹ for the whole Term of there Service 1780

| Mens Names | Commencement of Time | To what time Paid | Towns they Belong to | |
|---|---|---|---|---|
| Samll Steal Serj¹ | July 1 | Dec. 13 | Toland | Promoted to a Serjt Sep. 1 80 |
| William Eldridge | 15 | " | " | |
| Samuel Pierce | 1 | " | Danbury | |
| William Johnson | " | 8 | Tolland | |
| Bruster Harris | " | " | " | |
| Sam¹ Ellis | " | " | Farmington | |
| Allen Webster | 18 | " | Hartford | |
| Ezra Nicholas | 1 | " | Danbury | |
| Eleazer Hatch | Aug. 1 | " | Toland | |
| John Thompson | July 1 | 13 | " | |
| Ezra Raudin | " | " | " | |
| Aaron Dilyno | Aug. 1 | " | " | |
| Ebenezer Pinney | July 20 | " | East Windsor | |
| Sandrus Perry | 1 | 9 | Danbury | |
| Reubin Judd | " | " | " | |

## CONNECTICUT LINE, 1777-1781.

| Mens Names | Commencement of Time | | To what time Paid | | Towns they Belong to |
|---|---|---|---|---|---|
| Levi Barnam | July | 1 | Dec. | 9 | Danbury |
| John Steel | " | | " | | " |
| Job Hodgers | " | | " | | " |
| Daniel Gregory | " | | | 18 | " |
| Amos Lovland | " | | | 9 | Hartford |
| Sanford Williams | | 15 | | 18 | Norwich |
| Elisha Smith | " | | " | | " |
| Lott Burdges | | 1 | " | | Toland |
| Andrew Steel | | 15 | | 9 | East Windsor |
| Isaac Herrick | " | | | 18 | Fairfield |
| James Roberds | | 1 | " | | Farmington |
| Salvenas Gage | Aug. | 1 | | 9 | Toland |
| Luther Delyno | July | 1 | Sep. | 28 | " |

J. Hinckley Cap<sup>t</sup> Comd<sup>t</sup>

[*State Library, Revolution* 17, 37.]

## THIRD REGIMENT—COL. WYLLYS.

### FIRST COMPANY COL. WYLLYS.

Pay Roll of the Short Levy men who have Served in the Col[s] Company 3[d] Conn[t] Reg[t] for the Campaign 1780 December 22[d] 1780 Copied

| Names | Commencement of Pay | to what time paid | Towns they Belong to |
|---|---|---|---|
| Lansford White | July 1 | Dec. 9 | Bolton |
| John Ward | " | 5 | " |
| Gideon Whitaker | " | 3 | Killingly |
| Daniel Hudson | " | 12 | Woodstock |
| David Ames | " | 4 | Killingley |
| Joseph Foster | " | 12 | Pomfret |
| Weaver Brown | 2 | " | " |
| Ithamar Oney | 1 | " | Killingly |
| Eben[r] Atwood | " | " | " |
| Thomas Heath | Aug. 25 | Nov. 14 | Litchfield |

Reuben Pride Lieu[t]

[*State Library, Revolution* 17, 68.]

### SECOND COMPANY — LIEUT. COL. GROSVENOR.

Pay roll of the short levies who have served in L[t] Col. Grosvenor's C[o] 3[d] Connecticut Reg[t] in the Campaign of 1780

| Names | Com[t] of Service 1780 | Expirat of Service 1780 | From what Town |
|---|---|---|---|
| Aseph Burley | July 10 | Dec. 14 | Hartford |
| Hezk[h] Barret | 1 | 9 | " |
| Ceaser Boeny | Aug. 10 | 4 | Weathersfield |
| David Enos | July 1 | " | Simsbury |
| Timothy Fisher | Aug. 15 | 10 | Hartford |
| Nath[l] Merrills | July 1 | 13 | " |
| John Randol | " | " | Pomfret |
| Ely Seymour | Aug. 15 | 4 | Hartford |
| Elisha Seymour | " | 11 | " |
| Ardon Seymour | July 1 | 9 | " |
| W[m] Sedgwick | Aug. 15 | 11 | " |
| Charles Webster | July 1 | 18 | " |
| Daniel Wadsworth | 10 | 11 | " |
| Timothy Heart | 1 | 4 | Farmington |

Israel Johnson Serj[t]
Ex Sam Richards P Master

[*State Library, Revolution* 17, 62.]

CONNECTICUT LINE, 1777-1781.      193

### THIRD COMPONY MAJ. CLIFT.

Pay Roll of the Short Levy Men who have Served in Major Clifts Comp⁷ the 8ᵈ Connec' Reg' in the Campain of 1780 Dec' 22ᵈ   Copied

| Names | Commencement of Pay | | To What Time Paid | | Town they belong to |
|---|---|---|---|---|---|
| Abnor Brown | July | 1 | Dec. | 5 | New London |
| Elihew Benton | " | | " | 4 | Winsor |
| Sam¹ Cleaveland | " | | Nov. | 9 | Pomfret |
| Fredrick Cleaveland | " | | Dec. | 4 | " |
| Gardner Cleaveland | " | | " | " | " |
| Wardwill Green | " | | " | " | " |
| Benjⁿ Green | " | | " | " | " |
| Rufus Gibbs | " | | | 11 | Winsor |
| Soloman Gilbert | " | | | 18 | Pomfret |
| Peleg Havens | " | | | 4 | Winsor |
| Andrew Morrison | " | | | 18 | Pomfret |
| Noah Pinney | " | | | 4 | Winsor |
| Preserved Redway | " | | | " | Killingly |
| Peltiah Tuttel | " | | | 11 | New London |
| Daniel Thomson | " | | Oct. | 25 | " |
| Asa Cutter | Aug. | 8 | Dec. | 9 | Killingly |
| Cromwill Luther | July | 1 | | 10 | " |

Sylvᵃ Perry Lieu'

[*State Library, Revolution 17, 61.*]

### FOURTH COMPANY—CAPT. WARNER.

Pay Roll of the Short Levies that Have Served in the 4ᵗʰ Comp⁷ 8ᵈ Conn' Reg' Part of the Year 1780   Copied

| Names | Commenc' of Pay | | to What Time Paid | | Town Belonging to |
|---|---|---|---|---|---|
| Aseal Cheney | Sep. | 11 | Dec. | 12 | Chatham |
| Aseal Peck | June | 3 | | " | Norwich |
| Joseph Kingsbury | | 30 | | " | " |
| Jasper Bentley | " | | | 31 | " |
| Benjⁿ Greenslit | " | | | 12 | " |
| Aseal Bentley | " | | | 4 | " |
| Barnard Convise | " | | | " | " |
| Benjⁿ Babbet | Sep. | 14 | | 20 | Middletown |
| Manoah Hubbard | | 5 | | 4 | " |
| Thadias Bowe (? Boise) | " | | | " | " |
| Daniel Burton | July | 7 | | 14 | Chatham |

R. Warner Cap'

[*State Library, Revolution 17, 64.*]

### FIFTH COMPANY—CAPT. EELLS.

Pay Roll of the Short Levies in the 5 Comp⁷ 8ᵈ Connec' Reg' for the Campain the year 1780 Dec 1780   Cap' Eells's Cᵒ   Copied

| Names | Commence of Pay | | to what time paid | | Towns |
|---|---|---|---|---|---|
| Aloan Begilow | July | 15 | Dec. | 9 | Hartford |
| Elias Clark | | 1 | | " | Winsor |
| Solomon Dunham | " | | | 14 | Farmington |
| Lem¹ Fox | | 15 | | 9 | Glasonb⁷ |
| Eben' Gates | | 1 | | 14 | Colchest' |
| David Hollister | | 15 | | 9 | Glasenb⁷ |

18

| Names | Commence of Pay | to what time paid | Towns |
|---|---|---|---|
| John Plank | July 15 | Dec. 14 | |
| Sam¹ Welch | 1 | 10 | |
| David Canady | " | 14 | Glasenbʸ |
| Abner Maten | " | " | |
| Josiah Brooks | 15 | Oct. 25 | " |
| Asher Sexton | " | Dec. 10 | |
| Joseph Levenie (?)* | " | Sep. 1 | |
| Ebenʳ Ames | Sep. 1 | Dec. 9 | |

Wᵐ Tryon Sarjᵗ
Ex Sam¹ Richards Lieuᵗ

[*State Library, Revolution 17, 65.*]

*This name crossed out in original document.

## SIXTH COMPANY.

Pay Roll of the Short Levies who have served in the 6ᵗʰ Company 8ᵈ Connecᵗ Regᵗ for the Campaign 1780 December 26ᵗʰ 1780 Capᵗ Barnard's Co

| Names | Commencᵗ of pay | to what time paid | Town they Belong |
|---|---|---|---|
| Timothy Sedgwick | July 1 | Dec. 11 | Hartford |
| Horatio Wales | " | 31 | " |
| James Ensign | " | 4 | " |
| Wᵐ Hinsdale | " | 9 | " |
| Rosel Fox | " | 14 | Glastenbury |
| Jacob Augustus | " | Nov. 11 | Hartford |
| Asa Bunce | " | Dec. 9 | " |
| Sam¹ Martin | " | Jan. 1 '81 | |
| Ezra Ramsdil | " | " | |

Ashbil Riley Serjᵗ
Exᵈ Sam¹ Richards P Master

[*State Library, Revolution 17, 66.*]

## SEVENTH COMPANY.

Pay Roll of the Leveys in the 7 Compʸ 8ᵈ Connecᵗ Regᵗ in the Service of the United States, Commanded by Colᵒ Sam¹ Wyllys, December 24ᵗʰ 1780 Copied

| Names | Comᵗ of Pay | To what Time Payd | Town |
|---|---|---|---|
| John Blackmar | July 1 | Dec. 14 | Killingly |
| Abiel Chaffe | " | 11 | " |
| Charles Chaffe | " | 11 | " |
| Jonathan Congdon | " | 11 | N. London |
| Reuben Hamlin | " | 10 | Farmington |
| Reuben Harrison | Aug. 1 | 1 | Wethersfield |
| Sam¹ Short | July 15 | 5 | Killingly |
| Ezekiel Scott | 1 | 14 | Farmington |
| Lyman Clark | Aug. 20 | " | " |
| Josiah Clark | " | 17 | " |
| Sam¹ Starbord | July 1 | Nov. 8 | Newtown |

Thoˢ G. Alvord Serjᵗ
Exᵈ Sam¹ Richards Lieuᵗ

[*State Library, Revolution 17, 69.*]

## CAPT. STILWILL'S COMPANY.

Pay Rool of the Short Levies who have serv'd in Cap' Stilwills Comp⁷ Col° Wyllys's Reg' for the Campaign 1780 Copied

| Names | Comm' of Pay | To what Time Paid | Towns they Belong to |
|---|---|---|---|
| Lemuel Barrows | July 1 | Dec. 12 | Killingly |
| George Robertson | " | 8 | " |
| Ebenz' Tolbert | 15 | " | " |
| William Turner | " | " | Gloucenbury |
| Hezek\<sup>h</sup> Wadworth | " | 12 | Hartford |
| Sam\<sup>l</sup> Dealing | " | " | Gloucenbury |
| Nathan Day | " | Oct. 25 | Killingly |
| Sam\<sup>l</sup> Learnard | Aug. 1 | Dec' 9 | " |
| Joseph Levine | " | 12 | " |
| John Friswell | 15 | " | Woodstock |
| William Chafee | 1 | Oct. 25 | Bolton |
| Tho' Fox | " | 26 | Gloucenb⁷ |
| John Brock, Fifer | July 1 | Dec. 12 | Woodstock |

Camp Highlands Dec' 22ᵈ 1780    Elias Stilwill Cap'

[*State Library, Revolution* 17, 67.]

W<sup>m</sup> Clealand served in Capt Haits Co. 3ᵈ reg. July 6 to Dec. 2, 1780

[*State Library, Revolution* 17, 70.]

## FOURTH REGIMENT — COL. DURKEE.

### FIRST COMPANY — COL. DURKEE.

Pay Roll of the Short Levy Men in Col° Durkees Comp⁷ in the 4th Connecticut Regimemt Who have served the Camp⁵ⁿ '80

| Mens Names | Comm¹ of Pay | To what Time Paid | Town they Belong to |
|---|---|---|---|
| Philip Martin | July 7 | Dec. 10 | Waterbury |
| Roman Freman | 14 | 15 | Windham |
| David Sampson | " | 7 | " |
| Peter Tacomwase | 12 | Sep. 6 | Mohegan Deserted Sep. 6 |
| Joshue Cooper | " | Dec. 10 | " |
| Jacob Cooper | " | " | " |
| Joseph Squib | 14 | 1 | " |
| Cudgo Purkins | 13 | " | Windham |
| Jonson Sampson | 14 | 7 | " |
| Amon Fortin | 11 | Oct. 21 | Lebanon |
| Prince Moredock | 13 | Dec. 15 | Norwich |
| Pomp Negro | 7 | 7 | " |
| Mark Clark | Aug. 4 | 10 | Seabrook |
| John Lines | July 12 | Oct. 26 | Windham |
| Jubiter Negro | 7 | Sep. 11 | Norwich |
| Brister Negro | 11 | Dec. 10 | " |
| Ceasar Negro | 7 | " | " |
| John George | Aug. 4 | 1 | Mohegan |

John Reynolds Serj¹

[*State Library, Revolution 17, 39.*]

### SECOND COMPANY — LIEUT.-COL. SUMNER.

Pay Roll of the short Levys who have served in L¹ Col° Sumners Company 4th Connecticut Regiment for the Campaign 1780

| Names | Comm¹ of Pay | what time Paid | Towns to Which belong |
|---|---|---|---|
| Luke Flint | July 5 | Oct. 25 | Windham |
| William Hyde | 16 | Nov. 12 | Norich |
| Elias Upton | 1 | Dec. 3 | Windham |
| Othnell Luce | 10 | " | " |
| John Green | 6 | " | Norwich |
| David Canady | Aug. 15 | 4 | Windham |
| Ezenas Hall | July 16 | 9 | Ashford |
| Roger Burchard | 8 | " | Norwich |
| Eben' Gennings | 12 | 10 | Windham |
| Zackeus Flint | 10 | " | Pomfret |
| Levy Dean | Oct. 1 | " | Scotland |
| Jared Burgh | July 16 | " | Chesseir |
| Wᵐ Yarington | Aug. 8 | " | Scotland |

CONNECTICUT LINE, 1777–1791. 197

| Names | Comm't of Pay | what time Paid | Towns to Which belong |
|---|---|---|---|
| Elizer Cutler | July 9 | Dec. 10 | Norwich |
| Jabez Downs | 5 | " | " |
| Echabod Blackman | 10 | " | Lebinon |
| Ezekiel Cleary | 7 | " | " |
| Asher Merrils | Aug. 15 | 12 | Hebron |
| Richard Bostick | Sep. 7 | " | " |
| Sam¹ Mix | July 4 | " | Waterbury |
| Joshua Ripley | Aug. 15 | " | Windham |

Jo⁵ Chapman Capt⁺ L⁺

[*State Library, Revolution* 17, 60.]

## THIRD COMPANY—MAJ. THROOP.

Pay Roll of the short Levys in Major Throops Comp^y 4^th Connecticut Regiment who have served for the Campaign 1780

| Names | Comm't of Pay | To what time Paid | Towns they belong to |
|---|---|---|---|
| Elijah Chudle | July 1 | Oct. 30 | Narwich |
| Danil Buttan | " | 31 | Windham |
| Isaac Winter | " | Dec. 3 | Pamfritt |
| Christopher Hall | 28 | 6 | Killingly |
| James Bishop | 1 | " | Durham |
| Erastus Warthington | " | 10 | Colchester |
| Amos Green | " | " | Killingly |
| Eben' Sparks | 20 | " | " |
| Fraderick Goodell | 1 | " | Parmfrett |
| Seth Pope | " | 12 | Lebanan |
| Eben' Groo | " | " | Pamfritt |
| Eben' Brooks | " | 13 | Chisaher |
| Jeremiah Lockwood | Sep. 15 | 14 | Danbury |
| Thomas Patten | July 11 | " | Narwich (?) |
| George Harris | 1 | " | Sey Brook |
| Aaran Chamberlin | Sep. 15 | " | Colchester |
| David Belding | July 1 | " | East Hadam |
| Sims Edgerton | " | 6 | Narwich |
| Nell Whittaker | " | Oct. 22 | Killingly |
| Joseph Ensworth | " | Dec. 12 | Woodstock |
| Aaran Putnam | " | 2 | Fairfield |
| Justice Whitlock | Sep. 1 | 14 | |
| Thomas Perry | " | " | |
| Curtes Stodard | " | " | |
| Adanijah Root | " | " | |

Lebbeus Loomis Lieu⁺

[*State Library, Revolution* 17, 36.]

## CAPT. PHELPS COMPANY.

Pay Roll of the short Levy Men who have serv'd in the Late Cap⁺ Phelps's Company in the 4^th Connecticut Reg⁺ for the Campaig 1780

| Names | Comm't of Pay | What time Paid | Towns |
|---|---|---|---|
| W^m Clark | July 1 | Dec. 4 | N London |
| Ezra Loomis | Sep. 1 | 10 | |
| Solomon Loomis | July 1 | " | |

198          REVOLUTION LISTS AND RETURNS.

| Names | Comm¹ of Pay | What time Paid | Towns |
|---|---|---|---|
| Joseph Boyd, | Aug. 21 | Dec. 16 | |
| Thoˢ Simamons | " | 10 | |
| Samˡ Dart | July 1 | 3 | Bolton |
| Daniel Dorchester | " | 10 | " |
| Samˡ Talcut | " | " | " |
| Samˡ Tracy | 6 | " | Plainfield |
| Jesse Gilbert | 1 | 4 | Windham |
| Jno Thomas | Aug. 1 | 14 | |
| Moses Hutchinson | " | Nov. 28 | |
| Jnº Keggin | July 10 | Dec. 11 | Plainfield |
| Job Philps | " | 10 | " |
| Guy Beckwith | 1 | 9 | |
| Eleazer Lewis | 10 | 14 | Voluntª |
| Elnathan Stevens | 20 | 11 | |
| Thoˢ Addis | " | 5 | |
| Wᵐ Bishop | " | Oct. 26 | |
| Amos Davis | " | Dec. 14 | |
| David Franklin | " | 10 | |
| Amos Gustin | " | " | |
| Hugh Canady | " | 9 | |
| Aaron Buell | " | 14 | Stratford |
| Ishum Simons | Aug. 5 | 10 | |
| Nathˡ Rogers | July 1 | 3 | Bolton |
| Luther Gates Drumʳ | Aug. 1 | 9 | |
| Benjⁿ Wells Fifer | July 20 | 14 | Bolton |
| Joseph Loomis | 1 | Oct. 26 | |
| Highlands 20ᵗʰ Decʳ 1780 | S Holt Lieuᵗ | | |

[*State Library, Revolution 17, 15.*]

## CAPT. McGRIEGIER'S COMPANY.

Pay Roll of the short levies of Capᵗ McGriegiers Compʸ 4ᵗʰ Regᵗ

| Names | Commᵗ of Service | To what time paid | Towns |
|---|---|---|---|
| John Allin | July 8 | Dec. 4 | Pomfret |
| Danˡˡ Spencer | " | 11 | " |
| John White | " | 10 | " |
| Asa Beech | 10 | " | |
| Griegory Smith | " | " | |
| Alexʳ Miller | 12 | 4 | Voluntown |
| Abel Franklin | 18 | " | " |
| Wᵐ McRow | " | " | |
| Ruben Bryant | 14 | " | Plainfield |
| John Lovejoy | 15 | " | |
| Jeduthan Hurd | " | " | Plainfield |
| Charles White | 22 | 10 | Durham |
| Thoˢ Cooke | " | " | |
| Juvenal Winter | 8 | 11 | Pomfret |
| Ephraim Witter | Aug. 1 | " | |
| Danˡˡ Davisson | " | " | |
| Joshua Kendall | 4 | " | Woodstock |
| Alven Answorth | " | 4 | " |
| Asa Lamb | 6 | 10 | Groton |
| Walter Griswold | " | Nov. 6 | |
| Sluman Allin | July 8 | Dec. 4 | Pomfret |
| John Robinson | " | Nov. 5 | " |
| Enoch Post | " | 3 | Norwich |

[Arranged with rolls for 1780.]

[*State Library, Revolution, 17, 17.*]

CONNECTICUT LINE, 1777-1781.  199

## CAPT. CLIFT'S COMPANY.

Pay Roll of the Short Levies of Cap¹ Clifts Company 4ᵗʰ Conn¹ Reg¹

| Names | Comme¹ of Service 1780 | | Expiration of Service | | Towns |
|---|---|---|---|---|---|
| Simeon Robinson | July | 14 | Dec. | 10 | Windham |
| Daniel Ginnings | " | | " | | " |
| Thoˢ Rindge | " | | | 16 | " |
| John Walden | " | 12 | | 9 | " |
| Elijah Lilley | " | | | 10 | " |
| Seabury Manning | " | | " | | " |
| Garsham Hale | " | | " | | " |
| Garsham Hall 2ᵈ | " | | " | | " |
| Joseph Waldon | " | 5 | | 9 | " |
| Epaphras Curtis | " | | | 10 | " |
| Asa Benjamins | " | | | 9 | Norwich |
| Stephen Avery | " | | " | | " |
| Peter Roath | " | | | 16 | " |
| Amos Wentworth | " | | | 10 | " |
| Benjⁿ Durfee | " | | " | | Stonington |
| Hezekiah Clift | " | | | 5 | Preston |
| Rufus Johnson | " | | | 10 | Windham |
| Robert Snow | " | | " | | Ashford |
| Enos Robins | " | | | 15 | Windham |
| Caleb Faulkner | " | 14 | | 10 | " |
| Benjⁿ Cary | Aug. | 1 | " | | " |
| Joseph Rogers | " | | Nov. | 19 | Litchfield |
| Isaac Rerde (?) | " | | Dec. | 10 | Killingly |
| Jabez Bottom | | 15 | " | | Windham |
| James Fuller | " | | " | | Plainfield |
| Samuel Kimball | " | | Oct. | 26 | Killingly |
| Stephen Ginnings | " | | " | | Windham |
| Elijah Farnom | " | | " | | " |
| Thadˢ Burdseye (?) | July | 16 | Dec. | 10 | Stratford |

Camp Decʳ 28ᵗʰ 1780        William Glenney Ensign

[*State Library, Revolution* 17, 23.]

## CAPT. BUELL'S COMPANY.

Pay Roll for the Short Levy Men in Cap¹ Buells Company Light Infntry in the 4ᵗʰ Connecticut Reg¹ who have Searved for the Company 1780

| Mens Names | Commencement of Pay | | to what time paid | | Towns they belong to |
|---|---|---|---|---|---|
| Danel Allen | July | 9 | Dec. | 14 | Waterbury |
| Anthony Burningham | | 1 | | " | Killingly |
| Isreal Bolch | | 8 | | " | Mansfield |
| Thedeous Burdsey | | 9 | | 10 | Stradford |
| Eliphelet Coburn | | 8 | | 4 | Norwich |
| Elijah Cook | | " | | 10 | Windham |
| Belliel Camp | | 9 | | 14 | Waterbury |
| Bibe Cotton | | 1 | | " | Pomfret |
| Ward Cotton | | 7 | | 4 | |
| Semeon Carew | | 8 | [ | ] | Norwich |
| Samuel Hunn | | " | | 10 | " |
| Aseael Hotchkiss | | 9 | | 14 | Waterbury |
| Samuel Kimball | | 1 | | 10 | " |

| Mens Names | Commencement of Pay | | to what time paid | | Towns they belong to |
|---|---|---|---|---|---|
| Chester Lillee | July | 8 | Dec. | 2 | Windham |
| Jeremiah Meacham | " | " | | 14 | " |
| John Marshel | | 1 | " | | Bolten |
| Jerod Pritcket | | 9 | " | | Waterbury |
| Nethanel Rogers | | 1 | | 9 | Bolten |
| Pirum Ripley | " | " | | 10 | Norwich |
| Joseph Wright | | 8 | | 12 | Lebenon |
| David Saffard | | 1 | | 10 | Bolten |
| Samuel Taler | " | " | | 14 | Pomfrit |
| James Ball | | 2 | " | " | Bolten |

Andrew Hibbard Serj<sup>t</sup>

[*State Library, Revolution 17, 28.*]

## CAPT. FITCH'S COMPANY.

Pay Roll for the Short Levy men in Cap<sup>t</sup> Fitch<sup>s</sup> Company in the 4<sup>th</sup> Connec<sup>t</sup> Reg<sup>t</sup> who have served for the Campaign 1780,

| Mens Names | Commencement of Pay | | to what time Paid | | Town they belong to |
|---|---|---|---|---|---|
| Abel Baker | July | 1 | Dec. | 8 | Norwich |
| Eli Church | | 15 | | 10 | Mansfield |
| Phineas Corwin | " | " | | 14 | Norwich |
| Titus Canfield | " | " | Nov. | 9 | Durham |
| Nathan Coal | " | " | Dec. | 18 | " |
| W<sup>m</sup> Johnson Daley | | 1 | | 5 | Pomphret |
| Clement Fairchild | " | " | | 10 | Newtown |
| Zalmon Fairweather | " | " | | 31 | Stratford |
| W<sup>m</sup> Gardner | | 15 | | 10 | Colchester |
| George Hall | | 1 | | 8 | Stratford |
| Asa Harris | | 10 | | 10 | Lebanon |
| Sam<sup>ll</sup> Hyde | | 1 | | 14 | " |
| Eli Moffatt | " | " | | 5 | Killingly |
| Augustus Post | " | " | | 10 | Norwich |
| James Robinson | | 15 | | 18 | Durham |
| Clement Stoddard | | 1 | | 10 | Norwich |
| Asa Sawyer | " | " | | 8 | Waterbury |
| Dudley Squire | | 15 | | 5 | Durham |
| Hez<sup>h</sup> Terrell | | 1 | | 8 | Stratford |
| Marchant Wooster | " | " | | 14 | " |
| Thomas Wakeley | " | " | | 10 | " |
| Ezra Woodworth | | 15 | | 17 | Lebanon |
| Ardamus Stevens | | 1 | Oct. | 26 | Norwich |
| Ichabod Sparks | Aug. | 1 | Dec. | 10 | Killingly |

Connecticut Huts Decm<sup>r</sup> 24<sup>th</sup> 1780    A Fitch Cap<sup>t</sup>

[*State Library, Revolution 17, 40.*]

CONNECTICUT LINE, 1779–1781. 201

## COL. WEBB'S COMPANY.

Pay Roll of the Short Levy Men who have serv'd in Cap$^t$ Webbs Company in the 4$^{th}$ Coonn$^t$ Reg$^t$ for the Camp$^n$ 1780

| Names | Comm$^t$ of Service | | what time Paid | | Towns |
|---|---|---|---|---|---|
| Tho$^s$ Deane | July | 11 | Dec. | 8 | Windham |
| James Bell | " | | " | | Norwich |
| David Wheeler | | 1 | | 4 | Windham |
| Benj$^a$ Woodworth | | 24 | | 6 | Lebanon |
| Rodger Huntington | | 11 | " | | Norwich |
| Elisha Allin | June | 5 | " | | |
| Richard Robinson | July | 12 | | 9 | Windham |
| Solaman Lord | " | | | 8 | " |
| Darius Bottom | June | 11 | | 10 | Norwich |
| John Pengo | July | 6 | " | | " |
| Joseph Miller | | 12 | " | | Windham |
| Nath$^n$ Kanady | " | | " | | " |
| Joseph Marsh | June | 5 | " | | |
| Timothy Green | | 4 | " | | |
| Henry Waldow | | 2 | " | | |
| Prentice Pengo | July | 11 | " | | Norwich |
| Charles Waterman | Aug. | 28 | " | | Plainfield |
| Henry M$^c$Neal | July | 4 | | 14 | Ashford |
| John Huff | | 28 | Oct. | 10 | Norwich |
| Lenard Perkins | | 11 | Dec. | 14 | Plainfield |
| Nath$^l$ Allin (?) | June | 28 | | 10 | |
| And$^w$ Ealy | | 27 | | 14 | |

Charles Fanning

[*State Library, Revolution 17, 53.*]

## FIFTH REGIMENT—COL. BRADLEY.

### FIRST COMPANY—COL. BRADLEY.

Pay Roll of the Levies in Col° Bradleys Company 5th Conn<sup>t</sup> Regiment Commanded by Philip B Bradley Col°

| Names | Commencement of pay 1780 | | To what Time paid 1780 | | Towns |
|---|---|---|---|---|---|
| Jacob Craw | July | 1 | Dec. | 8 | N. Fairfield |
| John Jinnings | " | | | 9 | Summors |
| Enoch Blackman (?) | " | | [ | ] | (?) Ripton |
| Nehemiah Sharwood | " | | | 9 | Ridgefield |
| Sam<sup>ll</sup> Gilbert | " | | " | | Ripton |
| Reubin M<sup>c</sup>Craw | " | | " | | Windsor |
| John Parker | " | | | 8 | Summors |
| Will<sup>m</sup> Hamblin | " | | | 18 | " |
| Abraham Holcomb | " | | " | | Canaan |
| Nathaniel Root | " | | " | | " |
| Joseph Olmsted | " | | | 8 | Ridgefield |
| Elijah Kellogg | " | | | 13 | " |
| Isiah (?) Nash | " | | " | | " |
| Reubin Coley | " | | | 9 | Summors |
| Ammon Craw (?) | Aug. | 1 | | 8 | N. Fairfield |

[The remainder of this roll is missing.]

[*State Library, Revolution 17, 54a.*]

### SECOND COMPANY—LIEUT.-COL. JOHNSON.

A Pay Roll of the Levies in L<sup>t</sup> Col° Johnson's Company in the 5<sup>th</sup> Connecticut Reg<sup>t</sup> Commanded by Philip B Bradley Col°

| Names | Commencement of Pay | | To what Time Paid | | Towns |
|---|---|---|---|---|---|
| Elijah Blackman | July | 1 | Dec. | 12 | Stratford |
| Mills De Forest | " | | | 14 | " |
| Abel De Forest | " | | | 12 | " |
| Sherm<sup>n</sup> Fairchild | " | | | 9 | N. Milford |
| Andrew Gleson | " | | Sep. | 9 | Torrington |
| Mead Heard | " | | Dec. | 9 | Stratford |
| Elijah Heard | " | | Oct. | 26 | " |
| Amos Holiday | | 20 | Dec. | 9 | Simsbury |
| Ezekiel Whitney | | 1 | Oct. | 26 | Ridgebury |
| Benajah Hays | | 20 | " | | Simsbury |
| David Osmer | | 1 | Dec. | 18 | Farmington |
| John Parker | " | | | 9 | Stonington |
| Pet<sup>r</sup> Wilkinson | " | | | 18 | N. Milford |
| W<sup>m</sup> Thorn | | 20 | | 2 | Simsbury |
| Nath<sup>n</sup> Henman | Aug. | 5 | | 13 | Stratford |
| Ephraim Sherwood | " | | " | | " |
| Sam<sup>l</sup> Ogden | Sep. | 1 | " | | Fairfield |
| Nathan Fairchild | | 12 | | 9 | Stratford |
| Sam<sup>l</sup> French | July | 1 | " | | " |

Sam<sup>l</sup> Woodcock Saj<sup>t</sup>  No offiser present

[Indorsed] 1780

[*State Library, Revolution 17, 49.*]

CONNECTICUT LINE, 1777-1781.        203

## THIRD COMPANY—MAJ. CHAPMAN.

Pay Roll of the Short Levies in Major Chapmans Company 5th Conn[t] Reg[t] Comm[d] by Philip B. Bradly Col

| Names | Commencement of Pay | To what time paid | |
|---|---|---|---|
| Jehiel Burr | July 1 | Dec. 9 | Toringford |
| Champhilet (?) Stanliff | " | 3 | " |
| Elijah Bissell | " | 9 | " |
| Phenious Elmor | " | 13 | Windsor |
| Remembrance Sheldin | " | 9 | " |
| Fredrick Biggelow | " | " | Toringford |
| Seelah Woodruff | " | 14 | |
| Daniel Clark | " | 9 | Windsor |
| John Whiten | " | 13 | " |
| Gilbert Hart | " | Oct. 27 | |
| Benj[m] Gaylor | " | Dec. 8 | Goshan |
| Robert Fields | " | 9 | Symsbury |
| Samuel Lamson | " | 16 | " |
| Brigador Lowmas | " | 31 | Toringford |
| Shedrick Bostwick | Aug. 1 | 3 | N Milford |
| Andrew Canfield | " | 9 | " |
| Joel Ingersole | July 1 | 19 | " |
| Ephram Turrel | Sep. 1 | 3 | Fairfield |
| Joseph Hazie (?) | " | 18 | " |
| Elijah Mills | " | " | Windsor |
| Jonathan Strong | " | 9 | Toringford |
| Jonethan Demmon | " | 13 | Fairfield |
| Ezra Brown | July 1 | " | Windsor |
| Joel Cook | " | 9 | " |
| Elijah Kelcy | " | 3 | Torringford |

D Beach Ens[n]

[Indorsed] Pay Roll of Major Chapmans Company 5th Connec[t] Regiment 1780

[*State Library, Revolution 17, 20.*]

## CAPT. WRIGHTS' COMPANY.

Pay Roll of the Short Levies in Cap[t] J A Wrights Company 5th Conn Regiment Commanded by Phillip B. Bradley Col°

| Names | Commencement of Pay 1780 | To what time paid 1780 | Towns |
|---|---|---|---|
| Peleg Brown | July 1 | Dec. 13 | Groatton |
| Asa Chapen | " | " | Summers |
| John Corkins | " | 9 | " |
| Daniel Cheney | July 24 | " | Pomfret |
| Jobe Davis | July 1 | 13 | Summers |
| Thomas Green | " | " | Harington |
| Timothy Harrington | " | 9 | Stafford |
| Sam[ll] Hodgkis | " | 13 | Litchfield |
| Isriel Treman (?) | " | 3 | Summers |
| Benj[n] Orcott | " | 9 | " |
| Derias Orton | " | 13 | Litchfield |
| Sollomon Parsons | " | 9 | Summers |
| Jeremiah Phillips | " | " | " |

| Names | Commencement of Pay 1780 | To what time paid 1780 | Towns |
|---|---|---|---|
| Ellee Pratt | July 1 | Dec. 9 | Summers |
| Reuben Perry | " | 3 | " |
| James Redfield | " | " | Middletown |
| Clement Tuttel | 24 | 9 | Toringford |
| Asa Wood | 1 | 13 | Summers |
| Isaac Buck | " | Oct. 27 | " |

J Willcox Lieut

[*State Library, Revolution, 17, 7.*]

## CAPT. HAIT'S COMPANY.

Pay Roll of the Leavies in Capt Samuel Haits Company 5th Connect Regt Commanded by Colo Philip B. Bradley

| Names | Commencement of Pay 1780 | To what time paid | Towns |
|---|---|---|---|
| Elisha Andras | July 1 | Dec. 2 | Simsbury |
| William Andras | " | 9 | " |
| Richard Andras | " | 2 | " |
| Roswell Case | " | 13 | " |
| Abiel Cook | " | " | N Fairfield |
| David Goowin | " | 14 | Simsbury |
| William Graham | " | 2 | " |
| Dudley Miller | " | 13 | " |
| Phineas Palmer | " | 9 | Stonington |
| Thomas Palmer | " | " | Voluntown |
| Jonas Randall | " | 2 | " |
| Richard Edgerton | " | 9 | Simsbury |
| Joseph Hawley | " | " | Ridgefield |
| John Gilbert | " | 31 | " |
| Samuel Bradley | " | 13 | " |
| Prince Walley | " | 9 | Danbury |
| David Sturgis | " | 13 | " |
| Chanley Judd | " | 31 | Waterbury |
| Clemmans Handy | " | Oct. 28 | Windsor |
| Jehial Winchel | " | Nov. 5 | Simsbury Deserted |

Thadds Keeler Lieut

[*State Library, Revolution 17, 31.*]

## CAPT. ST. JOHN'S COMPANY.

A Pay Roll of the Levies in Capt John St Johns Company in the 5th Connecticut Regt Commanded by Philip B. Bradley Colo

| Names | Commencement of Pay 1780 | To What Time Paid | Towns |
|---|---|---|---|
| Saml Baldwin | July 1 | Dec. 13 | Cornwell |
| Bruen Beach | " | " | Goshen |
| Elihu Barnerd | " | " | Simsbury |
| Richd Bangs | 10 | " | Stratford |
| Judah Case | " | 4 | Simsbury |
| Caleb Case | " | 13 | " |
| Rulif Coon | " | 17 | N Milford |
| Domini Douglas | 1 | 27 | " |
| Saml Kellog | " | 4 | Goshen |

CONNECTICUT LINE, 1777-1781.

| Names | Commencement of Pay 1780 | To What Time Paid | Towns |
|---|---|---|---|
| Hicol{d} Hitchcock | July 19 | Dec. 13 | Stratford |
| Nehem{h} Olmstead | 1 | 9 | Ridgefield |
| Math{w} Olmstead | 16 | " | " |
| Willm Cummins | " | 4 | " |
| Willm Elton | 1 | " | Farmington |
| Abner Guilbert | " | 9 | Litchfield |
| Joseph Osborn | " | 13 | Ridgefield |
| Buel Sacket | " | 9 | Litchfield |
| Saml Stebins | 19 | 2 | Ridgefield |
| Timothy Ray | 1 | 9 | Torrinton |
| John Weeler | 16 | 2 | Stratford |
| Southmit Guernsey | 1 | 9 | Waterbury |

H. Rogers Leiut

[*State Library, Revolution 17, 38.*]

## CAPT. MORRIS' COMPANY.

Pay Roll of the Short Levys that Belonged to Capt James Morris's Company 5th Connec{t} Reg{t} Commanded by Colo Philip B Bradley

| Names | Commencement of Pay | To What time paid | Town |
|---|---|---|---|
| Moses Allin | July 1 | Dec. 16 | Windsor |
| Josiah Apley | " | 25 | Torrington |
| Daniel Bogue | " | 9 | Windsor |
| Ezekiel Buck | " | " | N Millford |
| Reuben Barber | " | 13 | Windsor |
| John Culver | " | 16 | |
| Oliver Coller | " | 2 | Hartford |
| Lory Drake | " | 9 | Windsor |
| Martin Dill | " | Oct. 25 | Goshen |
| James Eno | " | Dec. 13 | Windsor |
| Eliakim Gaylord | " | 2 | " |
| Belah Hills | 19 | 16 | Torrington |
| Luther Lawrance | " | 9 | Norfolk |
| John Hall | 1 | " | Suffield |
| Philander Moore | " | Oct. 25 | Windsor |
| Asa Moore | " | Dec. 16 | " |
| Peleg Sweet | 19 | " | Torrington |
| Willm Stanard | 1 | 2 | " |
| Jonathan Walling | " | 16 | Hartford |
| Isaac Wardwell | " | 2 | Windsor |
| Christopher Whitbrite (?) | " | 13 | Middletown |

No Officer Present Grove Rockwell Serj{t}

[Indorsed] Pay Roll of the Short Levys in Capt Morrisses Company 1780

[*State Library, Revolution 17, 42.*]

## CAPT. WARD'S COMPANY.

A Pay Roll of the Levies in Capt Thaddeus Weeds Company 5th Connecticut Regiment Commanded by Colo Philip B Bradley Decr 31st 1780

| Names | Commencement of Service | Expiration of Service | Towns to which they Belong |
|---|---|---|---|
| John Austen | July 1 | Nov. 22 | Simsbury |
| Achilles Comstock | " | Dec. 2 | New Milford |
| Abel Collins | " | " | Southington |

| Names | Commencement of Service | Expiration of Service | Towns to which they Belong |
|---|---|---|---|
| Andrew Calahan | July 1 | Dec. 18 | Simsbury |
| Ithimar Colton | " | 2 | " |
| Eliakim Colton | " | 9 | " |
| Daniel Hillyer | " | 18 | |
| Samuel Ives | " | 9 | Farmington |
| Alexander Phelps | " | 2 | Simsbury |
| Beebe Pangburn | " | 9 | Cornwell |
| Joseph Rockwell | " | 26 | Colbrook |
| John Russell | " | Aug. 14 | Windsor |
| Arial Strong | " | Dec. 9 | Norfolk |
| Ashbel Tillison | " | 18 | Farmington |
| Elias Tillison | " | " | Simsbury |
| Voluntine Whitman | " | Aug. 19 | Farmington |
| Jesse Wilcocks | " | Dec. 18 | " |
| Daniel Johnson | " | Aug. 1 | |
| Williston Hurd | Aug. 20 | Dec. 2 | Stratford |
| Seth Tolcott | July 1 | " | Hartford |
| John Fyler | Aug. 25 | 13 | Torrington |
| Edward Pellom | July 5 | 9 | Coventry |

Corn⁸ Russel Lieut

[State Library, Revolution 17, 51.]

## CAPT. CHAPMAN'S COMPANY.

Pay Roll of the Leavies in Cap' Chapmans Company 5th Conn' Reg' Commanded by Phillip B. Bradley Col°

| Names | Commencement of Pay 1780 | To What time Paid 1780 | Towns |
|---|---|---|---|
| Thomas Buck | July 1 | Dec. 2 | Summers |
| Thamer Bingham | " | 4 | Goshen |
| Isaas Benham | " | 8 | Torrington |
| Rice Beach | " | " | Goshan |
| Jonathan Bostwick | " | 13 | N. Milford |
| Ebenezar Chubbuck | " | " | Tolland |
| Orcemus Brunson | " | Oct. 1 | N. Milford |
| Gideon Dunham | " | 31 | Canaan |
| Jonathan Emmonds | " | Dec. 16 | |
| Luther Gleason | " | 14 | Torrington |
| Ury Hill | " | 8 | Goshan |
| Asa How | " | " | Torrington |
| Timothy Hummaston | " | 16 | Northbury |
| Daniel Johnson | " | 1 | N. Milford |
| Edward Knapp | 24 | Sep. 14 | Simsbury |
| Brainard Linsley | 1 | Dec. 13 | Woodbury |
| Charles Millard | " | " | Cornwall |
| Ezekel Moses | 24 | " | Simsbury |
| Theodore Manross | 1 | 2 | Farmington |
| Charles Pease | " | 8 | Summers |
| Daniel Palmer | " | " | Stonington |
| John Russell | Aug. 14 | 2 | Windsor |
| Sanford Richardson | July 1 | 8 | Summers |
| Abner Squires | " | 2 | Tolland |
| Elijah Towner | " | 8 | Goshan |
| Walliston Hurd | " | Aug. 20 | Stanford |

D Bradley Lieut

[State Library, Revolution 17, 55.]

## SEVENTH REGIMENT—COL. SWIFT.

### FIRST COMPANY—COL. SWIFT.

Pay Roll of the short levies that have served in Col° Swifts Comp⁷ 7 Conn Reg¹

| Mens Names | Towns to which they belong | Commencement of Pay | Discharged |
|---|---|---|---|
| Elephaz Jerrum Priv. | Farmington | July 10 | Oct. 10 |
| " Drmr | " | Oct. 18 | Dec. 7 |
| James Bonnum | New Hartford | July 1 | 18 |
| Jason Cruttenden | Southernton | " | 7 |
| Giles Curtiss | Canaan | " | 3 |
| Samuel Dean | Cornwell | June 24 | " |
| Horriss Day | Southernton | " | 13 |
| Otis Ensign | N Hartford | " | 16 |
| Elijah Gaylord | " | " | 7 |
| Caleb Hall | Wallingford | July 10 | 10 |
| Noah Higby | Canaan | " | 7 |
| Ezra Jones | " | June 26 | " |
| John Marsh | N Hartford | 24 | 13 |
| Roswell Marsh | " | " | 25 |
| Samuel Moss | Wallingford | July 10 | Oct. 31 |
| Jeremiah Osborn | N Haven | 1 | Dec. 8 |
| David Plum | Stratford | June 28 | 7 |
| Stephen Parker | Cheshire | 24 | 13 |
| Ebenezer Pardy | Canaan | July 1 | 3 |
| Luke Roberts | Danbury | " | " |
| David Sanford | Canaan | " | " |
| Jonathan Thomson | Norwalk | " | " |
| Lemuel White | N Hartford | June 24 | 7 |
| Daniel Wallen | " | " | 3 |

A Hall Serg¹ No officer Present

[*State Library, Revolution* 17, 2.]

### SECOND COMPANY.
### LIEUT.-COL. HOLDRIDGE.

Pay Roll of the Short Levies in L¹ Col° Holdridges Comy⁷ 7ᵗʰ Connecticut Reg¹ Commanded By Heman Swift Col° in the Service of the United States For 1780

| Mens Names | Commencement of Pay | Ditcharged | Town to which they Belong |
|---|---|---|---|
| Benjamin Fairchild Fifer | July 1 | Dec. 5 | Stratford |
| John Ayres | " | 13 | Reding |
| Asa Benjamin | " | 5 | Stratford |
| Silas Berto | " | 15 | Reding |
| Gershum Beers | " | 3 | " |
| John Bordslee | " | 13 | Stratford |
| Elnathan Beech | Aug. 18 | 9 | Cornwall |
| Hezekiah Berdslee | July 1 | 13 | Stratford |

208        REVOLUTION LISTS AND RETURNS.

| Mens Names | Commencement of Pay | Ditcharged | | Town to which they Belong |
|---|---|---|---|---|
| Dennis Burnett | Aug. 1 | Dec. | 8 | Groton |
| William Chedsey | " | | 9 | " |
| Phineas Gorham | July 1 | | 15 | Reding |
| Nathaniel Geers | 24 | | 12 | Kent |
| Henery Ingraham | " | | 5 | " |
| Solomon Johnson | Aug. 18 | | 9 | Cornwall |
| Lemuel Malery | July 1 | Nov. | 19 | Stratford |
| Daniel Kine | " | Dec. | 8 | " |
| Noah Smith | 24 | | 19 | Kent |
| Noah Spencer | 1 | | 8 | N Hartford |
| Hoyt Scofield | " | | 9 | Stratford |
| Abraham Thompson | " | | 17 | " |
| Obediah Taylor | " | | 8 | N Hartford |
| Levi Watson | " | | 9 | " |
| John Wells | " | Oct. | 31 | Stratford |
| Jesse Morgin | Aug. 1 | Dec. | 8 | Groton |
| Thomas Bidwell | 20 | | 5 | Glasten[   ] |
| John Barnes | " | | 8 | Wethersfield |
| Ephraim Bidwell | " | | " | Glastenbury |
| Innitt (?) Holister | 25 | | 15 | " |
| Robert Holdredge | July 1 | Oct. | 31 | Hebron |
| Norman Phelps | Aug. 22 | Dec. | 27 | " |
| William Wetherill | 25 | | 9 | Wethersfield |

John Phinney Serj&#116; No Officer Present

[*State Library, Revolution* 17, 11.]

## THIRD COMPANY—MAJ. WOODBRIDGE.

Pay Roll of the Short Levies in Major Woodbridge's Comp&#121; In the 7&#116;&#104; Conn&#116; Regiment Commanded by Col&#111; Swift Dec&#114; 31&#115;&#116; 80

| Names | Comment of Service | Expra of Service | | Towns to which They Belong |
|---|---|---|---|---|
| Levi Arnold | June 25 | Dec. | 13 | Haddam |
| Benj&#97; Butlor | July 10 | | 9 | Canaan |
| Zacheus Cande | June 24 | | " | " |
| Sam&#108; Dennison | 22 | | " | Saybrook |
| Nehemiah Dickerson | 26 | | 3 | Haddam |
| Sam&#108; Fox | July 1 | | 27 | |
| Minor Hellard | June 22 | Oct. | 31 | Saybrook |
| James Thetsey | " | Dec. | 3 | " |
| Sam&#108; King | 26 | | 17 | Haddam |
| Frances Lewis | " | | 13 | " |
| Oliver Mead | Aug. 4 | | 3 | N. Milford |
| Abner Porter | June 25 | | 7 | Haddam |
| Jn&#111; Pratt | " | | 27 | Saybrook |
| Job Stannard | 22 | | 7 | " |
| Joseph Schovel | 26 | | " | Haddam |
| Philip Smith | " | | 13 | Saybrook |
| Jonathan Smith | 25 | | " | Haddam |
| James Sellick | July 1 | | 3 | Danbury |
| Jesse Spencer | June 26 | | 4 | N. Hartford |
| Randolph Shaddee | July 7 | | 27 | |
| David Tiley | June 26 | | 9 | Saybrook |
| Ruben Tylor | July 28 | | 4 | Wallingford |

J Willcox Lieu&#116;

[*State Library, Revolution* 17, 9.]

CONNECTICUT LINE, 1777-1781. 209

## CAPT. CHAMBERLAIN'S COMPANY.

Pay Roll of the Short Levies that have Served in Captain Chamberlains Company 7ᵗʰ Connᵗ Regᵗ the present year, Decʳ 31ˢᵗ 1780

| Mens Names | Commencement of Pay | To What Time Paid | Towns to which They Belong |
|---|---|---|---|
| Zachariah Doud | June 26 | Dec. 18 | Guilford |
| Ira Adkins | " | 8 | " |
| Benajah Tracy | July 7 | " | Preston |
| Daniel Collins | June 26 | " | Guilford |
| Nathˡˡ Cramton | " | " | " |
| Bradoe Stedmon | July 7 | " | Preston |
| Elijah Stanard | June 28 | " | Guilford |
| James Welman | July 29 | " | Killingsworth |
| Ezra Bishop | June 26 | 13 | Guilford |
| Leonard Bishop | " | " | " |
| Abel Parker | July 7 | " | Preston |
| Elisha Tracy | " | " | " |
| Henry Bevins | June 26 | 9 | Guilford |
| Stephen Stone | " | " | " |
| Poffe Niger | " | " | " |
| Clear Lewis | July 7 | " | Wallingford |
| Titus Frances | June 30 | " | " |
| James Fitch | 9 | 13 | Kent |
| James Hart | 26 | 17 | Guilford |
| John Wheeler | " | 27 | |

James Bennit Lieuᵗ

[*State Library, Revolution 17, 5.*]

## CAPT. CONVERSE'S COMPANY.

Pay Roll of the Short levies in Capᵗ Converses Compʸ 7ᵗʰ Connect Regᵗ in the Service of the United States Commanded by Colᵒ Swift 1780

| Mens Names | Commencement of pay | To what time paid | Towns to which they belong |
|---|---|---|---|
| Benjᵃ Allyn | Sep. 1 | Dec. 18 | Fairfield |
| George Buckingham | July 1 | 17 | Seabrook |
| Daniel Baily | " | 9 | " |
| John B. Juddson | " | " | Stratford |
| Isaac Butler | " | 8 | Norfolk |
| Joseph Batterson | Sep. 2 | 18 | Fairfield |
| Abijah Batterson | Aug. 22 | 9 | " |
| Ichabud Chapin | June 26 | 18 | Goshen |
| Oliver Cone | July 1 | 9 | Seabrook |
| Samˡˡ Downs | Aug. 22 | 25 | Fairfield |
| Jehiel Hull | July 1 | 18 | Norfolk |
| Justice Hail | June 26 | " | Goshen |
| Samˡˡ Hase | July 1 | 8 | Danbury |
| William Leach | " | 9 | Norfolk |
| Elisha Mayo | June 26 | " | Goshen |
| John Miner | July 1 | 8 | Norfolk |
| John Norton | June 26 | 18 | Goshen |
| Daniel Piquet | " | 9 | " |
| Thaddeus Potter | " | " | " |
| James Sturdivent | July 1 | 8 | Norfolk |
| Elisha Stoddard | June 28 | 9 | Groton |
| Silas Seward | July 1 | 18 | Norfolk |

14

| Mens Names | Commencement of pay | To what time paid | Towns to which they belong |
|---|---|---|---|
| Sam<sup>ll</sup> Taylor | July 1 | Dec. 13 | Norfolk |
| Bates Turner | " | " | " |
| Amos Wood | " | " | Seabrook |
| Moses Wilcocks | June 26 | 9 | Goshen |
| Abraham Bardin | July 1 | Oct. 31 | Norfolk |

Tho<sup>s</sup> Converse Cap<sup>t</sup>

[*State Library, Revolution 17, 6.*]

## CAPT. BILLING'S COMPANY.

Pay Roll of the Short Levies in Capt<sup>s</sup> Billing Company 7<sup>th</sup> Connecticut Regiment Commanded by Col<sup>o</sup> Swift Dec<sup>r</sup> 31<sup>st</sup> 1780

| Names | Commencement of Service | Dates of Discharges | Towns to which They Belong |
|---|---|---|---|
| Edward Austen | June 29 | Dec. 13 | Preston |
| Daniel Braymon | July 1 | " | Norwich |
| Frances Danity (?) | June 29 | 9 | Preston |
| James Tylor | " | 18 | " |
| Joseph Lane | " | 9 | " |
| Joseph Guile | " | 18 | " |
| Josiah Bourougs (?) | July 10 | 8 | Stratford |
| Jared Baldwin | " | 10 | N Milford |
| John Morehouse | " | 17 | N Fairfield |
| John Gregory | Sep. 2 | 8 | N Milford |
| Joel Hurlbert | Aug. 20 | 9 | Woodbury |
| Nathan<sup>l</sup> Prentice | July 15 | 13 | Preston |
| Neel M<sup>c</sup>Neel | 1 | 14 | Stratford |
| Noah Bartrum | 10 | 9 | Reding |
| Gilbert Tracy | June 29 | 17 | Preston |
| Tho<sup>s</sup> Grant | " | 18 | " |
| Aaron Taylor | July 8 | 9 | N London |
| Samuel Couch | Aug. 1 | " | N Milford |
| Isaac Goodsell | July 15 | " | Washington |
| Truman Beeman | 10 | 18 | Kent |
| Prentice Gallop | June 28 | 16 | Groton |
| William Ward | July 10 | 9 | Stratford |
| Rubin Jones | June 29 | 17 | Preston |
| Steph Tylor | " | 18 | " |
| James Hubbert | July 10 | 9 | Stratford |

C M<sup>c</sup>Donald Serj<sup>t</sup>    No officer present

[*State Library, Revolution 17, 14.*]

## CAPT. HALL'S COMPANY.

Pay Roll of the Short Levies in Cap<sup>t</sup> Halls Company 7<sup>th</sup> Connecticut Reg<sup>t</sup> Commanded By Col<sup>o</sup> Swift Dec<sup>r</sup> 31<sup>th</sup> 1780

| Mens Names | Commencement of Service | To what time Paid | Towns to which they Belong |
|---|---|---|---|
| James Brooks | July 1 | Dec. 9 | Haddam |
| [           ] | [   ] | [   ] | [           ] |
| Luis (?) Burton | 5 | " | Stratford |
| Hezekiah Clark | " | 25 | Haddam |
| Lemuel Chatfield | 9 | 3 | Stratford |
| Elihu Crane | 5 | " | Durham |
| Jedediah Coe | 4 | 13 | Gilford |

CONNECTICUT LINE, 1777-1781.

| Mens Names | Commencement of Service | To what time Paid | Towns to which they Belong |
|---|---|---|---|
| Asa Cogswell | July 7 | Dec. 8 | Canaan |
| Rosel Grant | " | 9 | Norfolk |
| William Hawley | 5 | " | Stratford |
| Asa Hide | 7 | 18 | Canaan |
| Luther Killum | 5 | " | Presson |
| John Lane | 1 | " | Killingsworth |
| Chileab Palmer | 10 | " | N Milford |
| James Parmerly | " | " | Gilford |
| Joshua Root | 7 | " | Canaan |
| Nathan Rix | 5 | 9 | Presson |
| Wiliam Stevens | 1 | " | Killingsworth |
| Ebenezer Scovill | 7 | 18 | Winchester |
| Sutliff Seward | 5 | " | Durham |
| Abel Tharp | " | 3 | Wallingford |
| Caleb Turner | 1 | " | Killingsworth |
| George White | 7 | " | Canaan |

Solomon Pinto Ens<sup>n</sup>

[*State Library, Revolution 17, 22.*]

## CAPT. BALDWIN'S COMPANY.

Pay Roll of the Short Levies who have Serv'd in Cap<sup>t</sup> Baldwin's Comp<sup>y</sup> 7<sup>th</sup> Cone<sup>t</sup> Reg<sup>t</sup>

| Mens Names 31<sup>st</sup> Dec<sup>r</sup> 1780 | Commencement of Pay | To what time Paid | Town to which they belong |
|---|---|---|---|
| John Buel | June 27 | Dec. 8 | Killingsworth |
| Joseph Bishop | July 1 | 9 | Canaan |
| Zopher Betts | 18 | 8 | Sharon |
| Gideon Buel | 10 | " | Killingsworth |
| Joseph Buel | " | 14 | " |
| Peter Blacke | June 26 | 18 | Haddam |
| Oliver Clark | 27 | " | " |
| Cornelius Dunham | 28 | 16 | Canaan |
| Benj<sup>n</sup> Dibble | 20 | 4 | Cornwall |
| Richard Ellot | 27 | 8 | Killingsworth |
| Francis Griswould | 26 | " | " |
| Peter Wines | July 6 | 9 | Kent |
| Robert Newel | June 28 | Oct. 27 | Killingsworth |
| Samuel Merrit (?) | 27 | Dec. 3 | " |
| Levi Osborn | July 1 | 9 | Danbury |
| Ezra Porter | June 27 | 27 | Killingsworth |
| Benjamin Peck (?) | July 1 | 9 | Danbury |
| Jared Rice | 20 | " | Moodus |
| Luke Stevens | June 27 | 27 | Killingsworth |
| Peter Spencer | 21 | 9 | Haddam |
| Jonah Sutlief | 27 | 8 | " |
| Reuben Wright | 29 | " | Killingsworth |
| Joab Wright | 26 | 18 | " |
| Nathan Wright | 27 | 9 | " |
| Eleazer Warner | " | 18 | " |
| Zebulon Thomson | 29 | 27 | " |
| James Spencer | 28 | 9 | Haddam |
| Rufus Thrall | July 1 | " | Norfolk |
| Giles Thrall | 25 | " | " |

Eben<sup>r</sup> Daggett Ens<sup>a</sup>

[*State Library, Revolution 17, 24.*]

## CAPT. STEEVENS' COMPANY.

Pay Roll of the Short Leves Who have served in Cap' Steevens Company 7th Connecticut Reg' Dec' 31st 1780

| Mens Names | Commencement of Pay | Discharged | Towns to Which They Belong |
|---|---|---|---|
| Anthony Florous drum' | 1 Aug. | 9 Dec. 80 | Stoningtown |
| David Chapman priv. | 10 July | 8 | Coalchester |
| Samuel Cruttondon | 27 June | " | Killingworth |
| Joel Willcox | " | " | " |
| Moses Stoddard | 1 Aug. | 9 | Groton |
| Joseph Lane | 27 June | " | Killingworth |
| Joseph Furbs | " | " | Haddam |
| Ezra Crane | " | " | Killingworth |
| Elias Redfield | " | " | " |
| Elisha White | " | " | |
| John Willcox | " | 18 | Haddam |
| Abner Graves | 10 July | " | Killingworth |
| Will'm Loveridge | " | " | Coalchester |
| Thomas French | 27 June | " | Guilford |
| Nathan Pierson | 10 July | 17 | Killingworth |
| Joel Evats | 27 June | " | " |
| Silas Parmele | " | 25 | " |
| Jonathan Chatfield | 10 July | 31 Oct. | |
| John Widger | " | 20 Nov. | Saybrook |

Nathaniel Crane Serj' No officer Present

[*State Library, Revolution 17.*]

CONNECTICUT LINE, 1777-1781. 213

# EIGHTH REGIMENT—LIEUT.-COL. COM. SHERMAN.

## FIRST COMPANY—LIEUT.-COL. COM. SHERMAN.

Pay Roll for the short Levies Colonel Sherman's Company 8th Connecticut R[         ]

| Names | Comment of Service | Expiration of Service | Towns they belong to |
|---|---|---|---|
| John Adams | July 24 | Dec. 12 | Canterbury |
| David Craft | " | Nov. 4 | Woodstock |
| Phinias Cole | " | Dec. 12 | Woodbury |
| Benjamin Durfee | " | 8 | Canterbury |
| Asahel Herrick | " | 9 | " |
| Jared Hotchkiss | " | 31 | |
| Zenas Goodrich | June 7 | Oct. 11 | Farmington |
| Amaziah Ingram | 10 | Dec. 5 | Sharon |
| Jerod Mott | 7 | 12 | Woodstock |
| Phinias Palmer | 23 | " | Woodbury |
| Uriah Page | 10 | Oct. 25 | Branford |
| Peter Stephens | 13 | Dec. 9 | Canterbury |
| Charles Woodard | 8 | " | " |
| John Benjamens | Aug. 16 | 12 | Saybrook |
| Israil Douglass | " | Nov. 13 | " |
| Calvin Webb | 26 | Dec. 12 | " |
| Felix Griswould | " | Oct. 25 | Winchester |
| Roswell Catlin | " | Dec. 9 | " |
| Peter Corbion | " | 3 | " |
| Daniel Wright | Sep. 7 | 9 | |
| Joseph Frizbie | 3 | Oct. 29 | Branford |
| Ceasor Negro | " | Dec. 12 | " |
| John Wright | July 10 | " | Chatham |
| Joel Clark | " | Sep. 7 | Southington |

I. Sherman Lᵗ Col Comd

[Indorsed] Pay roll of the short Levies Col Shermans Company 8th Regᵗ Decʳ 22ᵈ 1780

[*State Library, Revolution* 17, 54.]

## CAPT. HODGE'S COMPANY.

Pay Roll for the Short Levies in Cap! Hodges Company 8th Connecticut Regiment

| Names | Commencement of Service 1780 | | Expiration of Service 1780 | | Towns they belong to |
|---|---|---|---|---|---|
| Luther Baldwin | July | 17 | Dec. | 8 | Colchester |
| David Cable | | 6 | | 12 | Fairfield |
| Samuel Cole | | 1 | | 8 | Farmington |
| David Culver | | " | | 10 | Colchester |
| Parson Crosby | | 17 | Oct. | 26 | |
| Asa Hyde | | " | Dec. | 8 | Woodstock |
| Oliver Kellogg | | 16 | | " | Colchester |
| Joseph Lyon | | 6 | | 14 | Fairfield |
| Moses Parsons | June | 27 | | 16 | Farmington |
| Aden Palmer | July | 16 | | 10 | Stonington |
| Nathan Roberts | | " | | 8 | Colchester |
| Timothy Smith | | 1 | | " | Farmington |
| Ebenezer Seely | Sep. | 6 | | 12 | Fairfield |
| Simeon Stoddard | | 14 | | 11 | Woodbury |
| Reuben Taylor | July | 16 | | 10 | Colchester |
| Peter Tharp | | 6 | | 8 | Fairfield |
| Amos Wells | | 16 | | 10 | Colchester |
| Nathan Wheeler | Sep. | 6 | | 6 | Woodbury |
| Nath'll Pritchard | | " | | 5 | " |

Camp Highlands Dec' 25th 1780 I Sherman L' Col Comd

[*State Library, Revolution 17, 21*]

## CAPT. MONSON'S COMPANY.

Pay Roll for the Short Levies in Cap! Monsons Company 8th Conecticut Reg!

| Names | Commencement of Service 1778 | | Expiration of Service 1780 | | Town they belong to |
|---|---|---|---|---|---|
| Fradrick Avery | July | 4 | Dec. | 8 | Groton |
| David Avery | | " | | 12 | " |
| Asa Boudish | | 6 | | 8 | Norwich |
| Zalmon Burrit | | 4 | | 4 | Newtown |
| John Bedient | | 6 | | 9 | Fairfield |
| Christopher Bailey | | 1 | | 12 | Haddam |
| Benjamin Chapman | | 6 | | 8 | Stratford |
| Jese Cook | | 7 | | 12 | Coventry |
| William Ellis | | " | | 8 | Milford |
| Williaam Huston | | 4 | | 8 | Vollontown |
| Nathanel Jeffer | | | | | Groton |
| Joseph Liman | | 6 | | 8 | Coventry |
| Solomon Lommis | | " | | 12 | Tolion |
| Joseph Mitchel | | 10 | | " | Fairfield |
| William Rose | | 7 | | 9 | Canaan |
| Enoch Sherman | | " | | 12 | Stratford |
| George Woodburn | | 5 | | 8 | Stonington |
| Selah Stanley | | | | | |

John Hobart Lieut

[*State Library, Revolution 17, 32*]

CONNECTICUT LINE, 1777-1781. 215

## CAPT. COMSTOCK'S COMPANY.

Pay Roll for the Short Levies in Cap<sup>t</sup> Comstock's Company 8<sup>th</sup> Connecticut Regiment

| Names | Commencement of Service 1780 | | Expiration of Service 1780 | | Towns they belong to |
|---|---|---|---|---|---|
| George Bissel | July | 8 | Dec. | 12 | |
| Eliphalet Carpenter | " | " | | 17 | Coventry |
| Isaac Hail | | 22 | | 12 | |
| Jedediah Harger | | 26 | | 5 | |
| Moses Kelley | | 1 | | 9 | Norwalk |
| Stephen Halt | | 10 | | 25 | " |
| Henry Hewit | | 20 | | 12 | Stoningtown |
| Parley Herwington | | 15 | | 10 | |
| Samuel Warren | | 22 | | 9 | |
| David Sullid | | 15 | | 10 | |
| Samuel Mallery | | 25 | | 12 | |
| Joel Sanford | | " | | 3 | |
| George Griffin | | 22 | | 12 | |
| Eldad Barbermore | Aug. | 1 | | 3 | |
| Ruben Hill | | 5 | | 11 | |
| Dudley Stone | | 1 | Sep. | 18 | |
| Abraham Bayley | | 8 | Dec. | 11 | |
| Edward Babbit | July | 27 | | 12 | |
| William Hough | Aug. | 1 | | 18 | |
| Ebenezer Tatchen | Sep. | 1 | | " | |

Sam<sup>ll</sup> Chmstock Cap<sup>t</sup>

[*State Library, Revolution 17, 33.*]

## CAPT. BENTON'S COMPANY.

Pay Roll for the Short Levies in Cap<sup>t</sup> Bentons Comp<sup>y</sup> eighth Connec<sup>t</sup> Reg<sup>t</sup> Com'd<sup>d</sup> by L<sup>t</sup> C Comd<sup>t</sup> Sherman

| Names | Commen<sup>t</sup> of service 1780 | | Expiration of service 1780 | | Towns they belong to |
|---|---|---|---|---|---|
| Sam<sup>ll</sup> Atkins | Aug | 1. | Dec. | 5 | Farmington |
| Thom<sup>s</sup> Brown | July | 20 | | 12 | Chatham |
| Isaac Bristol | | 18 | | 9 | Litchfield |
| Elijah Bill | | " | | 12 | " |
| W<sup>m</sup> Bartholomew | | 19 | | 10 | Lyme |
| Elijah Bartholomew | | " | | 12 | Hebron |
| Zachar<sup>h</sup> Coe | | 18 | | " | Litchfield |
| Cesar Cady | | 17 | | 9 | Killingly |
| Elaphaz Kilborn | | 19 | | 10 | Colchester |
| Humphrey Palmer | | " | | 5 | " |
| James Redfield | | " | | " | Seabrook |
| Miles Wright | | " | Oct. | 25 | Colchester |
| Joseph Stannard | | " | Dec. | 5 | Seabrook |
| Tho<sup>s</sup> Smith | | " | | 81 | Groton |
| Athin (?) Waters | | " | | 9 | Lyme |
| Asa Canada | | 1 | | 12 | Farmington |
| Daniel Chittenden | | " | Oct. | 25 | Guilford |
| Seth Strickland | | " | Dec. | 3 | Middletown |
| Hez<sup>h</sup> Post | | 6 | | " | Seabrook |
| Joshua Osborn | | 22 | | 12 | Waterbury |
| Shubal Painter | Sep. | 1 | | 9 | Newhaven |
| Asahel Ives | | 11 | | 12 | Woodbury |
| David Martin | | " | | 9 | " |

James Olmsted Lieu<sup>t</sup>

[*State Library, Revolution 17, 35.*]

## CAPT. BRIGHAM'S COMPANY.

Pay Roll of the Short Levies in Cap' Brighams Comp'y 8th Cone' Reg'
Com'd by I Sherman L' Col° Comd'

| Names | Commencement of Service 1780 | | Expiration of Service 1780 | | Place of Aboad |
|---|---|---|---|---|---|
| Asahel Woodworth | July | 18 | Dec. | 12 | Lebanon |
| Sam' Whitney | " | " | " | " | Killingworth |
| Edward Spergar (?) | | 24 | | 5 | Groaten |
| Elisha Thorington | | 18 | | 9 | E. Haddam |
| Will'm Spencer | | " | | 16 | " |
| Abraham Buckley | Sep. | 1 | | 9 | Seybrook |
| James Brown | July | 24 | | " | Ashford |
| Joseph Buird (?) | | 28 | | 8 | Farmington |
| Joseph Collins | Aug. | 11 | | 12 | Derbey |
| Gideon Jackson | | " | | " | " |
| Daniel Dorman | July | 5 | | 9 | Coventry |
| W'm Lucas | | 4 | | 3 | Middletown |
| Roswell Mallison | | 3 | | 5 | Groton |
| Nicholas Morgan | | 8 | | 11 | " |
| James Parker | | 5 | | 12 | Coventry |
| Chester Rogers | | 24 | | 9 | Ashford |
| George Sealy | | " | | " | Groton |
| Asehel Hull | | 18 | | 5 | Glastenbury |
| Seth Lovel | Aug. | 12 | | 16 | Mansfield |
| Gideon Tucker | Sep. | 1 | | 9 | Seybrook |
| John Bartoo | | 12 | | 8 | Farmington |
| Chatham Freeman | | " | | 12 | N. Haven |
| Joseph Goff | June | 10 | | 81 | Litchfield |
| Jesse Torry, Fifer | July | 18 | | 9 | Lebanon |

Nath' Thornton Serj'

[*State Library, Revolution 17, 45.*]

## CAPT. SANFORD'S COMPANY.

Pay Roll of the Short Levies of Cap' Sanfords Comp'y 8th Cone' Reg'
com'd by I Sherman L' Col Comd'

| Names | Commencement Ser'e 1780 | | Expiration of Service 1780 | | Place of Aboad |
|---|---|---|---|---|---|
| Dan Beaumont | July | 20 | Dec. | 8 | Lebanon |
| Elijah Battis | | 26 | | 10 | N. Haven |
| Richard Booge | | 15 | Nov. | 1 | E. Haddam |
| Sam' Blaksley | Sep. | 12 | Dec. | 5 | Southington |
| Stephen Chapel | June | 27 | | 9 | Coventry |
| Oliver Churchel | July | 26 | | " | Woodbury |
| Daniel Grover | June | 27 | | 8 | Coventry |
| Sam' Green | July | 27 | | " | Milford |
| Ebenez' Humberfield | | 26 | | 11 | N. Haven |
| Ichabod Peeva (?) | June | 24 | | 16 | Voluntown |
| Comfot Robinson | July | 19 | | 5 | Killensly |
| Jason Robinson | | " | | 10 | " |
| James Salley | | 15 | | 81 | E. Haddam |
| Jonathan Stone | | 19 | | 5 | Killensley |
| Moses Scofield | | 17 | | 12 | Lebanon |
| David Sanford | | 27 | | 5 | Milford |
| John Wottson | | 15 | | 9 | E. Haddam |
| Jonathan Willey | | " | | 16 | " |

Sam' Halt Ens'n

[*State Library, Revolution 17, 46.*]

## CAPT. RICE'S COMPANY.

Return of the Short Levies in Capt Rices Company in the 8ᵗʰ Connt Regᵗ Decʳ 22ᵈ 1780

| Names | Commencement of Service 1780 | Expiration of Service 1780 | Towns |
|---|---|---|---|
| Job Bester | July 8 | Dec. 16 | Cantibury |
| Jonah Bishop | Sep. 11 | 11 | N. Haven |
| Isaac Coopper | July 7 | 12 | " |
| Christopher Crandel | Sep. 15 | " | Plainfield |
| James Freeman | July 2 | 5 | Grotton |
| Nathael Gates | 17 | 9 | E. Haddam |
| Elijah Harger | 10 | " | Hartland |
| Asahel Harvey | 17 | 12 | E. Haddam |
| Crippen Hurd | " | 3 | " |
| Joseph Jackson | 10 | 5 | Windham |
| Samˡˡ Leavens | 16 | 9 | Killingly |
| Timothy Leek | 28 | 16 | N. Haven |
| John Lord | 17 | 12 | E. Haddam |
| Calvin Mallery | 28 | " | N. Haven |
| Ira Manvill | " | 3 | Woodbury |
| Philep Nickels | 15 | Nov. 10 | Ashford |
| Burdan Potter | 8 | Dec. 9 | Vollingtown |
| Daniel Purkens | 28 | " | Mansfield |
| Ezra Sumner | 13 | 8 | Ashford |
| Isaac Town | 16 | Oct. 25 | Killingsly |
| Wᵐ Tyler | 14 | Dec. 9 | Thomson |

David Dixson Serjᵗ

[*State Library, Revolution 17, 52.*]

## RETURNS FROM MILITIA, 1780.

### FIRST REGIMENT.

Col Storrs's Return of Recruits for ye Amarican Army July 20, 1780 To Brigadr Genll J. Douglas Esqr of ye 5th Brigade of Militia in the State of Connecticut. The following is a Return of Names of the Recruits for the Continental Service Inlisted or Detachd & from what Town & Compy & how Conveyd or Sent forward to the Army from the first Regt in Said Brigade.

| Mens Names | Of what Town | with whome sent |
|---|---|---|
| David Carpenter | Mansfield | Sent forward |
| Daniel Preston Jun | " | Capt Shumway |
| Ebenr Cary | " | at Home unwell |
| Levy Dow | Coventry | Sent on |
| Time Rose | " | not Joind |
| John Gove | " | Sent on |
| Asa Manly | " | not Joind |
| Elisha Rodgers | Ashford | Capt Shumway |
| Amos Dowset | " | " |
| Lawrance Dowset | " | " |
| Asa Mason | Mansfield | " |
| Joseph Limon | Coventry | Sent on pr Col Brown |
| Lemll Parke | " | " |
| Samll Porter | " | " |
| Noah Carpenter | " | " |
| Elisha Dunham | Mansfield | by Capt Shumway |
| Nathan Parker | " | " |
| Samll Millington | " | " |
| Moses Bicknal | " | Sent on |
| James Brown | Ashford | |
| David Allen | | |
| Thomas Wing | Ashford | |
| Peter Aspenwall | Mansfield | Sent on |
| Israel Balch Jun | " | |
| Benja Bugbe | " | Capt Webb |
| Jonathan Basset | " | Capt Shumway |
| Ely Church | " | |
| Richd Crosbey | " | Capt Shumway |
| Robart Hammon | " | " |
| Walter Cory | " | " |
| Elijah Porter | " | " |
| Daniel Preston | " | " |
| Rhodolfus Howkins | Coventry | Sent on pr Col Brown |
| Asa Boodish | " | " |
| Peter Dun | " | " |
| Edward Pelham | " | " |
| Fredk Woodward | " | " |
| Danll Dorman | " | " |
| Caleb Hende | Ashford | Capt Shumway |
| Wm Southworth | " | " |
| James Chandler | " | " |
| Simeon Snow | " | " |
| Elisha Royce | " | " |

CONNECTICUT LINE, 1777-1781.        219

| Mens Names | Of what Town | with whome sent |
|---|---|---|
| Samuel Utley | Ashford | Cap¹ Shumway |
| John Goold | " | " |
| Moses Fitts | " | " |
| Benjⁿ Barna | " | " |
| Jedadᵃʰ Ward | " | " |
| Chester Rogers | " | " |
| Jesse Cook | Coventry | pʳ Col Brown |
| Joseph Waldo | " | " |
| Joel Fowler | " | " |
| Elihue Benton | " | " |
| George Bissel | " | " |
| James Parker | " | " |
| Danˡˡ Grover | " | " |
| Jeduthan Dimok | Mansfield | Cap¹ Shumway |
| Varney Fellows | " | " |
| Jesse Waldo Jr | " | " |
| Jeremᵃ Hedges | " | " |
| Amasa Royce | " | " |
| John Bugbe | " | Sent on |
| Benjⁿ Peirce | " | Cap¹ Shumway |
| Phillip Nichols | Ashford | " |
| Elisha Royce | " | |
| Steaphⁿ Eaton | " | |
| Joshua Rindel | " | " |
| Robart Snow Jr | " | " |
| Joseph Tarbox | " | " |
| Danˡˡ B. Perkins | Mansfield | Cap¹ Shumway |
| Eleazʳ Barrows | " | " |
| Joel Davis | " | " |
| Asa Bowdish | " | Joined |
| Jonathan Baker | " | Cap¹ Shumway |
| Wᵐ Eaton | " | " |
| Thᵒ Atwood | " | " |
| Ethan Barrows | " | " |
| Nathˡˡ Conant | " | " |
| Nathˡˡ Fenton | " | " |
| Augustus Storrs | " | " |
| Amos Thomson | " | " |
| Jobe Robbens | Ashford | " |
| Samˡˡ Bass | " | |
| John Hill | " | Joinᵈ |

To the Honᵇˡᵉ Brigadʳ Genˡˡ Douglas Esqʳ The within & foregoing Return is made in Consequence of your Orders of the 20ᵗʰ July & Submitted by your honʳˢ most Obedᵗ humble Servᵗ

Exp Storrs Colᵒ

[*Connecticut Historical Society.*]

## NINTH REGIMENT.

A Bounty Roll for Recruits raised in the 9ᵗʰ Militia Regᵗ to serve in the Continental Army for three years

Archibald Mott          George States
John Robinson           Thomas Chapman
Jack Spry               John McNulty
Timothy Ford

John Mead Colᵒ & Muster Master of the Recruits & three Months Men from the 9ᵗʰ Regᵗ &c 1780

[*State Library, Revolution 17, 79.*]

## TWELFTH REGIMENT.

A Return of Inlisted & Detached Men to Serve in Continental Service untill yᵉ last day of Decʳ Next Certifying whether Inlisted or Detachᵈ yᵉ Compʸ to which they belong place of abode by whom receipted or how conveyed to yᵉ Army &c. Belonging to yᵉ 12ᵗʰ Regᵗ of foot in the Militia of the State of Connecticut.

| Inlisted or Detachᵈ | Mens Names | Place of Abode |
|---|---|---|
| Inlisted | Asahel Woodworth | Lebanon |
| | Joseph Squebb | |
| | Squire Gooff | Hebron |
| | Thoˢ Marvin | |
| | Abel Spicer | Lebanon |
| | John Porter | |
| | Jesse Lyman | |
| | Linus Pineo | |
| | Nathˡˡ Little | |
| | Ebenʳ Silden | |
| | James Lathrop | |
| | Etkanah Jones | Hebron |
| | Asa Blish | |
| | Lawrance Powers | |
| | Ezra Woodworth | Lebanon |
| | Bigelow Waters | Hebron |
| | Solomon Saveroy | Lebanon |
| | Isaac Owen | Hebron |
| | Samˡˡ Thomas | Lebanon |
| Detachᵈ | George Lampshire | |
| Inlisted | Joshua Rennolds | |
| | Elnathan Garcy | |
| | Benjⁿ Woodworth | |
| | Isaa Lyman | |
| | Jonah Thomas | |
| | Moses Scofield | |
| | Elihu Jones | |
| | Samˡˡ Woodbridge | |
| | Wᵐ Winslow | Hebron |
| | Jacob Cooper | |
| | Jonᵗʰ Metcalf | Lebanon |
| | Zadock Lee | |
| Detachᵈ | Charles Hyde | |
| | Benjⁿ Payne Junʳ | gone out yᵉ State &c |
| | Nathan Starkweather | |
| | Derias Dewey | |
| | Thoˢ Fitch | |
| | David Deans | |
| | Samˡˡ Lyman | |
| | Ezekiel Horton | Hebron |
| | Epafroditus Loveland | |
| | Joseph Smith | |
| Inlisted | Elisha Lyman | Lebanon |
| | Nathˡˡ Fitch | |
| | Simon Newcomb | |
| Inlisted | Timᵒ Clark | |
| | John Powers | Hebron |
| | Nero Tom | Lebanon |

CONNECTICUT LINE, 1777-1781.

| Inlisted or Detach'd | Mens Names | Place of Abode |
|---|---|---|
| | Joseph Bloss | Hebron |
| | Sol° Day | |
| | Sol° Hayward | |
| | Jon'th Hutchinson | |
| | Sam'll Jones | |
| | Uriah Phinney | Lebanon |
| | James Downer | |
| | Dan Beamount | |
| | Asehel Kingsley | |
| | Jon'th Hutchinson Jun'r | Hebron |
| | W'm Eldrige | |
| | Eben'r Clark | Lebanon |
| | Robert Holdrige | Hebron |
| | Nero Coss | Lebanon |
| | Roger Woodworth | |
| | Jared Phelps | Hebron |
| | Joseph Wright | Lebanon |
| | Asa Harris | |
| | Ezekiel Avery | |
| | Dan Lyman | |
| | Aaron Overton | Norwich |
| Detach'd | Dan'll Emons | Hebron |
| | Asa Willey | |
| | Bethuel Phelps | |
| | Asa Fullor | |
| | Sam'l Horton | |
| | Walter Hunt | Lebanon |
| | Jn° Patrige Bisset | |
| Inlisted | Jon'th Bill | |
| Detach'd | Ambrose Woodward | |
| Inlisted | Beriah Skinner | Hebron |
| | John Carrior | |
| | Joel Mack | |

Errors Excepted

Lebanon 10th Aug't 1780

A True Return of Drafted & Inlisted men &c as by the Returns Rec'd &c. Test P'r me, Jeremiah Mason Col°

Sundry of the within Named Detached men have Since the Date of this Return March'd on to Camp &c & have not Rec'd no Returns Since of the Cap't &c.  J. M. C°

[*Connecticut Historical Society.*]

## SIXTEENTH REGIMENT.

State of Connecticut To Nehemiah Beardsley Paymaster to the Recruits raised within the 16th Regiment to join the Connecticut Line in the Continental Army in the year 1780.  D'r.

Bounties paid them in July 1780, and for Blankets as follows

Job Hodges
Abel Guthrie
John Mooney
Levi Barnum
Reuben Judd
Ezekiel Whitney
Josiah Nichols
Daniel Anderson

Samuel Price
Daniel Gregory
Joseph Munrow
Frederick Tubbs
James Roberts
Joseph C. Hawley
Nehemiah Olmstead
Clement Fairchild

Mills Deforrest
John Carmon
Elijah Hurd
Jonathan Sherwood
Samuel Bradley
William Benedict
Abraham Vanshoik
Jacob Crow
Amon Crow
Nathaniel Porter
Matthew Clark
Zachᵉ Brush
Saunders Perry
Joseph Olmstead
Zalmon Burrit
Luke Roberts
Benjamin Peck
Levi Osborn
John Barnum
Henry Knap
Jared Baldwin
Joseph Starr
Phillip Wheeler
Elijah Kellogg
Uriah Nash
William Commins
Ebenezer Hawley
Samuel Stebben
Stephen Northrop
Abram Jillit
Junus Sillick
Isaac Blackman
James Beardsley
John Finch
Stephen Barnum
Jeremiah Lockwood
John Gilbert
Abijah Osburn
Jared Dunning
Matthew Olmstead
Timothy Barnum
Clark Hide
Stephen Bennet
Austin Bishop

[*State Library, Revolution* 17, 72.]

## TWENTY FIRST REGIMENT.

A Return of the Men Inlisted or Detached from the 21: Reg$^t$ To Join the Continental Army July 12$^{th}$ 1780.

| What Company | Mens Names | Place of Abode | Inlisted Detached | Term Engaged |
|---|---|---|---|---|
| Cap$^t$ Johnson | Archalus Ams Negro<br>Ebenezer Fitch | Canterbury<br>" | Inlisted<br>Detached | till last of Dec$^r$<br>" |
| Cap$^t$ Ransford | Adams Stevens hir$^d$ by norwich<br>Peter Stevens d$^o$ Colchester | Canterbury<br>" | Inlisted<br>" | till last of Dec$^r$<br>" |
| Cap$^t$ Butt | Job Barstow<br>Charles Fred$^c$ Woodard<br>Asahel Herrick<br>John Adams<br>Ebenezer Shaw<br>Jared Mott Hir$^d$ by y$^e$ lite Horse | "<br>"<br>"<br>"<br>"<br>" | "<br>"<br>"<br>"<br>"<br>" | "<br>"<br>"<br>"<br>"<br>" |
| Cap$^t$ Bacon | David Eanos<br>Charles Justin<br>Thomas Scranton | "<br>"<br>" | "<br>"<br>" | During y$^e$ War<br>"<br>three years |
| Cap$^t$ Hibberd | Benjamin Darfee<br>Epaphrus Curtiss hir$^d$ by lite horse<br>Nicholus Falkner<br>Paul Harriss | Canterbury<br>"<br>"<br>" | Inlisted<br>"<br>"<br>Detach$^d$ | till last of Dec$^r$<br>"<br>"<br>" |
| Cap$^t$ Woodard | Joseph Dunam Hir$^d$ by Preston | " | inlisted | " |
| Cap$^t$ Tyler | Sam$^{ll}$ Cleaveland hir$^d$ by Pomfred | " | " | " |
| Cap$^t$ Branch | John Jack Negro<br>Stephen Elsworth hir$^d$ by lite horse<br>Seth Lovell | Plainfield<br>"<br>" | "<br>"<br>" | for 8 years<br>till last of Dec$^r$<br>" |

| What Company | Mens Names | Place of Abode | Inlisted | Term Engaged |
|---|---|---|---|---|
| Cap¹ Waterman | Jonathan Whippal | Plainfield | Inlisted | till last of Dec' |
| | Charles Waterman | " | " | " |
| | Thomas Simmons | " | " | " |
| | Jabez Bottom | " | " | |
| | James Fuller | " | " | |
| Cap¹ Bottom | James Patrick hir⁴ by lite horse | | | |
| | Job Phillips | " | " | " |
| | Samuel Tracy | " | " | " |
| | John Fagins | " | " | " |
| | Daniel Herrington | " | " | " |
| | Joshua Patrick hir⁴ by lite Horse | " | " | " |
| Cap¹ Dunlap | Reuben Bryant | " | " | " |
| | Edward Sparger | " | " | " |
| | Jeduthun Herd | " | " | " |
| | John Lovejoy | " | " | " |
| | Isaac Herrick | " | " | " |
| | Abraham Culver | " | " | " |
| | Joseph Boyd hir⁴ by lite Horse | " | " | " |
| | David Welch | " | " | " |
| | Samuel Kingsbury | " | " | " |
| | Charles Waterman | " | " | " |
| Cap¹ Baley | Alexander Miller Jun' | Voluntown | Inlisted | till last of Dec' |
| | John Phillips | " | " | " |
| | William Alma | | | " |
| Cap¹ Edmond | Henry Hewett | " | " | " |
| | Hugh Canady | " | " | " |
| | George Griffeth | | | |

| | | | |
|---|---|---|---|
| Cap.t Campbell | Elijah Fayer | " | " |
| | Elisha Card | " | " |
| | Jonathan Parker | " | " |
| | Eleazer Lewis | " | " |
| | David Franklin | " | " |
| | Robert Jackson hir.d by norwich | " | " |
| Cap.t Dixson | Jonathan Jenks | " | " |
| | Abel Franklin | " | " |
| | Burden Potter | " | " |
| | Ichabod Peavy | " | " |
| | Jo.s Griffin hir.d by y.e lite horse | " | " |
| | Miles Jordon | " | " |
| | Daniel Dowd | " | " |
| | David Franklin | " | till last of Dec.r next |
| Cap.t Robbins | Thomas Palmer | " | " |
| | Daniel Palmer | " | " |
| | Jonas Randal | " | |
| | Will.m Heughston hir.d by Groton | | |
| Cap.t Cady | George Little | Killingley | " |
| | Paul Griffis | " | " |
| Cap.t Eaton | Canterbury July 24.th 1780 | | |

To Gen.ll Douglas

Obadiah Johnson Colo.

[*Connecticut Historical Society.*]

## MISCELLANEOUS RETURNS, 1780.

A Return of the Recruits Rased by the Defrant Towns to Fill up the Conn$^t$ Line of the Army for Durin the War or 3 years.

| Mens Names | Date of Inlistment | Tarm of Servis | Towns to which they Belong |
|---|---|---|---|
| Darius Orcutt | Nov$^m$ 23$^{rd}$ 1780 | 3 years | Ashford |
| Charles Repley | Dec$^r$ 27$^{th}$ 1780 | " | Windham |
| Jube Deyer | Jan$^{ry}$ 11$^{th}$ 1781 | " | " |
| Daniel Woodward | Nov 24$^{th}$ 1780 | " | " |
| John Dingley | Dec$^r$ 15$^{th}$ 1780 | " | " |
| Joseph Barrows | Dec$^r$ 26$^{th}$ 1780 | " | " |
| Jed$^{ah}$ Hebard | Dec$^r$ 4$^{th}$ 1780 | " | " |
| Roswell Simons | Dec$^r$ 27$^{th}$ 1780 | " | " |
| John Gilburt | Do 26$^{th}$ 1780 | War | " |
| Elijah Randall | Dec$^r$ 8$^{th}$ 1780 | 3 years | " |
| Zopher Roberson | Dec$^r$ 8$^{th}$ 1780 | " | " |
| Abner Lilley | Dec$^r$ 8$^{th}$ 1780 | " | " |
| Eliphalit Spafford | Dec$^r$ 28$^{th}$ 1780 | " | " |
| John Abbe | Jan 1$^{th}$ 1781 | " | " |
| Nathanel Abbe | Jan$^y$ 15$^{th}$ 1781 | " | " |
| Joseph Abbe | Jan$^y$ 17$^{th}$ 1781 | " | " |
| Stephen Hall | Jan$^y$ 10$^{th}$ 1781 | " | Fairfeld |
| Abner Hills | Feb$^y$ 8$^{th}$ 1781 | " | Lebanon |
| Joshua Bill | Feb$^y$ 8$^{th}$ 1781 | War | " |

Lebanon Feb$^y$ 9$^{th}$ 1781

A Trew Return Test John Ball L$^t$ & Recruiting Officer

[*Connecticut Historical Society.*]


A List of the Names of Six Months Men for the Town of Hartford Decm$^r$ 1780

Asa Bunce
William Hinsdel
James Ensign
James Duggans
Alvin Bigelow
George Blackburn
William Wickham
Daniel Roberts
Thomas Wadsworth 3$^d$
Seth Talcott
David Cannady
Daniel Brewer Jun$^r$
George Abbe
George Burk
Isaac Bellows
Horatio Wales
William Boardman
Hezekiah Wadsworth
Tim$^o$ Sedgwick
John Wilson Jun$^r$
Stephen Burnham

W$^m$ Robbarts
Tho$^s$ Keeney
Amos Loveland
Roderick Seymour
W$^m$ Sedgwick
Elnathan Keyes
W$^m$ Ellis
Elisha Seymour
Ardon Seymour
Daniel Wadsworth
Jacob Augustus
Asaph Burley
Benjamin Porter Jun$^r$
Tim$^o$ Anderson
James Olcott
Tim$^o$ Fisher
Zenas Burnham
Allen Webster
Samuel Dalliber
John Thomson
Josiah Gates

[*Connecticut Historical Society.*]

## CONNECTICUT LINE, 1777-1781.

A Return of the Names of the Noncommissioned Officers and Soldiers who have Inlisted from the Town of Salisbury into the Continental Service in the Connecticut Line and other Regiments during the War and are now in Service

In Meggs Regiment
  Serg$^t$ John McLean
  " W$^m$ Tupper
  " Henry Hull
  " Gamaliel Terry
  Corp$^l$ James Bradly
  " Daniel Hull
  " Amasa Grenoll
  Fif$^r$ Jacob McLean
  Isaac Cool
  Champion Ackly
  Artemus Blodget
  Nath$^l$ Emerson
  Henry FitzJeroll
  Joseph T. Fitch
  Salmon Bostwick
  Benj$^n$ Graves
  George Griswould
  Sam$^l$ Griswould
  Moses Hull
  Jonathan Hull
  Billy Munger
  Simmeon Meggs
  Eliphalet Owen
  Asa Owen
  Phineas Strong
  Martin Tubbs
  W$^m$ White
  Solo$^m$ Whitney
  Jobe Towsley
  W$^m$ Gates
  Hyman Cool

In Swift's Reg$^t$
  John Holly
  Hildrick Barret
  Peter Surdam
  Benj$^n$ Scovel
In Bradley's Reg$^t$
  Isaac Welden
In Sam$^l$ B. Webbs Reg$^t$
  Daniel Bostwick
In Warner's Reg$^t$
  Sam$^l$ Stoddard
  Tho$^s$ Chipman
  W$^m$ Eno
  John Coon   Prisoner
  James Coon
  Ozias Baker
  Reuben Strong
  George Whitman **Prisoner**
  John Field
  George McCarter **Presoner**
In Hazens Reg$^t$
  Serg$^t$ W$^m$ Baker
  W$^m$ Roberts
  Benj$^n$ Daverson
  Heber Griswould
  Jacob Parish
  Micael Welch
  Reuben Clemons
In Sheldon's Reg$^t$ of Light Dragoons
  Benj$^n$ Hows
  Benj$^n$ Everest
  David Owen
In Col$^o$ Baldwins Core of Artificers
  Aaron Swetland

Salisbury Nov$^r$ y$^e$ 27$^{th}$ 1780

[*State Library, Hebard Papers*, 51.]

Return of Men who have Deserted from the 2$^d$ Connecticut Brigade Since Jan$^y$ 1$^{st}$ 1778. Springfield Apr$^{ll}$ 25$^{th}$ 1778

| Mens Names | Places of Abode |
|---|---|
| Q$^r$ M$^r$ Serg$^t$ Stratton | Lyme |
| D$^m$ Maj$^r$ Buckingham | Saybrook |
| Will$^m$ Manning | Norwich |
| Noah Pease | " |
| Ebenez$^r$ Pelton | Groton |
| Jabaz Metcalf | Norwich |
| Jonath$^n$ Nicholas | Mansfield |
| Will$^m$ Hollowell | N. London |
| David Fenn | Colchester |
| George Manwaring | N London |
| D$^m$ Abraham Petenger | Lyme |
| Sam$^{ll}$ Stark | Colchester |

| Mens Names | Places of abode |
|---|---|
| 2ᵈ Regᵗ | |
| Amas Fuller | Fishkills N.Y. |
| John Widger | Saybrook |
| Daniel Evens | Woodstock |
| 5ᵗʰ Regᵗ | |
| Isaac Grant | Litchfield |
| Jacob Poson | Transient Person |
| James Stanton | Burlington |
| John Gould | Litchfield |
| Ephraim Whelor | Redding |
| James Hews | Hartford |
| Barack Taylor | Fairfield |
| Cash Africa | Litchfield Since Joined |
| Jabaz Williams | Redding |
| 7ᵗʰ Regᵗ | |
| John More | Branford |
| Edward Booth | N Milford |
| John Lawrance | Canaan |
| Christopher Blake | Mass. |

N.B. There is a mistake in the above date, it ought to be Janʸ 1ˢᵗ 80.

[*State Library, Revolution* 17, 89.]

## OFFICERS AND SOLDIERS MARRIED.

[This list is undated, but is placed following other lists of 1780 and preceding lists of 1781 in the volume of records as now bound.]

List of Officers & Soldiers Married

N. Haven
Akin James Sej't
Alley William
Alling Jon'th
Bains Sol'n Serj't
Baher Edward d°
Brown Henry Corp'l
Brochett Hez'h
Bishop Nathan'l
Blacksly Zelous
Britton Samuel
Bradly Oliver
Clerk David Serj't
Clark Joel
Coshall Thomas
Clark Martin
Doyle Hugh
Davis James
Dayton Israel
Dickerman Joseph
Eagelston David
Foot Isaac Serj't
Ford Daniel
Gibson Samuel
Huse Bodwell
Hoel Nicholas
Hull Samuel
Harding Frad'k
How Joshua
Hunt Richard
Johnson Abr'm Corp'l
Joslin John
King George
Levensworth Eli Maj'r
Lord Jabez
Lynds John
Mansfield Jo's Cap't
Munson W'm Cap't
Miles John Leu't
Mix Tim° Leu't
Moultrop Jo's Serj't
Mallery Amos Corp'l
Moltrop Stephen
Melone Daniel
Martin Lewis
Matthews Robert
Mansfield Dan

Moss John
Moss Daniel
Ohara Timothy
Prentice Jonas Cap't
Parmele Jer'h Cap't
Potter Israel Leiut
Potter Moses
Parker Edmond
Robinson Jared Leiut
Robinson Samuel
Robinson Thomas
Sherman W'm Cap't
Sherman John Leiut
Sporry Channcey
Smith Ambrose
Stevens William
Sugden Ab'm
Stockwell Abel
Squier Daniel
Sanford Thomas
Squier Stent Sam'l
Simpson Robert
Shepherd John
Trowbridge John Leiut
Troop John Leiut
Thomas John
    Samuel
Tolles Elnathan
Townsend Solomon
Thomas James
Todd Yale
Thomas Ephraim
Vorguson John
Wooster Thomas Cap't
Wood Elisha
Wilson John
White Sam'l Jun'r
Walter W'm
Wilds Jonathan
Zandor Gad

WINDHAM COUNTY*
Woodstock
Bartholomew John
Bruce Ely
Clark Asael Ens'n
Green John Corp'l

---

*The Woodstock names with their Windham County heading appear to have been inserted after the first writing of the document.

Hambden W<sup>m</sup>
Holmes David D<sup>r</sup>
Lyon Asa Q.M.
Manning W<sup>m</sup> Cap<sup>t</sup>
Powers Nathan
Smith Dan<sup>ll</sup> Corp<sup>l</sup>

### Waterbury

Barns Daniel
Basset W<sup>m</sup>
Camp Samuel
Calkins Israel
Clark Richard
Cole John
Cook Joel
Camp Sam<sup>ll</sup> Jun<sup>r</sup>
Curtis Stephen
Dunbar Amos
Dutton Titus Serj<sup>t</sup>
Davis Jon<sup>a</sup>
    · Stephen
Dunbar Miles
Edwards Nath<sup>ll</sup> Leiu<sup>t</sup>
Fallandon John
Fulford John Serj<sup>t</sup>
Graves Simeon
Gaylord Benj<sup>a</sup>
Hickok W<sup>m</sup> Jun<sup>r</sup>
Hubbel James
Hickok Elisha
Hall Nathaniel
Judd Stephen
    Bruster
Lewis Sam<sup>l</sup> Serj<sup>t</sup>
Parker Eliab
Pardey Jonathan
Prichard George Jun<sup>r</sup>
Parker Isaac
Pendleton Daniel
Pressen Amasa
Rice Nehemiah
Robarts Abiel
    Joel
Smith John
Southmaid W<sup>m</sup>
Sanford Ezekiel
Smith Lus (?)
Scovill Stephen
Smith Samuel
Smith David Maj<sup>r</sup>
Seward Nathan
Thair Asa
Tuttle Ezekiel
    Timothy
    Jabesh
    Timothy Ens<sup>n</sup>
    Hezekiah
Terril Joel

Upson Ezekiel Serj<sup>t</sup>
Welton Stephen Jun<sup>r</sup>
Williams Obed

### Durham

Cook Tho<sup>s</sup>
Hinman Husted Corp<sup>l</sup>
Jonson W<sup>m</sup>
Strong Eliakim Serj<sup>t</sup>
Squire Saxton J<sup>r</sup>
Seward Sam<sup>l</sup>
Squire Abiather

### Derby

Allin David
Baldwin Silas
Farmer Tho<sup>s</sup> Ens<sup>n</sup>
Foot Ezra
Freeman Frank
Humphry E. Cap<sup>t</sup>
Hotchkiss Levi Lieu<sup>t</sup> (?)
Hawken Zadock
Moses Jonas
Murry Abr<sup>m</sup>
O'Kane Jon<sup>h</sup>
Prichard James Serj<sup>t</sup>
Prindle J. Enos
Rigs Labor
Rigs James
Tomlinson David Ens<sup>n</sup>
Warner Eben<sup>r</sup> (?) Serj<sup>t</sup>
Woster Henry
Washburn Benj<sup>a</sup>
Watreus Rich<sup>d</sup>
White Jo<sup>s</sup>
Whitny Henry P.M.
Wakelee Jon<sup>th</sup>

### Wallingford

Antony John
Bradley Daniel
Barns Moses
Bristol Benj<sup>n</sup>
Barns David
Chamberlain Ep<sup>m</sup> Cap<sup>t</sup>
Francis John
Hart Benj<sup>a</sup>
Hall Rufus
Hastings John
Holt Samuel
Hitchcock Lem<sup>l</sup> Leiut
    Thomas
Johnson John
Jones Thomas
Lewis Ebenezar
Munson Levi Leiut
Mansfield John Leiut
Mix Thomas Jun<sup>r</sup>

CONNECTICUT LINE, 1777-1781.     231

Parker Elisha
Page Timothy
Peck Charles Serj' of Artill
Parker Benjamin
Shallor Joseph Leiut
Smith Daniel
Stone David
Webb Gideon
Yale Nash

### Branford
Barker Sam¹ Cap'
Bunnil Abrahᵐ
Bagdon Cesar
Foot Ebenʳ
Garrit (?) John
Hubbard John Ensⁿ
Harrison Jairus Serj'
Hoadley Sam¹ Serj'
Janes Joseph
Norton Benjⁿ Ensⁿ
Otis Joseph
Potter Stephen Capt
Smith Jordan
Turner Jacob
White John Ensⁿ

### Guilford
Ball John Leiut
Benton Edward Serj'
Bishop Thalmeno
Doud Moses
Fowler Caleb Corp.
Hall Stephen Cap'
Hall Philemon Leiut.
Handy Samuel Serj'
Hotchkiss Ira
Johnson Isaac
Norton Rufus Corpor.
Elon
Niger Phillip
Pelton Benjamin
Strong John Serj'
Thomson David Serj'
Teal Samuel
Whaler Thomas

### Milford
Bristol Jonathan
Ben Thomas
Beebe Joel
Belding John
Burk John
Davidson Isaac
Frost Samuel alias Cornelius Cahales
Hodg David
Hooker John

Hine Titus
Seward Daniel
Steward John
Sharp Joseph
Seward William
Sanford Sam¹ Cap'
Smith Wᵐ Leiuᵗ

## COUNTY OF NEW LONDON
### Norwich
Bill Bariah Cap'
Bishop Nathˡˡ Leiut
Bennet Benjⁿ
Bryant John
Brewster Hezʰ
Bebee Ammon
Bond John
Chapman Joˢ Leiut
Cook Case
Comstock Gideon
Carr James Miller
Corwin Jonᵗʰ
Corwin Selah
Clark Jacob
Durkee John Colᵒ
Downing Chrisʳ
Ellis John Chapⁿ
Fox Jacob Leiuᵗ
Fanning Charles Leiuᵗ
Gardner Sherman
Gardner D. Tubbs
Hide James Ensⁿ
Maning Wᵐ
Mitchel George
Olin William
Peck Darius Leiuᵗ
Perrigo William
Pollard Wᵐ
Plumb Peter
Qui Libeus
Read Ruben
Sydleman John
Spicer Samuel
Stillman Robert
Starkweather Asa
Troop Benjⁿ Majʳ
Tracy Hugh Leiuᵗ
Tracy Wᵐ Ensⁿ
Tracy Moses
Waterman Eberʳ Jʳ
Webb Jonathan
Wedge Joshua
Walton Silas

### Killingsworth
Baldwin Caleb Lieuᵗ
Crane John
Hall Sam¹ Corp'

Leet Allen
Rumbelo Thomas
Stephens Aaron Cap⁺
Stevens Peter

### Preston

Aldrige William
Burnham Asa
Eavan Isaac
Guyant Luke
Hollay Joseph
Jackson Thomas
Miles Charles Leiut
M⁰Daniel James
Meach Joshua
Roup Simeon
Storry Silas
Sears Obediah
Tyler Nathan

### Saybrook

Baldwin Henry
Butler Stephen
Chapman Daniel Serj⁺
Comstock Samuel
Dudley Zebulon
Graham Silas
Grimes Cyrus
Grant James
Hull Oliver
Harvey W^m
Jones Aaron
Kirkland             Cap⁺
Lord William
    Jeremiah Serj⁺
Lay Asa Leiut
Negro Briston
Newel Robort
Pratt Ethan
Shirman (?) Sam¹ Serj⁺
Shipman John
Stevens Elijah
Tooley Andrew
Thompson Epaphras
Warden Isaac
Waterhouse Stephen
White Oliver
Widger John
Wright Ezekiel

### Lyme

Anderson Tho⁸ Leiu⁺
Burnam Joseph
Beckwit Phin⁸
Boge Ichabod
Corwin Sela
Dodge Daniel
De Wolf Stephen

D Wolf Edward
Hyde Rufus
Herron John
Hayns Jonathan
Hudson Eleazer
Harrison W^m
Lee Elisha Cap⁺
Lee Ezra Leui⁺
Lay Richard
Marther Elias L⁺
Miller Nathan
M⁰Coy Alex^r
Peck Silas
Peck Silas J^r
Reed Enoch Cap⁺
Rogers Lemuel
Rogers Joseph
Roach John
Sill David Col⁰
Selden Ezra Cap⁺
Spencer Ichabad L⁺
Sanders John
Sawyer Asa
Sullard Jacob
Smith Enoch
Wade John
Wilson George
Wade Martin

### Groton

Avery Thomas Lie⁺
Avery Simeon Ens^n
Allen Robart Serj⁺
Annew Andrew
Andrews James
Billing Stephen Lie⁺
Brightman Henry
Davis Daniel
Dayton Richard
Davison Robart
Freeman Guy
Faning Elisha
Freeman Edward
Freeman Micael
Gray Elijah
Harrington Isaac
Hannabal Joseph
Holly Joseph
M⁰Lane Mathew
M⁰Donold John
Pomp Samuel
Pelton Ebenezer
Pomp Jacob
Pelton David
Stanton Amos Cap⁺
Swift Robart
Sunsemun Aaron
Speers John

## CONTINENTAL REGIMENTS, 1775.

States or Starks Joseph
Sharper Tuis
Sterry Silas
Solomon Amos
Shortman William
Showls Nathan
Williams Henry Li$^t$
Williams Uriah Serj$^t$
Whitman Lemual d$^o$
Yerington Jesse

### Stoningtown

Brown Charles
Brumly William
Brown Joshua
Billings James
Brown Oliver
Cottrel Nathan
Cadwell Simeon
Cade Darius
Cinnamon Tho$^s$
Davol John
Fellows Joseph Ens$^n$
Fellows Nath$^ll$
Griffen James
Herrick Libeus
Hazzard Jeffery
Hanaball Joseph
Hudson John
Hiscox Thomas
Hawks Hannah p Son
Jackwise Robart
Ingram Mary p Son
Leeds Thomas
Lewis Valentine
M$^c$Kinzey James
Newgent John
Palmer W. Jonathan Sej$^t$
Peters Peter
Russel Giles Col$^o$
Shaw Richard
Smith Daniel
Simmons James
Sowas Richard
Shelly Lemuel
Searl Constant
Tuncheman
West John [    ]
Warden Walter
Wheeler David

### For the County of Fairfield
### Fairfield

Allen Eben$^r$
  d$^o$ Thomas
  d$^o$ Moses
Burr Daniel

Buckley Seth
Bradley Eliphalet
    Nathan
Beers Hezekiah
Coggin David
Cable William
Durfree Thomas
Disborough Justus
    Joshua Serg$^t$
Dimon Moses
Fuller John
Fegoe Peter
Fowler Nehemiah
French Samuel
Green Josiah
Glover John
Goodsall Epphaphras
Hubbel W$^m$ Leiut
    Isaac Leiut
Hutonot Francis
Hilton Atkinson
Hall Stephen Serj$^t$
Jackson P. Nathan Leu$^t$
Johnson Nathaniel
Leverick Gabriel
Lyon Samuel
Lockwood Stephen
Morehouse David
Mitchel John Serj$^t$
Meeker Stephen
Mills Joseph
Meeker Daniel
Osburn Stratten
Patching Elisha Serj$^t$
Raymond William
    David
Sturgis Moses Serj$^t$
Tayler Barrack
Webb Hezekiah
Williams Richard

### Stanford

Blanchard Jacob
Bates David
Benton David
Cleaveland John
Fountain Eneas
Hickok Sam$^l$ Serj$^t$
Hoyt Joseph Col.
Halley Abraham
Johnson Nathaniel
Jones Isaiah
Knap Usel
    James
Lockwood Timothy
    Eliphlalet Srj$^t$
Lunsbury Peter
McAnotter John

234  REVOLUTION LISTS AND RETURNS.

Parkinton Dine
Scofield Selah
Smith Isaac
S⁺ John James
Smith Isaac Jun'
Wardwell Jacob
      William
Weed Benjamin
    Thad⁺ Leiut

### Danbury

Bishop David
Chapman Collins
Dixon George
Eames Everit
Hall David
Ludeman John
Lord John
Matthews James
Orian alias Ryan Jeremiah
  See Redding
Picket Thomas
Rossell Jeremiah

### Redding

Bigsby Elias
Cooley Nathan
Hopkins Henry
Meeker Stephen
Sherwood Nehemiah
Raymond Sam¹

### New Fairfield

Beardsley Phineas Cap⁺
Barns James Leiut
Brown Charles Corpl.
Hall Talmage Serj⁺
Jolly William
Knap James
Kinning Thomas
Lacy J. Fairchild Serj⁺
Nichols Samuel
Robarts Benjaman
Saunders Wᵐ Serj⁺
Trowbridge John Serj⁺
Wilder Aaron

### Greenwich

Adams Jonathan
Butler Walton
Davis Isaac
Fletcher Joseph
Hays Abraham
Hariot Israel
Holmes Nathˡˡ
Jessup Nathˡˡ
Johnstone Wᵐ

Lockwood Moses
    Sam¹ Cap⁺
Nickerson Arana
Parsons Theodosius
Rundel John
Ritch Edward
Rogers James
Town John
Waters William
Wessels Herculus
Wilson David
Waren Henry Leiut
Whiting Sam¹ Leiu⁺

### Stratford

Benjamins John Serjt
Burrows Josiah
Beebee James Cap⁺
Collins Wᵐ Lock
Gilbert Obediah
Grover Jacob
Gorham Samuel
Hallop Joseph
Jones Jasper
King Orry
Phillips Thomas
Parker Samuel
    John
Russel Wᵐ Jun'
Shelley Eben' Serj⁺
Sunderland John
Walker Robart Cap
Washbon Samuel

### Newtown

Botsford Joel
Foot Elijah
Kimberly      Leiut.
Lacey Josiah Cap⁺
Prindle Abijah
Sanford James

### Ridgfield

Bradley Col. Phil.
Cummes William
Perry Elisha
Remington Stephen
Smith Lewis

### LITCHFIELD COUNTY

### Salsbury

Blodget Artimus
Chappel Curtis
Clankhorn Eleaz' Leiu
Fitch Joseph Trumbu..
Forgerson Daniel
Fitsgeral Henery

## CONTINENTAL REGIMENTS, 1775.

Hull Giles Serj$^t$
Larnebe Willord
Maclane Jacobe Fif$^r$
Monger Billey
Owen Eliphalet
Tupper William Corp$^l$
Yates W$^m$
Strong Phin$^s$

### Kent

Barnum Leiut
    Steaphen Serj$^t$
    Amos Corp$^l$
Barlow John
Curtice George
Cheney Richard
Die Daniel
Hill Eben$^r$ Capt
Lambskins Benj$^n$
Mane John Jun$^r$
Murry Noah Serj$^t$

### Litchfield

Bottem John
Burnham Asa
Mason John
Munger Daniel
Palmer Benj$^n$
Plant Tim$^o$
Rossiter Sam$^{ll}$
Shelly John
Seelye David
Smith Henry
Smith Jonathan
Stannard Sam$^l$
Stone Josiah
Tuttle Levi
Wright James

### Cornwell

Lake Phineas
Price Levi
Swift Heman Col.
Simmons Sam$^l$
Tanner Toral Leiut
Wix Uriah

### Woodbury

Camp Phineas
Church Ebenezer
Demmon John
Easton Eliphalet
Franklin Jchiel
Filets Francis
Humphrey Elijah Cap$^t$
Hitchcock David
Hull Stephen

Judgson Joseph
Lee Abner
Olds Aaron
Pollard Isaac
Rood Simeon
Stoddard Nathan Cap$^t$
    Eli
Taylor Simeon
Walker Elisha
    Zachariah
Welch Luke

### Colebrook

Canfield Abiel
Phillips Samuel
Simmons Joseph
    Ely

### Torrington

Barber Nathaniel
Gaylord Benjamin
Frisby Benjamin

### Winchester

Fay Gershom
d$^o$ Timothy
d$^o$ William
Filley Remembrance
Mott Adam
Scovil Stephen
Wilkinson Jesse

### New Milford

Bostwick Eben$^r$
Bunts Josiah
Buel David
Buck Josiah Ens$^n$
Canfield Elijah
Dunwell William
Daley James
Drinkwater W$^m$
Hawley C. Joseph
Peet Lemuel
Starr Josiah Col.
Stillwell Stephen
Trowbridge Eben$^r$
Wilkinson Ichabod
Whitley William

### Goshen

Converse Thomas Cap
Deming Waite
Goold John
Knap Timothy
Layre Jacob
Miles Isaac Serj$^t$
Norton Joseph

REVOLUTION LISTS AND RETURNS.

Peck Zebulon
Seelye John
Wyard Thomas

### New Hartford
[No names given]

### Harrington
Elmore Calib
Hodg Asael L$^t$
Gridley Seth
Sott Elijah
Willcox James
Foot Eben$^r$
Griswold White
Marshel Elisha

### Washington
Beman Friend
Bunce Isaiah
Davidson John
Fenn Daniel
Jordan John
Newton Ezekiel
Olds Oliver
Welch Micael

### Sharon
Allen Amos
Cleveland Josiah
Elmore Daniel
Fisher Isaac
Foster Benj$^n$
Goodrich David
Gilson Eleazer
Johnson Robart
Kelcy Noah
Pettitt Enos
Rust Jonathan
Strong David L$^t$
Waneright Thomas
Yale Waite

### Norfolk
Aspenwall Aaron
Adams Asael
Aspenwell Calib
Hamblin Joel
Horskins Daniel
Orvis Eleazer
Plumb Amariah
Sturdevant Nathan
Tubbs Nathan
Watson Titus Cap$^t$

### Canaan
Culver Aaron
Chambers W$^m$

Freeman Elisha
Green Samuel
Higbee Elihu
Holombeck John L$^t$
Lester Andrew

### Hartland
Bushnul Daniel
Hays Titus
Phelps Charles
Reed Benj$^n$

## COUNTY OF WINDHAM

### Windham
Burnap Benj$^n$
Bingham John Serg$^t$
d$^o$    Abisha
Durkee Benj$^n$ L$^t$
Durkee Jere$^h$
Farnum Reuben
Holt Philemon
See Willington
Littlefield Eben$^r$
Martin George
Parish Eliphaz
Perry Eben$^r$ Serj$^t$
Robinson Elias Ens$^n$
Randal Elijah
Rouse Jabez Serj$^t$
Riplee Charles d$^o$
Robison Sam$^l$
Smith James
Webb Nath$^{ll}$ Cap$^t$
Waldo Albigence
West Joseph

### Mansfield
Abbe John
Allen Ashur
Bassett Joshua
Barrows Jacob
Bugbee John
Bennet Joshua
Conant Sam$^{ll}$
Conant Calib
Dexter John
Fenton Jon$^{th}$
Fenton Sol$^n$ Lie$^t$
Harris John
Porter Nathan
Reed Nathan
Smith Jn$^o$ Ju$^r$
Shumway Jn$^o$ Cap$^t$

### Ashford
Allen Daniel Cap$^t$
Brandum Charles

Cheeney Eben' Corp'
Hardy Nath'll
Hall William
Lyon Henry
Mercy Thomas
Pool Daniel
Smith Peter
Smith Abijah
Spalding Eph'm
Wales Eben' L'
Waters W'm

Lebanon
Buts James
Badcock Jn°
Ball Humphry
Blackman Jon'th
Butler John
Coleman Noah Doc'
Clerk Jn°
Chappel Amaz'h
Carter (?) James
Foster Zeph
Gross Sam'll
Hill Phillip
Jones Dan'l
Palmer Elijah
Polly Alpheus
Strong Benajah
Vaughn Daniel
Woodworth Jed'h
Ward W'm
Woodworth Benj'n

Plainfield
Cleft Lem'l Cap'
Johnson Benj'n
McGreeger John Cap'
Marsh Peter
Stoddard Joshua

Pomphret
Bacon Nehemiah
Goodale Jacob
Jones Thomas
Lyon Abiel
Reed Oliver
Shadden John
Sharp Benj'n
Smith Henery
Stoel Elisha

Voluntown
Bacon Henry
Dennison Amos
Green Robart
Robins Joseph
Summitt Prince

Union
Houghten James
Lilley Eben'
Moore W'm Jun'
Sprague James Leiu'
Taylor Thomas

Killingsley
Perry Silvanus
Grover Amasa
Mash Abner

Cantebery
Adams David J'r
Adams David Doc'
Adams Samuel
Bacon Abner Cap'
Cleveland John Serj'
Cade Abijah
Carter Reuben
Cleveland Tim° Lei'
Cleveland Moses Lei'
Coburn Sam'll
Cushman Daniel
Duggins James
Downing Stephen
Fitch Rufus
Gates Nath'll Serj'
Stevens Peter J'r
Shaw William
Shaw Jonathan
Shaw Benj'n
Tickings Tias

[   ]ventry
[   ]ham Paul Capt
Clap Nathan
[   ]day Joseph
Parker Eben'
Robison Eph'm
Thompson Nath'll Serj'

COUNTY OF HARTFORD

Hartford
Adams William L'
Abbe Eleazer
Abbe Jeduthan
Augustus Cesar
[   ]arnard John Cap'
Brewer Dan'l Serj'
Bevens Ebenezer
Buckland Stephen Cap'
Bull Epaphras d°
Combs W'm Serj'
  See Weathersfield
Case Richard

Clark Abraham Serjᵗ
Corne Malachi
Cadwell Mattʷ Serjᵗ
Curtis Daniel
Cole Samuel
Darrow Chrisʳ Majʳ
Delibar James
Day Wastebrook
Demming David Lᵗ
Evans Abiathar
Evans Samuel Jʳ
Evans Henry
Green William Capᵗ
Heath Peleg Lᵗ
Hadlock Reuben
Hooker Wᵐ
Jarrel Thoˢ Serjᵗ
Keene Benjamin
Lummis Israel
Lucus Samuel
Mattucks Samˡ Capᵗ
Miller Charles Lᵗ
Mahar James
Mize William
Olmstad James Ensⁿ
Pomroy Ralph Lᵗ
Rislee Stephen
Smith George Ensⁿ
Sedgwick Samˡˡ
Spencer Obediah
Thomas Patrick
Wyllys Samˡ Colᵒ
Wadsworth Roger Lᵗ
Walker Roswell Serjᵗ
Way Hammon
Waters Thomas

### Suffield

Austin Richard
Allen Samuel
Granger Samuel
Granger Phinehas
Harmon John Capᵗ
Nelson Daniel
Pearman Joseph
Rising James
Spear Elijah

### Summers

Brown Jacob
Coole Reuben
Elmore William
Gibbs Josiah
Jones Eleazer
Pratt Russell
Wood Thomas

### Bolton

Downer Ezra
How Zadock Lᵗ
Warren John

### Glossenbury

Canada David Serjᵗ
Crary Richard
Conlee John
Dealing Samuel
Freeman Samson
Fox Asa
Freeman Syphax alias Mosely
Grover Phinehas Lᵗ
Hill Daniel
Holden John
Lamb Joseph
Loveland Thomas
Loveland Elisha
Loveland Levi
McDowel Alexʳ Ensⁿ
Miller John
Peas Peter Serjᵗ
Smithers William
Stevens Timothy
Sambo Prince
Treat John
Tryon Ezra
Webster Joshua Serjᵗ

### Weathersfield

Andrus Asa Serjᵗ
Buckley Edward Capᵗ
Blinn Abrahᵐ
Blinn Justus
Brown Edward
Clark James
Crane Curtis
Comes Wᵐ Serjᵗ
 see Hartford
Davis Ebenʳ
Griffin Simon Serjᵗ
Goodrich Ephraim
Kilby Christopher
Lockwood Moses Serjᵗ
Miller Nathaniel
Mygatt Zebulon
Riley John Leiut
Russel Asher
Stoddard Enock
Weston Benjⁿ Ensⁿ
Williams Daniel Serjᵗ
Wells Joshua

### Hebron

Baxter Aaron
Culver David

Holdridge Hezek. Col.
Mack Orlander Leiut
Marble Thomas
Morril Asher
McJuborrough Jedd<sup>n</sup>
Pomroy Benj<sup>n</sup> Doct<sup>r</sup>
Porter Eleazer
Pieffer Lazarus
Starks Stephen
Taylor Ephraim
Wright Simeon
  Isaiah

### Willington
Dimick Joseph
Fenton John
Holt Philemon Serj<sup>t</sup>
 see Windham
Hatch Hayman Corp.
Orcut Caleb Serj<sup>t</sup>
Root Nathan Leiut
Rice David

### Tolland
Brown Eben<sup>r</sup>
Eaton Solomon
Hinkly Ichabod Capt
Johnson Elihu
Luce Jonathan
Miner Andrew
Newton Elias
Price Rufus Leiut
Preston Tyrus
Peterson Andrew
Sabins Nehemiah

### Farmington
Albert Thomas G. Serj<sup>t</sup>
Andrus Theodore
  Obediah
Adams John
Brown Jonathan Cap<sup>t</sup>
Barns Daniel Leiut
Brunson Roger
  Asa
Bates John
Cole John Leiut
Culver Timothy
Clark Lyman
Curtis Amos
Camp Isaac
Dutton Oliver Serj<sup>t</sup>
Dunnum Cornelius
Fox Elisha
Hosmer Timothy Doc<sup>r</sup>
Hart Jonathan Adj<sup>t</sup>
Hotchkiss Zad<sup>k</sup> Corp.
Howard George

Hayden David
Judd William Cap<sup>t</sup>
Johnson John Corp.
Mix John Ens<sup>n</sup>
Momosuck Daniel
Merrils Cyprian
Oswold  Col.
Parceval Paul Q.M.
Powers James
Potter Lemuel Serj<sup>t</sup>
Rows Amos
Steel Josiah
Squier S. Samuel
Smith Asaph
  David
Stevens Rosewell
Thompson Isaiah Leiut
Wainright Samuel
Wilcox James
Welton Benjamin
Warren Abraham

### Middletown
Anger George
Blackman Elijah
Barns Thomas
Boardman Moses
  A Samuel
Blake Ebenzar
Brown William
Bacon William
Clark Othniel Leiut
Cone Ozias
  Joseph
  Daniel
Crittenden Gideon
Dewey James
Ells Edward Cap<sup>t</sup>
Fisher Christopher
Francis James
Foster John
Graves William
Gilston Jacob
Henshaw W<sup>m</sup> Leiut
Hubbard Hezekiah Leiut
Hull David
Harris John
Hubbard Roswell
Johnson Jon<sup>n</sup> Col.
 d<sup>o</sup> Davis
Kimball Abra<sup>m</sup> T.
Lung Joseph
Meigs J. Return Col.
Marks Comfort
Matthews William
Peck Ariel
Powers Thomas
Robinson John

Sumner John Col.
Savage Abijah Cap\*
Starr David Leiut
Sizer Jonathan
Warner Robart Cap\*
Wyllys Eben\*
    Joseph

### East Windsor

Anderson W$^m$
Andrus W$^m$
Brown Jude
Baxter Francis
Bissel John
Brown Josiah L$^t$
Beman Jonathan
Churchill Elijah
Downer Caleb
Grant Azariah
Lomis Moses
Newton Isaac
Porter Hez$^h$
Pearce Daniel
Wallace Ab$^m$
Wadsworth J. B. Doc$^r$

### Chatham

Bowers Benajah Cor (?)
    Ephraim
    Benjamin
Butler Peter
Carter Aaron
Cole Marcus Lieu$^t$
Graham Joseph
Goodrich Levy
Goff Samuel
Geddens Richard
Hale Aaron Leiu$^t$
Higgens Heman
    Jesse
Hubbard Elihue
Jennings Elnathan
Johnston James
Miller Enoch
    Daniel
Markham Josep
McCorne W$^m$
Norten Jedadiah
Pelton George
Parks Daniel
Ranney Jabesh
    Steaphen
Smith Ezra Leiu$^t$
Schalena Abrah$^m$
Stocken Marshall
Thomas Steaphen
Verry Jonathan

Wood Jacobe
Wright John

### Haddam

Arnold Jehiel
Bailey Gideon Leiu$^t$
    Jacobe
    Robert
Bates Eleazer
    Amos
    Daniel
Bonfoy Benunuel
Brainord Encrease
Boardman Jonathan
Clark Samuel
Chase Walter
    Aaron
Church Samuel
Cone Elisha
Gladding William
Higgins Cornelius L$^t$
Porter Amos
Smith John Leiu$^t$

### Simsbury

Andrus James Leiut
Bodwell Benjamin
Hill John 2$^d$
Higley Josiah
Harrington Elisha
Phelps Thomas
Prince Zacheriah
Woodbridg Theophilus L$^t$
Woodward Oliver

### Infield

Abbe Thomas Cap$^t$
Booth Henery
Chandler Joseph
Earl William
Griswold Joseph
Hall Israel
Hager Simeon
Parsons David Cap$^t$
Parsons Jonathan
Perkins Daniel Jun$^r$
Simons Isaac
Ware Daniel Serj$^t$
Wood Lemuel
Geer Elihu

### Colchester

Bill Jonathan
Carter Edward
Fenn David
Farnsworth Nath$^{ll}$
Harris Champlen

CONNECTICUT LINE, 1777-1781.     241

Hun Isaiah
Freeman Jack
Fox John
Graves Peter
Judd Daniel Serj᷄ᵗ
Quash Cato
Rowley Jesse
Roberts Nathaniel
Stark Tim⁰
   Samuel
   Steaphen
Tarble William
Witney Dan¹¹ Sarj᷄ᵗ Maj᷄ʳ
Williams John

   Windsor
Bristor John
Chandler Isaac
Coy Samuel
Denslow Marten
Gibs Samuel Leiut
Gillit Abel Jun᷄ʳ
Griswold Phineas
Hoskens Tim⁰
Holcomb Matthew
Lamberton Obed
Lawrance Amos
Loomis Steaphen
Mather Nathaniel
Marshal Samuel
Maclane Niel
Pinney Aaron
Porter Daniel
Phelps Isaac

Prior Abner
Seymour Joseph
Thrall David
Thrall Isaac
Woodward Oliver
Wing Joseph
   Samuel
Wakefield Potashel

   E. Haddam
Andrews Thoˢ
Ackley Thomas
Clark Samuel
Fox Joshua
Holmes Eliph᷄ᵗ Cap᷄ᵗ
Hary Itha᷄ʳ Cap᷄ᵗ
Harvey Ezra
Mitchel Samuel
Murfe Thomas
Mino Elihue
Mott Samuel
Mobs Pierce
Spencer David Lei᷄ᵗ
Salley James
Watkens Ephraim
Willey Jonathan
Wheeler Joshua
Williams Thomas

   Stafford
Manning Phineas
Millington Sam¹¹
Walker Nath¹¹
Wallbridg Ames Maj᷄ʳ

[*State Library, Revolution* 30, 5.]

16

## NINTH REGIMENT—COL. WEBB.*

[See *Record of Connecticut Men in the Revolution*, page 245.]

## FIRST COMPANY—COL. WEBB.

Return of the Officers and Privates of the Col.° Comp.y Col.¹ Sam.¹ B Webb's Regm.t Engaged for Three Years or During the War, the time of their Service, Pay Due &c from the 1ˢᵗ Jan.y 1780 to the 1ˢᵗ Jan.y 1781

| | | Terms engaged for | Married | Towns engaged for | Commenc.t of Service | Expiration of Service |
|---|---|---|---|---|---|---|
| Samuel B. Webb | Col.¹ | | | Lebanon | 1ˢᵗ Jan.y 1780 | 1ˢᵗ Jan.y 1780† |
| Timothy Allyn | C Lieu.t | | | New Hartford | " | " |
| Elisha Flowers | Serj.t M.r | 3 years | | Wethersf.d | " | 1ˢᵗ March 1780 |
| John Burnham | Serj.t | " | Mar.d | Middletown | " | 15th May 1780 |
| Elisha Hubbard | " | " | | Windsor | " | 7th March 1780 |
| Leonard Munroe | " | " | | Wethersf.d | " | 15th March " |
| Thomas Holmes | Private | " | | Hartford | " | 1ˢᵗ Jan.y 1781 |
| William Hooker | Serj.t | " | M.d | | 16th May 1780 | 16th May 1780 |
| Lach.b Saymore | Corp.l | " | | Hartford | Jan.y 15th 1780 | 1ˢᵗ Jan.y 1781 |
| Alva West | " | " | | Stratford | " | 19th May 1780 |
| John Beers | Private | D War | | Stratford | " | 20th June " |
| " | Corp.l | " | | | " | 1ˢᵗ Oct " |
| Timothy Cale | Drum.r | 3 years | | Middletown | 1ˢᵗ Oct 1780 | 1ˢᵗ Jan.y 1781 |
| Aden Ames | " | " | | Groton | 1ˢᵗ Jan.y 1780 | 9th April 1780 |
| Walter Harris | Fifer | " | | Lebanon | " | 1ˢᵗ Jan.y 1781 |
| Cyrus Fish | " | " | | Stonington | " | 28th April 1780 |
| Abial Allin | Private | " | | Windsor | " | 1ˢᵗ Jan.y 1781 |
| Amherst Bartlet | | " | | Lebanon | " | 10th March 1780 |
| Abm Belding | | D War | | Wethersf.d | " | 4th May " |
| Sam.l Blackman | | 8 years | | Stratford | " | 1ˢᵗ Jan.y 1781 |
| David Blackman | | " | | Stratford | " | 30th April 1780 |
| Joseph Brewer | | D War | | Hartford | " | " |
| James Chadwick | | " | | Hartford | " | 10th Jan.y 1781 |

CONNECTICUT LINE, 1777-1781.

| Name | Term | Residence | | |
|---|---|---|---|---|
| Will<sup>m</sup> Chadwick | D War | Hartford | | 10<sup>th</sup> Jan<sup>y</sup> 1781 |
| Tim<sup>o</sup> Chapin | 3 years | Windsor | 1<sup>st</sup> Jan<sup>y</sup> 1780 | 10<sup>th</sup> March 1780 |
| Phinehas Chapin | " | New Hartford | " | 16<sup>th</sup> April " |
| Levi Crowell | " | Middletown | " | 26<sup>th</sup> May " |
| Robart Colefax | " | Middletown | " | 26<sup>th</sup> Feb<sup>y</sup> " |
| Diureha Elderkin | " | Groton | " | 23<sup>d</sup> May " |
| Josiah Gayland | " | New Hartford | " | 7<sup>th</sup> April " |
| Solomon Goodrich | " | Hebron | " | 11<sup>th</sup> April " |
| Asa Hull | " | Enfield | " | 8<sup>th</sup> Nov. " |
| Eliphulet Hill | " | East Hartford | " | 21<sup>st</sup> April " |
| Ebenezer Hoadley | D War | Guilford | " | 1<sup>st</sup> Jan<sup>y</sup> 1781 |
| Silas Hubbard | 3 years | Middletown | " | 22<sup>nd</sup> April 1780 |
| Stephen Hurlbert | " | Winchester | " | 1<sup>st</sup> Jan<sup>y</sup> 1781 |
| Fred<sup>k</sup>. Jackson | " | Middletown | " | 26<sup>th</sup> May 1780 |
| Epahrass Jones | " | Hartford | " | 20<sup>th</sup> May " |
| Will<sup>m</sup> Jones | " | Windsor | " | 25<sup>th</sup> May " |
| Joseph Johnson | D War | Wethersf<sup>d</sup> | 26<sup>th</sup> May 1780 | 1<sup>st</sup> Jan<sup>y</sup> 1781 |
| Levi Lattimer | 3 years | Wethersf<sup>d</sup> | 1<sup>st</sup> Jan<sup>y</sup> 1780 | 15<sup>th</sup> July 1780 |
| Tho<sup>s</sup> Marshall | " | Norwich | " | 15<sup>th</sup> April " |
| Stephen Moulton | " | Stafford | " | 24<sup>th</sup> June " |
| Gardon Munsill | " | Windsor | " | 19<sup>th</sup> May " |
| Normond Newell | " | Farmington | " | 1<sup>st</sup> Jan<sup>y</sup> 1780 † |
| Timothy Olmstead | " | Hartford | " | 1<sup>st</sup> May " |
| James Pratt | " | Hebron | " | 11<sup>th</sup> March " |
| Sam<sup>l</sup> Pulford | D War | Stratford | " | 1<sup>st</sup> Jan<sup>y</sup> 1781 |
| Daniel Robbarts | 3 years | Middletown | " | 26<sup>th</sup> Feb<sup>y</sup> 1780 |
| Ozwill Rockwill | " | Wethersf<sup>d</sup> | " | 18<sup>th</sup> March " |
| Thomas Haynure | " | Worcester | " | 8<sup>th</sup> July " |
| Ezra Smith | " | Middletown | " | 14<sup>th</sup> April " |
| Army Sperry | D War | New Haven | " | 1<sup>st</sup> Jan<sup>y</sup> 1781 |
| John Steele | 3 years | Hartford | " | 3<sup>d</sup> June 1780 |

*The "Short Term Levies" in this regiment which appear in the volume of "Rolls and Lists of Connecticut Men in the Revolution" (Connecticut Historical Society Collections volume VIII), pages 80-82, served in 1780, not in 1779 as is there stated.
†An error for 1781 as is shown by the "whole term of Service."

|  | Terms engaged for | Married | Towns engaged for | Commenc[t] of Service | Expiration of Service |
|---|---|---|---|---|---|
| Josiah Treadway | 3 years |  | Middletown | 1[st] Jan[y] 1780 | 28[th] May 1780 |
| Bates Turnor | " |  | Norfolk | " | 7[th] April " |
| Mathew Thomsen | " |  | Stratford | " | 16[th] Jan[y] 1781 |
| John Vibbard | " |  | Hartford | " | 20[th] March 1780 |
| Daniel Ward | D War |  | Wethersfield | " | 1[st] Jan[y] 1781 |

Tim[o] Allyn C L[t]

[Indorsed] Colo[s] Comp[y] Cap. Timothy Allen Jan[y] 1780.

[*State Library, Revolution 29, 1.*]

Muster Roll of the Colo[s] Company in the 9[th] Connect[tl] Reg[t] of Forces in the service of the United States Commanded by Sam[l] B Webb for October November & Decem[r] 1780
[The following names, abstracted from this roll, do not appear in the preceding roll or in the previously printed volumes.]

| Inlisted | Privates | Term | Remarks |
|---|---|---|---|
| Dec[r] 2[d] 1780 | Abijah Smith | 3 years | Reinlisted & on furlough |
| July 18[th] " | Nehemiah Higgins | 6 M Levie | Discharged 4[th] Dec[r] 1780 |
| Aug[t] 28[th] " | Ozias Landon | " | Discharged 16[th] Dec[r] 1780 |
| July 18[th] " | John Watson | " | Discharged 4[th] Dec[r] 1780 |

[*State Library. Revolution 29, 10.*]

## SECOND COMPANY — LIEUT.-COL. HUNTINGTON.

Return of the Officers and Privates of the Lt Colo Company Colo Saml B. Webbs Regt Engaged for three Years or during the War, the time of their Service, pay due, &c., from the 1st Jany 1780 to the 1st Jany 1781

| Names | Rank | Term engaged for | From what Town | Date of Marriage | Commencement of Service | Expiration of Service |
|---|---|---|---|---|---|---|
| Ebenezr Huntington | Lt Colo | | Norwich | | 1st Jany 1780 | 1st Jany 1781 |
| Nathan Beers | Lieut | | New Haven | | ? | ? |
| " | P. Mr | | " | | " | " |
| " | Clothr | | " | | " | " |
| Jared Bunce | Privt | D. War | Wethersfield | before 1st Jany 80 | | |
| " | Serjt | | " | | 16th May 1780 | 16th May 1780 |
| Jonathan Arnold | Corpl | D. War | Hartford | | 1st Jany 1780 | 1st Jany 1780 |
| " | Serjt | | " | | 6th Septr 1780 | 6th Septr 1780 |
| Stephen Risley | Corpl | D. War | Hartford | before 1st Jany 80 | 1st Jany 1780 | 1st Jany 1781 |
| Jacob Achor | Privt | " | St Pennsylvania | | | |
| Jonathan Arnold | | 3 years | New Hartford | | | |
| Daniel Bostwick | | D. War | Hartford | | | |
| Reuben Cadwell | | " | Hartford | | | |
| Allin Evens | | 3 years | Hartford | | | |
| Moses Fay | | " | New Hartford | | | |
| Asa Fox | | D War | Glastenbury | before 1st Jany 80 | | |
| Naniah Fox | | " | Hartford | | | |
| William Martin | | " | Hartford | | | |
| Zebilon Mygatt | | " | Wethersfield | before 1st Jany 80 | | |
| David Robarts | | " | Middletown | before 14th March 80 | | |
| Stephen Robarts | | " | Middletown | | | |
| Josep Rawlinson | | " | Wethersfield | | | |
| Joshua Welles | | " | Wethersfield | before 1st Jany 80 | | |

Garrison West Point Novr 7th 1780   Nathan Beers Lieut.

[Indorsed] Lt Colo January 1780 Exd N. B. Jany 1st 1780 to Jan 1st 1781

[State_Library, Revolution 39, 2.]

## THIRD COMPANY—MAJ. WYLLYS.

Return of the Officers & Privates of the Majors Compy Coll Saml B. Webbs Regt engaged for three Years or during the War, the time of their Service pay due &c from Jany 1st 1780 to Jany 1st 1781

| Names | Term engaged for | From what town | Date of Marriage | Commencement of Service | Expiration of Service | |
|---|---|---|---|---|---|---|
| John P. Wyllyss Major | | Hartford | | Jany 1st 1780 | Jany 1 17M1 | |
| John Meiggs Leiut | | Middletown | | " | " | |
| " Adjt | | " | | " | " | |
| Stephen Dormant Sergt | 3 years | East Windsor | | " | " | |
| Wyman Parker " | D War | Hebron | | " | " | { Procured Christopher Horton to serve in his stead D. Wood |
| Peter Phillips " | " | Hartford | before 1st Jany 1780 | " | May 6 1780 | |
| Elijah Bill " | 3 years | Say Brook | | " | May 12 " | |
| Benjamin Mack Corpl | " | Windsor | | " | Mar. 7 " | |
| David Wood " | " | Wethersfield | | " | Apr 10 " | |
| Benjamin Dix Private | D War | " | | May 16th 1780 | May 15 " | |
| " Corpl | " | " | | Jany 1st 1780 | Jany 1 1781 | |
| John Forbs Private | " | Say Brook | | Sepr 6 1780 | Sepr 6 1780 | |
| " Corpl | " | Windsor | | Jany 1 1780 | Jany 1 1781 | |
| James Foster Drumr | " | Lyme | | " | " | |
| William Throll " | " | Groton | | " | May 10 1780 | |
| Joseph Dreed Fifer | 3 years | Wethersfield | | " | July 8 1780 | |
| Daniel Stoddard " | " | Hartford | | " | Jany 1 1780 | |
| Prichard Beckley " | " | Windham | | " | " | |
| Allen Corning " | D War | Wethersfd | | " | " | |
| Hezekiah Cary | 3 years | | | | | |
| James Goodrich | | | | | | |
| Christopher Horton | D War | East Windsor | | May 6 1780 | " | { Hired by Serjt Phillips to serve During the War |

# CONNECTICUT LINE, 1777-1781.

| Name | Term | Residence | | | |
|---|---|---|---|---|---|
| Jonathan Hand | D War | Wethersfd | | Jany 1 1780 | Jany 1 1780 |
| Thomas Morgan | " | " | | " | " |
| Aaron Merrill | 3 years | New Hartford | before 1st Jany 1780 | " | " |
| Jabesh Norton | D War | Hartford | | " | " |
| Francis Olmstead | 3 years | New " | | " | " |
| John Phillips | " | Hartford | | " | " |
| Phillip Jabor | D War | Do | | | |
| Elihu Waters | " | " | | | |
| Alexander Hoy | 3 years | Jericho | | | Jany 7 1780 |
| Ebenezer Forquoir (?) | " | Litchfield | | | Jany 25 " |
| Eusebius Austin | " | Kent | | | Mar. 1 " |
| David Vibbard | " | Nw Hartford | Do | | Mar. 20 " |
| Joel Couch | " | Hartford | | | Apl. 11 " |
| Samuel Norton | " | Wethersfd | | | Apl. 28 " |
| Fitch Lamphier | " | Middletown | | | May 26 " |
| Hosea Burge | " | Lebanon | | | June 3d " |
| William Lewis | " | New London | | | Sept 20 " |
| Jehiel Chapin | " | Bolton | | | Jany 1 1781 |
| Richard Bacon | D War | Wethersfd | | | |

Camp Highlands Decemr 14th 1780 Jno P Wyllys Major

[*State Library, Revolution 29, 3.*]

[Indorsed] Return of Major Wyllys' Compy 9th Connl Regt Decr 14th 1780.

Muster Roll of the Major's Company in the 9th Connecticut Regt in the Service of the United States Commanded by Coll Samuel B Webb for the month of Octr 1780

[The following names, abstracted from this roll, do not appear in the preceding roll or in the previously printed volumes.]

| Inlisted | Privates | Term | Remarks |
|---|---|---|---|
| Augt 26th 1780 | Thomas Stone | 6 months | |
| " | Nathan Elwood | | Discharged 14th Decr 1780 |
| 1777 | Richard Bacon | | Prisoner of War |

[*State Library, Revolution 29, 12.*]

## FOURTH COMPANY—CAPT. BULKLEY.

Return of the Officers & Privates of the 1st Capt Company Col S. B. Webbs Regt engaged for three Years or during the War, the time of their service, Pay due &c from January 1st 1780 to Janr 1st 1781.

| Names | | Time engaged for | Date of Marriage | Commencet of Service | Expiration of Service | Town engaged for |
|---|---|---|---|---|---|---|
| Edward Bulkley | Capt | | | 1st Jany 1780 | 1 Jany 1781 | Wethersfield |
| Saml Mears | Lieut | | | " | 20 Nov 1780 | Hartford |
| Jonathn White | Sergt | D War | | " | 20 Mar 80 | New Haven |
| Simon Giffin | Sergt Majr | " | | 20 March 1780 | 1 Jany 1781 | Wethersfield |
| David Pratt | Qr Mr Sergt | " | before 1st Jany | 1st Jany 1780 | " | Glastonbury |
| Wm Patterson | Dr Majr | " | | " | " | New Haven |
| Elijah Boardman | Fife Majr | " | | " | " | Wethersfield |
| Ithurel Flowers | Sergt | " | | " | " | N Hartford |
| Amaziah Chappel | Corpl | 3 years | Do | " | " | Labanon |
| Rhoderick Hopkins | " | " | | " | " | N Hartford |
| Daniel Sizor | Private | " | | " | 7 May 1780 | Middletown |
| Moses Griswould | Corpl | D War | | 20 March 80 | 28 Febr 80 | " |
| | Private | " | | 1st Jany 1780 | 20 Mar 80 | Wethersfield |
| Moses Hatch | corpl | " | | 6 Sept 80 | 1st Jany 81 | " |
| Christopher Brown | Drmr | " | | 1st Janr 1780 | 6 Sept 1780 | " |
| Arunah Hackley | Fifer | " | | " | 1 Jany 81 | " |
| Daniel Puffer | " | " | | " | " | Groton |
| Moses Boardman | " | 3 years | | " | " | Norwich |
| Zebediah Briggs | Private | D War | | " | " | Labanon |
| Wm Beaeton | " | 3 years | | " | 18 June 80 | Middletown |
| Prince Freeman | " | D War | | " | 1 Jany 80 | Chatham |
| Gideon Goff | " | 3 years | | " | " | Stratford |
| Bazeleel Hamlin | " | D War | | " | " | Groton |
| Saml Harrington | " | " | | " | " | Wethersfield |
| Thos Loveland | " | " | | " | " | Sandwich Mass B. |
| Elisha Mygott | " | " | | " | " | Glastonbury |
| | | | | | | Hartford |

CONNECTICUT LINE, 1777-1781.       249

| | | | | |
|---|---|---|---|---|
| Simeon Puffer | 3 years | 1 Jany 81 | 1st Oct 1780 | Lebanon |
| Marshal Stocking | D War | " | 1st Jany 81 | Chatham |
| Joseph Treat | " | " | " | Wethersfield |
| Hezh Wheeler | " | " | " | Stafford |
| Christopher Avery | 3 years | " | 8 Mar 80 | Groton |
| Asa Butler | " | " | 11 " " | Stafford |
| Phenious Shepherd | " | " | 20 " " | N. Hartford |
| Alexandl Dochester | " | " | 20 " " | Farmington |
| George Hopkins | " | " | 7 Apr " | New Hartford |
| Ignatious Waterman | " | " | 28 " " | Lebanon |
| Justus Blin | " | " | 20 May 80 | Wethersfield |
| Jonathn Wood | " | " | 22 " " | Hartford |
| Nathl Moungomury | " | " | 13 June 80 | Chatham |
| Zebulon Bourrows | " | " | 1st July 80 | East Windsor |
| Felix Curtis | " | " | 8 Augt 80 | Waterbury |
| Elihu Stowe | " | " | 15 " " | Middletown |
| Noah Roberts Corpl | " | " | 20 May 80 | Lebanon |

Garrison West Point Novbr 17th 1780    Saml Mears Lieut.

[Indorsed] 1st Compy Capt: Edward Bulkley Exd N. B. Jany 1780

[*State Library, Revolution 39, 4.*]

Muster Roll of the 1st Captt Company in the 9th Connecticut Battalion in the service of the United States commanded by Coll Saml B. Webb for the months of Octr November and December 1780 [The following names, abstracted from this roll, do not appear in the preceding roll or in the previously printed volumes.]

| | Enlisted | | Term | Remarks |
|---|---|---|---|---|
| Privates | | | | |
| Zenus Lines | July 23d 1780 | | 31st Decr | discharged Decr 9th 1780 |
| David Willets | Aug. 16th " | | " | " 16th " |
| Elijah Mygott | | | | Transferd to the Regt Invaleads Octr 8d 1780 |

[*State Library, Revolution 39, 15.*]

## FIFTH COMPANY—CAPT. WALKER.

Return of the Officers & Privates of Capt Joseph Walker's Comp'y Col'l Sam'l B. Webbs Reg't Engaged for three or During the War, the time of their Service, Pay Due &c from the 1st of Jan'y 1780 to the 1st of January 1781.

| Names | | Term Engaged for | For what town | Date of Marriage | Commencement of service | Expiration of Service |
|---|---|---|---|---|---|---|
| Joseph Walker | Capt | | Stratford | | Jan'y 1st 1780 | Jan'y 1st 1781 |
| Stephen Ingham | Serj't | 3 years | Saybrook | | " | Ap'l 14th 1780 |
| Amos West | " | " | Lebanon | | " | May 27th 1780 |
| Francis Nicholson | " | D War | Glastonbury | | " | Jan'y 1st 1781 |
| Waitstill Dickinson | Corp | " | Weathersfield | | " | " |
| Simeon Holmes | " | " | " | | Sept'r 6th 1780 | Sept'r 6th 1780 |
| " | Serj't | " | " | | Jan'y 1st 1780 | Jan'y 1st 1781 |
| Elijah Porter | Drum'r | " | Hartford | | " | " |
| John Kirkum | Fif'r | " | Weathersfield | | " | " |
| Theodore Andruss | Private | 3 years | New Hartford | | " | Ap'l 10th 1780 |
| Lewis Anguine | | D War | Stratford | | " | Jan'y 1st 1781 |
| Joel Beers | | " | " | | " | " |
| Timothy Beevins | | " | Farmington | | " | " |
| Peter Butler | | 3 years | Chatham | before 1st Jan'y | " | June 16th 1780 |
| David Chapin | | " | New Hartford | | " | Jan'y 1st 1781 |
| William Fay | | " | Winchester | before 1st Jan'y | " | " |
| John Fay | | D War | New Hartford | | " | Ap'l 12th 1780 |
| Remembrance Filley | | 3 years | Winchester | before 1st Jan'y | " | Jan'y 1st 1781 |
| Theodore Gilbert | | D War | New Hartford | | " | April 7th 1780 |
| John Graves | | " | Hartford | | " | May 22nd 1780 |
| Jacob Griswold | | " | Weathersfield | | " | Jan'y 1st 1781 |
| George Hills | | 8 years | Simsbury | | " | " |
| Orry King | | D War | Stratford | before 1st Jan'y | " | March 26th 1780 |
| Garmaliel Olmsted | | 8 years | New Hartford | | " | Jan'y 1st 1781 |
| William Prier | | " | Enfield | | " | Nov'r 8th 1780 |
| Zeri Page | | " | Lebanon | before 1st Jan'y | " | April 28th 1780 |
| Asher Russel | | D War | Weathersfield | | " | Jan'y 1st 1781 |
| Samuel Smith | | 3 years | Stratford | | " | " |
| Thom's Stanley | | D War | Weathersfield | | " | " |

| | | | | |
|---|---|---|---|---|
| Aaron Stevens | D War | New Hartford | before 1st Jany | Jany 1st 1780 | Jany 1st 1781 |
| John Thomas | " | New Haven | | " | " |
| Ezra Tryon | " | Glastenbury | | " | |
| Moses Ward | 3 years | Middletown | | " | May 29th 1780 |
| Joel Welton | " | Farmington | | " | Feby 5th 1780 |
| James Wayland | D War | Stratford | | " | Jany 1st 1781 |
| Abel Burton | " | " | | Feby 8th 1780 | |

[Indorsed] 2d Company Jany 1780 Cap. Joseph Walker Highlands Decr 20th 1780 Francis Nicholson Serjt

[*State Library, Revolution* 59, 7.]

## SIXTH COMPANY — CAPT. WILLIAMS.

Return of the Officers & Privates of the 3rd Company in Col¹ Sam¹ B. Webbs Reg¹ Engaged for three years or during the War, the time of their service, Pay due &c from Jan⁷ 1ˢᵗ 1780

| Names | | Term Engaged for | Date of Marriage | Cmⁿˢ of Service | Expiration of Service | Remarks |
|---|---|---|---|---|---|---|
| Sam¹ W^m Williams | Capt^n | | | Jan⁷ 1ˢᵗ 1780 | Jan⁷ 1ˢᵗ 1781 | Wethersfield |
| Thomas Gerralls | Serg¹ | D War | | " | " | Hartford |
| W^m Chapman | " | 3 years | Married | " | March 3 | Say Brook |
| Joseph Gilbert | " | " | | " | Feb⁷ 20^th | N. Hartford |
| Matthew Cadwell | Corp¹ | D W | Married | " | Jan⁷ 1ˢᵗ 1781 | Hartford |
| Phineus Cadwell | " | 3 years | Married | " | March 7 | N. Hartford |
| Stephen Butler | | D War | | " | Jan⁷ 1ˢᵗ 1781 | Saybrook, promoted to Capt. 20ᵗʰ March |
| W^m Kircum | Dm^r | " | | " | " | Guilford |
| Rich^d Jones | fifer | 3 years | | " | June 20^th 80 | Hartford |
| John Andras | Priv^t | " | Married | " | Feb^y 4^th 80 | Farmington |
| Ezra Andrus | | " | Married | " | April 7^th 80 | N. Hartford |
| Abraham Blin | | " | Married | " | April 9^th 80 | Wethersfield |
| Charles Bulkley | | " | | " | March 26^ab 80 | " |
| Jonath^n Butler | | " | | " | Jan⁷ 1ˢᵗ 81 | Say Brook |
| Jesse Chalker | | " | | " | March 4^th 80 | " |
| Charles Churchill | | " | Married | " | June 2^d 80 | Wethersfield |
| W^m Clark | | " | Married | " | April 5^th 80 | New London |
| Sam¹ Cole | | " | | " | March 26^th 80 | Hartford |
| Elisha Cole | | D War | | " | Jan⁷ 1ˢᵗ 81 | |
| Gid^n Crittenden | | 3 years | Married | " | March 14^th 80 | Middle Town |
| Avuara (?) Copeland | | " | | " | Jan⁷ 1ˢᵗ 81 | Pomfrett |
| Josiah Bordman | | " | | " | June 20^th 80 | Bolton |
| Daniel Davis | | " | Married | " | July 12^th 80 | Groton |
| Peter Holt | | D War | Married | " | Jan⁷ 1ˢᵗ 81 | New London |
| Nath¹ Holt | | 3 years | | " | " | Groton |
| Eph^m Holdridge | | " | | " | " | " |
| Joseph Hawley | | " | Married | " | " | " |
| Thomas Hillet | | D War | | " | " | Preston |

## CONNECTICUT LINE, 1777-1781.

| Name | Term | | Enlisted | Residence |
|---|---|---|---|---|
| Silas Lamb | 3 years | | Jany 1ˢᵗ 1780 | Groton |
| Cyprian Morrills | " | Married | " | N. Hartford |
| Roger Morrills | " | " | " | |
| Sam¹ Parker | D W | Married | " | Stratford |
| Isaac Payne | 3 years | | " | N. Hartford |
| John Packer | " | | " | Groton |
| Sam¹ Phillips | " | | " | Colebrooke |
| Grʰᵐ Robertson | D War | Married | " | Coventry |
| Frederick Stoddard | " | " | " | Groton |
| Sam¹ Schoolcraft | " | | " | " |
| Stephen Scovil | 3 years | Married | " | Stonington |
| James Spencer | " | | " | Winchester |
| Lemuel Sperry | D War | | " | N Hartford |
| Jesse Obbard | 3 years | | " | Norfolk |
| Sam¹ Weaver | " | | " | Hartford |
| Jesse Williams | " | | " | Weathersfield |
| Peter Freeman | " | | " | Groton |
| Caesar Freeman | " | | July 12ᵗʰ 80 | C Windsor |
| | | | | Wethersfield |

The above is a true Copy of the original abstract sent to the Committee for settling the Depreciations for the year 1780

Camp at West Point Novᵇ 29ᵗʰ 1780    Sam¹ Wᵐ Williams Capt

[Indorsed] 3ʳᵈ Compy Cap. S. W. Williams    Depreciation Abstract for 1780

[*State Library, Revolution 39, 9.*]

Muster Roll of the 3ᵈ Company in the 9ᵗʰ Regiment of Connecticut Forces in the service of the United States Commanded by Colᵒ Sam¹ B Webb; for the Months of October November & Decemʳ 1780

[The following names, extracted from this roll, do not appear in the preceding roll or in the previously printed volumes.]

| Enlisted | Privates | Term | Remarks |
|---|---|---|---|
| Feby 11ᵗʰ 78 | Amasa Copeland | 3 years | Blacksmith |
| | Ephraim Robertson | D. War | |
| July 23ʳᵈ 80 | Jedediah Woodworth | 6 Months | Discharged Decʳ 3ʳᵈ and Enlisted for 3 years |

[*State Library, Revolution 39, 18.*]

## SEVENTH COMPANY—CAPT. HOPKINS.

Return, of the Officers and Privates of the 4th Capt's Company, Coll Sam'l B. Webbs Reg't engaged for three Years, or during the War, the time of their Service Pay due &c from the 1st January 1780 to the 1st January 1781

| Names | | Term Engaged for | From what Town | Date of Marriage | Comment of Service | Expiration of Service |
|---|---|---|---|---|---|---|
| Elisha Hopkins | Capt | | Hartford | | 1st Jan'y 1780 | 1st Jan'y 1781 |
| Eben' Frothingham | Lieut | " | Middletown | | " | " |
| | Qr Mr | | | | | |
| Jeremiah Lord | Serj't | D War | Saybrook | before 1st Jan'y 80 | 29th Mar'h 1780 | |
| Nathan Savage | " | " | Middletown | | 1st Jan'y 1780 | |
| Samuel Helmes | " | 3 years | Lebanon | | | 12th June 1780 |
| Prentice Stores | " | " | Wethersfield | | | 28th Ap'l 1780 |
| Benjamin Mix | Corp'l | " | N Hartford | | | 7th March 1780 |
| Aaron Jones | Private Corp'l | D War | Saybrook | Do | | 19th March 1781* |
| | " | | | | | 1st Jan'y 1781 |
| Joseph Bacon | Drum' | 3 years | Middletown | | 20th Mar'h 80 | 15th April 1780 |
| Aaron Abercrombie | Private | D War | Raisley (?) | | 1st Jan'y 1780 | 1st Jan'y 1781 |
| John Barnham | " | " | Danbury | | " | " |
| Curtis Crane | " | " | Wethersfield | Do | " | " |
| Joshua Howe | " | " | New Haven | Do | " | " |
| Stephen Kellogg | " | " | Wethersfield | | " | " |
| Seth Montague | " | " | Manchester | | " | " |
| Adam Mott | " | " | " | Do | " | " |
| Jesse Wilkerson | " | 3 years | Nine Partners | Do | " | " |
| William Winans | " | D War | Wethersfield | Do | " | " |
| { Richard Belding | " | " | Farmington | | " | " |
| { Chauncey Lewis | | | | | | |
| † Isaac Lewis | " | 3 years | Bolton | | " | 19th Sept' 1780 |
| Jerijah Thayer | " | D War | Bishopsgate | | " | 15th Ap'l 1780 |
| Samuel Vallitt | " | 8 years | Bolton | | " | 22d May 80 |
| Levitt Millard | " | " | Groton | Do | | |
| James Anderson | | | | Do | | |
| Thomas Barnes | | | Middletown | | | |

CONNECTICUT LINE, 1777-1781.

| | | | | |
|---|---|---|---|---|
| John Benham | 3 years | N. Hartford | 1st Jan' 1780 | 7th Ap' 80 |
| David Covil | " | " | " | 5th May 80 |
| Ebenezer Davis | " | Wethersfield | Do | 12th May 80 |
| Gurdon Geer | " | Groton | " | 20th Mar¹ 80 |
| Seth Kellogg | " | Hartford | Do | 22d Ap' 80 |
| Christopher Kilby | " | Wethersfield | Do | 3d Mar¹ 80 |
| Amos Porter | " | " | " | 10th May 80 |
| Boswill Richardson | " | Lebanon | " | 26th May 80 |
| Eli Simons | " | Colebrook | " | 24th April 80 |
| Jehosaphat Starr Ensign Q.M. | " | Middletown | " | 29th March 80 |

[Indorsed] 4th Comp'y Ex'd N. B. Elisha Hopkins Cap Garrison West Point Nov' 25th 1780 Eben' Frothingham Lieu*

[State Library, Revolution 39, 6.]

Muster Roll of the 4th Capt' Company in the 9th Connecticut Battalion in the Service of the United States Commanded by Col¹ Sam¹ B. Webb for Oct' Nov' and Dec' 1780.

[The following names, extracted from this roll, do not appear in the preceding roll or in the previously printed volumes.]

| Inlisted | Privates | Term | Remarks |
|---|---|---|---|
| July 23d 1780 | Ira Mott | | |
| | John Porter | 31st Dec' | Discharged Dec' 14th |

[State Library, Revolution 39, 14.]

---

* An Error for 1780 as the "Whole Term of Service" shows.
† "Joined ( ? ) from Coll Sherburnes Reg't"

## EIGHTH COMPANY — CAPT. HEART

Return of the Officers and Privates of the 5th Comp'y Col Sam'l B. Webbs Reg't engaged for 8 years or during the War, the time of their Service, Pay p'r Month &c from 1st of Jan'y 1780 to 1st of Jan'y 1781.

| Names | | Term engaged for | From what town | Date of Marriage | Commencement of Service | Expiration of Service |
|---|---|---|---|---|---|---|
| John Heart Cap'n | | | Say Brook | | 1 Jany 80 | 9 Ap'l 80 |
| Joseph Bentley | Ensg'n | | Groton | | " | " |
| Jabez H. Tomlinson | " | | Stratford | | | 1st Jany 81 |
| Richard Price | Serg't | 8 years | Wethersfield | | 5 Apr'l 80 | 23d Ap'l 80 |
| Jesse Starr | " | " | Groton | | 1 Jany 80 | 23d Ap'l 80 |
| Daniel Williams | | D War | Wethersfield | before 1 Jany | " | 1 Jany 81 |
| Joshua Cone | Corp'l | " | Middletown | | " | 23d Ap'l 80 |
| " | Serg't | " | Middletown | | 22 Ap'l | 1 Jany 81 |
| Prosper Hosmer | Private | " | N Haven | | 1 Jany 80 | 16 May 80 |
| " | Serg't | " | | | 16 May | 1 Jany 81 |
| Samuel Beamount | Corp'l | " | Say Brook | | 1 Jany | " |
| David Parks | " | " | Groton | | " | 23 Dec 80 |
| Will'm Zepsor | Drum'r | " | Middletown | | | 15 Ap'l |
| David Lindsay | " | " | Wethersfield | | 19 July 80 | 1 Jany 81 |
| Moses Clarck | Fifer | " | Labanon | | 1 Jany 80 | 31st May 80 |
| Reuben Brown | " | " | Groton | | " | 1 Jany 81 |
| Jabin Bennet | Private | " | N. Hartford | | " | 20 June 80 |
| Allen Bradley | " | " | N Haven | | " | 1st Jany 81 |
| Edward Brown | " | " | Wethersfield | before 1 Jany | " | " |
| Daniel Bushnell | " | " | Hartland | D° | " | " |
| Nehemiah Baron | " | 8 years | Groton | | " | " |
| James Barnard | " | " | " | | " | " |
| Joshua Basset | " | " | Mansfield | | " | " |
| Hezekiah Brewster | " | " | Norwich | before 1 Jany | " | 31st July 80 |
| Caleb Curtis | " | " | Northbury | | " | 26 May |
| Brewster Chappell | " | " | Labanon | | " | " |
| Joshua Carpenter | " | " | " | | " | " |
| Amos Chappman | " | " | Groton | | " | 1st Jany 81 |

## CONNECTICUT LINE, 1777–1781.

| Name | Term | Town | | Date 1 | Date 2 |
|---|---|---|---|---|---|
| Martin Dibble | 3 years | Say Brook | | 1 Jan<sup>y</sup> 80 | 4 June 80 |
| West Brook Day | " | Hartford | D° | " | 24 Aug<sup>t</sup> 80 |
| Jack Freeman | D War | Lyme | | 28 Sep<sup>t</sup> 80 | 1 Jan<sup>y</sup> 81 |
| Peter Freeman | 3 years | Groton | | 1 Jan<sup>y</sup> 80 | 11 Sept 80 |
| Elisha Faning | " | Wethersfield | D° | " | 1 Jan<sup>y</sup> 81 |
| Hezekiah Nott | D War | Lebanon | | " | " |
| Isaac Killogg | 3 years | Hartford | | " | 18 June 80 |
| Israel Loomis | " | Wethersfield | | " | 20 March |
| Josiah Robbins | D War | Hartford | | " | 1 Jan<sup>y</sup> 81 |
| Sam<sup>l</sup> Roberts | " | N Hartford | | " | 13<sup>th</sup> Ap<sup>l</sup> |
| Elisha Roberts | " | Wellington | | " | 14 June |
| Will<sup>m</sup> Stiles | " | Groton | | " | 7 July |
| Ralph Williams | " | Wethersfield | | " | 19 March |
| Gideon Welles | " | Say Brook | D° | " | 1 Jan<sup>y</sup> 81 |
| Isaac Wardin | " | Wethersfield | | " | 28 Ap<sup>l</sup> 80 |
| George Price | | | | | |

17

[Indorsed] 5<sup>th</sup> Comp<sup>y</sup> Ex<sup>d</sup> N. B. Cap<sup>t</sup> John Heart Jan<sup>y</sup> 1780

[*State Library, Revolution* 59, 5.]

Muster Roll of the 5<sup>th</sup> Company in the 9<sup>th</sup> Connecticut Battalion in the Service of the United States Commanded by Col° Sam<sup>l</sup> B Webb for the Months of October Nov<sup>r</sup> & December 1780.

[The following names, extracted from this roll, do not appear in the preceding roll nor in the previously printed volumes.]

John Riley Captain  Lately Exchanged not Joind
Nehemiah Barns  3 years

Mch 21<sup>st</sup> 1778

[*State Library, Revolution* 59, 15.]

## LIGHT INFANTRY COMPANY—CAPT. WELLS.

Return of the Officers & Privates of Cap.ⁿ Roger Wells's comp.ʸ of Light Infantry in the 9ᵗʰ Connecticut Reg.ᵗ Commanded by Col.ˡˡ Samuel B. Webb engaged for three years or during the War the time of their service pay due &c from January 1, 1780 to January 1, 1781.

| | | Term engaged for | from what Town | Date of Marriage | Comm't of service | Expiration of service |
|---|---|---|---|---|---|---|
| Roger Wells | Lieut | | Weatherford | | Jan⁷ 1 1780 | April 9ᵗʰ 1780 |
| " | Capt.ⁿ | | " | | April 9ᵗʰ 1780 | Jan⁷ 1ˢᵗ 1781 |
| Daniel Brewer | Serj.ᵗ | 3 years | Hartford | | Jan⁷ 1 80 | " |
| Bela Scovell | Corp | D War | Guilford | | " | " |
| " | Serj.ᵗ | " | " | | | |
| Joseph Day | Corp.ˡ | " | Hartford | | May 15 80 | May 15ᵗʰ 1780 |
| " | Serj.ᵗ | " | " | | Jan⁷ 1 80 | Jan⁷ 1ˢᵗ 1781 |
| Sam.ˡ Easton | Corp.ˡ | " | " | | May 15 80 | May 15ᵗʰ 1780 |
| Walter Booth | Private | " | New Haven | | Jan⁷ 1 80 | Jan⁷ 1ˢᵗ 1781 |
| " | Corp.ˡ | | " | | " | " |
| David Lounsbury | Private | " | " | | March 20ᵗʰ 80 | March 20 80 |
| " | Corp.ˡ | " | " | | Jan⁷ 1 1780 | Jan⁷ 1ˢᵗ 1781 |
| Ezekiel Winchel | Drum.ʳ | " | Weatherfield | | Aug.ᵗ 28 80 | Aug.ᵗ 28 1781 |
| Hough White | Fifer | 3 years | Middletown | | Jan⁷ 1 1780 | Jan⁷ 1ˢᵗ 1781 |
| Jn.ᵒ Allen | Private | D W | N Haven | | " | " |
| Noah Barnham | " | " | Danbury | | " | " |
| Timothy Fay | " | 3 years | N. Hartford | M.ᵈ | " | " |
| Ichabod Goodrich | " | D W | Wetherford | | " | " |
| Joseph Hand | " | " | " | | " | " |
| Joel Hoyt | " | " | Stamford | | " | " |
| Sam.ˡ Hull | " | " | N. Haven | M.ᵈ | " | " |
| Benjamin Kircum | " | " | Guilford | | " | " |
| Asa Leonard | " | 3 years | Balton | | " | " |
| Jonathan Miller | " | D War | Wetherfield | | " | " |
| Brian Montique | " | " | Stratford | | " | " |
| Thomas Norton | " | 3 years | Middletown | | " | " |

| | | | | |
|---|---|---|---|---|
| Moses Porter | D W | Hartford | Jan'y 1 1780 | Jan'y 1st 1781 |
| Josiah Savage | 3 years | Middletown | " | " |
| Joseph Simons | " | N. Hartford | " | " |
| Seth Stannard | D War | Winchester | | |

[Indorsed] L. Infantry Cap Roger Wells Ex'd N. B. Jan'y 1780

[*State Library, Revolution* 39, 8.]

# CONNECTICUT LINE, 1781 - 1783.

[See Record of Connecticut Men in the Revolution, pages 301-355.]

## SUPPLIES, 1781.

An Alphabetical List of the Names of the Officers and Soldiers in the Conne' Line who have rec⁴ Family Supplies from the several Towns for 1781.

|     | Names              | Rank  | Towns to which they belong |
|-----|--------------------|-------|----------------------------|
| 5   | Anderson Thomas    | Lieut.| Lyme                       |
|     | Atkins Josiah      | Priv. | Waterbury                  |
| 5   | Avery Simeon       | Lieut.| Groton                     |
| 2   | Allay William      | Priv. | New Haven A⁷               |
| 4(?)| Alling Jonathan    | "     | "                          |
| D   | Adams Samuel       | "     | Canterbury                 |
| [ ] | Archer Grippin     | "     | Hebron                     |
| Invᵈ| Auger George       | "     | Middletown  Invalid        |
| [ ] | Acley Thomas       | "     | East Haddam                |
| {   | Andreus Thomas     | "     | "                          |
| D   | Adams Rhodrick     | "     | Symsbury                   |
| 1   | Andrus Asa         | "     | Weathersfield              |
| 5   | Abbe Jeduthan      | "     | Hartford                   |
| 1   | Abbe Eleazer       | "     | "                          |
|     | Alverd Thomas G.   | Serg. | Farmington A⁷              |
| Invᵈ| Andrus Theodore    | "     | "        Invalids          |
| 1   | Andrus Obediah     | Priv. | "                          |
| 8   | Alling Abel        | "     | "        Sapper            |
| 1   | Arnold Seth        | "     | "                          |
| 5   | Aldredge Wᵐ        | "     | Preston   Disert Aug. 1 '81|
| 1   | Austin Phinehas    | "     | Suffield                   |
| D   | Barber Amaziah     | "     | Symsbury                   |
| 4   | Bacon William      | "     | Middletown                 |
| Inᵈ | Boardman Moses     | "     | "         Invalid          |
| 3   | Brown Benjamin     | "     | Canterbury                 |
| 4   | Baker Edward       | "     | New Haven                  |
|     | Bishop Simeon      | "     | "                          |
| A   | Barns Solomon      | "     | "                          |
| 4   | Blakeley Enos      | "     | "                          |
| A   | Bishop Nathˡˡ      | "     | "                          |
| 4   | Blakslee Jared     | "     | "                          |
| 1   | Brown Henry        | "     | "                          |
| 4   | Blakslee Zealous   | "     | "                          |
| 4   | Beeck Asa          | "     | "                          |
| 4   | Brocket Hezekiah   | "     | "                          |
| 2   | Billins Stephen Ju' | Capt. | Groton                    |
| 5   | Brightman Henry    | Priv. | "                          |
|     | Brice Robert       | "     | "                          |
| 5   | Bristor Stephen    | "     | Waterbury                  |
| 1   | Beckwith Phinehas  | Ens.  | Lyme                       |
|     | Burnham Joseph     | Conr⁷ | "                          |
| 5   | Butler William     | Priv. | "                          |
| 4   | Booth Henry        | "     | Coventry                   |
| 1   | Brown Ebenezer     | "     | Killingly                  |
| 5   | Bayden Elhanan     | "     | "                          |
| D   | Bugbee Pelatiah    | "     | Mansfield                  |
| 3   | Bordin Samuel      | "     | Norfolk                    |

## CONNECTICUT LINE, 1781-1783.

|   | Names | Rank | Towns to which they belong |   |
|---|---|---|---|---|
| 2 | Baldwin Caleb | Capt. | Killingsworth | |
|   | Brewster Hezeki[h] | Priv. | Norwich | |
| 1 | Briant John | " | " | |
| 4 | Bennet Benjamin | " | " | |
| [ ] | Beebee James | Capt. | Stratford Sapper | |
| 3 | Booth Nathaniel | Ens. | " | |
| 4 | Bayley Henry | Priv. | " | |
| 2 | Brown Charles | " | New Fairfield | |
|   | Beardsley S. Wheeler | " | " | |
| 1 | Barnum Timothy | " | " | |
| 2 | Bishop David | " | Danbury | |
| † | Benidict Ezra | " | " | |
| 1 | Blanch Robin | " | Colchester | |
| 5 | Beamon Cæsar | " | " | |
| 1 | Booth Henry | Serg. | Enfield | |
| 3 | Burges Ephraim | Priv. | " | |
| 1 | Bunnel Amos | " | Southington | |
| 2 | Brister John | " | Winsor | |
| 5 | Brown Elias | " | " | |
| Inv[d] | Barnes Moses | " | Wallingford | Invalid |
| 4 | Bradley Daniel | " | " | |
| 3 | Basset William | Serg. | Watertown | |
| 4 | Barnes David | Priv. | Cheshire | |
| 4 | Bristol Benjamin | " | " | |
| 4 | Beldin John | " | Milford | |
| H | Burk John | " | " | |
| 4 | Bebee Joel | " | " | |
| In[d] | Bristol Jonathan | " | " | Invalid |
| 3 | Bates Daniel | " | Haddam | |
| 4 | Baily Robert | " | " | |
|   | Bates Eleazer | " | " | |
| 1 | Bowers Ephraim | " | Chatham | |
| In[d] | Brown Edward | " | Weathersfield | Invalid |
| 4 | Ball John | Lieut. | Guilford | |
| 2 | Bishop Thalmeno | Priv. | " | |
| 4 | Benton Edward | " | " | |
| 4 | Buckley Job | " | Seabrook | |
| 2 | Bushnel Constant | " | " | |
| D | Bugbee John | " | Mansfield | |
|   | Bull Epaphras | Maj. | Hartford | |
| 1 | Belden Simeon | Lieut. | " | |
| 8 | Brewer Daniel | Serg. | " | |
|   | Bitons Timothy | Priv. | Farmington | |
|   | Brownson Roger | " | " | |
| 1 | Belden Ezra | " | " | |
| 4 | Bagdon Cezar | " | Branford | |
| 4 | Blodget Artemas | " | Salisbury | |
| D | Barns Steaphen | " | New Hartford | |
| 2 | Bennet Isaac | " | Ridgfield | |
| 2 | Beach David | Ens. | New Milford | |
| 2 | Bostwick Eben[r] | Serj. | " | |
| D | Bewel David | Priv. | " | |
| D | Bennet John | " | " | Deserted |
| A | Barlow John | " | Kent | |
| 2 | Barnum Amos | Serj. | " | |
| 2 | Barnum Stephen | " | " | |
| 3 | Bushnell Daniel | Priv. | Hartland | |

| | Names | Rank | Towns to which they belong |
|---|---|---|---|
| 3 | Brown Jonathan | Priv. | Norwalk |
| 5 | Ba[ ]ton John | " | " |
| 5 | Betts Elijah | " | " |
| 2 | Barnes Ambrose | " | " |
| 1 | Bacon Nehemi[h] | " | Pomfrett |
| 5 | Billins Peleg | " | Preston |
| 5 | Ball Humphry | " | Lebanon |
| 5 | Buck Frank | " | " |
|   | Bates David | " | Stamford |
| 2 | Batterson George | " | Fairfield |
| 2 | Chamberlain Ephr[m] | Capt. | Wallingford |
|   | Coedry Joseph | Priv. | Milford |
| 2 | Cohale Corn[s] alias Frost Sam[ll] | " | " |
| 4 | Clark Nathaniel | " | Durham |
| D | Churchill Elijah | " | Enfield |
| Inv[d] | Culver Timothy | " | Southington |
| 1 | Carter Edward | " | Colchester |
| † | Chapman Rufus | " | Stratford |
| † | Clark Ithurel | " | Danbury |
|   | Corts Richard | " | Winchester |
| 3 | Comstock Sirajah | " | Norfolk |
| 1 | Cleft Lemuel | Capt. | Plainfield |
| 4 | Clark Martin | Priv. | New Haven |
| † | Clarrage Francis | " | " |
| 5 | Chapman Edward | " | Hebron |
| 4 | Cleaveland John | Ens. | Canterbury |
| D | Cushman Daniel | Priv. | " |
| 5 | Carter Reuben | " | " |
| 3 | Cleaveland Curtis | " | " |
| 2 | Clark Othniel | Lieut. | Middletown |
| 2 | Cone Ozias | Priv. | " |
|   | Carrell John | " | Symsbury Deserted |
| 1 | Case Jeremiah | " | " |
|   | Crocker Grace | " | " |
| D | Cone Elijah - | " | East Haddam |
|   | Chapman Joseph | Lieut. | Norwich |
| 5 | Chatfield John | Priv. | Killingsworth |
| 5 | Caesar Bristol | " | New Town |
| † | Cone Samuel | " | Haddam |
| † | Carey George | " | Chatham |
| 1 | Carter Aaron | " | " |
| 1 | Coombs William | " | Weathersfield |
| 3 | Crane Curtis | " | " |
| 3 | Clark William | " | " |
| 4 | Comstock Samuel | " | Seabrook |
| 1 | Curtis Daniel | " | Hartford |
| 3 | Cadwell Mathew | Serj. | " |
| 5 | Clark Abraham | Priv. | " |
| 5 | Case Richard | " | " |
|   | Corning Malachi | " | " |
| A | Curtis Daniel | " | Farmington |
| 4 | Cooper James | " | Branford |
|   | Chipman John | Capt. | Salisbury Prisoner |
| 4 | Chappel Curtis | Priv. | " |
| D | Cook Nathan | " | " |
| 2 | Convers Thomas | Capt. | Goshen |

CONNECTICUT LINE, 1781-1783.

| | Names | Rank | Towns to which they belong |
|---|---|---|---|
| 2 | Caswell Ezra | Priv. | " |
| 2 | Carter Nathan | " | " |
| 5 | Comstock Samuel | Capt. | Norwalk |
| 5 | Chapel Russell | Priv. | Reading |
| 2 | Coley Nathan | Serj. | " |
| 3 | Duggan James | Priv. | Canterbury |
| [ ] | Doyl Hugh | " | New Haven |
| | Denison John Jr | " | "    Deserted |
| In⁴ | Davis James | " | "    Invalid |
| | Davis Daniel | " | Groton    Deserted |
| 1 | Dickenson George | " | Southington |
| 4 | Dudley Zebulon | " | " |
| 5 | Dodge Benjamin | " | Colchester |
| 5 | Dodge Elihu | " | " |
| 2 | Denslaw Martin | Ens. | Windsor |
| 5 | Davis Jonathan | Priv. | Watertown |
| † | Daniels Samuel | " | Milford |
| 4 | Davison Isaac | Serj. | Washington |
| 4 | Davison John | Priv. | " |
| A | Dickson George | " | Danbury |
| 3 | Dawns John | " | Stratford |
| In⁴ | Demmon John | " | Woodbury   Invalids |
| 1 | Durkee John | Col. | Norwich |
| | Doud Moses | Priv. | Guilford   Deserted |
| | Doud Zechariah | " | "    6 months man |
| 2 | Dota Benjamin | " | Seabrook |
| D | Dimmick Joseph | " | Mansfield |
| 1 | Dunham Cornelius | " | Farmington |
| D | Dorman Garsham | " | Sharon |
| 3 | Dayley James | " | New Milford   Sapper |
| 2 | Demming Wait | " | Goshen |
| 2 | D' Forest Samuel | Lieut. | Norwalk |
| 3 | Davis Joseph | Priv. | Preston |
| | Durfe Thomas | " | Fairfield |
| 4 | Elwood Joseph | " | " |
| 5 | Ellis Carpenter | " | Volunton |
| 4 | Egleston David | " | New Haven |
| 1 | Ells Edward | Capt. | Middletown |
| X | Ellis John | Rev⁴ | Norwich |
| 5 | Eldridge Samuel | Priv. | Willington |
| | Emmit John | " | N. Haven |
| | Ely John | Col. | Seabrook |
| 3 | Evens Abiather | Serj. | Hartford |
| 1 | Evens Henry | Priv. | " |
| 5 | Elmore Calib | " | Harwington |
| 1 | Elles Nathan | " | Preston |
| 1 | Fox John | " | Colchester |
| 2 | Fenn Daniel | " | Washington |
| 4 | Foot Ezra | " | Derby |
| 3 | Filley Remembrance | " | Winchester |
| In⁴ | Fulford, John | Serj. | Watertown  Invalid |
| 4 | Field Edmund | Priv. | Wallingford |
| A | Fryar Charles | " | New Haven |
| A | Foot Isaac | " | " |
| 2 | Franklin Sam¹¹ | " | Killingsworth |
| 1 | Fanning Charles | Lieut. | Norwich |
| 5 | Farnsworth Nath¹¹ | Priv. | " |

## REVOLUTION LISTS AND RETURNS.

| | Names | Rank | Towns to which they belong |
|---|---|---|---|
| 1 | Foster John | Priv. | Middletown |
| D | Fuller Jacob | " | Symsbury  alias Tullar |
| 3 | Fuller Ely | " | "  alias Tullar |
| | Farnham Abiel | " | Canterbury |
| 3 | Freeman Edward | " | Groton |
| 4 | Farmer Thomas | Lieut. | Derby |
| | Fayer Elijah | Priv. | Voluntown  Deserted |
| | Ford Daniel | " | New Haven |
| 5 | Ford Martin | " | " |
| 5 | Farnsworth Nath[ll] | " | Colchester |
| 3 | Fox Asa | " | Glastenbury |
| 1 | Fuller John | " | Chatham |
| 5 | Freeman Sam[ll] | " | " |
| | Flag Jonathan | " | Hartford |
| | Fisher Isaac | " | Sharon  Deserted |
| | Farnam Benj[a] | " | Ashford |
| 4 | Foot Eben' | " | Branford |
| 4 | Fits Gerrald Hen[y] | " | Salisbury |
| 4 | Fitch Joseph | " | " |
| 3 | Fox Simeon | " | New Hartford |
| 3 | Fuller James | " | Suffield |
| 2 | Fowler Nehemiah | " | Fairfield |
| | Feego Peter | " | " |
| 3 | Glass Silas | Priv. | Canterbury |
| 3 | Gates Nath[ll] | " | " |
| 4 | Gitston Jacob | " | Middletown |
| 8 | Graves William | " | "  Sapper |
| 3 | Gillet Jacob | " | Symsbury |
| In[d] | Gardner Sherman | " | Norwich  Invalid |
| | Gillet Benj[a] | " | New Haven |
| 3 | Grant Azariah | " | East Windsor |
| In[d] | Gibbs Samuel | Lieut. | Windsor  Invalid |
| | Gibbs William | Priv. | Colchester  Deserted |
| 3 | Gay Jason | " | New Fairfield |
| 5 | Gaylord Jonathan | " | Watertown |
| 4 | Goldsmith William | " | Milford |
| 5 | Gillet John | " | " |
| 1 | Grover Amaza | " | Killingly |
| 1 | Graves John | " | " |
| 5 | Griffeth George | " | Voluntown |
| 5 | Gladen William | " | Haddam |
| In[d] | Graham Joseph | " | Chatham  Invalid |
| 4 | Goodrich Levi | Ens. | " |
| 3 | Giffin Simon | Serj. | Weathersfield |
| 4 | Grant James | Priv. | Seabrook |
| 4 | Graham Cyrus | " | " |
| 2 | Gilson Eleazer | " | Sharon |
| [ ] | Goodrich David | " | " |
| 4 | Garrie John | " | Branford |
| [ ] | Griggory Mathew | Ens. | Norwalk |
| [ ] | Grant Luke | Priv. | Preston |
| [ ] | Granger Sam[ll] | " | Suffield |
| 3 | Gavet Steaphen | | Stonington |
| 4 | Hoskins Timothy | " | Windsor |
| 5 | Harris Champlin | " | Colchester |
| 5 | Hallimage John | " | Enfield |
| 5 (?) | Hall Hiram | " | " |

CONNECTICUT LINE, 1781–1783.

| | Names | Rank | Places to which they belong |
|---|---|---|---|
| 3 | Halley Nathan | Priv. | Stratford |
| 3 | Harrop Joseph | " | " |
| A | Harris Henry | " | " |
| † | Hewet Elisha | " | Danbury |
| 1 | Hawkins William | " | " |
|  | Hall (?) Samuel | " | Wallingford |
| 4 | Hooker John | " | Milford |
| 4 | Hine Titus | " | " |
| 5 | Hull Eliakim | " | Durham |
| 3 | Hamlin Joel | " | Norfolk |
|  | Howard Richard | " | Windham |
| 4 | Howel Nicholass | " | New Haven |
| 5 | Huse Bodwell | " | " |
| 3 | Hull Samuel | " | " |
| [ ] | Hide James y<sup>e</sup> 3<sup>d</sup> | Ens. | Norwich |
| 1 | Harrinton Elisha | Priv. | Symsbury |
| D | Humphry Timothy | " | " |
| D | Hunt John | " | " |
| 1 | Hill John | " | " Deserted |
|  | Harvey Ezra | " | East Haddam |
| 1 | Hubbard Hezekiah | Lieut. | Middletown |
| 2 | Henshaw William | " | " |
| 1 | Hull David | Priv. | " |
| 1 | Higgins William | Lieut. | Lyme |
| 4 | Hodge David | " | Milford |
| 5 | Hanes Jonathan | " | Lyme |
| I<sup>d</sup> | Holden John | " | Glastenbury Invalid |
| 3 | Holmes Simeon | " | Weathersfield |
| 3 | Howe Joshua | " | New Haven |
| 2 | Hall Philemon | Lieut. | Guilford |
| 2 | Handy Samuel | Priv. | " |
|  | Hall Eben | " | " |
| 4 | Hough Simon | " | Seabrook |
|  | Hadlack Reubin | " | Hartford |
| 1 | Hill Daniel | " | " |
| 1 | Jonathan Heart | Capt. | Farmington |
| 4 | Hobart John | Lieut. | Branford |
| 4 | Hoadley Sam<sup>ll</sup> | S<sup>t</sup> | " |
| 4 | Harrison Jarius | " | " |
| 2 | Hawley C. Joseph | " | New Milford |
| 5 | Hodg Asael | Capt. | Harwington |
| In<sup>d</sup> | Hills Ebenezer | " | Kent Invalid |
| 5 | Hubbell Seth | Priv. | Norwalk |
| D | Hatherway Seth | " | Suffield |
| D | Hatherway Willbre | " | " |
| 3 | Hills Phillip | " | Lebanon |
|  | Harvey Ephraim | " | Stonington |
| 5 | Hawley Abraham | " | Stamford |
| A | Hubbel Isaac | Capt. | Fairfield |
| 4 | Hall Steaphen | Serj. | " |
| H | Jones Thomas | Priv. | Wallingford |
| 4 | Johnson Abraham | " | New Haven |
|  | Joslin John | " | " |
| 1 | Johnson Bristol | " | Colchester |
| 2 | Johnson Jonathan | Lt. Col. | Middletown |
| 4 | Johnson William | Priv. | Durham |
| 4 | Jones Jasper | " | Stratford |

## REVOLUTION LISTS AND RETURNS.

|   | Names | Rank | Places to which they belong |
|---|---|---|---|
| [ ] | Johnson Isaac | Priv. | Guilford |
| 3 | Jones Aaron | " | Seabrook |
| 3 | Jarrels Thomas | Serj. | Hartford |
| H | Jones Joseph | Priv. | Branford |
| 5 | Johnson John | " | Norwalk |
| 2 | Jackson Jonathan | " |  |
| 5 | Jones Dan¹ | " | Lebanon |
|   | James Phillup | " | Fairfield |
| 3 | Kimball Jededeʰ | " | Norwich |
| 5 | Kimberley Ephraim | Lieut. | New Town |
| † | Knowles James | Priv. | Haddam |
| D(?) | Kneeland Jesse | " | Chatham |
|   | Kellcey Preson | " | Guilford 6 month man |
| † | Kenney Benjamin | " | Hartford |
| 2 | Kelsey Noah | " | Sharon |
| D | King Joseph | " | Suffield |
| 4 | Lillie Abner | " | Windham |
| 4 | Lord Jabez | " | New Haven |
| 5 | Lines John | " | Colchester |
| 5 | Lane (?) Joel | " | Waterbury |
| 1 | Lung Joseph | " | Middletown |
|   | Lawrence Amos | Serj. | Windsor Discharged |
| Inᵈ | Lamberton Obed | Priv. | " Invalid |
| Inᵈ | Ludiman John | " | Danbury Invalid |
| 1 | Laverrick Gabriel | " | Milford |
| 4 | Loveman Jonathan | " | Durham |
| 5 | Lee Ezra | Lieut. | Lyme |
| 5 | Lay Richard | Priv. | " |
| 4 | Lay John | " | " |
| 3 | Lewis Peter | " | Stratford |
| In | Loveland Thomas | " | Glastenbury Invalid |
| D | Lattemore Levi | " | Weathersfield |
| † | Lord Jeremiah | " | Seabrook Invalids |
| 4 | Lay Asa | Capt. | " |
| 4 | Lord William | Priv. | " |
| 1 | Lyon Henery | " | Ashford |
| 3 | Luce Jonathan | " | Tolland |
| H | Lee Noah | Capt. | Salisbury |
| D | Leach Hezekiah | Priv. | Harwington |
| 1 | Levorick Gabriel |  | Fairfield vide above |
| 4 | Mansfield T. | Lieut. | Wallingford |
| 1 | Mix Thomas Junʳ | Priv. | " |
| 1 | Mix Enos | " | " |
| D | Meriman Josiah | " | " |
| H | Munson William | Capt. | New Haven |
| A | Miles John | " | " |
| A | Mix Timothy | Lieut. | " |
| 4 | Mothrop Joseph | Priv. | " |
| Inᵈ | Mansfield Dan | " | " Invalid |
| S | Mathews Robert | " | " Sapper |
| 4 | Mallery Amos | " | " |
| 5 | Mallery Jonah | " | Waterbury |
| 3 | Meiggs John | Lieut. | Middletown |
| 4 | McCartee John | Priv. | Canterbury |
| 1 | Mack Abner | " | Hebron |
| 1 | Marble Thomas | " | " |
| 1 | Mason Rufus | " | Symsbury |

## CONNECTICUT LINE, 1781–1783.

| | Names | Rank | Places to which they belong |
|---|---|---|---|
| 4 | Mallery Amos | Priv. | Milford |
| 2 | Marshal Byard | " | " |
| | Murry Abraham | " | Derby    Deserted |
| † | Marchant John | " | Washington |
| D | Minor Elisha | " | Woodbury |
| † | Mathews Eliada | " | Cheshire |
| 5 | Mitchell Sam{11} | " | East Haddam |
| 1 | Mosely Syphax | " | Glastenbury |
| 3 | Maculpin Alexander | " | " |
| 1 | Miller Daniel | " | Chatham |
| D | Morrison William | " | Weathersfield |
| 8 | Maggot Zebulon | " | " |
| | Marks Abisha | " | " |
| 4 | M{c}Cullum Duncan | " | Seabrook |
| 1 | Millar Charles | Lieut | Hartford |
| 1 | Mize William | Priv. | " |
| 1 | Mahar James | " | " |
| 3 | Mix John | Lieut. | Farmington |
| 1 | Mossack Daniel | Priv. | " |
| 4 | M{c}Lane Jacobe | Serj. | Salisbury |
| | M{c}Cartee George | " | " |
| 4 | Munger Billa | " | " |
| 4 | Meigs Simeon | " | " |
| 3 | Meeker Steaphen | " | Ridgefield |
| | M{c}Coy John | Priv. | New Milford |
| 2 | Mix Elisha | " | Goshun |
| *4 | Moss Daniel | " | Norwalk |
| 1 | M{c}Daniel James | " | Preston |
| 3 | Meeker Stephen | " | Reading |
| 3 | Moor William | " | Union |
| 3 | M{c}Nulter John | " | Stamford |
| 2 | Morchouse David | " | Fairfield |
| 4 | Northrup Isaac | " | Milford |
| 3 | Nicholson Francis | Serj. | Glastonbury |
| A | Norton Jedediah | Priv. | Chatham |
| 2 | Norton Rufus | " | Guilford |
| 2 | Norton Elon | " | " |
| | Nigar Phillip | " | "        6 months man |
| 4 | Newel Robert | " | Seabrook |
| † | Norton Sam{11} | " | Hartford |
| A | Newell James | " | Farmington |
| 4 | Norton Benjn | Ens. | Branford |
| 5 | Nichols Samuel | Priv. | Norwalk |
| 3 | Nedson Robbin | | Stoningtown |
| 2 | Owen Alvan | Priv. | Windsor |
| 4 | Olds Oliver | " | Washington |
| 5 | Olds Aaron | " | Woodbury |
| S | Osborn Nath{11} | Serj. | Stratford    Sapper |
| 3 | Orcutt Caleb | " | Willington |
| 4 | Oates Joseph | Priv. | Branford |
| 4 | Owen Eliphalet | " | Salisbury |
| 3 | Olmsted Jesse | " | Norwalk |
| 4 | Ovit William | " | Stanford |
| 5 | Parker Nathan | Serj. | Coventry |
| 4 | Peirce John | Priv. | Wallingford |
| 3 | Pirkins Daniel | " | Enfield |
| 4 | Potter Moses | " | New Haven |

|   | Names | Rank | Places to which they belong |
|---|---|---|---|
| A | Parker Edward | Priv. | New Haven |
| 1 | Pawers Thomas | " | " |
|   | Paul Peter alias Peter Kellogg | " | Colchester |
| 4 | Pawers James | " | Southington |
| 1 | Perrigo William Jr. | " | Norwich |
| 5 | Patterson James | " | " |
| Inv<sup>d</sup> | Penhellow Richard | " | " |
| 4 | Prior Abner | Maj. | Windsor |
| 2 | Porter Daniel | Priv. | " |
| 1 | Parsons Thomas | Serj. | " |
| D | Phillips William | Priv. | Symsbury |
| H | Parmalee Jerem<sup>h</sup> | " | Milford |
| A | Prindle I Enos | " | Derby |
| 5 | Pumham Joseph | " | Lyme |
| 5 | Pollard Isaac | " | Woodbury |
| 3 | Preston Joseph | " | Winchester |
| † | Pendleton Daniel | Capt. | Watertown |
| 4 | Parker Isaac | Priv. | " |
| 4 | Phillips Thomas | " | Stratford |
| 5 | Prindle Abijah | " | New Town |
| Inv<sup>d</sup> | Palmer Isaac | " | Weathersfield |
| 2 | Pettet Enos | " | Sharon |
| 4 | Potter Steaphen | Capt. | Branford |
| † | Painter Gamaliel | " | Salisbury |
| 2 | Perry Elisha | Priv. | Ridgfield |
| 3 | Phinney Joseph | " | Lebanon |
| D | Patchen Elijah | " | Fairfield |
| 2 | Parrit David | " | " |
| 1 | Qui Libbeus | " | Norwich |
| 4 | Robinson Elias | Lieut. | Windham |
| † | Rexford Benj<sup>a</sup> | Priv. | Wallingford |
| H | Robinson Sam<sup>ll</sup> | Lieut. | New Haven |
| 5 | Rogers Josiah | Priv. | Colchester |
| 5 | Roberts Nathan | " | " |
| 2 | Ransdale Ezra | " | " |
| 3 | Roberts David | " | Middletown |
| † | Runnels John | " | Norwich { supposed to be Joshua |
| 4 | Rowlee John | " | Winsor |
| A | Rumbeglow Tho<sup>s</sup> | " | Killingsworth |
| 4 | Rozell Jeremiah | " | Danbury |
|   | Rude Samuel | " | Hebron |
| 5 | Rice John | " | " |
| 4 | Reed Enoch | Capt. | Lyme |
| 5 | Ransom David | Priv. | " |
| 4 | Robinson Cato | " | Groton |
| 5 | Reaves James | " | East Haddam |
| 5 | Rice Nehemiah | Capt. | Watertown |
| 5 | Russell William | Priv. | Stratford |
| 2 | Ray Daniel | " | Haddam |
| 1 | Ranney Stephen | Serj. | Chatham |
| 3 | Russell Asher | Priv | Weathersfield |
| 3 | Riley John | Capt. | " |
| 3 | Rowlanson Joseph | Priv. | " |
| 4 | Roulenson Reubin | " | Guilford |
| 2 | Reeves Puryer | " | Seabrook |

CONNECTICUT LINE, 1781-1783.

| | Names | Rank | Places to which they belong |
|---|---|---|---|
| 1 | Runnels John | Priv. | Hartford |
| 3 | Risley Stephen | " | " |
| D | Rich Amos | " | Farmington |
| 1 | Ruggs Solomon | " | " |
| 2 | Russ Jonathan | " | Sharon |
| | Riley Phillip | " | Colebrook   vid Original |
| 2 | Rust Epaphras | " | Cornwell |
| S | Raymond Sam[ll] | " | Reading  Sapper deserted |
| 5 | Sweets John | " | Killingly |
| 5 | Sherman Reubin | " | Coventry |
| 4 | Shaylor T | Lieut. | Wallingford |
| 5 | Smith Daniel | Priv. | " |
| 4 | Sherman John | Lieut. | New Haven |
| 4 | Smith Ambrose | Priv. | " |
| 4 | Sugden Abraham | " | " |
| 4 | Stockwell Abel | " | " |
| A | Sherman Edmund | " | " |
| 5 | Shote James | " | Colchester |
| 5 | Shon Simeon | " | " |
| A | Squire Samuel | " | Southington |
| 4 | Starr David | Capt. | Middletown |
| † | Sizer William | " | " |
| † | Savage Stephen | Priv. | " |
| 3 | Simons Jonathan | " | Canterbury |
| 1 | Shaw Benj[n] | " | " |
| 2 | Sanders William | " | New Fairfield |
| H | Stringham Peter | " | Danbury |
| 4 | Stewart John | " | Milford |
| 5 | Sandford Samuel | Capt. | " |
| 4 | Selden Ezra | " | Lyme |
| 5 | Spencer Ichabod | Lieut. | " |
| 4 | Swift Robert | Priv. | Groton |
| 3 | Sealy George | " | " |
| 5 | Stoddard Ely | " | Woodbury |
| 5 | Stewart Joseph | " | East Haddam |
| 5 | Smith David | Maj. | Watertown |
| † | Smith John | Priv. | " |
| 5 | Shilley Ebenezer | Serj. | Stratford |
| A | Simons Robert | Priv. | " |
| A | Sunderland John | " | " |
| 1 | Stevens Timothy | " | Glastenbury |
| In[d] | Simbo Prince | " | "   Invalid |
| 1 | Smith John | " | Haddam |
| † | Smith Joshua | " | " |
| 3 | Stocken Marshal | " | Chatham |
| | Smith Ezra | Lieut. | " |
| 3 | Sizar Daniel | Priv. | Weathersfield |
| 3 | Shelley Edmund | " | Guilford |
| 4 (?) | Shortman William | " | Hartford |
| [ ] | Spencer (?) John | Lieut. | " |
| D | Seward Jedediah | Priv. | Farmington |
| D | Smith Asaph | " | " |
| 1 | Stedman Thomas | " | " |
| 1 | Steel William | " | " |
| 2 | Strong David | Capt. | Sharon |
| D | Strong Phin[s] Ju[r] | | East Windsor |
| | Smith Abijah | Priv. | Ashford   Deserted |
| 4 | Smith Jordan | " | Branford |

| | Names | Rank | Places to whch they belong |
|---|---|---|---|
| D | Sheldon Elisha | Col. | Salisbury |
| † | Swetland Aaron | Serg. | " |
| 4 | Strong Phineas | Corp. | " |
| 2 | Smith Heman | Col. | Cornwell |
| D | Sereen James | Priv. | Suffield |
| 3 | Thompson David | " | Guilford |
| 5 | Taylor Elijah | Ens. | Norwalk |
| 5 | Tracy Perez | Priv. | Preston |
| 8 | Thompson James | " | Reading |
| H | Tisdale Eliph<sup>t</sup> | " | Lebanon |
| 5 | Tharp M Cornelius | " | Fairfield |
| 2 | Tredwell Cato | " | " |
| 1 | Talbut Benjamin | " | Killingly |
| 5 | Thompson Nath<sup>ll</sup> | Serj. | Coventry |
| A | Throop John | Lieut. | New Haven |
| 4 | Trobridge John | " | " |
| A | Todd Yale | Priv. | " |
| A | Thomas John | " | " |
| 4 | Tolles Elnathan | " | " |
| 1 | Townsend Solomon | " | " |
| 4 | Thomas Samuel | " | " |
| 4 | Thomas Ephraim | " | " |
| | Tarble William | " | Colchester |
| 5 | Talmage Icabad | " | Southington |
| 5 | Thair Asa | " | Waterbury |
| 5 | Throop Benjamin | Maj. | Norwich |
| | Tracy William | Ens. | " |
| 1 | Tracy Moses | Priv. | " |
| 8 | Tykan Tyas | " | Canterbury |
| | Turner Isaac | " | Killingsworth |
| 1 | Taylor Ephraim | " | Hebron |
| D | Tiffeny Humphry | " | Symsbury |
| 4 | Tolls Elnathan | " | Milford |
| D | Tucker Jarvis | " | " |
| 5 | Taylor Simeon | " | Woodbury |
| 5 | Taylor Josiah | " | " |
| 3 | Tubbs Nathan | " | Norfolk |
| † | Tryon Isaac | " | Glastenbury |
| 2 | Thomas Stephen | " | Chatham |
| D | Thomson Epaphras | " | Seabrook |
| A | Thomson Isaiah | Lieut. | Farmington |
| [ | ]ylor Jonathan | Priv. | Middletown |
| 4 | Towner Jacobe | " | Branford |
| 4 | Terry Gamalial | Serj. | Salisbury |
| 4 | Tupper William | " | " |
| D | Vanduser Thomas | Priv. | Windsor |
| 4 | Vangason John | " | Milford |
| | Verry Jonathan | " | Chatham |
| | Wright Jacob | " | Killingly |
| D | Wilson Barzillai | " | Woodstock for 1780 & 1781 |
| † | Wilcox Jarius | Capt. | Wallingford |
| 3 | Wolcutt Joseph | Priv. | " |
| 4 | Wilson John | " | New Haven |
| 4 | Wood Elisha | " | " |
| D | Wild Jonathan | " | " |
| 4 | White Samuel | " | " |
| | Wallis Abraham | " | East Windsor |
| 1 | Warner Robert | Capt. | Middletown |

## CONNECTICUT LINE, 1781-1783.

| | Names | Rank | Places to which they belong |
|---|---|---|---|
| 4 | Willis Joseph | Priv. | Middletown |
| In⁴ | Waterman Ebenezer Jr | " | Norwich Invalid |
| In⁴ | Waterman Jo⁸ | " | " Invalid |
| 1 | Wardwell Isaac | " | Windsor |
| In⁴ | Wilder Aaron | " | New Fairfield Invalid |
| 1 | Woodbridge Timothy | " | Symsbury |
| 1 | White John | " | " |
| | Wood Justus | " | Milford |
| 4 | White Joseph | " | Derby |
| 5 | Wilson George | " | Lyme |
| 5 | Wade John | " | " |
| 1 | Whitman Lemanuel | " | Groton |
| A | Webb Gideon | " | Cheshire |
| 3 | Walter Charles | " | Norfolk |
| 3 | Wheeler John | " | " |
| 2 | Warren John | " | Bolton |
| 2 | Watkins Ephraim | " | East Haddam |
| 5 | Williams Thomas | " | " |
| 1 | Warren John | Serj. | Glastenbury |
| 1 | Wright John | Priv. | Chatham |
| 3 | Williams Daniel | Serj. | Weathersfield |
| 3 | Wells Joshua | Priv. | " |
| D | Walton Silas | " | " |
| 4 | Wheeler Thomas | " | Guilford |
| 4 | White Oliver | " | Seabrook |
| | Whittlesey Nathan | " | " { in R Island Regᵗ |
| 1 | Waters Thomas | " | Hartford |
| 5 | Willcox Giles | " | " |
| 1 | Wilton Solomon | " | Farmington |
| 2 | Williox James | " | " |
| 1 | Wilton Benjamin | " | " |
| 1 | Welton Joel | " | " |
| D | Wainwright Samuel | " | |
| 3 | Whitney Peter | " | Ashford |
| In⁴ | Weterous Wᵐ | " | " Invalid |
| 4 | White John | Lieutˑ | Branford |
| 2 | Wier Thomas | Priv. | Goshen |
| In⁴ | Williams John | " | Norwalk Invalid |
| | Woodworth Jedediah | " | Lebanon Desertᵈ |
| 1 | Welch Ebenezer | " | Washington |
| A | Wilson David | " | Stamford |
| 3 | Wardwell Jacob | " | " |
| 5 | Waterbury Wᵐ | " | " |
| A | Williams Richard | " | Fairfield |
| 4 | Yale Nash | " | Wallingford |
| 2 | Young Ebenezer | " | Hebron |
| 4 | Yates William | " | Salisbury |
| 3 | York Richard | " | Preston |

N: B: 1, 2, 3, 4, 5 denotes the Regᵗ
    D              Dragoons
    In⁴           Invalids
    †              Artificers
    H              Hazens
    A              Artillery
        Family Supplies 1781

[*State Library, Revolution* 30, 6.]

## BOUNTIES, 1781.

The United States D$^r$ To the State of Connecticut, for Bounties granted to the Towns in said State for expence of recruiting the Continental Army in 1781.

[Each man received £30 bounty.]

| Date | Name of each Recruit | By what Town procured |
|---|---|---|
| 1781 | | |
| March 15 | Joshua Reynolds | Norwich |
| " | Solomon Andrews | " |
| " | Jabez Kirtland | " |
| " | Levi Munsell | " |
| " | James Bell | " |
| " | David Mattison | " |
| " | Comfort Chapman | " |
| " | Frederick Whipple | " |
| " | Jonas Ellis | " |
| " | Phineas Knight | " |
| " | Roger Edgerton | " |
| " | Benjamin Greenslit | " |
| " | John Munsell | " |
| " | Asa Squier | " |
| " | William Armstrong | " |
| " | Oliver Everett | " |
| " | Comfort Ames | " |
| " | Thomas Rathburn | " |
| " | Jacob Pettingall | " |
| " | John Patten | " |
| " | Benjamin Downs | " |
| " | Nathan Frink | " |
| " | Cato Derrick | " |
| " | Daniel Verguson | " |
| " | Benjamin Stoddard Jun$^r$ | " |
| " | Ozias Backus | " |
| " | James Miner | " |
| " | Jonathan Jer$^h$ Beebee | " |
| " | Daniel Hendricks | " |
| " | Isaac White | " |
| " | Ezra Hartshorn | " |
| " | Moses Tracy | " |
| " | Asaph Pettingell | " |
| " | Joel Hyde | " |
| " | Daniel Armstrong Jun$^r$ | " |
| " | Ephraim Story Jun$^r$ | " |
| " | Asa Patten | " |
| " | Jacob Wright | Killingly |
| " | Joseph Robbins | " |
| " | Clement Corbin | " |
| " | Stephen Blackmer | " |
| " | John Blackmer | " |
| " | Samuel Cheese | " |
| " | Abiel Chafee | " |
| " | Josiah D. Childs | " |
| " | Benjamin Adams | " |
| " | Joshua Fuller | " |

## CONNECTICUT LINE, 1781-1783.

| Date | Name of each Recruit | By what Town procured |
|---|---|---|
| March 15 | Chester Upham | Killingly |
| " | Justin Cady | " |
| " | John Graves | " |
| " | Amasa Grover | " |
| " | Ichabod Brooks | " |
| " | Abel Fling | " |
| " | Preserved Redway | " |
| " | John Peters | " |
| " | Jacob Wright Jun' | " |
| " | Gideon Martin Jun' | " |
| " | Ebenezer Corbin | " |
| " | David Peck | Ashford |
| " | William Chuble | " |
| " | Aaron Parks | " |
| " | Ezra Davidson | " |
| " | Jonathan Buttock | " |
| " | Peter Whitney | " |
| " | William Johnson | " |
| " | Elijah Smith | " |
| " | James Hittrel | " |
| " | Darius Orcutt | " |
| " | David Tucker | Derby |
| " | Joseph Derrimo | " |
| " | Reuben Chalman | " |
| " | Primas Freeman | " |
| " | Dan Chatfield | " |
| " | Richard Pitts | " |
| " | George Clark | " |
| " | Marchant Wooster | " |
| " | Amasa Scott | " |
| " | Thomas Lee | " |
| " | Eliphalet Tomlinson | " |
| " | James Fields | " |
| " | Jonathan Loveland | Durham |
| " | Nath¹ Clark | " |
| " | Ebenezer Carr | " |
| " | Clement Carr | " |
| " | Silas Stanbourgh | " |
| " | Lemuel Stanbourgh | " |
| " | Samuel Bardin | Norfolk |
| " | Eliakim Seward | " |
| " | Nathan Tubbs | " |
| " | Serajah Comstock | " |
| " | Hendrick Biel | " |
| " | Joel Hamlin | " |
| " | Charles Walter | " |
| " | Philemon Kirkum | " |
| 16th | John Wright | Killingworth |
| " | Cornelius Chittenden | " |
| " | Paul Pierson | " |
| " | Nathan Pierson | " |
| " | Joel Griffing | " |
| " | Eleazer Baldwin | " |
| " | Joseph Buell | " |
| " | Nathan Teal | " |
| " | James Elderkin | " |
| " | Caleb Elu | " |
| " | Jonah Carter | " |

18

| Date | Name of each Recruit | By what Town procured |
|---|---|---|
| March 16th | John Griswold | Killingworth |
| " | Joel Ixbel | " |
| " | Solomon Chittenden | " |
| " | Henry Stevens | " |
| " | Phineas Jones | " |
| " | Benjamin Gillet | " |
| " | Cornelius Thorp | Fairfield |
| " | Philip Hubbard | " |
| " | James Hubbard | " |
| " | Toney Gold | " |
| " | Nehemiah Fowler | " |
| " | Seth Burr | " |
| " | George Batterson | " |
| " | William Batterson | " |
| " | Caleb Disbrow | " |
| " | Tony Hill | " |
| " | Cato Treadwell | " |
| " | Dan Tooley | " |
| " | Solomon Culver | " |
| " | Jonathan Poor | " |
| " | Fortune Sanford | " |
| " | Benjamin Treadwell | " |
| " | Nehemiah Smith Odell | " |
| " | Thomas Solley | " |
| " | Thomas Banks | " |
| " | Josiah Patchin | " |
| " | Stephen Hall | " |
| " | John Polley | " |
| " | James Whipple | " |
| " | Joseph Elwood | " |
| " | Aaron Fox | " |
| " | Peter Montgomery | " |
| " | Elijah Patchen | " |
| " | Gideon Morehouse | " |
| " | Jedidiah Sherwood | " |
| " | Daniel Westcott | " |
| " | David Parrot | " |
| " | Samuel Taylor | " |
| 15 | | Woodstock |
| " | | " |
| " | | " |
| " | | " |
| " | | " |
| " | | " |
| " | | " |
| 16th | Michael Clark | Haddam |
| " | Daniel Ray | " |
| " | Joseph Forbes | " |
| " | Andrew Southworth | " |
| " | Peter Black | " |
| " | Solomon Wadhams | Goshen |
| " | Aaron Merrills | " |
| " | Cyprian Collins | " |
| " | David Francis | " |
| " | Elisha Peck | " |
| " | Jesse Royce | " |
| " | Jonathan Deane | " |
| " | Job Willcox Jun' | " |

| Date | Name of each Recruit | By what Town procured |
|---|---|---|
| March 16th | Thomas Wyar | Goshen |
| " | Julius Beach | " |
| " | Caleb Munson | " |
| " | Seth Munson | " |
| " | Nathan Carter | " |
| " | James Crane | " |
| 20th | Asahel Holcomb 3d | Symsbury |
| " | David Enos Junr | " |
| " | Agar Bonton | " |
| " | Ezekiel Davis | " |
| " | William Philips | " |
| " | Levi Wadsworth | " |
| " | Ezekiel Messenger | " |
| " | James Aldridge | " |
| " | Johnson Tiff | " |
| " | Morris F. Gerald | " |
| " | David Parkhurst | " |
| " | Eli Fuller | " |
| " | William Shepard Junr | " |
| " | Ezra Roberts | " |
| " | Jacob Fuller | " |
| " | Amaziah Barker | " |
| " | Jacob Holiday | " |
| " | John G. Holcomb | " |
| " | John Slater | " |
| " | Jeremiah Case | " |
| " | David Taylor | " |
| " | Ebenezer Edgerton | " |
| " | Zebulon Wallace | " |
| " | Rufus Mason | " |
| " | David Eggleston | " |
| " | Thomas Phelps | " |
| " | Jacob Gillet | " |
| " | Timothy Woodbridge | " |
| " | John Hunt | " |
| " | John White | " |
| " | Timothy Humphry | " |
| " | Philip Gregory | " |
| " | Jared Touser | " |
| " | Francis Stanley | Somers |
| " | Samuel Burges | " |
| " | Isaac Colton | " |
| " | Joel Pelton | " |
| " | William Hamlin | " |
| 23d | William Merritt | Hebron |
| " | Jesse Thomson | Cheshire |
| " | Joel Barns | " |
| " | Dick Bristol | " |
| " | Cezar Doolittle | " |
| 26th | John Abbee | Mansfield |
| " | Elihu Reed | " |
| " | Benajah Brown | " |
| " | David Brown | " |
| " | Stephen Reed | " |
| " | Jesse Badcock | " |
| " | Anthony Needham | " |
| " | William Mooney | " |
| " | Oliver Smith Junr | " |

| Date | Name of each Recruit | By what Town procured |
|---|---|---|
| March 26th | Hezekiah Wailey | Fairfield |
| " | Ebenezer Patchin | " |
| " | John Andrews | " |
| " | Abijah Hubbel | " |
| " | Levi Mallery | " |
| 27th | Ichabod West | Tolland |
| " | James Covil | " |
| " | Moses Coy | " |
| " | Silvanus Gage | " |
| " | Reuben Robinson | " |
| " | Joel Barnard | " |
| " | Abel Stimson | " |
| 28th | Daniel Cone 3d | East Haddam |
| " | James Reeves | " |
| " | Thomas Williams | " |
| " | Samuel Mobbs | " |
| " | Pierce Mobbs | " |
| " | Nathan Luther | " |
| " | Nathl Warner Junr | " |
| " | Ansell Patterson | " |
| " | Ephriam Watkins | " |
| " | Ebenezer Post | " |
| " | Isaac Williams | " |
| " | David Hattuck | " |
| " | Abel Bingham | " |
| " | Robert Hull | " |
| " | Eli Hull | " |
| " | Cuff Negro | " |
| " | Richard Mack | " |
| " | Samuel Buckett | " |
| " | Stephen Sparrow 2d | " |
| " | Judah Warner | " |
| " | Joel Spencer Junr | " |
| " | Charles Goodwin | " |
| " | Asael Hervey | " |
| " | Robert Watkins | " |
| " | Isaac Wardwell | Windsor |
| " | Jabez Colt | " |
| " | Peter Roberts | " |
| " | James Eggleston | " |
| " | Allen Prior | " |
| " | Timothy Horskins | " |
| " | Remembrance Sheldon | " |
| " | Reuben Hill | " |
| " | Calvin Willson | " |
| " | Elihu Mather | " |
| 29th | Jack Negro | Hebron |
| " | Samuel Tyler | " |
| " | Seth Smith | New Hartford |
| " | Simeon Fox | " |
| " | Bassett Fox | " |
| " | Ichabod Talmadge | Southington |
| " | Jonathan Case | " |
| " | Luke Hart | " |
| " | George Dickinson | " |
| " | Amos Bunnel | " |
| " | Robert Cook | " |
| " | Archibald Cook | " |
| " | William Jones | " |

| Date | Name of each Recruit | By what Town procured |
|---|---|---|
| March 29th | Zebulon Dudley | Southington |
| " | Adonijah Rose | " |
| " | Abraham Tuttle | " |
| " | David Andrews | " |
| " | Bordle Hoose | " |
| 30th | Benjamin Brown | Canterbury |
| " | David Spencer | " |
| " | Jedidiah Adams | " |
| " | John Maccarty | " |
| " | Curtis Cleaveland | " |
| " | Silas Glass | " |
| " | Nathl Gates | " |
| " | Benjamin Durfee | " |
| " | Jonathan Simons | " |
| " | Mason Green | " |
| " | James Duggens | " |
| " | J. Smith | " |
| " | John Cremer | " |
| " | Abiel Farnam | " |
| " | Javan Negro | " |
| " | Jedidiah Green | " |
| " | Rowland Cotton | Pomfret |
| " | Alfred Dresser | " |
| " | Nathl Stowell | " |
| " | Joseph Ross | " |
| " | Paul Davison | " |
| " | Ichabod Downing | " |
| " | Abijah Downing | " |
| " | Enoch Hurlbutt | " |
| " | John Ballard | " |
| " | Jonathan Stevens | " |
| April 2d | Moses George | Cornwall |
| " | Jacob Young | " |
| " | John Carter Junr | " |
| " | Samuel Scovill Junr | " |
| " | Jack Freedom | " |
| " | Abner Lazel | " |
| " | Deliverance Stow | " |
| " | Rolin Jeffery | " |
| " | Elijah Holcomb | Windsor |
| " | Solomon Ruggs | Farmington |
| " | Aaron Hart | " |
| " | Solomon Ruggs Junr | " |
| " | Seth Arnold | " |
| " | William Steele | " |
| " | Ashble Merrills | " |
| " | Thomas Stedman | " |
| " | Gad North | " |
| " | Ezra Belding Junr | " |
| " | Prince Negro | " |
| " | Abel Allen | " |
| " | Sage Churchill | " |
| " | Solomon Welton | " |
| " | Timothy Fox | " |
| " | Moses Parsons | " |
| " | Thomas F. Bishop | " |
| " | Matthew Lee | " |
| " | Joel Welton | " |

| Date | Name of each Recruit | By what Town procured |
|---|---|---|
| April 2d | Roswell Cook | Farmington |
| " | Uri Hungerford | " |
| " | Isaac Tillotson | " |
| " | Amos Couch | " |
| " | Seth Root | " |
| " | Lemuel Lane | " |
| " | Robert Carr | " |
| " | Solomon Woodruff | " |
| " | Asael Tollotson | " |
| " | Gedar Woodruff | " |
| " | Obed. Gridley | " |
| " | James Gridley Junr | " |
| " | Jesse Shepard | " |
| " | Peter Rose | " |
| " | Reuben Hamlin | " |
| " | Obadiah Andrus | " |
| " | Isaac Nelson | " |
| " | Timothy Seward | " |
| " | Abner Tuttle | " |
| " | Isaac Bartholemew | " |
| " | Amos Rich | " |
| " | Abraham Bartholemew | |
| 4th | Daniel Roley | East Haddam |
| " | Thomas Green | Harwinton |
| " | Hezekiah Catlin | " |
| " | Shubael Crow | New Hartford |
| " | John Norwash | Glassenbury |
| " | Cuff Acklin | " |
| " | Thomas Brewer | " |
| " | William Peck | Somers |
| " | Reuben Perry | " |
| " | Jacob Granger | Suffield |
| 5th | Alexander McCulpin | Glassenbury |
| " | Jacob Strong | East Windsor |
| 6th | Joseph Willson | Willington |
| " | Reuben Dodge | " |
| " | Samuel Eldridge | " |
| " | Joseph Jacobs | " |
| " | Heman Hatch | " |
| " | Abel Stowell | " |
| " | Samuel Stowell | " |
| " | Alexander Ewing | " |
| " | Ebenezer Nye | " |
| " | Ezra Sibley | " |
| " | George Hatch | " |
| " | Cyrus Fenton | " |
| " | John George | Lebanon |
| " | Joseph Shantop | " |
| " | Reuben Tatson | " |
| " | Ezekiel Mazzeen | " |
| " | Elimath Elderkin | " |
| " | Ives Huntington | " |
| " | Philip Hill | " |
| " | Jedidiah Woodworth | " |
| " | Chester Waterman | " |
| " | Samuel Rice | " |
| " | Benjamin Cuthbert | " |
| " | Joshua Bill | " |

| Date | Name of each Recruit | By what Town procured |
|---|---|---|
| April 6th | Joseph Tinney | Lebanon |
| " | Daniel Beamont | " |
| " | Joel Clark | " |
| " | Uriah Palmer | " |
| " | John Clark 3d | " |
| " | Abner Hill | " |
| " | David Davison | " |
| " | William Fish | " |
| " | Marlack Tang | " |
| " | Lemuel Stancliff | Torrington |
| " | John Barns | Canaan |
| " | Annanias Porridge | " |
| " | Samuel Porridge | " |
| " | David Beebe | " |
| " | John Onkshun | " |
| " | Gideon Jonathan | " |
| " | Thomas Studson | " |
| " | Jeremiah Wheedon | " |
| " | Joseph Johnson | " |
| " | Asa Hyde | " |
| " | David Jones | " |
| 7th | John Crocker | Symsbury |
| " | Roderick Adams | " |
| " | Gad Alderman | " |
| 10th | Benjamin Herrington | Enfield |
| " | Daniel Perkins 2d | " |
| " | John Mooney | " |
| " | Briant Brown | " |
| " | Thomas Ward | " |
| " | Oliver Field | " |
| " | Ephraim Burges | " |
| " | Ephraim Burges Junr | " |
| " | Joseph Sheeker | " |
| 11th | Joel Doane | Saybrook |
| " | Reuben Bushnell | " |
| " | Cornelius Teigh | " |
| " | Job Bulkley | " |
| " | Benjamin Wilcox | " |
| " | Jesse Gorham | " |
| " | Gideon Buckingham | " |
| " | Richard Doane | " |
| " | Constant Chapman | " |
| " | Jude Pratt | " |
| " | Solomon Goff | " |
| " | David Haines | " |
| " | George Harris | " |
| " | George Buckingham | " |
| " | Amos Stephens | " |
| " | Samuel Lynde Junr | " |
| " | Puryer Reeves | " |
| " | Constant Bushnell | " |
| " | Zebulon Bushnell | " |
| " | Benjamin Doty | " |
| " | Jack Tobey | " |
| " | Joseph Whiteley | " |
| " | James Grant | " |
| " | Robert Newell | " |
| " | John George Wisetman | " |

| Date | Name of each Recruit | By what Town procured |
|---|---|---|
| April 11th | George Clark | Saybrook |
| " | George Wright Jun' | " |
| " | Duncan McCullum | " |
| " | Samuel Comstock | " |
| 12th | Seth Baldwin | Hebron |
| " | Daniel Polly | " |
| " | Samuel Rude | " |
| " | Reuben Rolingson | Guilford |
| " | Joel Johnson | " |
| " | Ira Atkins | " |
| " | Edmund Shelly | " |
| " | Reuben Evarts | " |
| " | Gilbert Graves | " |
| " | Jehiel Willcox | " |
| " | Eber Hall | " |
| " | Timothy Shelly | " |
| 13th | Brigadier Loomis | Torrington |
| 17th | Jeremiah Cunnel | Ashford |
| " | Pelatiah Bugbee | Mansfield |
| 19th | James Walker | Union |
| " | Perly Coy | " |
| " | William Moore | " |
| " | George Dillaby | " |
| " | David Thomson | " |
| " | Nehemiah Parker | " |
| " | Joseph Lawson | " |
| " | Peter Marsh | Plainfield |
| " | Stephen Bennet | " |
| " | Reuben Briant | " |
| " | Jeremiah Bennet | " |
| " | John Fagins | " |
| " | Daniel Dunham | " |
| " | Frederick Waldon | " |
| " | Amos Simons | " |
| " | Nath¹ Price | " |
| 23d | Frank Buck | Lebanon |
| 26th | Ebenezer Walker | Bolton |
| " | Richard Lawrence | Hebron |
| " | James Thomson | Union |
| " | David Butler | Harwinton |
| " | Timothy Rossetter | " |
| " | Caleb Elmour | " |
| " | Andrew Peters | Coventry |
| " | Simeon Commins | " |
| " | Jonathan Ball | " |
| " | Job Leason | " |
| " | Caleb Turner | Killingworth |
| 28th | Samuel Fargo | Willington |
| " | Seth Dodge | " |
| " | Zephon Flower | New Hartford |
| 30th | Elijah Cone 2d | East Haddam |
| " | Shubael Welton | Watertown |
| " | Jonathan Gaylord | " |
| " | Isaac Levingston | " |
| " | Lemuel Cook | " |
| " | Zarah Cook | " |
| " | Jn° Whitney | " |
| " | James Fulford | " |

## CONNECTICUT LINE, 1781–1783.

| Date | Name of each Recruit | By what Town procured |
|---|---|---|
| April 30th | Josiah Preston | Winchester |
| " | Richard Coit | " |
| " | Richard Wares | Guilford |
| " | Bartlet Rowlinson | " |
| May 2d | John Love | Somers |
| " | Thomas Watson | Stonington |
| " | Thomas Worden | " |
| " | Ephraim Harry | " |
| " | Anthony Defloris | " |
| " | Kudjoe Helmes | " |
| " | Jacob Sawas | " |
| " | Robbin Nedson | " |
| " | Benidict Eggleston | " |
| " | Ichabod Worden | " |
| " | Cato Jessup | " |
| " | Edward Nedson | " |
| " | Stephen Gavitt | " |
| " | Thomas Lambert | " |
| " | William Skesuck | " |
| " | Cato Cuff | " |
| " | Lodewick Paul | " |
| " | Benjamin George | " |
| " | Nath¹ Cottril | " |
| " | Christopher Avery | " |
| " | Jabez Morton | " |
| " | Daniel Hary | " |
| " | Thomas Paucheage | " |
| " | Jacob Robin | " |
| " | William Hudson | " |
| " | Samuel Peters | " |
| " | William Foster | " |
| " | Peter Apes | " |
| " | Isaac Herd | " |
| " | John Robertson | " |
| 5th | John Bloss | Hebron |
| 9th | Eleazer Hatch | Tolland |
| 12th | John Rowley | Windsor |
| " | Samson Cuff | " |
| " | Eli Kelsey | Killingworth |
| " | Lyman Isbell | " |
| " | Josiah Chatfield 2d | " |
| " | Jonathan Ward | " |
| " | Elias Stevens | " |
| " | Joseph Hull | " |
| " | Abraham Hurd Junr | " |
| " | James Wellman | " |
| " | Joseph Teal | " |
| " | John Carter Junr | " |
| " | Gideon Buell | " |
| " | William Jones | " |
| " | Nath¹ Chittenden | " |
| " | Joel Willcox | " |
| 14th | Hubbard Burrows | Groton |
| " | Nath¹ Chapman | " |
| " | Jesse Holt | " |
| " | Jacob Lamb | " |
| " | Edward Freeman | " |
| " | John Mills | " |

| Date | Name of each Recruit | By what Town procured |
|---|---|---|
| May 15th | Jabez Cook | New Hartford |
| " | Nathan Mallery | Kent |
| " | Nathan Wheeler | " |
| " | Philetus Swift | " |
| " | Roger Luke | " |
| " | Samuel Ingraham | " |
| " | John Lay | Lyme |
| " | Nath¹ Smith | " |
| " | Sam¹ Bartholemew | " |
| " | John Lay 2d | " |
| " | Joseph Ransom | " |
| " | John Trube | " |
| " | William I. White | " |
| " | Amaziah Corwin | " |
| " | Joseph Pumham | " |
| " | William Butler | " |
| " | George W. Shepman | " |
| " | Isaac Scipis | " |
| " | Edward DeWolf | " |
| " | Ezekiel Beckwith | " |
| " | Benidict Minor | " |
| 16th | Stephen Barnes | New Hartford |
| " | Solomon W. Beardsley | New Fairfield |
| " | Benjamin Knapp | " |
| " | Abel Guthrie | " |
| " | Calvin Bulkley | " |
| " | James Tilly | " |
| " | John Randall | " |
| " | Stephen Fox | " |
| " | Jason Gay | " |
| " | Moses Dutton | " |
| " | Heman Carter | " |
| " | Humphrey Gilbert | Mansfield |
| " | Marshal Keyes | " |
| " | John Bugbee | " |
| " | Titus Beadle | " |
| " | Joseph Dimick | " |
| 17th | Skeen Douglass | New Milford |
| " | Daniel Utter | " |
| " | John Summers | " |
| " | John McCoy | " |
| " | David Blacknee | " |
| " | Joseph C. Hawley | " |
| " | William Whiteley | " |
| " | Samuel Hull | " |
| " | Daniel Johnson | " |
| " | Joel Sturdivant | " |
| " | Bostwick Ruggles | " |
| " | Ebenezer Steloon | " |
| " | Daniel Ower | " |
| " | Joseph Douglass | " |
| " | Isaac Lockwood | " |
| " | William Spear | " |
| " | David Buell | " |
| " | John Barnet | " |
| " | Frederick Slain | " |
| " | John Bartoo | " |
| " | Esquier Davenport | " |

| Date | | Name of each Recruit | By what Town procured |
|---|---|---|---|
| May | 17th | William Luke | New Milford |
| | 18th | Jonathan Newman | Ridgfield |
| | " | Patrick Ambrose | " |
| | " | John Dennison | " |
| | " | Joseph Hawley | " |
| | " | Isaac Bennet | " |
| | " | Doge Williams | " |
| | " | Solomon Benn | " |
| | " | Nehemiah Olmstead | " |
| | " | Hezekiah Boutin | " |
| | " | Robert Willson | " |
| | " | Talcott Hawley | " |
| | 21st | Sherry Reed | Coventry |
| | " | Samuel Goodell | " |
| | " | Ebenezer Youngs | Hebron |
| | " | John Wright | " |
| | " | Thomas McGuire | " |
| | " | Peter Allen | " |
| | 22d | Henry Pollester | Voluntown |
| | " | David Coy | " |
| | " | Christopher Wier | " |
| | " | John Desiton | " |
| | " | John Kelly | " |
| | " | Bryan Gordon | " |
| | " | Jonathan Rogers | " |
| | " | Daniel Dowd | " |
| | " | John Frederick Jone | " |
| | " | Andrew Hensley | " |
| | " | Henry Pond | Colchester |
| | " | James Shoat | " |
| | " | Peter Kellogg | " |
| | " | Josiah Rogers | " |
| | " | Abner Hills Junr | " |
| | " | John Lines | " |
| | " | Richard Beebe | " |
| | " | David Waters | " |
| | " | Cezar Beman | " |
| | " | Nathan Roberts | " |
| | " | Gideon Quass | " |
| | " | William Gibbs | " |
| | " | Elihu Dodge | " |
| | " | Peter Meguire | " |
| | " | Comfort Beebe | " |
| | " | Tony Edor | " |
| | " | Israel Ransom | " |
| | " | Simeon Shon | " |
| | " | John Godfrey | " |
| | " | Henry Hawton | " |
| | " | Champlin Harris | " |
| | " | James Freeman | " |
| | " | Daniel Wright | " |
| | " | Martin Stiles | " |
| | " | Jasper P. Sears | " |
| | " | Russell Williams | " |
| | " | John Roberts | " |
| | " | Derby Goff | " |
| | " | Alpheus Wright | " |
| | " | James French | " |

| Date | Name of each Recruit | By what Town procured |
|---|---|---|
| May 23d | Jeremiah Booth | Colchester |
| 24th | Jeremiah Parmerlee | Milford |
| " | Joseph Cowdry | " |
| " | Samuel Wier | " |
| " | Levi Lattimer | Wethersfield |
| " | Wilber Hathaway | Suffield |
| " | Seth Hathaway | " |
| " | Levi French | " |
| " | Ready Lareey | " |
| " | Josiah Rising | " |
| " | Joseph King | " |
| " | James Screen | " |
| 25th | Samuel Mott | Danbury |
| " | Henry Goslee | Chatham |
| " | Levi Benidict | Torrington |
| 28th | Zechariah Waldo | Pomfret |
| " | Edward Crandell | " |
| " | Luther Grover | " |
| " | Samuel Lyon | " |
| " | Gardiner Cleaveland | " |
| " | John Robertson | " |
| " | David Dick | " |
| " | Ebenezer Grow | " |
| " | James McFarland | " |
| " | Cato | " |
| " | William Obriant | " |
| " | John Pearle | " |
| " | Richard Weax | " |
| " | Asa Gear | " |
| " | John Kimball | " |
| " | Benjamin Cady | " |
| " | Jared Kimball | " |
| " | Joseph Cheeney | " |
| " | Reuben Sharp | " |
| " | Joseph Craft | " |
| " | Archelaus Arney | " |
| " | Daniel Spencer | " |
| " | Ward Cotton | " |
| " | Stephen Barns | New Fairfield |
| " | John Katon | Windsor |
| 30th | Jesse Kneeland | Chatham |
| " | William Gladding | Haddam |
| " | Daniel Bates | " |
| " | Aaron Stevens | Woodbury |
| " | Timothy Closby | " |
| " | John Tyler | " |
| " | John White | " |
| " | John Glazier | " |
| " | Zuar Bradley | " |
| " | Elnathan Miner | " |
| " | Electus M. Backus | " |
| " | Ezekiel Root | " |
| " | Gideon W. Mider | " |
| " | James Stoddard | " |
| " | Amos Davis | " |
| " | Gideon Curtiss | " |
| " | Samuel Cowell | " |
| 31st | Benjamin Farnum | Ashford |

## CONNECTICUT LINE, 1781-1783.

| Date | Name of each Recruit | By what Town procured |
|---|---|---|
| May 31st | Thomas Simons | Stafford |
| " | Silas Blodget | " |
| " | David Gardiner | Groton |
| " | George Sealy | " |
| " | Elihu Babcock | " |
| " | Abraham Neils | " |
| " | Anthony Goodsell | " |
| " | Robert Brice | " |
| " | Cary Latham | " |
| June 1st | Jacob Patching | Redding |
| 2d | Inis Harper | Groton |
| " | Joseph Barrows | " |
| " | James Anderson | " |
| " | Jabez Edgcomb | " |
| " | Henry Brightman | " |
| 4th | Stephen DeWolf | Hebron |
| " | James Leason | Ridgfield |
| " | Cato Freedom | Woodstock |
| 5th | Josiah Hendrick | Redding |
| " | Daniel Couch Junr | " |
| " | John Springer | " |
| " | Whala Springer | " |
| " | John Lines | " |
| " | James Dixon | " |
| " | Henry Hopkins | " |
| " | James Thomson | " |
| " | William Eldridge | Tolland |
| " | Timothy Halsted | Harwinton |
| " | Ebenezer Talker | Kent |
| " | Swift Chamberlain | " |
| " | Thomas Prows | Lebanon |
| " | Jona. Danquegen | " |
| 6th | Thomas Van Dunsen | Windsor |
| " | David H. Potter | Winchester |
| " | Humphrey Tiffany | Symsbury |
| " | Edward Crow | Ridgfield |
| " | William Kenn | New Milford |
| 7th | Elias Carpenter | Woodstock |
| " | Eliphalet Carpenter | " |
| " | Isaiah Pratt | " |
| " | Ebenezer Bacon | " |
| " | Nathl Johnson | " |
| " | David Hammond | " |
| " | Stephen Child | " |
| " | William Westcott | " |
| 8th | Thomas Manning | Stafford |
| " | Amasa Dimmick | " |
| " | Daniel Davis | Groton |
| " | David Chester | " |
| " | Jesse Williams | " |
| " | Daniel Morley | Glassenbury |
| 9th | Reuben Sherman | Coventry |
| 11th | Stephen Ben Davis | Newtown |
| " | Thomas Taylor | Norwalk |
| " | Thomas Wasson | " |
| " | Jesse Olmstead | " |
| " | Jonathan Brown | " |
| " | Daniel St John | " |

| Date | Name of each Recruit | By what Town procured |
|---|---|---|
| June 11th | Elijah Betts | Norwalk |
| " | Isaiah Grant | Colchester |
| " | Nathl Roberts | Chatham |
| 13th | John Wheeler | Norfolk |
| " | Bristo Johnson | Colchester |
| " | Benjamin Dodge | " |
| 15th | John Trumbull | Preston |
| " | William Ely | " |
| " | Simeon Guile | " |
| " | James Brand | " |
| " | John Whitman | " |
| " | Joseph Davis | " |
| " | John Gates | " |
| " | Elias Meson | " |
| " | Silas Jacobs | " |
| " | James Nedson | " |
| " | Richard York | " |
| " | Joseph Quochetts | " |
| " | Joseph Hanniball | " |
| " | James Simons | " |
| " | Abraham Guile | " |
| " | Peleg Billings | " |
| " | Joseph S. Champlin | East Haddam |
| " | Joseph Stewart | " |
| 16th | Jeremiah Hutchen | Torrington |
| 19th | Adoniram Benton | East Windsor |
| " | Phineas Strong Junr | " |
| " | Elijah Benton | " |
| " | Henry Booth | Coventry |
| " | Samuel Burdon | " |
| 20th | Solomon Bixly Junr | Stafford |
| 21st | Eton Jones Junr | Litchfield |
| " | Asa Gillet | " |
| " | Reuben Smith Junr | " |
| " | Ebenezer Seeley | " |
| " | Roswell Kilborn | " |
| " | John Welch 2d | " |
| " | Midian Griswold | " |
| " | Orange Barnes | " |
| " | Solomon Lindsley Junr | " |
| " | George Negro | " |
| " | Samuel Jones | " |
| " | James Jones | Harwinton |
| 26th | George Griffith | Voluntown |
| " | Ephraim Tucker | " |
| " | Elijah Fayer | " |
| " | Daniel Palmer | " |
| " | Reuben Bryant | " |
| " | Miles Jordan | " |
| " | Eliab Egleston | " |
| " | John Gray | " |
| " | Zadock Hurd | " |
| " | Alexander Knox | " |
| " | Reuben Adams | " |
| " | Samuel Palmer | " |
| " | Pharis Barnard | Coventry |
| July 5th | Ephraim White | Stafford |
| 6th | Joseph Pease | East Windsor |

## CONNECTICUT LINE, 1781-1783.

| Date | Name of each Recruit | By what Town procured |
|---|---|---|
| July 6th | Hazard Negro | East Windsor |
| " | William Jackson | Newtown |
| 11th | John Royce | Hebron |
| 12th | Joseph Wheeler | Stafford |
| 17th | Benjamin Elsworth | East Windsor |
| 19th | David Brown | Mansfield |
| 31st | Daniel Miller | " |
| Augt 1st | John Lee | Ashford |
| 8th | Charles Barnes | New Fairfield |
| 16th | Edward Chapman | Hebron |
| 20th | Solomon Eaton | Tolland |
| 28 | Nathan Chadwick | Lyme |
| " | Benjamin DeWolf | " |
| Septr 6th | Christopher Youngs | Redding |
| 14th | Obadiah Taylor | New Hartford |
| " | Amos Tylor | " |
| 25th | Cato Negro | East Windsor |
| 27th | John Danielson | Newtown |
| " | Edward Jessup | " |
| " | Ezekiel Bennet | " |
| Octr 3d | William Lement | Washington |
| " | Justus Taylor | " |
| " | Ephraim Doane | " |
| " | Simon Rose | " |
| 15th | David Plummer | Redding |
| " | Isaac Stedman | Groton |
| " | John Downer | " |
| 16th | Thomas Hutchinson | Ridgfield |
| 20th | Frederick Storrs | Mansfield |
| Novr 8 | William Short | Killingly |
| " | John Sweet | " |
| " | Ebenezer Brown | " |
| " | Benjamin Talbutt | " |
| " | William Burrus | " |
| " | Jeremiah Robinson | " |
| 9th | Seth Baldwin | Hebron |
| 17th | Ezra Ramsdell | Colchester |
| " | Moses Loomiss | Coventry |
| 20th | Thomas Fitz Simmons | Hebron |
| 28th | Jedediah Kimball | Norwich |
| " | Thomas Brooks | " |
| " | Josiah Doane | Saybrook |
| 29th | Jethro Freeman | Derby |
| " | Marshall Bayard | Washington |
| 30th | Noah Merrill | New Hartford |
| " | James Benham | " |
| Decr 11th | Jeff Liberty | Washington |
| 19th | Lemuel Stancliff | Torrington |
| " | Andrew Fester | " |
| " | Nicholas Bosher | " |
| 1782 | | |
| Jany 21st | Samuel Shelly | Stratford |
| 24th | Isaac Olmstead | Redding |
| 28th | Daniel Smith | Norwich |
| 29th | Enoch Crovel | Willington |
| 30th | John Jenks | Coventry |
| Febry 7th | Elijah Atwood Junr | Woodbury |
| 13th | Ebenezer Shaw | Canterbury |

| Date | Name of each Recruit | By what Town procured |
|---|---|---|
| Feb 13th | Archelaus Ame | Canterbury |
| 14th | Daniel G. Raymond | Norwalk |
| " | Jacob Hayden | " |
| March 1st | Isaac Higgins | Fairfield |
| 6th | Selah Hart | Farmington |
| " | Josiah Barns Jun' | " |
| " | David Hayden | " |
| " | David Hayden Jun' | " |
| " | Zephaniah Hull | " |
| " | Jedidiah Seward | " |
| 7th | Francis Barnard | Lyme |
| " | John Lay 4th | " |
| 8th | Daniel Rider Jun' | Stafford |
| 12th | William Peck | Symsbury |
| " | John Allen | |
| April 1st | Cazar Landing | Guilford |
| May 15th | John Pensyl | Stonington |
| 30th | Isaac Avery | Groton |
| Aug't 12th | Robert Johnson | Coventry |
| Sep't 20th | Jos. Paro, alias Liberty | Haddam |
| Oct' 23rd | Joshua Northrup Jun' | Newtown |
| 25th | Abijah Smith | Coventry |
| Dec' 31st | William Osborn | Haddam |
| 1783 | | |
| Jan'y 15th | John Warson | Torrington |
| 21st | Ruel Africa | Coventry |
| May 24th | John Smith | Woodstock |
| June 3d | Eliphalet Spafford | Windham |
| " | Aaron Kingsley | " |
| " | Stephen Bennet | " |
| " | Lathrop Frink | " |
| " | Eleazer Robertson | " |
| " | Jedidiah Hebard | " |
| " | Daniel Woodward | " |
| " | John Dingley | " |
| " | Roswell Simons | " |
| " | Joseph Barrows | " |
| " | Charles Ripley | " |
| " | Juba Dyer | " |
| " | Jesse Gilbert | " |
| " | Elisha Back | " |
| " | James L. Dean | " |
| " | Ethiel London | " |
| " | Seth Laraba | " |
| " | Joseph Abbe | " |
| " | Nath'l Abbe | " |
| " | John Abbe | " |
| " | Zophar Robinson | " |
| " | Abner Lilley | " |
| " | Elijah Randall | " |
| 1784 | | |
| March 15th | Samuel Ames | Waterbury |
| " | David Davis | " |
| " | Moses Wooster | " |
| " | Asael Parker | " |
| " | Bethel Camp | " |
| " | Truman Hotchkiss | " |
| " | Stephen Bristol | " |

## CONNECTICUT LINE, 1781–1783.

| Date | Name of each Recruit | By what Town procured |
|---|---|---|
| March 15th | Humphry Potter | Waterbury |
| " | James Prout | " |
| " | Jacob Morgan | " |
| " | Richard Lawrence | " |
| " | Levi Bronson | " |
| " | Joel Lane | " |
| " | Josiah Atkins | " |
| " | Osi Hitchcocks | " |
| " | Benjamin Burnham | " |
| " | Rozel Hotchkiss | " |
| " | John Flair | " |
| Septr 30th | Samuel Taylor Junr | Fairfield |

[*Comptroller's Office, Haskill's Receipts, 35.*]

# RETURNS FROM TOWNS, 1781.

## NEW LONDON RETURN.

A Return of Inlisted Soldiers into the Continental Army by the Town of New London For the year 1781, viz;

Adi Chapman
Bliss Wilabey
Samuel Rogers
William Matterson
Jese Ward
William Clark
Joshua Kendal

A Return of Inlisted Soldiers in the Continental Army before the year 1781, viz,

James Gray
Sylvester Miner
Benj{o} Brooks
James Douglass Junr
Benjamin Darrow
John Minard
William Prentice
Ichabod Beckwith
David Goodfaith
Joseph Copp Junr
Roland Swift
Peter Holt
Daniel Plumb
Joseph Morgan
Simon Georgay
James Robertson
John Rogers 4th
Thomas Harris
Solomon Douglass
Samuel Weever

Robert Frasher
William Chappell
Nathan Douglass Junr
Boanerges Beebe
James Giddis hired a man in his Room [Peter Holt]
John Daniels
John Butler
Daniel Henry
Alpheus Chappell
George Manwaring
Noah Chappell
Tim{o} Beckwith Junr
Benjn Chappell Junr

Capt George Hurlbut
Capt Richd Douglass
Capt Wm Colfax
Capt Wm Richards
Lieut Peter Robenson

The above is Copy delivered into the Com{tte} New London Mar 20 1782

[Besides the above, another list contains the following additional names.]

Wm Fargo Junr
Danl Comin
John Stewart.

[*Connecticut Historical Society.*]

## LEBANON RETURN.

List of Soldiers of Lebanon now in ye Con{l} army as allowed by the Assembly May 1781

Elip{t} Tisdale
Richd Woodworth
Nathl Porter
Humphrey Ball
Thos Earl
Cash Palatine
Elip{t} Dower
Uriah Polley

Wm Bentley
Dan. Jones
Nero Cross
Elijah Bill
Recomp{e} Woodworth
Dav{d} Lewis
Nathl Fitch Artif{r}
Allen Prat a [    ]

CONNECTICUT LINE, 1781-1783.

Wᵐ Williams
Beriah Badcock
Dennis Torney
Jez Palmer
Jnᵒ Whiteley Artifʳ
Jnᵒ Allen

Towns Quota    81
in Service    45
   —
Deficient    36

Recruits, raisᵈ 1781

Jos. Shantop
Reuben Tatson
Ezˡ Mazzeen
Elemoth Elderkin
Jos. Huntington
Phillip Hill
Jed. Woodworth
Chester Waterman
Samˡ Bill
Benj Cuthburt
Joshua Bill

Jos. Finney
Dan Beumont
Joel Clark
Uriah Palmer
Jnᵒ Clark 8ᵈ
Davᵈ Davison
Wᵐ Fish
Marleck Jany
Frank Buck
Jnᵒ Danquenen
Thoˢ Brown

[*Connecticut Historical Society.*]

Names of Men belonging to the Town of Lebanon, engaged in the Continental Army during the War, as returnd lately by Genˡ Washington

Uriah Polley
Thoˢ Earl
Humphy Ball
Beriah Badcock
Nathˡˡ Porter
Wᵐ Williams
Cash Palatine

Dennis Torney
Wᵐ Jones
Richᵈ Woodworth
Cuff Wells
Jacob Rannee
Elipˡ Downer

Beside the above We have in yᵉ Conˡˡ [                      ]
Persons Viz

Jabez Palmer for yᵉ War
John Whiteley Artifʳ
John Allen, an old Country Man
Wᵐ Bentley, for yᵉ W. (Norwich)
Danˡˡ Jones for yᵉ W. (Colchester)
Allen Pratt
Alpheus Polley

Thoˢ Baker, hird by Jonᵃ Bill
Ezra Downer (Bolton)
Nero Cross, inlisted last Spring for 3
  years
Elijah Bill, at home on Furlough
Recompence Woodworth

Lebanon Mar 5 1781

Upon the most carefull & mature Enquiry & Consideration, We Judge That We have full & sufficient Reason to claim, also, the next foregoing Persons belonging to this Town, as actually & bona fide engaged & serving in yᵉ Continental Army. (We have also missd & loose two or three, who were in our first Return which is lost & we cannot find their Names)

Test in behalf of yᵉ Town of Lebanon

Wᵐ Williams     ⎫
Wᵐ Huntington  ⎬ Select Men
Silas Phelps      ⎭

add David Lewis inlisted p Capˡ Fitch & received Cloathˢ & Refreshments from Lebanon

also Jnᵒ Polley who listed at Fairfield

[*Connecticut Historical Society.*]

[Another list dated Feb. 28, 1781, gives the following additional names.]

John Bray Deserted now Lives at or Near Winsor
Hezekiah Buel Artʳ
Nathaniel Fitch artificer

[*Connecticut Historical Society.*]

## REDDING RETURN.

£30 Bounties for Sundry Soldiers bel$^\text{g}$ to Reading

| Date | Names of Soldiers | Date | Names of Soldiers |
|---|---|---|---|
| 1781 | | June 5 | James Dixon |
| June 1 | Jacob Vatching | " | Henry Hopkins |
| 5 | Josiah Hendrick | " | James Thomson |
| " | Daniel Couch J$^r$ | Sep. 6 | Christopher Youngs |
| " | Jn$^o$ Springer | Oct. 15 | David Plummer |
| " | Whala Springer | 1782 | |
| " | Jn$^o$ Lines | Jan. 24 | Isaac Olmsted |

[*State Library, Revolution 23.*]

## KILLINGLY RETURN.

These certify that the following Persons was Raised by the Town of Killingly for their Quota of Recruits to fill up the Continental Army Are as follows Viz

| | |
|---|---|
| Clement Corbin | Abil Flingg |
| Chester Upham | Justin Cady |
| Joshua Fuller | John Peters |
| Benjamin Adams | Ichabod Brooks |
| Josiah D. Child | William Barrows |
| Ebenezer Corbin | Amasa Grover |
| Abial Chaffee | Benja Taulburt |
| Samuel Cheese | Preserved Redaway |
| Jacob Wight Jr | Steven Blackmore |
| Gideon Martin | John Sweat |
| Jacob Wight | Ebenezer Brown |
| Joseph Robins | Asa Copeland for 1 year |
| John Blackmore | Elhanon Boydon " |
| William Short | Ithamer Olney " |
| Jeremiah Robinson | Pline Greensar 6 months |
| John Graves | |

Killingly July the 6$^{th}$ 1781

these Certify that the above 31 Recruits Were Raised by the Town of Killingly and certificates have Ben Received from the Recriuting officers for the Same they all being duly Musterd and Marchd in order to Join the Army

Will$^m$ Danielson  
Pain Converse  } Selectmen  
Eleaz$^r$ Moffitt  } of Killingley

[*State Library, Revolution 25.*]

## WALLINGFORD RETURN.

Acct of Supplies for the Officers & Soldiers Families Belonging to Wallingford from Apl 1 1781 until Jan 1 1782

| | | |
|---|---:|---:|
| Capt Eph Chamberlain . . . . | £13 | 10 |
| Capt Jarius Wilcox . . . . . | 4 | 10 |
| Lt Jno Mansfield . . . . . | 13 | 10 |
| " Jos Shailor . . . . . . | 13 | 10 |
| Nath Yale . . . . . . | 9 | |
| Benj Rexford . . . . . . | 3 | |
| Moses Barns . . . . . . | 9 | |
| Thos Jones . . . . . . | 9 | |

Edmond Field . 9
Dan¹ Smith . 9
 " Bradley . 9
Thos Mix . 9
Jos. Wollcott . 9
Saml Holt . 12
Enos Mix . . 7 14
Josiah Merriman 9
John Pierce . 9

[*George M. Curtis, Meriden.*]

## RETURNS FROM MILITIA, 1781.

### FIFTH BRIGADE.

The following is a Return of those who have Engaged in the Continental service in the 5th Brig$^d$ of militia after the sesions of assembly in may last their Names the Time they Engaged in service the Term they Inlisted for and the Town they count for and whether marcht or not

[All except the six noted below are described as having Marcht or Joined.]

| Names 5th Reg$^t$ | Time when Inlisted or Detached | Time for which Engaged | For the Quota of what Town |
|---|---|---|---|
| Enos Stebbins | June 26 1781 | one year | Mansfield |
| Asa Cleaveland | 29 | to y$^e$ last Dec | " |
| Robert Hale | 28 | year | " |
| John Fanton | July 2 | last Dec | " |
| Solomon Fenton | 3 | year | " |
| Augustus Storrs | 2 | " | " |
| James Dunham | 2 | last Dec | " |
| Fredrick Storrs | June 12 | 3 years | " |
| Consider Hanks | 28 | last Dec | " |
| Joseph Whitemore | 30 | year | " |
| Chester (?) Southworth | July 2 | " | " |
| James Church | 5 | " | " |
| Joseph Cushman | 3 | " | " |
| Joseph Tufts | June 28 | " | " |
| Daniel Miller | July 5 | 3 years | " |
| Jon$^a$ Dowset | 7 | year | " |
| Jon$^a$ Ammedown | June 27 | " | " |
| David Drown | 30 | 3 years | " |
| Elisha Fenton | 30 | Last Dec | " |
| Calvin Chafee | 10 July | year | " |
| Robart Eldrig | 10 | " | " |
| Phillip Perkins | 20 July | " | " |
| Daniel Heff | July 3 | Last Dec | Windham |
| James Hovey | 3 | " | " |
| Uriah Luce | 3 | " | " |
| John Neff | July 27 | " | " |
| Jesse Peck | June 30 | " | " |
| Chester Lillie | 30 | " | " |
| Elisha Back | March [ ] | 3 years | " |
| James Luddington | 20 | " | " |
| John Quigley | | " | " |
| Moses Ryce | July 10 | year | Coventry |
| Charles Warnor | 1 | Last Dec | " |
| Elijah Hunt | 1 | " | " |
| Sam$^{ll}$ Carpenter | 1 | " | " |
| Step$^a$ Long | 1 | " | " |
| W$^m$ Porter | 1 | " | " |
| Joseph Bacon | 2 July | " | " |
| Oliver Kingsbury | 1 | " | " |
| Jon$^a$ Fitch | 28 June | " | " |

| Names 5th Regt | Time when Inlisted or Detached | Time for which Engaged | For the Quota of what Town |
|---|---|---|---|
| Mosess Loomis | 25 | 3 years | Coventry |
| John Jinks | 20 Aug | During war | " |
| **11 Regt** | | | |
| John Smith | | 3 years | Woodstock |
| Amos Morse | | 6 months | " |
| Harbe Childs | | " | " |
| Abner Richmand | | " | " |
| John Badger | | " | " |
| Thoª Spencer | | 1 year | " |
| John Comba | | 6 months | ", |
| Sylvenos Smith | | " | " |
| Asa Copland | | 1 year | Killingly |
| Pleney Greene | | 6 months | " |
| Ishecor Onley | | 1 year | " |
| Ebnr Brown | | 3 years | " |
| James Boyd | | 1 year | " |
| Stephen Utley | | 6 months | Pomfret |
| **12th Regt** | | | |
| Benjª Russell | | 1 year | Lebanon |
| Jonah Sweatland | | | " |
| Benjª Bennet | | | " |
| Jabez Woodworth | | | " |
| Stephn Buckingham | | | " |
| Jesse Wright | | | " |
| John Williams Jr | | | " |
| Benjª Bissell | | | " |
| Benjª Wood Jr | | | " |
| Elezr Woodward | | | " |
| Wm Woodworth | | | " |
| Comfort Babe | | | " |
| Enos Gray | | | " |
| John Marin | | | " |
| John Clark | | | " |
| Ezekiel Lyman Jr | | | " |
| Samll Hills Jr | | | " |
| Benjª Bissell | | | " |
| Prince Williams | | | " |
| Joseph Allin | | | " |
| Daniel Puffor | | | " |
| Nathn Hovey | | | " |
| David Nucomb | | | " |
| Gurden Molton | | | " |
| Thoª Newcomb | | | " |
| Heman Woodworth | | | " |
| Zebadial Hide | | | " |
| Elisha Blackman | | | " |
| Nathn Hovey | | | " |

The above named men are Continentals

| | | | |
|---|---|---|---|
| Joshua Goff | | | Lebanon |
| John Colman Jr | | | " |
| Nathan Law | | | " |
| Daniel Perkins | | | " |
| Charls Hunt | | | " |

# REVOLUTION LISTS AND RETURNS.

| Names 12th Regt | Time when Inlisted or Detached | Time for which Engaged | For the Quota of what Town |
|---|---|---|---|
| Joseph Bartlet | | | Lebanon |
| Ichd Miner | | | " |
| Saml Lamfeer | | | " |
| Jabez Strong | | | " |
| John Jinkins | | | " |
| Philip Harris | | | " |

For the 2 state Battallions from Leabanon

| Names | Time when Inlisted or Detached | Time for which Engaged | For the Quota of what Town |
|---|---|---|---|
| Daniel Vaughan | first March | | Leabanon |
| Paul Hutsheson | " | | " |
| Behuel Newcomb | " | | " |
| Eleazer Richardson | " | | " |
| Dan Bliss | " | | " |
| Saml Bliss | " | | " |
| Jason Youpon (? Jonson) | " | | " |
| Saml Hayward | " | | " |
| Dan Lyman | " | | " |
| Philip Harris Jr | " | | " |
| Caleb Gaspe | " | | " |
| Dan Wattles | " | | " |
| Wm Baxter | " | | " |
| Beriah Bliss | " | | " |
| Saml Bliss | " | | " |
| John Rice | Continental | | Hebron |
| Wm Merit | " | | " |
| John Carver | " | | " |
| Abner Hatch | " | | " |
| Elisha Man | " | | " |
| Appleton Holliston | " | | " |
| Thos Brown Jr | " | | " |
| Elijah Norton | " | | " |
| Abel Wright | " | | " |
| Sawyer Ellis | " | | " |
| John Hutchison | " | | " |
| Joas Dunham Jr | " | | " |
| John Ellis 3d | " | | " |
| Stephn Cumings | " | 6 months | " |
| Moses Loomis | " | 3 years | " |
| Benja Wood | " | | " |
| Eazar Woodward | " | | " |
| John Hutcheson | " | | " |
| Larance Dowswet | " | | " |
| Oliver Parish | " | | " |
| Saml Goff | " | | " |
| Daniel Folley | " | | " |
| John Rice | " | | " |
| Benja Steward | | first March State Service | " |
| John Hibbard | | " | " |
| Jabez Wotters | | " | " |
| Squire Goff | | " | " |
| Elijah Foller | | " | " |
| Thos Mack | | " | " |
| Thos Brown | | " | " |
| John Powers | | " | " |

CONNECTICUT LINE, 1781-1783.

| Names 12th Regt | Time when Inlisted or Detached | Time for which Engaged first March | For the Quota of what Town |
|---|---|---|---|
| Jared Philips | | State Service | Hebron |
| Norman Philips | | " | " |
| **21 Regit** | | | |
| Joseph Whipple | Detd | Last Dec | Plainfield |
| Amasa Brown | " | " | " |
| Isaac Wight | " | " | " |
| Wm Watterman | " | " | " |
| George Dunworth | " | " | " |
| Benja Gallup | " | " | " |
| Andrew Clark | " | " | " |

[The six next above are not noted as having Marcht]

| | | | |
|---|---|---|---|
| Joseph Pratt | Inlisted | " | " |
| John Green | " | " | " |
| Saml Bruster | " | " | " |
| Thos Beckus | " | " | " |
| Darbe Dunners (?) | " | " | " |
| Cuggo Negro | " | " | " |
| Alexr Knox | " | 3 yers | Voluntown |
| Samll Palmer | " | " | " |
| Daniel Palmer | " | " | " |
| Ephm Tucker | " | " | " |
| Elijah Foster | " | " | " |
| Joseph Smith | " | " | Canterbury |
| Elezr Shaw | " | " | " |
| Benja Rathbon | " | " | " |
| Archalus Ama | " | " | " |
| Prince Negro | " | " | " |
| Thos Cranton | " | " | " |
| John Ormsbury | " | " | " |
| David Eanous | " | " | " |
| Daniel Herrick | " | first March | " |
| Berrey Boing | " | " | " |
| Elisha Balding | " | " | " |
| Jerh Parrish | " | " | " |
| Joseph Herrick | " | " | " |
| Samll Cleavland Jr | " | " | " |
| Joseph Munrow | " | " | " |
| John Adams | " | " | " |
| Charles Woodward | " | " | " |
| Samll Adams | " | " | " |
| Bethuel Bond | " | " | " |
| Joseph Hibbard | " | " | " |

12th Sepr 1781

The following is A return of the men inlisted into the Massachusets Line in the Continental army from the Town of ashford for three years which by act of Congress said ashford hath a just Right to Count Viz

Wm Danscey                James Brown
Benja Davison             Origin Eatton
John Davison              Natha Ward
Roger Crane               Ambros Brown
Phileman Eatton           Elisha Roy[ ]
Oliver Ellis              Chester Rogers

Moon Dimmuck          Th⁰⁸ Morey
Jn⁰ Wintchester       Sam¹ Perey

The above men are muster⁴ in the Countes of Suffolk Worster & middlesix certified July 1781

P' Edward Green    ⎫
John Gleason       ⎬ Muster masters
Barth" Woodbury    ⎭

We whose Names are hereunto subscribed certifie that the above named men are Legal inhabitants of the state of Connecticut & Belong to the Town of Ashford & the bigest Part of them was born in s⁴ Town & have resided in the same Ever since Till inlisting

Dated at Ashford
11ᵗʰ Sep' 1781

Elijah Whiton     ⎫ Justices
Benjᵃ Sumner     ⎭

Benjᵃ Clark       ⎫
Joseph Woodward   ⎬ Selectmen
Squier Hills      ⎭

[*State Library, Hebard Papers, 55*].

# MISCELLANEOUS RETURNS, 1781.

A Return of the recruits rec[d] and forwarded to Join The Connecticut Line in the Continental Army Hartford March 1st 1781
[Each man engaged for three years]

| Soldiers Names | From what Regiment | For what Town |
|---|---|---|
| John Norwash | Col. Woodbridge | Glasenbury |
| Cuff Acklin | " | " |
| Ruel Affrican | Col. Storrs | Mansfield |
| Philip Gregory | Col. Phelps | Simsbury |
| John Slater | " | " |
| Ready Larey | Col. Newbury | Suffield |
| Remembrance Sheldon | " | Windsor |
| Jabish Colt | " | " |
| James Eggleston | " | " |
| Petor Roberts | " | " |
| David Eggleston | Col. Phelps | Simsbury |
| Abel Allyn | Col. Hooker | Farmington |
| Sage Churchell | " | " |
| Solomon Welton | " | " |
| Timothy Fox | " | " |
| Moses Persons | " | " |
| Thomas F. Bishop | " | " |
| Mathew Lee | " | " |
| Joel Welton | " | " |
| Roswell Cook | " | " |
| Uri Hungerford | " | " |
| Isaac Tillitson | " | " |
| Amos Couch | " | " |
| Lemuel Lane | " | " |
| Ruben Carr | " | " |
| Obed Gridley | " | " |
| Asel Tillitson | " | " |
| Gider Woodruff | " | " |
| Solomon Woodruff | " | " |
| James Gridley | " | " |
| Jessy Shepard | " | " |
| Seth Root | " | " |
| Peter Rose | " | " |
| Ruben Hamtin | " | " |
| David Taylor | Col. Phelps | Simsbury |
| John Griffin Holcom | " | " |
| Ebenezer Edgerton | " | " |
| Jeremy Cass | " | " |
| John White | " | " |
| Ruben Mason | " | " |
| Jacob Halladay | " | " |
| Zebulon Walles | " | " |
| Robert Cook | Col. Hooker | Southington |
| Archibel Cook | " | " |
| Bodwell H[  ] | " | " |
| Luke Hart | " | " |

# REVOLUTION LISTS AND RETURNS.

| Soldiers Names | From what Regiment | For what Town |
|---|---|---|
| George Dickerson | Col. Hooker | Southington |
| Clement Andrus | " | " |
| David Andrus | " | " |
| William Jones | " | " |

Simeon Belding Lieu[t]

*[State Library, Hebard Papers, 68.]*

A Return of the Recruits to fill the Conn[t] Line of the Army

| Mens Names | Towns to which they Belong |
|---|---|
| Henery Booth | Coverntry |
| Joseph Teal | Killingworth |
| Richard Weers | Guilford |
| William Poust | Killingworth |
| Eli Keley | " |
| Nathaniel Chittindan | " |
| Samuel Lynde Jur | Say Brook |
| Puryer Reeves | " |
| Zebelon Thompson | " |
| Benj[n] Doty | " |
| Park Toby | " |
| Jonathan Ward | Killingworth |
| Joel Isbell | " |
| Joseph Whitley | Say Brook |
| Cornelus Chapman | Say Brook |
| James Grant | " |
| Chester Bushnel | " |
| Amos Stevens | " |
| Richard Done | " |
| George Buckingham | " |
| George Harris | " |
| Solomon Goff | " |
| David Hains | " |
| Jude Pratt | " |
| Gideon Buckingham | " |
| Ruben Bushnal | " |
| Jese Graham | " |
| Benj[n] Wilcocks | " |
| John Bucley | " |
| Cornelius Tiegh | " |
| Joel Done | " |
| John Griswold | Killingworth |
| Joner Chester | " |
| Lymon Isbell | " |
| John Wright | " |
| Henery Stevens | " |
| Solomon Chittindan | " |
| Paul Pirson | " |
| Phinehus Jones | " |
| Caleb Elie | " |
| Joel Griffen | " |
| Nathan Person | " |
| Joseph Beull | " |
| Josiah Chatfield | " |
| Isaac Turner | " |
| Constant Bushnel | Say Brook |

CONNECTICUT LINE, 1781–1783.        301

| Mens Names | Towns to which they Belong |
|---|---|
| Jonathan Bullock | Ashford |
| William Cubb | " |
| William Jonson | " |
| James Hatrel ( ? ) | " |
| Peter Whitney | " |
| Ezra Daverson | " |
| Abijah Smith | " |
| Aaron Parks | " |
| Jonathan Ball | Coventry |
| Amesey Scott | Darby |
| David Davison | Lebanon |

Middletown March 7th 1781

John Ball Lieut, & Recruiting Officer
of the 4th Conn' Reg'

[*Connecticut Historical Society.*]

Return of Recruits for the Continental Army Received or forward⁴ to Camp since last Return    March 29th 1781

| Names of the Men Rec⁴ since last Return | Term Engaged for | By what Town procured |
|---|---|---|
| Jedediah Kimball | 3 Ys | Norwich |
| Thomas Brooks | " | " |
| Men forward⁴ since last Return | | |
| Thomas McGuire | 3 Ys | Hebron |
| Reuben Talsen | " | Lebanon |
| Phillup Hills | " | " |
| Joseph Phinney | " | " |
| Gideon Martin | " | Killingly |
| Cato Negroe | D. W. | Pomfret |
| David Coy | 3 Ys | Voluntown |
| John Fredk Tone | " | " |
| Andrew Hensey | " | " |
| Gideon Quas (? Tuas) | " | Colchester |
| Dan¹ Armstrong | " | Norwich |
| Wm Armstrong | D. W. | " |
| James Bell | 8 Ys | " |
| Jabez Kirttend | " | " |
| Phinehas Knight | " | " |
| Moses Tracy | " | " |
| Jonth Jerh Beebe | " | " |
| John Patten | " | " |
| Asa Patten | " | " |
| Asa Squier | " | " |
| Thomas Brooks | " | " |
| Oliver Everit | D. W. | " |

A Size Roll of the following Men (Including The Deserters) Specifying the Towns Engag⁴ for &c Left with L' Pride, Accounting for the Whole I have Rec⁴

Joseph Ross
Isaac White
Comfort Eams

Henry Pollister  
John Kelley } were Return'd Deserted  
Richard Weir  
Sam<sup>l</sup> Rude  
Crippin Archer  
Eliab Eaglesten  
John Bloss  
John Wright  
Dan<sup>l</sup> Dowd  
Ephraim Story  
Reuben Bryant  
Stephen Bennet  
Jeremiah Bennet  
John Fagens  
Tho<sup>s</sup>. Fitz Simmons  
Amas Simons  
Jed<sup>h</sup> Kimball

Joel Clark who Engag'd for Lebanon has Been to Camp & Return'd by Order of Col<sup>o</sup> Grosvenor
Solomon Andrus of Norwich Muster'd out by Col<sup>o</sup> Swift

      James Hyde Ens<sup>n</sup>
       late R. Officer 1<sup>st</sup> Conn. Regm<sup>t</sup>

His Excellency
 Gov<sup>r</sup> Trumbull,—

          [*Connecticut Historical Society.*]

A Return of Deserters from the present 1<sup>st</sup> Connecticut Reg<sup>t</sup> since the Return for Settlem<sup>t</sup> of their Pay for Service of 1781.

| Names | Time When | Towns they belong to |
|---|---|---|
| William Jones Fifer | 1 Jan. '82 | Branford |
| Gerard Leverick | " | Fairfield |
| John Grant | 15 Jan. 82 | Lyme |
| Samuel Goff | 1 Jan. 82 | Chatham |
| Samuel Thompson | 21 Feb. 82 | Canterbury |
| Hezekiah Phelps | 30 Mar. 82 | Symsbury |
| Jehiel Gibbs | " | Somers |
| John Gray | " | Voluntown |
| John Casey D<sup>m</sup> | " | Providence |
| William Racke | 1 Apr. 82 | Bolton |
| James Brown | " | Westmoreland |
| William Flowers | 10 Apr. 82 | Hartford |
| Henry Walton | 11 Apr. 82 | Danbury |
| Gilbert Whitney | " | Symsbury |
| Andrew Gray | " | Stonington |
| Joseph Evans | " | Hartford |
| John Hamilton | 20 Apr. 82 | New Fairfield |
| Gideon Church | 9 May 82 | Westmoreland |
| Enos Mix | 21 June 82 | Wallingford |
| Austin Brown | 25 July 82 | Hebron |

The above is a true Extract from the Regimental Book
    Thos Grosvenor Lieut Col Com 1<sup>st</sup> Conn. Regt.

         [*State Library, Revolution 25, 41*]

# THIRD REGIMENT — COL. WEBB, 1782.

[See Record of Connecticut Men in the Revolution, page 330.]

## FIELD AND STAFF.

[The muster rolls of the field and staff for February, March, May, June, July, September and October 1782 are preserved. Only the earliest of these is here copied, with such changes noted as appear on any of the later rolls.]

Muster Roll of the Field, Staff and Commissioned Officers in the 3d Connecticut Regiment in the service of the United States Commanded by Col Saml B. Webb for Feby 1782.

| Appointed | Names | Rank | Remarks |
|---|---|---|---|
| Jan. 1, 1777 | Saml B. Webb | Col. | |
| Oct. 10, 1778 | Ebenr Huntington | Lt. Col. | |
| Oct. 10, 1778 | John P. Wyllys | Maj. | |
| Mar. 23, 1778 | Nathan Beers | Lt. P. Master | |
| June 1, 1778 | John Meigs | Lt. Adj. | |
| May 27, 1779 | Ebenr Frothingham | Lt. Q. Master | |
| Mar. 30, 1778 | Jeremiah West | Surgeon | in arrest Feb. 28, 1782. Vacant March 1782 |
| Aug. 1, 1778' | John Rose | Mate | Promoted to Surgeon March 8, 1782 |
| | Jonathan White | Serj. Maj. | On muster rolls for May 1782 and later |
| | Simon Griffin or Giffin | Qr. Mr. Serj. | " " |
| | David Pratt | Drum Maj. | " " |
| | John Kircum | Fife Maj. | " " |

### Light Infantry

| Apr. 9, 1780 | Roger Welles | Capt. | |
| Apr. 9, 1780 | Wm Linn | Lieut. | |
| July 26, 1780 | Jacob Kingsbury | Ens. | |

### 1st Company

| Jan. 1, 1777 | Edward Bulkley | Capt. | Recruiting Officer March 1782, but not noted later in that capacity. |
| July 20, 1780 | Daniel Bradley | Lieut. | |

| Appointed | Names | Rank | Remarks |
|---|---|---|---|
| | **6th Company** | | |
| Oct. 10, 1778 | Elisha Hopkins | Capt. | |
| Sep. 1, 1779 | Eli Barnum | Lieut. | |
| Dec. 28, 1781 | Nathan Gregory | Lieut. | |
| | **4th Company** | | |
| Aug. 23, 1777 | Joseph Walker | Capt. | Aid de Camp to Gen¹ Parsons |
| Dec. 17, 1781 | Martin Denslow | Lieut. | In arrest Feb. 28, 1782 |
| | **8th Company** | | |
| Feb. 10, 1781 | Timothy Allyn | Capt. | |
| Dec. 8, 1781 | William Lord | Lieut. | |
| Apr. 3, 1780 | Jaques Harman | Ens. | |
| | **3d Company** | | |
| Jan. 1, 1779 | Stephen Betts | Capt. | |
| Aug. 1, 1779 | Isaac Keeler | Lieut. | doing the duty of Adj. |
| | **7th Company** | | |
| July 10, 1779 | John Biley [Riley] | Capt. | |
| June 16, 1778 | John Mix | Lieut. | Q. Master Gen¹ Department |
| | **5th Company** | | |
| Mar. 22, 1778 | Sam¹ Wm Williams | Capt. | |
| Feb. 10, 1781 | Nathan H. Whiting | Lieut. | |
| | **2d Company** | | |
| Nov. 15, 1781 | Hezekiah Rogers [Rogers] | Capt. | Aid de Camp to Gen. Huntington. |
| May 4, 1781 | Benjamin Dimmick | Lieut. | |

[*State Library. Revolution 29, 12.*]

CONNECTICUT LINE, 1781–1783. 305

## LIGHT INFANTRY COMPANY—CAPT. WELLES.

[The muster rolls of this company for February, May, June, July, September and October 1782 are preserved. Only the earliest of these is here copied, with such changes noted as appear on any of the later rolls.]

Muster Roll of Capt Roger Welles's Company of Light Infantry in the 3d Connecticut Regiment in the Service of the United States Commanded by Col Sam¹ B. Webb, For the Month of Feby 1782.

| Inlisted | Term | | | |
|---|---|---|---|---|
| Apr. 9, 1780 | | Roger Wells | Capt. | Transfered 1st Co. June 1, 1782 |
| Apr. 9, " | | Wm Linn or Lim | Lieut. | |
| July 25 " | | Jacob Kingsbury | Ens. | |
| | D. W. | Lewis Hurd | Serj. | |
| | " | Silas or Elias Phelps | " | Not on muster roll for May 1782 or later |
| | " | Reubin Beach | " | |
| | " | John Downs | " | |
| | " | Stephen Butler | " | Promoted from Corp. Feb. 9, 1782 |
| | " | David Bullin | Corp. | |
| | " | Benjn Dire or Dix | " | Reduced June 1, 1782 |
| | " | David Lounsbury | " | |
| | " | Joseph Clinton | " | Not on muster roll for May 1782 or later |
| | " | John Dixon | " | |
| | " | Daniel Winchel | Drum. | |
| | " | Jacob Achor | Fifer | |
| | " | John Allyn | | |
| Dec. 20, 1780 | 3 years | Hendrick Bail | | Not on muster roll for May 1782 or later |
| | D. W. | John Barnum | | |
| | " | Noah Barnum | | Deserted Oct. 24, 1782 |
| | " | Nathl Beach | | Transferred 6th Co. July 1, 1782 |
| July 1, 1780 | 3 years | Edward Burges | | " 2d Co. " " " |
| | D. W. | Reubin Gadwell | | |
| | " | Jeret Chamberlain | | Not on muster roll for May 1782 or later |
| | " | Allyn Corning | | " " " " " " " |
| Dec. 22 " | 3 years | Jeret Cunnell | | " " " " " " " |
| | D. W. | Allyn Evins | | " " " " " " " |
| | " | Rememberence Filley | | |

20

| Inlisted | Term | Name | Rank | Remarks |
|---|---|---|---|---|
| | D. W. | Vaniah or Variah Fox | | |
| | " | Ichabod Goodrich | | |
| | " | Sam¹ Hennin or Hennan | | |
| | " | David Ward | | Not on muster roll for May 1783 or later |
| | " | James Hyde | | Not on muster roll for May 1783 or later |
| Mar. 18, 1781 | 3 years | Joseph Johnson | | " " |
| | D. W. | Jedediah Kimball | | " " |
| | " | Benj⁰ Kircum | | |
| | " | Jonath⁰ Miller | | Not on muster roll for May 1783 or later |
| | " | Joel Mosher | | |
| | " | Stephen Meeker | | |
| | " | Brion Montigue | | |
| | " | Shelden Potter | | |
| | " | David Roberts | | Not on muster roll for May 1783 or later |
| | " | Isaiah Smith | | |
| | " | Justin St. John | | Not on muster roll for May 1783 or later |
| | " | Ezra Tryon | | " " |
| | " | Sam¹ Vallett | | |
| | " | Benj⁰ Waklee | | |
| | " | Joshua Wheeler | | |
| | " | Sam¹ Whitney | | Transfered 1ˢᵗ Co. June 1, 1783 |
| July 11, 1780 | 8 years | Seth Grigory | Serj. | Not on muster roll for May 1783 or later |
| | D. W. | Thomas Wood | | Dead Feb. 21, 1783 |
| | | Elihu Spear | | Received from 4ᵗʰ Co. June 1, 1783 |
| | | Selah Scoviel or Scofield | Corp | "  3ᵈ Co. " " |
| | 1y. 8m. 16d. | Arehelus Amis or Ames | | "  8ᵗʰ Co. " " |
| | 1y. 9m. 19d. | Ebenezer or Eben Bacon | | "  7ᵗʰ Co. " " |
| | 1y. 6m. 25d. | Elias Carpinter | | "  8ᵗʰ Co. " " |
| | 1y. 7m. 20d. | Calvin Chaffe | | "  7ᵗʰ Co. " " |
| | D. W. | James Chadwick | | "  3ᵈ Co. " "   Transfered 3ᵈ |
| | " | Asa Copeland | | Co. July 1, 1783 |
| | 1y. 7m. | Ward Cotton | | "  from 6ᵗʰ Co. " " |
| | | | | "  1ˢᵗ Co. " " |

CONNECTICUT LINE, 1781–1783.    307

| Term | Name | Company | Status |
|---|---|---|---|
| 1y. 6m. 8d. | Roger Edgerton | " 5th Co. " | " Transfered |
| D. W. | Thomas Evans | 5th Co. July 1, 1783 | " " |
| " | Mason Green | from 1st Co. " | " Deserted |
| 1y. 6m. 21d. | Andrew Hansey or Haney | June 18, 1783 | " " |
| 1y. 6m. 3d. | Philemon Kirkum | from 8th Co. " | " " |
| 1y. 7m. 4d. | Joseph Lauson | " 4th Co. " | " " |
| 1y. 6m. 16d. | Theophilus Luther | " 2d Co. " | " Deserted |
| 1y. 7m. 14d. | John Munsell | July 16, 1783 | " " |
| 1y. 7m. 27d. | Abijah Olmsted | from 6th Co. " | " Deserted |
| | | " 2d Co. " | |
| D. W. | Lemuel Raymont or Raymond | July 16, 1782 | " " |
| " | Elias Shaw | from 8th Co. " | " " |
| 1y. 7m. 4d. | David Spencer | " 7th Co. " | " " |
| D. W. | Lemuel Sperry | " 5th Co. " | " " |
| 1y. 6m. 14d. | Samuel Stowell | " 4th Co. " | " " |
| 1y. 5m. 14d. | Charles Walter | " 1st Co. " | " " |
| D. W. | Elihu Waters | " 4th Co. " | " " |
| " | | " 5th Co. " | " Transfered |
| " | Seth Stannard | 5th Co. July 1, 1783 | Trans- |
| | | Joined from desertion May 28, 1783. | fered 4th Co. July 1, 1783 |
| 1y. 8m. 27d. | Nathl or Nathan Stowell | Received from 1st Co. June 1, 1782 | |
| 1y. 7m. 6d. | Selah Harke or Hearts or Hartee or Harte | " 4th Co. July 1, 1783 | |
| D. W. | Chancey Lewis | " 4th Co. " | " " |
| " | Ira Mott | " 5th Co. " | " " |
| 1y. 6m. 7d. | Levi Munsell | " 5th Co. " | " " |
| 1y. 7m. 1d. | Reuben Sharpe | " 6th Co. " | " " |
| 1y. 4m. 14d. | Chester or Christopher Upham | " 7th Co. " | " " |
| 1y. 2m. 16d. | Hazard Prior | " 3d Co. " | " " |
| D. W. | Nathn or Nathanl Smith | on muster roll for Sept. 1782 | " " |

[*State Library, Revolution* 39 ; 50, 67, 77, 88, 96, 104.]

## FIRST COMPANY—CAPT. BULKLEY.

[The muster rolls of this company for February, May, June, July, September, and October, 1782, are preserved. Only the earliest of these is here copied, with such changes noted as appear on any of the later rolls.]

Muster Roll of Captain Edward Bulkley's Company 3d Connecticut Regiment in the Service of the United States commanded by Col. Samuel B. Webb for the Month of February 1782.

| Time Appointed | Term of Inlistment | | | |
|---|---|---|---|---|
| | | Edward Bulkley | Capt. | |
| | | Daniel Bradley | Lieut. | |
| Mar. 20, 1780 | D. W. | Jonathan White | Serj. Maj. | not on muster roll of May 1782 or later |
| May 17, 1778 | " " | Simeon Giffin | Qr. Mr. Serj. | " " " " " " |
| Aug. 22 " | " " | David Pratt | Drum Maj. | " " " " " " |
| | | John Kircum | Fife Maj. | " " " " " " |
| | | Elijah Bordman | Serj. | |
| Nov. 3, 1780 | 3 years | Darius Orcutt or Oniott | " | |
| | D. W. | Moses Griswold | Serj. | |
| | | Daniel Sizer | " | |
| | | Samuel Easton | " | Discharged Feb. 18, 1782. |
| | | Lewis Hurd | " | Received from the Light Co. June 1, 1782. Discharged Sept. 1, 1782. |
| | | Hezekiah Nott | Corp | |
| | | Thomas Stanley | " | |
| | | Gideon Goff | " | |
| | | Moses Hatch | Drum | |
| | | David Lindsey | " | not on muster roll of May 1782 or later |
| | | Asa Squire | Fifer | " " " " " " |
| | | William Armstrong | " | |
| | | Daniel Bushnell | | |
| | | Abraham Belding | | |
| Jan. 1, 1782 | 3 years | Jonathan Bullock | | |
| Jan. 2 " | " " | Simeon Barns | | Time expires Apr. 13, 1782 |
| Apr. 3, 1781 | " " | Jeremiah Bennet | | |
| Jan. 17 " | " " | John Ballard | | |
| | | Ward Cotton | | Transferred to the Light Co. July 1, 1782 |

CONNECTICUT LINE, 1781-1783.    309

| Name | Date | Term | Notes |
|---|---|---|---|
| Moses Coy | Feb. 18 | | |
| Robert Chandler | Jan. 20 | | |
| Daniel Dunham | Jan. 11 | | |
| Joseph Douglas | Feb. 5 | | |
| Alphred Dresser | Jan. 17 | D. W. | |
| Jack Freeman | Dec. 14, 1780 | 3 years | |
| Prince Freeman | June 1, 1781 | " | |
| Stephen Fox | | | |
| Cato Freeman | | D. W. | |
| Samuel Herington | | " | |
| Arunah Hackley | | | |
| Samuel Lyon | Jan. 17, 1781 | 3 years | |
| Daniel Morley or Muley | Dec. 1, 1780 | D. W. | |
| David Peck | March 10, 1781 | 3 years | |
| Nathaniel Price | Feb. 10, " | " | |
| Joseph Preston | June 29, " | " | |
| Joseph Pease | | | |
| Samuel Roberts | Mar. 5, " | D. W. | |
| Reuben Roberson or Robinson | Jan. 1, " | 3 years | |
| Abel Stowell | Jan. 1, " | " | |
| Samuel Stowel | Mar. 13, " | " | Transfered to the Light Co. June 1, 1782 |
| Nathaniel Stowel | June 1, " | " | not on muster roll of June 1782 or later |
| John Smith | | | Joined from desertion May 24, 1782. Not on muster roll for Sept. 1782 or later |
| Joseph Treat | | D. W. | not on muster roll for Sept. 1792 or later |
| Hezekiah Wheeler | Jan. 8, " | " | |
| Peter Whitney | Dec. 20, 1780 | 3 years | not on muster roll of May 1782 or later |
| Joseph Wilson | Jan. 1, 1781 | " | Died Feb. 22, 1782 |
| Ebenezer Nye | Apr. 30, 1782 | " | Joined May 16, 1782 |
| Nehemiah Seely | Apr. 15, " | 6m. 15d. | Fool transferred June 26, 1782 |
| Joseph Clark | Apr. 27, " | 6m. 0d. | |
| George Foot | Apr. 10, " | 6m. 12d. | |
| Joseph Bunnel | Apr. 10, " | 5m. 25d. | Joined May 16, 1782 |
| Thomas Evins | | | Transfered to the Light Co. June 1, 1782 |

310  REVOLUTION LISTS AND RETURNS

| Time Appointed | | Term of Inlistment | | |
|---|---|---|---|---|
| May 8, 1782 | William Wetherll | 6m. 23d. | | with his Excellencys Barge June 5, 1782 and later. |
| | Joshua Wheater | D. W. | | Received from the Light Co. June 1, 1782. Not on muster roll for Sept. 1782 or later |
| Apr. 1, 1782 | Eleazer Cutler or Cutter | 8m. 10d. | | Joined June 10, 1782. Discharged Dec. 10, 1782 |
| " " " | Amos Gustin or Griffin | 5m. 10d. | | Joined June 10, 1782. |
| May 1 " | Daniel Knight | " | | Discharged Dec. 26, 1882 |
| Apr. 1 " | Christopher Kilby | 8m. 10d. | | Joined June 20, 1782 |
| May 1 " | Benoni Robins | 5m. 10d. | | Joined June 20, 1782. Discharged Dec. 27, 1782. |

[*State Library, Revolution 39; 45, 63, 74, 82, 91, 100.*]

## SECOND COMPANY — CAPT. ROGERS.

[The muster rolls of this company for February, March, May, June, July, September, and October, 1782, are preserved. Only the earliest of these is here copied, with such changes noted as appear on any of the later rolls.]

Muster Roll of Captain Rogers' Company in the 3rd Connecticut Regiment of Foot in the Service of the United States commanded by Colonel Samuel B. Webb for the Month of February 1782

| Inlisted | | Term | | | |
|---|---|---|---|---|---|
| | Hezekiah Rogers | | Capt. | | Aid to Gen. Huntington |
| | Benjamin Dimmick | | Lieut. | | Transfered to 6th Co. Sep. 23, 1782 |
| | Nathan H. Whiting | | Lieut. | | Joined from 4th Co. Aug 1, 1782 |
| | Richard Lord | | Serj. | | |
| | William Bassett | | " | | |
| | Abiathar Evans | | " | | |
| | Peter Stalker | | " | | |
| | Ebenezer Stoddart | | " | | Discharged for Simeon C. Stoddart in his room Feb. 26, 1782 |
| Dec. 20, 1780 | Jesse S¹ John | 3 years | Corp. | | |
| | James Crane | " | " | | |
| | John Avery | | | | |
| | Frederick Whipple | | Drum. | | |
| Mar. 1, 1781 | Antselus or Archelus Ames | " | Fifer | | Transfered to L. Co. June 1, 1782 |

CONNECTICUT LINE, 1781-1783.

| Date | Name | | Remarks |
|---|---|---|---|
| Dec. 21, 1780 | Reuben Adams | " | |
| Feb. 1, 1781 | Ephraim Burges | " | |
| Jan. 1, " | William Burrus or Burns | " | |
| Jan. 9, " | Elias Carpenter | " | |
| Jan. 2, " | Eliphelet Carpenter | " | Transfered to L. Co. June 1, 1782 |
| Feb. 1, " | Comfort Chapman | " | |
| Jan. 1, " | James Duggan | " | Deserted Aug. 1, 1782 |
| | Moses Elsworth | " | Deserted April 10, 1782; but appears on later rolls. |
| Feb. 1 | Joseph Finney or Phinney or Skinney | " | |
| | John Gimson | | not on muster roll for May 1782 or later |
| | Asa Haze or Hays | | name crossed from Sept 1782 roll and does not appear later |
| Feb. 14 | Joel Hait or Hart | " | |
| | Samuel Hull | | not on muster roll for May 1782 but appears on June 1782 and later |
| Dec. 18, 1780 | Jacob Halladay | " | |
| Mar. 18, 1781 | Abraham Murry | D. W. | Returned from desertion Feb. 27, 1782 |
| Jan. 5, " | David Hammond | 8 years | |
| Mar. 1, " | Andrew Hensey | " | not on muster roll for May 1782 or later |
| | Phillip Hills | | |
| | Samuel Jinkins | | |
| Feb. 1, " | David Mattison or Matheson | " | |
| July 5, " | Cato Negro | " | |
| Mar. 6, " | Aaron Parks or Parker | " | |
| Feb. 1, " | William Short | " | |
| | Reuben Smith | | not on muster roll for May 1782 or later |
| | Benjamin Stoddard | | Died Dec. 27, 1782 |
| Jan. 11, " | Johnson Tiff | " | |
| Jan. 11, " | Darius Truesdell or Tinsdell | " | |
| Jan. 21, " | Eli Tuller or Fuller | " | |
| Jan. 15, " | John F. Tone | " | |
| | William Woolcut | | Died Feb. 5, 1783 |
| | Simeon Curtis Stoddart | | In room of Ebenezer Stoddard not on muster roll for Sept. 1782 or later |

312    REVOLUTION LISTS AND RETURNS.

| Inlisted | Term | | Name | | Notes |
|---|---|---|---|---|---|
| | D. W. | | Reubin Beach | Serj. | appears on muster roll for May 1782 and later |
| | 1y. 7m. 17d. | | Ephraim Bates | | " " " " " " " |
| | D. W. | | Joel Mosher | | " " " " " " " |
| Apr. 10, 1782 | 2y. 10m. 17d. | | Tho⁸ Palmer | | Joined April 27, 1782 |
| | 1y. 9m. 8d. | | Jedediah Kimball | | appears on muster roll for May 1782 and later |
| | 10m. 17d. | | Ebenezer Platt | | Joined May 15, 1782. |
| | 6m. 17d. | | Miles Bennet | | not on muster roll for June 1782, but appears on July and later |
| | 10m. 5d. | | Aaron Eaton | | " " " " " " |
| | 6m. 17d. | | Daniel Jackson | | " " " " " " |
| | D. W. | | Justin St. John | | appears on muster roll for May 1782 and later |
| | 1y. 6m. 22d. | | Andrew Treusey | | " " " " Transfered to L. Co. June 1, 1782 |
| | 6m. 28d. | | David Shelton | | Joined May 15 and deserted June 1, 1782 |
| | 7m. 24d. | | Esaias Butts | | Joined June 6, 1782 |
| | D. W. | | Jonathan Edwards | | Joined June 14, 1782 |
| | 5m. 9d. | | Nathan¹ Fenton | | Joined June 20, 1782 |
| | 7m. 24d. | | James Raymond or Braymon | | Joined June 6, 1782 |
| | 5m. 9d. | | Sasal or Saral Squires | | Joined June 20, 1782 |
| | " | | Nath¹ Connant | | Joined July 17, 1782 |
| | 4m. 20d. | | Jonathan Bamon or Beaumont | | appears on muster roll for Sept. 1782 and later |
| | D. W. | | David Clark | | |

[*State Library, Revolution* 39; 48, 57, 65, 75, 84, 93, 102.]

## THIRD COMPANY—CAPT. BETTS.

[The muster rolls of this company for February, March, May, June, July, September, and October, 1782, are preserved. Only the earliest of these is here copied, with such changes noted as appear on any of the later rolls.]

Muster Roll of Captain Betts Company 3rd Connecticut Regiment in the service of the United States, Commanded by Colonel Samuel B. Webb for the Month of February 1782

| Enlisted | Term | Name | Rank | Notes |
|---|---|---|---|---|
| Jan. 1, 1777 | | Stephen Betts | Capt. | Transferred 3ᵈ Co. July 31, 1782 |
| Aug. 1, 1779 | | Isaac Keeler | Lieut. | Transferred July 31, 1782 from 7ᵗʰ Co. Called Lieut. Sept. 1782. |
| | | Jacques Harmon | Ens. | |
| | D. W. | Aaron Raymond | Serj. | |
| | " | Joseph Hait | " | |
| | " | Uzel Knap | " | |
| | " | Elihu Spear | " | |
| | " | Selah Scofield | Corp. | not on muster roll for June 1782 or later |
| | " | James Downs | " | not on muster roll for June 1782 or later |
| | " | George Hubbard or Hubert | | |
| | " | Anthony Floris or De Flovis | Drum. | |
| | " | Reuben or Martin Reynolds or Rannals | Fifer | |
| Jan. 18, 1781 | 8 years | Thomas Blake | Brigade baker | |
| | D. W. | David Betts | | |
| | " | Jacob Bosworth | | |
| | " | Jonathan Brown | | |
| Jan. 1, 1781 | 8 years | Parley Coy | | not on muster roll for March 1782 or later |
| Jan. 19, " | " | Joseph Davies | | not on muster roll for March 1782, but reappears as Joseph Davis on muster roll May 1782. An entry against his name has been cut from the roll for Oct. 1782 |
| Dec. 4, 1780 | | | | |
| July 7, 1781 | 1 year | Jonathan Dowsit | | |
| July 5, " | " | Lawrence Dowsit | | Discharged July 7, 1782 |
| Dec. 28, 1780 | 8 years | David Dicks or Dickers | | Discharged July 5, 1782 |
| Mar. 17, 1781 | " | Edward or Ned Freeman | | |

314    REVOLUTION LISTS AND RETURNS.

| | Term | Name | |
|---|---|---|---|
| Feb. 8, 1781 | 3 years | Benjamin Greenalit | |
| Dec. 10, 1780 | " | John Gates | |
| Nov. 19, " | " | Abel Guthire | |
| Feb. 1, 1781 | " | Jason Gay | |
| Dec. 26, 1780 | " | Robert Holdridge | |
| July 19, 1781 | 1 year | William Huse or Hughes | confined Provost Guard muster roll for June 1782, but not so noted on July 1782 roll |
| Apr. 1 | D. W. | David Jackson | |
| " " | 3 years | Theophillus Luther | joined from desert" May 31, 1782 not on muster roll for June 1782 or later |
| Jan. 19 " | " | Joseph Lawson | transferred to L. I. Comp. June 1, 1782 |
| July 19 " | 1 year | John Mills | Discharged Dec. 19, 1782 |
| July 17 " | " | Abraham Mills | Discharged Dec. 19, 1782 |
| July 19 " | " | Gabriel Mills | Discharged Dec. 19, 1782 |
| July 1, 1780 | 3 years | John McNulty | |
| July 11 " | " | Abijah Olmsted | transferred to L. I. Comp. June 1, 1782 |
| July 11 " | " | Justus Olmsted | not on muster roll of Sept. 1782 or later |
| Jan. 1, 1781 | " | Jesse Olmsted | Deserted Sept. 1, 1782. |
| Feb. 6 " | " | Jacob Pettingell or Pettersgill | |
| Feb. 6 " | " | Asaph Pettingell or Pettersgill | |
| Dec. 10, 1780 | " | Samuel Peters | |
| Jan. 29, 1781 | D. W. | Jack Spry | Dead Feb. 8, 1782. |
| Apr. 2 " | 3 years | Abel Stimson | Field Officers servant. Invalided June 21, 1782 not on muster roll of May 1782 or later |
| Jan. 1 " | " | Feeviah or Tuis Sharper | |
| Jan. 19 " | " | Daniel St. John | |
| Jan. 19 " | " | David Thompson | |
| . " | " | James Thompson | discharged July 25, 1782 |
| Dec. 16, 1780 | D. W. | Jacob Wardwell | |
| Jan. 19, 1781 | 3 years | Chester Waterman | |
| Mar. 10 " | " | Thomas Worden | |
| " " | " | Jesse Williams | |
| Mar. 12, 1783 | 18m. 15d. | Elexander Dermant or Deurant or Duvan | Joined May 12, 1783 |
| May 1 " | 6m. 17d. | Jacob Haskel | "    "   31    "    " |
| May 6 " | 6m. 17d. | Samuel Bliss | "    "    "    "    " |

CONNECTICUT LINE, 1781-1783.    315

| Inlisted | Term | | |
|---|---|---|---|
| April 20 | 6m. 17d. | Samuel Parks | " " " |
| May 6 | 6m. 17d. | John Bliss | " " " |
| April 17 | 6m. 17d. | Moses Barnard | " " " |
| April 27 | 6m. 17d. | Beriah Bliss | " " " |
| April 27 | 6m. 17d. | Dan Lyman | " " " |
|  | D. W. | John Berry | " " " |
|  |  | Edward Burghes | Rec'd from L. Co. July 1, 1782 |
| June 5, 1782 | " | John Haskal | Joined July 17, 1782 |
| March 13 | " | Ichabod Case | " " " |
| May 6 | " | Andrew Hazen | " " " |

[*State Library, Revolution 59; 44, 54, 68, 71, 81, 90, 99.*]

## FOURTH COMPANY – CAPT. WALKER.

[The muster rolls of this company for February, March, May, June, July, September and October 1782 are preserved. Only the earliest of these is here copied, with such changes noted as appear on any of the later rolls.]

Muster roll of Captain Joseph Walker's Company 3d Connecticut Regiment of foot in the Service of the United States, Commanded by Col'o Sam'l B. Webb for the month of Feb'y 1782.

| Inlisted | Term | | | |
|---|---|---|---|---|
| Aug. 22, 1777 |  | Joseph Walker | Capt. | Aid de Camp to Maj. Gen. Parsons. B. Major on Oct. roll |
| Dec. 6, 1781 |  | Martin Denslow | Lieut. | In arrest on Feb. roll only. Retired upon a resolution of Congress July 11, 1782. |
|  | D. W. | Isaac Keeler | Lieut. | Joined from 2d Co. July 31, 1782. |
|  | " | Francis Nicholson | Serj't |  |
|  |  | Jonathan Arnold |  | Name given as Jonathan Steuben on muster roll for June 1782 and later |
|  | " | Simeon Holmes | " |  |
|  | " | Waitsoll or Waitstill Dickenson | " |  |
|  | " | Stephen Risley or Prisley | Corp. |  |
|  | " | Moses Porter | " |  |
|  | " | Army Sperry | " |  |
|  | " | Elijah Porter | Drum. | Discharged Mar. 28, 1782. |

# REVOLUTION LISTS AND RETURNS.

| Enlisted | Term | Name | Remarks |
|---|---|---|---|
| Mar. 21, 1781 | D. W. | Timothy Bevens | Servant to Gen. Parsons or to Capt. Walker Dec. 4, 1780 |
| Dec. 28, 1780 | 3 years | Hubbard Burrows | Invalided June 27, 1782 |
| " | D. W. | Samuel Bardon | Transfered to Light Co. June 1, 1782, but entered on muster roll for July and later. |
| " | " | James Chadwick | |
| Dec. 13 | 8 years | John Clark | |
| Nov. 29 | " | Benjamin Durfee or Duffee | |
| " | " | Reuben Dodge | |
| " | " | Seth Dodge | |
| Jan. 29, 1781 | " | John Fagins | |
| Feb. " | " | Joshua Fuller or Tusler | |
| " | D. W. | Isaac Ford | |
| " | " | Azariah Grant | |
| " | " | Mason Green | Transfered to Light Co. June 1, 1782 |
| " | " | Ebenezer Hadley or Hoadley or Hodley | |
| Dec. 20, 1780 | 8 years | Joel Hamlin | Deserted Apr. 10, 1782 |
| Dec. 26, " | " | Herman or Hemen Hatch | |
| May " 1781 | " | David Hayden | |
| Jan. 11, " | " | Jabez Mortars | |
| | D. W. | Michael Minthern | Deserted Nov. 1, 1782 |
| | 8 years | Henry Ponds | |
| | D. W. | Asher Russell | |
| | | Lemiel Manclift or Lemuel Stanclift | Waggoner |
| Mar. 1, " | " | Jonathan Simonds | |
| Feb. 4, " | " | William Skeericks | called Serj. on muster roll for Sept. 1782 and later. |
| Dec. 16, 1780 | D. W. | John Thomas | Transfered to L. Inf. July 1, 1782 |
| " " | 8 years | Chester Upham | not on muster roll for Sept. 1782 or later |
| Dec. 16 | D. W. | James Wayland | |
| " | 3 years | Jacob Weight 1st | |
| " | D. W. | Jacob Weight 2d | |
| July 10, 1781 | 1 year | Calvin Chaffee | Discharged Mar. 12, 1783 |
| July 1, " | 6 m. | Oliver Kingsbury | Died Dec. 11, 1781 |

CONNECTICUT LINE, 1781–1783.

| Name | Term | Rank/Notes | Muster roll notes |
|---|---|---|---|
| David Lindsey | D. W. | Drum. | on muster roll for March and later. Received from 1st Co. |
| Asa Squire | 1y. 11m. | Fifer | on muster roll for March and later. Received from 1st Co. |
| Jeremiah Chamberlin | D. W. | | on muster roll for May 1782 only and later |
| John Goodrich | " | | " " " " " " |
| David Hurd | " | | " " " " " " |
| Alexander McColpin | 1y. 10m. | | " " " " Invalided June 27, 1782 and later |
| Elijah Molley or Morley | 2y. 11m. | | " " " " " " |
| Nathan Potter | 7m. | | " " " " Not on muster roll for Oct. 1782 |
| David Robarts | D. W. | | " " " " " " |
| Judah Robarts | 11m. | | " " " " " " |
| Ezra Tryon | D. W. | | " " " " " " |
| Samuel Whitney | " | | " " " " Not on muster |
| Daniel Evit | " | | roll Sept 1782 and later |
| Royal Marter or Mantor | 3 years | | Joined from desertion June 7, 1782 on muster roll for June 1782 and later Deserted Nov. 7, 1782 |
| Joshua Olmsted | 6m. | | on muster roll for June 1782 and later Discharged Dec. 30, 1782 |
| Jeremiah West | 3 years | | on muster roll for June 1782 Deserted July 27, 1782 |
| Benjamin Yerred | " | | " " " " " " |
| David Hubbell | 4m. 20d. | | Joined July 20, 1782. |
| Noah Norton or Noah U. Norton | 2m. 20d. | | Joined July 20, 1782. |
| Isaac Beers | | | on roll for Sept. 1782 and later. |

[State Library, Revolution 39; 49, 58, 68, 76, 85, 94, 103.]

## FIFTH COMPANY—CAPT. WILLIAMS.

[The muster rolls of this company for February, March, May, June, July, September and October 1782 are preserved. Only the earliest of these is here copied, with such changes noted as appear on any of the later rolls.]

Muster roll of Captain Samuel William Williams Company in the 3rd Connecticut Regiment in the service of the United States commanded by Colonel Samuel B. Webb for the month of February 1782.

| Enlisted | Term | | | |
|---|---|---|---|---|
| | | Samuel William Williams | Capt. | Transferred to 3d Co. Aug. 1, 1782. |
| | | Nathan H. Whiting | Lieut. | |
| | D. W. | Joshua Cone | Serj. | |
| | " | Jared Bunce | " | |
| | " | John Forbes | " | |
| | " | Thomas Wood | " | not on muster roll for June 1782 or later |
| | " | Walter Booth | " | Discharged Dec. 16, 1782 by hiring a man |
| | " | Daniel Ward | Corp. | |
| | " | Zebulon Mygatt | " | |
| | " | Frederick Stoddard | " | |
| | " | William Kirkum | Drum. | |
| | " | Joel Clark | Fifer | |
| Nov. 22, 1780 | 3 years | Jeddediah Addams | | |
| Feb. 2, 1781 | " | Christopher Avary | | |
| Apr. 14, " | " | Elihu Babcock | | Waggoner |
| Jan. 6, 1778 | " | Zebedee Brown | | Discharged July 24, 1782 |
| Feb. 3, 1781 | " | Joseph Borrows or Burrows | | Deserted Apr. 16, 1782. On May roll and later sick in hospital never mustered |
| Jan. 29, " | " | Hezekiah Catlin | | |
| Apr. 18, " | " | Stephen Childs | | |
| Dec. 20, 1780 | " | Serajah Comstock | | |
| July 2, 1781 | 1 year | James Church | | |
| June 30, " | " | Abner Coe | | |
| Jan. 1, " | 3 years | Samuel Fargo | | Deserted July 27, 1782, but continued on later rolls |
| | D. W. | Asa Fox | | Discharged July 2, 1782 |
| July 12, 1780 | 3 years | Caesar Freman | | Discharged June 29, 1782 |
| Nov. 22, " | " | Nathaniel Gates | | |

## CONNECTICUT LINE, 1781–1783.

| Date | Term | Name | Rank | Notes |
|---|---|---|---|---|
| Nov. 22, 1780 | 3 years | Silas Glass or Silas G. Cass | | Transferred to L. I. Co. July 1, 1782 |
| Mar. 5, 1781 | D. W. | Selah Hart | | Servant to Col. Huntington on muster roll for June 1782 |
| | | Thomas Hallet | | |
| Apr. 17, " | 3 years | Nathaniel Holt | | |
| Mar. 2, " | " | Jesse Holt | | |
| July 19, " | 1 year | Stephen Hurlbut | | Discharged June 29, 1782 |
| Dec. 26, 1780 | 3 years | Philliman Kirkum | | Transferred to L. I. Co. June 1, 1782 |
| | D. W. | William Martin | | |
| | " | Stephen Roberts | | Promoted to Corp. Sept. 21, 1782 |
| | " | Ephraim Robertson | | |
| | " | Joseph Rowlandson | | |
| | " | Samuel Schoolcraft | | |
| | | Lemuel Sperry | | |
| Apr. 23, 1781 | 3 years | Jonathan Stevens | | Transferred to L. I. Co. June 1, 1782 |
| July 2, " | 1 year | Chester Southwoth | | Discharged July 2, 1782 |
| Dec. 1, 1780 | 3 years | Charles Walter | | Transferred to L. I. Co June 1, 1782 |
| | D. W. | Joshua Welles | | |
| Dec. 8, " | 3 years | Zedediah or Jedediah Woodworth | | |
| Jan. 1, 1781 | | Elimkin Seward | | Dead Feb. 6, 1782 |
| | 1y. 6m. 8d. | Jeremiah Cunnell | | on muster roll for May 1782 and later |
| | 1y. 8m. 17d. | Elijah Fayer | | " " " |
| Mar. 22, 1782 | 9m. 8d. | Oliver Coe | | Joined June 10 |
| Apr. 1, " | 9m. 16d. | Daniel Heddy | | " " " |
| May 1, " | 9m. 16d. | Janna Wilcox | | " " " |
| Apr. 15, " | 6m. 14d. | Adrin or Adino Chapman | | Deserted Oct. 2. |
| May 23, " | 5m. 14d. | Elisha Catlin | | Joined June 6. |
| Mar. 15, " | 5m. | Josiah Butt | | not on muster roll for Oct. 1782. |
| May 4, " | 5m. 14d. | Levi Hall | | Joined June 10 |
| | D. W. | Seth Stannard | Lieut. & Adj. | Transferred from L. I. Co. July 1, 1782 |
| June 1, 1778 | | John Meiggs | | Transferred from Staff Aug. 1, 1782. |
| Apr. 28, 1782 | 4m. 20d. | Ebenezer Durfee | | Joined July 7 |
| May 13, " | 4m. 20d. | Elijah Durfee | | " " " |
| | 4m. 20d. | William Cook | | Joined July 24, Deserted Oct. 2. |
| June " " | D. W. | Joseph Freat or Treat | | on muster roll for Sept. 1782 and later. |

[*State Library, Revolution 39; 51, 59, 68, 78, 87, 94, 105.*]

## SIXTH COMPANY—CAPT. HOPKINS.

[The muster rolls of this company for February, March, May, June, July, September and October, 1782, are preserved. Only the earliest of these is here copied, with such changes noted as appear on any of the later rolls.]

Muster roll of Captain Elisha Hopkins's Company 3 Connec' Regiment of Foot in service of the United States, commanded by Colonel B. Webb for February 1780*

| Inlisted | | Term | | | |
|---|---|---|---|---|---|
| | | | Elisha Hopkins | Capt. | |
| | | | Eli Barnham | Lieut. | |
| | | | Matthew Gregory | Lieut. | |
| | | D W | Stephen Dormant | Serj. | |
| | | " | Nathan Savage | " | |
| | | " | Joseph Day | " | |
| | | " | John Beers | " | |
| Jan. | 4, 1782 | " | Thomas Stone | Corp. | |
| | | " | Aaron Jones | " | Deserted July 21 |
| | | " | W<sup>m</sup> Winans | " | |
| | | " | Rich<sup>d</sup> Belding | Drum. | |
| | | " | William Thrall | Fifer | |
| | | " | Isaac Finch | | |
| May | 1, 1781 | 3 years | James Anderson | | |
| Nov. | 21, 1780 | D. W. | Aaron Abercrumbie | | |
| | | 8 years | Benjamin Brown | | |
| | | D. W. | Richard Baker or Bacon | | Servant to Col. Webb |
| Apr. | 20, 1781 | 8 years | Daniel Baits or Baits or Bates or Betts | | |
| Feb. | 27 " | " | Thomas Brewer or Brown | | not on muster roll for Oct. 1782 |
| May | 15 " | " | Josiah Barns | | |
| July | 1 " | 1 year | Daniel Betts or Bates | | Discharged July 21 |
| Nov. | 22, 1780 | 3 years | Curtice Cleavland | | |
| Jan. | 1, 1781 | " | Gardiner Cleavland | | |
| May | 1 " | " | Ichabod Downing | | |
| Dec. | 20, 1780 | " | Roger Edgerton | | On Lord Sterlings Guard Fish-hill, Transfered to L. Inf. June 1, and returned July 1, 1782 |
| Jan. | 16, 1781 | " | Stephen Gavit | | |

CONNECTICUT LINE, 1781-1783.

| Date | Term | Name | Remarks |
|---|---|---|---|
| Dec. 7, 1780 | D. W. 3 years. | Joshua Howe | |
| | | Ephraim Harry | not on muster roll for June 1782. Appears on July 1782 muster roll and later |
| | D. W. " | Stephen Kellogg | |
| | | Chancey Lewis | Deserted Feb. 27, 1783. Appears on muster roll for May and June Transferred to Light Inf. July 1. |
| | " | Sith Montague | |
| | " | Ira Mott | |
| | | Jabez or Tabor Norton | Transferred to Light Inf. July 1 |
| July 4, 1781 | 3 years | Hazard Prior | comm'd conn't with Col. Webb Dec. 18ᵈ 1781 not on muster roll for Sept 1782 or later |
| | D. W. | Will= Rainvolt or Rain Volt or Reinvault | |
| Dec. 1, 1780 | 8 years | David Spencer | not on muster roll for Sept 1782 or later Transferred to L. Inf. June 1, 1782 |
| Feb. 1, 1781 | " | Jacob Strong | not on muster roll for May 1782 but appears on June 1782 and later |
| Feb. 18 " | " | Edmond Shelley or Thelly | |
| Nov. 28, 1780 | " | Joseph Smith | not on muster roll for May 1782 or later |
| | D. W. | John Swaddle | |
| July 1, 1781 | 1 year | Thos Spencer | |
| | D. W. | Hezekiah Cary | Discharged July 1 |
| | " | Elihu Waters or Warren | |
| Apr. 9, 1782 | D. W. | Jonathan Crutie | Joined from desertion Feb. 2, 1782. Transferred to L. Inf. June 1, and returned July 1, 1782 |
| | " | Allen Corning | Deserted June 12, 1782 |
| | | Joseph Johnston | on muster roll for May 1782 and later |
| Apr. 1 | 1y. 6m. 5d. | Hendrick Bail | " |
| " " | 9m. 15d. | Ruben Clark | " |
| Apr. 19 " | 6m. 15d. | Noah Kelsey | Joined May 18, with Geographer July 12, 1782. Not on muster roll for Sept. 1782 or later |
| Mar. 22 " | 9m. 7d. | Samuel Stantliff | Joined May 18 |
| Apr. 27 " | 9m. 6d. | Nathan Edgerton | " " 20 |

* Signed and indorsed 1782, and later rolls of this company are dated 1782.

322   REVOLUTION LISTS AND RETURNS.

| | Inlisted | | Term | | |
|---|---|---|---|---|---|
| May | 24 | 1782 | 5m. 9d. | Ebenezer Chapman | Joined June 5 Deserted Oct. 2, 1782 |
| Apr. | 18 | " | " | Daniel or David Gardner | "   "   10   "        "      "   " |
| Apr. | 29 | " | " | Jacob Fenton | "   "   20   "        "      "   " |
| May | 15 | " | 8m. 24d. | James Bliss | "   "   20   "        "      "   " |
| Apr. | 15 | " | " | Jabez or Tabor Cole | "   "   20   "        "      "   " |
| Apr. | 30 | " | 2y. 8m. 20d. | Wilson Commins | "   July 8 |
| | | | | Frank Negro | Joined Apr. 7, 1782 Servant. not on muster roll for Oct. 1782 |
| | | | D. W. | Daniel Bostwick | Joined from desertion Sep. 24, 1782 |
| | | | " | William Daskim | "      "        "        "    "   " |
| | | | " | Simion C. Stoddard | appears on muster roll for Sep. 1782 |

[*State Library, Revolution* 39 ; 46, 55, 64, 75, 83, 92, 101.]

## SEVENTH COMPANY—CAPT. RILEY.

[The muster rolls of this company for February, March and June 1782 are preserved. Only the earliest of these is here copied, with such changes noted as appear on any of the later rolls.]

Muster Roll of Captain John Rileys Company of the 3rd Connecticut Regiment in the service of the United States commanded by Colonel Samuel B. Webb For the month of February 1782

| Inlisted | Term | | |
|---|---|---|---|
| | | John Riley | Capt. |
| | | John Mix | Lieut. |
| | D. W. | William or Thomas Holmes | Serj. |
| | " | William Taylor | " |
| | " | David Webb | " |
| | " | William Patterson | Corp. |
| | " | Dan¹ Potter | " |
| | " | Christopher Horton | " |
| | " | Ezekiel Winchal | " |
| | " | Joseph Wolcutt | Drum |
| | " | Samuel Bush | Fifer |
| Sep. 1, 1779 | 8 years | Job Boomer | |

With the Quarter Master General since July 19, 1781.

CONNECTICUT LINE, 1781–1783.

|  | | |  |  |
|---|---|---|---|---|
| Feb. | 6, | 1781 | Ozias Bachus | |
| Apr. | 22, | " | Joseph Cheem or Cheney | |
| Jan. | 8, | " | David Cheater | |
| June | 30, | " | Asa Copeland | 1 year |
| Dec. | 1, | 1780 | Benjamin Cady | 3 years Transfered to L. Inf. June 1, 1782 |
| Feb. | 1, | 1781 | Silvenus Gage | " |
| Feb. | 5, | " | Joel Hyde | " |
| Feb. | 1, | " | Amos Harris | |
| | | | Eleazar Hatch | |
| | | | Peter Johnson | |
| Feb. | 1, | " | John or Richard Kimball | " |
| Feb. | 1, | " | Jared Kimball | " |
| Dec. | 10, | 1780 | Marshall Kyes | " |
| Jan. | 27, | 1781 | Jabez Kirtland Brigade Waggoner | " |
| Feb. | 3, | " | Phinehas Knight | " |
| | | | Jonathan Luce | |
| Feb. | 6, | " | Levi Munsill | " |
| Feb. | 1, | " | John Munsill | " Transfered to L. Inf. June 1, 1782 |
| Feb. | 28, | " | Benoni Moss | " |
| Jan. | 15, | " | James Miner | " |
| May | 16, | " | Noah Merrills | " |
| | | | Gallaway Peters | D. W. |
| | | | David Potter | 8 years Transfered to L. Inf. June 1, 1782 |
| Feb. | 3, | " | Lemuel Raymond | |
| | | | Joshua Reynolds | |
| | | | Peter Shopp | |
| | | | Thadeus Scofield | |
| | | | Toney Turney | |
| Dec. | 20, | 1780 | Nathan Tubbs | " Deserted Apr. 10, 1782. Joined from desertion May 18, 1782 |
| Mar. | 5, | 1781 | John Wheeler | |
| Feb. | 1, | " | Ichabod West | |
| Jan. | 1, | " | Ichabod Warden | |
| | | | Thomas Wilson | Servant to Gen. Parsons Aide |

| | Inlisted | Term | | |
|---|---|---|---|---|
| Nov. | 1, 1782 | 3 years | Richard York | |
| " | " | 1y. 9m. | George Seeley | Corp. |
| " | " | D. W. | Joseph Clinton | |
| May | 6 | 34m. 21d. | David Heyden | |
| April | 22 | 6m. 8d. | Nathaniel Silliman | not on muster roll for March 1782 or later |
| Mar. | 25 | 8m. 22d. | Oliver Scott | appears on muster roll for March 1782 and later |
| Feb. | 3 | 3m. 22d. | Simon Stimson | appears on muster roll for June 1782 |
| Apr. | 12 | 5m. 28d. | Robert Welsh | Joined May 9 |

[State Library, Revolution 39; 47, 66, 74.]

## EIGHTH COMPANY—CAPT. ALLYN.

[The muster rolls of this company for February, March, May, June, July, September, and October, 1782, are preserved. Only the earliest of these is here copied, with such changes noted as appear on any of the later rolls.]

Muster Roll of Captain Allyns Company in the 3rd Connecticut Regiment in the service of the United States Commanded by Col¹ Samuel B. Webbs for the Month of February 1782.

| Appointed | Term | | Name | |
|---|---|---|---|---|
| | | Capt. | Timothy Allyn | not on muster roll Oct. 1782 |
| | | Lieut. | William Lorl | " " |
| | | Ens. | Jacquess Harmon | Transfered to 2d Co. July 31 |
| | | Serj. | Wyman Parker | |
| | D. W. | " | Abraham Hawley | |
| | " | " | Enoch Merriman | |
| | " | " | John Downe | not on muster roll May 1782 or later on muster roll for May and later |
| July 11, 1780 | 3 years | Corp. | Hezekiah Betts | |
| | D. W. | " | Nathan Hawley | |
| | " | Drum. | Curtis Crane | Deserted April 10 |
| | " | Fifer | Thomas Brown | |
| | 1m. 10d. | Fifer | David Coy | |
| | | | Matthew Jackson | reduced from fifer April 1 Hired by Isaiah Pratt to serve in his stead March 21, 1782 |
| | D. W. | | John Ammit | |

## CONNECTICUT LINE, 1781–1783.

| Date | Name | Term | Remarks |
|---|---|---|---|
| Apr. 4, 1781 | Ebenezer Bacon | 3 years | Transferred to Capt. Wells L. I. Co. June 1, 1782 |
| Jan. 29, " | Comfort Beebee | " | |
| Jan. 29, " | Richard Beebee | " | |
| Feb. 26, " | Abial Chaffee | D. W. | |
| July 18, " | John Churchill | 3 years | Discharged July 18, 1782 |
| July 18, " | William Clark | D. W. | Transferred to Invalid Corps June 21, 1782 |
| July 18, " | Cesar Edwards | 3 years | |
| Mar. 1, " | Jabez Edgecomb | " | |
| Jan. 1, " | Benedick Eggleston | " | |
| July 15, " | Benjamin Ellsworth | " | |
| Jan. 3, " | Basset Fox | " | |
| Jan. 29, " | Simeon Fox | " | |
| March | James Eggleston | " | Servant to Col. Verrick Nov. 18, 1781 |
| Jan. 17, " | David Garner | " | |
| Jan. 29, " | Jacob Gillet | " | |
| Jan. 29, " | Henry Horton | " | |
| Jan. 29, " | Cudjo Helms | " | Transferred to Invalid Corps June 21, 1782 |
| Dec. 18, 1780 | John G. Holcomb | " | |
| Jan. 16, 1781 | Aaron Kingsley | " | |
| | Peter Lewis | D. W. | not on muster roll Sept. 1782 or later |
| | Eliel London | " | |
| | Stephen Ludlow | " | |
| | Nathaniel or Nathan Mallery | | |
| Nov. 25, 1780 | Elias Measom or Meason | 3 years | |
| Nov. 25, " | John Mills | " | |
| Jan. 8, 1781 | James Nedson | " | |
| Dec. 27, 1780 | Robert Nedson | " | Not on muster roll March 1782 or later |
| Dec. 27, 1781 | Issac Neilson | " | |
| Mar. 5, " | Daniel Perkins | " | |
| Jan. 1, " | Isaiah Pratt | " | |
| Mar. 1, " | Adonijah Rose | " | |
| | John Robertson | D. W. | |
| | Comma Simonds | " | |
| | Elias Shaw | " | Transferred to Capt. Wells L. I. Co. June 1, 1782 |

| Name | Term | Appointed | |
|---|---|---|---|
| Ebenezer Shaw | 3 years | Feb. 1, 1781 | Transferred to Light Infantry Co. July 1, 1782. |
| Reuben Sharp | " | Mar. 1, " | |
| David Taylor | | | |
| Calvin Chaffee | " | Dec. 14, 1780 | hired by Abial Chaffee to serve in his stead March 1782. Transferred to Capt. Wells L. I. Co. June 1, 1782. |
| Isaac Beers | 6m. 16d. | Apr. 24, 1782 | Joined June 8  Deserted July 18, 1782 |
| Hezekiah Terrill or Turnill | " " | Apr. 24 " | "  "  8 |
| Nehemiah Barns | 5m. 9d. | June 29 " | "  July 17 |
| Edward Dunkin | " " | May 11 " | "  June 17 |
| Daniel Hawley | " " | May 11 " | "  "  17 |
| Charles Lewis | " " | May 11 " | "  "  17 |
| Aaron Waley | " | June 3 " | "  "  17 |

[*State Library, Revolution* 39; 45, 53, 61, 70, 80, 89, 98.]

# CONNECTICUT LINE, 1783.

## THIRD REGIMENT—COL. WEBB.

[*See Record of Connecticut Men in the Revolution, page 367.*]

### FIELD AND STAFF.

[The muster rolls of the Field and Staff for Dec. 1782–Jan. 1783 and Feb. 1783 are preserved. Only the earlier of these is here printed, with such changes noted as appear on the later.]

Muster Roll of the Field and Staff Officers, of the 3rd Connecticut Reg't with such Noncommissioned Officers as are not attached to any Company

| Ranks | Names | |
|---|---|---|
| Colonel | Samuel B. Webb | |
| Lieut. Col. | Ebenezer Gray | |
| Maj. | Joseph A. Wright | |
| Adjnt | John Meigs | |
| Quarter Master | Ebenezer Frothingham | |
| Pay Master | Nathan Beers | |
| Recruit Officer | | |
| Surgeon | John Rose | |
| Mate | Jedediah Ensworth | Resigned Jan. 15, 1783 |
| | Aeneas Monson | Joined Jan. 15, 1783 |
| Serj. Majors | Edward Miller | |
| | Jonathan White | Deserted Jan. 4, 1783 |
| Qr. Mr. Serjeants | Simon Griffin or Giffin | |
| | William Tupper | |
| Drum Major | David Pratt | |
| Fife Majors | John Kircum | |
| | George Cook | |

I certify the Present Muster Roll to be true in all its contents
Inspection of December 1782 & January 1783

W Barber Major & Ass't Inspector of the North'n Army

[*State Library, Revolution 39; 105, 116.*]

## LIGHT INFANTRY COMPANY—CAPT. WELLES.

[The muster rolls of this company for Dec. 1782–Jan. 1783 and Feb. 1783 are preserved. Only the earlier of these is here printed, with such changes noted as appear on the later roll.]

Roll and Muster of the Light Infantry Company in the 3rd Regiment of Connecticut Troops Commanded by Col¹ Sam¹ B. Webb

| Ranks | Names | Term of Enlistment | |
|---|---|---|---|
| Capt | Roger Welles | | |
| Lieut | John Trowbridge | | Transf⁴ 1ˢᵗ Co Feb 1ˢᵗ 1783 |
| " | William Linn | | Transfer⁴ to 8ᵗʰ Comp⁷ 1ˢᵗ Jany 1783 |
| Ensⁿ | Jacob Kingsbury | | Transf⁴ 6ᵗʰ Co Feb 1ˢᵗ 1783 |
| Sergts | Stephen Butler | D W | |
| | Elihu Spear | " | |
| | Silas Phelps | | |
| | Moses Griswould | " | Rec⁴ from 3ᵈ Comp⁷ 1ˢᵗ Jany 1783 |
| | Thomas Wood | " | Deserted Jany 10ᵗʰ 1783 |
| Corporals | Selah Scofield | | |
| | David Lounsbury | " | |
| | Benjamin Dix | " | |
| Drummer | John Dixon | " | |
| fifer | Daniel Winchel | " | |
| Privates | Jacob Achor | " | |
| | John Allyn | " | |
| | Archelus Ames | 1  1 15 | |
| | John Barnum | D W | |
| | David Bullen | " | |
| | Ebenezer Bacon | 1  2  8 | |
| | Reuben Cadwell | D W | |
| | Elias Carpenter | 0 11 13 | |
| | Calvin Chaffee | 0 11  9 | |
| | Asa Copeland | D W | |
| | Ward Cotton | 0 11 18 | |
| | Benjamin Dix | D W | promoted to Corp¹ 1 Jan⁷ 1783 |
| | Allyn Evins | " | |
| | Thomas Evins | " | |
| | Remembrance Filley | " | |
| | Vaniah Fox | " | |
| | Ichabod Goodrich | " | |
| | Samuel Gookins | " | |
| | Andrew Hansey | 0 11 10 | |
| | Selah Harte | 1  1  8 | |
| | Samuel Hinman | D W | |
| | James Hyde | " | |
| | Benjamin Kircum | " | |
| | Philemon Kircum | 0 11 22 | |
| | Joseph Lawson | 0 11 23 | |
| | Chansey Lewis | D W | |
| | Stephen Meeker | " | |
| | Jonathan Miller | " | |
| | Ira Mott | " | |
| | Brion Montigue | " | |
| | John Munsill | 1  0  4 | |

CONNECTICUT LINE, 1783.

| Ranks | Names | Term of Enlistment | |
|---|---|---|---|
| Privates | Levi Munsell | 1 0 10 | |
| | Sheldon Potter | D W | |
| | Lemuel Raymond | " | |
| | Reuben Sharpe | 1 1 3 | |
| | Elias Shaw | D W | |
| | Isaiah Smith | " | |
| | Nathan Smith | " | |
| | David Spencer | 1 0 4 | |
| | Lemuel Sperry | D W | |
| | Samuel Stowel | 0 11 3 | |
| | Nathaniel Stowel | 1 1 15 | |
| | Samuel Vallit | D W | Deserted Jan⁷ 31, 83 |
| | Chester Upham | 0 10 19 | |
| | Benjamin Waklee | D W | |
| | Charles Walter | 0 10 8 | |
| | Hazard Pryor | 1 5 8 | transf$^d$ 1$^{st}$ Comp$^y$ 1$^{st}$ Jany 1783 |

I certify the above Roll to be the true State of said Comp$^y$ this 26$^{th}$ day of Jan$^y$ 1783

J. Kingsbury Ens$^n$

[*State Library, Revolution 39; 115, 125.*]

## FIRST COMPANY—CAPT. BETTS.

[The muster rolls of this company for Dec. 1782–Jan. 1783 and Feb. 1783 are preserved. Only the earliest of these is here printed, with such changes noted as appear on the later roll.]

Roll and muster of the 1$^{st}$ Company 3$^{rd}$ Regiment of Connecticut Troops Commanded by Colonel Sam$^l$ B. Webb for Dec$^r$ & Jan$^y$ 1782 & 3

| Ranks | Names | Term of Enlistment | Casualties & Alterations |
|---|---|---|---|
| Captain | Stephen Betts | | on Furlough |
| Lieu$^t$ | John Mix | | Comm$^d$ Q. M. G. Rec$^d$ from the 8 Company transferred to the 8$^{th}$ Comp$^y$ Feb. 1, 83 |
| Lieut | John Trowbridge | | Rec$^d$ from the Light Compy Feb$^y$ 1 82-3 |
| Ens$^n$ | Jaques Harmon | | |
| Lieu$^t$ | Ebenezer Frothingham | | Transfered to the Reg$^{al}$ Staff |
| Serjeants | Jesse Smith | D War | |
| " | Joseph Clark | " | |
| " | Aaron Raymond | " | |
| " | Torey Scranton | " | |
| " | Joseph Hait | " | |
| " | Uzal Knapp | " | |
| " | Luther Reeves | " | |
| Corporals | James Downs | " | |
| " | Abel Hitchcock | " | |
| " | George Hubbard | " | |
| " | Enoch Thomas | " | |
| " | Samuel Jackson | " | |
| Drum | Anthony DeFloris | 11m. 6d. | |
| " | Lemuel Sanborough or Samuel Stanborugh | 12 7 | |

| Ranks | Names | Term of Enlistment | | Casualties & Alterations |
|---|---|---|---|---|
| Fife | Reuben Rennolds | War | | |
| " | John Dauset | " | | |
| Privates | Roger Avory | " | | |
| | Thomas Blake | " | | |
| | David Betts | " | | |
| | Jacob Bosworth | " | | |
| | John Bary | " | | |
| | James Coburn | " | | |
| | Joseph Davis | 9 | 29 | |
| | Juline Eston | War | | |
| | Primas Freeman | " | | |
| | Sirus Graham | " | | |
| | Joseph Goldsmith | " | | |
| | Silas Glasco or Glasses | " | | |
| | William Hanson | " | | |
| | Ebenezer Hill | " | | |
| | James Freeman | " | | |
| | David Jackson | " | | |
| | Alexander Judd | " | | |
| | Abner Lee | " | | |
| | Job Leason | " | | |
| | Robert Marsh | " | | |
| | Anthony McDaniel | " | | |
| | Reuben Parks | " | | |
| | Nathaniel Pardy | " | | |
| | Jeremiah Rozell | " | | |
| | Ambrose Smith | " | | |
| | Aaron Tuttle | " | | |
| | Samuel Thomas | " | | |
| | Jacob Wardwell | " | | |
| | Benjamin Welton | " | | |
| | Edward Burges | 8m. | 9d. | |
| | Jonathan Brown | 10 | 25 | |
| | Alexander Durand | 10 | 23 | |
| | Benjamin Dodge | 10 | 25 | |
| | David Dicks | 10 | 23 | |
| | Edward Freeman | 10 | 12 | |
| | John Gates | 11 | 5 | |
| | Benjamin Greenslit | 11 | 28 | |
| | Jaison Gay | 11 | 26 | |
| | Able (?) Guthrey | 9 | 14 | |
| | Gilbert Graves | | | |
| | Robert Holdridge | 10 | 21 | |
| | William Hughes | 11 | 25 | |
| | Clement Handy | 28 | 7 | |
| | William Lament | 17 | 7 | |
| | John McNulty | 4 | 25 | |
| | Aseph Pettengall | 11 | 26 | |
| | Jesse Olmstead | 11 | 3 | |
| | Jacob Pettengall | 12 | 1 | |
| | Hazard Prior | 17 | 8 | Rec[d] from the L[t] Inf[y] Com[y] Jan[y] 1 1783 Serv[t] to Col[l] Webb in Conn[t] |
| | Adonijah Rose | 9 | 16 | Rec[d] from the 6 Comp[y] |
| | Tuis Sharper | 13 | 27 | |
| | Ephraim Story | 15 | 7 | |
| | Shubel Snow | 28 | 7 | |

CONNECTICUT LINE, 1783. 331

| Ranks | Names | Terms of Enlistment | | Casualties & Alterations |
|---|---|---|---|---|
| Privates | Daniel S[t] John | 10 | 25 | |
| | James Thompson | 11 | 25 | |
| | Thomas Worden | 18 | 2 | |
| | Jesse Williams | 12 | 25 | |
| | Chester Waterman | 11 | 11 | |
| | Josiah Rogers | | transf[d] to the 6 Company Jan 1[st] 83 |
| | John Bliss | | Dich[d] Dec[r] 29[th] 82 Time expired |
| | Beriah Bliss | " | " 29 | " |
| | Samuel Bliss | " | " 29 | " |
| | Moses Barnard | " | " 29 | " |
| | Abijah Bloggett | " | " 29 | " |
| | Ichabod Case | 1 | 3 | |
| | John Haskal | | Disch[d] Dec[r] 29[th] 82 Time expired |
| | Jacob Haskal | " | " " | " |
| | Andrew Hazen | " | " " | " |
| | Dan Lyman | " | " " | " |
| | Charles Miner | " | " " | " |
| | Reubin Cree | " | " " | " |
| | Sam[l] Parks | " | " " | " |
| | John Porter | " | " " | " |
| | Oziah (?) Prentice | " | " " | " |
| | John Meeker | | Discharged by his Excellencys order Jan[y] 4[th] 83 for Inability |

I certify the above Roll to be the true State of said Company this day of Jan[y] 1783

J. Harmon Ens[n]

[*State Library, Revolution 39: 107, 117.*]

## SECOND COMPANY—CAPT. WALKER.

[The muster rolls of this company for Dec. 1782–Jan. 1783, and Feb. 1783 are preserved. Only the earlier of these is here printed, with such changes noted as appear on the later roll.]

Roll and Muster of 2[nd] Company 3[rd] Connecticut Regiment of Foot by Col[l] S. B. Webb for Dec[r] 82 & Jan[y] 1783

| Ranks | Names | Term of Inlistment | |
|---|---|---|---|
| Capt. | Joseph Walker | | Brigade Major |
| Lieu[t] | Aron Benjamin | | |
| Ensign | Joseph Clark | | |
| Serjeants | Jonathan Steuben | D W | |
| " | Francis Nickelson | " | |
| " | Simeon Holmes | " | |
| " | Waitstill Dickinson | " | |
| " | Ezbon Hubbell | " | |
| " | Elijah Demming | " | |
| " | Elihu Mather | " | |
| Corporals | Stephen Risley | " | |
| " | Moses Porter | " | |
| " | Armey Sperry | " | |
| " | John Thomas | " | |
| " | Benjamin Wheeler | " | |
| Drumer | David Linsly | " | |
| " | John Jinks | " | |

| Ranks | Names | Term of Inlistment | | |
|---|---|---|---|---|
| Drumer | John Vaughn | D. W. | | Joined from late 5th Reg't Discharged 1st Jan'y 83 |
| Fifer | Asa Squires | " | | Died 24th Jany 1783 |
| Privates | Henry Bivens | " | | |
| | Abel Batchlor | " | | |
| | James Chadwick | " | | |
| | Benjamin Craft | " | | |
| | Jehiel Doude | " | | |
| | Daniel Evett | " | | |
| | Reuben Everts | 14m | | |
| | Isaac Ford | D War | | |
| | Jonathan Finch | " | | |
| | Plymouth Freeman | " | | |
| | Azariah Grant | " | | |
| | John Goodrich | " | | |
| | Prince George | " | | |
| | Ebenezer Hodley | " | | |
| | David Hurd | " | | |
| | Titus Hine | " | | |
| | Jonathan Haynes | " | | |
| | Reuben Lake | " | | |
| | Silvester Miner | " | | |
| | Uriah Polly | " | | |
| | Ashur Russell | " | | |
| | David Roberts | " | | |
| | Samuel Stone | " | | |
| | Ezra Tryon | " | | |
| | Jacob Wright 2nd | " | | |
| | Silas Wood | " | | |
| | James Grant | " | | |
| | Hubbard Burras or Burrows | 18m | 9d | |
| | Isaac or James Beers | 28 | 8 | |
| | William Butler | 12 | 0 | deserted 8 Feby 83 |
| | Elisha Back | 14 | 0 | |
| | Thomas Burrell | 2 | 0 | with the Geographer |
| | John Clark | 10 | 10 | |
| | Benjamin Durffee | 9 | 16 | |
| | Reuben Dodge | 9 | 18 | |
| | Seth Dodge | 9 | 18 | |
| | Joshua Fullar | 11 | 8 | |
| | John Faggins' | 11 | 9 | |
| | David Hayden | 15 | 27 | |
| | Heman Hatch | 10 | 14 | |
| | Rufus Holdridge | 18 | 0 | |
| | Bodwell Hughes | 25 | 0 | |
| | Joel Johnson | 12 | 0 | |
| | Prince Johnson | 10 | 0 | |
| | Jabez Morters | 11 | 28 | |
| | Elijah Morley | 26 | 28 | |
| | Henry Pond | 18 | 25 | |
| | Jacob Patchen | 18 | 0 | |
| | Richard Pitts or Potts | 11 | 0 | |
| | Judah Roberts | 1 | 18 | |
| | Lemuel Stancliff | 12 | 15 | |
| | Jonathan Simons | 12 | 18 | |

CONNECTICUT LINE, 1783.   333

| Ranks | Names | Terms of Inlistment | | | | |
|---|---|---|---|---|---|---|
| | William Sheericks | 11 | 25 | | | |
| | Joshua Turner | 25 | 0 | | | |
| | Jacob Wight | 12 | 23 | | | |
| | Joseph Wakely | 12 | 15 | | | |
| | David Hubbell | | | Disch<sup>d</sup> Dec<sup>r</sup> | 9<sup>th</sup> | 1782 |
| | Noah U. Norton | | | " | " | " |
| | Joshua Olmsted | | | " | " | 30 82 |
| | Amos Clark | | | " | " | 9 " |
| | David Hubbard | | | " | " | 30 " |
| | David Joice | | | " | " | 20 " |
| | Solomon Ranney | | | " | " | 30 " |
| | Nathan Wheeler | | | " | " | 30 " |
| | Walter Smith | | | " | " | 9 " |
| | Benjamin Webster | | | " | " | 6 " |
| | Ashbel Webster | | | " | " | 6 83 |
| | John Clark 2<sup>d</sup> | | | " | " | 31 83 |

I certify the above Roll to be the true state of said Company this 26<sup>th</sup> day of January 1783.

Joseph Clark Ens<sup>n</sup>

[*State Library, Revolution 39; 114, 124.*]

## THIRD COMPANY—CAPT. SELDEN.

[The muster rolls of this company for Dec. 1782–Jan. 1783 and Feb. 1783 are preserved. Only the earlier of these is here printed, with such changes noted as appear on the later roll.]

Roll and Muster of the third Company of the 3<sup>rd</sup> Connecticut Regiment Commanded by Col<sup>l</sup> Sam<sup>l</sup> B. Webb for Dec<sup>r</sup> 1782 & Jan<sup>y</sup> 1783.

| Ranks | Names | Term of Inlistment | |
|---|---|---|---|
| Capt | Ezra Selden | | |
| Lieu<sup>t</sup> | John Meigs | | Transf<sup>d</sup> to y<sup>e</sup> Reg<sup>l</sup> Staff Jan<sup>y</sup> 1<sup>st</sup> 1783 |
| " | John Mix | | Rec<sup>d</sup> from the 1<sup>st</sup> Co 1<sup>st</sup> Feby |
| Ens<sup>n</sup> | Abner Cole | | |
| Lieu<sup>t</sup> | John Hobart | | Rec<sup>d</sup> from y<sup>e</sup> 4<sup>th</sup> Reg<sup>t</sup> Jan<sup>y</sup> 1<sup>st</sup> 1783 transf<sup>d</sup> to 8<sup>th</sup> Co 1<sup>st</sup> Feby |
| Serj<sup>ts</sup> | Daniel Sizer | D War | |
| " | Elijah Boardman | " | |
| " | Darius Orcutt or Oniott | 8m 20d. | |
| " | Moses Griswold | D War | Transfd to the L I Comp<sup>y</sup> 1<sup>st</sup> Jan<sup>y</sup> |
| " | Allen Prior | " | |
| " | Ebenezer Shelley | " | |
| " | Phineas Squires | " | |
| Corporals | Hezekiah Nott | " | |
| " | Thomas Stanley | " | Reduced 8 March 83 |
| " | Gideon Goff | " | |
| " | Reuben Moss | " | |
| " | Abraham Parker | " | |
| Drum | Moses Hatch | " | |
| " | Miles Cook | " | |
| Fife | William Armstrong | " | |

| Ranks | Names | Terms of Inlistment | | |
|---|---|---|---|---|
| Fife | Silas Stanbrough | 13m | | |
| Privates | Daniel Morley | D War | | |
| | Hezekiah Wheeler | " | | |
| | Prince Freeman | " | | |
| | Jack Freeman | " | | |
| | Samuel Roberts | " | | |
| | Abraham Belding | " | | |
| | Benajah Bracket | " | | |
| | David Barnes | " | | |
| | Peter Lyon | " | | |
| | Jabez Lord | " | | |
| | David Hull | " | | |
| | John Lerow or Scrow | " | | |
| | John Bishop | " | | |
| | Linus Morse | " | | |
| | Eliacom Hull | " | | |
| | Enoch Kellogg | " | | |
| | Abdiel Flowers | " | | |
| | Samuel Lee | " | | |
| | Othniel Branard | " | | |
| | Seth Hubbell | " | | |
| | John Packard | " | | |
| | Solomon Williams | " | | |
| | Ezra Harvey | " | | |
| | Samuel Cheese | " | | |
| | Cezar Negro | 18m. | | deserted 26 Feb. 83 |
| | Joseph Pease | 16 | 14d. | |
| | Cato Freeman | 16 | 1 | |
| | John Ballard | 13 | 20 | |
| | Moses Coy | 12 | 3 | |
| | Nathan Frinck | 12 | | |
| | Nathaniel Price | 13 | | |
| | Reuben Robinson | 12 | 20 | |
| | Samuel Lyon | 12 | 3 | |
| | Robert Chandler | 12 | | |
| | Joseph Douglass | 11 | 22 | |
| | Alfred Dressor | 11 | 5 | |
| | Joseph Preston | 11 | 27 | |
| | Peter Whitney | 10 | 25 | |
| | Daniel Dunham | 10 | 28 | |
| | Abel Stoel | 10 | 17 | |
| | Jeremiah Bennet | 10 | 17 | |
| | Jonathan Bullock | 10 | 17 | |
| | Stephen Fox | 10 | 1 | |
| | Benjamin Brown | 10 | | |
| | David Peck | 9 | 17 | |
| | Joseph Abby | 11 | 21 | |
| | Gideon Dunham | 2 | | |
| | Joseph Bunnel | 1 | 28 | |
| | Eleazer Cutler | 1 | 19 | |
| | Christopher Kelby | 1 | 19 | |
| | Nathaniel Hardy | 1 | | Disch$^d$ 8$^{th}$ Febr 1783 |
| | William Witherel | | | Discharged Jan$^y$ 18$^{th}$ 1783 |
| | Neal McNeal | | | " Dec$^r$ 6$^{th}$ 1782 |
| | Gideon Russell | | | " " 27$^{th}$ |
| | Jesse Thomas | | | " " 9$^{th}$ |
| | George Foot | | | " " 20$^{th}$ |

CONNECTICUT LINE, 1783.   335

| Ranks | Names | Term of Inlistment | |
|---|---|---|---|
| Privates | Amos Gustin | | Discharged Dec' 10th 1782 |
| | Benoni Robins | | " " 22d |
| | Ephraim Webster | | " " 9th |
| | John Downing | | " Jany 2d 1783 |
| | John Tucker | | " Dec' 10th 1782 |
| | Daniel W Knight | | " " 26th |
| | Daniel Stevens | | Transferred to ye 2nd Reg't Jany 1st 1783 |
| | Nehemiah Seley | | Discharged Dec' 9th 1782 |
| | Daniel Bushnell | | " Jany 6th 1788 |
| | William Saivers | D War | Joined from the late 4th Feb 19,83 |
| | Samuel Herrington | " | Found only on Feb. roll |

I certify the above Roll to be the true State of said Company this 26th day of January 1783

Ezra Selden Capt

[*State Library, Revolution 39; 111, 122.*]

## FOURTH COMPANY—CAPT. TEN EYCK.

[The muster rolls of this company for Dec. 1782–Jan. 1783 and Feb. 1783 are preserved. Only the earlier of these is here printed, with such changes noted as appear on the later roll.]

Roll and Muster of the 4th Company 3rd Conn't Regiment Commanded by Col'l Sam'l B. Webb

| Ranks | Names | Term of Inlistment | | |
|---|---|---|---|---|
| Capt | Henry Ten Eyck | | | |
| Lieut | Isaac Keeler | | | |
| Serj't | Jared Bunce | D War | | |
| | John Forbes | " | | |
| | Joshua Cone | " | | Adj't Gen'l Guard July 12th 82 |
| | Walter Booth | | | Dischd Dec' 6th by hiring a man |
| | Ahimaaz Punderson | " | | |
| | Constant Chapman | 11m 16d | | |
| | Phinehas Squires | D War | | Transferd to the 3d Compy Jany 1st 83 |
| | David Dixon | " | | |
| Corp'ls | Zebulon Mygott | " | | Reducd to a private 1 Mch 83 |
| | Daniel Ward | " | | |
| | Frederick Stoddard | " | | |
| | Stephen Roberts | " | | |
| | Jiles Wilcox | " | | |
| Drummers | William Kerkum | " | | |
| | Elijah Peeksley | " | | |
| Fifer | Joel Clark | " | | |
| | Samuel Shelley | " | | |
| Privates | Jedediah Adams | 9m | 17d | |
| | Christopher Avery | 17 | 7 | |
| | Elihu Babcock | 14 | 9 | |
| | Joseph Borrows | 13 | 7 | |
| | Joseph Branch | D War | | |
| | David Brown | 10 | 5 | |
| | Solomon Bigsby | 15 | 27 | |
| | John Boughton | D War | | |
| | Jeremiah Cunnell | 10 | 27 | |

| Ranks | Names | Term of Inlistment | |
|---|---|---|---|
| Privates | Serajah Comstock | 10 | 23 |
| | Joseph Chamberlin | 10 | 16 |
| | Curtis Chapel | D War | |
| | Stephen Childs | 14 | 22 |
| | Hezekiah Catlin | 12 | 2 |
| | Joel Dolittle | D War | |
| | William Davis | " | |
| | James Dinah | " | |
| | Jonas Elis | " | |
| | Asa Fox | " | |
| | Elijah Fayer | 18 | 5 |
| | Sam¹ Fargo | 11 | 1 |
| | Caesor Freeman | 5 | 17 |
| | Cuffee Freeman | D War | |
| | Silas Glass | 9 | 27 |
| | Nath¹ Gates | 9 | 27 |
| | Sam¹ Green | D War | Rec⁴ from 7ᵗʰ Compʸ Janʸ 10ᵗʰ 83 |
| | Nath¹ Holt | 14 | 21 |
| | Jesse Holt | 12 | 27 |
| | Pratt Jones | D War | |
| | Eli King | " | |
| | Willᵐ Martin | " | |
| | Thomas Meach | " | Transf⁴ to the 7ᵗʰ Compʸ Janʸ 1ˢᵗ 83 |
| | Clemont Miner | " | Inlisted Decʳ 6ᵗʰ 1782 hired by Serjᵗ Booth |
| | Robert Newel | | |
| | William Ovitt | " | |
| | Joseph Otis | " | |
| | Daniel Purkins | 10 | 25 |
| | Isaac Roberts | D War | |
| | Joseph Rowlandson | " | |
| | Isaac Raymond | " | |
| | Ephᵐ Robertson | " | |
| | Seth Stannard | " | |
| | Philliman Stedmon | " | |
| | Isaac Stedmon | 16 | 16 |
| | Sam¹ Schoolcraft | D War | |
| | Abel Stockwell | " | Deserted Decʳ 17ᵗʰ 82 |
| | Andrew Simons | " | |
| | Jonathan Stevens | 14 | 27 |
| | Joseph Treat | D War | |
| | Job Uffoot | " | |
| | Jedediah Woodworth | 9 | 7 |
| | Joshua Welles | D War | |
| | Congo Zado | " | |
| | Josiah Butt | 1 | 21 |
| | Daniel Heddy or Healdy | 2 | 20 |
| | Oliver Coe | 1 | 20 |
| | Elijah Durfy | | Disch⁴ Decʳ 9ᵗʰ 82 |
| | Sam¹ Convirs | | " Janʸ 3ᵈ 83 |
| | Elijah Andros | | " Decʳ 6ᵗʰ 82 |
| | James French | | " " " |
| | Amos Green | | " " " |
| | Edmond J Dunning | | " " 17ᵗʰ 82 |
| | Levi Hall | | " Janʸ 11ᵗʰ 83 |

CONNECTICUT LINE, 1783.

| Ranks | Names | Term of Inlistment | | |
|---|---|---|---|---|
| Privates | Roswell Lamphere | Disch$^d$ | Dec$^r$ | 9$^{th}$ 82 |
| | Stephen Squires | " | Dec$^r$ | 7$^{th}$ 82 |
| | James Wilcox | " | Dec$^r$ | 28$^{th}$ 82 |
| | Elisha Catlin | " | Dec$^r$ | 28$^{th}$ 82 |

I certify the above Roll to be the true State of said Company This 26$^{th}$ day of January 1783

Hen$^y$ Ten Eyck Capt$^a$

[Indorsed] Roll & Muster of 4$^{th}$ Company 3$^{rd}$ Reg$^t$ of Connecticut For Decem$^r$ 82 & Jan$^y$ 1783

[*State Library, Revolution 39; 115, 123.*]

## FIFTH COMPANY—CAPT. HOPKINS.

[The muster rolls of this company for Dec. 1782–Jan. 1783, and Feb. 1783 are preserved. Only the earlier of these is here printed, with such changes noted as appear on the later roll.]

Roll and Muster of the 5$^{th}$ Company in the 3$^d$ Connecticut Regiment Commanded by Col$^l$ Sam$^l$ B. Webb for Decemb$^r$ 82 & Jan$^y$ 83

| Ranks | Names | Term of Inlistment | | | |
|---|---|---|---|---|---|
| Capt | Elisha Hopkins | | | | |
| Lieu$^t$ | Daniel Bradley | | | | |
| Serjeants | Stephen Dormant | D | War | | |
| | Nathan Savage | " | | | |
| | Joseph Day | " | | | |
| | John Beers | " | | | |
| | Thomas Stone | " | | | |
| | Daniel Bradley | " | | | |
| | Isaac Parker | " | | | |
| Corporal | William Wimans | " | | | Reduced, the 6$^{th}$ March 1782 |
| | Richard Belding | " | | | |
| | Jonathan Hull | " | | | |
| | Warren Murry | " | | | |
| | Asher Heacox | " | | | |
| Drummer | William Thrall | " | | | |
| Fifers | Isaac Finch | " | | | |
| | James Satterly | " | | | |
| | James Anderson | 1 | 2 | 23 | |
| | Aaron Abber·rumbie | D | War | | |
| | Benjamin Brown | 0 | 9 | 13 | |
| | Richard Bacon | D | War | | |
| | Daniel Baits | 1 | 2 | 13 | |
| | Josiah Barnes | 1 | 2 | 18 | |
| | Hendrick Bail | 0 | 10 | 13 | |
| | Curtice Cleaveland | 0 | 9 | 15 | |
| | Guardner Cleaveland | 0 | 10 | 23 | |
| | Allen Corning | D | War | | |
| | Wilson Commins | 2 | 2 | 23 | |
| | Ichabod Downing | 1 | 2 | 23 | |
| | William Daskin | D | War | | |
| | Roger Edgerton | 0 | 10 | 12 | |
| | Stephen Gavit | 0 | 11 | 8 | |
| | Joshua How | D | War | | |
| | Ephraim Harry | 0 | 10 | 9 | |

| Ranks | Names | Term of Inlistment | | | |
|---|---|---|---|---|---|
| Privates | Seth Montague | D War | | | |
| | Jabez Norton | " | | | |
| | John Swaddle | " | | | |
| | Jacob Strong | 0 | 9 | 23 | |
| | Edmond Sholly or Shelly | 1 | 0 | 6 | |
| | Simeon C Stoddard | D War | | | |
| | Elihue Warters | " | | | |
| | Joseph Johnston | " | | | |
| | Samuel Stanklift or Stancliff | 0 | 1 | 15 | |
| | Nathan Edgerton | 0 | 2 | 19 | |
| | Jabez Cole | 0 | 2 | 7 | |
| | William Beardsley | D War | | | |
| | Bristol Caesar | " | | | |
| | Moses Evens | " | | | |
| | Robert Freeman | " | | | |
| | Samuel D. Goff | 1 | 0 | 9 | |
| | Boswell or Roswell Hotchkiss | 0 | 11 | 11 | |
| | Joseph Kent | 1 | 5 | 9 | |
| | Elijah Lord | D War | | | |
| | Elnathan Minor | " | | | |
| | Mills or Milo Palmer | 2 | 3 | 9 | |
| | Eliphilet Parrish | 2 | 2 | 18 | |
| | Cash Pallintine | D War | | | |
| | William Russel | " | | | |
| | Alexander Williams | " | | | |
| | Nathaniel Warner | 0 | 11 | 6 | |
| | Jack Arabus | D War | | | |
| | Lewis Martin | " | | | |
| | John Nayls | " | | | |
| | Shany or Sparry Reed | 0 | 11 | 8 | |
| | Ebenezer Carr | 0 | 11 | 8 | |
| | David Jones | D War | | | |
| | Israel Dodge | " | | | |
| | Abraham Johnston | " | | | |
| | John Lay | 0 | 11 | 4 | |
| | Eleazer Robertson | D War | | | |
| | Jared Palmer | " | | | |
| | Daniel Bostwick | " | Deserted Jan'y 22d 83 | | |
| | Hezekiah Cary | " | " " " | | |
| | Stephen Kellogg | " | Discharged Jan'r 5th 83 | | |
| | Noah Kelsug | " | Dec'r 24th 82 | | |
| | Jacob Fenton | " | " 9th | | |
| | James Bliss | " | " 5th | | |
| | John Taylor | " | " 9th | | |
| | Samuel Minor | " | " 5th | | |
| | Freeman Gates | " | 6th Jan'y 83 | | |
| | Benoni Pendal | " | 29th Decem 82 | | |
| | James Dunning | " | 10th | | |
| | Thomas Anderson | " | 5th | | |
| | Sedgwick Orter | " | 9th | | |

I certify the above Roll to be the true State of said Comp'y this 26th day of January 1783

Dan. Bradley Lieu't

[*State Library, Revolution 39; 110, 120.*]

CONNECTICUT LINE, 1783.    339

## SIXTH COMPANY—CAPT. DORRANCE.

[The muster rolls of this company for Dec. 1782–Jan. 1783 and Feb. 1783 are preserved. Only the earlier of these is here printed, with such changes noted as appear on the later roll.]

Roll and Muster of the 6th Company 3d Connecticut Regiment Commanded by Col. Samuel B. Webb for Decr 82 & Jany 1783.

| Ranks | Names | Term of Inlistment | |
|---|---|---|---|
| Capt | David Dorrance | | |
| Lieu<sup>t</sup> | Joshua Whitney | | |
| Ensign | Jacob Kingsbury | | Joined from the Light Company Febr 1783 |
| Serj<sup>ts</sup> | Elihu Sanford | D War | |
| | Hyman Parker | " | |
| | Abraham Hawley | " | |
| | John Kindle | " | |
| | Augustus Clark | " | |
| | John Downs | " | Deserted 11 March 1783 |
| | Jehiel Bradley | " | |
| | Hezekiah Betts | 4m 15d | |
| [Corporals] | John Daboll | D War | |
| | Nathan Hawley | " | |
| | Curtee Craen | " | |
| | Abijah Hubell | 1y 1m | |
| | Alexander Mills | D War | |
| Drum Fif<sup>r</sup> | Thomas Brown | " | |
| | Robert Bartlet | " | |
| | Mathew Jackson | 1 0 25 | |
| | Samuel Wardell | D War | |
| Privates | John Ammit | " | |
| | Comfort Becks or Beebe | 11 16 | |
| | Richard Beebe | 11 16 | |
| | John Curchel | D War | |
| | Eli Denslow | " | |
| | Jones or Jeames Egleston | 1 0 11 | |
| | Benedick Egleston | 10 18 | |
| | Jabez Edgcomb | 1 0 18 | |
| | Benjamin Elsworth | 1 4 18 | |
| | Basel or Basset Fox | 11 5 | |
| | Jacob Gillet | 11 5 | |
| | David Gardner | 1 0 18 | Serv<sup>t</sup> to Gen<sup>l</sup> M<sup>c</sup>Dougal |
| | Henery Horton | 11 3 | |
| | John Holcomb | 9 2 | |
| | Cudjo Helmes | 10 18 | |
| | Aaron Kingsley | 11 4 | |
| | Ebel or Eliel London | D War | |
| | Nathan Maleny or Mallery | " | |
| | Elias Meason | 9 14 | |
| | James Nodson | 9 12 | |
| | Isaac Nelson | 10 14 | |
| | Robert Neason | 1 0 46 | |
| | John Robertson | 1 0 18 | |
| | Ebenezer Shaw | " " " | |

| Names | Term of Inlistment | |
|---|---|---|
| Comma Simons | D War | |
| David Taylor | 10 2 | |
| Simeon Fox | 9 21 | |
| John Mills | 11 18 | |
| Josiah Rogers | 11 6 | |
| Asa Rathburn | D War | |
| Aron Olds | " | |
| Ezekiel Butler | " | |
| Uriah Hungerford | " | |
| Georg Wilson | " | Deserted 9 March 1783 |
| David Goodfaith | " | |
| Samuel Chapman | " | |
| Philo Gibbs | 2 25 | |
| Charles Repley or Risley | 2 25 | |
| Samuel Elwell | 23 | Deserted Feby 7 1783 |
| Thomas Simons | 1 1 0 | |
| Barnabas Mitahel | D War | |
| Oliver Rouse | " | |
| Elijah Bryan | " | |
| Joseph Hawkins | " | |
| Amos Tharp or Sharp | " | |
| Timothy Johnston | " | |
| James Ceabury | " | |
| Martin Ford | " | |
| Daniel Moss | " | |
| Josiah Taylor | " | |
| Jonathan Ford | " | |
| Adonijah Ross | | Transfer[d] to the 1 Com[y] 1 Jan 83 |
| Nathan Lane | | Discharged 1 Jan[y] 83 |
| Edward Dunker (?) | | " " |
| Nehemiah Barns | | " " |
| David Hawly | | Deserted 1[st] Dec[r] 1782 |
| Charles Lewis | | Discharged 1 Jany 1783 |
| Hezekiah Turnill | | " " |
| Aron Wayley | | " " |
| Amos Westland | | " " |
| Reuben Martin | | " " |
| David Coy | D War | " " |
| Elijah Kiplee | | Deserted 4[th] Jany 83 |
| Jason Hitchcock | | Discharg[d] 1 Jan[y] 83 |
| James Patchen | | |
| William Reed | | |
| George Mitchel | | |
| Rufus Hyde (?) | | |

I Certify the above Roll to be the true State of said Company this Twenty sixth Day of January 1783

David Dorrance Capt[a]

[*State Library, Revolution 39; 108, 113.*]

## SEVENTH COMPANY—CAPT. DOUGLASS.

[The muster rolls of this company for Dec. 1782–Jan. 1783 and Feb. 1783 are preserved. Only the earlier of these is here printed, with such changes noted as appear on the later roll.]

Roll and Muster of the 7th Company 3d Connecticut Regt Commanded by Col Saml B. Webb for Decr 1782 and Jany 1783

| Ranks | Names | Term of Inlistment | |
|---|---|---|---|
| Capt | Richd Douglass | | |
| Lieut | Saml Hait | | |
| Serjt | Thos Holmes | D War | |
| " | Willm Taylor | " | |
| " | Abraham Clark | " | |
| " | David Webb | " | |
| " | Benjn Brooks | " | |
| " | Willm Patterson | " | Deserted Jany 3d 1783 |
| Corporal | Danl Potter | " | |
| " | Joseph Clinton | " | |
| " | Isaac Northrop | " | |
| " | Christr Horton | " | |
| " | James Hooker | " | |
| Drumer | Ezekiel Winchel | " | |
| " | Anthony Needham | " | |
| Fifer | David Phelps | " | |
| " | Joseph Woolcot | " | |
| Pt | Benjn Avery | " | |
| | Saml Bush | " | |
| | Nathl Beach | " | |
| | Benjn Bennet | " | |
| | David Bradley | " | |
| | Hezekiah Bracket | " | |
| | Azias Bowen or Ozias Backers | 1y | Waiter to Col Webb in Connt |
| | Willm Carr | D War | |
| | David Chester | 11m | |
| | Benjn Cady | 10m | |
| | Costor Freeman | D War | Waiter to Capt Sill Aid de Camp |
| | Saml Rich | " | |
| | Thos Meach | " | Recd from the 4th Compy Jany 1st |
| | Sylvanus Gage | 1y | |
| | Amos Harris | D War | |
| | David Hyden or Hayden | 2y 4m | |
| | Joel Hyde | 1y | |
| | Eliezer Hatch | 1y | |
| | Peter Johnson | D War | |
| | Willm Johnson | " | |
| | Richd Kimball | 1y | |
| | Jared Kimball | 1y | |
| | Marshal Keyes or Hayes | 10m | |
| | Phineas Knight | 1y | |
| | Jabez Kirtland | 1y | |
| | Jonathan Luce | D War | Deserted Decr 11th 1782 |
| | James Miner | 1y 1m | |
| | Noah Merils | 11m | |
| | Benoni Moss | D War | |

| Ranks | Names | Term of Inlistment | | | |
|---|---|---|---|---|---|
| | Simeon Meigs | D War | | | |
| | David Potter | 1y 3m | | | |
| | Moses Potter | D War | | | |
| | Levi Risley | " | | | |
| | Levi Robertson or Ralinson | " | | | |
| | Joshua Rynolds | 1y | | | |
| | George Seely | " | | | |
| | Peter Shopp | D War | | | |
| | Ichabod Schofield | " | | | |
| | Tony Turney | " | | | |
| | Nathan Tubbs | 11m | | | |
| | Philip White | D War | | | |
| | Benj$^n$ Watrous | " | | | |
| | Tho$^s$ Wilson | " | | | |
| | Ichabod West | 11m | | | |
| | Ichabod Worden | " | | | |
| | Oliver Scott | | | | |
| | Elijah Woolcot | 1m | | | |
| | Cato Robertson or Robinson | D War | | | |
| | | " | | | |
| | Sam$^l$ Green | | Transf$^d$ to the 4$^{th}$ Comp$^y$ 1$^{st}$ Jan$^y$ | | |
| | Rich$^d$ Case | | Discharg$^d$ 31$^{st}$ Dec$^r$ 1782 | | |
| | Sam$^l$ Mitchel | | " | " | " |
| | Elijah Pike | | " | " | " |
| | John Wheeler | | " | " | " |
| | Eliphalet Burnham | | " | 6$^{th}$ Jan$^y$ 83 | |
| | Dan$^l$ Barns | | " | 10$^{th}$ Dec$^r$ 82 | |
| | Jeremiah Chapman | | " | 6$^{th}$ | " " |
| | Benj$^n$ Gaylord | | " | 13$^{th}$ | " " |
| | Stacy Evans | | " | 15$^{th}$ | " " |
| | Jos$^h$ Kenny | | " | 6$^{th}$ | " " |
| | Rich$^d$ Kenny | | " | 10$^{th}$ | " " |
| | Dan$^l$ Root | | " | 6$^{th}$ | " " |
| | Sam$^l$ Peck | | " | 6$^{th}$ | " " |
| | Cornelius Phelps | | " | 29$^{th}$ | " " |
| | Nath$^l$ Sylliman | | " | 6$^{th}$ Jany 83 | |
| | Zaccheus Gillet | | " | 10$^{th}$ Dec$^r$ 82 | |
| | Benoni Gillet | | " | 10$^{th}$ " " | |
| | Ebenez$^r$ Elwell | | Deserted 13$^{th}$ Jan$^y$ 1783 | | |

I Certify the above Roll to be the true State of said Company this day of Jan$^y$ 1783

Rich$^d$ Douglass Capt$^n$

[*State Library, Revolution 39; 109, 119.*]

CONNECTICUT LINE, 1783.

## EIGHTH COMPANY—CAPT. ROGERS.

[The muster rolls of this company for Dec. 1782–Jan. 1783 and Feb. 1783 are preserved. Only the earlier of these is here printed, with such changes noted as appear on the later roll.]

Roll and Muster of the 8th Company in the 3rd Connecticut Regiment Commanded by Col¹ Samuel B. Webb; for Dec' 1782 & Jan' 1783

| Ranks | Names | Term of Inlistment | |
|---|---|---|---|
| Captain | Hezekiah Rogers | | Rec⁴ from 3ᵈ Compy Feby 1, 83 |
| Lieut. | John Hobart | | Received from 3ᵈ Company |
| " | William Lynn | | Transf⁴ to 1ˢᵗ Lt. Co. |
| Ensn | Aron Keeler | | |
| Serjeants | Richard Lord | D W | |
| " | William Bassett | " | |
| " | Abiather Evans | " | |
| " | Peter Stalker | " | |
| " | Reuben Beach | " | |
| " | Henery Hull | " | |
| " | Thomas Wells | " | |
| Corporals | Jesse Sᵗ John | | |
| " | James Crane | 10m 12d | |
| " | Amasy Grenold | D W | |
| " | Nicholas Howell | " | |
| " | Reuben Carter | " | |
| Drummer | John Avery | | |
| " | William Kane or Thane | 12  6 | |
| Fifer | Frederick Whipple | D W | |
| " | Isaac Higgans or Wiggins | 17  6 | |
| Private | Uriah Keeler | D W | |
| | Johnson Tiff | 11  4 | |
| | Thomas Palmer | 26  23 | |
| | Anor Adee | D W | |
| | Cato Negro | 16  28 | |
| | Jonathan Edwards | D W | |
| | Joel Shirt | " | Not on Feb. roll. |
| | Stephen Meigs | " | |
| | Aron Eaton | 2  11 | |
| | Nathan Walker | D W | |
| | Amos Holden | 28  0 | |
| | Moses Elsworth | D W | |
| | Weight Lewis | " | |
| | Enos Tuttle | " | |
| | John Durgley or Dingly | " | |
| | Joel Mosher | " | |
| | Philip Hill | 12  28 | |
| | Justin Sᵗ John | D W | |
| | James Liberty | " | |
| | Peter Mix | " | |
| | James Duggan | 10  28 | |
| | Uthiel or Ethiel Scott | D W | |
| | Aron Parks | " | |
| | David Hodge | " | |
| | Abner Lord | " | |
| | Cato Wilborow | " | |

| | | | |
|---|---|---|---|
| Private | Samuel Jenkins | D W | |
| | John F Tone | 11 8 | |
| | David Hammond | 18 6 | |
| | Esaias Butts | 1 7 | |
| | Eli Tuller or Fuller | 11 18 | |
| | Ebenezer Platt | 2 13 | |
| | Chandler or Charles Judd | 2 0 | Burning Lime |
| | Ephraim Burgess | 11 23 | |
| | Jedediah Kimball | 18 9 | |
| | Reuben Adams | 10 11 | |
| | Amos Temple | D W | |
| | David Clark | " | Not on Feb. Roll |
| | William Short | 18 6 | |
| | Samuel Hull | 11 23 | |
| | William Waterbury | D W | |
| | Thomas Frink | " | |
| | Jacob Haladay | 10 9 | |
| | Ephraim Bates | 11 23 | |
| | Stephen Thompson | D W | |
| | Eliphalet Carpenter | 10 26 | |
| | Joseph Plinney or Pheney | 11 23 | |
| | William Burras | 10 23 | |
| | James Raymond | 1 7 | |
| | Samuel Eells | D W | |
| | Darius Trussedell | 11 4 | |
| | Abram Murrey | D W | |
| | David Matterson | 11 23 | |
| | Jethro Toney | D W | Recd Novr 18th 1782 from the late 5th C Regt left out of the Muster Rolls for Novr thro' Mistake |
| | Amasy Stephenson | | Discharged Dec 10th 1782 |
| | Jonathan Beaumont | | " " " |
| | Nathaniel Couant | | " " " |
| | Joseph C Stubbs | | " " " |
| | Thomas Leads | | " " " |
| | William McFall | | " " " |
| | Jesse Torrey | | " " " |
| | Daniel Jackson | | " " " |
| | Thomas Marble | | " " " |
| | George Dameson (?) | | " " " |
| | Nathan Fenton | | " " " |
| | Miles Bennet | | " " " |
| | Samuel Gorden | | " " " |
| | Comfort Chapman | | " Jan 1st 83 |
| | Sariel Squires | | " " " |
| | Ephraim Coy | | " " 19th |
| | Bristor Negro | | Private Servt Gen. Huntington |
| | Frank Buck | D W | Not on Jan. roll |
| | Joel Hait | " | " " " |

I certify the above Roll to be the true state of said Company this 26th day of January 1783

Aaron Keeler Ensign

[*State Library, Revolution 39 ; 112, 121.*]

# CONNECTICUT LINE.

## MISCELLANEOUS.

### HARTFORD COUNTY RETURNS.

A List of the Names of Men taken from the Returns from the Continental Army & those Claim{d} by & allow{d} to the Several Towns by the Committee for Hartford County

#### Hartford

| | |
|---|---|
| Cesar Augustus | Elijah Porter |
| Daniel Curtis | James Chadwick |
| Ockelow Porter | John Hosmer |
| Nathaniel Merrils | Thos Spencer |
| Thomas Kittle | Elijah Demming |
| Josiah Stulee | Abraham Clark |
| Seth Kellogg | Thos Wells |
| Samuel Simons | John Kendall |
| Daniel Hill | David Crosly |
| Jesse Taylor | Philemon Stedman |
| William Flowers | Jeduthan Abbey |
| William Shortman | Levi Risley |
| Jupeter Stephens | Moses Evans |
| James Maharr | Richard Case |
| William Mize | Ephraim Prescott |
| Henry Evans   Dead | Hezekiah Goodwin |
| Josiah Evans | Asa Saymour |
| Benjamin Webster | Seth Kneeland |
| Joseph Whipple | Simeon Goodrich |
| Jeremiah Barrett | John Raynolds |
| Samll Easton  Discharg{d} | Samuel Dorr |
| Samll Robarts | Charles Raynolds |
| Joseph Day | Ashbel Easton |
| Jabez Norton | Elnathan Smith |
| Abiather Evans | Eliphelet Abbey |
| David Williams | Richard Risley |
| Reuben Cadwell | John Knowles |
| Elisha Cowls | Asa Risley |
| Jonathan Arnold | Theodore Treet |
| Stephen Risley | William Tryon |
| Moses Porter | Amos Shepherd |

the following not Return{d} from the army but Claim{d} and allow{d} to Hartford

| | |
|---|---|
| Paul M{c}Kinstry | Thos Waters |
| Allen Evans | Eleazar Abbey } Disch{d} |
| Allen Corning | Francis Psalter } |
| Reuben Toney | Thos Wilson   Dead |

Matthew Cadwell
Vaniah Fox
Joseph Brewer   Dead
Tho[s] Jarrall
William Martin
William Matthews
Sam[l] Norton
Jonathan Flagg   Disch[d]
James Gray
Peter Surkee
Benjamin Keney
Tho[s] Obrian
David Taylor
William Lewis
Phillip Tabor

Giles Easton
Theodore Chamberlain
Ashbel Fox
Daniel Millar
William Combs
Henry Walton
Reuben Hadlock
Pattrick Marr
Ebenezar Haman
Samuel Holmes
William Anderson
Elisha Mygatt
John Foster
Nathaniel Fenton

### Middletown

Sam[ll] Simons
Jacob Wood
Charles Loveland
Lamberton Clark
Francis Wright
Aaron Ward
Ebenezar Hubbard
Joseph Copp
David Butler
Jonathan Goff   Dead
John Foster
David Hull
Joseph Lung
Daniel Morgan
Christopher Middletown
Sawney Baston
Exter Freeman
Peter Middletown
Grove Rockwell
Naboth Lewis
Christopher Welch
Ozias Cone
Peter Torminer
Richard Cornwell
David Freeman
Elijah Phelps
Stephen Robarts
David Robarts
Edward Millor
Oliver Monn   Dead
George Doolittle
Jabez Adkin

William Bacon
Samuel Frothingham   Disch[d]
Jonathan Taylor
Joseph Willis
Aaron Rowley
Lem[ll] Wilcocks
Jonathan Hubbard
Josiah Smith
Nathaniel W Benton
Jacob Gilson
Isaac Robarts
Peter Freeman
Cuff Liberty
Phillemon Freeman
Cuff Freeman
Zachariah Stow
James Fosdick
David Gallipin
Jehiel Hurlbutt
Henry Hart
Joseph Bates
James Johnson
Abijah Hubbard
Daniel Robbison
Richard Down[d]
David Adkins
Elijah Clark
James M[c]David
Allen Gilbart
Tho[s] Petland
Jacob Rash
Stephen Salvage.

The following not Return[d] from the army

William Hall
John Trat
Sam[ll] Johnson
Abraham T. Kimball
Aaron Clark
Sam[ll] Cook

Moses Boardman
Sumner Banks
William Salvage
John Swift
William Millar
James White

Moses Collins
James Hurlbutt
John Barson
Kay Cambridge
Allen Pratt
Robert Stephens
William Cook

William Graves
Cuff Negro
Enoch Cornwell
Elisha Driggs
Jonathan Hurlbutt
George Anger
Seth Knowles

### Farmington

Aaron Hart
Solomon Rugg   Disch[d]
Solomon Rugg Ju[r]
Tho[s] Stedman
William Steel
Seth Arnold
Ezra Belding
Ashbel Merrill
Gad North
Matthew Lee
Seth Root
Solomon Welton
Sage Churchel
Tho[s] F. Bishop
Isaac Tillotson
Ashbel Tillotson
Gedur Woodruff
Amos Couch
Salmon Root
James Gridley
Daniel Mosock   Dead
George Walton
Obed Gridley
Aaron Morce
John Robbison
Gideon Andrus
Free Love Robart
Prince Dennison
Hosea Gridley
Reubin Hamlin
Obadiah Andras
Jonathan Barns
Joseph Teal
Solomon Woodruff
Jesse Shepard
Joel Welton
Tho[s] Stanley
Nathan Savage
Josiah Barns

Isaac Nelson
Selah Hart
Tim[o] Bevens
Daniel Winchell
David Haydon
Simeon Barns
Ira Hungerford
Roswell Cook
Ichabod Bailey
Josiah Cowl
Jesse Matthews
Lem[ll] Lane
Timothy Fox
Simeon Parsons
Asher Hecock
William Woodruff
Levi Parson
Barnabas Mitchel
Tho[s] G Olvard
Tho[s] G Olvard Ju[r]
Nath[ll] Lownsbury
Tho[s] Warner
John Smith
Giles Abanathy
John Welch
Joseph Hunt
James Newel
Benjamin Cole
Jedediah Seward
Ebenezer Tuttle
Chancey Curtiss
Clark Curtiss
Asaph Smith
Sam[ll] Wain Wright
Isaac Bartholimew
Tim[o] Seward
Abraham Bartholimew
Aaron Rich

The following not Return[d] from the army but allow[d] to Farmington

Zachariah Hull
Abel Allen
Robart Carr
James Wilcocks
William D. Mott
James Evans
Roger Brunson
Cambridge Negro

Stephen Chapman Ju[r]
Constant Robarts
Joseph Andras
Peter Negro
Sam[ll] Stebbens
John Platner
Andrew Dowley
Cornelius Gordin

Amos Barns
Thos Collet
James Taylor
Cornelius Dunham } Dischd
Liverpool Wadsworth }

Abel Scipio     Dead
James H Hurlbutt "
Hartwell Barns Dischd
Prince Negro

## Windsor

Ebenezer Welch
Barzilli Henry
Richard Cook
Alvin Hurlbutt
Thos Parsons
William Cook
Isaac Wardwell
Clark Robarts
Ebenezar Wolworth
John Bristor
Alvin Owen
Daniel Porter
Sherman. Rowland
Robart Westland
Peter Robarts
Remembrance Sheldon
David Daniels
Zebulon Hoskins

Eppaphras Lotwell
James Egleston
Allen Pryar
Timothy Hoskins
Calvin Wilson
Elihu Mather
John Rowley
Samson Cuff
John Dewset
Elias Brown
Joseph Holcomb
Burden Davis
John Keton
Reuben Hill
Elijah Holcomb
Zephaniah Webster
Jonathan Pinny
Thos Vanduzar

These not Returned from the army

Jabez Colt
Plymouth Negro
Amos Lawrence    Dischd
Thos Bunc
Joseph Egleston

Joseph Westland
Ebenezar Drake
William Taylor
Obed Lamberton

## Wethersfield

Ashbel Riley
Abner Andras
Moses Belding
Jonathan Millar
Dick Loomis
Thos Wilson
Simeon Holms
Waitstill Dickerson
John Kirkum
Arthur Russell
Ezekiel Winchel
Stephen Dormont
Richard Belding
Stephen Kellogg
Seth Montague
Jared Bunce
Daniel Ward
Joshua Wells
Joseph Rowlison
Cesar Freeman
Simeon Griffin
Elijah Boardman
Hezekiah Knot
Thos Holmes
Gideon Goff

Moses Hatch
David Linsey
Abraham Belding
Joseph Treet
Benjamin Dix
Ichobad Goodrich
Joseph Johnson
John Forbs
Richard Bacon
Curtiss Crane
Moses Griswold
Solomon Williams
Samuel Wells
Samuel Kirkum
Levi Lattimore
Edmond Weatherhead
William Clark
Jonathan Dallibier
Joseph Waters
Jabez Sizer
Charles Treet
Caleb Miller
William Morrison
Daniel Sizer

CONNECTICUT LINE. 349

The following not Return<sup>d</sup> from the army but allow<sup>d</sup> to Weathersfield

Peter Mohawk
Simeon Griffin
Tho<sup>s</sup> Morgan
Zebulon Mygatt
Edward Brown
John Dowl
Joshua Cone

Josiah Robins
William Ware
Asa Andras
Isaac Palmer
Jared Goodrich
Ebenezar Stoddard
Samuel Weaver

### Simsbury

Phillip Grigory
Jacob Davis
Benjamin Hayse
Stephen Langatha
Timothy Woodbridge
James Slaughter
Consider Holcomb
Rufus Mayson
John White
Jeremiah Case
Elisha Harrington
Elijah Clark
Zebulon Wallace
Joseph Wallace
Asa Hayze
Jacob Hollidy
Eli Fuller
William Taylor
Johnson Tiff
John G. Holcomb
Jacob Gillet
David Taylor
John Herlihy
James Aldridge

David Egleston
John Crocker
Gad Alderman
John Hunt
David Enos
Levi Woolworth
Roderick Addams
Azer Bowton
Ebenezar Edgerton
Timothy Humphry
Jacob Fuller
William Phillips
Jared Towser
Solomon Parkharst
Levi Addams
Abel Case
Enum Moses
Furbuss More
Humphry Tiffeny
David Parkharst
Asahel Holcomb 3<sup>rd</sup>
Hezekiah Phelps
Gilbert Whitney

The following not in the army Return

Owin Rewick
John Huxley
George Sweet
William Andras   Disch<sup>d</sup>
David Jones
John Hill 2<sup>nd</sup>   Disch<sup>d</sup>
John Carrell
Charles Spencer
Josiah Linsley
Robart Linsley
Erastus Hatch
John Pooler
Ezekiel Davis
Jonathan Andras

Phillip Negro
Morris Jarrold
William Shepard
Amaziah Barber
John Slaughter
Jeremiah Parmerly
William Peck
John Allen
Ithamer Granger
Edward Knap
Israel Humphry
Joseph Segar 3<sup>rd</sup>   Disch<sup>d</sup>
Joseph Sharp
Cuff Negro

### East Windsor

Jude C. Brown
Jacob Strong
Mark Philly
Cato Negro
Hazard Prior
Azariah Grant
Joseph Pease

Stephen Ellis
Israel Osborn
Reuben Raynolds
Elijah Benton
Phinehas Strong
Adoniram Benton

## Those below not in the army Return

Elijah Churchil
Stephen Dormŏnd
Theodore Smith
Moses Elsworth
Ezra Elsworth
Oliver Hills
Benoni Hills

Christopher Horton
David Clark
Josiah Grovener
Sam<sup>ll</sup> Hadlock
Jeptha Hills
Benjamin Elsworth

### Tolland

George Hubberd
Abel Stimson
Reuben Robinson
Moses Coy
Job Booman
Amos Harriss
Ichabod West
Ebenezar Hatch

Jonathan Luce
Joel Barnard
James Covel
Solomon Eaton
William Eldridge
Isaac Squires
Benjamin Butler

## Those below not Return<sup>d</sup> from the army

John George
John William Hendrick
Phinehas Heth

Silvanus Gage
William Kinsey

### Southington

Robart Cook
Archibald Cook
George Dickerson
Amos Bunnal
William Jones
David Andras
James Powers

Zebulon Dudley
Ichabod Talmage
Chancey Lewis
Isaac Lewis
Adonijah Roze
Samuel Root

## Those below not in the army Return

Timothy Culver
Jason Hitchcock
Daniel Munson
Elijah Rice
Samuel Grannis
John Ukhart
Daniel Hitchcock

Moses Barker
Isaac Fisk
Barnabas Clark
Luke Hart
Bordle Hoose
Abraham Tuttle
Clemont Andras

### Enfield

Benjamin Harrington
Henry Booth
John Hallamagee
John Jimpson
Ephraim Burges
Daniel Pirkins

David Bullin
Hiram Hall
Elijah Mecham
Levi French
Simeon Hager   Disch<sup>d</sup>
Jonathan Parsons D<sup>o</sup>

## Those below not return<sup>d</sup> from the Army

Justin Davis
Lemuel Wood
Jonathan Terry
Alexander Banter

John Herman
Johannes Mecham
Oliver Field
John Moony

### Colchester

Joshua Isham
Samuel Loomis
Lewis Ackley
Robart Bland   Disch⁴
John Fox
William Isham
Joseph McHood
Ezekiel Danields
Bristol Johnston
Frederick Bowman
Israel Ransom
Esau Carter
Edward Carter
Israel Johnson
Ezra Ramsel
John Godfrey   Dead
James Shoot   D°
John Lines
Cesar Bement

Josiah Rogers
Champlin Harris
Benjamin Dodge
Elihu Dodge
Tony Edor
David Waters   Dead
Simeon Shon
Peter Beguine (?)
Sam¹¹ D. Goff
James Freeman
Peter Kellogg
Nathan Robarts
Daniel Wright
Josiah Grant
Martin Stiles
Roswell Chapell
John Robarts
Nicholas Ackley

Those below not Return⁴ from the army

Nathan Scovil   Dead
Joseph Thompson
Dolphin Dart
Daniel Whitney   Disch⁴
William Jones
Martin Canary

Comfort Bebee
Henry Horton
Richard Bebee
Jeremiah Booth   Dead
Henry Loud (? Lord)
James French

### Glastenbury

Peter Forriss
Daniel Loveland
Nathan Hill
Peter Foster
Daniel Wright
Joseph Wright
Cuff Acklin
John Johnson   Disch⁴
Samuel Fox
Cyphax Mosley
Newport Hale
Timothy Stephens
Aaron Ward
David Pratt

Daniel Morley
Thoˢ Brewer
Alexander McCulpin
Frances Nicholson
Asa Fox
William Peters
John House
George House
Ezra Tryon Jun ͬ
James Stephens
Isaac Tryon
Abisha Marks
Elias Wares

Those below not Return⁴ from the Army

Thos˙ Loveland
John Holding
James Dougharty
Ezra Tryon
Prince Simber

Josiah Hollister
Joseph Hills
Levius Eddy
Elisha Stephens

### Suffield

Phinehas Austin
Lewis Leach
Narcissus Graham
Apollus Answitz
Samuel Thistle

Peletiah Pumroy
Dan¹¹ Wheeler
Silas Pease
Leucius Hurlbutt
Jeremiah Newbury

Phebus Pomroy
Michael Towsley
John Laphland
Joshua Spear
Sam[ll] Gookins
James Fuller
Jeremiah Chamberlain
Samuel Granger
David Addams
John Russell

Edy Coy
Josiah Rising
Jacob Granger
James Serene
Joseph King
Darius Dunlay
Seth Hathaway
Wilber Hathaway
Titus Kent

The following not Return[d] from the Army

James Dada
Filo Stoddard
Richard Austin
Eliphelet Phillips
Cesar Negro
Tho[s] Watson

Phinehas Granger
John Spencer
Thada Larry
Jabiel Spencer
Matthew Goldwin

## East Haddam

Sam[ll] Chapman
Levi Fox
Richard Mack
Abel Bingham
David Shattock
Daniel Rols
Isaac Williams
Sam[ll] Mobbs
Ephraim Wadkins
Asahel Hervy
Crppin Hurd
Robert Hull
Eli Hull
Samuel Rusket
Joel Spencer
Robart Wadkins
Cuff Smith
Judah Warner   Dead

Asahel Patterson
Israel Cone
Ebenezar Hinkley
Elihu Church
Nathan W. Minor
John Marsh
Stephen Sparrow
Daniel Thornton
Tho[s] Williams
Phillip White
Tho[s] Ackley
Sam[ll] Mitchel
Zacheus Rols
Israel Rowley
Elijah Cone
William Lee
Daniel Cone

Those below not Return[d] from the army

Ezra Harvey
John Ashley
Tho[s] Andras
Charles Clark
Noah Huntly

Sam[ll] Reves
Nathaniel Warner
Joseph Stewart
Joseph Chamberlain

## Haddam

Loudon Bailey
Daniel Ray
Joseph Forbs
Peter Black
Michael Clark

Andrew Southard
James Wilcox   Time out July
  Next
William Bailey
Daniel Bates

## CONNECTICUT LINE.

Those below not Return⁴ from the army

Jarius Congdon
William Osburn
Joseph Paro
Joshua Smith
Jonathan Smith   Dead

John Smith
Cesar Chapman
London Sawyer
William Gladding

### Willington

Ezra Sibble
Samˡˡ Eldridge   Dead
Alexander Evans
Abel Stoel
Samuel Stoel

Cyrus Fenton   Dead
Reuben Dodge
Seth Dodge
Heman Hatch
Samuel Firgo

Those below not Return⁴ from the army

Joseph Wilson
Ebenezar Nye
Richard Lord

Caleb Olcott
Gideon Noble

### Chatham

John Parks
Ephraim Bowers
Stephen Ranney
James Shield
Bathuel Goodrich
Joab Bowers
Samuel Goff
Charles O. Martin
John Wright   Dischᵈ
Jabez Wetmore
Samˡˡ Wood
Jacob Woods
Timothy Chapman
John Fuller
Jonathan Stocking
William Cook
Joel Doolittle

Othniel Brainard
Samuel Rich
Lend Rich
Samˡˡ Freeman
Lemuel Goodrich
Jedediah Norton
Elij. Whiting
George Carry
Jonathan Very
Samuel Cowdy
Henry Goseley
Jessie Kneeland
Josiah Davis
Eber Stocking
Stephen Thomas
Daniel Bliss

Those below not Return⁴ from the army

Abner Cowl
Joseph Graham
Marshal Stocking
Stephen Tubbs
Aaron Carter

Oliver Graham
Thomas Snow
Nathaniel Robarts
Daniel Pelton

### Bolton

William Rock
Ebenezar Walker

John Warren

Those below not Return⁴ from the army

Samuel Addams   Dead
Ezra Downer
John Smith

Benajah Abrow
William Beach

### Hebron

Robart Cox
Stephen D: wolf
Jack Demming
Abner Mack
Seth Baldwin
Abijah Gardner
Joseph Belcher
Matthew Ford
Ebenezer Youngs

Robart Holdridge
Wyman Parker
John Royce
Cyprian Archer
Daniel Polly
Walker Tiffiny
Cesar Scipio
Thomas Marble   Disch[d]

Those below not in the army Return

Austin Brown
John Winship
William Merrit
Israel Jillit
Barzilla Mack
John George
Thomas McQuire
Richard Lawrence
Peter Pease

Rodowick Morrison
Edward Chapman
*Lawrence Dowsch time out 5[th] July next
*Nathan Reed time out 5[th] July next
*Roger Loomis time out August 1[st]

### Sommers

Jehiel Gibbs
Joel Pelton

Reuben Perez
William Hamlin

Those below not in the Army Return

John Love
William Beke
Isaac Colton

William Quirk
Edward Burges

### Stafford

Solomon Bebce
Hezekiah Wheeler
Joshua Wheeler
Joseph Harrop
Daniel Rider Ju[r]
Tho[s] Simons

Amasa Dimmuk
Tho[s] Manning
Silas Blotchet
Josiah Wheeler
Ephraim White

Jonathan Wells } Committee
Howel Woodbridge }

[*State Library, Hebard Papers, 81.*]

## FAMILY SUPPLIES.

An Alphabetical List of the Officers and Soldiers who have received Family Supplies whose names are not found in the Returns from the Army.

| Names | Towns |
|---|---|
| Arnold Jehiel | Haddam |
| Austin Richard | Suffield |
| Bull Epaph[m] Major | Hartford |
| Buckland Stephen Capt | " |
| Brownson Roger | Farmington |

---

* These names have been crossed out.

# CONNECTICUT LINE.

| Names. | Towns. | |
|---|---|---|
| Barnes Moses | Wallingford | |
| Bradley Eliphalet | Fairfield | |
| Beebe James  Capt | Stratford | |
| Blakesley Jerem[h] | Danbury | |
| Burnap Benj[a] | Windham | |
| Comstock Gideon | Norwich | |
|     Samuel | Saybrook | |
| Cheney Richard | Kent | |
| Cone Joseph | Middletown | In Service of Elijah Hubbard Es[q] States Comissary or of Gen[l] Parsons |
|     Ozias | " | |
| Carrill John | Simsbury | |
| Carter Aaron | Chatham | |
| Clark Lyman | Farmington | |
|     Joel | New Haven | |
| Dunbar Miles | Watertown | |
| Downing John | Fairfield | |
| Desborough Joshua | " | |
| Dickerman Joseph | New Haven | deserted  Whip[d]  shot thro discharged on procuring one Ebenez[r] Warner  Substitute accepted & now in Service |
| Durkee Jeremiah | Windham | |
| Dickinson George | Danbury | |
| Davidson Robert | Groton | |
| Edwards Nathaniel Lieut | Watertown | |
| Fitch Nehem[h] | Lebanon | |
| Ford Matthew | New Haven | |
| Flagg Jonathan | Hartford | |
| Gillet Adna | New Hartford | |
|     Zechariah  Serjt | Southington | |
| Gibson Samuel | New Haven | |
| Goold John | Goshen | |
| Gladding William | Haddam | In the army not Returned |
| Hull Giles | Salisbury | Supplies due at his Death |
| Hargar Simeon | Enfield | |
| Hovey Ezra | East Haddam | |
| Higgins Corn[s]  Lieut | Haddam | Supplies due before Discharged |
| Hotchkiss Zadock | Farmington | |
| Huse Boardwell | New Haven | |
| Johnson Robert | Sharon | |
| Lion Ezra | Ashford | |
| Lines John | New Haven | |
| Morgan Joshua | Salisbury | Balance due when Discharged |
| Munger Daniel | Litchfield | Discharged from Invalids 26 Feby 1780 |
| M[c]Donald John | Groton | |
| Meeker Daniel | Hartford | |
| Nash Eben[r] | Norwalk | |
| Osborn Nath[l] | Stratford | |
| Olmsted Isaac | Norwalk | |
| Parker Benj[a] | Wallingford | |
| Pickett Thomas | Danbury | |
| Patchin Elijah | Fairfield | Hired David Patchen in his room & Supplyd untill about Oct[r] last |
| Persival Paul  Q M | Farmington | |

# REVOLUTION LISTS AND RETURNS.

| Names. | Towns. | |
|---|---|---|
| Palmer Benj[a] | Litchfield | Died 9 April 1780 at Litchfield |
| Powers James | Southington | |
| Polley Alpheus | Lebanon | Returned by Gen Washington |
| Pool Daniel | Ashford | |
| Porter Daniel | Windsor | |
| Raymong Sam[l] | Reading | |
| Rose Samuel | Coventry | Never Returned from the Town nor in Con[tl] Service nor Counted in the quota of s[d] Town |
| Remington Stephen | Ridgfield | |
| Sullard Jacob | Lime | |
| Smith Enoch | " | |
|     John | Watertown | |
| Stillwell Stephen | New Milford | |
| Smith Job | Ridgfield | |
| Stanard Elijah | Guilford | |
| Stark Samuel | Colchester | |
|     Timothy | " | |
| Tarble William | " | |
| Wording Isaac | Saybrook | |
| Yarington Jesse | Groton | |

[*State Library, Revolution 20, 362.*]

## RETURNS FROM MILITIA.

| Names 5 Regt | Time for which Engaged | The Quota of What Town |
|---|---|---|
| John Woodward | first march | Windham |
| Shubeel Snow | " | " |
| Jed. Peck | " | " |
| Eph[m] Robinson | " | " |
| Abel Robinson | " | " |
| Frances West | " | " |
| Richard Robinson | " | " |
| Jn[o] Pettingal | " | " |
| Tube Negro | " | " |
| W[m] Yerington | " | " |
| Nath[n] Clark | " | Mansfield |
| Amos Conant | " | " |
| Nath[n] Marten | " | " |
| Isaac Arnold | " | " |
| Elias Burchard | " | " |
| Tho[s] Barrows Jr. | " | " |
| Oliver Smith | " | " |
| Elijah Davis | " | " |
| Joel Davis | " | " |
| Nath[ll] Eatton Jr | " | " |
| James Parker Jr | " | " |
| Bezeleel Balch | " | " |
| Eben[r] Fenton Jr | " | " |
| Gemaliel Fenton | " | " |
| John Redington | " | Coventry |
| Amos Dog | " | " |
| Nath[n] Bassett | " | " |
| Nath[ll] Conent | " | " |
| Jonath[n] Fenton | " | " |
| Steap[n] Chappee | " | " |

| Names 5 Regt | Time for which Engaged | The Quota of What Town | |
|---|---|---|---|
| Don Carlos Brigham | first march | Coventry | |
| Tim<sup>y</sup> White | " | " | |
| Sam<sup>ll</sup> Dreston | " | Ashford | Deserted |
| Sam<sup>ll</sup> Robbins | " | " | |
| Clark Robbins | " | " | |
| Benj<sup>a</sup> Perey | " | " | |
| Sam<sup>ll</sup> Crocker | " | " | |
| W<sup>m</sup> Snell | for West Point | " | |
| Archable Knox | " | " | |
| Step<sup>n</sup> Russell | " | " | |
| Eben<sup>r</sup> Eastman | " | " | |
| John Frink | " | " | |
| Sam<sup>ll</sup> Walker | " | " | |
| Sam<sup>ll</sup> Whipple | " | " | |
| John Abbett | " | " | |
| Amosiah Snow | " | " | |
| Abraham Ford | " | Windham | |
| James Flint | " | " | |
| David Jinins | " | " | |
| Daniel Robbins | " | " | |
| Tho<sup>s</sup> Gray | 3 months | " | |
| Alfeas Bingham | " | " | |
| Perez Hibard | " | " | |
| Nath<sup>n</sup> Kennedy | " | " | |
| W<sup>m</sup> Wales | " | " | |
| W<sup>m</sup> Burnam | " | " | |
| Jesse Burnam | " | " | |
| Tim<sup>y</sup> Warner | " | " | |
| Eben<sup>r</sup> Devotion | " | " | |
| James Bicknal | " | Mansfield | |
| Joshua Barrows | " | " | |
| Asa Hanks | " | " | |
| Joseph Grover | " | " | |
| Peter Cambell | " | " | Des<sup>t</sup> |
| James Hylys (? Wylys) Jr. | " | " | |
| Bej<sup>a</sup> Collins | " | " | |
| Eben<sup>r</sup> Badcock | " | " | |
| Lyman Back | " | " | |
| Josiah Squire | " | " | |
| Eben<sup>r</sup> Carey | " | " | |
| Robert Badcock | " | Coventry | |
| Tim<sup>y</sup> Brown | " | " | |
| W<sup>m</sup> Dean | " | " | |
| Elea<sup>r</sup> Root | " | " | |
| Asa Lyman | " | " | |

[Each man except the deserters is noted as having "marcht."]

[*State Library, Hebard Papers,* 77.]

## NEW LONDON RETURNS.

Memorandoms Concerning Continental Soldiers from the Town of New London that are disputed.

  James Gray
  Moses Tracy
  Benony Condle
  Benja Brooks
  W<sup>m</sup> Fargo Jun
  Backus Fox
  Andrew Harris
  Simon Hubbard
  Christo<sup>r</sup> Leech
  Ezekiel Beckwith Jun
  Aaron Jones
  John Paul of Preston
  John Swaddle
  Daniel Davis
  James Barnerd
  Ichab<sup>d</sup> Beckwith Claim<sup>d</sup> by Norwich
  Tho<sup>s</sup> Hallet Claim'd by Preston
  Rufas Chappel
  John Truby Claim'd by Lyme
  Benj<sup>a</sup> Darrow Claim'd by Hartford
  Tho<sup>s</sup> Harris Claim'd by Canterbury
  Robert Frazier Claim'd by Norwich
  Rob<sup>t</sup> Price Claim'd by Preston

           [*Connecticut Historical Society.*]

List of Men in the Continental Army belonging to the Town of New London

| | |
|---|---|
| Lost | Ethel Plant |
| | James Grey |
| | Benjamin Brooks his Mother Grandmother & himself lived in this Town |
| Lost | Simeon Hubbard an Ind living with Pardon Tabor Enlisted with Collins 1777 |
| | James Douglass Jun<sup>r</sup> |
| | Benjamin Darrow |
| | John Maynard |
| | William Prentice |
| | Ichabod Beckwith was born and always lived in New London |
| | Timothy Beckwith Jun<sup>r</sup> |
| | David Goodfaith |
| | Joseph Copp Jun<sup>r</sup> |
| | Rowland Swift |
| | Peter Holt. |
| | James Robertson |
| | Danie<sup>l</sup> Plumb called David in the return from the Army |
| | Joseph Morgan |
| Lost | William Fargoe Jun<sup>r</sup> |
| Lost | Backus Fox |
| | Simon Gorgay |

The above are return'd from the Army

## CONNECTICUT LINE. 359

| | |
|---|---|
| alow<sup>d</sup> | Alpheus Chappel |
| | George Monworring |
| | Daniel Cornin a Transient Person, hired by this Town, in Durkees Reg<sup>t</sup> |
| | John Stewart a Transient Person hired by this Town, in Durkees Reg<sup>t</sup> |
| | Benjamin Chappel of this Town in Livingstons Reg<sup>t</sup> in New York Line |
| alow<sup>d</sup> | Daniel Hendry of this Town, now attending the Hospital at Danbury |
| | William Whiting a Transient Person hired by this Town in Webb's Reg<sup>t</sup> Discharg<sup>d</sup> |
| Disputed | Thomas Hallet of Preston hired by this Town in Sherburns Reg<sup>t</sup> |
| | William Chappel of this Town unknown what Reg<sup>t</sup> |
| | Stephen Oliver of this Town unknown what Reg<sup>t</sup> |
| Lost | Christopher Leech, born in this Town and an Apprentice here when he Enlisted in Lamb's Reg<sup>t</sup> Artillery adjudged to Lime |
| | Isaac Beckwith J<sup>r</sup> of this Town unknown what Reg<sup>t</sup> |
| | Josiah Smith of this Town hired by this Town who has since hir'd Andrew Harris of Norwich |
| Lost | John Tooby of this Town hir'd by Lyme |
| to be refer<sup>d</sup> to the Govenour & Council | Ezekiel Beckwith Jun<sup>r</sup> of this Town hired by Lyme he Lives in New London bounds but in a Lyme Company. |
| Stonington | William Hudson |
| | Levi Lee |
| | W<sup>m</sup> Lane |
| | James Derrick, was a Servand to Isaiah Bolles of this Town in New Hampshire Line |
| alow<sup>d</sup> | John Rogers 4<sup>th</sup> was born and liv'd in this Town when he enlisted in Sheldons Reg<sup>t</sup> Light Horse |
| | Asa Crandal of this Town in Rhode Island Line |
| | Dennis Dewis (an Indian) in Col. Durkees Reg<sup>t</sup> |
| adjudg<sup>d</sup> to Norwich | Moses Tracy, formerly of Norwich he Married his Wife & Settled in this Town sometime before he Enlisted where his Wife & Child now lives. |
| | Thomas Harriss of this Town where he has a Wife & Interest in the 1<sup>st</sup> Reg<sup>t</sup> |
| | Amariah Lyon of this Town unknown what Reg<sup>t</sup> |
| | Curtis Chappel of this Town unknown what Reg<sup>t</sup> |
| | Henry Jones of this Town in Glovers Brigade |
| ad<sup>d</sup> to Seabrook | Aaron Jones of this Town where he has a wife & Family unknown what Reg<sup>t</sup> |
| ad<sup>d</sup> lost | James Barnard of Groton hir'd by this Town unknown what Reg<sup>t</sup> |
| | John Nicolls, Transient Person hir'd by this Town in Chandler's Reg<sup>t</sup> |
| | John Wheaton Transient Person hir'd by this Town in Col Durkee's Reg<sup>t</sup> |
| | Samuel Brooks a Transient Person hired by this Town in S. B. Webbs Reg<sup>t</sup> |
| alow<sup>d</sup> | Solomon Douglas of this Town, hired last Summer during the Warr |
| alow<sup>d</sup> | Samuel Weaver of this Town, hired last Summer for three Years |
| | John Grant transient Person Hired by this town |

| | |
|---|---|
| allow[d] | Robert Frassier of this Town where he had Married and lived Some Years before and at the time of his Enlisting hired last Summer During the Warr |
| alow[d] | William Chapel 3[d] at home on furlough being unwell of this Town |
| alow[d] | Nathan Douglass Jun[r] of this Town an Invalid |
| alow[d] | Boanerges Beebee of this Town where he has a wife and family in New York Line |
| | David Wilson a Transient Person in Durkees Reg[t] |
| | Benjamin Beebee of this Town in the Light Horse |
| alow[d] | James Gidias of this Town in the 1[st] Reg[t] |
| | Robert Brice a Transient Person hir'd by this Town in Storrs Reg[t] |
| | John Paul Indian hired by this Town in Durkees Reg[t] |
| | Russel Handy a Transient Person hired by this Town Starrs Reg[t] |
| | Thomas Handy d[o] d[o] & d[o] |
| alow[d] | John Daniels of this Town in Durkees Reg[t] |
| allow[d] | John Butler of this Town in Starrs Reg[t] |
| | Thomas Mitchell a Transient Person hired by this Town in Durkees Reg[t] |
| ad[d] to Nor[h] Lost | Benoni Congdol his Mother & he living in this Town — he Inlisted at the age of 15 Years while he was at Norwich for the Term of three Weeks on Trial as an apprentice |

[*Connecticut Historical Society.*]

# MILITIA REGIMENTS

## SEVENTH REGIMENT, 1777.

### CAPT. PLATT'S COMPANY.

A Pay Roll of Cap¹ Dan¹ Platts C° of the 7ᵗʰ Reg¹ in the State of Conn¹ commanded by Wᵐ Worthington Esq Col¹ who marchᵈ as far as New Haven on Ap¹ 27 1777
[Each man was five days in service.]

| | | |
|---|---|---|
| Dan¹ Platt | Cap | Ebenezer Williams |
| Elijah Scovel | Lieut | Noah Scovel Jʳ |
| Sam¹ Doty | Ensⁿ | Jered Buckingham |
| Israel Done ( ? ) | Serg¹ | Taber Pratt |
| Asa Pratt | " | George Shaw |
| Ruben Pratt | " | Bemond Clark |
| Jesse Pratt | " | Jaˢ Utter |
| Jaˢ Comstock | Corp¹ | Wᵐ Bulkley |
| Dan¹ Pratt | " | Nathⁿ Southard |
| Sam¹ Burnel | " | Davᵈ Beebe Pratt |
| Sam¹ Parker | " | Jaˢ Hamblen |
| Benj Williams Jʳ | | Martin Debble |
| Jaˢ (or Francis) Bushnell | | Josiah Payt |
| Jesse Pratt 2 | | Isaac Webb |
| Ashbel Clark | | Wᵐ Southard |
| Zephʰ Pratt | | Gid° Pratt |
| Phinas Pratt | | John Williams 2 |
| Abrᵐ Pratt Jʳ | | Jaˢ Shaw |
| Stephⁿ Starkey | | Ezra Pratt |
| Joˢ Glading | | Abrᵐ Bulkley |

[*Comptroller's Office, Copy 2*, 17.]

## SEVENTEENTH REGIMENT, 1777.

### ENS. CORBIN'S COMPANY.

A pay Abstract of Ens. Peter Corbins Co. it being the 7ᵗʰ Co. of the Alarm list in the 17ᵗʰ Regt. of the State of Conn. Fish-kill Oct 27 day. A.D. 1777. Marched Oct. 6ᵗʰ day. Discharged Oct 27. including 4 days for returning Home

| Mens Name and Rank | | time when marched | Discharged. |
|---|---|---|---|
| Peter Corbin, | Ens. | Oct. 6 | Oct. 31 |
| Jonathan Coe, | Sergt. | " | " |
| Eliphaz Alvord, | Sergt. | " | " |
| Robert McCune, | Sergt. | " | " |
| Philip Priest, | Corp. | " | 29 |
| Joel Roberts | | " | 31 |

362        REVOLUTION LISTS AND RETURNS.

| Mens Name and Rank | time when marched | Discharged |
|---|---|---|
| Darius Gibbs | Oct. 6 | Oct. 31 |
| Samuel Clark | " | " |
| Samuel McCune | " | " |
| Nathan Blackman | " | 22 |
| Daniel Andrews | " | 31 |
| Nathaniel Balcan | " | " |
| Samuel Preston | " | 14 |
| Ichabod Loomis | " | " |

Test Peter Corbin Ens
   Eliphaz Alvord S. Clerk
[*Green Woods Chapter D. A. R., Winsted.*]

## COL. JOHNSON'S REGIMENT, 1778.

### CAPT. BRANCH'S COMPANY.

[*See Record of Connecticut Men in the Revolution, page 527.*]

A Pay Roll of Cap$^t$ Moses Branch's Company in Col$^o$ Johnson's Regiment of Militia from the State of Connecticut now in Service in the State of Rhode-Island from the First of February 1778 untill the 15$^{th}$ of March 1778 both Days Inclusive.

| Mens Names | | february first 1778 | Finished Service |
|---|---|---|---|
| Moses Branch | Capt | Feb$^y$ 1$^{st}$ | March 15$^{th}$ |
| Joseph Burges | Lieut | " | " |
| Ebenezer Lathrop | " | " | " |
| Jacob Tuckerman | Ensign | " | " |
| Nathaniel Phillips | Serj$^t$ | " | " |
| Nicholas Randall | " | " | " |
| Elijah Simons | " | " | " |
| Comfort Titus | " | " | Feb$^y$ 4$^{th}$ |
| John Burnap | " | " | March 15$^{th}$ |
| Archabel Jackson | " | 4 | " |
| Benjamin Palmer | Corp$^l$ | 1 | " |
| Archabel Jackson | " | " | Feb$^y$ 4$^{th}$ |
| Samuel Adams | " | " | March 15$^{th}$ |
| Jonathan Chilson | " | " | " |
| Elijah Kimball | " | 4 | " |
| Luther Bingham | fifer | " | " |
| Jesse Ensworth | | " | " |
| Joshua Finney | | " | " |
| John Munrow | | " | " |
| Henry Head | | " | " |
| Benjamin Chace | | " | " |
| Caleb Hall | | " | " |
| George Mordock | | " | " |
| Samuel Brown | | " | " |
| Willard Pierce | | " | " |
| Noah How | | " | " |
| James Briggs | | " | " |
| Jedediah Johnson | | " | " |
| Samuel Brown Jur | | " | " |
| John Burt | | " | " |
| Samuel Marshall | | | |

## MILITIA REGIMENTS. 363

| Mens Names | february first 1778 | Finished Service |
|---|---|---|
| Squre Cleaveland | Feb<sup>y</sup> 1 | Feb<sup>y</sup> 28<sup>th</sup> |
| Jonathan Fish | " | March 15<sup>th</sup> |
| Israel Fitts | " | " |
| Philip Utley | " | " |
| Adam Treadwell | " | " |
| Abraham Herrinton | " | " |
| David Kenedy | " | " |
| Zacheriah Maynord | " | " |
| Chester Lilley | " | " |
| Jared Webb | " | " |
| Sebuary Manning | " | " |
| Joseph Holland | " | " |
| Asaph Adams | " | " |
| Jonathan Sprague | " | " |
| Daniel Fairman | " | " |
| Charles Burges | . | " |
| Jedediah Adams | " | " |
| Josiah Butts | " | " |
| Fuller Smith | " | " |
| Elkany Smith | " | " |
| Daniel Downing | " | " |
| Ebenezer Parks | " | " |
| Samuel Palmer | . | " |
| Asahel Herrick | " | " |
| Dyer Williams | " | " |
| James Alexander | " | " |
| James Campbel | " | " |
| Archabel Campbel | " | " |
| James Tuller | " | " |
| Shubel Huchens | " | " |
| Zebediah Holt | " | " |
| Alexander Miller | " | " |
| John Whitney | " | " |
| Elijah Kimbal | " | Febu<sup>y</sup> 4<sup>th</sup> |
| Mark Eames | " | March 15<sup>th</sup> |
| Simeon Stevens | " | " |
| Joseph Eaglestone | " | " |
| Ichabod Randal | " | " |
| Cyrus Maynord | " | " |
| Elisha Pirkins | " | " |
| Benjamin Williams | " | " |
| Silas Glass | " | " |
| Asa Stevens | " | " |
| Joseph Raymond | " | " |
| Stephen Durkee | " | " |
| Thomas Jewett | " | " |
| Benj<sup>a</sup> Colegrove | " | " |
| Philemon Adams | " | " |
| Thomas Bradford | " | " |
| Samuel Adams Jr | " | " |
| Josiah Collins | " | 8<sup>th</sup> |
| Josiah Bradford | 3<sup>rd</sup> | 15<sup>th</sup> |
| David Enos | 14<sup>th</sup> | 18 |
| Joshua Pattrick | 1 | Febu<sup>y</sup> 5<sup>th</sup> |
| Thomas Foster | 4<sup>th</sup> | March 15<sup>th</sup> |

Moses Branch Cap<sup>t</sup>

[*State Library, Drake Papers, 33.*]

## THIRTEENTH REGIMENT, 1779.

### CAPT. FULLER'S COMPANY.

A Pay Abstract of the Company commanded by Cap$^{tn}$ Abraham Fuller in the thirteenth Regiment of Militia Commanded by Co$^{ll}$. Increase Mosley belonging to the State of Connecticut Who marched into the continental Service at Fredericksborough in the State of New york June y$^e$ 4$^{th}$ 1779

| Names of Officers and Privates | Time of marching | Days in Service | |
|---|---|---|---|
| Cap$^n$ Abraham Fuller | June 4 | 9 | |
| Sar$^t$ Joseph Bates | " | " | |
| Corp$^{ll}$ Abraham Wilcox | " | " | |
| Corp$^{ll}$ Joseph Eaton | " | " | |
| Fif Bartlet Chamberlin | " | " | |
| Nathaniel Gear | " | " | |
| Asa Parish | " | " | |
| Timothy Stevens | " | " | |
| Timothy Hatch | " | " | |
| Aaron Sacket | " | " | |
| Stephen Eaton | " | " | |
| Abel Lamphere | " | " | |
| Ebenezer Lion | " | " | |
| Jirah Chamberlin | " | " | |
| Daniel Beebe | " | " | |
| Aaron Case | " | " | |
| Isaac Coller | " | " | |
| Norise Coller | " | " | |
| Newcomb Raymond | 5 | 8 | |
| Robert Brownell | " | " | |
| Manasah Martins (?) | 4 | 18 | Who was Draughted from my Company to go to Hartford with Prisoners |

[*State Library.*]

# NAVAL RECORD.

## FRIGATE TRUMBULL.

[See *Record of Connecticut Men in the Revolution*, page 588.]

Ship Trumbull's Muster Book 1777

[The roll in Record of Connecticut Men in the Revolution was evidently printed from this document. Data are here given that were not included in the former printing.]

| Name | Place Ship'd at | Place born at | Age | Height | Complex" |
|---|---|---|---|---|---|
| Dudley Saltonstall | | New London | | | |
| Jonathan Maltbie | | Fairfield | | | |
| David Phipps | | | | | |
| Jacob White | | | | | |
| James Morris | | Stratford | | | |
| John Crocker | | | | | |
| Joseph Cheilds | | England | | | |
| Alex<sup>r</sup> P. Adams | | New London | | | |
| Jona<sup>th</sup> Gaylord | | Middletown | | | |
| Elisha Bennet | | | | | |
| Samuel Roberts | New London | Scotland | 28 | 5 9 | Fair |
| Robert Halladay | Conn. | England | 26 | 5 6 | Dark |
| Robert Saunders | New London | New London | | | |
| Aurther Robertson | " | Ireland | | | |
| Thomas Fitz Gerald | Fairfield | Fairfield | | | |
| Peter Whitney | New Haven | New Haven | | | |
| Jona<sup>th</sup> Sabin | Middletown | Middletown | | | |
| Samuel Stow | Cambridge, Mass. | | 14 | 5 | Brown |
| Edward Prentis | Middletown | | 21 | 6 | Fair |
| James Knapp | " | Middletown | 39 | 5 8 | Brown |
| Jedediah Norton | | Guilford | | | |

| Name | Place Ship'd at | Place born at | Age | Height | Complex |
|---|---|---|---|---|---|
| James Ward | New Haven | New London | 24 | 5 7 | Fair |
| Jabin Sperry | " | New Haven | 28 | 5 9 | " |
| Philo Sperry | " | " | 23 | 5 5 | " |
| James Jeffery | " | Scotland | 19 | 5 6 | " |
| Moses Cook | " | New Haven | 28 | 5 9 | " |
| Will. Baird Nicholson | " | Rhoad Island | 20 | 5 5 | " |
| William West | " | Ireland | 28 | 5 8¼ | Dark |
| Trueman Loveland | " | Darby | 16 | 5 9 | Fair |
| Bowars French | " | " | 19 | 5 11 | " |
| John Stubbs | " | England | 18 | 5 5 | " |
| William Turner | " | " | 18 | 5 5 | " |
| John Huggins | " | Brantford | 18 | 5 4 | " |
| Edmund Taylor | Lyme | England | 17 | 5 7 | " |
| James Richardson | Wethersfield | Devonshire | 20 | 5 2 | " |
| Richard Wear | " | Dublin | 48 | 5 5 | " |
| John Emmitt | " | Lancashire | 26 | 5 8 | " |
| Thomas Clark | " | Liverpool | 21 | 5 6 | " |
| John Burnham | " | Wethersfield | 18 | 5 8¼ | " |
| Samuel Caverle | N Haven | New Haven | 19 | 5 3 | Dark |
| Freeman Badger | " | Wallingford | 20 | 5 8 | Fair |
| John Thomson | " | Bristol | 48 | 5 6 | Brown |
| Thomas Jones | Lyme | England | 24 | 5 8 | Fair |
| Henry Peck | New Haven | New Haven | 23 | 5 6 | " |
| Elisha White | " | " | 16 | 5 5 | " |
| Samuel Wise | " | " | 17 | 5 4 | " |
| Samuel Tory | Middletown | Middletown | 17 | 5 6 | Brown |
| Jonathan Setchell | New Haven | Ipswich Mass. | 19 | 5 11 | " |
| Robert Aitkins | " | Scotland | 19 | 5 4 | Fair |
| Michael Creamer | Middletown | Middletown | 17 | 5 4 | Blemish in one eye |
| Thomas Johnson | " | " | 21 | 5 0 | Brown |
| Thomas Bazzill | " | " | 23 | 5 8 | " |
| Thomas Scott | Glastenbury | Glastenbury | 23 | 5 10 | " |
| George Stow | Middletown | Middletown | 39 | 5 6 | " |
| Joseph Miller | Glastenbury | Glastenbury | 18 | 5 2 | Fair |

| Name | Residence | Birthplace | Age | Ft | In | Complexion |
|---|---|---|---|---|---|---|
| Noah Brooks | Middletown | Middletown | 21 | 5 | 8 | Brown |
| Will<sup>m</sup> Putnam | New London | Boston | 24 | 5 | 5 | Fair |
| John Brown | Fairfield | England | 25 | 5 | 4 | " |
| John Brice | East Haddam | Scotland | 23 | 5 | 6 | Brown |
| Thomas Wendover Jr. | " | New York | 19 | 5 | 9 | " |
| Levy Hodge | Glastenbury | Glastenbury | 30 | 5 | 11 | " |
| Joseph Scott | " | " | 21 | 5 | 6 | " |
| Joseph Peck | Wethersfield | Wallingford | 16 | 5 | 5 | Fair |
| Aron White | Middletown | Middletown | 23 | 5 | 5 | Brown |
| Samuel Collins | " | " | 21 | 5 | 10 | " |
| Ebenezer Miller | " | Chatham | 30 | 5 | 8 | Fair |
| Ebenezer Sage | " | Middletown | 17 | 5 | 9 | Brown |
| Samuel Johnson | East Haddam | New York | 53 | 5 | 6 | Brown |
| Bouton Knapp | " | Stanford | 26 | 5 | 10 | Light |
| Joseph Merris | " | Killingsworth | 15 | 5 | 4 | Brown |
| David Miller | Middletown | Middletown | 12 | 5 | | Fair |
| Isaac Knapp | " | Newbury | 28 | 5 | 9 | " |
| Abijah Collins | " | Wethersfield | 28 | 5 | 2 | Brown |
| Levy Holmes | Wethersfield | " | 24 | 5 | 5 | Dark |
| Bennett Eaglestone | Middletown | Middletown | 50 | 5 | 6 | Fair |
| Stephen Eaglestone | " | " | 15 | 5 | † | |
| Justus Starr | " | " | | | | |
| William Goodrich | Glastenbury | Glastenbury | 21 | 6 | 2 | Fair |
| Samuel Dunham | East Haddam | Colchester | 25 | 5 | 7 | Brown |
| Nehemiah Storer | New Haven | New Haven | 28 | 5 | 7 | Fair |
| Nathan Gould | Fairfield | Fairfield | 20 | 5 | 6 | " |
| Edmund Burr | " | " | 17 | 5 | 9 | " |
| Samuel Adams | " | " | 17 | 5 | 9 | " |
| John House | New Haven | New York | 15 | 5 | 4 | " |
| Nathaniel Warren | " | New Haven | 22 | 5 | 7 | " |
| Eber Sperry | " | " | 25 | 5 | 9 | " |
| Jonathan Smith | " | " | 19 | 5 | 10 | Brown |
| John Jeffery | E Haddam | Pachaug | 22 | 5 | 7 | Indian |
| Robert Upham | N Haven | West of England | 22 | 5 | 8 | Brown |
| Elisha Forbes | " | New Haven | 21 | 5 | 4 | " |

| Name | Place Ship'd at | Place born at | Age | Height | Complex |
|---|---|---|---|---|---|
| Christian Hanson | N Haven | Denmark | 31 | 5 2 | Fair |
| William Presher | " | Cortlands Manor | 21 | 5 7 | " |
| Richard Goff | E Haddam | N London | 13 | 4 10 | Brown |
| Roger Robins | Wethersfield | Wethersfield | 16 | 5 2 | " |
| Samuel Davis | " | Worcester Eng. | 41 | 5 9 | " |
| John Giles | " | Somersdsh " | 22 | 5 6 | " |
| Mitchel Kingman | New Haven | Norwich | 32 | 5 6 | " |
| Stephen Oliver | " | New London | | | |
| Thomas Oliver | | Scotland | | | |
| Will. Taylor | Lyme | Long Island | | | Fair |
| Silas Sanford | Wethersfield | England | 30 | 5 4 | " |
| William Webb | " | Mass. | | 6 1 | Sandy |
| Asael Bush | New Haven | New Haven | | | Brown |
| John Daggett | New London | New London | | | Negro |
| Brittain | | | | | |
| Daniel Porter | New Haven | | | | Negro |
| Daniel Peterson | Lyme | England | 21 | 5 9¼ | Fair |
| Josiah Wood | | | | | |

[*State Library, Gurley Papers, 4.*]

# MISCELLANEOUS.

## HARTLAND RETURN.

Asa Andrews
Jonathan Bill Jun<sup>r</sup>
Samuel Benjamin Ju<sup>r</sup>
Daniel Benjamin
John Damels
Festus Giddings
Benjamin Giddings
Phinehas Kingbury Ju<sup>r</sup>
Zebulon Mack
Eliphas Pirkins
Jason Pirkins
Gideon Pirkins
Reuben Daniels
Ebenezer Dimock
Thomas Jones
Moses Cowdrey
Asa Cowdrey
Noah Chappel
Jessa Gates
Abner Waters
Titus Allen Ju<sup>r</sup>

Oliver Bates
Hendale Bates
Timothy Crosby
Daniel Driggs
Ephraim Fox
Nathan Fox
Haris Fox
Daniel Beman
Joseph Gilbert
James Hungerford
Josiah Meeker
Aaron Meeker
John Porter
George Treet
Childes Taylor
Gamaliel Wilder
Erastus Hil s
Dan Monrow
Isaac Meacham
Thomas Wilder

Hartland Jenuary y<sup>e</sup> 26<sup>th</sup> AD 1778

This is to Certify that the above Named was in actual Service in the Year AD 1776

[Although this Return is stated to be for service in 1776 it seems probable that that date is an error of the writer for 1775.]

[*State Library, Revolution 6, 9.*]

In the Record of Connecticut Men in the Revolution, page 528, Capt. Jehiel Bryant's company, Sergeant John Downs is noted as having marched Oct. 5 and deserted Oct. 15, 1777. John Downes of Milford who served in the Revolution kept a diary, now in the possession of William H. Downes of Boston, which contains the following among other entries for Oct. 1777.

5 Alarm made. I march off.
8 I march towards Fishkill
15 Marched to North River
18 I Joined Lieut Col Fenn's Regt at Peekskill.

In printing the volume of Rolls and Lists of Connecticut Men in the Revolution (Collections, vol. 8) several rolls were, unfortunately, printed from a volume of copied rolls in the Comptroller's office instead of from the original rolls in the State Library. The following changes should be made in the printed volume to conform to the original rolls.

Capt. Miller's Company, page 160.

| For | Sol<sup>n</sup> Phelps | read | Solomon Phelps Jr. |

For Sol<sup>n</sup> Phelps    read Solomon Phelps Jr.
" W<sup>m</sup> Burt    " William Buel.
" Sam<sup>l</sup> Finley    " Samuel Finley Jr.
" David Blush    " David Blush Jr.
" Libbius Hills    " Lebbeus Hills Jr.
" Ja<sup>s</sup> Mackarel    " James Mackaul.

Capt. Hutchinson's Company, page 161.

For Adam Bingham    read Aaron Bingham.
" Asariah Bell    " Azariah Bill.
" Ja<sup>s</sup> House    " Joseph House.
" Isabel Jones    " Asahel Jones.
" Jon<sup>a</sup> Savary    " Jn<sup>o</sup> Savary.
" Jon<sup>a</sup> Townsen    " Jn<sup>o</sup> Townsen.

Capt. Dewey's Company, page 161.

For Annis Fitch    read Ammi Fitch.
" Ja<sup>s</sup> Tickour    " James Tickner.
" Rodolph<sup>s</sup> Wacker    " Rodolphus Thacher

Capt. Phelps' Company, page 162.

For Sam<sup>l</sup> Tyler    read Samuel Fyler.
" Beniah Phelps    " Beriah Phelps.

Capt. Carpenter's Company, page 162.

For Ja<sup>s</sup> Gay    read Joseph Gay.

[*State Library, Revolution 6 ; 137, 148, 149, 151, 155.*]

The following corrections should be made in the volume of Rolls and Lists of Connecticut Men in the Revolution (Collections, vol. 8).

Page 80. For Short Term Levies, 1779, read Short Term Levies, 1780.
Page 160. For Joseph Bartlet Jr., read Josiah Bartlet Jr.
Page 163. For Sam<sup>ll</sup> Boston, read Sam<sup>ll</sup> Bastow.
Page 209. Kezin Gridley should be Rezin Gridley.

---

## ERRATA.

Page 48. Add at bottom of page — East Windsor Apr<sup>ll</sup> 6<sup>th</sup> 1779.
Page 136. The document ending here should be credited to *Connecticut Historical Society.*
Pages 233, 235. The headline should read — Connecticut Line, 1777–1781.

# INDEX.

Aames, Ebenezer, 49.
Abanathy, Giles, 347.
Abbe, Eleazer, 22, 163, 237, 260.
Abbe, George, 226.
Abbe, Jeduthan, 22, 163, 237, 260.
Abbe, John, 22, 54, 55, 73, 129, 163, 226, 236, 288.
Abbe, Joseph, 226, 288.
Abbe, Mason, 85, 127.
Abbe, Nathaniel, 226, 288.
Abbe, Thomas, 22, 66, 240.
Abbee, John, 182, 275.
Abbercrumbie, Aaron, 337.
Abberhart, John Lodewick, 2.
Abbett, John, 357.
Abbey, Eleazar, 345.
Abbey, Eliphelet, 345.
Abbey, Jeduthan, 345.
Abbot, 143.
Abbot, John, 12.
Abbot, John, Jr., 130.
Abbot, Stephen, 134.
Abby, Eleazer, 70.
Abby, Elezr, 143.
Abby, George, 180.
Abby, Joseph, 334.
Abby, Richard, 189.
Abel, Abel, 65.
Abell, Rufus, 74.
Abenathy, James, 61.
Abercrombie, Aaron, 254.
Abercrumbie, Aaron, 320.
Abernerthy, James, 102.
Abey, 80.
Abrow, Benajah, 59, 353.
Acaly, Samuel, 5.
Achor, Jacob, 245, 305, 328.
Ackley, Aeral, 118.
Ackley, Barzileel, 3.
Ackley, Champeon, 78.
Ackley, Lewis, 87, 351.
Ackley, Nicholas, 87, 351.
Ackley, Silas, 3.
Ackley, Thomas, 241, 352.
Ackley, Warren, 3.
Acklin, Cuff, 278, 279, 351.
Ackly, Champion, 227.
Ackly, Thomas, 21, 163.
Acley, Ariel, 80.
Acley, Azerial, 57.
Acley, Thomas, 260.
Acley, Uriah, 153.
Adams, 138.
Adams, Abel, 10.
Adams, Alexander P., 365.
Adams, Asael, 21, 177, 236.
Adams, Asaph, 363.
Adams, Benjamin, 11, 106, 272, 292.
Adams, Charles, 75.
Adams, David 21, 64, 146, 157, 163, 237.
Adams, David, Jr., 21, 237.
Adams, Elisha, 132.
Adams, James, 89.
Adams, Jed⁴, 146.
Adams, Jedediah, 64, 157, 277, 335, 363.
Adams, John, 21, 52, 70, 213, 223, 239, 297.
Adams, Jonathan, 21, 234.
Adams, Jonathan, Jr., 116, 144.
Adams, Oliver, 10.
Adams, Parker, 71, 136.
Adams, Permenio, 10.
Adams, Philemon, 363.
Adams, Reuben, 286, 311, 344.
Adams, Rhodrick, 10, 260, 279.
Adams, Samuel, 21, 49, 64, 157, 163, 237, 260, 297, 302, 367.
Adams, Samuel, Jr., 363.
Adams, Simion, 50.
Adams, William, 21, 70, 72, 82, 136, 160, 163, 237.
Adams, William, Jr., 148.
Addams, Abner, 19.

Addams, Asael, 74.
Addams, David, 19, 352.
Addams, Jeddediah, 318.
Addams, Joshua, 8.
Addams, Levi, 349.
Addams, Roderick, 349.
Addams, Samuel, 353.
Addis, Thomas, 198.
Adee, Aner, 61.
Adee, Anor, 343.
Adhins, David, 51.
Adkin, Jabez, 346.
Adkins, David, 346.
Adkins, Ira, 209.
Adkins, Josiah, 51.
Adkins, Luther, 50.
Adrus, Theodore, 163.
Adye, Aner, 99.
Aery, Ephriam, 46.
Affrica, Ruel, 60.
Affrican, Ruel, 299.
Africa, Cash, 53, 228.
Africa, Ruel, 288.
Aitkins, Robert, 366.
Akely, Samuel, 163.
Aken, James, 22.
Akerly, Samuel, 51.
Akin, James, 163, 229.
Albert, Thomas G., 22, 239.
Alcock, Giles, 53.
Alderman, Eppaph, 144.
Alderman, Gad, 279, 349.
Alderman, John, 10.
Alderman, Timothy, 188.
Aldin, 188.
Aldredge, William, 260.
Aldrich, Timothy, 184.
Aldrich, William, 163.
Aldridge, James, 275, 349.
Aldridge, Thomas, 10.
Aldridge, Jonathan, 137.
Aldridge, William, 232.
Aldrish, William, 77.
Alexander, James, 363.
Alger, Aaron, 137.
Allas, Phinehas, 148.
Allay, William, 260.
Allen, Abel, 277, 347.
Allen, Amasa, 49, 66.
Allen, Amos, 21, 236.
Allen, Asher, 72, 129, 163.
Allen, Ashur, 21, 54, 55, 236.
Allen, Benjamin, 67, 98, 113.
Allen, Daniel, 21, 199, 236.
Allen, David, 21, 218.
Allen, Diarca, 54, 72, 129.
Allen, Ebenezer, 21, 67, 163, 233.
Allen, Ebenezer, Jr., 96.
Allen, Eliphalet, 67.
Allen, Eseck, 10.
Allen, Gabrel, 4.
Allen, Ichabod, 182.
Allen, John, 47, 75, 139, 258, 288, 291, 349.
Allen, Jonathan, 21.
Allen, Lemuel, 46, 86, 130.
Allen, Minor, 119, 153, 154.
Allen, Moses, 21, 67, 163, 233.
Allen, Othniel, 49, 66.
Allen, Peter, 283.
Allen, Phineas, 54, 72, 129.
Allen, Robart, 232.
Allen, Samuel, 21, 46, 131, 132, 163, 238.
Allen, Thomas, 21, 67, 97, 233.
Allen, Timothy, 244.
Allen, Titus, Jr., 369.
Allen, William, 8.
Alley, William, 22, 163, 229.
Allin, Abel, 48, 242.
Allin, Amasa, 12.
Allin, Amos, 57, 79.
Allin, Arch, 14.
Allin, David, 230.
Allin, Ebenezer, 8.
Allin, Elisha, 201.
Allin, John, 198.
Allin, Joseph, 295.
Allin, Lemuel, 133.
Allin, Moses, 205.
Allin, Nathaniel, 201.
Allin, Sluman, 198.
Alling, Abel, 260.
Alling, John, 150.
Alling, Jonathan, 163, 229, 260.
Alling, Nathaniel, 6.
Alling, Titus, 6.
Alling, William, 8.
Allis, Nathaniel, Jr., 4.
Allyn, Abel, 299.
Allyn, Benjamin, 209.
Allyn, Daniel, 49.
Allyn, Ellihu, 189.
Allyn, Job, 14.
Allyn, John, 305, 328.
Allyn, Jonathan, 189.
Allyn, Joseph, 185.
Allyn, Miner, 51, 69.
Allyn, Robert, 50, 68.
Allyn, Theophilus, 189.
Allyn, Thomas, Jr., 14.
Allyn, Timothy, 242, 304, 324.
Alma, William, 224.
Aloord, Hewet, 65.

# INDEX. 373

Alton, Joseph, 135.
Alverd, Thomas G., 260.
Alvord, Eliphaz, 361, 362.
Alvord, Thomas G., 163, 194.
Alvord, see Aloord.
Ama, Archalus, 223, 297.
Ambrose, Patrick, 283.
Ame, Archelaus, 288.
Amedown, Jonathan, 186.
Ames, Aden, 75, 242.
Ames, Alven, 128.
Ames, Antielus, 310.
Ames, Archelus, 310, 328.
Ames, Arehelus, 306.
Ames, Asa, 128.
Ames, Comfort, 272.
Ames, Cyrus, 9.
Ames, David, 192.
Ames, Ebenezer, 66, 194.
Ames, Ezra, 77.
Ames, John, 64, 156.
Ames, Matthias, 9.
Ames, Nathaniel, 182.
Ames, Samuel, 288.
Ames, Zebulon, 78.
Amis, Arehelus, 306.
Ammedown, Jonathan, 294.
Ammit, John, 324, 339.
Amos, 58.
Ancraman, John Frederick, 75.
Andeson, Thomas, 21.
Andeson, William, 21.
Anderson, Daniel, 221.
Anderson, J., 116.
Anderson, James, 254, 285, 320, 337.
Anderson, John, 136.
Anderson, Robert, Jr., 124.
Anderson, Thomas, 163, 180, 232, 260, 338.
Anderson, Timothy, 188, 226.
Anderson, William, 48, 163, 186, 240, 346.
Anderwood, Elius, 131.
Andras, Abner, 348.
Andras, Asa, 349.
Andras, Clemont, 350.
Andras, David, 350.
Andras, Elisha, 204.
Andras, John, 252.
Andras, Jonathan, 349.
Andras, Joseph, 347.
Andras, Obadiah, 347.
Andras, Richard, 204.
Andras, Thomas, 352.
Andras, William, 204, 349.
Andreus, Thomas, 260.

Andrews, Amos, 60, 83, 187.
Andrews, Andrew, 59, 82.
Andrews, Asa, 6, 369.
Andrews, Daniel, 362.
Andrews, David, 277.
Andrews, James, 232.
Andrews, John, 8, 276.
Andrews, Joshua, 65.
Andrews, Nathaniel, 186.
Andrews, Phil⁰, 179.
Andrews, Richard, 186.
Andrews, Solomon, 272.
Andrews, Thomas, 241.
Andrews, Timothy, 84.
Andros, Elijah, 336.
Andrss, 48.
Andrus, Asa, 21, 163, 238, 260.
Andrus, Clement, 300.
Andrus, Daniel, 189.
Andrus, David, 300.
Andrus, Ezra, 21, 163, 252.
Andrus, Gideon, 347.
Andrus, Hezekiah, 11.
Andrus, James, 11, 21, 68, 80, 163, 240.
Andrus, John, 50.
Andrus, Jonathan, 145.
Andrus, Obediah, 21, 239, 260, 278.
Andrus, Richard, 10.
Andrus, Solomon, 302.
Andrus, Theodore, 21, 239, 260.
Andrus, Thomas, 21, 163.
Andrus, Timothy, 163.
Andrus, William, 10, 21, 163, 240.
Andruss, Ezra, 55.
Andruss, Theodore, 250.
Andruss, Timothy, 52, 70.
Andruss, William, 10.
Anew, Andrew, 163.
Angar, George, 163.
Anger, George, 239, 347.
Anguine, Lewis, 250.
Angur, George, 22.
Anibell, David, 3.
Anjevine, Lewis, 58, 92.
Annew, Andrew, 22, 68, 232.
Answitz, Apollus, 351.
Answorth, Alven, 198.
Anthony, John, 13, 60, 83.
Antoney, John, 22.
Antony, John, 230.
Apes, Peter, 281.
Apley, Josiah, 205.
Aply, Rozel, 147.
Arabus, Jack, 338.

Archer, Benjamin, Jr., 142.
Archer, Crippin, 302.
Archer, Cyprian, 354.
Archer, Grippin, 260.
Armstrong, Daniel, 301.
Armstrong, Daniel, Jr., 272.
Armstrong, Ebenezer, 76, 112.
Armstrong, Joseph, 95.
Armstrong, Josiah, 67, 97.
Armstrong, William, 272, 301, 308, 333.
Arnall, Jonathan, 51.
Arney, Archelaus, 284.
Arnold, 5.
Arnold, Abijah, 108.
Arnold, Gideon, 129.
Arnold, Isaac, 356.
Arnold, Jehiel, 22, 69, 163, 240, 354.
Arnold, John, 5, 132.
Arnold, Jonathan, 52, 70, 245, 315, 345.
Arnold, Josiah, 5.
Arnold, Levi, 208.
Arnold, Oliver, Jr., 74.
Arnold, Seth, 6, 260, 277, 347.
Arven, William, 71.
Arvin, William, 77, 135.
Ashford, 21, 22, 25, 27, 30, 33, 34, 36, 39, 42, 43, 46, 88, 130, 133, 138, 166, 169, 170, 173, 175, 177, 179, 181, 182, 183, 184, 185, 196, 199, 201, 216, 217, 218, 219, 226, 236, 264, 266, 269, 271, 273, 280, 284, 287, 297, 298, 301, 355, 356, 357.
Ashley, Abner, 129.
Ashley, John, 114, 352.
Ashly, John, 103.
Aspenwall, Aaron, 22, 177, 236.
Aspenwall, Caleb, 22, 177.
Aspenwall, Peter, 218.
Aspinwell, Aaron, 74.
Aspinwell, Caleb, 74, 236.
Asten, Banjmin, 15.
Astin, Thomas, 146.
Athington, Thomas, 67.
Atkins, Chancy, 189.
Atkins, Ira, 280.
Atkens, Joseph, 132.
Atkins, Josiah, 7, 260, 289.
Atkins, Josiah, Jr., 163.
Atkins, Samuel, 215.
Attwood, John, 3.
Attwood, Thomas, 182.
Atwater, Titus, 60.
Atwood, Ebenezer, 192.
Atwood, Elijah, Jr., 287.
Atwood, Isaac, 135.
Atwood, Thomas, 219.
Auger, George, 260.
Augustus, Bristo, 75.
Augustus, Caesar, 22, 70, 237, 345.
Augustus, Jacob, 194, 226.
Augustus, Zezar, 163.
Auldredg, William, 22.
Austen, Edward, 210.
Austen, John, 77, 205.
Austen, Richard, 22.
Austin, Amos, 13.
Austin, Benjamin, 13.
Austin, David, 115.
Austin, Ezra, 190.
Austin, Eusebius, 247.
Austin, Joshua, 144.
Austin, Phinehas, 260, 351.
Austin, Richard, 163, 238, 352, 354.
Austin, Thomas, 64, 156.
Austin, Uriah, 18.
Avered, Ambrose, 14.
Averet, Thadeous, 13.
Averies, Daniel, 90.
Averill, Jacob, 10.
Averill, Jonathan, 10.
Averill, Thomas, 9.
Avery, Amos, 66.
Avery, Benjamin, 61, 99, 341.
Avery, Charles, 34, 74.
Avery, Christopher, 77, 249, 281, 318, 335.
Avery, Constant, 51, 69, 78.
Avery, Daniel, 80.
Avery, David, 214.
Avery, Elisha, 50, 68.
Avery, Ephraim, 131.
Avery, Ezekiel, 221.
Avery, Frederick, 75, 214.
Avery, George, Jr., 50, 68.
Avery, Isaac, 288.
Avery, John, 310, 343.
Avery, Miles, 74.
Avery, Prentis, 9.
Avery, Roger, 76, 148.
Avery, Simeon, 68, 163, 183, 232, 260.
Avery, Stephen, 199.
Avery, Thomas, 232.
Avory, Amos, Jr., 132.
Avory, Roger, 330.
Avory, Simeon, 22.
Avory, Thomas, 22.
Ayer, John, 78.

INDEX. 375

Ayers, Peter, 183.
Ayres, John, 207.
Ayres, Nathan, 77.

Ba[ ]ton, John, 262.
Babbet, Benjamin, 193.
Babbit, 7.
Babbit, Benjamin, 7.
Babbit, Edward, 215.
Babcock, Amos, 12.
Babcock, Christopher, 15.
Babcock, Elihu, 285, 318, 335.
Babcock, John, 140.
Babe, Comfort, 295.
Bacchus, Delucena, 99.
Baccus, Elijah 127.
Bachus, Ozias, 323.
Back, Elisha, 288, 294, 332.
Back, Lyman, 357.
Backer, Andrew, 50.
Backer, Samuel, 50.
Backers, Ozias, 341.
Backon, Henry, 148.
Backon, John, 145.
Backus, Abner, 85.
Backus, Electus M., 284.
Backus, Elijah, 85.
Backus, Ozias, 272.
Backus, Timothy, 149.
Bacon, 19, 223.
Bacon, Abner, 22, 64, 237.
Bacon, B., 157.
Bacon, Benjamin, 146.
Bacon, Eben, 306.
Bacon, Ebenezer, 285, 306, 325, 328.
Bacon, Henry, 22, 82, 149, 160, 237.
Bacon, Jabez, 99.
Bacon, Joseph, 254, 294.
Bacon, Nehemiah, 22, 76, 138, 165, 237, 262.
Bacon, Richard, 247, 320, 337, 348.
Bacon, William, 22, 74, 164, 239, 260, 346.
Badcock, Beriah, 291.
Badcock, Ebenezer, 357.
Badcock, Jesse, 275.
Badcock, John, 23, 237.
Badcock, Joseph, 65, 132.
Badcock, Robert, 357.
Badger, Freeman, 366.
Badger, John, 295.
Bagdon, Cezar, 22, 164, 231, 261.
Baher, Edward, 229.
Bail, Hendrick, 305, 321, 337.
Bailey, Aaron, 74.

Bailey, Christopher, 214.
Bailey, Elisha, 50.
Bailey, Gideon, 24, 240.
Bailey, Ichabod, 50, 347.
Bailey, Jacobe, 24, 240.
Bailey, Loudon, 352.
Bailey, Robert, 24, 164, 240.
Bailey, William, 352.
Bails, Daniel, 320.
Baily, 6.
Baily, Amos, 5.
Baily, Christopher, 52, 70.
Baily, Daniel, 209.
Baily, Gideon, 5, 69.
Baily, Gideon, Jr., 5.
Baily, Gurdon, 52, 69.
Baily, Jabez, 6.
Baily, Jacob, 6, 69.
Baily, Jacob, Jr., 5.
Baily, Jeremy, 51, 69.
Baily, John, 51, 69.
Baily, John, Jr., 5.
Baily, Loudon, 52, 69.
Baily, Robert, 69, 261.
Baily, Timothy, 5, 52, 69.
Baily, William, 5, 51, 70.
Bains, Solomon, 229.
Baits, Daniel, 320, 337.
Baits, Zepheniah, 48.
Baker, Abel, 200.
Baker, Andrew, 4, 68.
Baker, Bartholemew, 24, 89, 120, 162, 164.
Baker, Edward, 24, 164, 260.
Baker, James, 8.
Baker, John, 54, 73, 97, 159, 184.
Baker, Jonas, 136.
Baker, Jonathan, 130, 219.
Baker, Joshua, 4, 183.
Baker, Ozias, 63, 78, 227.
Baker, Phinehas, 102.
Baker, Richard, 320.
Baker, Rufus, 19.
Baker, Thomas, 291.
Baker, William, 87, 227.
Balcan, Nathaniel, 362.
Balch, Bezeleel, 356.
Balch, Henery, 129.
Balch, Israel, Jr., 218.
Balch, John, 129.
Balch, John, Jr., 54, 73.
Balcom, John, 188.
Balding, Elisha, 297.
Baldwin, 211, 227.
Baldwin, Aaron, 1.
Baldwin, Abel, 8, 124.
Baldwin, Abel, Jr., 154.

Baldwin, Abraham, 123.
Baldwin, Asa, 12.
Baldwin, Caleb, 72, 231, 261.
Baldwin, Eleazer, 273.
Baldwin, Elisha, 77.
Baldwin, Henry, 232.
Baldwin, Isaac, 123, 154.
Baldwin, Jared, 210, 222.
Baldwin, Levi, 1.
Baldwin, Luther, 214.
Baldwin, Samuel, 204.
Baldwin, Seth, 280, 287, 354.
Baldwin, Silas, 230.
Baldwin, William, 1.
Baldwin, Calib, 22, 164.
Baldwine, Elijah, 54, 72, 129.
Baldwine, Henery, 22.
Baldwine, Silas, 22.
Baley, 224.
Baley, Asa, 50.
Ball, Caleb, 8.
Ball, Humphry, 23, 237, 262, 290, 291.
Ball, James, 200.
Ball, John, 5, 164, 226, 231, 261, 301.
Ball, Jonathan, 280, 301.
Ball, Umphry, 163.
Ball, Vmphrey, 140.
Ballard, John, 277, 308, 334.
Ballen, Benjamin, 133.
Bamon, Jonathan, 312.
Bangs, Richard, 204.
Banjmin, Jese. 15.
Banks, Gershom, 4.
Banks, Samuel, 118.
Banks, Sumner, 346.
Banks, Thomas, 274.
Bannister, George, 61.
Banter, Alexander, 350.
Barber, Amaziah, 10, 260, 349.
Barber, Daniel, 10, 11, 143.
Barber, David, Jr., 85.
Barber, Elijah, 10.
Barber, Job, 11.
Barber, John, Jr., 144.
Barber, Jonathan, 186.
Barber, Nathaniel. 22, 235.
Barber, Reuben, 205.
Barber, Shubel, 14.
Barber, Stephen, 119, 142.
Barber, W., 327.
Barbermore, Eldad, 215.
Barbor, Simon, 6.
Barbur, Benjamin. 6.
Barbur, Simion, 6.
Barbur, Timothy, 6.

Bardin, Abraham, 210.
Bardin, Samuel, 273.
Bardon, Samuel, 316.
Bardsley, Abijah, 151.
Bardsley, Garsham, 47.
Bardsley, Gawham, 47.
Bardsly, Phineas, 7.
Barham, 95.
Barker, Amaziah, 275.
Barker, Ethen, 179.
Barker, James, Jr., 2.
Barker, John, 56, 77.
Barker, Joshua, 117.
Barker, Moses, 350.
Barker, Samuel, 22, 231.
Barker, Timothy, 1.
Barkhamsted, 145, 189.
Barlow, Daniel, 58, 67, 93.
Barlow, David, 68, 92.
Barlow, David, Jr., 58.
Barlow, John, 23, 107, 165, 235, 261.
Barlow, Micah, 134.
Barlow, Silas, 123.
Barna, Benjamin, 219.
Barnabee, James, 65.
Barnam, Levi, 191.
Barnard, 143, 194.
Barnard, Edward, Jr., 14.
Barnard, Francis, 288.
Barnard, James, 52, 70, 256, 359.
Barnard, Joel. 276, 350.
Barnard, John, 23, 70, 164, 237.
Barnard, Joseph, 86.
Barnard, Moses, 315, 331.
Barnard, Pharis, 286.
Barnard, Samuel, 10.
Barnard, Willial, 187.
Barnee, Frederick, 61.
Barnerd, Elihu, 204.
Barnerd, James, 358.
Barnes, Ambrose, 262.
Barnes, Charles, 287.
Barnes, David, 261, 334.
Barnes, James, 162.
Barnes, John, 140, 208.
Barnes, Josiah, 337.
Barnes, Moses, 261, 355.
Barnes, Orange, 286.
Barnes, Stephen, 282.
Barnes, Thomas, 254.
Barnet, John, 282.
Barnet, William, 123, 154.
Barnett, William, 8.
Barney, Luther, 3.
Barnham, Eli, 320.
Barnham, John, 254.

Barnham, Noah, 258.
Barnibee, James, 140.
Barns, 19.
Barns, Abel, 13.
Barns, Abraham, 55, 106.
Barns, Abram, 74.
Barns, Ambrose, 53, 165.
Barns, Amos, 49, 348.
Barns, Benjamin, 19.
Barns, Daniel, 23, 84, 164, 230, 239, 342.
Barns, David, 23, 83, 164, 230.
Barns, Eliphalet, 8.
Barns, Enos, 2, 53.
Barns, Enos, 3d, 53.
Barns, Ethel, 162.
Barns, Hartwell, 49, 348.
Barns, Ithiel, 122.
Barns, Jacob, 8.
Barns, James, 23, 162, 234.
Barns, Joel, 275.
Barns, John, 279.
Barns, Jonathan, 347.
Barns, Josiah, 320, 347.
Barns, Josiah, Jr., 288.
Barns, Lemuel, 71.
Barns, Moses, 23, 83, 164, 230, 292.
Barns, Nehemiah, 7, 257, 326, 340.
Barns, Simeon, 61, 100, 189, 308, 347.
Barns, Solomon, 23, 164, 260.
Barns, Stephen, 261, 284.
Barns, Thomas, 23, 71, 164, 239.
Barns, Wise, 49.
Barnum, 23, 235.
Barnum, Amos, 23, 104, 165, 235, 261.
Barnum, Comfort, 124.
Barnum, Ebenezer, 47, 123.
Barnum, Eli, 304.
Barnum, Ephraim, 153.
Barnum, Isaac, 119.
Barnum, John, 47, 118, 153, 222, 305, 328.
Barnum, Levi, 221.
Barnum, Noah, 47, 118, 153, 305.
Barnum, Richard, 154.
Barnum, Samuel, 118, 153, 165.
Barnum, Stephen, 23, 103, 165, 222, 235, 261.
Barnum, Thomas, 154.
Barnum, Timothy, 222, 261.
Barnum, Zenus, 104.
Baron, Nehemiah, 256.
Barr, G., 96.
Barret, Hezekiah, 192.

Barret, Hildick, 227.
Barrett, Batholomew, 71.
Barrett, Jeremiah, 345.
Barrett, Thomas, 183.
Barrot, Hildrick, 78.
Barrow, Josiah, 93.
Barrows, Eleazer, 179, 219.
Barrows, Ethan, 179, 219.
Barrows, Isaac, 72, 129, 135.
Barrows, Jacob, 24, 54, 55, 73, 130, 163, 236.
Barrows, Joseph, 226, 285, 288.
Barrows, Joshua, 357.
Barrows, Josiah, 72, 135.
Barrows, Lemuel, 135, 195.
Barrows, Thomas, 136.
Barrows, Thomas, Jr., 356.
Barrows, William, 292.
Barrus, Thomas, 161.
Barry, Michael, 139.
Barson, John, 347.
Barss, Joseph, 7.
Barstow, Job, 223.
Bartholemew, Abraham, 278.
Bartholemew, Isaac, 278.
Bartholemew, John, 24.
Bartholemew, Samuel, 282.
Bartholimew, Abraham, 347.
Bartholimew, Isaac, 347.
Bartholomew, Benjamin, 1.
Bartholomew, Elijah, 215.
Bartholomew, Gideon, 1.
Bartholomew, Ira, 13.
Bartholomew, John, 86, 134, 229.
Bartholomew, Joseph, 134.
Bartholomew, William 79, 215.
Bartlet, Amherst, 139, 242.
Bartlet, Isaac, 140.
Bartlet, Joseph, 296.
Bartlet, Joseph, Jr., 370.
Bartlet, Josiah, Jr., 304.
Bartlet, Robert, 76, 339.
Bartlet, Stephen, 48.
Bartoo, John, 216, 282.
Bartrum, Noah, 210.
Bary, John, 330.
Baskam, Elias, 187.
Bass, Samuel, 219.
Basset, Abel, 69.
Basset, Abraham, 2.
Basset, Edward, 2.
Basset, Isaac, 64, 146, 157.
Basset, John, 92.
Basset, Jonathan, 218.
Basset, Joshua, 24, 54, 55, 72, 129, 163, 256.
Basset, Joshua, Jr., 129.

Basset, William, 24, 163, 230, 261.
Bassett, Joshua, 236.
Bassett, Joshua, Jr., 73.
Bassett, Nathan, 365.
Bassett, William, 310, 343.
Bassey, Peleg, 8.
Bassey, Silas, 8.
Bassit, Jonathan, 179.
Bassit, William, 84.
Bassitt, John, 58.
Baston, Sawney, 346.
Bastow, Samuel, 370.
Batchlor, Abel, 332.
Bate, Eleazer, 5.
Bates, Amos, 23, 70, 164, 240.
Bates, Daniel, 23, 70, 164, 240, 261, 284, 320, 352.
Bates, David, 23, 165, 233, 262.
Bates, Eleazer, 23, 70, 164, 240, 261.
Bates, Ephraim, 53, 312, 344.
Bates, Ezra, 108.
Bates, Hendale, 369.
Bates, John, 23, 239.
Bates, Joseph, 346, 364.
Bates, Oliver, 369.
Bates, Reuben, 6.
Bates, Samuel, 103.
Bath, John, 70.
Batterson, Abijah, 209.
Batterson, George, 262, 274.
Batterson, George, Jr., 4.
Batterson, James, Jr., 67, 96.
Batterson, John, 4.
Batterson, Joseph, 4, 67, 96, 209.
Batterson, Stephen, 67, 96.
Batterson, William, 4, 274.
Battis, Elijah, 216.
Baxter, Aaron, 23, 75, 141, 238.
Baxter, Alexander, 80.
Baxter, Benjamin, 49, 66.
Baxter, Francis, 23, 48, 164, 240.
Baxter, William, 296.
Bayard, Marshall, 287.
Bayden, Elhanan, 260.
Bayley, Abraham, 215.
Bayley, Henry, 93, 261.
Bayley, William, 51.
Bazzill, Thomas, 366.
Beach, Asa, 60, 83.
Beach, Benjamin, 58.
Beach, Bruen, 204.
Beach, D., 203.
Beach, David, 55, 261.
Beach, Ezekel, 6.
Beach, James, 144.
Beach, John, 58.
Beach, Julius, 275.
Beach, Lazarus, 89.
Beach, Nathaniel, 58, 90, 305, 341.
Beach, Obil, 69.
Beach, Reuben, 90, 305, 312, 343.
Beach, Rice, 206.
Beach, Roswel, 59, 83.
Beach, William, 353.
Beadle, Titus, 282.
Beadle, William, 51.
Beaeton, William, 248.
Beaher, John, 67.
Beaman, 48.
Beamon, Caesar, 261.
Beamont, Daniel, 279.
Beamont, Samuel, 256.
Beamont, Samuel, Jr., 79.
Beamont, William, 61.
Beamount, Dan, 221.
Beard, Abijah, 2.
Beard, Timothy, 73.
Beardsee, Gersham, 151.
Beardsle, Philo, 8.
Beardslee, Abijah, 58.
Beardslee, John, 4.
Beardslee, John, Jr., 58.
Beardslee, N., 162.
Beardsley, 98, 100, 126.
Beardsley, Abijah, 93.
Beardsley, Elijah, 122, 154.
Beardsley, James, 222.
Beardsley, John, 93.
Beardsley, Nehemiah, 221.
Beardsley, Phineas, 234.
Beardsley, Solomon W., 282.
Beardsley, Wheeler S., 261.
Beardsley, William, 338.
Beardsly, 118, 119, 120, 124.
Beardsly, Nehemiah, 162.
Beardsly, S., 91.
Bears, Hezekiah, 4.
Bearsley, Georshom, 2.
Bearzal, William, 161.
Beaumont, Dan, 216.
Beaumont, Jonathan, 312, 344.
Beazel, William, 82.
Bebe, Ammon, 165.
Bebe, James, 165.
Bebe, Joe, 164.
Bebee, Amon, 7, 231.
Bebee, Comfort, 351.
Bebee, Joel, 73, 261.
Bebee, Nathan, 181.
Bebee, Richard, 351.
Bebee, Solomon, 354.
Beckley, Prichard, 246.

INDEX. 379

Becks, Comfort, 339.
Beckus, Thomas, 297.
Beckwit, Phineas, 232.
Beckwith, Ezekiel, 282.
Beckwith, Ezekiel, Jr., 358, 359.
Beckwith, Ezra, 3, 86.
Beckwith, Guy, 198.
Beckwith, Ichabod, 23, 290, 358.
Beckwith, Isaac, Jr., 359.
Beckwith, Phineas, 23, 164, 260.
Beckwith, Timothy, Jr., 290, 358.
Beckwith, William, 3.
Bectley, Ephraim, 89.
Beden, William, 58.
Bedient, John, 214.
Bedient, Mordecai, 25, 109, 165.
Bedson, Daniel, 99.
Beebe, 88.
Beebe, Ammon, 24.
Beebe, Boanerges, 24, 290.
Beebe, Comfort, 283, 339.
Beebe, Daniel, 364.
Beebe, David, 279.
Beebe, James, 24, 355.
Beebe, Joel, 24, 231.
Beebe, Jonathan Jeremiah, 301.
Beebe, Naomi, 87.
Beebe, Nathan, 3.
Beebe, Nathaniel, 3.
Beebe, Richard, 283.
Beebee, Ammon, 76.
Beebee, Benjamin, 360.
Beebee, Boanerges, 360.
Beebee, Comfort, 325.
Beebee, James, 234, 261.
Beebee, Jonathan Jeremiah, 272.
Beebee, Nathaniel, 93.
Beebee, Richard, 325, 339.
Beech, Asa, 198.
Beech, Ashbell, 6.
Beech, David, Jr., 105.
Beech, Ebenezer, 97.
Beech, Elnathan, 207.
Beeck, Asa, 260.
Beeman, Elisha, 106.
Beeman, Ezekiel, 189.
Beeman, Friend, 24, 103.
Beeman, Jonathan, 24.
Beeman, Lemuel, 106.
Beeman, Matthias, 106.
Beeman, Samuel, 107.
Beeman, Truman, 210.
Beeny, John, 106.
Beers, Ephraim, 68, 96.
Beers, Gershum, 207.
Beers, Hezekiah, 22, 233.
Beers, Isaac, 317, 326, 332.

Beers, James, 92, 105, 382.
Beers, Jesse, 25, 109.
Beers, Joel, 58, 93, 250.
Beers, John, 92, 242, 320, 337.
Beers, John, Jr., 58.
Beers, Nathan, 245, 303, 327.
Beers, Thiah, 98.
Beers, Zachariah, 100.
Beevins, Ebenezer, 70, 164.
Beevins, Timothy, 250.
Begilow, Aloan, 193.
Beguine, Peter, 351.
Beke, William, 354.
Belcher, Elish, 10.
Belcher, Gill, 142.
Belcher, Joseph, 141, 354.
Belcher, Nathan, 10.
Belden, Ezra, 261.
Belden, John, 24, 73.
Belden, Simeon, 261.
Beldin, John, 261.
Belding, Abraham, 242, 308, 334, 348.
Belding, David, 197.
Belding, Ezra, 347.
Belding, Ezra, Jr., 277.
Belding, John, 164, 231.
Belding, Moses, 164, 348.
Belding, Richard, 254, 320, 337, 348.
Belding, Simeon, 300.
Beley, Asa, 68.
Bell, Asariah, 370.
Bell, Francis, 113.
Bell, J., 113.
Bell, James, 201, 272, 301.
Bellamy, Asa, 60, 83.
Bellows, Isaac, 185, 226.
Bellows, Nathaniel, 51, 69.
Bellows, Thomas, 15.
Bellus, Daniel, 10.
Bellus, Thomas, 10.
Belshaserhes, John, 118.
Beman, Cesar, 283.
Beman, Daniel, 369.
Beman, Friend, 236.
Beman, Jonathan, 240.
Beman, Uriah, 10.
Bement, Cesar, 351.
Bement, Jonathan, 189.
Bemont, Olliver, 140.
Bemus, Ephraim, 141.
Ben, Solomon, 121.
Ben, Thomas, 231.
Bend, John, 24.
Benedic, Derias, 162.
Benedict, Amos, 8.

Benedict, Asahel, 124.
Benedict, Comfort, 119.
Benedict, Daniel, 56.
Benedict, Darius, 78, 120.
Benedict, Ebenezer, 108.
Benedict, John, Jr., 8.
Benedict, Thomas, Jr., 8.
Benedict, William, 222.
Beneduk, Daniel, 59.
Benham, Isaas, 206.
Benham, James, 287.
Benham, Jared, 13.
Benham, John, 255.
Benham, Samuel, 13.
Benidict, Ezra, 261.
Benidict, Jeames, 74.
Benidict, Levi, 284.
Benjaman, Phinihas, 57.
Benjamen, J., 91.
Benjamen, John, Jr., 92.
Benjamens, John, 213.
Benjamens, Phin., 80.
Benjamin, Abial, Jr., 15.
Benjamin, Aron, 331.
Benjamin, Asa, 207.
Benjamin, Benjamin, 58, 65.
Benjamin, Daniel, 369.
Benjamin, David, 15.
Benjamin, Ezra, 15.
Benjamin, James, 8.
Benjamin, Jesse, 150.
Benjamin, John, 10, 165.
Benjamin, Rozel, 10.
Benjamin, Samuel, Jr., 369.
Benjamin, Stephen, 154.
Benjamins, Asa, 199.
Benjamins, Jesse, 77, 165.
Benjamins, John, 24, 234.
Benjamon, Daniel, 6.
Benn, Solomon, 283.
Bennedick, 88.
Bennedict, Eleazer, 124.
Bennedict, William, 102.
Bennet, Amos, 56, 76, 147, 159.
Bennet, Benjamin, 24, 75, 165, 231, 261, 295, 341.
Bennet, Benjamin, Jr., 7.
Bennet, David, 183.
Bennet, Elisha, 305.
Bennet, Ezekiel, 287.
Bennet, Isaac, 261, 283.
Bennet, Jaben, 81, 256.
Bennet, James, 19.
Bennet, Jeremiah, 280, 302, 308, 334.
Bennet, Job, 12.
Bennet, John, 12, 261.

Bennet, Joshua, 24, 54, 55, 130, 236.
Bennet, Miles, 312, 344.
Bennet, Nathaniel, 128.
Bennet, Stephen, 76, 148, 158, 222, 280, 288, 302.
Bennet, William, 12.
Bennett, Benjamin, 78, 120.
Bennett, Daniel, 75.
Bennett, John, 92.
Bennit, Abel, 10.
Bennit, Benjamin, 57, 68, 162.
Bennit, Daniel, 67.
Bennit, James, 55, 209.
Bennit, Nathaniel, 85.
Bennitt, 97.
Bennitt, Andrew, 4.
Bennitt, Benjamin, 3d, 93.
Bennitt, Daniel, 4, 95.
Bennitt, Hezekiah, 4.
Bennitt, James, 8, 101.
Bennitt, John, 58.
Bennitt, Tobe, 154.
Bennitt, Wolcutt, 4.
Bens, Thomas, 24.
Benson, William, 147.
Bentley, Aseal, 193.
Bentley, Jasper, 193.
Bentley, Joseph, 68, 256.
Bentley, William, 140, 290, 291.
Bently, Joseph, 50.
Benton, 215.
Benton, Adoniram, 185, 286, 349.
Benton, Azariah, 12.
Benton, David, 233.
Benton, Ebenezer, 17.
Benton, Edward, 24, 164, 231, 261.
Benton, Elihew, 193.
Benton, Elihue, 219.
Benton, Elijah, 82, 128, 286, 349.
Benton, Jonathan, 12, 187.
Benton, Josiah, 12.
Benton, Nathaniel W., 346.
Benton, Samuel, 12.
Benton, Zadock, 186.
Benton, Zebulon, 5, 51.
Berber, Shubel, 86.
Berdslee, Hezekiah, 207.
Berdsley, Phineas, 24.
Berry, John, 315.
Berto, Silas, 207.
Bester, Abel, 186.
Bester, Job, 217.
Bettis, James, Jr., 140.
Betts, 187.
Betts, Daniel, 320.
Betts, David, 313, 330.

INDEX. 381

Betts, Elijah, 262, 286.
Betts, Hezekiah, 324, 339.
Betts, Isaiah, 111.
Betts, James, 8, 23.
Betts, Peter, 116.
Betts, Rheuben, 8.
Betts, Stephen, 304, 313, 329.
Betts, Thomas, 8.
Betts, Thomas, Jr., 8.
Betts, Zopher, 211.
Beull, Joseph, 300.
Beumont, Dan, 291.
Bevens, Ebenezer, 23, 237.
Bevens, Timothy, 316, 347.
Bevin, Thomas, 4.
Bevins, Henry, 209.
Bewel, Daniel, 80.
Bewel, David, 24, 261.
Bewel, Matthew, 11.
Bewil, David, 163.
Bibbins, Timothy, 49.
Bicknal, James, 357.
Bicknal, Josiah, 131.
Bicknal, Moses, 218.
Bicknall, Josiah, 46.
Bidd, Bruster, 113.
Bidwell, Ephraim, 188, 208.
Bidwell, Jonathan, 14.
Bidwell, Jonathan, Jr., 86.
Bidwell, Joseph, 17.
Bidwell, Thomas, 208.
Biel, Hendrick, 273.
Bigelow, Alvin, 226.
Biggelow, Eli, 22.
Biggelow, Fredrick, 203.
Bigsbe, Elias, 24.
Bigsby, Elias, 89, 234.
Bigsby, Solomon, 335.
Biley, John, 304.
Bill, Azariah, 370.
Bill, Berinh, 22, 74, 231.
Bill, Daniel, 6.
Bill, Elijah, 139, 215, 246, 290, 291.
Bill, John, 66, 132.
Bill, Jonathan, 22, 139, 221, 240, 291.
Bill, Jonathan, Jr., 369.
Bill, Jont, 64.
Bill, Joshua, 142, 226, 278, 291.
Bill, Judah, 165.
Bill, Jude, 57, 80.
Bill, Samuel, 291.
Billens, James, 23.
Billens, Steaphen, 23.
Billing, 210.
Billing, Christopher, 149.

Billing, Ezekiel, 50, 68.
Billing, Joseph, 77.
Billing, Roger, 15.
Billing, Stephen, 68, 232.
Billings, Ebenezer, 47.
Billings, James, 233.
Billings, Joseph, 10.
Billings, Peleg, 10, 286.
Billings, Samuel, 189.
Billings, Steaphen, 165.
Billins, Peleg, 262.
Billins, Stephen, Jr., 260.
Bingham, Aaron, 141, 370.
Bingham, Abel, 276, 352.
Bingham, Abishai, 24, 85, 165, 236.
Bingham, Adam, 370.
Bingham, Alfeas, 357.
Bingham, Bartlet, 64, 146, 157.
Bingham, Elias, 85.
Bingham, John, 24, 85, 127, 165, 236.
Bingham, Levy, 127.
Bingham, Luther, 362.
Bingham, Maltier, 128.
Bingham, Samuel, 128.
Bingham, Thamer, 206.
Binns, Thomas, 73.
Birdsly, J., 91, 92.
Bishop, Almeno, 164.
Bishop, Austin, 222.
Bishop, Daniel, 2.
Bishop, David, 22, 120, 123, 154, 165, 234, 261.
Bishop, Elisha, 60, 83.
Bishop, Ezra, 209.
Bishop, James, 4, 197.
Bishop, Joel, 51.
Bishop, John, 66, 113, 334.
Bishop, John, Jr., 75.
Bishop, Johnson, 5.
Bishop, Jonah, 217.
Bishop, Joseph, 211.
Bishop, Leonard, 209.
Bishop, Nathaniel, 8, 22, 74, 164, 229, 231, 260.
Bishop, Nerinh, 5.
Bishop, Richard, 46, 63.
Bishop, Simeon, 260.
Bishop, Thalmeno, 5, 231, 261.
Bishop, Thalmenus, 22.
Bishop, Thomas F., 277, 299, 347.
Bishop, William, 198.
Bishopp, Austin, 186.
Bishopsgate, 254.
Bissel, 48, 88.
Bissel, Benjamin, 163.

Bissel, Elihu, 48.
Bissel, George, 215, 219.
Bissel, John, 24, 48, 240.
Bissel, Justice, 190.
Bissell, Benjamin, 54, 295.
Bissell, Daniel, Jr., 85.
Bissell, Elijah, 203.
Bissell, John, 111.
Bisset, John Patrige, 221.
Bitons, Timothy, 261.
Bivens, Henry, 332.
Bixby, Jacob, 71, 136.
Bixly, Solomon, Jr., 286.
Blachly, Stephen, 53.
Black, Benjamin, 48.
Black, Jesper, 9.
Black, Peter, 274, 352.
Black, Tom, 71.
Blackburn, George, 189, 226.
Blacke, Peter, 211.
Blackley, Joseph, 103.
Blacklidge, 88.
Blackman, 80.
Blackman, Andrew, 123, 154.
Blackman, Dan, 141.
Blackman, Daniel, 4.
Blackman, David, 93, 242.
Blackman, Echabod, 197.
Blackman, Elihu, 58.
Blackman, Elijah, 23, 202, 239.
Blackman, Elisha, 295.
Blackman, Enoch, 202.
Blackman, Isaac, 222.
Blackman, Jeremiah, 58, 93.
Blackman, John, 58, 97.
Blackman, Jonathan, 23, 237.
Blackman, Nathan, 362.
Blackman, Samuel, 58, 93, 242.
Blackman, Timothy, 58, 93.
Blackmar, John, 194.
Blackmer, John, 272.
Blackmer, Stephen, 272.
Blackmore, John, 292.
Blackmore, Steven, 292.
Blacknee, David, 282.
Blacksly, Zelous, 229.
Blaisdell, Roger, 104.
Blake, Christopher, 228.
Blake, Ebenezer, 6, 23, 239.
Blake, Freelove, 7.
Blake, Reuben, 47.
Blake, Thomas, 313, 330.
Blakeley, David, 102.
Blakeley, Enos, 260.
Blakeley, Jonathan, 102.
Blakely, James, 118.
Blakesley, Jared, 164.

Blakesley, Jeremiah, 355.
Blakesley, Joseph, 61.
Blakesly, Jeremiah, 165.
Blakesly, Zealus, 164.
Blakman, John, 4.
Blakslee, Jared, 260.
Blakslee, Samuel, 59, 83.
Blakslee, Zealous, 24, 260.
Blaksley, Samuel, 216.
Blanch, Robin, 261.
Blanchard, Jacob, 114, 233.
Blanchard, Jedediah, 189.
Blanchard, Robbins, 164.
Blanchard, William, 71, 84, 105, 136.
Blancher, Jacob, 116.
Blancherd, Jacobe, 22.
Blancherd, Robbin, 22.
Bland, Robart, 351.
Blenney, Barnabas, 61.
Blin, Abraham, 164, 252.
Blin, Justus, 164, 249.
Blinn, Abraham, 24, 238.
Blinn, Justus, 24, 238.
Blish, Asa, 220.
Bliss, Beriah, 296, 315, 331.
Bliss, Dan, 296.
Bliss, Daniel, 353.
Bliss, Eli, 185.
Bliss, Elias, 141.
Bliss, James, 322, 338.
Bliss, John, 315, 331.
Bliss, Samuel, 15, 296, 314, 331.
Blodget, Artemas, 24, 163, 227, 234, 261.
Blodget, Phinias, 189.
Blodget, Silas, 285.
Bloget, Artemus, 78.
Blogget, Samuel, 18.
Blogget, Silas, 57.
Bloggett, Abijah, 331.
Bloodgood, Isaac, 8.
Bloom, Isaac, 61.
Bloss, John, 281, 302.
Bloss, Joseph, 221.
Blotchet, Silas, 354.
Blush, David, 370.
Blush, David, Jr., 370.
Bly, Rouse, 10.
Boardman, Elijah, 248, 333, 348.
Boardman, Hezekiah, 15.
Boardman, Jonas, 10.
Boardman, Jonathan, 23, 64, 240
Boardman, Moses, 23, 164, 239, 248, 260, 346.
Boardman, Samuel A., 23, 164, 239.

# INDEX. 383

Boardman, William, 226.
Boardmun, John, 77.
Bobinson, Benjamin, 71.
Bocor, Hemon, 12.
Bodwel, Benjamin, 10.
Bodwell, Benjamin, 240.
Bodwill, Benjamin, 81.
Bocny, Ceaser, 192.
Boge, Ichabod, 232.
Boge, Oliver, 187.
Bogers, Hezekiah, 304.
Bogue, Daniel, 205.
Bogue, Ickabud, 23.
Boing, Berrey, 297.
Boise, Thadias, 193.
Bolch, Israel, 199.
Boles, Jeremiah, 142.
Bolles, Isaiah, 359.
Bolles, James, 24.
Bolles, Samuel, 76.
Bolls, Richard, 134.
Bolls, Samuel, 131.
Bolt, Benjamin, 103.
Bolton, 1, 27, 30, 43, 63, 66, 169, 192, 195, 198, 200, 238, 252, 254, 258, 271, 280, 291, 302, 353.
Bond, Bethuel, 297.
Bond, John, 74, 130, 231.
Bond, Joseph, 64, 147.
Bond, Stephen Moulton, 81.
Bonds, Joseph, 150.
Bondy, William, 61.
Boney, Javis, 69.
Bonfoey, Benanual, 164.
Bonfoy, Benanuel, 69.
Bonfoy, Benunuel, 23, 240.
Bonfoy, Henry, 7.
Bonfoy, Jerathmel, 52, 69.
Bonney, Peres, 47.
Bonnum, James, 207.
Bonton, Agar, 275.
Boodish, Asa, 218.
Booge, Richard. 216.
Booman, Job, 350.
Boomer, Job, 322.
Booth, 336.
Booth, Abell, 123.
Booth, David, 186.
Booth, Edward, 228.
Booth, Ernstus, 48.
Booth, Henry. 22, 66, 164, 240, 260, 261, 286, 300, 350.
Booth, J., 92.
Booth, Jeremiah, 284, 351.
Booth, John, 14, 102, 186.
Booth, Joseph, 8.
Booth, Nathaniel, 58, 90, 261.

Booth, Prosper, 153.
Booth, Salvanus, 185.
Booth, Walter, 150, 258, 318, 335.
Bordin, Samuel, 260.
Bordman, David, 15.
Bordman, Elijah, 308.
Bordman, Jonathan, 5, 70.
Bordman, Joseph, 15.
Bordman, Josiah, 63, 252.
Bordslee, John, 207.
Borrows, Joseph, 318, 335.
Bosher, Nicholas, 287.
Bostick, Richard, 197.
Boston, Samuel, 370.
Boston, Toby, 122, 154.
Boston, 14, 367, 369.
Bostwic, Levi, 8.
Bostwick, B., 100.
Bostwick, Daniel, 79, 227, 245, 322, 338.
Bostwick, David, 55, 105.
Bostwick, Ebenezer, 24, 55, 73, 105, 163, 235, 261.
Bostwick, Jonathan, 206.
Bostwick, Jos., 106.
Bostwick, Oliver, 55, 101.
Bostwick, Salmon, 227.
Bostwick, Shedrick, 203.
Bostwick, Solomon, 105.
Bostwick, William, 122.
Bosworth, Aaron, 131.
Bosworth, Daniel, 54, 73, 130.
Bosworth, Jacob, 130, 313, 330.
Botchford, Joel, 7.
Botsford, Abel, 154.
Botsford, Clement, 8.
Botsford, Elijah, 154.
Botsford, Jabez, 8.
Botsford, Jack, 154.
Botsford, Joel, 24, 123, 154, 162, 234.
Botsford, John. 8, 154.
Botsfords, Elijah, 162.
Botsfords, Jabez, 162.
Bottom, 159, 224.
Bottom, Darius, 201.
Bottom, Jabez, 199, 224.
Bottom, John. 24, 53, 235.
Bottom, Joshua. 147.
Boudish, Asa. 214.
Boughton, John. 335.
Bourn, Rawswold. 140.
Bourns, William, 66.
Bourougs, Josiah, 210.
Bourrows, Zebulon. 249.
Bouten, David, 24, 108.
Bouten, John, 109.

Bouten, Joseph, Jr., 111.
Bouten, Simeon, 108.
Boutin, Hezekiah, 283.
Bouton, Eleazor, 8.
Bouton, John, 24, 165.
Bowdish, Asa, 78, 219.
Bowdish, Joseph, 12.
Bowdril, Barzil, 74.
Bowe, Thadias, 193.
Bowen, 133.
Bowen, Azias, 341.
Bowen, Daniel, 86.
Bowen, John, 134.
Bowen, Michael, 98.
Bowers, Benajah, 22, 65, 164, 240.
Bowers, Benjamin, 22, 64, 164, 240.
Bowers, Ephraim, 22, 65, 164, 240, 261, 353.
Bowers, Joab, 353.
Bowers, Zepheniah, 79.
Bowing, Michael, 68.
Bowman, Frederic, 47, 351.
Bowman, Robert, 118.
Bowton, Azer, 349.
Boyd, James, 295.
Boyd, Joseph, 198, 224.
Boydon, Elhanon, 292.
Boyinton, Joseph, 114.
Brace, David, 18.
Bracket, Benajah, 334.
Bracket, Hezekiah, 164, 341.
Brackitt, Hezekiah, 73.
Bradford, 88.
Bradford, Josiah, 363.
Bradford, Thomas, 363.
Bradley, 55, 78, 80, 151, 227.
Bradley, Allen, 256.
Bradley, Ashbel, 69.
Bradley, Asa, 4.
Bradley, D., 206.
Bradley, Dan, 338.
Bradley, Daniel, 22, 67, 164, 230, 261, 293, 303, 308, 337.
Bradley, David, 4, 341.
Bradley, Elijah, 12.
Bradley, Eliphalet, 22, 67, 98, 165, 233, 355.
Bradley, Elisha, 4.
Bradley, James, 78.
Bradley, Jehiel, 61, 100, 339.
Bradley, Joseph, 4.
Bradley, Justice, 4.
Bradley, Nathan, 22, 67, 98, 165, 233.
Bradley, Oliver, 22.
Bradley, Onesimus, 4.
Bradley, Phil., 234.
Bradley, Philip B., 22, 165, 202, 203, 204, 205, 206.
Bradley, Samuel, 4, 204, 222.
Bradley, Zuar, 61, 99, 284.
Bradly, 151.
Bradly, Ashbil, 52.
Bradly, Charls, 151.
Bradly, Daniel, 83.
Bradly, James, 227.
Bradly, Josiah, 18.
Bradly, Oliver, 229.
Bradly, Reuben, 18, 186.
Bradshaw, William, 103.
Bragg, Ebenezer, 5.
Brainard, 88.
Brainard, Gideon, 3.
Brainard, Jonah, 3.
Brainard, Othniel, 65, 353.
Brainerd, Aaron, 5.
Brainerd, David, 6.
Brainerd, Reuben, 6.
Brainerd, Thomas, 6.
Brainerd, Timothy, 51, 70.
Brainord, Encrease, 23, 240.
Braizier, William, 95.
Branard, Othniel, 334.
Branch, 147, 158, 223.
Branch, Joseph, 75, 335.
Branch, Moses, 362, 363.
Branch, William, 74.
Brand, James, 286.
Brandon, Charles, 22, 131.
Brandum, Charles, 236.
Branford, 1, 22, 28, 29, 30, 32, 36, 39, 42, 43, 150, 164, 167, 168, 170, 172, 173, 175, 177, 179, 213, 228, 231, 261, 262, 264, 265, 266, 267, 268, 269, 270, 271, 302, 366.
Brath, Jonas, 7.
Braughton, John, 12.
Bray, John, 139, 291.
Braymon, Daniel, 190, 210.
Braymon, James, 312.
Brayzer, Benjamin, 58.
Breck, John, 54.
Breed, Jabez, 183.
Brewer, Benjamin, 81.
Brewer, Daniel, 23, 70, 164, 186, 237, 258, 261.
Brewer, Daniel, Jr., 226.
Brewer, Joseph, 242, 346.
Brewer, Thomas, 278, 320, 351.
Brewster, 88.
Brewster, Amos, 64, 75.
Brewster, Hez., 165.
Brewster, Hezekiah, 24, 75, 231, 256, 261.

Brewster, Justus, 66, 132.
Brewster, Silas, 9.
Brian, Patrick, 123.
Briant, John, 24, 75, 77, 86, 137, 165, 261.
Briant, Reuben, 76, 159, 280.
Briant, William, 155.
Brice, John, 367.
Brice, Robert, 260, 285, 360.
Briggs, James, 362.
Briggs, Perez, 12.
Briggs, Zebediah, 65, 248.
Brigham, 216.
Brigham, Don Carlos, 357.
Brigham, Jonathan, 50.
Brigham, Paul, 22, 65, 163.
Brightman, Henry, 24, 165, 232, 260, 285.
Brigs, Ephraim, 65.
Brind, Edward, 24.
Brinsmaid, 90.
Brisler, John, 164.
Brister, 141.
Brister, John, 86, 261.
Bristol, Benjamin, 24, 83, 164, 230, 261.
Bristol, Caesar, 166.
Bristol, Dick, 275.
Bristol, Gedeon, 13.
Bristol, Gideon, Jr., 61, 100.
Bristol, Isaac, 215.
Bristol, John, 24.
Bristol, Jonathan, 24, 164, 231, 261.
Bristol, Ruben, 14.
Bristol, Stephen, 288.
Bristol, 366.
Bristoll, Jonathan, 73.
Bristoll, Peter, 73.
Bristor, John, 241, 348.
Bristor, Stephen, 260.
Britman, Henery, 68.
Brittain, 368.
Britton, Samuel, 24, 229.
Brochett, Hezekiah, 229.
Brock, John, 86, 134, 195.
Brocker, Samuel, 186.
Brocket, Hezekiah, 24, 260.
Brockitt, Ebenezer, 60.
Brockitt, Titus, 13.
Brockway, Timothy, 57, 80.
Bronson, Levi, 289.
Brook, Samuel, 154.
Brooks, Abijah, Jr., 46, 131.
Brooks, Abraham, Jr., 6.
Brooks, Asa, 69.
Brooks, Benja, 358.

Brooks, Benjamin, 76, 290, 341, 358.
Brooks, David, 183.
Brooks, Ebenezer, 197.
Brooks, Ichabod, 273, 292.
Brooks, James, 51, 70, 210.
Brooks, Josiah, 17, 194.
Brooks, Noah, 367.
Brooks, Samuel, 5, 119, 359.
Brooks, Samuel Lewis, 94.
Brooks, Thomas, 17, 119, 154, 287, 301.
Brothwell, Fayweather, 4.
Broughton, Ebenezer, 76.
Brown, 218, 219.
Brown, Abnor, 193.
Brown, Abraham, 76, 132.
Brown, Alexand, 12.
Brown, Amasa, 87, 297.
Brown, Ambros, 297.
Brown, Asa, 2.
Brown, Austin, 302, 354.
Brown, Barzilla, 7.
Brown, Benajah, 275.
Brown, Benjamin, 260, 277, 320, 334, 337.
Brown, Briant, 133, 279.
Brown, Charles, 23, 47, 122, 154, 163, 233, 234, 261.
Brown, Christopher, 82, 148, 161, 248.
Brown, Daniel, 8, 48, 111, 134, 151.
Brown, David, 66, 275, 287, 335.
Brown, Dyer, 46.
Brown, Ebenezer, 10, 23, 81, 130, 164, 239, 260, 287, 292, 295.
Brown, Ed., 115.
Brown, Edward, 23, 164, 238, 256, 261, 349.
Brown, Eleazer, 142.
Brown, Elias, 14, 15, 86, 164, 261, 348.
Brown, Elisha, 87.
Brown, Ephraim, 182.
Brown, Ezra, 203.
Brown, Gashom, 66.
Brown, George, 65.
Brown, Gershom, 51, 69.
Brown, Henry, 23, 164, 229, 260.
Brown, Isaac, 58, 87, 92, 115.
Brown, Israel, 51.
Brown, Jacob, 11, 23, 80, 164, 238.
Brown, James, 59, 61, 69, 83, 99, 216, 218, 297, 302.
Brown, Jedidiah, 64, 146, 157.
Brown, Jesse, 47.

Brown, John, 51, 66, 69, 76, 106, 117, 122, 132, 162, 367.
Brown, Jonathan, 2, 8, 22, 77, 151, 239, 262, 285, 313, 330.
Brown, Joshua, 23, 233.
Brown, Josiah, 23, 48, 164, 240.
Brown, Judah, 23.
Brown, Jude, 48, 240.
Brown, Jude C., 349.
Brown, Lucus, 162.
Brown, Luke, 74.
Brown, Nathan. 8, 24, 108.
Brown, Nathaniel, 66, 117.
Brown, Obadiah, 56, 77, 131, 138.
Brown, Oliver, 23, 181, 233.
Brown, Osten, 142.
Brown, Pearly, 15.
Brown, Peleg, 203.
Brown, Philip, 134.
Brown, Reuben, 66, 256.
Brown, Robert, 179.
Brown, Samuel, 66, 85, 127, 128, 362.
Brown, Samuel, Jr., 86, 362.
Brown, Solomon, 121, 162.
Brown, Stephen, 56, 113, 138.
Brown, Thomas, 65, 215, 291, 296, 320, 324, 339.
Brown, Thomas, Jr., 296.
Brown, Timothy, 357.
Brown, Weaver, 102.
Brown, William, 23, 48, 57, 118, 164, 239.
Brown, Zebada, 153.
Brown, Zebedee, 79, 318.
Brownel, Aaron, 63, 64.
Brownell, Robert, 364.
Brownson, Asa, 189.
Brownson, Phineas, 186.
Brownson, Roger, 261, 354.
Bruce, David, 140.
Bruce, Eli, 24, 86.
Bruce, Ely, 133, 229.
Bruce, Robert, 78.
Bruister, Samuel, 141.
Brumbly, Bethuel, 10.
Brumbly, Preserved, 9, 15.
Brumly, William, 24. 233.
Brunson, Asa, 23, 239.
Brunson, Asa, Jr., 49.
Brunson, Benoni, 49.
Brunson, Joel, 27.
Brunson, Orcemus. 206.
Brunson, Roger, 23, 164, 239, 347.
Brunson, Stephen. 49.
Brush, Gibbart, 162.
Brush, Gibbert, 57, 78, 120.
Brush, Zach$^s$, 222.
Bruster, Amos, 147, 150.
Bruster, Samuel, 297.
Bryan, Elijah, 73, 340.
Bryant, Jehiel, 369.
Bryant, John, 56, 231.
Bryant, Reuben, 56, 147, 198, 224, 286, 302.
Bryant, William, 102.
Buck, Amisa, 11.
Buck, Ezekiel, 205.
Buck, Frank, 262, 280, 291, 344.
Buck, George, 189.
Buck, Isaac, 204.
Buck, Josiah, 24, 101, 163, 235.
Buck, Solomon, 49.
Buck, Thomas, 206.
Buckett, Samuel, 276.
Buckin, Nehemiah, 77.
Buckingham, 227.
Buckingham, Gideon, Jr., 79.
Buckingham, George, 209, 279, 300.
Buckingham, Gideon, 279, 300.
Buckingham, Gideon, 2$^d$, 152.
Buckingham, Hezekiah, 152.
*Buckingham, Hezekiah, Jr., 79.
Buckingham, Jered, 361.
Buckingham, Joseph, 141.
Buckingham, Reuben, 152.
Buckingham, Stephen, 295.
Buckland, 63.
Buckland, Stephen, 23, 70, 163, 237, 354.
Buckley, Abraham, 216.
Buckley, Edward, 22, 238.
Buckley, Job, 261.
Buckley, Matthew, 69.
Buckley, Seth, 22, 92, 233.
Buckmaster, George, 50.
Bucley, John, 300.
Buel, Asa, 52, 72.
Buel, Benjamin, 61.
Buel, David, 235.
Buel, Gideon, 211.
Buel, Hezekiah, 291.
Buel, John, 211.
Buel, Joseph, 211.
Buel, Solomon, 10.
Buel, William, 370.
Buell, 199.
Buell, Aaron, 198.
Buell, Benjamin. Jr., 132.
Buell, David, 282.
Buell, Gideon, 281.
Buell, Joseph, 273.
Buffington, Benjamin, 77.

## INDEX.

Buffington, Benjamin, 137.
Bufinton, Benjamin, 56.
Bugbe, Benjamin, 54, 72, 218.
Bugbe, John, 24, 54, 55, 72, 130, 163, 219.
Bugbee, Abijah, 133.
Bugbee, Benjamin, 49, 66.
Bugbee, John, 183, 236, 261, 282.
Bugbee, Pelatiah, 260, 280.
Bugbee, Peter, 189.
Bugbee, Samuel, 56, 77, 138.
Buird, Joseph, 216.
Bulford, John, 61, 100.
Bulkley, Abraham, 361.
Bulkley, Calvin, 282.
Bulkley, Charles, 252.
Bulkley, Edward, 164, 248, 249, 303, 308.
Bulkley, Job, 279.
Bulkley, Nathan, Jr., 68.
Bulkley, Seth, 68, 95, 165.
Bulkley, William, 361.
Bull, Epaphras, 237, 261, 354.
Bull, Eppiphras, 23, 163.
Bull, John, 23.
Bullen, David, 328.
Bullen, David, Jr., 49, 66.
Buller, Asa, 57.
Buller, Benjamin, 57, 59.
Buller, Solomon, 6.
Buller, Zebulon, 190.
Bullin, Benjamin, 82.
Bullin, David, 305, 350.
Bullock, Jonathan, 46, 56, 77, 131, 138, 301, 308, 334.
Bunc, Thomas, 348.
Bunce, Asa, 52, 70, 194, 226.
Bunce, Isaiah, 55, 74, 106, 163, 236.
Bunce, Jared, 245, 318, 335, 348.
Bunday, Joshua, 78.
Bunday, William, 102.
Bunde, Simeon, 128.
Bundy, Nathaniel, 135.
Bundy, Thomas, 78.
Bunn, Paul, 6.
Bunnal, Amos, 86, 350.
Bunnel, Abraham, 2, 22.
Bunnel, Amos, 261, 276.
Bunnel, John, 2.
Bunnel, Joseph, 309, 334.
Bunnel, Levi, 60.
Bunnell, Abraham, 164.
Bunnil, Abraham, 231.
Bunnil, Samuel, 14.
Buns, Isaiah, Sr., 24.
Buns, Isaiah, Jr., 24.

Buntin, William, 60.
Bunts, Josiah, 235.
Burchard, Daniel, 11.
Burchard, Elias, 356.
Burchard, Roger, 196.
Burden, Benjamin, 13.
Burden, Samuel, 65, 132.
Burdges, Lott, 191.
Burdon, Samuel, 286.
Burdsey, Thedeous, 199.
Burdseye, Thads, 199.
Burge, Hosea, 140, 247.
Burges, Asa, 19.
Burges, Charles, 363.
Burges, Edward, 186, 305, 330, 354.
Burges, Ephraim, 261, 279, 311, 350.
Burges, Ephraim, Jr., 279.
Burges, Joseph, 362.
Burges, Samuel, 275.
Burgess, Ephraim, 344.
Burgh, Jared, 196.
Burghes, Edward, 315.
Burk, Elackander, 73.
Burk, George, 226.
Burk, John, 24, 164, 231, 261.
Burley, Aseph, 192, 226.
Burley, John, 116.
Burlington, 228.
Burn, Benjamin, 73.
Burn, Thomas, 81.
Burnal, Amos, 134.
Burnam, Asa, 10.
Burnam, David, 186.
Burnam, Elijah, 146.
Burnam, Jesse, 357.
Burnam, John, 68, 84.
Burnam, Joseph, 232.
Burnam, Nathan, 84.
Burnam, William, 357.
Burnan, Zeanas, 185.
Burnap, Benjamin, 24, 84, 165, 236, 355.
Burnap, Calvin, 85.
Burnap, James, 84.
Burnap, John, 362.
Burnel, Samuel, 361.
Burnet, James, 128.
Burnett, Dennis, 208.
Burnham, 88.
Burnham, Asa, 71, 77, 232, 235.
Burnham, Benjamin, 289.
Burnham, Eliphalet, 342.
Burnham, John, 50, 242, 366.
Burnham, Joseph, 260.
Burnham, Josiah, 64, 85, 128, 157.

Burnham, Stephen, 226.
Burnham, William, 87.
Burnham, Zenas, 226.
Burningham, Anthony, 199.
Burns, James, 121.
Burns, John, 87, 100.
Burns, Jules, 66.
Burns, Julius, 132.
Burns, William, 132, 311.
Burnside, Henry, 78.
Burnum, Asa, 23.
Burnum, Joseph, 23.
Burr, Andrew, 1.
Burr, Daniel, 22, 67, 95, 233.
Burr, David, 3d, 3.
Burr, Edmund, 367.
Burr, G., 95.
Burr, Jehiel, 203.
Burr, Seth, 274.
Burr, Stephen, 52, 69.
Burr, Zebinah, 11.
Burras, Hubbard, 332.
Burras, William, 344.
Burrell, Thomas, 332.
Burret, Abijah, 89.
Burret, Israel, 154.
Burrill, Joseph, 11.
Burrit, Charles, 66.
Burrit, Israel, 119.
Burrit, Zalmon, 214, 222.
Burritt, Charles, 58, 94.
Burritt, Isael, 8.
Burroos, Zebulon, 48.
Burros, Jonathan, 12.
Burroughs, 92.
Burroughs, Samuel, 164.
Burrows, Hubbard, 281, 316, 332.
Burrows, J. Procter, 81.
Burrows, Joseph, 318.
Burrows, Josiah, 234.
Burrus, John Proct, 59.
Burrus, Josiah, 24.
Burrus, William, 287, 311.
Burt, John, 362.
Burt, Josiah, 54, 73, 129.
Burt, William, 370.
Burton, Abel, 251.
Burton, Daniel, 193.
Burton, Henry, 15.
Burton, Isaac, 15.
Burton, Jacob, 10, 77.
Burton, Luis, 210.
Burton, Nathan, 15.
Burton, Robert, 104.
Bush, Asael, 368.
Bush, John, 136.
Bush, Samuel, 114, 322, 341.

Bushnal, Daniel, 23.
Bushnal, Ruben, 300.
Bushnel, Chester, 300.
Bushnel, Constant, 261, 300.
Bushnel, Daniel, 6.
Bushnell, Constant, 279.
Bushnell, Daniel, 71, 256, 261, 308, 335.
Bushnell, Francis, 361.
Bushnell, James, 361.
Bushnell, Reuben, 279.
Bushnell, Zebulon, 279.
Bushnul, Daniel, 236.
Butlar, John, 13.
Butler, Asa, 81, 249.
Butler, Benjamin, 1, 49, 66, 81, 139, 350.
Butler, David, 280, 346.
Butler, Ely, 7.
Butler, Ezekiel, 340.
Butler, Isaac, 209.
Butler, Isaiah, Jr., 6.
Butler, Israel, 57, 81.
Butler, John, 22, 121, 140, 162, 237, 290, 360.
Butler, Jonathan, 71, 79, 252.
Butler, Matthew, 2.
Butler, Peter, 22, 65, 164, 240, 250.
Butler, Solomon, 6.
Butler, Stephen, 22, 67, 79, 182, 232, 252, 305, 328.
Butler, Walter, 1, 22.
Butler, Walton, 234.
Butler, William, 6, 9, 260, 282, 332.
Butler, Zebulon, 185, 186, 187, 188, 189, 190.
Butlor, Benjamin, 208.
Buts, James, 237.
Butt, 156, 223.
Butt, Josiah, 319, 336.
Buttan, Danil, 197.
Buttock, Jonathan, 273.
Buttolph, Daniel, 11.
Buttolph, Joel, 145.
Button, Joshua, 186.
Button, Josiah, 186.
Butts, Esaias, 312, 344.
Butts, Josiah, 363.
Butts, Sherebiah, 146.
Byington, Benjamin, 112.
Byington, Isaac, 49.
Byintun, Ebenezer, 2.
Byintun, Jonathan, 2.
Byne, Jeremiah, 89.
Byshup, David, 154.

Cable, David, 214.
Cable, Elijah, 4.
Cable, Josiah, 97.
Cable, Nehemiah, 4.
Cable, Wheeler, 4.
Cable, William, 25, 96, 233.
Caby, Isaac, 79.
Cade, Abijah, 237.
Cade, Darius, 233.
Cadwell, Matthew, 26, 70, 166, 238, 252, 262, 346.
Cadwell, Phineas, 252.
Cadwell, Reuben, 144, 245, 305, 328, 345.
Cadwell, Simeon, 26, 233.
Cady, 225.
Cady, Abner, 181.
Cady, Abijah, 25, 64, 146, 156.
Cady, Benjamin, 135, 284, 323, 341.
Cady, Benjamin, 3d, 71.
Cady, Cesar, 215.
Cady, D., 136, 161.
Cady, Daniel, 60, 83.
Cady, Darius, 25.
Cady, David, 82.
Cady, J., 135.
Cady, Jedediah, 181.
Cady, Justin, 273, 292.
Cady, Penual, 135.
Cady, Samuel, 56, 77, 138.
Caesar, Bristol, 262, 338.
Cage, Nehemiah, 59.
Cahales, Cornelius, 26, 29, 231.
Calahan, Andrew, 206.
Cale, Timothy, 242.
Calif, Steaphen, 128.
Calihan, Thomas, 102.
Calkens, Israel, 26.
Calkin, Abner, 80.
Calkin, Derias, 57.
Calkin, Stephen, 75.
Calkins, Israel, 84, 230.
Call, John, 71.
Cambell, John, 77.
Cambell, Peter, 357.
Camberlin, Plina, 183.
Cambridge, Kay, 347.
Cambridge, Mass., 365.
Cammell, Daniel, 78.
Camp, Aaron, 2.
Camp, Belliel, 199.
Camp, Bethel, 288.
Camp, Eldad, 53.
Camp, Isaac, 26, 166, 239.
Camp, John, 59.
Camp, Phineas, 26, 99, 235.

Camp, Samuel, 26, 84, 166, 230.
Camp, Samuel, Jr., 26, 84, 230.
Camp, Simeon, 56, 77, 86, 134.
Camp Highlands, 195, 214.
Camp Highlands, see Highlands.
Campbel, 160.
Campbel, Archabel, 363.
Campbel, James, 363.
Campbel, William, 129.
Campbell, 225.
Campbell, David, 12.
Campbell, John, 138.
Campbell, Moses, 148.
Campbell, Noble, 12.
Campbell, Robert, 12, 82, 148, 160.
Campbill, William, 179.
Canada, Asa, 215.
Canaan, 25, 28, 29, 30, 46, 63, 189, 202, 206, 207, 208, 211, 214, 228, 236, 279.
Canada, David, 26, 238.
Canada, Seth, 190.
Canady, David, 194, 196.
Canady, Hugh, 198, 224.
Canndy, William, 112, 113.
Canary, Martin, 351.
Cande, Gideon, 2.
Cande, Zacheus, 208.
Canfield, Abial, 53, 65, 235.
Canfield, Andrew, 203.
Canfield, Azariah, 101.
Canfield, Daniel, 98, 120, 162.
Canfield, David, 2.
Canfield, Elijah, 26, 55, 74, 101, 166, 235.
Canfield, Ezekel, 3.
Canfield, Ichabod, 3.
Canfield, Reuben, 2.
Canfield, Titus, 200.
Cannady, David, 226.
Cannan, Thomas, 155.
Cant,, 33.
Canterbury, 19, 21, 22, 25, 27, 28, 29, 39, 42, 64, 138, 146, 150, 151, 156, 157, 158, 159, 161, 163, 166, 171, 175, 176, 181, 213, 217, 223, 225, 237, 260, 262, 263, 264, 266, 269, 270, 277, 287, 288, 297, 302, 358.
Can[ ]y, 158.
Capron, Jeremiah, 75.
Car, James, 26.
Card, Elisha, 225.
Carew, Semeon, 199.
Carey, Ebenezer, 357.
Carey, George, 262.
Carey, Walter, 180.

Carlton, Darius, 12.
Carlton, John, 12.
Carlton, Richard, 12, 66, 82, 132.
Carmon, John, 222.
Carpenter, 370.
Carpenter, Allen, 84.
Carpenter, Comfort, 12.
Carpenter, David, 179, 218.
Carpenter, Elias, 285, 311, 328.
Carpenter, Elijah, 133.
Carpenter, Eliphalet, 215, 285, 311, 344.
Carpenter, Henry, 136, 149, 160.
Carpenter, John, 18.
Carpenter, Joshua, 139, 256.
Carpenter, Nathan, 84.
Carpenter, Noah, 133, 218.
Carpenter, Samuel, 294.
Carpentor, Comfort, 183.
Carpentor, Henry, 82.
Carpinter, Elias, 306.
Carr, Clement, 273.
Carr, Ebenezer, 273, 338.
Carr, James, 75.
Carr, James Miller, 231.
Carr, Robert, 278, 347.
Carr, Ruben, 299.
Carr, William, 341.
Carr, William, Jr., 66.
Carrel, Joseph, 136.
Carrell, John, 262, 349.
Carril, John, 166.
Carril, Nathaniel, 137.
Carrill, John, 355.
Carrior, John, 221.
Carry, George, 353.
Cart, William, 56, 77.
Carter, Aaron, 25, 65, 166, 240, 262, 353, 355.
Carter, Asher, 47.
Carter, Daniel, 53.
Carter, Edward, 25, 166, 240, 262, 351.
Carter, Enoch, 63.
Carter, Esau, 351.
Carter, Heman, 282.
Carter, J., 106.
Carter, James, 25, 237.
Carter, John, Jr., 277, 281.
Carter, Jonah, 273.
Carter, Nathan, 263, 275.
Carter, Reuben, 25, 64, 146, 157, 166, 237, 262, 343.
Carter, Thadeous, 13.
Carter, William, 3.
Cartwright, Cyrus, 56.
Carver, John, 206.

Carver, Joseph, 1.
Carver, Nathaniel, 19.
Carwin, Selah, 166.
Cary, Benjamin, 199.
Cary, Benjamin, Jr., 85, 128.
Cary, Ebenezer, 218.
Cary, Ezra, 149.
Cary, George, 166.
Cary, Hezekiah, 85, 246, 321, 338.
Cary, Jabez, 180.
Cary, Levi, 85.
Cary, Nathaniel, Jr., 54, 73, 129.
Cary, Oliver, 85.
Case, Aaron, 364.
Case, Abel, 349.
Case, Abraham, Jr., 11.
Case, Amasa, Jr., 143.
Case, Amos, 145.
Case, Asa, 144.
Case, Caleb, 204.
Case, Elisha, 81.
Case, Ezekiel, 14.
Case, Ezekil, Jr., 86.
Case, Ichabod, 315, 331.
Case, Jeremiah, 262, 275, 349.
Case, Jonah, 139.
Case, Jonathan, 276.
Case, Joseph Wain, 142.
Case, Judah, 204.
Case, Lemuel, 139.
Case, Lumey, 73, 130.
Case, Lummin, 54.
Case, Martin, 10.
Case, Micah, 11.
Case, Nehemiah, 59.
Case, Oliver, 10.
Case, Pliney, 11.
Case, Reuben, 143.
Case, Richard, 26, 70, 165, 237, 262, 342, 345.
Case, Ros, 144.
Case, Roswell, 204.
Case, Rufus, 143.
Case, William, 11.
Casey, John, 302.
Cash, 139.
Cass, Jeremy, 209.
Cass, Silas G., 319.
Caswell, Ezra, 263.
Caswell, Ezrael, 140.
Catlin, Abraham, 6.
Catlin, Eli, 6, 55.
Catlin, Elisha, 319, 337.
Catlin, Hezekiah, 279, 318, 336.
Catlin, Putnam, 53.
Catlin, Roswell, 71, 213.
Catling, Aling, 187.

INDEX.   391

Cato, 284.
Caverle, Samuel, 366.
Cay, David, 154.
Ceabury, James, 340.
Ceaser, 58.
Ceaser, Negro, 12.
Cebra, James, 73.
Center, John, 183.
Cesar, 56, 141.
Chace, Benjamin, 362.
Chace, Joseph, 65.
Chadwick, James, 52, 70, 242, 306, 316, 332, 345.
Chadwick, John, 26.
Chadwick, Nathan, 287.
Chadwick, William, 243.
Chafe, Cyrus, 130.
Chafe, Serel, 18.
Chafee, Abiel, 272.
Chafee, Calvin, 294.
Chafee, James, Jr., 134.
Chafee, William, 195.
Chaffe, Abiel, 194.
Chaffe, Calvin, 306.
Chaffe, Charles, 194.
Chaffee, Abial, 292, 325, 326.
Chaffee, Calvin, 316, 326, 328.
Chaffee, Samuel, 183.
Chamberlane, Ephriam, 165.
Chaimberlane, Luther, 54.
Chaimberlen, Luther, 130.
Chaimberlen, Seth, 130.
Chaise, Walter, 85.
Chalker, Isaac, 5.
Chalker, Jesse, 79, 252.
Chalman, Reuben, 273.
Chamberlain, 209.
Chamberlain, Eph, 292.
Chamberlain, Ephraim, 82, 230, 262.
Chamberlain, Jeremiah, 352.
Chamberlain, Jeret, 305.
Chamberlain, Joseph, 352.
Chamberlain, Samuel, 104.
Chamberlain, Swift, 285.
Chamberlain, Theodore, 52, 70, 346.
Chamberlin, Aaron, 87, 197.
Chamberlin, Bartlet, 364.
Chamberlin, Ephraim, 13, 26.
Chamberlin, Esre, 133.
Chamberlin, Jeremiah, 317.
Chamberlin, Jirah, 364.
Chamberlin, Joseph, 336.
Chambers, John, 78.
Chambers, William, 25, 63, 236.
Champen, Samuel, 150.

Champhilet, Stanliff, 203.
Champion, 145.
Champlin, Joseph S., 286.
Chandler, 46, 135, 359.
Chandler, Isaac, 86, 241.
Chandler, James, 181, 218.
Chandler, Joseph, 25, 66, 166, 240.
Chandler, Robert, 86, 134, 309, 334.
Chanler, 150.
Chapel, Curtis, 336.
Chapel, Guy, 181.
Chapel, Russell, 76, 263.
Chapel, Stephen, 216.
Chapel, William, 3d, 360.
Chapell, Roswel, 351.
Chapen, Asa, 203.
Chapen, Ezra, 63.
Chapen, Hiel, 63.
Chapens, Daniel, 18.
Chapin, David, 250.
Chapin, Ichabud, 209.
Chapin, Jehiel, 247.
Chapin, Oliver, 18.
Chapin, Phinehas, 243.
Chapin, Timothy, 243.
Chapin, Tomo, 48.
Chapman, 80, 203, 206.
Chapman, Abner, 56, 77, 87, 138.
Chapman, Adi, 290.
Chapman, Adino, 319.
Chapman, Adrin, 319.
Chapman, Albert, 67, 165.
Chapman, Amos, 159.
Chapman, Benjamin, 214.
Chapman, Cesar, 51, 70, 353.
Chapman, Collaris, 153.
Chapman, Collins, 25, 47, 124, 165, 234.
Chapman, Comfort, 272, 311, 344.
Chapman, Constant, 79, 279, 335.
Chapman, Cornelus, 300.
Chapman, Dan, 79, 150.
Chapman, Dan[   ], 25.
Chapman, Daniel, 232.
Chapman, David, 47, 69, 151, 212.
Chapman, Ebenezer, 322.
Chapman, Edward, 262, 287, 354.
Chapman, Elijah, 81, 103.
Chapman, Elisha, 153.
Chapman, Elius, 131.
Chapman, Gideon, 47.
Chapman, James, 67, 165.
Chapman, Jediah, Jr., 79.
Chapman, Jeremiah, 1, 342.
Chapman, John, 25.
Chapman, Jonathan, 158.

Chapman, Joseph, 25, 74, 142, 165, 197, 231, 262.
Chapman, N., 102.
Chapman, Nathaniel, 281.
Chapman, Oliver, 183.
Chapman, Reuben, 4.
Chapman, Rufus, 262.
Chapman, Samuel, 3, 97, 340, 352.
Chapman, Stephen, 49.
Chapman, Stephen, Jr., 347.
Chapman, Thomas, 219, 227.
Chapman, Timothy, 58, 353.
Chapman, William, 79, 252.
Chapman, Zach[b], 179.
Chapmon, Elijah, 12.
Chappee, Steaphen, 356.
Chappel, Alpheus, 359.
Chappel, Amaziah, 26, 139, 237, 248.
Chappel, Benjamin, 359.
Chappel, Bruister, 140.
Chappel, Comfort, 26.
Chappel, Curtice, 26, 78.
Chappel, Curtis, 234, 262, 359.
Chappel, Joshua, 26.
Chappel, Noah, 369.
Chappel, Roswel, 87.
Chappel, Rufas, 358.
Chappel, Solomon, 63.
Chappel, William, 359.
Chappel. William 3[d], 26.
Chappell, Alpheus, 290.
Chappell, Benjamin, Jr., 290.
Chappell, Brewster, 256.
Chappell, Noah, 65, 290.
Chappell, William, 290.
Chapple, Noah, 132.
Chappman, Amos, 256.
Chaps, John, 92.
Chard, Joseph, 8.
Chard, Samuel, 8.
Charter, Levi, 48, 86.
Chase, Aaron, 240.
Chase, Jared, 8.
Chase. Lot, 76, 147, 159.
Chase, Samuel, 188.
Chase, Walter, 26, 70, 127, 240.
Chatfield, Caleb, 2, 58, 91.
Chatfield, Dan, 273.
Chatfield, John, 53, 72, 166, 262.
Chatfield, Jonathan, 212.
Chatfield, Josiah, 300.
Chatfield, Josiah, 2[d], 281.
Chatfield, Lemuel, 210.
Chatfield, Levi, 48.
Chatfield, Oliver, 2.
Chatham, 22, 25, 29, 30, 32, 34, 36, 38, 39, 41, 42, 43, 64, 88, 164, 166, 167, 168, 171, 172, 173, 175, 176, 193, 213, 215, 240, 248, 249, 250, 261, 262, 264, 266, 267, 268, 269, 270, 271, 284, 286, 302, 353, 355, 367.
Chatman, Timothy, 91.
Cheapeak, Simon, 68.
Chedsey, William, 208.
Cheem, Joseph, 323.
Cheeney, Ebenezer, 237.
Cheeney, Joseph, 284.
Cheese, Samuel, 272, 292, 334.
Cheets, Isaac, 130.
Cheilds, Joseph, 365.
Cheney, Aseal, 193.
Cheney, Daniel, 203.
Cheney, Ebenezer, 25, 77, 131, 138, 166.
Cheney, Elijah, 56, 77, 137.
Cheney, John, 56, 77, 137.
Cheney, Joseph, 323.
Cheney, Richard, 25, 165, 235, 355.
Cheshire, Joseph, 114.
Cheshire, 164, 170, 172, 176, 196, 197, 207, 261, 267, 271, 275.
Chester, Christopher, 50, 69.
Chester, David, 285, 323, 341.
Chester, Jones, 300.
Chester, Lemuel, 51, 69.
Chester, 171.
Chidsey, Ephraim, 1.
Chidsey, Roswell, 1.
Child, Josiah, 136.
Child, Josiah D., 292.
Child, Pennel, 71.
Child, Penuel, 135.
Child, Stephen, 285.
Childs, Harbe, 295.
Childs, Josiah D., 272.
Childs, Stephen, 318, 336.
Chilson, Jonathan, 13, 362.
Chipman, John, 165, 262.
Chipman, Thomas, 78.
Chipman, Timothy, 65.
Chipman, Jonathan, 147.
Chittenden, Benjamin, 13.
Chittenden, Cornelius, 273.
Chittenden, Daniel, 215.
Chittenden, Daniel Jr., 5.
Chittenden, Eber, 53.
Chittenden, Gideon, 2.
Chittenden, James, 52, 72.
Chittenden, Jared, 5, 51.
Chittenden, John, 53, 72.
Chittenden, Nathaniel, 281, 300.
Chittenden, Reuben, 52, 72.

INDEX. 393

Chittenden, Simeon, 4.
Chittenden, Simeon, Jr., 5.
Chittenden, Solomon, 274, 300.
Chittenden, William, 51.
Chmstock, Samuel, 215.
Choat, Jabez, 76.
Choichoi, Simon, 76.
Chops, John, 58.
Chrittendon, Gideon, 66.
Chubbuck, Ebenezar, 206.
Chuble, William, 273.
Chudle, Elijah, 197.
Church, Benedict, 181.
Church, Ebenezer, 26, 63, 103, 165, 235.
Church, Eli, 200.
Church, Elihu, 352.
Church, Ely, 218.
Church, Euriah, 6.
Church, Gideon, 302.
Church, James, 294, 318.
Church, Lemuil, 190.
Church, Moses, 61.
Church, Samson, 73.
Church, Samuel, 26, 69, 80, 145, 166, 240.
Church, Willard, 54, 73, 129.
Churchel, Elijah, 25.
Churchel, Jesse, 17.
Churchel, Joseph, 17.
Churchel, Oliver, 216.
Churchel, Sage, 347.
Churchell, John, 325.
Churchell, Sage, 299.
Churchet, Paschal, 97.
Churchil. Elijah, 48, 350.
Churchill, Charles, 252.
Churchill, Elijah, 166, 240, 262.
Churchill, Moses, 103.
Churchill, Sage, 277.
Cinnamon, Joshua, 159.
Cinnamon, Thomas, 233.
Claghorn, Eleazer, 165.
Claghorn, Elezer, 78.
Clain, Amos, 147, 158.
Clanghorn, Eleazer, 26.
Clankhorn, Eleazer. 234.
Clap. Nathan, 166, 237.
Clapham, George, 154.
Clapp. Nathan, 25.
Clarage, Francis. 152.
Clarck, Moses, 256.
Clark, 88.
Clark, Aaron, 25, 69, 83, 166, 346.
Clark, Abel, 60, 83.
Clark, Abraham, 25, 70, 165, 238, 262, 241, 345.

Clark, Amos, 73, 103, 185, 333.
Clark, Andrew, 297.
Clark, Asael, 25, 133, 229.
Clark, Ashbel, 361.
Clark, Augustus, 339.
Clark, Barabas, 50.
Clark, Barnabas, 350.
Clark, Bemond, 361.
Clark, Benjamin, 130, 298.
Clark, Charles, 352.
Clark, Daniel, 203.
Clark, David, 25, 48, 81, 312, 344, 350.
Clark, Dimond, 83.
Clark, Divan, 60, 83.
Clark, Ebenezer, 221.
Clark, Elias, 193.
Clark, Elijah, 73, 81, 150, 346, 349.
Clark, Ephram, 2.
Clark, Ezekiel, Jr., 86.
Clark, Flaviel, 140.
Clark, George, 73, 273, 280.
Clark, George, Jr., 150.
Clark, Hezekiah, 52, 69, 210.
Clark, Hugh, 8.
Clark, Ithurel, 262.
Clark, Jacob, 2, 25, 76, 165, 231.
Clark, James, 25, 64, 147, 153, 156, 238.
Clark, Joel, 25, 166, 213, 229, 279, 291, 302, 318, 335, 355.
Clark, John, 25, 147, 159, 166, 295, 316, 332.
Clark, John, Jr., 139.
Clark, John, 2d, 333.
Clark, John, 3d, 279, 291.
Clark, Jonathan, 6.
Clark, Joseph, 5, 58, 59, 83, 101, 139, 180, 309, 329, 331, 333.
Clark, Josiah, 194.
Clark, Lamberton, 346.
Clark, Lyman, 25, 166, 194, 239, 355.
Clark, Mark, 196.
Clark, Martin, 8, 25, 150, 166, 229, 262.
Clark, Matt, 8.
Clark, Matthew, 124, 154, 222.
Clark, Michael, 274, 352.
Clark, Nathan, 356.
Clark, Nathaniel, 262, 273.
Clark, Oliver, 14, 211.
Clark, Othniel, 6, 25, 166, 239, 262.
Clark, Pinkerman, 91.
Clark, Reuben, 11, 321.

Clark, Richard, 25, 68, 84, 230.
Clark, Robert, 5.
Clark, Samuel, 25, 75, 113, 165, 240, 241, 362.
Clark, Samuel, Jr., 79.
Clark, Solomon, Jr., 14.
Clark, Sylvenus, 6.
Clark, Thomas, 366.
Clark, Timothy, 183, 220.
Clark, Uriah, 118.
Clark, William, 2, 25, 52, 70, 81, 197, 252, 262, 290, 325, 348.
Clark, Zebulon Lewis, 2.
Clark, Zepheniah, 53.
Clarke, John, 61.
Clarke, Joseph, 55.
Clarke, Moses, Jr., 139.
Clarrage, Francis, 262.
Clarriage, Francis, 166.
Clase, Odle, 117.
Clealand, William, 195.
Cleary, Ezekiel, 197.
Cleaveland, 88.
Cleaveland, Asa, 294.
Cleaveland, Curtice, 337.
Cleaveland, Curtis, 262, 277.
Cleaveland, Dyar, 53.
Cleaveland, Fredrick, 193.
Cleaveland, Gardner, 193, 284, 337.
Cleaveland, John, 15, 25, 166, 233, 262.
Cleaveland, Jonas, 25.
Cleaveland, Josiah, 25, 79, 165.
Cleaveland, Moses, 25.
Cleaveland, Samuel, 56, 193, 223.
Cleaveland, Squre, 363.
Cleaveland, Timothy, 25.
Cleaveland, William, 56.
Cleavland, Curtice, 320.
Cleavland, Gardner, 320.
Cleavland, Jacob, 146.
Cleavland, John, 147.
Cleavland, John, Jr., 146.
Cleavland, Samuel, 77.
Cleavland, Samuel, Jr., 297.
Cleavland, William, 77.
Cleff, Lemuel, 26.
Cleft, Lemuel, 76, 166, 237, 262.
Cleft, Wills, 76.
Clemons, Reuben, 227.
Clemons, Richard, 71.
Clenton, Joseph, 8.
Clergio, Francy, 156.
Clerk, Amos, 61.
Clerk, David, 11, 229.
Clerk, John, 237.
Clerk, Neil, 7.
Clerk, Stephen, 68.
Clerk, William, Jr., 12.
Cleveland, Curtis, 19.
Cleveland, Jacob, 64.
Cleveland, Joen, 64.
Cleveland, John, 80, 108, 157, 158, 237.
Cleveland, John, Jr., 64.
Cleveland, Josiah, 236.
Cleveland, Moses, 64, 237.
Cleveland, Samuel, 158.
Cleveland, Solemn, 19.
Cleveland, Timothy, 64, 237.
Cleveland, Tracy, 19.
Clevland, William, 137.
Clift, 193, 199.
Clift, Hezekiah, 199.
Clinton, Joseph, 305, 324, 341.
Clinton, Levi, 111.
Clorck, Elifelet, 72.
Closby, Timothy, 284.
Close, Samuel, 115.
Clough, Isaac, 53.
Clough, Uriah, 18.
Coal, James, 4.
Coal, Nathan, 200.
Coals, Benjamin, Jr., 131.
Coble, Thomas, 145.
Cobom, Samuel, 147.
Coburn, Edward, 85, 128.
Coburn, Eliphelet, 199.
Coburn, James, 60, 83, 330.
Coburn, Joseph, 60, 83.
Coburn, Samuel, 25, 64, 158, 237.
Cocheits, Isaac, 76.
Cockran, Christopher, 101.
Coe, Abner, 318.
Coe, Eh., 92.
Coe, Jedediah, 210.
Coe, Jonathan, 361.
Coe, Oliver, 189, 319, 336.
Coe, Robert, 187.
Coe, Samuel, 49.
Coe, Zachariah, 215.
Coedry, Joseph, 262.
Cofrin, Samuel, 61.
Cogin, David, 25, 233.
Coggins, David, 67, 165.
Coggins, John, 68.
Cogswell, Asa, 211.
Cogswell, John, 15.
Cogswell, Nathan, 15.
Cogswell, Samuel, 85.
Cogswell, W., 106.
Cohale, Cornelius, 166, 167, 262.
Coit, Daniel, 77.

INDEX. 395

Coit, Farewell, 10.
Coit, George, 179.
Coit, Isaac, 77.
Coit, Richard, 281.
Coit, Roger, 10.
Colchester, 22, 25, 27, 28, 29, 32, 33, 36, 38, 40, 42, 43, 47, 87, 88, 138, 150, 164, 166, 167, 168, 173, 175, 177, 181, 182, 193, 197, 200, 212, 214, 215, 223, 227, 240, 261, 262, 263, 264, 265, 266, 268, 269, 270, 283, 284, 286, 287, 291, 301, 356, 367.
Cole, Abin, 109.
Cole, Abner, 64, 333.
Cole, Alben, 27, 165.
Cole, Alvin, 8.
Cole, Benjamin, 347.
Cole, David, 55, 101.
Cole, Elisha, 252.
Cole, Jabez, 322, 338.
Cole, James, 49, 96.
Cole, John, 25, 84, 230, 239.
Cole, Josiah, 50.
Cole, Marcus, 25, 64, 240.
Cole, Phinias, 213.
Cole, Reubin, 49.
Cole, Samuel, 25, 214, 238, 252.
Cole, Tabor, 322.
Colebrook, 40, 65, 175, 206, 235, 253, 255, 269.
Colefax, Robart, 243.
Colefox, Jonathan, 76.
Colefox, William, 26.
Colegrove, Andrew, 179.
Colegrove, Benjamin, 363.
Colegrove, Christopher, 148.
Coleman, Noah, 26, 237.
Coley, Nathan, 89, 263.
Coley, Reuben, 80, 202.
Colfax, William, 290.
Colkin, Abner, 57.
Colkin, Derias, 80.
Collar, Isaac, 153.
Collen, Isaac, 119, 123.
Coller, Isaac, 364.
Coller, Norise, 364.
Coller, Oliver, 205.
Collet, Thomas, 49, 348.
Collings, Joseph, 8.
Collins, 358.
Collins, Abel, 205.
Collins, Abijah, 367.
Collins, Benjamin, 357.
Collins, Cyprian, 274.
Collins, Daniel, 209.
Collins, Joseph, 216.

Collins, Josiah, 363.
Collins, Moses, 347.
Collins, Pell, 182.
Collins, Samuel, 13, 60, 83, 367.
Collins, William L., 165.
Collins, William Lock, 26, 234.
Collon, Rowland, 137.
Collyer, Joseph, 53.
Colman, John, Jr., 295.
Colt, Jabez, 276, 348.
Colt, Jabish, 299.
Colton, Eliakim, 206.
Colton, Isaac, 275, 354.
Colton, Ithimar, 206.
Columbus, James, 53.
Colver, David, 142.
Colver, John, 142.
Colver, Joseph, 51.
Comba, John, 295.
Combs, William, 26, 70, 237, 346.
Comes, John, 18.
Comes, William, 238.
Comestock, Gideon, 26.
Comestock, John, 26.
Comstock, Samuel, 26, 165.
Comey, Allen, 165.
Comey, Mallehi, 165.
Comin, Daniel, 290.
Commins, Simeon, 280.
Commins, William, 222.
Commins, Wilson, 322, 337.
Comstalk, Cuff, 103.
Comstalk, Theophilus, 101.
Comstick, Samuel, 50.
Comstock, 215.
Comstock, Achilles, 205.
Comstock, Gideon, 75, 165, 231, 355.
Comstock, James, 361.
Comstock, Samuel, 25, 165, 232, 262, 263, 280, 355.
Comstock, Samuel, Jr., 79.
Comstock, Serajah, 262, 273, 318, 336.
Comstock, Simn, 50.
Comstock, Simeon, 68.
Comstock, Theophilus, 55.
Conant, Amos, 179, 356.
Conant, Caleb, 26, 54, 55, 56, 72, 77, 129, 138, 236.
Conant, Ebenezer, 179.
Conant, Eleazer, 129.
Conant, Josiah, Jr., 54, 72, 130.
Conant, Nathan, 180.
Conant, Nathaniel, 219, 344.
Conant, Samuel, 26, 54, 55, 129, 236.

Condle, Benony, 358.
Condrick, John, 56, 78.
Condruy, John, 162.
Cone, Daniel, 26, 166, 239, 352.
Cone, Daniel, 3d, 276.
Cone, Elias, 5.
Cone, Elijah, 181, 262, 352.
Cone, Elijah, 2d, 280.
Cone, Elisha, 26, 69, 166, 240.
Cone, Giles, 5.
Cone, Henery, 3.
Cone, Israel, 3, 352.
Cone, James, 5.
Cone, Jesse, 52, 69.
Cone, Jonah, Jr., 3.
Cone, Joseph, 26, 166, 239, 355.
Cone, Joshua, 256, 318, 335, 349.
Cone, Noadiah, 52, 70.
Cone, Oliver, 3, 52, 69, 209.
Cone, Ozias, 26, 166, 239, 262, 346, 355.
Cone, Phenihas, 3.
Cone, Samuel, 6, 262.
Conent, Nathaniel, 356.
Cones, William, 165.
Coney, Edward, 181.
Congdol, Benoni, 76, 360.
Congdon, Jarius, 353.
Congdon, Jonathan, 194.
Conkling, Deliverance, 113.
Conkling, Silvenus, 117.
Conlee, John, 26, 238.
Connant, Nathaniel, 312.
Connecticut Huts, 200.
Convers, 135.
Convers, Chostor, 135.
Convers, Thomas, 26, 165, 262.
Converse, 209.
Converse, Israel, 18.
Converse, Pain, 292.
Converse, Thomas, 69, 210, 235.
Convirs, Samuel, 336.
Convise, Barnard, 193.
Cook, Aaron, 143.
Cook, Abel, 86.
Cook, Abiel, 204.
Cook, Abraham, 2.
Cook, Archibald, 186, 276, 299, 350.
Cook, Benajah, 15.
Cook, Case, 25, 75, 165, 231.
Cook, Daniel, 6.
Cook, Ebenezer, 12, 51.
Cook, Elihu, 59, 83.
Cook, Elijah, 147, 199.
Cook, George, 59, 83, 327.
Cook, Giles, 14.
Cook, Isaac, Jr., 13.
Cook, Jabez, 282.
Cook, Jesse, 214, 219.
Cook, Joel, 25, 59, 83, 84, 203, 230.
Cook, John, 68.
Cook, John, Jr., 15.
Cook, Johnson, 59, 83.
Cook, Jonathan, 6.
Cook, Joseph, 187.
Cook, Lemuel, 280.
Cook, Miles, 333.
Cook, Moses, 14, 366.
Cook, Nathan, 52, 262.
Cook, Nathaniel, 65, 70.
Cook, Ozem, 71.
Cook, Richard, 86, 348.
Cook, Robert, 50, 276, 299, 350.
Cook, Roswell, 278, 299, 347.
Cook, Samuel, 346.
Cook, Shubel, 86.
Cook, Thomas, 25, 47, 66, 166, 230.
Cook, Warren, 59, 83.
Cook, William, 59, 65, 83, 86, 152, 319, 347, 348, 353.
Cook, Zarah, 280.
Cooke, 88.
Cooke, Barton, 15.
Cooke, Thomas, 198.
Cool, Hyman, 227.
Cool, Isaac, 78, 227.
Coole, Himan, 63.
Coole, Reuben, 238.
Cooley, Nathan, 26, 234.
Cooley, Ruben, 26, 166.
Cooly, Nathan, 165.
Cooly, Reuben, 18.
Coombs, William, 262.
Coon, Jacob, 78.
Coon, James, 57, 165, 227.
Coon, John, 227.
Coon, Rulif, 204.
Cooper, Abraham, 152.
Cooper, Jacob, 196, 220.
Cooper, James, 262.
Cooper, John, 122.
Cooper, Joshua, 196.
Cooper, William, 79.
Coopper, Isaac, 217.
Copeland, Amasa, 56, 253.
Copeland, Asa, 292, 306, 323, 328.
Copeland, Avuara, 252.
Copland, Amasa, 138.
Copland, Asa, 295.
Copp, Joseph, 346.
Copp, Joseph, Jr., 290, 358.
Corbin, Clement, 272, 292.
Corbin, David, 155, 162.

INDEX.    397

Corbin, Ebenezer, 273, 292.
Corbin, Peter, 361, 362.
Corbion, Peter, 213.
Corbit, James, 13.
Corkins, John, 203.
Corne, Malachi, 238.
Cornell, Ashbell, 7.
Cornell, Prince, 154.
Corner, John, 49.
Corney, Malachi, 70.
Corney, Maleciah, 26.
Cornin, Daniel, 359.
Corning, Allen, 246, 321, 337, 345.
Corning, Allyn, 305.
Corning, Jason, 75.
Corning, Malachi, 144, 262.
Cornish, Elisha, Jr., 10.
Cornish, Joseph, 50.
Cornwall, 33, 36, 40, 42, 43, 47, 88, 171, 173, 174, 204, 206, 207, 208, 211, 235, 269, 270, 277.
Cornwell, Daniel, 7.
Cornwell, Elisha, 7.
Cornwell, Enoch, 347.
Cornwell, Richard, 346.
Cortlands Manor, 368.
Corts, Richard, 262.
Cortwhrite, Cyrus, 77.
Corwin, Amaziah, 182, 282.
Corwin, Jonathan, 26, 75, 231.
Corwin, Phineas, 200.
Corwin, Selah, 26, 75, 231, 232.
Corwin, Selah, 26, 75, 231, 232.
Coshall, Thomas, 26, 166, 229.
Cosher, Abel, 7.
Coss, Nero, 221.
Cossit, Timothy, 11.
Cotten, Thomas, 19.
Cotton, Bibe, 199.
Cotton, Rowland, 56, 77, 277.
Cotton, Ward, 199, 284, 306, 308, 328.
Cottrel, Nathan, 26, 233.
Cottril, Nathaniel, 281.
Cottrill, Nathan, 180.
Couch, 88.
Couch, Abraham, 67, 96.
Couch, Amos, 278, 299, 347.
Couch, Daniel, Jr., 285, 292.
Couch, E., 106.
Couch, James, 49.
Couch, Joel, 247.
Couch, John, 67, 96.
Couch, Jonathan, 11.
Couch, Joshua, 4.
Couch, Samuel, 210.
Couch, Steven, 17.

Couch, Thomas, 4.
Couch, Timothy, 6.
Coussland, Amasa, 77.
Covel, Elijah, 17.
Covel, James, 350.
Covel, Jonathan, 17.
Covel, Salos, 137.
Covel, Silas, 56, 77.
Coventry, 22, 25, 27, 38, 42, 65, 132, 133, 160, 163, 166, 173, 176, 187, 206, 214, 215, 216, 218, 219, 237, 253, 260, 267, 269, 270, 280, 283, 285, 286, 287, 288, 294, 295, 300, 301, 356, 357.
Covil, David, 255.
Covil, James, 276.
Cowdrey, Asa, 369.
Cowdrey, Moses, 369.
Cowdry, Edward, 71.
Cowdry, Joseph, 115, 284.
Cowdy, Ambras, 189.
Cowdy, Samuel, 353.
Cowell, Samuel, 284.
Cowl, Abner, 353.
Cowl, John, 53.
Cowl, Josiah, 347.
Cowles, Joseph, 46, 63.
Cowles, Silas, 74.
Cowls, Elisha, 13, 345.
Cowls, Joel, 13.
Cowls, Samuel, 166.
Cox, Robert, 142, 354.
Coy, Abraham, 11.
Coy, David, 82, 123, 148, 283, 301, 324, 340.
Coy, Edy, 352.
Coy, Ephraim, 10, 344.
Coy, Mathew, 10.
Coy, Moses, 276, 309, 334, 350.
Coy, Nathan, 12, 82, 148, 160.
Coy, Parley, 313.
Coy, Perly, 280.
Coy, Samuel, 26, 86, 241.
Coye, David, 160.
Coye, Ephraim, 77.
Coye, Nehemiah, 82.
Cozier, Benjamin, 119.
Craen, Curtee, 339.
Craft, Benjamin, 75, 332.
Craft, David, 213.
Craft, Joseph, 284.
Craft, Samuel, 185.
Crafts, 138.
Crain, Jonathan, 56.
Crain, Rufus, 190.
Craine, Jonathan, 77.
Crammer, Adam, 79, 99.

Crampton, Benjamin, 51.
Crampton, Calvin, 51.
Cramton, Nathaniel, 209.
Cran, Amon, 162.
Cran, Ruben, 162.
Crandal, Abel, 81.
Crandal, Asa, 359.
Crandal, John, 81.
Crandel, Abel, 59.
Crandel, Christopher, 217.
Crandell, Edward, 284.
Crandol, John, 139.
Crane, Amarah, 72.
Crane, Amariah, 54, 129.
Crane, Curtice, 26.
Crane, Curtis, 165, 238, 254, 262, 324, 348.
Crane, Daniel, 52, 70.
Crane, Elihu, 210.
Crane, Elijah, 7.
Crane, Enos, 66.
Crane, Ezra, 212.
Crane, James, 275, 310, 343.
Crane, Joel, 53, 72.
Crane, John, 52, 72, 231.
Crane, Jonathan, 46, 131.
Crane, Nathaniel, 52, 72, 212.
Crane, Roger, 297.
Cranton, Thomas, 297.
Crary, Richard, 26, 166, 238.
Crary, William, 148.
Craw, Ammon, 202.
Craw, Haman, 121.
Craw, Jacob, 202.
Craw, Reuben, 53, 121.
Crawferd, Jason, 86.
Crawfoot, John, 90.
Crawford, Jason, 134.
Crawford, John, 58.
Crawford, Newton, 113.
Crawford, William, 123, 154.
Creamer, Michael, 366.
Cree, Reubin, 331.
Cremer, John, 277.
Crissey, Truman, 100.
Crittenden, Gideon, 26, 239, 252.
Crittendon, Gideon, 166.
Crocker, Grace, 262.
Crocker, John, 279, 349, 365.
Crocker, Rozwel, 76.
Crocker, Samuel, 357.
Crofford, Jason, 46.
Cromwell, Prince, 123.
Crosbey, Richard, 218.
Crosby, Levi, 3.
Crosby, Michel, 136.
Crosby, Obed, 6, 71.

Crosby, Parson, 214.
Crosby, Richard, 182.
Crosby, Simon, 53.
Crosby, Timothy, 369.
Crosby, David, 345.
Cross, Jonathan, 18.
Cross, Joseph, 57, 81.
Cross, Nero, 290, 291.
Crossman, John, 96.
Croswell, Mark, 12, 82, 148, 160.
Crovel, Enoch, 287.
Crow, Amon, 222.
Crow, Edward, 285.
Crow, Elias, 86.
Crow, Jacob, 222.
Crow, Shubael, 278.
Crowel, Enoch, 190.
Crowel, Manoah, 185.
Crowell, Edward, 7.
Crowell, Levi, 243.
Crowell, Solomon, 7.
Crowfoot, Samuel, 124.
Crudock, William, 117.
Crutie, Jonathan, 321.
Cruttenden, Gilbert, 4.
Cruttenden, Jason, 207.
Cruttenden, Jedidiah, 4.
Cruttenden, Salmon, 4.
Cruttenden, Zebulon, 5.
Cruttondon, Samuel, 212.
Cubb, William, 301.
Cuff, Abel, 58.
Cuff, Cato, 281.
Cuff, Samson, 281, 348.
Cuffe, Cato, 180.
Cuggo, 148.
Culbert, Robert, 52, 70.
Culver, Aaron, 25, 63, 64, 236.
Culver, Abel, 53.
Culver, Abraham, 224.
Culver, Daniel, 25.
Culver, David, 25, 214, 238.
Culver, John, 205.
Culver, Moses, 82, 149, 160.
Culver, Samuel, Jr., 14.
Culver, Solomon, 274.
Culver, Timothy, 25, 166, 239, 262, 350.
Cumber, Lemon, 60, 83.
Cumings, Stephen, 296.
Cummes, William, 26, 234.
Cummins, William, 162, 165, 205.
Cummus, Williams, 78.
Cumstalk, Aaron, 110.
Cunnel, Jeremiah, 280.
Cunnell, Jeremiah, 319, 335.
Cunnell, Jeret, 305.

Curchel, John, 339.
Curtice, Amos, 25.
Curtice, Daniel, 25.
Curtice, Frederick, 146.
Curtice, George, 26, 235.
Curtice, Steaphen, 26.
Curtis, Amos, 239.
Curtis, Caleb, 81, 256.
Curtis, Daniel, 70, 166, 238, 262, 345.
Curtis, Daniel, Jr., 166.
Curtis, Eliphilit, 11.
Curtis, Elisha, 13.
Curtis, Epaphras, 199.
Curtis, Ezekial, 49.
Curtis, Felix, 144, 249.
Curtis, Fraderick, Jr., 157.
Curtis, George, 165.
Curtis, Giles, 60, 83.
Curtis, John, 19, 46, 47, 63, 154.
Curtis, Seth, 63.
Curtis, Solomon, 11.
Curtis, Stephen, 84, 230.
Curtis, Stephen, 3d, 84.
Curtiss, Aaron, 61, 107.
Curtiss, Chancey, 347.
Curtiss, Clark, 347.
Curtiss, Epaphrus, 223.
Curtiss, Frederick, 64.
Curtiss, George, 106.
Curtiss, Gideon, 284.
Curtiss, Giles, 207.
Curtiss, Isreal, Jr., 100.
Curtiss, John, 119, 123.
Curtiss, P., 91.
Curtiss, Samuel, 93.
Curtiss, Stiles, 58.
Cushman, Daniel, 19, 25, 64, 166, 237, 262.
Cushman, Eliphelit, 84.
Cushman, Jonah, 182.
Cushman, Joseph, 84, 294.
Cushman, Thomas, 64.
Cushmon, Isaac, 57, 81.
Cushmon, Nanh[ll], 81.
Cushmon, Nathaniel, Jr., 57.
Cuthbert, Benjamin, 278.
Cuthburt, Benjamin, 291.
Cutler, 19.
Cutler, Eleazer, 310, 334.
Cutler, Elizer, 197.
Cutter, Asa, 193.
Cutter, Eleazer, 310.
Cynamon, Thomas, 26.
Cyrus, Pomp, 73.

Dabol, John, 68.

Dabol, John, 3d, 50.
Daboll, Benjamin, 183.
Daboll, John, 339.
Dada, James, 352.
Daggett, Ebenezer, 211.
Daggett, John, 368.
Dailey, James, 27, 166, 235.
Daley, William Johnson, 200.
Daily, James, 73, 101.
Dains, David, 107.
Dalliber, Samuel, 226.
Dallibier, Jonathan, 348.
Dalton, Richard, 167.
Daly, Jacob, 135.
Daniels, John, 369.
Damenery, Richard, 58.
Dameson, George, 344.
Damewood, Followdan, 65.
Danbury, Richard, 94.
Danbury, 22, 25, 27, 28, 30, 33, 34, 36, 38, 39, 47, 88, 118, 120, 121, 123, 124, 126, 153, 154, 165, 167, 169, 171, 172, 173, 174, 185, 186, 187, 188, 189, 190, 191, 197, 204, 207, 208, 209, 211, 234, 254, 258, 261, 262, 263, 265, 266, 268, 269, 284, 302, 355, 359.
Danield, Stephen, 78.
Danields, Ezekiel, 351.
Daniels, David, 86, 348.
Daniels, Ezekiel, 28, 47.
Daniels, John, 290, 360.
Daniels, Nehemiah, 47.
Daniels, Peletiah, 189.
Daniels, Reuben, 369.
Daniels, Samuel, 17, 166, 182, 263.
Daniels, William, 183.
Danielson, John, 287.
Danielson, William, 134, 137, 138, 141, 292.
Danity, Frances, 210.
Danquegen, Jona., 285.
Danquenen, John, 291.
Danscey, William, 297.
Danwell, William, 101.
Danzy, William, 28.
Daras, Philip, 79.
Darfee, Benjamin, 223.
Darling, Benjamin, 71.
Darren, Ebenezer, 49.
Darrow, Benjamin, 290, 358.
Darrow, Christopher, 27, 70, 167, 238.
Dart, Dolphin, 351.
Dart, Ebenezer, 63.
Dart, Samuel, 198.
Dascomb, William, 90.

Daset, John, 86.
Daskam, William, 58.
Daskim, William, 322.
Daskin, William, 337.
Daton, Ezekiel, 116.
Daton, Israel, 13, 27.
Daton, Richard, 27, 68.
Dauset, John, 330.
Davel, John, 27.
Davenport, Bernard, 106.
Davenport, Esquier, 282.
Davenport, John, 61, 95, 99.
Davenport, Richard, 66.
Davenport, Stephen, 109, 114.
Davenport, Thomas, 106.
Daverson, Benjamin, 227.
Daverson, Ezra, 301.
Davice, Martin, 81.
Davice, William, 14, 49.
David, Sill, 232.
Davidson, Ezra, 273.
Davidson, Isaac, 73, 166, 231.
Davidson, John, 153, 236.
Davidson, Robert, 355.
Davies, Joseph, 313.
Davies, Josiah, 65.
Davinson, Isaac, 27.
Davinson, John, 27.
Davinson, Peter, 129.
Davinson, Robert, 27.
Davinson, William, 27.
Davis, Amos, 2, 13, 66, 198, 284.
Davis, Burden, 348.
Davis, Daniel, 27, 68, 167, 232, 252, 263, 285, 358.
Davis, David, 288.
Davis, Ebenezer, 27, 167, 238, 255.
Davis, Elijah, 356.
Davis, Ezekiel, 275, 349.
Davis, Isaac, 27, 115, 234.
Davis, Jacob, 80, 349.
Davis, Jacob, Jr., 10.
Davis, Jacob, 34, 145.
Davis, James, 27, 124, 154, 167, 229, 263.
Davis, Jobe, 203.
Davis, Joel, 183, 219, 356.
Davis, John, 81.
Davis, Jonathan, 27, 84, 129, 166, 263.
Davis, Jonn, 230.
Davis, Joseph, 263, 286, 313, 330.
Davis, Joshua, 54, 129.
Davis, Josiah, 353.
Davis, Justin, 350.
Davis, Lathrop, 76, 140.
Davis, Lemuel, 18.

Davis, Martin, 59.
Davis, Robert, 68.
Davis, Samuel, 18, 182, 368.
Davis, Stephen, 27, 84, 230.
Davis, Stephen Ben, 285.
Davis, Thomas, 60.
Davis, Thomas Justus, 49, 66.
Davis, William, 50, 68, 76, 336.
Davison, Asa, 46, 131.
Davison, Benjamin, 297.
Davison, David, 279, 291, 301.
Davison, Isaac, 263.
Davison, John, 263, 297.
Davison, Paul, 46, 277.
Davison, Robert, 167, 232.
Davison, William, 131, 166.
Davisson, Daniel, 198.
Davol, John, 233.
Dawner, Caleb, 27.
Dawner, Ezra, 27.
Dawns, Benjamin, 121.
Dawns, John, 263.
Day, David, 95, 148, 160.
Day, Horriss, 207.
Day, Isaac, 59.
Day, Joseph, 52, 70, 258, 320, 337, 345.
Day, Nathan, 195.
Day, Solomon, 221.
Day, Wastebrook, 238.
Day, Westbrook, 27, 257.
Dayley, James, 263.
Dayton, Israel, 167, 229.
Dayton, Richard, 232.
Deains, Levi, 76.
Dealing, Samuel, 27, 195, 238.
Dean, 98.
Dean, Benjamin, 92.
Dean, Bradley, 98.
Dean, James L., 288.
Dean, Jeremiah, 120, 162.
Dean, Levy, 128, 196.
Dean, Samuel, 207.
Dean, Solomon, Jr., 132.
Dean, William, 357.
Deane, Jonathan, 274.
Deane, Thomas, 201.
Deans, David, 220.
Deans, Levi, 85.
Deaolph, Amasa, 138.
Deates, Samuel, 76.
Deathic, Ephraim, Jr., 47.
Deavenport, Richard, Jr., 132.
Debble, Martin, 361.
Defloris, Anthony, 281.
De Floris, Anthony, 329.
De Floris, see Floris.

# INDEX. 401

De Flovis, Anthony, 313.
De Forest, Abel, 202.
Deforest, David, 8.
De Forest, Mills, 202.
Deforest, Samuel, 28, 110, 167.
Deforrest, Mills, 222.
Delaney, John, 49, 66.
Delano, Jonathan, 66, 81.
Delibar, James, 27, 70, 238.
Deliber, Samuel, 180.
Delyno, Luther, 191.
Deming, David, 70.
Deming, Waite, 235.
Demming, David, 27, 238.
Demming, Elijah, 331, 345.
Demming, Jack, 354.
Demming, Jonathan, 69.
Demming, Phinehas, 99.
Demming, Wail, 27, 69, 263.
Demmon, John, 167, 235, 263.
Denison, John, Jr., 263.
Demmon, Jonethan, 203.
Demmon, Wait, 167.
Demmonds, Davis, 100.
Deneson, Amos, 148.
Denisen, Amos, 82.
Denison, Jediah, 79.
Denison, Prince, 50.
Denmark, 368.
Dennison, Amos, 27, 160, 237.
Dennison, John, 283.
Dennison, Nathan, 12.
Dennison, Prince, 347.
Dennison, Samuel, 208.
Densey, William, 75.
Denslow, Eli, 152, 339.
Denslow, Joel, 85.
Denslow, Martin, 14, 27, 86, 166, 241, 263. 304, 315.
Denslow, Philander, 18.
Densmore, William, 17.
De Pew, Abraham, 115.
De Pew, Francis, 116.
De Pew, Henry, 115.
De Pew, John, 115.
Derby, 2, 21. 22, 28, 30, 31, 35, 36, 38, 42, 43, 47, 88, 91, 126, 151, 167, 170, 172, 176, 182, 216, 230, 263, 264, 267, 268, 271, 273, 287, 301, 366.
Dernant, Elexander, 314.
Derrick, Cato, 272.
Derrick, James, 359.
Derrimo, Joseph, 273.
Desborough, Joshua, 355.
Desiton, John, 283.
Deurant, Elexander, 314.

26

Devenport, William, 51.
Devonshire, 366.
Devotion, Ebenezer, 357.
Dewey, 370.
Dewey, Derias, 220.
Dewey, James, 7, 27, 239.
Dewey, Silas, 179.
Dewis, Dennis, 359.
De Wolf, Benjamin, 287.
De Wolf, Edward, 27, 282.
De Wolf, Joseph, 144.
De Wolf, Peter, 186.
Dewolf, Samuel, 11.
De Wolf, Stephen, 27, 166, 232, 285.
De Wolf, see Dwolf, Wolf.
Dewset, John, 348.
Dexter, John, 236.
Dexter, Samuel, 159.
Dextor, Darius, 54, 130.
Dextor, James, 54, 72, 130.
Dextor, John, 27, 54, 55, 72, 130, 167.
Deyer, Jube, 226.
D'Forest, Samuel, 263.
Dibble, Benjamin, 211.
Dibble, Daniel, 119.
Dibble, Martin, 79, 152, 257.
Dibble, Nehemiah, 119.
Dibble, Samuel, 124.
Dibble, Silas, 47.
Dibol, Aaron, 143.
Dibol, Dan, 143.
Dibol, Levi, 10.
Dick, 56, 77.
Dick, David, 284.
Dick, James, 147, 159.
Dickeman, Jonathan, 47.
Dickeman, Stephen, 98.
Dickenson, George, 263.
Dickenson, Samuel, 112.
Dickenson, Waitstill, 315.
Dickenson, Waitsoll, 315.
Dickerman, Isaac, 91.
Dickerman, Jesse, 91.
Dickerman, Joseph, 152, 167, 229, 355.
Dickermon, Joseph, 27.
Dickers, David, 313.
Dickerson, George, 300, 350.
Dickerson, Isaac, 59.
Dickerson, Joseph, 6.
Dickerson, Nehemiah, 208.
Dickerson, Samuel. 73, 151.
Dickerson, Waitstill, 348.
Dickins, Martin, 1£9.
Dickinson, George, 167, 276, 355.

Dickinson, Jesse, 58.
Dickinson, Waitstill, 250, 331.
Dickison, Jesse, 187.
Dicks, David, 313, 330.
Dickson, George, 263.
Dickson, John, 113.
Dickson, Joseph, 4.
Dickson, Miles, 94.
Die, Daniel, 27, 235.
Diggins, Benjamin, 183.
Dike, 135.
Dikeman, Daniel, 119.
Dikeman, Frederick, 118.
Dikeman, Jonathan, 119.
Dileno, Jonathan, 132.
Dill, Martin, 205.
Dillaba, George, 59.
Dillabur, George, 82.
Dillaby, George, 280.
Dilyno, Aaron, 190.
Dimick, Joseph, 84, 239, 282.
Dimmick, Amasa, 285.
Dimmick, Benjamin, 304, 310.
Dimmick, Jeduthan, 183.
Dimmick, John, 18.
Dimmick, Joseph, 263.
Dimmick, Phillip, 183.
Dimmick, Shoball, 81.
Dimmick, Solomon, 183.
Dimmick, Timothy, 180.
Dimmock, Benjamin, 131.
Dimmock, Elias, 131.
Dimmok, Joseph, 27.
Dimmuck, Benjamin, 46.
Dimmuck, Elias, 46.
Dimmock, Moon, 298.
Dimmuck, Simeon, 18.
Dimmuk, Amasa, 354.
Dimock, Ebenezer, 369.
Dimock, Edward, 12.
Dimock, Shubal, 59.
Dimok, Jeduthan, 219.
Dimon, Gold, 98.
Dimon, John, 27.
Dimon, Moses, 4, 27, 96, 233.
Dinah, James, 336.
Dingley, John, 226, 288.
Dingly, John, 343.
Dire, Benjamin, 305.
Disherow, Simon, 67.
Disborough, Henry, 67,
Disborough, Joshua, 27, 233.
Disborough, Justus, 27, 233.
Disborow, Joshua, 67, 167.
Disborow, Justice, 67.
Disborow, Justin, 167.
Disbrow, Caleb, 274.

Disbrow, Henry, 96.
Disbrow, Isaac, 96.
Disbrow, Joshua, 96.
Disbrow, Justin, 96.
Disbrow, Russell, 4.
Disbrow, Simon, 4, 96.
Diteman, Fradrick, 153.
Diteman, Jon[n], 154.
Dix, Benjamin, 246, 305, 328, 348.
Dixon, David, 61, 103, 335.
Dixon, George, 27, 54, 234.
Dixon, James, 64, 148, 285, 292.
Dixon, Jared, 61, 103.
Dixon, John, 305, 328.
Dixon, Joseph, 104.
Dixon, Miles, 58.
Dixson, 225.
Dixson, David, 217.
Dixson, James, 147.
Dixson, John, 148.
Dixson, R., 160.
Dixson, Robert, 149.
Doan, Prince, 79.
Doane, Ephraim, 287.
Doane, Joel, 279.
Doane, Josiah, 287.
Doane, Richard, 279.
Dochester, Alexander, 249.
Dodg, Daniel, 27.
Dodg, James, 133.
Dodg, Nathan, 27.
Dodg, William, 54, 73, 129.
Dodge, 162.
Dodge, Benjamin, 263, 286, 330, 351.
Dodge, Daniel, 232.
Dodge, Elihu, 263, 283, 351.
Dodge, Israel, 59, 64, 75, 83, 158, 338.
Dodge, James, 47.
Dodge, Jeriel, 64.
Dodge, Peregreen, 87.
Dodge, Perigree, 83.
Dodge, Reuben, 278, 316, 332, 353.
Dodge, Seth, 280, 316, 332, 353.
Dody, Jeriel, 147, 158.
Doel, Shem, 61.
Dog, Amos, 356.
Doghardy, Andrew, 113.
Dolittle, Joel, 336.
Donatis, Francis, 167.
Done, Israel, 361.
Done, Joel, 300.
Done, Richard, 300.
Donity, Francis, 75.
Donnety, 62.
Donvon, Daniel, 147.

Donwon, Daniel, 158.
Doolittle, Cezar, 275.
Doolittle, George, 153, 346.
Doolittle, Isaac, 14.
Doolittle, Joel, 65, 353.
Dorance, 182.
Dorchester, Daniel, 198.
Dorchester, Elixr, 50.
Dorman, Daniel, 216, 218.
Dorman, David, 150.
Dorman, Gershom, 167, 263.
Dorman, Stephen, 48.
Dormant, Stephen, 246, 320, 337.
Dormond, Stephen, 350.
Dormont, Stephen, 348.
Dorner, Ezrah, 141.
Dorr, Samuel, 345.
Dorrance, David, 12, 182, 339, 340.
Dota, Benjamin, 263.
Doty, Benjamin, 279, 300.
Doty, Samuel, 361.
Doty, Samuel, Jr., 79, 152.
Doty, William, 79.
Doubleday, Joseph, 27, 65, 132.
Doubleday, Joseph, Jr., 65, 132.
Doubledee, Abner, 140.
Doubledee, Ammi, 140.
Doubledee, Seth, 140.
Doud, Jehial, 51.
Doud, John, 5.
Doud, Moses, 167, 231, 263.
Doud, Ruben, 5.
Doud, Solomon, 51.
Doud, Zachariah, 5, 209, 263.
Doude, Jehiel, 332.
Dougharty, James, 351.
Doughtey, Daniel, 128.
Douglas, 219, 225.
Douglas, Domini, 204.
Douglas, J., 133, 218.
Douglas, Joseph, 309.
Douglas, Robert, 47.
Douglas, Solomon, 359.
Douglass, 151, 181.
Douglass, Israil, 213.
Douglass, James, Jr., 290, 358.
Douglass, Joseph, 282, 334.
Douglass, Nathan, Jr., 290, 360.
Douglass, Nathaniel, 63.
Douglass, Richard, 28, 290, 341, 342.
Douglass, Skeen, 282.
Douglass, Solomon, 28, 290.
Dow, John, 47.
Dow, Levy, 218.
Dowd, Daniel, 225, 283, 302.
Dowd, Moses, 5, 27.

Dower, Eliphalet, 290.
Dowl, John, 349.
Dowley, Andrew, 347.
Down$^d$, Richard, 346.
Downe, John, 324.
Downer, Caleb, 240.
Downer, Eliphalit, 291.
Downer, Ezra, 63, 141, 238, 291, 353.
Downer, James, 221.
Downer, John, 287.
Downer, Stephen, 78.
Downer, Thaddeus, 10.
Downes, James, 58.
Downes, John, 58, 369.
Downes, William H., 369.
Downia, John, 68.
Downing, Abijah, 277.
Downing, Christopher, 27, 76, 231.
Downing, Daniel, 363.
Downing, Ichabod, 277, 320, 337.
Downing, John, 91, 167, 335, 355.
Downing, Rufus, 19.
Downing, Stephen, 27, 237.
Downs, Benjamin, 162, 272.
Downs, Chancey, 4.
Downs, Eliphalet, 61.
Downs, Jabez, 197.
Downs, James, 90, 313, 329.
Downs, John, 90, 305, 339, 369.
Downs, Patrick, 106.
Downs, Samuel, 209.
Dowsch, Lawrence, 354.
Dowset, Amos, 130, 218.
Dowset, Jonathan, 294.
Dowset, Lawrence, 218.
Dowset, Lemuel, 130.
Dowsett, Amos, 46.
Dowsett, Lawrence, 46.
Dowsit, Amos, 179.
Dowsit, Jonathan, 313.
Dowsit, Lawrence, 179, 296, 313.
Doyl, Hugh, 263.
Doyle, Hugh, 27, 167, 229.
Doyle, Thomas, 139.
Drake, Ebenezer, 81, 348.
Drake, Francis, 8.
Drake, John, Jr., 11.
Drake, Lory, 205.
Drake, Moses, 14.
Drake, Phenihas, 3d, 14.
Dreed, Joseph, 246.
Dresser, Alfred, 277, 309, 334.
Dreston, Samuel, 357.
Drew, Peter, 89.
Driggs, Daniel, 369.
Driggs, Elisha, 247.

Driggs, Joseph, Jr., 7.
Drinkwater, Ebenezer, 55, 101.
Drinkwater, John, 187.
Drinkwater, William, 27, 55, 74, 101, 235.
Drown, David, 294.
Drummonds, John, 100.
Dubbs, Cyrus, 71.
Dublin, 366.
Dubury, Joseph, 7.
Duclos, David, 58.
Dudley, Abisha, 106.
Dudley, David, 34, 5.
Dudley, Gilbert, 95.
Dudley, Thomas, 5, 13.
Dudley, Zebulon, 27, 232, 263, 277, 350.
Dudly, Joel, 5.
Dudly, Thomas, 60, 83.
Duffee, Benjamin, 316.
Duffey, Thomas, 4.
Dugan, John, 77.
Duggan, James, 157, 158, 263, 311, 343.
Duggans, James, 226.
Duggen James, 186.
Duggen, James, 186.
Duggens, James, 277.
Duggin, James, 64, 138, 156.
Duggins, James, 27, 237.
Duggins, John, 77.
Dulford, Alexander, 105.
Dun, Peter, 218.
Dunam, Joseph, 223.
Dunbar, Amos, 27, 84, 230.
Dunbar, Miles, 27, 166, 230, 355.
Dunham, Asael, 54, 72, 130.
Dunham, Cornelius, 27, 166, 211, 263, 348.
Dunham, Cornelius, Jr., 49.
Dunham, Daniel, 280, 309, 334.
Dunham, David, 189.
Dunham, Edward, 155, 162.
Dunham, Elisha, 218.
Dunham, Ezekiel, 85, 127.
Dunham, Gershom, 85, 127.
Dunham, Gideon, 206, 334.
Dunham, James, 294.
Dunham, Joas, Jr., 296.
Dunham, Samuel, 141, 186, 367.
Dunham, Solomon, 193.
Dunham, Steaphen, 54, 72.
Dunker, Edward, 340.
Dunkin, Edward, 326.
Dunlap, 159, 224.
Dunlap, Epheram, 147.
Dunlap, Joshua, 147.

Dunlay, Darius, 352.
Dunn, Timothy, 66, 166.
Dunners, Darbe, 297.
Dunning, David, 107.
Dunning, Edmond J., 336.
Dunning, James, 338.
Dunning, Jared, 222.
Dunnum, Cornelius, 239.
Dunwell, William, 55, 73, 166, 235.
Dunwill, William, 27.
Dunworth, George, 297.
Durand, Alexander, 330.
Durand, Ebenezer, 48, 151.
Durand, Eleazer, 47.
Durand, Elezer, 2.
Durand, Isaac, 2.
Durand, Samuel, 2.
Durfe, Thomas, 27, 167, 263.
Durfee, Benjamin, 199, 213, 277, 316, 332.
Durfee, Daniel, 64.
Durfee, Ebenezer, 319.
Durfee, Elijah, 319.
Durfee, Thomas, 67, 92.
Durfey, Daniel, 146, 157.
Durfey, Ephraim, 75.
Durfree, Thomas, 233.
Durfy, Elijah, 336.
Durfy, William, 136.
Durgley, John, 343.
Durham, 2, 25, 31, 32, 40, 66, 166, 168, 170, 175, 197, 198, 200, 210, 211, 230, 262, 265, 266, 273.
Durgy, 150, 151.
Durke, Benjamin, 27, 84.
Durke, Jeremiah, 27, 167.
Durke, John, 27, 167.
Durkee, 82, 150, 156, 157, 158, 159, 160, 161, 196, 359, 360.
Durkee, Asa, 104.
Durkee, Benjamin, 236.
Durkee, Jeremiah, 236, 355.
Durkee, John, 74, 231, 263.
Durkee, John, Jr., 74.
Durkee, John Hyde, 75.
Durkee, Nathaniel, 101.
Durkee, Phinehas, 74.
Durkee, Stephen, 363.
Dutton, Joseph, 187.
Dutton, Moses, 282.
Dutton, Oliver, 27, 239.
Dutton, Titus, 27, 84, 166, 230.
Duvant, Elexander, 314.
Dwolf, Daniel, 53, 79.
D'Wolf, Edward, 232.
D:wolf, Stephen, 354.

INDEX. 405

Dyar, Benjamin, 11.
Dye, Daniel, 101, 104.
Dye, Richard, 183.
Dyer, Juba, 288.

Eadwards, Bildad, 68.
Eady, Caleb, 136.
Eagelston, David, 229.
Eagleston, David, 28, 167.
Eagleston, Eliab, 302.
Eagleston, Elisha, 13.
Eaglestone, Bennett, 367.
Eaglestone, Joseph, 363.
Eaglestone, Stephen, 367.
Ealy, Andrew, 201.
Eames, Anthony, Jr., 12.
Eames, Everit, 234.
Eames, Isaac, 13.
Eames, John, 147.
Eames, Mark, 363.
Eames, Mark, Jr., 13.
Eams, Asa, 75.
Eams, Comfort, 301.
Eams, Everet, 28, 75.
Eanos, David, 223.
Eanous, David, 297.
Earl, Jesse, 138.
Earl, Thomas, 140, 290, 291.
Earl, William, 28, 77, 137, 240.
Earles, Jesse, 77.
Earls, Jesse, 56.
Earls, William, 56.
East Haddam, 3, 21, 25, 28, 31, 34, 38, 40, 42, 43, 88, 163, 165, 169, 171, 172, 176, 179, 180, 181, 183, 197, 216, 217, 241, 260, 262, 265, 267, 268, 269, 271, 276, 278, 280, 286, 352, 355, 367, 368.
East Hartford, 88, 143, 243.
Eastman, Ebenezer, 357.
Easton, Ashbel, 345.
Easton, Eliphalet, 28, 99, 167, 235.
Easton, Giles, 346.
Easton, Julian, 61, 99.
Easton, Norman, 100.
Easton, Samuel, 52, 70, 258, 308, 345.
East Windsor, 21, 23, 24, 25, 27, 30, 33, 36, 37, 43, 48, 163, 164, 166, 172, 176, 190, 191, 240, 246, 249, 253, 264, 269, 270, 278, 286, 287, 349, 370.
Eaten, Daniel, 187.
Eaton, 136, 225.
Eaton, Aaron, 312, 343.

Eaton, J., 161.
Eaton, James, 46, 131, 138.
Eaton, Joseph, 364.
Eaton, Luther, 54, 72, 130.
Eaton, Samuel, 18.
Eaton, Solomon, 28, 81, 167, 239, 287, 350.
Eaton, Stephen, 46, 131, 181, 219, 364.
Eaton, William, 183, 219.
Eatton, Nathaniel, Jr., 356.
Eatton, Origin, 297.
Eatton, Phileman, 297.
Eavan, Isaac, 232.
Eddy, Levius, 351.
Edgcom, Gilbert, 50, 69.
Edgcomb, Ezra, 28, 56.
Edgcomb, Jabez, 285, 339.
Edgecomb, Jabez, 325.
Edgerton, Ebenezer, 275, 299, 349.
Edgerton, Jonathan, 139.
Edgerton, Nathan, 321, 338.
Edgerton, Richard, 204.
Edgerton, Roger, 272, 307, 320, 337.
Edgerton, Simeon, 142.
Edgerton, Sims, 197.
Edgett, George, 116.
Edmond, 224.
Edmonds, Andrew, 112.
Edmonds, William, 160.
Edor, Tony, 283, 351.
Edson, Benjamin, 18.
Edson, Eliab, 182.
Edson, Joseph, 18, 57.
Edson, Josiah, 18, 57, 81.
Edson, Nathan, 18, 57, 81.
Edson, Samuel, 18.
Edward, 28.
Edward, Bildad, 50.
Edwards, 88.
Edwards, Cesar, 325.
Edwards, Daniel, 64, 66, 132.
Edwards, Henry, 11.
Edwards, John, 58.
Edwards, Jonathan, 68, 99, 115, 312, 343.
Edwards, Nathaniel, 28, 64, 84, 146, 157, 158, 167, 230, 355.
Eells, 88, 193.
Eells, Edward, 167.
Eells, Nathaniel, 133.
Eells, Samuel, 344.
Eells, Samuel, Jr., 73.
Egelston, Isaac, 86.
Egelston, Joseph, 86.
Egelston, Nathaniel, Jr., 86.

Egelston, Timothy, 86.
Egelstone, David, 81.
Eggleston, Benedick, 325.
Eggleston, Benidict, 281.
Eggleston, David, 275, 299.
Eggleston, James, 276, 299, 325.
Egleston, Benedick, 339.
Egleston, David, 263, 349.
Egleston, Eliab, 286.
Egleston, James, 339, 348.
Egleston, Jones, 339.
Egleston, Joseph, 348.
Elderkin, 19.
Elderkin, Diariah, 50.
Elderkin, Diarka, 68.
Elderkin, Diureha, 243.
Elderkin, Elemoth, 291.
Elderkin, Elimath, 278.
Elderkin, James, 273.
Elderken, Vine, 28.
Eldredg, John, 54, 72.
Eldredg, Jonothan, 130.
Eldridge, Samuel, 263, 278, 353.
**Eldridge, William,** 190, 285, 350.
Eldrig, Robart, 294.
Eldrige, Daniel, 46.
Eldrige, William, 221.
Eley, Daniel, 14.
Elie, Caleb, 300.
Elies, Nathan, 78.
Eliot, Thomas, 135.
Elis, Jonas, 336.
Elles, J. Bard, 8.
Elles, Nathan, 263.
Ellington, 48.
**Ellis, Carpenter,** 78, **263.**
Ellis, John, 28, 74, 167, 231, 263.
Ellis, John, 34, 296.
Ellis, Jonas, 272.
Ellis, Oliver, 297.
Ellis, Peter, 9.
Ellis, Phenis, 82.
Ellis, Phineas, 160.
Ellis, Samuel, 190.
Ellis, Sawyer, 296.
Ellis, Stephen, 181, 349.
Ellis, William, 214, 226.
Ellot, Richard, 211.
Ells, Edward, 28, 239, 263.
Ellsworth, Benjamin, 325.
Elmer, Calib, 28.
Elmer, Daniel, 28, 79, 119, 154.
Elmer, Daniel, Jr., 57, 80.
Elmer, William, 11, 28, 80.
Elmon, Calib, 167.
Elmor, Phenious, 203.
Elmore, Caleb, 71, 236, 263.

Elmore, Daniel, 167, **336.**
Elmore, Joseph, 188.
Elmore, William, 238.
Elmour, Caleb, 280.
Elsworth, Hez, 48.
Elsworth, Benjamin, 190, 287, 339, 350.
**Elsworth, Ezra,** 350.
Elsworth, John, 180.
Elsworth, Moses, 48, 311, **343,** 350.
Elsworth, Stephen, 223.
Elton, William, 205.
Elu, Caleb, 273.
Elwell, Ebenezer, 342.
Elwell, Samuel, 340.
Elwood, Isaac, 67, 96.
Elwood, Joseph, 4, 263, 274.
Elwood, Nathan, 67, 247.
Elwood, Thomas, 3.
Ely, Elisha, 167.
Ely, Gabriel, 3.
Ely, John, 263.
Ely, William, 286.
Emerson, Joseph, 180.
Emerson, Nathaniel, 227.
Emmeson, Nathanael, 78.
Emmit, John, 263.
Emmitt, John, 366.
Emmonds, Jonathan, 206.
Emmons, Noadiah, 3.
Emons, Daniel, 221.
Enfield, 22, 25, 28, 29, 30, 31, **37,** 40, 43, 49, 66, 164, 166, 168, 169, 173, 177, 180, 185, 186, 189, 190, 240, 243, 250, **261, 262,** 264, 267, 279, 350, 355, **365.**
England, 366, 367, 368.
Engle, Joseph, 131.
Eno, David, Jr., 81.
Eno, Elisha, 144.
Eno, Isaac, 144.
Eno, James, 10, 205.
Eno, Joel, 143.
Eno, Levi, 187.
Eno, Samuel, 145.
Eno, William, 227.
Enoe, Joab, 131.
Enos, David, 49, 192, 349, **363.**
Enos, David, Jr., 275.
Ensign, James, 104, 226.
Ensign, Otis, 207.
Ensworth, Jedediah, 15, 327.
Ensworth, Jesse, 362.
Ensworth, Joseph, 197.
Ephraim, Joshua, 59, 82.
Erl, James, 49.

INDEX. 407

Erl, Jams, 66.
Erl, William, 67.
Ervin, William, 56.
Eston, Juline, 330.
Eumun, Stedly, 112.
Eustace, Francis, 101.
Evan, Isaac, 28.
Evans, Abiather, 28, 70, 167, 238, 310, 343, 345.
Evans, Alexander, 353.
Evans, Allen, 345.
Evans, Benonia, 71.
Evans, Daniel, 86, 134.
Evans, Henry, 28, 167, 238, 345.
Evans, James, 347.
Evans, Joseph, 302.
Evans, Josiah, 345.
Evans, Moses, 345.
Evans, Samuel, Jr., 28, 70, 238.
Evans, Stacy, 342.
Evans, Thomas, 307.
Evarts, Daniel, 78.
Evarts, Jensourah, 53.
Evarts, Reuben, 280.
Evats, Joel, 212.
Evens, 66.
Evens, Abiather, 263.
Evens, Allin, 245.
Evens, Daniel, 228.
Evens, Elijah, 11.
Evens, Henry, 263.
Evens, Isaac, 77, 146, 157.
Evens, Moses, 338.
Evens, Samuel, 132.
Evens, Stephen, 68.
Everest, Benjamin, 227.
Everet, Richard, 108.
Everett, Oliver, 272.
Everit, Eliphalit, 80.
Everit, Oliver, 301.
Everts, Reuben, 332.
Eves, David, 58.
Evett, Daniel, 332.
Evins, Allyn, 305, 328.
Evins, Thomas, 309, 328.
Evis, Daniel, 167.
Evit, Daniel, 317.
Ewen, Edward, Jr., 76.
Ewing, Alexander, 278.
Exton, William, 65.

Fabrique, Abraham, 93.
Fagens, John, 302.
Faggins, John, 332.
Fagins, John, 224, 280, 316.
Fagins, William, 181.
Failor, Stephen, 12.

Faiman, Richard, 29.
Fairbanks, Barachiah, 6.
Fairbanks, Benjamin, 136.
Fairchield, Alexander, 58, 91.
Fairchild, Benjamin, 207.
Fairchild, Clement, 200, 221.
Fairchild, Edmund, 7.
Fairchild, Gershom, 90.
Fairchild, James, Jr., 8.
Fairchild, Jesse, 8.
Fairchild, Joseph, 47.
Fairchild, Nathan, 202.
Fairchild, Peter, 154.
Fairchild, Samuel, 104.
Fairchild, Sherman, 202.
Fairfield, 3, 21, 22, 25, 27, 28, 29, 30, 31, 32, 33, 34, 35, 36, 37, 38, 40, 41, 43, 67, 92, 94, 95, 96, 97, 98, 125, 126, 151, 163, 165, 167, 168, 169, 171, 172, 174, 176, 188, 189, 191, 197, 202, 203, 209, 214, 226, 228, 233, 262, 263, 264, 265, 266, 267, 268, 270, 271, 274, 276, 288, 289, 291, 302, 355, 365, 367.
Fairfield Co., 233.
Fairman, Daniel, 363.
Fairman, Elezar, 136.
Fairman, Henry, 8.
Fairman, John, 12.
Fairman, Richard, 67.
Fairweather, Samuel, 123.
Fairweather, Zalmon, 200.
Falkner, Aaron, 146.
Falkner, Nicholus, 223.
Fallandon, John, 230.
Fallows, Isaac, 12.
Fancher, Rufus, 53.
Faning, Elisha, 232, 257.
Fanning, 88.
Fanning, Charles, 28, 74, 168, 231, 263.
Fanning, David, 51, 69.
Fanning, Elisha, 28, 69, 168.
Fanning, Frederick, 51, 69, 76.
Fanning, John, 74.
Fanning, Nathan, 51, 69.
Fanning, Thomas, 51, 69.
Fanning, Walter, 9.
Fanton, Hezekiah, 97.
Fanton, John, 294.
Fareweather, Samuel, 154.
Fargo, Aaron, 48.
Fargo, Samuel, 280, 318, 336.
Fargo, William, 76.
Fargo, William, Jr., 290, 358.
Fargoe, William, 28.

Fargoe, William, Jr., 358.
Farguson, Charles, 162.
Farmen, Daniel, 59.
Farmer, Thomas, 28, 167, 230, 264.
Farmington, 21, 22, 23, 25, 26, 27, 28, 31, 32, 33, 34, 35, 36, 37, 38, 39, 40, 42, 43, 49, 88, 145, 151, 163, 164, 166, 167, 169, 170, 171, 172, 173, 175, 177, 185, 186, 187, 188, 189, 190, 191, 192, 193, 194, 202, 205, 206, 207, 213, 214, 215, 216, 239, 243, 249, 250, 251, 252, 254, 260, 261, 262, 263, 265, 267, 269, 270, 271, 277, 278, 288, 299, 347, 354, 355.
Farnam, Abial, 64, 77, 85, 137, 147, 157, 277.
Farnam, Benjamin, 264.
Farnam, John, 53.
Farnam, Ruben, 85, 129.
Farnam, Stephen, 64, 146, 157.
Farnam, Thomas, 85.
Farnham, Abiel, 264.
Farnom, Elijah, 199.
Farnsworth, Joseph, 6.
Farnsworth, Nathan, 167.
Farnsworth, Nathaniel, 29, 240, 263, 264.
Farnum, Benjamin, 284.
Farnum, Bezellel, 78.
Farnum, Reuben, 29, 236.
Farrand, J., 104.
Farron, John, 81.
Fattendon, John, 29.
Faulkner, Aaron, 64, 157.
Faulkner, Caleb, 199.
Fay, Elijah, 18.
Fay, Gershom, 29, 61, 64, 144, 168, 235.
Fay, John, 84, 250.
Fay, Moses, 168, 245.
Fay, Timothy, 29, 59, 60, 84, 168, 235, 258.
Fay, William, 29, 60, 84, 168, 235, 250.
Fayer, Elijah, 225, 264, 286, 319, 336.
Fayr, Elijah, 12.
Feego, Peter, 264.
Fegoe, Peter, 28, 233.
Fegro, Peter, 67.
Felch, Ebenezer, 64, 146, 156.
Felen, John, 134.
Fellows, Joseph, 29, 233.
Fellows, Nathaniel, 29, 233.
Fellows, Varney, 183, 219.

Fellows, William, 63.
Felows, John, 140.
Fenn, 369.
Fenn, Aaron, 19.
Fenn, Daniel, 29, 104, 236, 263.
Fenn, David, 29, 227, 240.
Fenn, Thomas, 106.
Fenton, Adonijah, 84.
Fenton, Cyrus, 278, 353.
Fenton, Ebenezer, Jr., 356.
Fenton, Elisha, 294.
Fenton, Gemaliel, 356.
Fenton, Jacob, 322, 338.
Fenton, John, 29, 239.
Fenton, Jonathan, 29, 54, 55, 72, 130, 167, 236, 356.
Fenton, Joshua, 131.
Fenton, Nathan, 344.
Fenton, Nathaniel, 179, 219, 312, 346.
Fenton, Solomon, 29, 55, 72, 84, 167, 236, 294.
Ferguson, Francis, 122.
Ferinan, John, 18.
Ferman, John, 80.
Ferris, Abraham, 117.
Ferrol, George, 5.
Fervin, Zebulon, 179.
Fester, Andrew, 287.
Field, Ebenezer, 7.
Field, Edmond, 87, 293.
Field, Edmund, 263.
Field, Edward, 67.
Field, Francis, 102.
Field, George, 102.
Field, John, 227.
Field, Luke, 5.
Field, Oliver, 279, 350.
Field, Timothy, 5.
Fields, Edmond, 82.
Fields, Edmund, 168.
Fields, Francis, 168.
Fields, George, 61.
Fields, James, 273.
Fields, Robert, 203.
Filets, Francis, 29, 235.
Fillean, John, 112.
Filley, David, 14.
Filley, Elnathan, 14.
Filley, Remembrance, 29, 59, 61, 84, 168, 235, 250, 263, 305, 328.
Filly, Mark, 48.
Finch, Isaac, 320, 337.
Finch, Jeremiah, 116.
Finch, John, 222.
Finch, Jonathan, 332.
Finch, Samuel, 115, 116.

INDEX. 409

Finchley, George, 115.
Finkins, Edward, 106.
Finley, Samuel, 370.
Finley, Samuel, Jr., 370.
Finney, John, 106.
Finney, Joseph, 291, 311.
Finney, Joshua, 362.
Finnigham, John, 123.
Finnington, John, 154.
Firgo, Samuel, 353.
Fish, Cyrus, 242.
Fish, James Denison, 139.
Fish, John, 101.
Fish, Jonathan, 363.
Fish, William, 279, 291.
Fisher, Christopher, 29, 167, 239.
Fisher, Darius, 105.
Fisher, Isaac, 29, 79, 168, 236, 264.
Fisher, Timothy, 192, 226.
Fishkill, 228, 320, 361, 369.
Fisk, Isaac, 50, 350.
Fisk, James, 187.
Fisk, Samuel, 78.
Fitch, 88, 200, 291.
Fitch, A., 200.
Fitch, Ammi, 370.
Fitch, Annis, 370.
Fitch, Asa, 76.
Fitch, Caleb, 85, 127.
Fitch, Daniel, 64, 75, 146, 157.
Fitch, Dick, 9.
Fitch, Ebenezer, 223.
Fitch, Elnathan, 48.
Fitch, James, 209.
Fitch, James Paine, 56, 77, 158.
Fitch, Jonathan, 294.
Fitch, Joseph, 14, 264.
Fitch, Joseph T., 227.
Fitch, Joseph Trumbull, 28, 78, 168, 234.
Fitch, Nathaniel, 141, 181, 220, 290, 291.
Fitch, Nehemiah, 167, 355.
Fitch, Prentice. 104.
Fitch, Roger, 75.
Fitch, Rufus, 28, 64, 146, 156, 237.
Fitch, Thomas, 220.
Fitcher, John, 123.
Fitsgeral, Henery, 234.
Fits Gerald, Henery, 28.
Fits Gerald, Heny, 264.
Fitsjareld, Thomas, 128.
Fits Jerell, Henery, 78.
Fitts, Israel, 363.
Fitts, Moses. 179, 219.

Fitz Gerald, Thomas, 365.
Fitz Gerald, see Gerald.
Fitz Jeroll, Henry, 227.
Fitz Simmons, Thomas, 287.
Fitz Simons, Thomas, 65.
Flag, Jonathan, 168, 264, 346, 355.
Flair, John, 289.
Fleet, William, 121.
Fleng, Abijah, 137.
Fletcher, John, 10.
Fletcher, Joseph, 28, 115, 234.
Fling, Abel, 273.
Fling, Lemuel, 56, 77, 138.
Flingg, Abil, 292.
Flint, 153.
Flint, Jabez, 84.
Flint, James, 357.
Flint, James L., 85.
Flint, Jonathan, 85.
Flint, Joshua, 63.
Flint, Luke, 128, 196.
Flint, Zackeus, 196.
Flisher, John, 154.
Floris, Anthony, 313.
Floris. see De Floris.
Floro, Peter, 153.
Florous, Anthony, 212.
Flower, Elijah, 55.
Flower, Zephon, 280.
Flowers, Abdiel, 52, 70, 334.
Flowers, Benjamin, 52, 70.
Flowers, Elijah, 29, 167.
Flowers, Elisha, 242.
Flowers, Ithurel, 59, 248.
Flowers, William, 302 345.
Focher, Ebenezer, 106.
Foller, Elijah, 296.
Folley, Daniel, 296.
Fooks, Amos, 2.
Foot, Ebenezer, 2, 28, 167, 231, 236, 264.
Foot, Elijah, 28, 124, 154, 234.
Foot, Ezra, 28, 167, 230, 263.
Foot, George, 309, 334.
Foot, Isaac, 28, 167, 229, 263.
Foot, Samuel, 166, 167.
Foot, William, 55. 101.
Forbes, Elisha, 367.
Forbes, John, 318, 335.
Forbes, Joseph, 274.
Forbs, John, 246, 348.
Forbs, Joseph, 352.
Force, Ebenezer, 138.
Ford, Abraham, 357.
Ford, Benjamin, 60, 83.
Ford, Cephas, 19.

Ford, Daniel, 29, 152, 167, 229, 264.
Ford, Isaac, 150, 316, 332.
Ford, John, 187.
Ford, Jonathan, 60, 83, 340.
Ford, Martin, 167, 264, 340.
Ford, Matthew, 354, 355.
Ford, Timothy, 219.
Foreseth, Andrew, 68.
Forgarson, Daniel, 29.
Forgerson, Daniel, 78, 234.
Forgo, Peter, 168.
Forquoir, Ebenezer, 247.
Forriss, Peter, 351.
Forsdich, 88.
Forseth, Andrew, 50.
Forsyth, Jesse, 76.
Fortin, Amon, 196.
Fosbury, John, 14.
Fosbury, Stephen, 14.
Fosdick, James, 346.
Foster, Ben, 80.
Foster, Benjamin, 29, 168, 236.
Foster, Chancy, 48.
Foster, Christopher, 5.
Foster, Comfort, 85, 128.
Foster, Elijah, 297.
Foster, Francis, 162.
Foster, James, 49, 79, 153, 246.
Foster, John, 29, 70, 167, 239, 264, 346.
Foster, Jonah, 162.
Foster, Joseph, 192.
Foster, Nathaniel, 57, 81.
Foster, Peter, 351.
Foster, Thomas, 363.
Foster, Warham, 48.
Foster, William, 281.
Foster, Zephaniah, 29, 139, 237.
Fountain, Eneas, 233.
Fountain, Enos, 114.
Fountaine, Enos, 28.
Fowler, 5.
Fowler, Abiathar, 2.
Fowler, Amos, 2.
Fowler, Caleb, 28, 167, 231.
Fowler, Elisha Adams, 3.
Fowler, Joel, 219.
Fowler, Jonath, 48.
Fowler, Josiah, 5.
Fowler, Josiah, Jr., 2, 5.
Fowler, Matthew, 122, 162.
Fowler, Nehemiah, 3, 28, 67, 233, 264, 274.
Fowler, William, 5.
Fox, Aaron, 53, 274.
Fox, Amos, 47, 48.

Fox, Asa, 28, 168, 238, 245, 264, 318, 336, 351.
Fox, Ashbel, 346.
Fox, Backus, 75, 358.
Fox, Basel, 339.
Fox, Bassat, 325.
Fox, Basset, 276, 339.
Fox, David, Jr., 3.
Fox, Ebenezer, 168.
Fox, Elisha, 28, 167, 239.
Fox, Ephraim, 6, 369.
Fox, Gideon, 47.
Fox, Harris, 71, 369.
Fox, Jacob, 28, 74, 231.
Fox, Joel, 87, 141.
Fox, John, 28, 241, 263, 351.
Fox, Jonathan, 8.
Fox, Joseph, 76.
Fox, Joshua, 3, 28, 241.
Fox, Lemuel, 193.
Fox, Levi, 352.
Fox, Naniah, 245.
Fox, Nathan, 189, 369.
Fox, Robert, 130.
Fox, Rosel, 194.
Fox, Samuel, 208, 351.
Fox, Sariah, 143.
Fox, Simeon, 264, 276, 325, 340.
Fox, Stephen, 52, 70, 282, 309, 334.
Fox, Thomas, 195.
Fox, Timothy, 277, 299, 347.
Fox, Vaniah, 306, 328, 346.
Fox, Variah, 306.
Frame, John, 85.
Frances, Amos, 14.
Frances, James, 13, 29.
Frances, John, 14, 29.
Frances, Titus, 209.
Francis, Christopher, 12.
Francis, David, 274.
Francis, James, 167, 239.
Francis, John, 82, 168, 230.
Franck, Joshua, 139.
Frank, Joshua, 47.
Frank, Mical, 162.
Franklen, Jehial, 29.
Franklin, Abel, 76, 148, 158, 159, 198, 225.
Franklin, David, 198, 225.
Franklin, Jehiel, 107, 168, 235.
Franklin, Samuel, 28, 72, 167, 263.
Fransway, Anthony, 73.
Fraser, Samuel, 152.
Frasher, Robert, 290.
Frassier, Robert, 360.
Frazier, Robert, 358.
Freat, Joseph, 319.

INDEX.   411

Frederick, John, 87.
Fredericksborough, N. Y., 364.
Free, Arkelaus, 87.
Free Body, London, 143.
Freedom, Cato, 285.
Freedom, Chatham, 60.
Freedom, Dick, 60, 83.
Freedom, Jack, 277.
Freeman, Amos, 97.
Freeman, Benjamin, 9.
Freeman, Caesar, 253, 336, 348.
Freeman, Cato, 309, 334.
Freeman, Chatham, 83, 216.
Freeman, Costor, 341.
Freeman, Cuff, 346.
Freeman, Cuffee, 336.
Freeman, Cult, 103.
Freeman, Daniel, 9.
Freeman, David, 346.
Freeman, Edward, 28, 168, 232, 264, 281, 313, 330.
Freeman, Elisha, 28, 236.
Freeman, Exter, 346.
Freeman, Frank, 28, 230.
Freeman, Gager, 9.
Freeman, Gift, 153.
Freeman, Guy, 28, 232.
Freeman, Jack, 28, 91, 241, 257, 309, 334.
Freeman, James, 217, 283, 330, 351.
Freeman, Jethro, 287.
Freeman, Joseph, 76.
Freeman, Micael, 28, 168, 232.
Freeman, Mosely, 28.
Freeman, Nathan, 9.
Freeman, Ned, 313.
Freeman, Peter, 253, 257, 346.
Freeman, Phillemon, 346.
Freeman, Phineas, 9.
Freeman, Plymouth, 332.
Freeman, Primas, 273, 330.
Freeman, Prince, 248, 309, 334.
Freeman, Providence, 28.
Freeman, Robert, 58, 338.
Freeman, Roger, 54, 73, 130.
Freeman, Sampson, 28, 168.
Freeman, Samson, 238.
Freeman, Samuel, 65, 264, 353.
Freeman, Shubael, 91.
Freeman, Sifax, 28.
Freeman, Syphax, 238.
Freeman, Toney, 93.
Freman, Caesar, 318.
Freman, Elish, 64.
Freman, Elisha, 63.
Freman, Robert, 91.

Freman, Roman, 196.
French, Abner, 56, 77, 85, 128, 138.
French, Abner, Jr., 75.
French, Bowars, 366.
French, Isaac, 49, 67.
French, James, 283, 336, 351.
French, Jehiel, 58.
French, John, 147.
French, Josiah, 58, 94.
French; Levi, 189, 284, 350.
French, Samuel, 28, 97, 202, 233.
French, Thomas, 212.
French, Truman, 93.
Frenchman, Philip, 67, 95.
Frinck, Nathan, 334.
Frink, Elisha, 77.
Frink, Jabez, 182.
Frink, James, Jr., 78.
Frink, John, 357.
Frink, Lathrop, 288.
Frink, Nathan, 272.
Frink, Seth, 77.
Frink, Silas, 85, 127.
Frink, Theophilas, 77.
Frink, Thomas, 77, 344.
Frisbey, Benjamin, 28.
Frisbey, Jabez, 6.
Frisbie, Caleb, 1.
Frisbie, Hooker, 2.
Frisbie, Titus, 1.
Frisby, Benjamin, 235.
Frisby, Levi, 11, 49.
Frissel, Amasa, 86.
Frissell, 133.
Friswell, John, 195.
Frizbie, Joseph, 213.
Frost, Ephraim, 181.
Frost, Joseph, 4.
Frost, Samuel, 26, 29, 73, 231, 262.
Frost, Stephen, 111.
Frothingham, Ebenezer, 254, 255, 303, 327, 329.
Frothingham, John, 101, 105.
Frothingham, Samuel, 346.
Fryar, Charles, 167, 263.
Fulford, James, 280.
Fulford, John, 29, 84, 167, 230, 263.
Fullar, Joshua, 332.
Fuller, 158.
Fuller, A., 104.
Fuller, Abraham, 364.
Fuller, Amas, 228.
Fuller, Barnabas, 17.
Fuller, Bethuel, 3.

Fuller, David, 187.
Fuller, Edward, 74, 105.
Fuller, Eli, 275, 311, 344, 349.
Fuller, Ely, 264.
Fuller, Jacob, 264, 275, 349.
Fuller, James, 199, 224, 264, 352.
Fuller, John, 3, 28, 67, 85, 95, 97, 138, 167, 233, 264, 353.
Fuller, Joshua, 272, 292, 316.
Fuller, Natn, 18.
Fuller, Timothy, 3.
Fuller, Timothy, 2d, 3.
Fuller, William, 187.
Fullers, Aaron, 147.
Fullor, Asa, 221.
Funning, Charles, 201.
Furbs, Joseph, 212.
Fyler, Ambros, 59.
Fyler, John, 206.
Fyler, Norman, 86.
Fyler, Samuel, 370.

Gage, Salvenas, 191.
Gage, Silvanus, 276, 350.
Gage, Silvenus, 323.
Gage, Sylvanus, 341.
Gage, Tom, 61.
Gainer, James, 150.
Gains, Daniel, 144.
Gains, Jonathan, 17.
Gallet, James, 81, 141.
Gallipin, David, 346.
Gallop, Prentice, 210.
Gallup, Benjamin, 149, 297.
Gallup, Prentice, 51, 69.
Gallup, Thomas, 51.
Gallup, Wheler, 148.
Galord, Joel, 69.
Galpen, Peet, 7.
Garcy, Elnathan, 220.
Gardiner, David, 29, 168, 285.
Gardiner, De Tubs, 29.
Gardiner, Sherman, 29, 168.
Gardiner, Thomas, 8.
Gardner, 183.
Gardner, Abijah, 142, 354.
Gardner, D. Tubbs, 231.
Gardner, Daniel, 322.
Gardner, David, 74, 322, 339.
Gardner, Dennis, 87.
Gardner, George, 69.
Gardner, Nathaniel, 74.
Gardner, Peregrine, 76.
Gardner, Septimer, 138.
Gardner, Sherman, 75, 231, 264.
Gardner, Thomas, 75.
Gardner, Thomas, 75.

Gardner, William, 47, 200.
Garner, David, 325.
Garner, William, 111.
Garret, John, 29.
Garret, Samuel, 181.
Garrie, John, 264.
Garrison, Lewis, 95.
Garrit, John, 56, 168, 231.
Gaspe, Caleb, 296.
Gates, Daniel, 3d, 3.
Gates, Ebenezer, 193.
Gates, Freeman, 338.
Gates, Jessa, 369.
Gates, John, 10, 286, 314, 330.
Gates, Jonah, 3.
Gates, Jonas, 153.
Gates, Jonathan, 148.
Gates, Josiah, 226.
Gates, Luther, 77, 198.
Gates, Nathaniel, 29, 64, 237, 264, 277, 318, 336.
Gates, Nathael, 217.
Gates, Samuel, 8, 110.
Gates, Silas, 19, 64, 146, 156.
Gates, Steven, 10.
Gates, Uriah, 189.
Gates, William, 227.
Gates, Zechariah, 3.
Gaunecy, Timothy, 94.
Gauney, Timothy, 58.
Gavit, Stephen, 264, 320, 337.
Gavitt, Stephen, 281.
Gay, Jaison, 330.
Gay, James, 370.
Gay, Jason, 264, 282, 314.
Gay, Joseph, 370.
Gay, Richard, Jr., 11.
Gayland, Josiah, 243.
Gaylor, Benjamin, 203.
Gaylor, John, 190.
Gaylor, William, 52, 72.
Gaylord, Benjamin, 30, 230, 235, 342.
Gaylord, Eleazer, 14.
Gaylord, Eliakim, 205.
Gaylord, Elijah, 207.
Gaylord, John, 48, 75.
Gaylord, Jonathan, 264, 280, 365.
Geanings, Elnathan, 64.
Gear, Asa, 284.
Gear, Nathaniel, 364.
Gearham, Nehemiah, 94.
Geddens, Richard, 240.
Geer, Allen, 10.
Geer, Benajah, 54, 73, 128, 130.
Geer, Elihu, 20, 240.
Geer, Gideon, 140.

Geer, Gurdon, 255.
Geer, Lemuel, 10.
Geer, Samuel, 76.
Geers, Benaijn, 85.
Geers, Nathaniel, 208.
Gellett, Nathan, 50.
Gellit, Jeremiah, Jr., 72.
Gellitt, John, 73.
Gelson, Eleazer, 168.
Gennings, Ebenezer, 196.
Georgay, Simon, 290.
George, Benjamin, 281.
George, Francis, 75.
George, John, 196, 278, 350, 354.
George, Moses, 277.
George, Prince, 332.
Gerald, Morris F., 275.
Gerald, see Fitz Gerald.
Gerrald, Thomas F., 85.
Gerralls, Thomas, 252.
Giants, Luke, 168.
Gibbard, Elisha, 162.
Gibbs, Darius, 362.
Gibbs, David, 14, 85.
Gibbs, Ichiel, 80.
Gibbs, Jehiel, 302, 354.
Gibbs, Josiah, 18, 80, 168, 238.
Gibbs, Philo, 340.
Gibbs, Rufus, 193.
Gibbs, Samuel, 14, 86, 168, 264.
Gibbs, Timothy, 100.
Gibbs, William, 264, 283.
Gibs, Josiah, 30.
Gibs, Samuel, 30, 241.
Gibson, Samuel, 30, 168, 229, 355.
Gibson, William, 133.
Giddens, Richard, 29.
Giddinge, Benjamin, 71.
Giddings, Benjamin, 7, 369.
Giddings, Elisha, 6.
Giddings, Festus, 369.
Giddings, Jonathan, 122.
Giddings, Joshua, 6.
Giddins, Richard, 64.
Giddis, James, 290.
Gideons, Jabez, 145.
Gideons, Josph, 78.
Gidias, James, 360.
Giffin, Simeon, 308.
Giffin, Simon, 30, 168, 248, 264, 303, 327.
Gifford, John, 180.
Gilbart, Allen, 346.
Gilbart, John, 136.
Gilbert, Amus, 6.
Gilbert, Burr, 67, 92, 94.
Gilbert, Butler, 7.

Gilbert, Ebenezer, 56, 77, 97, 137.
Gilbert, Elisha, 120.
Gilbert, Garner, 142.
Gilbert, Gershom, 8, 110.
Gilbert, Humphrey, 282.
Gilbert, Ichabod, 143.
Gilbert, Jesse, 7, 198, 288.
Gilbert, Joel, 98.
Gilbert, John, 58, 67, 90, 97, 152, 204, 222.
Gilbert, Joseph, 29, 55, 71, 168, 252, 369.
Gilbert, Moses, 110.
Gilbert, N., 110.
Gilbert, Neziah, 142.
Gilbert, Obediah, 29, 168, 234.
Gilbert, Samuel, 142, 202.
Gilbert, Soloman, 193.
Gilbert, Thadeus, 8, 110.
Gilbert, Theodore, 29, 55, 168, 260.
Gilbord, Joel, 4.
Gilbord, John, 4.
Gilburt, John, 226.
Gile, Richard, 133.
Giles, John, 368.
Giles, Mingo, 154.
Gill, John, 65.
Gillet, Abel, Jr., 86.
Gillet, Adna, 168, 355.
Gillet, Asa, 286.
Gillet, Benjamin, 264, 274.
Gillet, Benoni, 342.
Gillet, Israel, Jr., 142.
Gillet, Jacob, 264, 275, 325, 339, 349.
Gillet, Jeremiah, 129.
Gillet, Joab, 143.
Gillet, John, 264.
Gillet, Jonah, Jr., 14.
Gillet, Jonathan, 14.
Gillet, Nath, 144.
Gillet, Nathan, 151.
Gillet, Othaniel, 11.
Gillet, Thomas, 14.
Gillet, Zechariah, 355.
Gillett, Jeremiah, 50.
Gillis, Tint, 61.
Gillit, 88.
Gillit, Abel, Jr., 241.
Gillit, Isaac, 187.
Gillit, Jeremiah, 54.
Gillit, Zacheriah, 168.
Gillit, Zacheus, 188, 342.
Gillson, Eleazer, 30.
Gilson, Ebenezer, 79.
Gilson, Eleazer, 236, 264.
Gilson, Jacob, 168, 346.

Gilston, Jacobe, 30, 239.
Gimson, John, 311.
Ginning, Joseph, Jr., 85.
Ginnings, Daniel, 199.
Ginnings, Stephen, 199.
Gitston, Jacob, 264.
Gladding, Jediah, 79.
Gladding, William, 168, 240, 284, 353, 355.
Gladen, William, 69, 264.
Gladin, Jedidiah, 153.
Glading, Joseph, 361.
Glading, William, 29, 183.
Glasco, Silas, 330.
Glasgow, Silas, 92.
Glass, Samuel, 56, 64, 77, 146, 157.
Glass, Silas, 264, 277, 319, 336, 363.
Glasses, Silas, 330.
Glassgow, Silus, 58.
Glastonbury, 17, 26, 27, 28, 30, 31, 33, 34, 35, 37, 39, 40, 42, 43, 88, 143, 166, 168, 169, 170, 171, 175, 176, 177, 193, 194, 195, 208, 216, 238, 245, 248, 250, 251, 264, 265, 266, 267, 269, 270, 271, 278, 285, 299, 351, 366, 367.
Glasten[ ], 208.
Glazier, John, 284.
Gleason, James, 187.
Gleason, John, 298.
Gleason, Jonn, 76.
Gleason, Luther, 206.
Glenney, William, 199.
Gleson, Andrew, 202.
Glover, 359.
Glover, Christopher, 119.
Glover, John, 30, 168, 233.
Goar, Elijah, 136.
Goarham, Isaac, 124.
Godard, Edward, 153.
Goddard, Skiler, 66.
Godfrey, 98.
Godfrey, Cresterfey, 4.
Godfrey, John, 283, 351.
Godfrey, Nathaniel, Jr., 4.
Goff, Derby, 283.
Goff, Gideon, 5, 248, 308, 333, 348.
Goff, Hezekiah, Jr., 7.
Goff, Jonathan, 346.
Goff, Joseph, 216.
Goff, Joshua, 65, 87, 295.
Goff, Richard, 368.
Goff, Samuel, 29, 65, 168, 240, 296, 302, 353.
Goff, Samuel, Jr., 65.
Goff, Samuel D., 338, 351.
Goff, Solomon, 279, 300.
Goff, Squire, 296.
Gold, John, 102.
Gold, Toney, 274.
Gold, William, 67, 97.
Goldsmith, James, 73.
Goldsmith, Joseph, 73, 330.
Goldsmith, William, 73, 264.
Goldwin, Matthew, 352.
Gomer, Pharoah, 49.
Goodale, Alvin, 138.
Goodale, Elez, 17.
Goodale, Ezra, 137.
Goodale, Jacobe, 30, 138, 237.
Goodale, John, Jr., 133.
Goodale, Silas, 74.
Goodell, Alvin, 77.
Goodell, Ezra, 56, 77.
Goodell, Fraderick, 197.
Goodell, Jacob, 76.
Goodell, Oliver, 56.
Goodell, Samuel, 283.
Goodfaith, David, 29, 290, 340, 358.
Good Luck, London, 58.
Goodrich, Abel, 187.
Goodrich, Bethuel, 65, 353.
Goodrich, David, 79, 168, 236, 264.
Goodrich, Ephraim, 238.
Goodrich, Ichabod, 258, 306, 328, 348.
Goodrich, James, 246.
Goodrich, Jared, 349.
Goodrich, John, 65, 80, 317, 332.
Goodrich, Lemuel, 65, 352.
Goodrich, Levi, 64, 168, 264.
Goodrich, Levy, 240.
Goodrich, Simeon, 345.
Goodrich, Solomon, 74, 243.
Goodrich, William, 367.
Goodrich, Zenas, 213.
Goodsall, Epphaphras, 233.
Goodsel, Eppaphras, 67.
Goodsel, James, 4.
Goodsel, Thomas, 4.
Goodsell, Anthony, 285.
Goodsell, Epaphras, 95.
Goodsell, Isaac, 210.
Goodsill, Anthony, 60, 83.
Goodsill, Eppiphras, 30.
Goodwell, Jonathan, 95.
Goodwin, Charles, 276.
Goodwin, Hezekiah, 52, 70, 345.
Goodyear, Edward, 107.

INDEX. 415

Gooff, Squire, 220.
Gookins, Samuel, 306, 328, 352.
Goold, Hezekiah, 3.
Goold, John, 30, 219, 235, 355.
Goold, Samuel, 75.
Gooldsmith, William, 168.
Goowin, David, 204.
Goraham, Shubal, 4.
Goram, Ephraim, 19.
Gorddin, William, 112.
Gorden, Samuel, 344.
Gordia, Cornelius, 347.
Gordon, Bryan, 283.
Gordon, George, Jr., 12.
Gordon, James, 149.
Gordon, Joseph, 12.
Gore, Amos, 148.
Gore, Richard, 150.
Gorgay, Simon, 358.
Gorham, Isaac, 153.
Gorham, Jesse, 279.
Gorham, Phineas, 208.
Gorham, Samuel, 234.
Gorum, Samuel, 30.
Gosard, Ebenezer, 144.
Gosard, John, 144.
Gosard, Nicholas, 144.
Goshen, 26, 27, 30, 33, 34, 35, 36, 37, 40, 44, 50, 69, 165, 167, 168, 170, 172, 177, 185, 203, 204, 205, 206, 209, 210, 235, 262, 263, 267, 271, 274, 275, 355.
Goslee, Henry, 284.
Gosely, Henry, 353.
Goslin, Henry, 141.
Goudy, John, 18.
Goudy, Samuel, 18.
Goudy, William, 18.
Gould, James, 134.
Gould, John, 69, 168, 182, 228.
Gould, Nathan, 367.
Gove, 88.
Gove, John, 218.
Gove, Nathaniel, 9.
Gowdy, Hills, 189.
Gowdy, Samuel, 189.
Graham, Cyrus, 168, 264.
Graham, Jese, 300.
Graham, John, 49, 65, 66, 106.
Graham, Joseph, 29, 168, 240, 264, 353.
Graham, Joshua, 65.
Graham, Narcissus, 351.
Graham, Oliver, 152, 353.
Graham, Silas, 29, 232.
Graham, Sirus, 330.
Graham, William, 204.

Grainger, Phineas, 168.
Grainger, Samuel, 168.
Granger, Ithamer, 349.
Granger, Jacob, 278, 352.
Granger, Peter, 74.
Granger, Phineas, 30, 238, 252.
Granger, Samuel, 30, 238, 264, 352.
Grannis, Samuel, 350.
Granger, Thamar, 189.
Grant, 48, 88.
Grant, Azariah, 30, 240, 264, 316, 332, 349.
Grant, David, 190.
Grant, Ebenezer, 12.
Grant, Isaac, 53, 228.
Grant, Isaiah, 286.
Grant, James, 30, 46, 56, 77, 79, 130, 138, 168, 232, 264, 279, 300, 332.
Grant, John, 302, 359.
Grant, Josiah, 351.
Grant, Luke, 264.
Grant, Noah, 132.
Grant, Oliver, 188.
Grant, Oliver, 2d, 188.
Grant, Reuben, 187.
Grant, Rosel, 211.
Grant, Thomas, 210.
Grant, William, 60, 83.
Grates, Edward, 105.
Gratis, Jesse, 107.
Gratis, Prince, 101.
Graves, Abner, 212.
Graves, Benjamin, 78, 227.
Graves, Gilbert, 280, 330.
Graves, John, 250, 264, 273, 292.
Graves, Peter, 29, 168, 241.
Graves, Simeon, 30, 84, 230.
Graves, Sylvanus, 53.
Graves, William, 30, 168, 239, 264, 347.
Gray, Andrew, 302.
Gray, Derias, 57, 80.
Gray, Ebenezer, 85, 327.
Gray, Elijah, 29, 68, 232.
Gray, Eliphalet, 4, 68, 98.
Gray, Enos, 295.
Gray, James, 29, 290, 346, 358.
Gray, John, 82, 148, 160, 286, 302.
Gray, Liman, 4.
Gray, Samuel, 57, 80.
Gray, Thomas, 357.
Gray, William, 12, 82, 148, 160.
Grayham, Simeon, 14.
Great Britain, 8.

Green, 136.
Green, Amos, 75, 197, 336.
Green, Asahel, 108.
Green, B., 115.
Green, Benjamin, 183, 193.
Green, David, 10, 57.
Green, David, Jr., 81.
Green, Edward, 298.
Green, Ezra, 115.
Green, Francis, 75.
Green, Frederick, 86, 134.
Green, Jack, 71.
Green, Jacob, Jr., 57.
Green, James, 89.
Green, Jedd, 146.
Green, Jedediah, 157, 277.
Green, Jeremiah, Jr., 39.
Green, Joel, 65.
Green, John, 29, 133, 147, 196, 229, 297.
Green, Joseph, 57, 168.
Green, Joseph, Jr., 4.
Green, Joshua, 81.
Green, Josiah, 29, 68, 98, 109, 233.
Green, Mason, 277, 307, 316.
Green, Robert, 29, 82, 149, 160, 237.
Green, Roger, 64, 146, 156.
Green, Samuel, 29, 63, 73, 98, 110, 216, 236, 336, 342.
Green, Solomon, 4.
Green, Thomas, 49, 71, 203, 278.
Green, Timothy, 201.
Green, Wardwill, 193.
Green, William, 18, 29, 70, 238.
Green, Zach, 57.
Greene, John, 86.
Greene, Pleney, 295.
Greenfield, Archibald, 179.
Grenold, Amasy, 343.
Greensar, Pline, 292.
Greenslit, Benjamin, 193, 272, 314, 330.
Greenwich, 21, 22, 27, 28, 31, 32, 33, 36, 37, 38, 42, 43, 44, 88, 115, 116, 118, 126, 234.
Greer, James, 74.
Gregory, Daniel, 191, 221.
Gregory, Elias, 9.
Gregory, Ezra, 9.
Gregory, Isaac, 9.
Gregory, J., 111.
Gregory, Jack, 185.
Gregory, John, 210.
Gregory, Matthew, 110, 320.
Gregory, Matthew, Jr., 111.
Gregory, Nathan, 304.

Gregory, Philip, 275, 299.
Gregory, Stephen, 7.
Grenoll, Amasa, 227.
Grey, James, 358.
Grey, William, 65.
Gregory, Benjamin, 154.
Gridley, Hosea, 49, 347.
Gridley, James, 299, 347.
Gridley, James, Jr., 278.
Gridley, Kezin, 370.
Gridley, Obed, 299, 347.
Gridley, Obed., 278.
Gridley, Rezin, 370.
Gridley, Seth, 30, 71, 236.
Gridly, Seth, 168.
Griffen, Abner, 144.
Griffen, James, 30, 233.
Griffen, Joel, 300.
Griffen, John, 144.
Griffen, Nathaniel, 11.
Griffeth, George, 224, 264.
Griffeth, William, 47.
Griffin, Amos, 310.
Griffin, Cornelius, 76.
Griffin, Edward, 53, 72.
Griffin, George, 215.
Griffin, Joseph, 77, 137, 225.
Griffin, Joseph, Jr., 56.
Griffin, Matthew, 143.
Griffin, Simeon, 348, 349.
Griffin, Simon, 238, 303, 327.
Griffin, William, 118.
Griffing, Joel, 273.
Griffis, Paul, 225.
Griffith, George, 286.
Griffith, William, 8, 153.
Griggory, Mathew, 264.
Griggs, Paul, 19.
Grigory, Phillip, 349.
Grigory, Seth, 306.
Grimes, Abraham, 47.
Grimes, Cyrus, 29, 79, 232.
Grimes, Joseph, Jr., 10.
Grimes, Silus, 29.
Grinall, Amasa, 78.
Grisson, Lewis, 67.
Griswell, Giles, 13.
Griswold, 15.
Griswold, Andrew, 74.
Griswold, Benjamin, 1.
Griswold, Cesar, 183.
Griswold, Elijah, 14.
Griswold, Elisha, 143.
Griswold, Ezra, 5.
Griswold, George, 52, 72.
Griswold, Jacob, 250.
Griswold, John, 274, 300.

Griswold, Joseph, 30, 66, 168, 240.
Griswold, Midian, 286.
Griswold, Moses, 308, 348.
Griswold, Phin, 86.
Griswold, Phineas, 241.
Griswold, Simeon, 1, 12.
Griswold, Thomas, 5.
Griswold, Walter, 198.
Griswold, White, 30, 236.
Griswold, Zenas, 52, 72.
Griswould, Asa, 6.
Griswould, Felix, 213.
Griswould, Francis, 211.
Griswould, George, 78, 227.
Griswould, Heber, 227.
Griswould, John, 13.
Griswould, Moses, 248, 328, 333.
Griswould, Samuel, 78, 227.
Griswould, White, 6.
Grizwould, Warren, 46.
Gro, John, 19.
Groo, Ebenezer, 138, 197.
Groos, John, 139.
Groos, Jonah, 140.
Groos, Samuel, 139.
Gross, Samuel, 30, 237.
Grosvenor, 192, 302.
Grosvenor, Thomas, 56, 138, 302.
Groto, Eleazer, 76.
Groton, 21, 22, 23, 24, 27, 28, 29, 31, 35, 36, 37, 40, 43, 44, 50, 68, 73, 129, 130, 136, 148, 158, 159, 160, 163, 165, 167, 168, 171, 173, 175, 177, 179, 180, 181, 183, 198, 203, 208, 209, 210, 212, 214, 215, 216, 217, 225, 227, 232, 242, 243, 246, 248, 249, 252, 253, 254, 255, 256, 257, 260, 263, 264, 268, 269, 271, 281, 285, 287, 288, 355, 356, 359.
Grovener, Josiah, 350.
Grover, Amasa, 30, 71, 135, 237, 264, 273, 292.
Grover, Benjamin, 66, 132.
Grover, Cato, 74.
Grover, Daniel, 216, 219.
Grover, Jacob, 30, 91, 234.
Grover, Joseph, 357.
Grover, Luther, 284.
Grover, Phineas, 30, 168, 238.
Grow, Ebenezer, 56, 77, 284.
Grummon, Nehemiah, 3.
Guernsey, Southmit, 205.
Guient, Luke, 81.
Guilbert, Abner, 205.
Guile, Abraham, 286.
Guile, Elisha, 15.

Guile, James, 86.
Guile, Joseph, 210.
Guile, Richard, 86.
Guile, Simeon, 286.
Guilford, 4, 22, 23, 24, 27, 28, 30, 31, 32, 36, 40, 42, 43, 51, 163, 164, 167, 169, 170, 172, 175, 177, 209, 210, 211, 212, 215, 231, 243, 252, 258, 261, 263, 265, 266, 267, 268, 269, 270, 271, 280, 281, 288, 300, 356, 365.
Gunner, Joseph, 56, 77.
Gustin, Amos, 198, 310, 335.
Gutherie, James, 154.
Guthery, James, 47.
Guthire, Abel, 314.
Guthra, James, 123.
Guthrey, Able, 330.
Guthrie, Abel, 221, 282.
Gutrich, David, 29.
Gutrich, Ephraim, 29.
Gutrich, Levey, 29.
Guttrege, Solomon, 141.
Guy, 28.
Guy, John, 2.
Guyant, Duke, 77.
Guyant, Luke, 30, 77, 232.
Guyar, Stephen, 3.

H[ ], Bodwell, 299.
Hackley, Arunah, 76, 248, 309.
Haddam, 5, 22, 23, 24, 25, 26, 29, 30, 36, 39, 51, 69, 88, 163, 164, 166, 168, 169, 172, 174, 181, 183, 208, 210, 211, 212, 214, 2'0, 261, 262, 264, 266, 268, 269, 274, 284, 288, 352, 354, 355.
Hadley, Ebenezer, 316.
Hadlock, John, 48.
Hadlock, Reuben, 31, 70, 169, 238, 265, 346.
Hadlock, Samuel, 48, 350.
Hadlock, Thomas, 187.
Hagar, Simeon, 31.
Hager, Simeon, 66, 169, 240, 350.
Hail, Isaac, 215.
Hail, Justice, 209.
Hail, Ruben, 71.
Hail, Samuel, 18.
Haines, David, 279.
Hains, David, 300.
Hait, 186, 195.
Hait, Daniel, 111.
Hait, Ebenezer, 113.
Hait, Garret, 117.
Hait, Joel, 115, 311, 344.
Hait, Joseph, 32, 170, 313, 329.

Hait, Nehemiah, 109.
Hait, S., 112.
Hait, Samuel, 113, 204, 216, 341.
Hait, Stephen, 108, 215.
Haladay, Jacob, 344.
Halchet, John, 151.
Hale, Aaron, 30, 64, 240.
Hale, Garsham, 199.
Hale, James, 46, 85, 131.
Hale, Joseph, 188.
Hale, Newport, 351.
Hale, Robert, 46, 131, 294.
Hale, Thomas, Jr., 49, 66.
Halkins, Samuel, 189.
Hall, 55, 88, 210.
Hall, A., 207.
Hall, Aaron, 60, 82.
Hall, Abram, 14.
Hall, Amos, 51, 142.
Hall, Andrew, 129.
Hall, Asa, 13, 67.
Hall, Benajah, 59, 83.
Hall, Benjamin, 4.
Hall, Caleb, 207, 362.
Hall, Charles, 13.
Hall, Christopher, 197.
Hall, Daniel, 13.
Hall, Daniel Johnson, 60, 83.
Hall, David, 30, 47, 83, 119, 154, 169, 224.
Hall, Eben, 265.
Hall, Ebenezer, 3, 71.
Hall, Eber, 5, 280.
Hall, Eleazer, 97.
Hall, Elisha, 60, 83.
Hall, Enos, 13.
Hall, Ezenas, 196.
Hall, Garsham, 2ᵈ, 199.
Hall, George, 93, 200.
Hall, Henrey, 82.
Hall, Hiland, 74.
Hall, Hiram, 49, 66, 264, 350.
Hall, Irael, 66.
Hall, Isaac, 49, 129.
Hall, Israel, 13, 30, 169, 240.
Hall, Jatham, 83.
Hall, Jedediah, 97.
Hall, Joel, 14.
Hall, John, 47, 53, 205.
Hall, Josiah, 188.
Hall, Jotham, 60.
Hall, Levi, 319, 336.
Hall, Moses, 83.
Hall, Moses, 2ᵈ, 13.
Hall, Moses, 3ᵈ, 13, 60.
Hall, Nathan, 3.
Hall, Nathaniel, 30, 84, 129, 230.

Hall, Philemon, 5, 30, 169, 231, 265.
Hall, Robert, 169.
Hall, Rufus, 13, 30, 83, 169, 230.
Hall, Samuel, 13, 30, 71, 136, 170, 231, 265.
Hall, Simeon, 50, 69.
Hall, Stephen, 30, 58, 67, 93, 117, 139, 169, 226, 231, 233, 265, 274.
Hall, Street, 14.
Hall, Talmage, 7, 30, 234.
Hall, Thomas, 51.
Hall, Titus, 13, 169.
Hall, Timothy, 19.
Hall, William, 30, 131, 237, 346.
Halladay, Jacob, 144, 299, 311.
Halladay, Robert, 365.
Hallamagee, John, 350.
Hallet, Thomas, 78, 319, 358, 359.
Hallett, John, 68.
Halley, Abraham, 233.
Halley, Edmond, 184.
Halley, Joseph, 160.
Halley, Manchester, 184.
Halley, Nathan, 265.
Halley, Robart, 10.
Hallimage, John, 264.
Hallop, Joseph, 32, 234.
Halloway, William, 32.
Hallowell, William, 75.
Hally, Abraham, 31.
Halsey, Jeremiah, 9.
Halsted, Joseph, 71.
Halsted, Timothy, 285.
Haman, Ebenezar, 346.
Hambden, William, 32, 230.
Hamblen, James, 361.
Hamblen, Levi, 12.
Hambleton, John, 8, 122.
Hamblin, Joel, 169, 236.
Hamblin, John, 80.
Hamblin, Levi, 80.
Hamblin, William, 202.
Hamhidon, James, 94.
Hamilton, George, 53.
Hamilton, James, 112.
Hamilton, John, 155, 302.
Hamlin, Bazeleel, 248.
Hamlin, Cornelius, 57, 80.
Hamlin, Joel, 32, 74, 265, 273, 316.
Hamlin, John, 18.
Hamlin, Levi, 18, 50.
Hamlin, Reuben, 194, 278, 347.
Hamlin, Richard, 6.
Hamlin, William, 275, 354.
Hammon, Robart, 218.

Hammond, David, 285, 311, 344.
Hammond, Robert, 184.
Hamtin, Reuben, 299.
Hanaball, Joseph, 233.
Hancy, Samuel, 70.
Hand, Jonathan, 247.
Hand, Joseph, 79, 153, 258.
Handcox, John, 66.
Handee, Caleb, 183.
Handey, Samuel, 169.
Handy, 5.
Handy, Clement, 330.
Handy, Clemmans, 204.
Handy, Jairus, 5.
Handy, Jonathan, 5.
Handy, Richard, 58, 94.
Handy, Russel, 360.
Handy, Samuel, 31, 231, 265.
Handy, Thomas, 360.
Hanes, Jonathan, 170, 265.
Hanes, Silas, 4.
Haney, Andrew, 307.
Hanford, Eleazor, 9.
Hanford, Ozias, 109.
Hanford, Stephen, 9.
Hanford, Theophilus, Jr., 9.
Hanford, Theophilus, 34, 9.
Hanford, Timothy Hathorly, 108.
Hanks, Asa, 357.
Hanks, Consider, 294.
Hannabal, Joseph, 31, 232, 286.
Hansen, Samuel, 79.
Hansey, Andrew, 307, 328.
Hanson, Christian, 368.
Hanson, Samuel, 153.
Hanson, William, 330.
Haradan, Paul, 86.
Hard, David, 91.
Harde, John, 130.
Harde, Nathaniel, 130, 169.
Harden, Frederick, 32, 169.
Hardey, Nathaniel, 72.
Harding, Fradk, 229.
Harding, Frederick, 8.
Hardy, Nathaniel, 30, 237, 334.
Hargar, Simeon, 355.
Harger, Elijah, 217.
Harger, Jedediah, 215.
Harington, Elisha, 10.
Harington, Stephen, 10.
Hariot, Israel, 234.
Harke, Selah, 307.
Harlop, Joseph, 169.
Harman, Jaques, 304.
Harmon, J., 331.
Harmon, Jacques, 313, 324, 329.
Harmon, John, 32, 238.

Harper, Inis, 285.
Harret, Israel, 117.
Harrington, Andrew, 75.
Harrington, Benjamin, 350.
Harrington, Elisha, 80, 240, 349.
Harrington, Isaac, 232.
Harrington, Samuel, 248.
Harrington, Timothy, 203.
Harrinton, Elisha, 31, 170, 265.
Harrinton, Isaac, 31.
Harriot, Israel, 31.
Hurris, Amos, 59, 82, 323, 341.
Harris, Andrew, 358, 359.
Harris, Asa, 200, 221.
Harris, Bruster, 190.
Harris, Champlin, 32, 168, 246, 264, 283, 351.
Harris, George, 197, 279, 300.
Harris, Henry, 169, 265.
Harris, Jason, 71.
Harris, John, 5, 32, 54, 55, 129, 169, 236, 239.
Harris, Joseph, 7.
Harris, Nathaniel, 66, 132, 140.
Harris, Paul, 181.
Harris, Philip, 296.
Harris, Philip, Jr., 296.
Harris, Thomas, 64, 290, 358, 359.
Harris, Walter, 139, 242.
Harrison, Asahel, 2.
Harrison, Champlin, 168.
Harrison, Jairus, 2, 30, 231, 265.
Harrison, Jarus, 170.
Harrison, John, 71, 111.
Harrison, Reuben, 194.
Harrison, William, 30, 76, 232.
Harrison, Wooster, 2.
Harriss, Amos, 350.
Harriss, Andrew, 76.
Harriss, Jason, 136.
Harriss, Paul, 223.
Harriss, William, 76.
Harrop, Joseph, 169, 265, 354.
Harry, Ephraim, 281, 321, 337.
Harscall, David, 135.
Hart, Aaron, 277, 347.
Hart, Benjamin, 31, 83, 169, 230.
Hart, Gilbert, 203.
Hart, Henry, 346.
Hart, James, 209.
Hart, Joel, 311.
Hart, John, 79.
Hart, Jonathan, 31, 169, 239.
Hart, Luke, 276, 299, 350.
Hart, Selah, 288, 319, 347.
Hart, Timothy, 13, 60, 83.
Hart, Titus, 14, 60, 82.

Hart, Tucker, 53.
Harte, Selah, 307, 328.
Hartee, Selah, 307.
Hartford, 21, 22, 23, 25, 26, 27, 28, 29, 31, 33, 34, 35, 36, 37, 38, 39, 40, 41, 43, 44, 52, 66, 70, 88, 143, 163, 164, 165, 166, 167, 168, 169, 170, 171, 172, 173, 175, 177, 179, 180, 185, 186, 187, 189, 190, 191, 192, 193, 194, 195, 205, 206, 226, 228, 237, 238, 242, 243, 244, 245, 246, 248, 249, 250, 252, 253, 254, 255, 257, 258, 259, 260, 261, 262, 263, 264, 265, 266, 267, 269, 271, 299, 302, 345, 354, 355, 358, 364.
Hartford Co., 237, 345.
Harthaway, Zenas, 56, 138.
Hartland, 6, 23, 31, 37, 38, 71, 144, 145, 189, 217, 236, 256, 261, 369.
Hartshorn, Diah, 74.
Hartshorn, Ezra, 272.
Hartshorn, John, 72, 130.
Hartshorn, John, Jr., 54.
Hartshorn, Joshua, 47.
Hartshorn, Rufus, Jr., 75.
Hartshorn, William, 15.
Harvey, Asahel, 217.
Harvey, Ephraim, 265.
Harvey, Ezra, 3, 31, 169, 241, 265, 334, 352.
Harvey, Ithamar, 31.
Harvey, John, 3.
Harvey, Nathan, 3.
Harvey, Robert, 3.
Harvey, William, 3, 31, 79, 169, 232.
Harwinton, 6, 28, 30, 31, 35, 40, 43, 71, 167, 168, 169, 187, 203, 236, 263, 265, 266, 278, 280, 285, 286.
Hary, Daniel, 281.
Hary, Ithas, 241.
Hase, Samuel, 209.
Haskal, Jacob, 81, 314, 331.
Haskal, John, 315, 331.
Hastens, 152.
Hastens, John, 87.
Hasting, John, 83.
Hastings, John, 32, 230.
Hatch, Abner, 12, 296.
Hatch, Dan, 12.
Hatch, Eastus, 187.
Hatch, Ebenezar, 350.
Hatch, Ede, 188.
Hatch, Edy, 59, 81.

Hatch, Eleazer, 190, 281, 323.
Hatch, Eliezer, 341.
Hatch, Erastus, 349.
Hatch, George, 278.
Hatch, Haman, 84.
Hatch, Hayman, 239.
Hatch, Heman, 278, 332, 353.
Hatch, Hemen, 316.
Hatch, Hemon, 32.
Hatch, Herman, 316.
Hatch, James, 15.
Hatch, Joseph, 123, 154.
Hatch, Moses, 248, 306, 333, 348.
Hatch, Timothy, 364.
Hatchcock, Levi, 49.
Hatchet, John, 48.
Haters, Ritchard, 2.
Hathaway, Seth, 284, 352.
Hathaway, Wilber, 284, 352.
Hathaway, Zenus, 136.
Hatherway, Seth, 265.
Hatherway, Willbre, 265.
Hathway, Abner, 18.
Hathway, Zenas. 77.
Hatrel, James, 301.
Hattuck, David, 276.
Haughton, Jonas, 134.
Hauley, Joseph, 154.
Hauley, Lyberias, 154.
Havens, Cornelius, 71, 136.
Havens, John, 78.
Havens, Peleg, 193.
Havey, Jacob, 138.
Haward, Joseph, 134.
Hawes, Samuel, 106.
Hawken, Zadock, 230.
Hawkins, 136.
Hawkins, Edward, 141.
Hawkins, Joseph, 340.
Hawkins, Moses, 61, 108.
Hawkins, William, 265.
Hawkins. Zadock, 31, 100.
Hawkins, Zadock, Jr., 100.
Hawks, 32, 233.
Hawks, Hannah, 32, 233.
Hawley, Abraham, 58, 91, 108, 265, 324, 339.
Hawley, Clauson, 124.
Hawley, Daniel. 58, 75, 326.
Hawley, E., 103.
Hawley, Ebenezer, 222.
Hawley, Ezekiel, 98.
Hawley, Ezra, 58.
Hawley, Gideon, 90.
Hawley. Hezekiah, 57, 78, 100, 120, 162.
Hawley, Ichabod, 49.

INDEX. 421

Hawley, Israel, 91.
Hawley, James, 102, 104.
Hawley, John, 78.
Hawley, Joseph, 120, 204, 252, 283.
Hawley, Joseph C., 6, 31, 55, 71. 74, 221, 235, 265, 282.
Hawley, Liverius, 55.
Hawley, Liverus, 120.
Hawley, Nathan, 90, 169, 324, 339.
Hawley, Nathan, Jr., 58.
Hawley, Ozias, 188.
Hawley, Peter, 54.
Hawley, Richard, 58, 94.
Hawley, Stephen, Jr., 8.
Hawley, Talcott, 283.
Hawley, Talmage, 122.
Hawley, Wallaston, 92.
Hawley, William, 4, 211.
Hawton, Henry, 283.
Hayden, David, 31, 239, 288, 316, 332, 341.
Hayden, David, Jr., 288.
Hayden, Jacob, 288.
Hayden, Thomas, 31.
Haydon, Alyn, 6.
Haydon, David, 347.
Haydon, Thomas, 14.
Hayes, John, 121.
Hayes, Marshal, 341.
Hayley, John, 128.
Haynes, Jonathan, 332.
Hayns, Jonathan, 31, 232.
Hays, Abraham, 31, 234.
Hays, Asa, 80, 311.
Hays, Asahel, 11.
Hays, Benajah, 202.
Hays, Benjamin, 80, 144, 349.
Hays, Jacob, 11, 144.
Hays, John, 162.
Hays, Luke, 11.
Hays, Micah, 144.
Hays, Oliver, 11.
Hays, Seth, 11.
Hays, Titus, 31, 71, 236.
Hays, William, 3d, 11.
Hays, Zenos, 144.
Hayse, Abraham, 117.
Hayward, Samuel, 296.
Hayward, Solomon, 221.
Hayze, Asa, 349.
Hazard, Jeffry, 32.
Haze, Asa, 311.
Haze, Enoch, 188.
Hazelton, Arnold, 5.
Hazelton, Charles, Jr., 5.

Hazen, 178, 227, 271.
Hazen, Andrew, 315, 331.
Hazie, Joseph, 203.
Hazzard, Jeffery, 233.
Heacock, David, 32.
Heacock, Elisha, 32.
Heacock, Samuel, 32.
Heacock, William, Jr., 32.
Heacox, Asher, 49, 337.
Head, Henry, 362.
Healdy, Daniel, 336.
Heard, Elijah, 202.
Heard, Isaac, 147.
Heard, Jacob, 56, 147.
Heard, Jeduthen, 82, 148.
Heard, Mead, 202.
Heard, Robert, 148.
Heart, 88:
Heart, Bliss, 49.
Heart, Elijah, 50.
Heart, Elisha, 49.
Heart, John, 256, 257.
Heart, Jonathan, 265.
Heart, Reuben, 50.
Heart, Timothy, 49, 192.
Hearts, Selah, 307.
Heath, John, 73.
Heath, Peleg, 31, 70, 238.
Heath, Peleg L., 169.
Heath, Thomas, 192.
Hebard, Jedediah, 226, 288.
Hebbard, Aaron, 86, 134.
Hebbard, Andrew, 64, 147.
Hebbard, Asa, 134.
Hebbard, Elihu, 86, 134.
Hebbard, Timothy, 86, 134.
Hebbard, William, 146.
Hebbern, Francis, 67.
Hebron, 23, 25, 31, 34, 35, 37, 40, 42, 141, 142, 169, 171, 176, 185, 197, 208, 215, 220, 221, 238, 243, 246, 260, 262, 266, 268, 270, 271, 275, 276, 280, 281, 283, 285, 287, 296, 297, 301, 302, 354.
Hecock, Asher, 347.
Hecock, Daniel, 173.
Hecock, David, 61.
Hecox, E., 168.
Heddy, Daniel, 319, 336.
Hedges, Jeremiah, 183, 219.
Heerd, Isaac, 159.
Heerd, Jacob, 159.
Heff, Daniel, 294.
Heldrig, William, 113.
Hellard, Minor, 208.
Hellermegy, John, 190.
Helmes, Cudjo, 339.

Helmes, Kudjoe, 281.
Helmes, Samuel, 140, 254.
Helms, Cudjo, 325.
Hende, Caleb, 131, 218.
Hendee, Caleb, Jr., 46.
Hendreck, David, 9.
Hendric, Benjamin, 60.
Hendrick, Eleazer, 55, 106.
Hendrick, John, 7.
Hendrick, John William, 350.
Hendrick, Josiah, 285, 292.
Hendrick, Nathan, 9.
Hendrick, Nathaniel, 110.
Hendricks, Daniel, 272.
Hendry, Daniel, 32, 359.
Henington, Benjamin, 49.
Henman, Nathan, 202.
Henman, Samuel, 58.
Henmin, Hust., 66.
Henmin, Samuel, 306.
Hennan, Samuel, 306.
Henries, Zadock, 107.
Henry, Barzil, 86.
Henry, Barzilli, 348.
Henry, Daniel, 290.
Henry, William, 52, 70.
Hensey, Andrew, 301, 311.
Henshaw, Benjamin, 2.
Henshaw, William, 31, 169, 239, 265.
Hensley, Andrew, 283.
Hepburn, Joseph, 119.
Hepburn, Peter, 73.
Herd, Isaac, 281.
Herd, Jeduthan, 224.
Herick, Amos, 53.
Herington, Clark, 146.
Herington, Ezekiel, 146.
Herington, Samuel, 309.
Herington, Timothy, 57.
Herlihy, John, 349.
Herman, John, 350.
Hernden, Paul, 133.
Herreck, Isaac, 9.
Herren, Perley, 71.
Herrick, Asahel, 213, 223, 363.
Herrick, Daniel, 297.
Herrick, Ebenezer, 15.
Herrick Isaac, 191, 224.
Herrick, Israel, 15.
Herrick, John, 61, 99.
Herrick, Joseph, 181, 297.
Herrick, Lemuel, 77.
Herrick, Libens, 32, 233.
Herrick, Robert, 64, 146, 156.
Herrin, Perley, 136.
Herrington, Abraham, 148.

Herrington, Benjamin, 66, 279.
Herrington, Clark, 64, 156.
Herrington, Daniel, 224.
Herrington, Ezekiel, 64, 156.
Herrington, Samuel, 73, 335.
Herrington, Timothy, 81.
Herrinton, Abraham, 363.
Herrinton, Samuel, 129.
Herris, Thomas, 146.
Herron, John, 232.
Hervey, Asael, 276.
Hervy, Asahel, 352.
Herwington, Parley, 215.
Hesket, James, 68.
Heth, Phinehas, 350.
Heughston, William, 225.
Hewet, Elisha, 265.
Hewett, Henry, 224.
Hewit, Henry, 215.
Hewit, Nathaniel, 184.
Hewit, Robert, 184.
Hewlett, John, 133.
Hews, James, 228.
Heyden, David, 169, 324.
Heyden, David, Jr., 49.
Heydon, Charles, 60, 83.
Hibard, Perez, 357.
Hibbard, 157, 158.
Hibbard, Andrew, 156, 200.
Hibbard, Asa, 85, 86, 127.
Hibbard, Dyar, 85.
Hibbard, Eben, 85.
Hibbard, Elish, 7.
Hibbard, John, 296.
Hibbard, Joseph, 297.
Hibbard, Levi, 85.
Hibbard, Timothy, 85.
Hibbard, Uriah, 85.
Hibberd, 223.
Hibberd, Dier, 127.
Hibberd, Ebenezer, 127.
Hibberd, Hez, 128.
Hibberd, Timothy, 127.
Hibberd, Vriah, 128.
Hibbert, Francis, 67.
Hiccock, Samuel, 170.
Hickcox, Elisha, 84.
Hickcox, William, Jr., 84.
Hickock, Bethel, 108.
Hickok, Elisha, 230.
Hickok, Samuel, 233.
Hickok, William, Jr., 230.
Hickox, Joseph, 66.
Hickox, Samuel, 114.
Hicks, John, 152.
Hicock, David, 100.
Hicock, Thads, Jr., 105.

INDEX. 423

Hide, Asa, 211.
Hide, Clark, 222.
Hide, James, 58, 91, 94, 169, 231.
Hide, James, 3d, 265.
Hide, Nathaniel, 18.
Hide, Theophilus, 11, 14.
Hide, William R., 169.
Hide, Zebadial, 295.
Higbee, Elihu, 236.
Higby, Elihu, 30.
Higby, Isaac, 63.
Higby, Lemuel, 190.
Higby, Noah, 207.
Higgans, Isaac, 343.
Higgens, Heman, 240.
Higgens, Jesse, 240.
Higgins, Cornelius, 30, 69, 240, 355.
Higgins, Cornelius, Jr., 5.
Higgins, Cornetuis, 169.
Higgins, Heman, 30, 65.
Higgins, Isaac, 288.
Higgins, Jesse, 30, 65.
Higgins, Jesse, Jr., 65.
Higgins, Nehemiah, 244.
Higgins, William, 169, 265.
Highlands, 182, 198, 247, 251.
Highlands, see Camp Highlands.
Higley, Benjamin, 68.
Higley, Eben, 188.
Higley, Josiah, 81, 143, 240.
Higley, Ozias, 144.
Hill, 98.
Hill, Abner, 279.
Hill, Daniel, 31, 89, 238, 265, 345.
Hill, David, 11, 89.
Hill, Ebenezer, 31, 106, 169, 235, 330.
Hill, Eli, 9.
Hill, Elijah, 188.
Hill, Eliphulet, 243.
Hill, Henry, 79.
Hill, John, 5, 170, 187, 219, 265.
Hill, John, 2d, 11, 31, 80, 240, 349.
Hill, Jonah, 13.
Hill, Jonathan, 56, 77, 137.
Hill, Moses, 5, 51.
Hill, Nathan, 351.
Hill, Nathaniel, 75.
Hill, Philip, 31, 237, 278, 291, 343.
Hill, Reuben, 187, 215, 276, 348.
Hill, Squier, 131.
Hill, Thomas, 56, 77, 137.
Hill, Tony, 274.
Hill, Ury, 206.
Hill, William, 112.

Hillard, Azariah, 179.
Hillard, Jonathan, 149.
Hillet, Thomas, 252.
Hills, Abner, 226.
Hills, Abner, Jr., 283.
Hills, Belah, 205.
Hills, Benoni, 48, 350.
Hills, Daniel, 169.
Hills, Ebenezer, 49, 265.
Hills, Eliphalet, 52, 70.
Hills, Erastus, 188, 369.
Hills, George, 81, 250.
Hills, Jacob, 180.
Hills, Jeptha, 350.
Hills, Joseph, 351.
Hills, Lebbeus, Jr., 370.
Hills, Libbius, 370.
Hills, Oliver, 350.
Hills, Phillip, 139, 265, 310, 311.
Hills, Samuel, Jr., 17, 295.
Hills, Squier, 298.
Hills, William, 141.
Hillton, Atkisson, 67.
Hillyer, Daniel, 206.
Hilton, Atkinson, 31, 98, 169, 233.
Hilton, Benjamin, 58.
Hinckley, David, 84.
Hinckley, Iccabud, 169.
Hinckley, Ichd, 81.
Hinckley, J., 185, 186, 187, 188, 189, 190, 191.
Hinckley, Jared, Jr., 139.
Hinckley, John, 84.
Hinde, Caleb, 131.
Hine, Ambrose, 60, 83.
Hine, Isaac, 162.
Hine, N., 99, 100, 105, 106.
Hine, Titus, 32, 73, 170, 231, 265, 332.
Hinkley, Ebenezar, 352.
Hinkly, Ichabod, 32, 239.
Hinkston, Joseph, 11.
Hinman, Benjamin, 3d, 61.
Hinman, D., 100.
Hinman, E., 107, 108.
Hinman, Enos, 100.
Hinman, Houghton, 168.
Hinman, Husted, 3, 31, 230.
Hinman, Joel, 100.
Hinman, Jonas, 100.
Hinman, Samuel, 90, 328.
Hinman, Timothy, 61, 107.
Hinsdale, William, 52, 70, 194.
Hinsdel, Elisha, 71.
Hinsdel, Samuel, 71.
Hinsdel, William, 226.
Hinson, William, Jr., 76.

Hiscox, Thomas, 32, 233.
Hitchcock, Abel, 53, 73, 329.
Hitchcock, Ambras, 188.
Hitchcock, Daniel, 350.
Hitchcock, David, 235.
Hitchcock, Hicol$^d$, 205.
Hitchcock, Ichabod, 83.
Hitchcock, Jarel, 73.
Hitchcock, Jason, 49, 340, 350.
Hitchcock, John, 57, 78, 80, 121, 162.
Hitchcock, Lemuel, 32, 60, 82, 230.
Hitchcock, Levi, 60, 83, 182.
Hitchcock, Samuel, 49, 188.
Hitchcock, Thomas, 32, 60, 230.
Hitchcocks, Osi, 289.
Hitchcox, Abel, 150.
Hitchcox, Jared, 150.
Hitchkook, Ebenezer, 2.
Hittrel, James, 273.
Hoadley, Ebenezer, 51, 243, 316.
Hoadley, Samuel, 30, 231, 265.
Hoadly, Ralph, 1.
Hoadly, Samuel, Jr., 1.
Hobart, Elisha, 100.
Hobart, John, 100, 170, 214, 265, 333, 343.
Hobart, Mason, 1.
Hobbey, 88.
Hobby, J., 117.
Hobs, John, 127.
Hodg, Asael, 169, 236, 265.
Hodg, David, 170, 231.
Hodge, 214.
Hodge, Asael, 31.
Hodge, Asahel, 71.
Hodge, David, 31, 73, 265, 343.
Hodge, Elijah, 12.
Hodge, Levy, 367.
Hodge, Thomas, 65.
Hodgers, Job, 191.
Hodges, Job, 221.
Hodges, Joseph, 122.
Hodgkis, Samuel, 203.
Hodley, Ebenezer. 316, 332.
Hoel, Nicholas, 229.
Hogins, Benjamin, 3.
Hoit, Samuel, 5.
Hokhins, William, 119.
Holaday, Amos, 11.
Holaday, Azriah, 11.
Holbrook, Joseph, 151.
Holcom, Benjamin, 10.
Holcom, John Griffin, 299.
Holcom, Joseph, 85.
Holcomb, Abraham, 202.

Holcomb, Amos, 144.
Holcomb, Asahel, 3$^d$, 275, 349.
Holcomb, Benj$^a$, 144.
Holcomb, Consider, 349.
Holcomb, Consider, Jr., 81, 145.
Holcomb, Ebenezer, 143.
Holcomb, Eli, 11.
Holcomb, Elijah, 11, 145, 277, 348.
Holcomb, Elishama, 11.
Holcomb, Ezra, Jr., 144.
Holcomb, Joel, 143, 189.
Holcomb, John, 339.
Holcomb, John G., 275, 325, 349.
Holcomb, Joseph, 348.
Holcomb, Joshua, Jr., 144.
Holcomb, Martin, Jr., 14.
Holcomb, Matthew, 86, 241.
Holcomb, Moses, 11.
Holcomb, Noadiah, 10.
Holcomb, Noah, 145.
Holcomb, Seth, 11.
Holcum, Enos, 188.
Holcumb, Ezekiel. 188.
Holden, Amos, 343.
Holden, John, 31, 169, 238, 265.
Holding, John, 351.
Holdredge, Robert, 208.
Holdredge, Rufus, 51, 69.
Holdridge, 207.
Holdridge, Ephraim, 252.
Holdridge, Hezekiah. 31, 169, 239.
Holdridge, Robert, 221, 314, 330, 354.
Holdridge, Rufus, 332.
Holdridge, William, Jr., 75.
Holebrook, Nathaniel, Jr., 140.
Holembok, John, 30.
Holibod, Stephen, 4.
Holibord, Gideon, 3.
Holiday, Amos, 202.
Holiday, Jacob, 275.
Holister, Innitt, 208.
Holland, Joseph, 363.
Hollay, Joseph, 232.
Holley, Abraham, 170.
Holley, Joseph, 31, 68.
Holley, Joseph C., 6.
Hollidy, Jacob, 349.
Hollis, Joseph, 169.
Holliss, John, 85.
Hollister, Aaron, 17.
Hollister, David, 193.
Hollister, Josiah, 17, 351.
Hollister, Thomas, 17, 185.
Holiston, Appleton, 296.
Holloday, Jacob, 81.
Hollowell, William, 227.

## INDEX. 425

Holly, John, 85, 227.
Holly, Joseph, 77, 232.
Holmes, Aaron, 87.
Holmes, David, 31, 133, 230.
Holmes, Eliphat, 31.
Holmes, Eliphalet, 169, 241.
Holmes, John, 179.
Holmes, Joseph, 77, 137.
Holmes, Levy, 367.
Holmes, Nathaniel, 31, 116, 234.
Holmes, Peleg, 106.
Holmes, Samuel, 110, 346.
Holmes, Simeon, 250, 265, 315, 331.
Holmes, Thomas, 242, 322, 341, 348.
Holmes, William, 322.
Holms, David, 69.
Holms, Joe, 56.
Holms, Simeon, 348.
Holms, Walter, 190.
Holombeck, John, 63, 236.
Holster, Appleton, 187.
Holt, Jesse, 281, 319, 336.
Holt, Lavinas, 6.
Holt, Nathaniel, 78, 157, 252, 319, 336.
Holt, Peter, 252, 290, 358.
Holt, Philemon, 85, 128, 130, 187, 236, 239.
Holt, S., 198.
Holt, Samuel, 87, 230, 293.
Holt, Silas, 56, 138.
Holt, Zebediah, 363.
Holway, Daniel, 51, 69.
Hoodley, Samuel, 170.
Hooker, 299, 300.
Hooker, James, 103, 341.
Hooker, John, 31, 73. 170, 231, 265.
Hooker, William, 31, 70, 238, 242.
Hoose, Bordle. 277, 350.
Hopkins, Daniel, 12.
Hopkins, Elisha, 254, 255, 304. 320, 337.
Hopkins, George, 249.
Hopkins, Henry, 32, 90, 234, 285, 292.
Hopkins, John, 92.
Hopkins, Maturen, 184.
Hopkins, Rhoderick, 248.
Hopkins, Richard, 136.
Hopkins, William, 12. 154.
Hoppen, 4.
Hoppen, Gideon. 4.
Hopson, Linus, 14, 169.
Hopson, Pren, 14.

Hopson, Samuel, Jr., 14.
Hopson, Simeon, 13.
Horron, John, 31.
Horseey, 151.
Horskins, Daniel, 236.
Horskins, Timothy, 276.
Horton, Christopher, 48, 246, 322, 341, 350.
Horton, Ezekiel, 220.
Horton, Henry, 325, 339, 351.
Horton, Moses, 18.
Horton, Samuel, 221.
Hoskins, Timothy, 241.
Hoskins, Timothy, 86, 264, 348.
Hoskins, Zeb., 86.
Hoskins, Zebulon, 348.
Hosmer, John, 345.
Hosmer, Prosper, 256.
Hosmer, Simeon, 52, 70.
Hosmer, Timothy, 3, 31, 169, 239.
Hotchkiss, Aseael, 199.
Hotchkiss, Boswell, 338.
Hotchkiss, Eldad, 8.
Hotchkiss, Ira, 31, 169, 231.
Hotchkiss, Isaac, 51.
Hotchkiss, Jared, 213.
Hotchkiss, Levi, 34, 230.
Hotchkiss, Mark, 5.
Hotchkiss, Medad, 53.
Hotchkiss, Prince, 83.
Hotchkiss, Reuben, 100.
Hotchkiss, Roswell, 338.
Hotchkiss, Rozel, 289.
Hotchkiss, Samuel S. B., 59, 83.
Hotchkiss, Stephen, 49.
Hotchkiss, Truman, 288.
Hotchkiss, Zadock, 31, 169, 239, 355.
Hough, Phenihas, 13.
Hough, Samuel, 13.
Hough, Simon, 265.
Hough, William, 215.
Houghton, James, 32, 82, 237.
House, Asael, 65, 132.
House, Eliphalet, 186.
House, George, 351.
House, James, 370.
House, John, 351, 367.
House, Jonathan, 132.
House, Joseph, 370.
Hovey, Ezra, 355.
Hovey, Ichabod, 54, 73, 130.
Hovey, Jacob, 56, 77, 85, 128.
Hovey, James, 294.
Hovey, Nathan, 85, 128, 295.
How, 69.
How, Asa, 206.

How, Israel, 18.
How, J., 117, 118.
How, Jaazaniah, 56, 77, 137.
How, John, 17.
How, Joshua, 229, 337.
How, Noah, 362.
How, Zadock, 1, 63, 169, 238.
Howard, Benjamin, 17.
Howard, Elijah, 63.
Howard, George, 32, 169, 239.
Howard, Jonathan, 131.
Howard, Richard, 85, 127, 169, 265.
Howard, William, 129.
Howd, Joel, 2.
Howe, George, 103.
Howe, Joshua, 30, 169, 254, 265, 321.
Howe, Silas, 117.
Howe, Zadock, 30.
Howel, Nicholas, 32, 265.
Howell, John, 74.
Howell, Nicholas, 169, 343.
Howkins, Rhodolfus, 218.
Hows, Benjamin, 227.
Hows, George, 61.
Hoy, Alexander, 247.
Hoyt, Comfort, 153.
Hoyt, Joel, 258.
Hoyt, Joseph, 233.
Hoyt, Joseph, Jr., 9.
Hoyt, Justice, 9.
Hoyt, Nathan, Jr., 9.
Hoyt, Peter, 32.
Hoyt, Philemon, 32.
Hoyt, Samuel, 32.
Hoyt, Thomas, 9.
Hrreck, Sanford, 9.
Hubbard, Aaron, 17.
Hubbard, Abijah, 346.
Hubbard, Benjamin, 48.
Hubbard, David, 17, 333.
Hubbard, Dean, 7.
Hubbard, Ebenezar, 346.
Hubbard, Elihu, 30, 65, 240.
Hubbard, Elijah, 17, 355.
Hubbard, Elisha, 242.
Hubbard, Eliz, 17.
Hubbard, George, 59, 82, 313, 329, 350.
Hubbard, Hezekiah, 30, 169, 239, 265.
Hubbard, Hezekiah, Jr., 7.
Hubbard, James, 274.
Hubbard, Joel, 6.
Hubbard, John, 7, 30, 68, 231.
Hubbard, Jonas, 74.

Hubbard, Jonathan, 346.
Hubbard, Joseph, 90.
Hubbard, Manoah, 193.
Hubbard, Philip, 274.
Hubbard, Roswell, 30, 169, 239.
Hubbard, Selah, 7.
Hubbard, Silas, 243.
Hubbard, Simeon, 358.
Hubbard, Simon, 358.
Hubbard, Solomon, 7.
Hubbard, Timothy, 7.
Hubbart, John, 61.
Hubbel, Abijah, 276.
Hubbel, Amos, 7.
Hubbel, Enoch, 8.
Hubbel, Ezra, 7.
Hubbel, Isaac, 31, 67, 68, 169, 233, 265.
Hubbel, James, 230.
Hubbel, Seth, 169.
Hubbel, William, 31, 169, 233.
Hubbell, Aaron, 3.
Hubbell, David, 317, 333.
Hubbell, Ezbon, 331.
Hubbell, Gershom, 4.
Hubbell, Isaac, 4, 92, 94.
Hubbell, Isband, 97.
Hubbell, Isbon, 67.
Hubbell, Jos., Jr., 4.
Hubbell, Lemuel, 154, 162.
Hubbell, Nathan, 123, 154.
Hubbell, Primus, 103.
Hubbell, Samuel, 104.
Hubbell, Seth, 109, 265, 334.
Hubbell, William, 4, 67.
Hubbell, William G., 162.
Hubbert, Elisha, 61.
Hubbert, James, 210.
Hubbert, Joseph, 59.
Hubble, Thadeus, 9.
Hubell, Abijah, 339.
Hubert, George, 313.
Huchens, Shubel, 363.
Hucker, James, 61.
Hudson, Daniel, 192.
Hudson, David, 61.
Hudson, Eleazer, 31, 232.
Hudson, George, 84.
Hudson, John, 31, 233.
Hudson, Joshua, 18.
Hudson, William, 281, 359.
Huff, John, 201.
Huggins, John, 366.
Hughes, Bodwell, 332.
Hughes, William, 314, 330.
Huit, Leuis, 10.
Hubbard, John, 7.

Hulbart, Raphel, 13.
Hulbert, Gideon, 67.
Hulbert, John, 59.
Hulburd, Ithriel, 7.
Hulburt, Stephen, 9.
Hulet, Phinehas, 76, 147.
Hull, Aaron, 13.
Hull, Abel, 52, 72.
Hull, Asa, 243.
Hull, Asehel, 216.
Hull, Caleb, 13.
Hull, Daniel, 78, 227.
Hull, David, 5, 7, 31, 47, 169, 239, 265, 334, 346.
Hull, Eli, 276, 352.
Hull, Eliakim, 66, 265, 334.
Hull, George, 53, 72.
Hull, Giles, 31, 78, 168, 235, 355.
Hull, Henry, 78, 227, 343.
Hull, James, 31.
Hull, Jehiel, 209.
Hull, Job, 83.
Hull, Jonathan, 78, 227, 337.
Hull, Joseph, 53, 72, 281.
Hull, Moses, 78, 227.
Hull, Oliver, 31, 79, 169, 232.
Hull, Robert, 276, 352.
Hull, Samuel, 2, 31, 72, 169, 229, 258, 265, 282, 311, 344.
Hull, Stephen, 31, 99, 235.
Hull, Talmage, 154.
Hull, Wakeman, 67, 95.
Hull, Zachariah, 347.
Hull, Zephaniah, 288.
Humberfield, Ebenezer, 216.
Hummaston, Timothy, 206.
Hummerston, Daniel, 83.
Humph, Jonathan, Jr., 10.
Humpr, Theophilus, 10.
Humphrey, Elijah, 235.
Humphrey, Israel, 144.
Humphrey, John, 141.
Humphry, E., 30, 230.
Humphry, Elijah, 30, 170.
Humphry, George, 11.
Humphry, Israel, 80, 349.
Humphry, John, 80.
Humphry, Joel, 10.
Humphry, Jonathan, 143.
Humphry, Oliver, 11.
Humphry, Solomon, Jr., 11.
Humphry, Timothy, 10, 265, 275, 349.
Humphrys, Lott, 186.
Hun, Isaiah, 241.
Hungerford, David, 174.
Hungerford, Ira, 347.
Hungerford, James, 6, 269.
Hungerford, Uri, 278, 299.
Hungerford, Uriah, 340.
Hunn, David, 74.
Hunn, Samuel, 199.
Hunt, Cato, 71.
Hunt, Charles, 184, 295.
Hunt, Elijah, 294.
Hunt, John, 265, 275, 349.
Hunt, John, Jr., 102.
Hunt, Joseph, 347.
Hunt, Richard, 32, 229.
Hunt, Rusel, 63.
Hunt, Samson, 46.
Hunt, Samson R., 63.
Hunt, Samuel, 63.
Hunt, Simeon, 102.
Hunt, Theophilus, 188.
Hunt, Walter, 221.
Hunter, Joseph, 46, 131, 137.
Hunter, Robert, 112.
Hunting, 157.
Huntingdon, Ebenezer, 245.
Huntington, 82, 150, 156, 158, 159, 160, 161, 181, 304, 310, 319, 344.
Huntington, Ebenezer, 74, 303.
Huntington, Eleazer, 129.
Huntington, Hezekiah, 188.
Huntington, Hiram, 76.
Huntington, Ives, 278.
Huntington, Jedidiah, 74.
Huntington, John, 12, 85, 128, 140.
Huntington, Joseph, 291.
Huntington, Rodger, 201.
Huntington, Samuel, 10, 76.
Huntington, William, 59, 81, 291.
Huntley, Elihu, 3, 180.
Huntley, Solomon, 75.
Huntly, Noah, 3, 352.
Hurburt, A., 102.
Hurd, Abraham, Jr., 281.
Hurd, Calvin, 105.
Hurd, Crippen, 217, 352.
Hurd, David, 58, 317, 332.
Hurd, Elijah, 222.
Hurd, Gideon, Jr., 61, 99.
Hurd, Jacob, 76.
Hurd, Jeduthan, 160, 198.
Hurd, Jonathan, 8.
Hurd, Joseph, 104.
Hurd, Lewis, 61, 107, 305, 308.
Hurd, Walliston, 206.
Hurd, Williston, 206.
Hurd, Zadock, 286.
Hurlbert, Joel, 210.

Hurlbert, John, 83.
Hurlbert, Stephen, 243.
Hurlburt, Cuff, 181.
Hurlburt, Gideon, 96.
Hurlburt, Gideon, Jr., 102.
Hurlburt, Noah, 104.
Hurlburt, Reuben, 144.
Hurlburt, Robert, 102.
Hurlburt, S., 104.
Hurlburt, Steave, 84.
Hurlburt, Steaven, 60.
Hurlburt, Stephen, 98.
Hurlbut, 61.
Hurlbut, Abner, 76.
Hurlbut, Alvin, 86.
Hurlbut, Aseph, 61.
Hurlbut, David, 69.
Hurlbut, George, 290.
Hurlbut, Stephen, 319.
Hurlbut, Thomas, 128.
Hurlbutt, Alfred, 85.
Hurlbutt, Alvin, 348.
Hurlbutt, Aseph, 102.
Hurlbutt, Enoch, 277.
Hurlbutt, James, 347.
Hurlbutt, James H., 348.
Hurlbutt, Jehiel, 346.
Hurlbutt, Jonathan, 347.
Hurlbutt, Leucius, 351.
Huse, 8.
Huse, Boardwell, 169, 355.
Huse, Bodwell, 32, 229, 265.
Huse, Freeman, 8.
Huse, William, 314.
Huston, William, 214.
Hutchen, Jeremiah, 286.
Hutchenson, Thomas, 78.
Hutcherson, Thomas, 57.
Hutcheson, John, 296.
Hutchinson, 370.
Hutchinson, Amos, 15.
Hutchinson, Asa, 142.
Hutchinson, Ebenezer, 142.
Hutchinson, Elijah, 141.
Hutchinson, Jonathan, 221.
Hutchinson, Jonathan, Jr., 221.
Hutchinson, Moses, 198.
Hutchinson, Thomas, 121, 162, 287.
Hutchison, John, 296.
Hutchson, Amos, 15.
Hutenot, Francis, 169.
Hutinock, Frances, 4.
Hutonet, Francis, 31.
Hutonot, Francis, 67, 233.
Hutsheson, Paul, 296.
Hutternock, Francis, 98.

Huxley, John, 349.
Hyat, Abraham, 9.
Hyat, Alvin, 9.
Hyatt, Samuel, 111.
Hyde, Asa, 214, 279.
Hyde, Charles, 220.
Hyde, James, 31, 302, 306, 328.
Hyde, James, 34, 74.
Hyde, Jedidiah, Jr., 74.
Hyde, Joel, 272, 323, 341.
Hyde, Ollever, 140.
Hyde, Rufus, 31, 232, 340.
Hyde, Samuel, 200.
Hyde, William, 196.
Hyden, David, 341.
Hylys, James, Jr., 357.

Indian, 4.
Indian, James, 138.
Indian, John, 48.
Indian, Joseph, 141.
Indian, Samson, 156.
Indian, Tom, 104.
Ingals, 138.
Ingersole, Joel, 203.
Ingham, Samuel, 49.
Ingham, Stephen, 79, 250.
Ingly, Joseph, 46, 113.
Ingraham, Daniel, Jr., 140.
Ingraham, Eleazer, 104.
Ingraham, Henry, 208.
Ingraham, Samuel, 282.
Ingraham, William, 104.
Ingram, 33, 233.
Ingram, Amaziah, 213.
Ingram, Jared, 10.
Ingram, Mary, 33, 233.
Ipswich, Mass., 366.
Ireland, 365, 366.
Isbell, Joel, 300.
Isbell, Lyman, 281, 300.
Isbell, Peruda, 104.
Isham, Ebenezer, 87.
Isham, Jona, 87.
Isham, Joshua, 47, 351.
Isham, William, 87, 351.
Ivers, Thomas, 58.
Ives, Aaron, 13.
Ives, Abij., 83.
Ives, Asahel, 215.
Ives, Elnathan, 19.
Ives, Lazarus, 19.
Ives, Levi, 13.
Ives, Samuel, 206.
Ixbel, Joel, 274.

Jaaroms, David, 49.

INDEX. 429

Jabor, Phillip, 247.
Jack, 58.
Jack, John, 147, 158, 223.
Jackknife, Robert, 33.
Jacklin, Ebenezer, 120, 162.
Jacklin, Lewis, 56, 78, 120, 162.
Jacklin, Thomas, 94.
Jackson, Archabel, 362.
Jackson, Daniel, 97, 312, 344.
Jackson, David, 58, 68, 94, 314, 330.
Jackson, Frederick, 243.
Jackson, George, 182.
Jackson, Gideon, 216.
Jackson, John, 73.
Jackson, Jonathan, 266.
Jackson, Joseph, 118, 153, 162, 217.
Jackson, Joseph, 2d, 120.
Jackson, Levi, 58.
Jackson, Matthew, 137, 324, 339.
Jackson, Moses, 110.
Jackson, N. Peet, 67.
Jackson, Nathan, 110.
Jackson, Nathan, Jr., 109.
Jackson, Nathan P., 4, 33, 233.
Jackson, Richard, 52, 53, 70, 72.
Jackson, Robert, 181, 225.
Jackson, Samuel, 61, 103, 329.
Jackson, Stephen, 182.
Jackson, Thomas, 33, 77, 170, 232.
Jackson, William, 67, 97, 109, 287.
Jackson, Zebulon, 111.
Jackwise, Robart, 233.
Jacobs, Joseph, 278.
Jacobs, M., 33.
Jacobs, Silas, 286.
Jambers, James, 4.
James, Amos, 188.
James, Freeman, 188.
James, Jeffrey, 73.
James, Phillup, 266.
James, Thomas, 100.
Jameson, Robert, Jr., 12.
Janes, Elias, 132.
Janes, Joseph, 231.
Janes, Thomas, 13, 83.
Jany, Marleck, 291.
Jarols, Amos, 59.
Jarrall, Thomas, 346.
Jarrel, Thomas, 238.
Jarrell, Thomas, 70.
Jarrels, Thomas, 33, 266.
Jarrold, Morris, 349.
Jeacocks, Gershom, 67.
Jeacocks, Joshuah, 67.

Jecocks, Joshua, 96.
Jecox, Gershom, 96.
Jeffards, John, 64.
Jeffer, Nathanel, 214.
Jeffery, James, 366.
Jeffery, John, 367.
Jeffery, Rolin, 277.
Jeffords, John, 157, 158.
Jemison, William, 115.
Jenings, Eliphalet, 4.
Jenings, Joal, 4.
Jenings, Josiah, 4.
Jenings, Justice, 4.
Jenings, Lyman, 3.
Jenings, William, 3.
Jenkes, Jonathan, 137.
Jenkins, Calvin, 109.
Jenkins, Samuel, 344.
Jenkins, William, 109.
Jenks, John, 287.
Jenks, Jonathan, 225.
Jennings, Elnathan, 32, 240.
Jennings, Isbon, 68.
Jennings, John, Jr., 68.
Jennings, Joseph, Jr., 128.
Jennison, Pender, 19.
Jepson, William, 86.
Jeralls, Thomas, 170.
Jerrum, Elephaz, 207.
Jervis, Isaac, 3.
Jervis, Nathan, 109.
Jessup, Cato, 281.
Jessup, Edward, 287.
Jessup, Nathaniel, 117, 234.
Jesup, Nathaniel, 33.
Jewett, Thomas, 363.
Jiles, Mingo, 123.
Jillit, Abram, 222.
Jillit, Israel, 354.
Jillson, Andrew, 13.
Jimpson, John, 350.
Jinins, David, 357.
Jinkes, Joseph, 137.
Jinkins, John, 296.
Jinkins, Samuel, 311.
Jinks, John, 205, 331.
Jinks, Oliver, 71.
Jinnings, John, 202.
Joans, Jesse, 72.
Job, Benjamin, 70.
Jobb, Benjamin, 52.
Jocelin, John, 8, 33.
John, 75.
Johnson, 156, 202, 223, 362.
Johnson, Abner, 190.
Johnson, Abraham, 32, 170, 229, 265.

Johnson, Artemas, 1.
Johnson, Benjamin, 32, 60, 76, 83, 148, 158, 237.
Johnson, Bristo, 286.
Johnson, Bristol, 265.
Johnson, Caleb, 181.
Johnson, Caleb, Jr., 7.
Johnson, Dan, 13.
Johnson, Daniel, 10, 116, 206, 282.
Johnson, Davice, 70.
Johnson, David, 32, 84.
Johnson, Davis, 52, 239.
Johnson, Eliakim, 60, 83.
Johnson, Elihu, 32, 81, 170, 239.
Johnson, Elijah, 10, 12.
Johnson, Grant, 59.
Johnson, Isael, 83.
Johnson, Isaac, 32, 231, 266.
Johnson, Israel, 47, 60, 192, 351.
Johnson, James, 7, 32, 64, 84, 146, 346.
Johnson, James, Jr., 65.
Johnson, James, 2d, 7.
Johnson, Jedediah, 362.
Johnson, Jeremiah, 4.
Johnson, Joel, 280, 332.
Johnson, John, 4, 9, 32, 53, 67, 77, 83, 96, 110, 146, 150, 170, 230, 239, 266, 351.
Johnson, John, Jr., 5.
Johnson, Jonathan, 32, 170, 239, 265.
Johnson, Joseph, 85, 128, 243, 279, 306, 348.
Johnson, Luther, 60.
Johnson, Nathaniel, 4, 11, 32, 67, 98, 114, 233, 285.
Johnson, Obadiah, 158, 159, 161, 225.
Johnson, Peter, 61, 323, 341.
Johnson, Phinehas, 73.
Johnson, Prince, 332.
Johnson, Reuben, 1.
Johnson, Robert, 32, 170, 236, 288, 355.
Johnson, Rufus, 199.
Johnson, Samuel, 6, 13, 117, 346, 367.
Johnson, Samuel, 2d, 13.
Johnson, Solomon, 72, 135, 208.
Johnson, Thomas, 366.
Johnson, Timothy, 73.
Johnson, William, 3, 32, 59, 66, 67, 81, 96, 117, 170, 190, 265, 273, 341.
Johnston, Abraham, 338.
Johnston, Bristol, 351.
Johnston, James, 240.
Johnston, Jonathan, 132.
Johnston, Joseph, 321, 338.
Johnston, Timothy, 340.
Johnstone, William, 234.
Johson, Isaac, 170.
Joice, David, 333.
Jole, William, 162.
Jolly, William, 33, 122, 155, 234.
Jona, 162.
Jonas, Jonah, 154.
Jonathan, Gideon, 279.
Jone, John Frederick, 283.
Jones, Aaron, 32, 79, 170, 232, 254, 266, 320, 358, 359.
Jones, Asa, 76, 147, 159.
Jones, Asahel, 370.
Jones, Charles, 170.
Jones, Dan, 290.
Jones, Daniel, 32, 58, 90, 140, 170, 237, 266, 291.
Jones, David, 279, 338, 349.
Jones, Eleazer, 32, 80, 238.
Jones, Elezer, 18.
Jones, Elias, 56, 77, 137.
Jones, Elihu, 220.
Jones, Epahrass, 243.
Jones, Etkanah, 220.
Jones, Eton, Jr., 286.
Jones, Ezra, 207.
Jones, George, 6.
Jones, Henry, 32, 359.
Jones, Isaac, 63.
Jones, Isahel, 370.
Jones, Isaiah, 32, 114, 170, 233.
Jones, Issacher, 18.
Jones, James, 56, 77, 137, 286.
Jones, Jasber, 170.
Jones, Jasper, 32, 93, 234, 265.
Jones, Jesse, 52.
Jones, John, 2, 90, 95, 97, 136.
Jones, Jonah, 122.
Jones, Joseph 2, 32, 170, 266.
Jones, Manual, 147.
Jones, Morris, 74, 79.
Jones, Nathan, 80.
Jones, Phineas, 274.
Jones, Phinehus, 300.
Jones, Pratt, 336.
Jones, Richard, 252.
Jones, Rubin, 210.
Jones, Samuel, 59, 60, 83, 221, 286.
Jones, Stephen, 12, 18.
Jones, Thomas, 9, 32, 76, 77, 137, 170, 230, 237, 265, 292, 366, 369.

# INDEX. 431

Jones, William, 47, 48, 71, 135, 243, 276, 281, 291, 300, 350, 351.
Jonson, Christopher, 6.
Jonson, Ephraim, 18.
Jonson, Jason, 296.
Jonson, Joseph, 152.
Jonson, Noah, 152.
Jonson, Robert, 79.
Jonson, Samuel, 6.
Jonson, William, 230, 301.
Jordan, John, 33, 105, 236.
Jordan, Miles, 286.
Jordon, Miles, 225.
Joseph, 58.
Joslen, Jose, 137.
Joslin, John, 170, 229, 265.
Josselin, Pember, 5.
Judd, 143, 144.
Judd, Alexander, 330.
Judd, Brewster, 33, 84, 170, 230.
Judd, Calvin, 187.
Judd, Chandler, 344.
Judd, Chanley, 204.
Judd, Charles, 344.
Judd, Daniel, 33, 185, 241.
Judd, Ebenezer, 124.
Judd, Ephraim, 87.
Judd, Freeman, 61, 99.
Judd, Jacob, 14.
Judd, Phinehas, 49.
Judd, Reuben, 124, 190, 221.
Judd, Stephen, 33, 84, 170, 230.
Judd, W., 144, 145.
Judd, William, 33, 143, 170, 239.
Juddson, John B., 209.
Judgson, Joseph, 33, 235.
Judson, Brester, 154.
Judson, Chapman, 99.
Judson, Chapman, Jr., 100.
Judson, Joseph, 102, 116, 170.
Judson, S., 92.
Judson, T., 99.
June, James, 108.
June, Stephen, 115.
Jurden, Stephen, 8.
Justin, Charles, 223.
Justin, Walcott, 64, 157.

Kafin, 78.
Kanady, Nathan, 201.
Kafin, 78.
Kane, William, 343.
Karril, John, 33.
Kasson, William, 12.
Kath, John, 135.
Katon, John, 284.
Keach, Philip, 71, 136.

Kedar, 75.
Kee, John, 13.
Kee, Nathaniel, 136.
Keehole, Peter, 50.
Keeler, 56, 88, 162.
Keeler, Aaron, 110, 111, 343, 344.
Keeler, David, 108.
Keeler, Ebenezer, 55, 120, 154.
Keeler, Henry, 110.
Keeler, Hezekiah, 61, 103.
Keeler, Isaac, 9, 304, 313, 315, 335.
Keeler, Jeremiah, 56, 78, 120, 162.
Keeler, Levi, 56, 78, 120, 162.
Keeler, Lockwood, 9.
Keeler, Samuel, 3d, 9.
Keeler, Thodds, 204.
Keeler, Thomas, 56, 78, 120.
Keeler, Uriah, 109, 343.
Keelsoy, Nathan, 66.
Keene, Benjamin, 238.
Keeney, Benjamin, 33.
Keeney, Thomas, 226.
Keeny, Benjamin, 70.
Keggin, John, 198.
Keigwin, Amos, 12.
Keigwin, James, 12.
Keigwin, Thomas, 12.
Keith, John, 71.
Kelby, Christopher, 334.
Kelcey, John, 52, 72.
Kelcey, Joshua, 53, 72.
Kelcey, Oliver, 52.
Kelcy, Elijah, 203.
Kelcy, Noah, 236.
Kelcy, Peter, 53.
Keley, Eli, 300.
Keley, Samuel, Jr., 59.
Kellcey, Preson, 266.
Kelley, John, 170, 302.
Kelley, Moses, 215.
Kellis, Peter, 61, 121.
Kellog, Enoch, 111.
Kellog, Isaac, 132.
Kellog, Samuel, 204.
Kellog, Stephen, 111.
Kellogg, Dolphin, 47.
Kellogg, Elijah, 202, 222.
Kellogg, Enoch, 334.
Kellogg, Esau, 47.
Kellogg, Grove, 52, 70.
Kellogg, Horrace, 52, 70.
Kellogg, Isaac, 66, 141.
Kellogg, Jonathan, 9.
Kellogg, Oliver, 214.
Kellogg, Peter, 268, 283, 351.

Kellogg, Seth, 52, 70, 255, 345.
Kellogg, Stephen, 254, 321, 338, 348.
Kelly, John, 40, 53, 283.
Kelsey, Eli, 281.
Kelsey, Noah, 33, 80, 170, 266, 321.
Kelsey, Oliver, 72.
Kelsug, Noah, 338.
Kelue, Peter, 162.
Kendal, Daniel, 19.
Kendal, Joshua, 290.
Kendall, John, 345.
Kendall, Joshua, 198.
Kendol, Noadiah, 144.
Kendrich, Benjamin, 87.
Kenedy, David, 363.
Keney, Benjamin, 170, 346.
Keney, Thomas, 180.
Kenn, William, 285.
Kennedy, Joseph, 12.
Kennedy, Nathan, 357.
Kenney, Benjamin, 266.
Kenning, Thomas, 122.
Kenny, Jonas, 184.
Kenny, Joshua, 342.
Kenny, Richard, 342.
Kent, Abel, 18.
Kent, Benajah, 18.
Kent, Joseph, 180, 338.
Kent, Nathan, 57.
Kent, Oliver, 179.
Kent, Titus, 352.
Kent, 23, 25, 26, 27, 31, 34, 35, 103, 104, 106, 107, 126, 165, 169, 170, 189, 208, 209, 210, 211, 235, 261, 265, 282, 285, 355.
Keny, 143.
Keny, James, 143.
Kerkum, William, 335.
Kerns, Luke, 60.
Ketcham, Ezra, 47.
Ketchem, Daniel, 4.
Ketchum, Ezra, 119, 154.
Ketchum, Samuel, 109.
Keton, John, 348.
Keyes, Aaron, 46.
Keyes, Elnathan, 226.
Keyes, Marshal, 282, 341.
Keys, Elnathan, 181.
Kibbe, Bildad, 11.
Kibbe, Daniel, 11.
Kibbe, James, 2d, 11.
Kibbe, Philip, 57, 81.
Kidder, James, 130.
Kilbey, Christopher, 170.
Kilborn, Abraham, 53.

Kilborn, David, 53.
Kilborn, Elaphaz, 215.
Kilborn, Roswell, 286.
Kilborn, Samuel, 53.
Kilby, Anthony, 188.
Kilby, Christopher, 33, 238, 255, 310.
Killam, Cyrus, 51.
Killingly, 30, 35, 37, 71, 134, 135, 136, 137, 138, 161, 173, 183, 190, 192, 193, 194, 195, 197, 199, 200, 215, 216, 217, 225, 237, 260, 264, 269, 270, 272, 273, 287, 292, 295, 301.
Killingworth, 22, 28, 30, 34, 38, 39, 52, 72, 150, 151, 164, 166, 167, 170, 173, 174, 188, 209, 211, 212, 216, 231, 261, 262, 263, 268, 270, 273, 274, 280, 281, 300, 367.
Killogg, Isaac, 257.
Killum, Luther, 211.
Kiltam, Cyrus, 69.
Kimbal, Abraham, 33.
Kimbal, Elijah, 363.
Kimball, Abraham T., 170, 239, 346.
Kimball, Elijah, 362.
Kimball, Jared, 284, 323, 341.
Kimball, Jedede, 266.
Kimball, Jedediah, 287, 301, 302, 306, 312, 344.
Kimball, John, 284, 323.
Kimball, Richard, 323, 341.
Kimball, Samuel, 199.
Kimberlee, John, 154.
Kimberley, Ephraim, 266.
Kimberly, 33, 234.
Kimberly, Charles, 60.
Kimberly, E., 170.
Kimberly, John, 123.
Kimboe, Charles, 131.
Kinball, Charles, 185.
Kindle, John, 339.
Kine, Daniel, 208.
King, Eli, 336.
King, George, 33, 75, 170, 229.
King, Hez, 170.
King, John, 152.
King, Joseph, 266, 284, 352.
King, Orry, 33, 93, 170, 234, 250.
King, Samuel, 4, 208.
King, Theodore, 187.
Kingbury, Phinehas, Jr., 369.
Kingley, Asael, 181.
Kingman, Mitchel, 368.
Kingsberry, Jabez, 75.
Kingsberry, Joseph, 48.

Kingsbury, Andrew, 132.
Kingsbury, J., 329.
Kingsbury, Jabez, 71, 136, 161.
Kingsbury, Jacob, 303, 305, 328, 339.
Kingsbury, Joseph, 193.
Kingsbury, Michael, 113.
Kingsbury, Oliver, 136, 294, 316.
Kingsbury, Samuel, 224.
Kingsley, Aaron, 288, 325, 339.
Kingsley, Asehel, 221.
Kingsley, Elipaz, 85.
Kingsley, Hezekiah, 159.
Kingsley, James, 75.
Kingsley, Ebenezer, 19.
Kinne, Asa, 10.
Kinne, Benoni, 12, 148.
Kinne, Ezra, 15.
Kinne, Jacob, 10.
Kinne, James, 149.
Kinne, Spencer, 15.
Kinney, Joseph, 182.
Kinning, Thomas, 33, 234.
Kinsey, William, 350.
Kiplee, Elijah, 340.
Kircum, Benjamin, 258, 306, 328.
Kircum, John, 303, 308, 327.
Kircum, Philemon, 328.
Kircum, William, 252.
Kirkham, Benjamin, 51.
Kirkham, William, 51.
Kirkland, 232.
Kirkum, John, 250, 348.
Kirkum, Philemon, 273, 307, 319.
Kirkum, Samuel, 348.
Kirkum, William, 318.
Kirtland, 33.
Kirtland, Jabez, 272, 323, 341.
Kirtland, James, 81.
Kirttend, Jabez, 301.
Kittle, Thomas, 345.
Knap, Aaron, 119, 154.
Knap, Abraham, 74.
Knap, Benjamin, 121.
Knap, Borden, 114.
Knap, Charles, 116.
Knap, David, 121.
Knap, Ebenezer, 3.
Knap, Edward, 349.
Knap, Elijah, 74.
Knap, Henry, 222.
Knap, James, 33. 57, 80, 115, 233, 234.
Knap, John, 3, 55, 105.
Knap, John, Jr., 121.
Knap, Jonas, 57.
Knap, Jones, 80.

Knap, Lemuel, 137.
Knap, Moses, 7, 89.
Knap, S., 114.
Knap, Samuel, 116.
Knap, Timothy, 33, 69, 170, 235.
Knap, Usel, 33, 233.
Knap, Uzel, 313.
Knapp, Benjamin, 282.
Knapp, Bouton, 367.
Knapp, Edward, 206.
Knapp, Isaac, 367.
Knapp, James, 365.
Knapp, Jared, 53.
Knapp, Nathan, 115.
Knapp, Ushal, 114.
Knapp, Uzal, 329.
Kneel, Robart, 66.
Kneeland, Jesse, 266, 284, 353.
Kneeland, Jonathan, 3.
Kneeland, Samuel, 87.
Kneeland, Seth, 345.
Knight, Daniel, 310.
Knight, Daniel W., 335.
Knight, Elijah, 75.
Knight, Phineas, 272, 301, 323, 341.
Knight, Squier, 136.
Knight, Squir. 71, 148.
Knight, Squire, 160.
Knight, William, 82, 147, 159.
Knolton, Joseph, 3.
Knot, Hezekiah, 348.
Knowles, Charles, 7.
Knowles, Giles, 65.
Knowles, James, 266.
Knowles, John, 345.
Knowles, Seth, 65, 347.
Knowlton, 88.
Knowlton, Joshua, 46.
Knox, Alexander, 286, 297.
Knox, Archable, 357.
Koberling, Cornelus, 14.
Kyes, Aaron, 130.
Kyes, Marshall, 323.

Lacey, Fairchild F., 34.
Lacey, John F., 154.
Lacey, Josiah, 34, 67, 234.
Lacey, Richard, 4.
Lacy, J. Fairchild, 234.
Lacy, John, 7.
Lacy, John Fairchild, 122.
Lacy, Josiah, 171.
Lacy, Seth, 8.
Lad, Eliab, 12.
Ladd, John, 132.
Ladd, Oliver, 132.

## 434  REVOLUTION LISTS AND RETURNS.

Ladd, Samuel, Jr., 75.
Laflen, James, 82.
Laflen, John, Jr., 82.
Laflin, Abraham, 82.
Laflin, James, 59.
Laflin, John, 59, 61.
Lair, Jacob, 69.
Lake, Phineas, 171, 235.
Lake, Reuben, 332.
Lamb, 150, 152, 359.
Lamb, Asa, 51, 69, 198.
Lamb, Benjamin, 128.
Lamb, Jacob, 281.
Lamb, Joseph, 33, 183, 238.
Lamb, Silas, 253.
Lambart, Samuel, 6.
Lambert, Thomas, 281.
Lamberton, Obed, 34, 170, 241, 266, 348.
Lamberton, Obed, Jr., 85.
Lambkins, Benjamin, 170.
Lambskins, Benjamin, 34, 235.
Lament, William, 330.
Lamfear, Samuel, 61.
Lamfeer, Samuel, 296.
Lamphere, Abel, 364.
Lamphere, Roswell, 337.
Lamphere, Samuel, 108.
Lamphier, Fitch, 247.
Lamphier, Roswell, 182.
Lampshire, George, 220.
Lamson, Ebenezer, 11.
Lamson, Samuel, 203.
Lancashire, 366.
Landing, Cazar, 288.
Landon, Ozias, 244.
Lane, Amos, 80.
Lane, Joel, 266, 289.
Lane, John, 46, 131, 211.
Lane, Joseph, 210, 212.
Lane, Lemuel, 278, 299, 347.
Lane, Nathan, 340.
Lane, Robert, 65, 132.
Lane, William, 33, 359.
Lanfere, Oliver, Jr., 2.
Langatha, Stephen, 10, 349.
Langathe, Stephen, 80.
Langdon, Philip, 18, 80.
Langly, David, 69.
Lankton, Jonathan, 50.
Lanord, Asa, 63.
Lanphear, Fitch, 140.
Laphland, John, 352.
Laraba, Seth, 288.
Larabe, Nathaniel, 9.
Larabee, John, 154.
Laraby, Asa, 54.

Laraby, Willet, 54.
Lareey, Ready, 284.
Larey, Ready, 299.
Larnebe, Willord, 235.
Larned, 135.
Larnord, Joseph, 141, 142.
Larow, John, 53.
Larrebee, Willard, 78.
Larrebee, Willet, 34.
Larribe, Seth, 85.
Larrobe, Seth, 127.
Larroby, Thomas, 180.
Larry, Thada, 352.
Lashbrooks, William, 56, 77, 137.
Latham, Amos, 50, 68.
Latham, Cary, 285.
Lathrop, Ebenezer, 362.
Lathrop, James, 179, 220.
Lathrop, Joseph, 75.
Lathrop, Samuel, 76.
Lattemore, Levi, 266.
Lattimer, Levi, 243, 284.
Lattimore, Levi, 348.
Laughlin, James, 80.
Laurance, Edward, 11.
Lauson, Joseph, 307.
Lauton, Joshua, 134.
Laverrick, Gabriel, 266.
Law, Nathan, 205.
Lawin, Joseph, 93.
Lawrance, Amos, 86, 170, 241.
Lawrance, Bille, 46, 63, 64.
Lawrance, John, 135, 228.
Lawrance, Luther, 205.
Lawrence, Amos, 34, 266, 348.
Lawrence, David, 86, 134.
Lawrence, Luthar, 10.
Lawrence, Richard, 280, 289, 354.
Laws, Joseph, 139.
Lawson, David, 179.
Lawson, Joseph, 280, 314, 328.
Lay, Asa, 34, 79, 171, 232, 266.
Lay, Elias, 3.
Lay, John, 179, 266, 282, 338.
Lay, John, 2d, 282.
Lay, John, 4th, 288.
Lay, Richard, 34, 170, 232, 266.
Layre, Jacob, 34, 235.
Lazel, Abner, 277.
Leach, 151.
Leach, Ebenezer, 59.
Leach, Hezekiah, 6, 266.
Leach, Jabez, 71, 137.
Leach, Lewis, 351.
Leach, William, 60, 84, 209.
Leads, Thomas, 344.
Leaming, George, 93.

Learnard, Samuel, 195.
Leason, James, 285.
Leason, Job, 280, 330.
Leathercoat, John, 85, 127.
Leavens, Jacob, 137.
Leavens, Samuel, 217.
Leavenswth, 93.
Leavenswth, D, 102.
Leavensworth, Gideon, 91.
Leavenworth, Eli, 171.
Lebanon, 22, 23, 25, 26, 29, 30, 31, 32, 37, 40, 42, 44, 132, 137, 139, 140, 141, 142, 163, 166, 167, 170, 173, 176, 179, 180, 181, 182, 183, 184, 196, 197, 200, 201, 216, 220, 221, 226, 237, 242, 248, 249, 250, 254, 255, 256, 257, 262, 265, 266, 268, 270, 271, 278, 279, 280, 285, 290, 291, 295, 296, 297, 301, 302, 355, 356.
Lebbeus, 75.
Lebret, Charles, 71, 135.
Lee, Abner, 33, 171, 235, 330.
Lee, David, 187.
Lee, Ebenezer, 49.
Lee, Elias, 46, 63, 64.
Lee, Elisha, 33, 232.
Lee, Enos, 89.
Lee, Ezra, 33, 170, 181, 183, 232, 266.
Lee, Horton, 140.
Lee, John, 287.
Lee, Jonathan, 135.
Lee, Lemuel, 7.
Lee, Levi, 5, 33, 359.
Lee, Matthew, 277, 299, 347.
Lee, Noah, 57, 171, 266.
Lee, Samuel, 61, 103, 334.
Lee, Stephen, 75.
Lee, Thomas, 273.
Lee, William, 49, 352.
Lee, Zadock, 181, 220.
Leech, Christopher, 358, 359.
Leeds, Thomas, 34, 184, 233.
Leek, Timothy, 217.
Leet, Allen, 34, 72, 170, 232.
Leman, George, 58.
Lement, William, 287.
Lenord, Asa, 1.
Lenord, Jedediah, 1.
Lenord, Simeon, 71.
Lensley, Josiah, 49.
Leonard, Asa, 258.
Leonard, Benajah, 105.
Leonard, Ezra, 48.
Leonard, Simeon, 137.
Lerone, John, 67.

Lerow, John, 334.
Leson, Jesse, 66.
Leson, Job, 66.
Lester, Andrew, 33, 63, 64, 236.
Lester, Elijah, 15.
Lester, Guy, 180.
Lester, Nathan, 64, 146, 157.
Levenie, Joseph, 194.
Levensworth, Eli, 229.
Leverick, Gabriel, 34, 73, 171, 233.
Leverick, Gerard, 302.
Levine, Joseph, 195.
Levingston, Isaac, 280.
Levingsworth, Eli, 34.
Levorick, Gabriel, 266.
Lewes, John, 53, 72.
Lewis, 56, 77.
Lewis, Abel, 60, 83.
Lewis, Andrew, 79.
Lewis, Augustus, 5.
Lewis, Chauncey, 60, 83, 254, 307, 321, 328, 350.
Lewis, Clear, 209.
Lewis, David, 290, 291.
Lewis, Ebenezer, 34, 60, 69, 83, 230.
Lewis, Eleazer, 198, 225.
Lewis, Eli, 92.
Lewis, Elihu, 13.
Lewis, Elisha, 73.
Lewis, Frances, 208.
Lewis, Isaac, 254, 350.
Lewis, Jabez, 57, 80.
Lewis, Naboth, 346.
Lewis, Peter, 58, 90, 93, 171, 266, 325.
Lewis, Philip, 66.
Lewis, Philo, 48, 151.
Lewis, Phinies, 148.
Lewis, Robert, 131.
Lewis, Roger, 49.
Lewis, Samuel, 34, 84, 230.
Lewis, Samuel, Jr., 91.
Lewis, Thomas, 78, 113.
Lewis, Valentine, 34, 233.
Lewis, Wait, 154, 162.
Lewis, Weight, 343.
Lewis, William, 247, 346.
Liberty, 288.
Liberty, Cuff, 346.
Liberty, Jeff, 287.
Liberty, James, 343.
Liley, Moses, 10.
Lilington, Samuel, 63.
Lille, Benjamin, 130.
Lille, John, 138.
Lille, Turner, 85.

Lillee, Chester, 200.
Lilley, Abner, 226, 288.
Lilley, Benjamin, 72.
Lilley, Chester, 363.
Lilley, Ebenezer, 171, 237.
Lilley, Elijah, 199.
Lilley, John, 77, 157, 171.
Lilley, Prince, 158.
Lilley, Reuben, 157.
Lilley, Turnor, 128.
Lillie, Abner, 266.
Lillie, Chester, 294.
Lillie, Ebenezer, 82.
Lillie, John, 64.
Lillie, Prince, 64.
Lilliee, Reuben, 64.
Lilly, Ebenezer, 34.
Lilly, John, 56.
Lim, William, 305.
Liman, Joseph, 214.
Limon, Joseph, 218.
Linch, Patrick, 68.
Lincoln, Elisha, 56, 78, 121, 162.
Lindsay, David, 256.
Lindsey, David, 308, 317.
Lindsley, Solomon, Jr., 286.
Lines, John, 34, 171, 196, 266, 283, 285, 292, 351, 355.
Lines, Zenus, 249.
Linkon, Elijah, 85, 127.
Linkton, Elisha, 50.
Linn, David, 188.
Linn, William, 52, 72, 303, 305, 328.
Linsey, David, 348.
Linsey, Josiah, 80.
Linsey, Roland, 80.
Linsley, Abiel, 61.
Linsley, Abiel, Jr., 99.
Linsley, Brainard, 206.
Linsley, Josiah, 349.
Linsley, Robart, 349.
Linsly, David, 331.
Linsly, Simeon, 2.
Lion, Ebenezer, 364.
Lion, Ezra, 355.
Litchfield, Elisha, 64.
Litchfield, James, 64, 158.
Litchfield, 23, 24, 35, 37, 38, 39, 40, 42, 53, 88, 163, 170, 171, 173, 175, 177, 192, 199, 203, 205, 215, 216, 228, 235, 286, 355, 356.
Litchfield Co., 234.
Little, George, 225.
Little, John, 146.
Little, Nathan, 124.
Little, Nathaniel, 8, 154, 181, 220.

Little, Prince, 146.
Little, Ruben, 146.
Little, William, 77.
Littlefield, Ebenezer, 34, 236.
Liverpool, 366.
Livingston, 178, 359.
Loaring, Joseph, 58.
Loatwall, Ephriah, 86.
Lock, William, 95.
Lockwood, Amos, 116.
Lockwood, David, 9, 116.
Lockwood, E., 109.
Lockwood, Eliphalet, 33, 115, 233.
Lockwood, Gershom, 34, 109.
Lockwood, Isaac, 282.
Lockwood, J., 113, 114.
Lockwood, James, 9.
Lockwood, Jared, 116.
Lockwood, Jeremiah, 197, 222.
Lockwood, Joseph, Jr., 116.
Lockwood, Josiah, 181.
Lockwood, Moses, 33, 116, 171, 234, 238.
Lockwood, Samuel, 33, 234.
Lockwood, Stephen, 33, 67, 96, 98, 233.
Lockwood, Timothy, 33, 114, 233.
Lockwood, Timothy, Jr., 116.
Login, Cato, 153.
Lombord, Juston, 18.
Lomis, Ezekiel, 137.
Lomis, Moses, 240.
Lomis, Oliver, 186.
Lomiss, Ezekiel, 77.
Lommis, Solomon, 214.
London, Charles, 59, 83.
London, Ebel, 339.
London, Eliel, 325, 339.
London, Ethiel, 288.
London, Pomp, 61.
Long, James, 153.
Long, Stephen, 294.
Long Island, 88, 368.
Loomis, Abel, 144.
Loomis, Andrew, 63.
Loomis, Brigadier, 280.
Loomis, Dick, 348.
Loomis, Eleazer, 65.
Loomis, Ezekiel, 56, 140.
Loomis, Ezra, 197.
Loomis, George, 86.
Loomis, Ichabod, 362.
Loomis, Israel, 33, 70, 170, 257.
Loomis, Jonathan, 14.
Loomis, Joseph, 198.
Loomis, Lebbeus, 87, 197.
Loomis, Luthar, 59, 82.

INDEX. 437

Loomis, Moses, 33, 295, 296.
Loomis, Roger, 63, 354.
Loomis, Ruben, 14.
Loomis, Samuel, 63, 351.
Loomis, Samuel, Jr., 47.
Loomis, Solomon, 197.
Loomis, Steaphen, 241.
Loomis, Stephen, Jr., 86.
Loomiss, Elijah, 6.
Loomiss, George, 6.
Loomiss, Moses, 287.
Lord, [ ]ben, 153.
Lord, Abner, 343.
Lord, Amos, 79.
Lord, Elijah, 338.
Lord, Eliphalet, 48.
Lord, Henry, 351.
Lord, Jabez, 33, 171, 229, 266, 334.
Lord, James, 74.
Lord, Jeremiah, 33, 79, 153, 171, 232, 254, 266.
Lord, John, 33, 217, 234.
Lord, Richard, 84, 310, 343, 353.
Lord, Solaman, 201.
Lord, William, 33, 79, 153, 232, 266, 304, 324.
Lorian, Joseph, 95.
Lorthup, Azariah, 78.
Loswell, Mark, 159.
Lothrop, Solomon, 75.
Lotroop, David, 188.
Lotwell, Eppaphras, 348.
Loud, Henry, 351.
Loughlin, James, 57.
Lounbuary, David, 150.
Lounsbury, David, 258, 305, 328.
Lounsbury, Peter, 114.
Love, John, 281, 354.
Lovegoy, Nathaniel, 136.
Lovejoy, John, 198, 224.
Lovel, Seth, 216.
Loveland, Amos, 226.
Loveland, Charles, 346.
Loveland, Daniel, 351.
Loveland, Elijah, 7.
Loveland, Elisha, 33, 170, 238.
Loveland, Epafroditus, 220.
Loveland, Isaac, 143.
Loveland, Jonathan, 3, 17, 273.
Loveland, Levi, 33, 238.
Loveland, Thomas, 33, 170, 238, 248, 266, 351.
Loveland, Trueman, 366.
Lovell, Seth, 223.
Loveman, Jonathan, 266.
Loveridge, William, 212.

Lovland, Amos, 191.
Low, William, 57, 80.
Lowden, John, 12.
Lowil, Willobe, 12.
Lowmas, Brigador, 203.
Lownsbury, Nathaniel, 347.
Loyd, Clement, 114.
Lucas, Ichabod, 65.
Lucas, Samuel, 3, 66, 70.
Lucas, William, 7, 66, 216.
Luce, Jonathan, 34, 81, 170, 239, 266, 323, 341, 350.
Luce, Othnell, 196.
Luce, Timothy, 57.
Luce, Uriah, 294.
Luch, James, 48.
Lucus, Samuel, 238.
Luddington, James, 294.
Ludeman, John, 33, 123, 234.
Ludiman, John, 153, 171, 266.
Ludlow, Stephen, 79, 153, 325.
Lung, Joseph, 346.
Luis, Benjamin, 139.
Luis, Simeon, 79.
Luke, Phineas, 33.
Luke, Roger, 282.
Luke, William, 283.
Lukus, Samuel, 34.
Lum, Joseph, 2.
Lumis, Josiah, 17.
Lumis, Samuel, 150.
Lummis, Israel, 238.
Lummis, Nathan, 154.
Lung, Joseph, 7, 34, 170, 239, 266.
Lunsbury, Peter, 34, 233.
Lusk, Solomon, 186.
Luther, Cromwill, 193.
Luther, Crumel, 135.
Luther, Crummil, 71.
Luther, Elisha, 140.
Luther, Nathan, 276.
Luther, Theor, 86.
Luther, Theophilus, 134, 307, 314.
Lylley, Benjamin, 54.
Lyman, 88.
Lyman, Asa, 357.
Lyman, Dan, 141, 221, 296, 315, 331.
Lyman, Elihu, 7.
Lyman, Elisha, 180, 220.
Lyman, Ezekiel, Jr., 141, 295.
Lyman, Isaa, 220.
Lyman, Isaac, 179.
Lyman, Jesse, 220.
Lyman, Jonathan, 2.
Lyman, Phenihas, 13.
Lyman, Richard, 75.

Lyman, Richard, 2⁴, 139.
Lyman, Richard, 3⁴, 139.
Lyman, Samuel, 220.
Lyme, 21, 23, 26, 27, 31, 33, 34, 35, 37, 38, 39, 40, 43, 44, 163, 164, 166, 167, 169, 170, 171, 173, 174, 177, 179, 180, 181, 182, 183, 184, 190, 215, 227, 232, 246, 257, 260, 265, 266, 268, 269, 271, 282, 287, 288, 302, 356, 358, 359, 366, 368.
Lynde, Gideon, 78.
Lynds, John, 229.
Lynde, Samuel, Jr., 279, 300.
Lynn, William, 343.
Lyon, 97, 98, 134.
Lyon, Aaron, 3, 14.
Lyon, Abiel, 33, 76, 138, 237.
Lyon, Amariah, 359.
Lyon, Asa, 33, 86, 134, 230.
Lyon, Ezra, 170.
Lyon, Henry, 33, 131, 237, 266.
Lyon, Isaac, 104.
Lyon, John, 97, 134.
Lyon, Joseph, 214.
Lyon, Joseph, Jr., 68.
Lyon, Nathan, 89.
Lyon, Pelatiah, 110.
Lyon, Peter, 334.
Lyon, Samuel, 33, 97, 233, 284, 309, 334.
Lyon, Stephen, 97, 134.
Lyon, Thomas, 33.
Lyon, Tony, 96.

McAnotter, John, 35, 233.
McCannack, John, 151.
McCartee, George, 267.
McCartee, John, 266.
McCarter, George, 227.
Maccarty, John, 277.
McCensey, George, 35.
McCensey, James, 35.
McClain, James, 78.
McCluer, James, 18.
McColpin, Alexander, 317.
McCorn, William, 34.
McCorne, William, 65, 240.
McCowen, Neal, 118.
McCoy, Alexander, 35, 74, 232.
McCoy, John, 267, 282.
McCraw, Reuben, 202.
McCullum, Duncan, 267, 280.
McCulpin, Alexander, 278, 351.
McCune, Robert, 361.
McCune, Samuel, 362.
McDaniel, Anthony, 54, 330.
McDaniel, Daniel, 71.

McDaniel, James, 232, 267.
McDaniel, John, 171.
McDanield, James, 35.
McDanields, James, 77.
McDaniels, Jams, 171.
McDaniels, Samuel, 9.
McDavid, James, 346.
McDonald, C., 210.
McDonald, Charles, 55, 120, 154.
McDonald, John, 35, 113, 355.
McDonel, John, 68.
McDonold, John, 232.
McDougal, 339.
McDowel, Alexander, 35, 238.
MacFall, William, 34, 344.
McFarland, James, 284.
McFee, Anguis, 73.
McGlaflin, John, 153.
McGreeger, John, 237.
McGregor, John, 35, 171.
McGregory, Aaron, 8.
McGregory, Samuel, 189.
McGriegier, 198.
McGriegier, John, 76.
Mcgriggay, Joel, 66.
Mcgriggry, Joel, 49.
McGuire, Thomas, 283, 301.
McHood, Joseph, 351.
McIntire, Abel, 48.
McIntosh, Timothy, 181.
McJuborrough, Jedd ⁿ, 239.
Mack, Abner, 141, 171, 266, 354.
Mack, Barzilla, 354.
Mack, Benjamin, 79, 246.
Mack, Daniel, 186.
Mack, Hezekiah, 3.
Mack, Joel, 141, 221.
Mack, Orlander, 239.
Mack, Richard, 276, 352.
Mack, Samuel, 142.
Mack, Thomas, 296.
Mack, Zebulon, 369.
Mackarel, James, 370.
Mckartey, James, 139.
Mackaul, James, 370.
Mackaul, Walter, 141.
McKay, James, 3.
McKeine, Barnabas, 5.
McKensey, John, 58.
McKenzie, John, 94.
McKey, Wyllin, 190.
Mackinborough, Benjamin, 142.
Mackinborough, Jedadiah, 142.
McKinstry, Paul, 345.
Mackintire, Henery, 57, 80.
McKinzey, James, 233.
Mackrady, John, 117.

INDEX. 439

Macks, Jeremiah, 171.
McLane, Jacobe, 35, 235, 267.
McLane, Matthew, 35, 232.
McLane, Moredock, 63.
Maclane, Niel, 241.
McLarlene, John, 158.
McLean, David, 52, 70.
McLean, Jacob, 78, 227.
McLean, John, 78, 227.
McLean, Neil, Jr., 86.
McLean, William, 47, 118, 153.
McLorey, Andrew, 77.
McMullin, John, 67.
McNale, Archabel, 14.
McNeal, Henry, 201.
McNeal, Neal, 334.
McNeel, Neel, 210.
McNeil, Neil, 63.
McNulter, John, 267.
McNulty, John, 219, 330.
McNulty, John, 314.
McNunlly, John, 113.
McNutters, John, 171.
MacOrlander, 35.
McQueen, William, 2.
McQuire, Thomas, 354.
McRenneck, John, 73.
McRow, William, 198.
Maculpin, Alexander, 267.
Maggot, Zebulon, 171, 267.
Mahar, James, 35, 70, 171, 238, 267.
Maharr, James, 345.
Maksfield, Caleb, 154.
Main, John, 104.
Malcom, Thomas, 75.
Maleny, Nathan, 339.
Malery, Lemuel, 208.
Malison, Thomas, 50, 68.
Mallary, A., 99.
Mallary, David, 102.
Mallerson, Benjamin, 34.
Mallery, Amos, 35, 73, 172, 229, 266, 267.
Mallery, Calvin, 217.
Mallery, David, 73.
Mallery, Giles, 9.
Mallery, John, 1.
Mallery, Jonah, 84, 171, 266.
Mallery, Levi, 276.
Mallery, Levey, 3.
Mallery, Nathan, 282, 325, 339.
Mallery, Nathaniel, 325.
Mallery, Samuel, 215.
Mallery, Simeon, 66.
Mallet, Abell, 93.
Mallison, Roswell, 216.

Maltbie, Jonathan, 365.
Maltbie, Zaccheus, 1.
Maltby, David, 115.
Malthrop, Joseph, 172.
Malthrop, Steaphen, 172.
Man, Elisha, 296.
Man, Zadock, 142.
Manchester, 254.
Manclift, Lemiel, 316.
Mane, John, Jr., 235.
Maning, Samuel, 58.
Maning, William, 80, 231.
Manjent, Nicholas, 54.
Manley, William, 14.
Manly, Asa, 218.
Manly, John, 147.
Manning, Bille, 134.
Manning, Dyar, 74.
Manning, Phin., 81.
Manning, Phineas, 35, 241.
Manning, Roger, 74.
Manning, Samuel, 91.
Manning, Seabury, 199.
Manning, Sebuary, 363.
Manning, Thomas, 285, 354.
Manning, William, 35, 133, 171, 227, 230.
Manning, William, Jr., 75.
Manross, Theodore, 206.
Mansfield, Charles, 152.
Mansfield, Dan, 35, 172, 229, 266.
Mansfield, John, 13, 35, 82, 171, 230, 292.
Mansfield, Josh, 35.
Mansfield, Joseph, 172, 229.
Mansfield, Mathew, 189.
Mansfield, Richard, 152.
Mansfield, T., 266.
Mansfield, 21, 22, 24, 26, 27, 29, 32, 37, 38, 39, 41, 54, 55, 72, 73, 88, 129, 133, 138, 163, 167, 173, 174, 179, 180, 181, 182, 183, 184, 199, 200, 216, 217, 218, 219, 227, 236, 256, 260, 261, 263, 275, 280, 282, 287, 294, 299, 356, 357.
Mantor, Royal, 317.
Manvill, Ira, 217.
Manwaring, George, 34, 227, 290.
Marble, Thomas, 35, 141, 171, 239, 266, 344, 354.
Marchant, John, 267.
Marchant, Stephen, 73.
Marcy, Thomas, 34.
Margaro, John, 112.
Marin, John, 295.
Markham, Isaac, 49, 66.
Markham, Joseph, 34, 171, 240.

Markham, Joshua, 65.
Markham, Samuel, 7.
Marks, Abisha, 267, 351.
Marks, Comfort, 7, 35, 239.
Marks, Hezekiah, 142.
Marr, Pattrick, 346.
Marsh, Abner, 35, 71, 135.
Marsh, John, 207, 352.
Marsh, Joseph, 201.
Marsh, Peter, 35, 76, 159, 172, 237, 280.
Marsh, Robert, 330.
Marsh, Roswell, 207.
Marsh, Samuel, 6.
Marshal, Byard, 267.
Marshal, Elisha, 35.
Marshal, Samuel, 241.
Marshall, Elijah, 14.
Marshall, Joseph, 118.
Marshall, Mead, 115.
Marshall, Samuel, 86, 362.
Marshall, Samuel Bryan, 73.
Marshall, Thomas, 243.
Marshall, William, 117.
Marshel, Alexander, 143.
Marshel, Elisha, 236.
Marshel, John, 200.
Marshell, Amos, 68.
Martain, Gidion, 72.
Martain, Hewlett, 133.
Marten, George, 35.
Marten, John, 54.
Marten, John, Jr., 72.
Marten, Lewis, 35.
Marten, Nathan, 356.
Marter, Royal, 317.
Marther, Elias, 232.
Martin, Charles, 65.
Martin, Charles O., 353.
Martin, David, 215.
Martin, George, 85, 171, 236.
Martin, Gideon, 135, 292, 301.
Martin, Gideon, Jr., 273.
Martin, John, 75.
Martin, John, Jr., 129.
Martin, Joseph, 140.
Martin, Lewis, 229, 338.
Martin, Nathaniel, 85.
Martin, Philip, 196.
Martin, Reuben, 340.
Martin, Samuel, 194.
Martin, William, 134, 245, 319, 336, 346.
Martins, Manasah, 364.
Marus, Moses, 87.
Marvin, Barnabas, 111.
Marvin, Matthew, 108, 154.

Marvin, O., 109.
Marvin, Ozias, 9.
Marvin, Thomas, 220.
Masa, Joseph, 127.
Mash, Abner, 237.
Mason, Asa, 179, 218.
Mason, Ashbel, 53.
Mason, Jeremiah, 142, 221.
Mason, John, 35, 53, 150, 171, 235.
Mason, Reuben, 299.
Mason, Rufus, 11, 266, 275.
Massachusetts, 99, 126, 228, 297, 368.
Masters, Nicholas, 100.
Maten, Abner, 194.
Mather, Elias, 35, 171.
Mather, Elihu, 86, 276, 331, 348.
Mather, Increase, 14.
Mather, John, 114.
Mather, Nath, 86.
Mather, Nathaniel, 241.
Matheson, David, 311.
Mathews, Eliada, 267.
Mathews, Hubbard, 49.
Mathews, James, 153.
Mathews, Jese, 49.
Mathews, Robert, 266.
Mathews, William, 50.
Matson, John, 11.
Matterson, David, 344.
Matterson, William, 290.
Mattherson, William, 78.
Matthews, Eliada, 171.
Matthews, James, 34, 118, 234.
Matthews, Jesse, 347.
Matthews, John, 11.
Matthews, Robert, 34, 172, 229.
Matthews, William, 34, 239, 346.
Mattison, David, 272, 311.
Mattocks, Samuel, 35, 70.
Mattoon, Joel, 13.
Mattoon, Samuel, 13.
Mattucks, Samuel, 238.
Mauenborough, Jedadiah, 35.
Maxfield, Caleb, 118.
May, John, 14.
Maynard, John, 358.
Maynord, Cyrus, 363.
Maynord, Zacheriah, 363.
Mayo, Elisha, 135, 209.
Mayson, Rufus, 349.
Mazuzen, Mark, 2.
Mazzeen, Ezekiel, 278, 291.
Meach, Joshua, 35, 232.
Meach, Thomas, 76, 336, 341.
Meach, William, 76, 147, 158.

INDEX. 441

Meacham, Ichabod, Jr., 67.
Meacham, Isaac, 369.
Meacham, Jeremiah, 200.
Meacham, Jonathan, 128.
Meachum, Philip, 181.
Mead, 93, 95, 108, 110, 112, 114, 116, 118, 126.
Mead, Elias, 9.
Mead, Elijah, 117.
Mead, Jasper, 36, 110.
Mead, Jeremiah, 110.
Mead, John, 219.
Mead, Jonathan, 117.
Mead, Mathew, 9.
Mead, Oliver, 208.
Mead, Samuel, 110, 116.
Mead, Theophilus, 109.
Mead, Uriah, 109.
Meaker, Daniel, 95, 97.
Meaker, Ebenezer, 4, 67, 92.
Meaker, Hezekiah, 154.
Meaker, John, 66.
Meaker, Stephen, 78, 89, 109.
Mears, Samuel, 248, 249.
Measom, Elias, 325.
Meason, Elias, 78, 325, 339.
Meason, John, 71.
Meason, John, Jr., 71.
Meason, Joseph, 68, 85.
Meazon, John, 161.
Meazon, John, Jr., 161.
Mecham, Elijah, 350.
Mecham, Johannes, 350.
Mecker, Stephen, 171.
Meech, Elkanah, 75.
Meech, Joshua, 9, 77, 150.
Meech, Thomas, 9.
Meecham, Jeremiah, 85.
Meecham, Jonathan, 85.
Meed, Jasper, 171.
Meed, Jeremiah, 171.
Meegan, John, 136.
Meeker, Aaron, 309.
Meeker, Daniel, 34, 171, 233, 355.
Meeker, Hezekiah, 68.
Meeker, John, 2, 331.
Meeker, Josiah, 6, 369.
Meeker, Stephen, 9, 34, 35, 57, 233, 234, 267, 306, 328.
Meggs, Simmeon, 227.
Megs, Nathan, 51.
Meguire, Peter, 283.
Meiggs, John, 246, 266, 319.
Meigs, 63, 150, 151, 152, 156, 157, 158, 160, 227.
Meigs, John, 303, 327, 333.
Meigs, Marks Comfort, 35.
Meigs, Nathan, 5.
Meigs, R., 150.
Meigs, Return, 35, 153.
Meigs, Return J., 7, 171, 239.
Meigs, Simeon, 78, 267, 342.
Meigs, Stephen, 343.
Meleck, Ebed, 54.
Melone, Daniel, 35, 229.
Mercy, Thomas, 237.
Merefield, Abraham, 139.
Merells, Aaron, 59.
Mereman, Ebenezer, 11.
Meriam, Ephraim, 60.
Meriam, John, 13.
Meriden, 187.
Merils, Ashur, 142.
Merils, Noah, 341.
Meriman, Josiah, 266.
Merit, William, 296.
Merriam, Asaph, 60, 83.
Merriam, Edmund, 60, 83.
Merriam, Ephraim, 13, 83.
Merriam, Erastus, 190.
Merriam, Ichabod, 13.
Merrill, Jared, 143.
Merrill, Aaron, 56, 247.
Merrill, Ashbel, 347.
Merrill, Cyperon, 55.
Merrill, Daniel, 10.
Merrill, Isaac, 52.
Merrill, John, 142.
Merrill, Noah, 287.
Merrills, Aaron, 274.
Merrills, Ashble, 277.
Merrills, Isaac, 70.
Merrills, Nathaniel, 192.
Merrills, Noah, 323.
Merrils, Aaron, 34, 171.
Merrils, Asher, 34, 197.
Merrils, Asnur, Jr., 142.
Merrils, Cyprian, 34, 171, 239.
Merrils, Cypron, 34.
Merrils, Jonathan, 185.
Merrils, Joseph, 367.
Merrils, Nathaniel, 345.
Merrils, Reuben, 142.
Merriman, Charles, 60, 83.
Merriman, Enoch, 60, 83, 324.
Merriman, Josiah, 293.
Merriman, Moses, 49.
Merrit, Samuel, 211.
Merrit, William, 354.
Merritt, Peter, 112.
Merritt, William, 275.
Merrium, Asaph, 190.
Merry, Sylvanus, 53.
Mershal, Thomas, 139.

Mertin, Joseph Plum, 73.
Merwin, David, 55, 105.
Merwin, Jesse, 104.
Mesenger, Aron, 11.
Mesenger, David, 11.
Mesenger, Israel, 11.
Mesenger, Ruben, 11.
Meson, Elias, 286.
Meson, Joseph, 50.
Messenger, Ezekiel, 80, 275.
Mesum, Joseph, 75.
Metcalf, Dan, 139.
Metcalf, Jabez, 139, 227.
Metcalf, Jonathan, 181, 220.
Micael, 28.
Micha, 75.
Middlesex Co., 298.
Middleton, William, 179.
Middletown, Christopher, 346.
Middletown, Peter, 346.
Middletown, 6, 22, 23, 25, 26, 27, 28, 29, 30, 31, 32, 33, 34, 35, 37, 38, 41, 43, 44, 88, 163, 164, 166, 167, 168, 169, 170, 171, 172, 173, 174, 176, 188, 193, 204, 205, 215, 216, 239, 242, 243, 244, 245, 246, 248, 249, 251, 252, 254, 255, 256, 258, 259, 260, 262, 263, 264, 265, 266, 268, 269, 270, 271, 301, 346, 355, 365, 366, 367.
Mider, Gideon W., 284.
Miel, Charles, 77.
Mielkin, John, 184.
Miels, Charles, 171.
Migat, Zebulon, 36.
Miggs, Phinehas, 66.
Mildrum, Mark, 49.
Miles, Caleb, 69.
Miles, Charles, 9, 35, 232.
Miles, Isaac, 35, 69, 235.
Miles, James, 60, 83.
Miles, John, 8, 35, 172, 229, 266.
Miles, Samuel, 13.
Miles, Thomas, 166.
Milord, 24, 26, 27, 29, 31, 32, 39, 40, 41, 73, 88, 150, 151, 164, 166, 167, 168, 170, 172, 174, 175, 176, 214, 216, 231, 261, 262, 263, 264, 265, 266, 267, 268, 269, 270, 271, 284, 369.
Millar, Charles, 267.
Millar, Daniel, 65, 346.
Millar, Jonathan, 348.
Millar, Samuel, 11.
Millar, William, 346.
Millard, Charles, 206.
Millard, Levit, 63, 254.
Miller, 370.
Miller, Abner, 46, 63, 64.
Miller, Alexander, 198, 363.
Miller, Alexander, Jr., 224.
Miller, Caleb, 348.
Miller, Charles, 34, 70, 171, 238.
Miller, Daniel, 34, 52, 70, 171, 240, 267, 287, 294.
Miller, David, 142, 367.
Miller, Dudley, 204.
Miller, Ebenezer, 367.
Miller, Edward, 327.
Miller, Enoch, 240.
Miller, James, 26, 75.
Miller, John, 34, 238.
Miller, Jonathan, 258, 306, 328.
Miller, Joseph, 201, 366.
Miller, Nathan, 34, 232.
Miller, Noah, 186.
Miller, Nathaniel, 7, 34, 171, 233.
Millet, Jonathan, 12.
Millington, Samuel, 36, 56, 137, 218, 241.
Millington, Samuel, 34, 81.
Millinton, Samuel, 77.
Millor, Edward, 346.
Mills, 103, 104.
Mills, Abraham, 314.
Mills, Alexander, 61, 103, 116, 339.
Mills, Elihu, 86.
Mills, Elijah, 203.
Mills, Ephraim, 11.
Mills, Gabriel, 314.
Mills, George, 114.
Mills, Gideon, 11.
Mills, John, 4, 281, 314, 325, 340.
Mills, Joseph, 35, 67, 96, 233.
Mills, Roger, 14.
Mills, Samuel, 35, 171.
Mills, Samuel Riggs, 94.
Mils, Nathaniel, Jr., 135.
Minard, John, 290.
Miner, Andrew, 34, 239.
Miner, Charles, 180, 331.
Miner, Christopher, 184.
Miner, Clement, 81, 336.
Miner, Elihu, 34.
Miner, Elnathan, 284.
Miner, Ichabod, 296.
Miner, James, 34, 272, 323, 341.
Miner, John, 209.
Miner, Sylvester, 34, 290, 332.
Miner, Rausel, 81.
Miner, Timothy, 180.
Mingo, 50.
Mino, Elihue, 241.

# INDEX. 443

Minor, Andrew, 12.
Minor, Andrew, Jr., 12.
Minor, Benidict, 282.
Minor, Clement, 73, 130, 186.
Minor, Elihu, 3, 171.
Minor, Elisha, 171, 267.
Minor, Elnathan, 338.
Minor, Nathan W., 352.
Minor, Rowswold, 139.
Minor, Samuel, 338.
Minot, David, 92.
Minthern, Michael, 316.
Mitchel, Barnabas, 60, 83, 347.
Mitchel, Eliph, 143.
Mitchel, George, 34, 76, 231, 340.
Mitchel, James, 49, 183.
Mitchel, John, 7, 34, 67, 95, 233.
Mitchel, John Benjamin, 58, 93.
Mitchel, Joseph, 214.
Mitchel, Samuel, 34, 172, 241, 342, 352.
Mitchel, Thomas, 61, 112, 113.
Mitchel, William, 121, 162.
Mitchel, Zephaniah, 182.
Mitchel, Zephaniah, 2d, 181.
Mitchell, Samuel, 267.
Mitchell, Thomas, 300.
Mitchell, William, 7.
Mitshel, Barnabas, 340.
Mix, Abell, 99.
Mix, Amos, 60, 83.
Mix, Benjamin, 254.
Mix, Brister, 150.
Mix, Eli, 53.
Mix, Elisha, 69, 107, 267.
Mix, Enos, 13, 59, 82, 266, 293, 302.
Mix, John, 35, 171, 239, 267, 304, 322, 329, 333.
Mix, Josiah, 14.
Mix, Peter, 343.
Mix, Samuel, 197.
Mix, Stephen, 50, 69, 172.
Mix, Thomas, 82, 293.
Mix, Thomas, Jr., 14, 35, 75, 171, 230, 266.
Mix, Timothy, 35, 172, 229, 266.
Mix, William, 46, 63, 64.
Mize, William, 35, 70, 171, 238, 267, 345.
Mobbs, Pierce. 276.
Mobbs, Samuel, 181, 276, 352.
Mobs, Pierce, 241.
Mobs, Piercey. 34.
Moffatt, Eli, 200.
Moffit, Mathew, 71.
Moffitt, Eleazer, 292.

Moffitt, Matthew, 136, 161.
Moger, Abijah, 55, 73, 105.
Mohawk, Peter, 349.
Mohegan, 196.
Molatto, Adam, 60.
Molatto, Job, 104.
Molatto, Michael, 100.
Molattow, Newport, 73.
Mollato, Ephraim, 59.
Molley, Elijah, 317.
Molton, Gurden, 295.
Moltrop, Stephen, 229.
Moltrop, Timothy, 14.
Momosuck, Daniel, 35, 239.
Monger, 4.
Monger, Billey, 235.
Monger, Wait, 4.
Mongo, Jonathan, 51.
Monn, Oliver, 346.
Monossuk, Daniel, 171.
Monroe, Daniel, 89.
Monrow, Dan, 369.
Monrow, Elijah, 146.
Monrow, Isiah, 147.
Monrow, Nehemiah, 146.
Monson, 214.
Monson, Aeneas, 327.
Monson, Ephraim, 187.
Montague, Seth, 254, 321, 338, 348.
Montecu, Jonathan, 10.
Montecue, Bryan, 58.
Montegue, Briant, 92.
Montgomery, Nathaniel, 64.
Montgomery, Peter, 274.
Montique, Brian, 258, 306, 328.
Monworring, George, 359.
Moodus, 211.
Mooney, Absalom, 185.
Mooney, John, 185, 221, 279, 350.
Mooney, William, 275.
Moor, Andrus, 60.
Moor, Luke, 143.
Moor, Ozias, 144.
Moor, William, 267.
Moor, William, Jr., 82.
Moore, Arunah, 11.
Moore, Asa, 205.
Moore, Edward, 75.
Moore, Kitt, 50.
Moore, Philander, 205.
Moore, Simeon, Jr., 86.
Moore, William, 75, 171, 280.
Moore, William, Jr., 237.
Moores, Elias, 74.
Moot, Adam, 60.
Morce, Aaron, 347.

Mordock, George, 362.
Mordock, Samuel, 140.
More, Furbuss, 349.
More, John, 228.
More, John, Jr., 35.
More, Nathaniel, 185.
More, William, Jr., 35.
Moredock, Ariel, 140.
Moredock, Jonathan, 140.
Moredock, Prince, 196.
Moree, Aaron, 50.
Morehouse, 111, 112.
Morehouse, David, 4, 34, 67, 94, 171, 233, 267.
Morehouse, Euriah, 4.
Morehouse, Ezra, 4.
Morehouse, G., 89, 90.
Morehouse, Gideon, 274.
Morehouse, John, 210.
Morehouse, Michael, 9.
Morehouse, Peter, 3.
Morehouse, Thomas, 9.
Morey, Thomas, 130, 298.
Morgan, Daniel, 346.
Morgan, Ebenezer, 50, 68.
Morgan, Ephraim, 78.
Morgan, Jacob, 289.
Morgan, James, Jr., 47.
Morgan, Jonathon, 11.
Morgan, Joseph, 290, 358.
Morgan, Joshua, 65, 355.
Morgan, Nathan, 85.
Morgan, Nath¹, 89.
Morgan, Nicholas, 216.
Morgan, Thomas, 247, 349.
Morgen, Nathan, 128.
Morgin, Jesse, 208.
Morley, Daniel, 285, 309, 334, 351.
Morley, Elijah, 317, 332.
Morley, John, 17.
Morley, Thomas, 17.
Morras, Peter, 82, 149.
Morril, Asher, 239.
Morrills, Cyprian, 253.
Morrills, Roger, 253.
Morris, 134.
Morris, Andrew, 2.
Morris, Asa, 134.
Morris, James, 205, 365.
Morris, John, 73.
Morris, Peter, 160.
Morris, Robert, 69.
Morrison, Andrew, 56, 193.
Morrison, Rodowick, 354.
Morrison, William, 171, 267, 349.
Morrisson, Andrew, 77.

Morrisson, John, 137.
Morrow, Thomas, 184.
Morse, Amos, 295.
Morse, Chester, 57.
Morse, David, 5.
Morse, James, 64, 75, 146.
Morse, John, 133.
Morse, Linus, 334.
Mortars, Jabez, 316.
Morters, Jabez, 332.
Morton, Jabez, 281.
Moseley, 126.
Moseley, Increase, 364.
Mosely, 28, 99, 100, 102, 104, 106, 108.
Mosely, Ebenezer, 128.
Mosely, Samuel, 131.
Mosely, Sifax, 171.
Mosely, Syphax, 238, 267.
Moser, George, 4.
Moses, Abel, 6.
Moses, Enum, 349.
Moses, Ezekel, 206.
Moses, John, 144.
Moses, Jonas, 35, 230.
Moses, Shubal, 10.
Mosher, Joel, 306, 312, 343.
Mosher, Stephen, 181.
Mosier, Daniel, 93.
Mosier, Joel, 90.
Mosier, Joseph, 67, 98.
Mosley, Cyphax, 351.
Mosock, Daniel, 347.
Moss, Barnibas, 13.
Moss, Benoni, 60, 83, 323, 341.
Moss, Daniel, 35, 229, 267, 340.
Moss, Isaiah, 60, 83.
Moss, John, 35, 229.
Moss, Linas, 69.
Moss, Pompy, 58.
Moss, Reuben, 60, 83, 333.
Moss, Samuel, 207.
Mossack, Daniel, 267.
Mothrop, Joseph, 266.
Mott, Adam, 34, 84, 235, 254.
Mott, Archibald, 219.
Mott, Benjamin, 75.
Mott, Edward, 9.
Mott, Elihu, 65.
Mott, Ira, 255, 307, 321, 328.
Mott, Jacob, 146.
Mott, Jared, 223.
Mott, Jarib, 151.
Mott, Jerod, 213.
Mott, Jarub, 156.
Mott, Jerub, 64.
Mott, Jerule, 64.

INDEX.  445

Mott, Samuel, 9, 34, 189, 241, 284.
Mott, William D., 347.
Moulthrop, Joseph, 8.
Moulton, Stephen, 57, 81, 243.
Moultrop, Joseph, 229.
Moultrup, Joseph, 35.
Moultrup, Steaphen, 35.
Moungomury, Nathaniel, 249.
Mountique, Jonathan, 144.
Mournouse, John, 7.
Mulet, Phinehas, 159.
Muley, Daniel, 309.
Mullin, Daniel M., 13.
Munger, Billa, 267.
Munger, Billey, 35, 78, 227.
Munger, Daniel, 35, 54, 171, 235, 355.
Munger, Jonathan, 61, 103.
Munger, Wait, 5.
Munn, Isaiah, 36.
Munraw, [ ]h, 156.
Munro, John, 34.
Munro, Joseph, 185.
Munro, Leonard, 48.
Munro, Nehem, 157.
Munro, Noah, 187.
Munroe, Daniel, 92.
Munroe, Elijah, 64.
Munroe, John, 91.
Munroe, Josiah, 64.
Munroe, Leonard, 242.
Munroe, Nehemiah, 64.
Munrow, Daniel, Jr., 58.
Munrow, Elijah, 157.
Munrow, John, 58, 362.
Munrow, Joseph, 221, 297.
Munrow, Samuel, 14.
Munrow, Will, 86.
Munrow, William, 14.
Munsell, Alpheus, 14.
Munsell, John, 272, 307.
Munsell, Levi, 272, 307, 329.
Munsil, Gurdon, 48.
Munsill, Garden, 243.
Munsill, John, 323, 328.
Munsill, Levi, 323.
Munson, Almond, 59, 83.
Munson, Caleb, 275.
Munson, Daniel, 350.
Munson, Lent, 59, 83.
Munson, Levi 82, 171, 230.
Munson, Levy, 35.
Munson, Orange, 59, 83.
Munson, Seth, 275.
Munson, William, 35, 172, 229, 266.
Murdock, Samuel, 85, 128.
Murfe, Thomas, 34, 241.

Murfey, Edmun, 11.
Murphy, Thomas, 172.
Murray, Daniel, 5.
Murray, George, 119.
Murray, Joel, 106.
Murray, Jonathan, 5.
Murray, Noah, 106.
Murrey, Abraham, 172.
Murrey, Abram, 344.
Murry, Abraham, 35, 151, 230, 267, 311.
Murry, George, 8, 154.
Murry, Isaul, 154.
Murry, Noah, 35, 235.
Murry, Saul, 123.
Murry, Warren, 337.
Murry, Warrop, 66.
Mygatt, Elisha, 346.
Mygatt, Zebulon, 238, 245, 318, 349.
Mygott, Elijah, 249.
Mygott, Elisha, 248.
Mygott, Zebulon, 335.


N. Fairfield, 88, 202, 204, 210.
Nailor, Robert, 123.
Nails, John, 61, 154.
Nalor, Robart, 154.
Names, Thomas, 118.
Nash, 96.
Nash, Ebenezer, 36, 172, 355.
Nash, Ebenezer, Jr., 9, 112.
Nash, Isiah, 202.
Nash, Nathaniel, 108.
Nash, Uriah, 222.
Naugason, John, 73.
Nayls, John, 338.
Neagro, Prince, 61, 84.
Neason, Robert, 339.
Ned., 75, 147.
Nedson, Edward, 281.
Nedson, James, 286, 325.
Nedson, Robbin, 267, 281.
Nedson, Robert, 325.
Needham, Anthony, 275, 341.
Neff, John, 294.
Negor, 80.
Negro, 56, 59, 81, 113, 138, 160.
Negro, Abel, 48.
Negro, Amos, 153.
Negro, Boston, 60, 83.
Negro, Brister, 196.
Negro, Briston, 36, 232.
Negro, Bristor, 344.
Negro, Caesar, 77, 82, 90, 112, 138, 196, 213, 334, 352.
Negro, Cambridge, 347.

Negro, Cato, 66, 69, 86, 133, 287, 311, 343, 349.
Negro, Cudjo, 52, 70, 76.
Negro, Cuff, 36, 51, 276, 347, 349.
Negro, Cuggo, 158, 297.
Negro, Cummy, 107.
Negro, Dick, 50, 138.
Negro, Edward, 86.
Negro, Frank, 322.
Negro, Gad, 50, 51.
Negro, Galloway, 107.
Negro, George, 286.
Negro, Gift, 79.
Negro, Hazard, 287.
Negro, Jack, 51, 54, 69, 118, 124, 153, 276.
Negro, James, 61, 107.
Negro, Javan, 277.
Negro, Jem, 107.
Negro, Job, 60.
Negro, Joseph, 91.
Negro, Josman, 91.
Negro, Jube, 73.
Negro, Jubiter, 196.
Negro, Limbo, 79.
Negro, Lively, 91.
Negro, Mark, 132.
Negro, Ned, 76, 112, 158, 162.
Negro, Nero, 90.
Negro, Peter, 60, 68, 73, 104, 347.
Negro, Phelix, 86.
Negro, Phillip, 349.
Negro, Plymouth, 348.
Negro, Pomp, 91, 196.
Negro, Pompy, 51.
Negro, Porter, 48.
Negro, Prince, 49, 60, 277, 297, 348.
Negro, Roben, 47.
Negro, Sampson, 124.
Negro, Samson, 83.
Negro, Sharp, 60, 66.
Negro, Shem, 102.
Negro, Sipeo, 159.
Negro, Tite, 99.
Negro, Titus, 131.
Negro, Tobe, 162.
Negro, Toby, 124.
Negro, Tom, 50.
Negro, Tony, 50, 83, 90, 107.
Negro, Tube, 356.
Negro, Uriah, 153.
Negro, Variah, 47.
Negro, William, 153.
Negro, York, 50.
Negroe, Cato, 301.
Negroe, Jack, 90.
Negroe, Ned, 90.
Negroe, Robin, 103.
Negroo, Cato, 135.
Negrow, Cuff, 50.
Negrow, David, 134.
Negrow, Jack, 137.
Negrow, Luis, 138.
Negrow, Robin, 61.
Negrow, Titus, 61.
Negrow, Tom, 135.
Negus, Jesse, 144.
Negus, John, 1.
Neils, Abraham, 285.
Nellson, Isaac, 325.
Nelson, Daniel, 36, 238.
Nelson, Isaac, 278, 339, 347.
Nettelton, Hollum, 53.
Nettelton, William, 53.
Nettleton, Samuel, 52, 72.
Newbury, 299, 367.
Newbury, Jeremiah, 351.
Newbury, Joshua, 189.
Newcomb, Behuel, 296.
Newcomb, Eleazer, 141.
Newcomb, James, Jr., 140.
Newcomb, Simon, 182, 220.
Newcomb, Thomas, 295.
Newel, James, 172, 347.
Newel, John, 48.
Newel, Robert, 36, 172, 211, 232, 267, 336.
Newell, James, 267.
Newell, Mark, 49.
Newell, Norman, 49.
Newell, Normond, 243.
Newell, Rivaous, 59.
Newell, Riverius, 50.
Newell, Robert, 79, 153, 279.
Newell, Robert, Jr., 79.
New Fairfield, 7, 23, 24, 30, 33, 34, 36, 38, 40, 42, 44, 122, 126, 154, 155, 162, 163, 171, 173, 175, 177, 234, 261, 264, 269, 271, 282, 284, 287, 302.
New Hampshire, 122, 359.
Newgent, John, 233.
New Hartford, 21, 28, 29, 34, 38, 39, 41, 55, 163, 167, 168, 173, 175, 177, 188, 207, 208, 236, 242, 243, 245, 248, 249, 250, 251, 252, 253, 254, 255, 256, 257, 258, 259, 261, 264, 276, 278, 280, 282, 287, 355.
New Haven, 8, 21, 22, 23, 24, 25, 26, 27, 28, 29, 30, 31, 32, 33, 34, 35, 36, 37, 38, 39, 40, 41, 42, 43, 44, 88, 150, 151, 152, 163, 166, 167, 168, 169, 170, 171, 172, 174, 175, 176, 185, 187, 207, 215, 216,

INDEX. 447

217, 229, 243, 245, 248, 251, 254,
256, 258, 260, 262, 263, 264, 265,
266, 267, 268, 269, 270, 355, 361,
365, 366, 367, 368.
New London, 18, 23, 24, 25, 26, 28,
29, 30, 32, 33, 34, 38, 41, 42, 66,
68, 119, 126, 137, 139, 158, 180,
181, 187, 193, 194, 197, 210, 227,
252, 290, 358, 359, 365, 366, 367,
368.
New London Co., 231.
Newman, Jonathan, 283.
Newman, Thomas, 114.
New Milford, 24, 26, 27, 31, 37, 41,
42, 44, 55, 73, 100, 101, 102, 105,
106, 120, 123, 126, 163, 166, 173,
175, 176, 177, 186, 187, 188, 202,
203, 204, 205, 206, 208, 210, 211,
228, 235, 261, 263, 265, 267, 282,
283, 285, 356.
Newport, 75.
Newport, Jonas, 56, 77.
Newton, Asahel, Jr., 47.
Newton, Cyrus, 66.
Newton, Elias, 12, 36, 66, 81, 132,
239.
Newton, Ezekiel, 36, 104, 236.
Newton, Isaac, 36, 148, 240.
Newton, William, 121, 162.
Newtown, 8, 24, 28, 33, 34, 36, 100,
119, 123, 124, 125, 126, 154, 162,
166, 170, 173, 174, 185, 194, 200,
214, 234, 262, 266, 268, 285, 287,
288.
New York, 19, 359, 360, 367.
New York State, 92, 122.
Nichalson, Frances, 17.
Nichalson, Nathan, 17.
Nicholas, Ezra, 190.
Nicholas, Jonathan, 227.
Nichols, 90, 93.
Nichols, Abraham, 7, 162.
Nichols, Daniel, 47, 151.
Nichols, Eli, 55, 58, 93, 105.
Nichols, Gershom, 55, 105.
Nichols, John, 70, 79.
Nichols, Jonathan, 72, 110.
Nichols, Jonathan, Jr., 54, 129.
Nichols, Josiah, 221.
Nichols, Phillip, 219.
Nichols, Robert, 101.
Nichols, Samuel, 7, 36, 111, 122,
129, 162, 172, 234, 267.
Nicholson, Francis, 250, 251, 267,
315, 351.
Nicholson, William Baird, 366.
Nickels, John, 152.
Nickels, Philep, 217.

Nickelson, Francis, 331.
Nickerson, Arana, 234.
Nickerson, Barack, 56, 78, 120.
Nickerson, Barret, 172.
Nickerson, Eliaphas, 121.
Nickerson, Eliphaz, 56, 78.
Nickerson, Iran, 117.
Nickerson, Urana, 36.
Nickols, John, 52.
Nickols, Silus, 59.
Nicolls, John, 359.
Nicols, Bether, 48.
Nicoson, Baruch, 162.
Nicoson, Eliphas, 162.
Nigar, Phillip, 267.
Niger, Phillip, 36, 172, 231.
Niger, Poffe, 209.
Nigh, David, 17.
Nikerson, Daniel, 50, 68.
Niles, Abraim, 183.
Niles, James, 188.
Nine Partners, 254.
No[ ]h, 173.
Noacoke, James, 144.
Nobel, Elijah, 10.
Noble, Abraham, 92.
Noble, Gideon, 84, 353.
Noble, Goodman, 55, 105.
Noble, Joel, 18.
Noble, Timothy, 18.
Nobles, John, 92.
Nocak, James, 81.
Nodson, James, 339.
Nonesuch, Jonathan, 51.
Norfolk, 21, 22, 32, 36, 37, 41, 42,
44, 74, 169, 176, 177, 205, 206,
209, 210, 211, 236, 244, 253, 260,
262, 265, 270, 271, 273, 286.
Norten, Benjamin, 36.
Norten, Elon, 36.
Norten, Jedadiah, 36, 240.
Norten, Joseph, 36.
Norten, Rufus, 36.
North, Gad, 277, 347.
Northbury, 206, 256.
North River, 369.
Northrop, Andrew, 8.
Northrop, Isaac, 73, 150, 341.
Northrop, Joseph, 10.
Northrop, Stephen, 222.
Northrup, Isaac, 172, 267.
Northrup, Joshua, Jr., 288.
Norton, Ambrous, 51.
Norton, Benjamin, 2, 5, 172, 231,
267.
Norton, Charles, 5.
Norton, Elijah, 296.
Norton, Elon, 172, 231, 267.

Norton, Jabesh, 247.
Norton, Jabez, 321, 338, 345.
Norton, Jedediah, 172, 267, 353, 365.
Norton, John, 209.
Norton, Joseph, 69, 172, 235.
Norton, Levi, 74.
Norton, Noah, 317.
Norton, Noah U., 317, 333.
Norton, Rufus, 172, 231, 267.
Norton, Samuel, 172, 247, 267, 346.
Norton, Shadrach, 18.
Norton, Tabor, 321.
Norton, Thomas, 258.
Norwalk, 8, 24, 25, 27, 28, 34, 36, 41, 42, 44, 88, 95, 108, 109, 110, 111, 112, 126, 151, 165, 167, 169, 171, 172, 175, 177, 207, 215, 262, 263, 264, 265, 266, 267, 270, 271, 285, 286, 288, 355.
Norwash, John, 278, 299.
Norwich, 22, 24, 25, 26, 27, 28, 29, 31, 33, 34, 35, 36, 37, 38, 41, 42, 43, 44, 74, 88, 137, 148, 159, 165, 167, 168, 169, 171, 172, 173, 176, 179, 180, 181, 182, 183, 184, 185, 186, 191, 193, 196, 197, 198, 199, 200, 201, 210, 214, 221, 223, 225, 227, 231, 243, 245, 248, 256, 261, 262, 263, 264, 265, 266, 268, 270, 271, 272, 287, 291, 301, 302, 355, 358, 359, 360, 368.
Nott, Epaphras, 13.
Nott, Hezekiah, 257, 308, 333.
Nottingham, George, 59, 118.
Noys, Nathaniel, 50.
Noyse, Nathaniel, 69.
Nucomb, David, 295.
Nugent, John, 36.
Numes, Benjamin, 153.
Nutton, Ezekiel, 172.
Nye, Ebenezer, 278, 309, 353.

Oates, Joseph, 267.
Oatis, Joseph, 172.
Obbard, James, 253.
Obrian, Thomas, 346.
OBriant, John, 152.
Obriant, William, 284.
OCain, Jeremiah, 151.
Odell, Isaac, 4, 67, 94.
Odell, Nehemiah Smith, 274.
Ogden, Edman, 4.
Ogden, Edmon, 4.
Ogden, Joseph, 98.
Ogden, Samuel, 202.
Ohara, Timothy, 229.

Oharra, Timothy, 36.
O'Kane, Jonh, 230.
Okeain, Jeremiah, 36.
Olcott, Caleb, 353.
Olcott, James, 226.
Olcut, James, 6.
Olcut, James, Jr., 6.
Olds, Aaron, 36, 103, 235, 267, 340.
Olds, Oliver, 36, 104, 236, 267.
Olford, Eber, 188.
Olin, William, 36, 231.
Oliver, Stephen, 359, 368.
Oliver, Thomas, 368.
Olmstad, James, 238.
Olmstead, Abijah, 111.
Olmstead, Francis, 247.
Olmstead, Isaac, 110, 172, 287.
Olmstead, James, 36, 172.
Olmstead, Jeremiah, 120.
Olmstead, Jesse, 285, 330.
Olmstead, Joseph, 222.
Olmstead, Matthew, 205, 222.
Olmstead, Nehemiah, 120, 205, 221, 283.
Olmstead, Timothy, 243.
Olmsted, Abijah, 307, 314.
Olmsted, Ashbel, 81.
Olmsted, Francies, 81,
Olmsted, Garmaliel, 250.
Olmsted, Isaac, 292, 355.
Olmsted, James, 70, 215.
Olmsted, Jeremiah, 162.
Olmsted, Jesse, 267, 314.
Olmsted, Joseph, 202.
Olmsted, Joshua, 317, 333.
Olmsted, Justus, 314.
Olmsted, Nehemiah, 56, 78.
Olmsted, Silas, Jr., 9.
Olmsted, Gemalial, 59.
Olmstid, David, 162.
Olmstid, Nehh, 162.
Olney, Ithamer, 292.
Olvard, Thomas G., 347.
Olvard, Thomas G., Jr., 347.
Oney, Ithamar, 192.
Oniott, Darius, 308, 333.
Onkshun, John, 279.
Onley, Isheoor, 295.
Orcott, Benjamin, 203.
Orcott, John, 80.
Orcut, 88.
Orcut, Caleb, 36, 239.
Orcut, Ben Jon, 57.
Orcutt, Benjamin, 81.
Orcutt, Caleb, 84, 172, 267.
Orcutt, Darius, 226, 273, 308, 333.
Orcutt, Jacob, 12.

INDEX. 449

Orcutt, John, 12.
Orian, Jeremiah, 234.
Ormsbury, John, 297.
Orsborn, Israel, 48.
Orsburn, Samuel, 13.
Orter, Sedgwick, 338.
Orton, Derias, 203.
Orvis, Eleazer, 36, 236.
Orvis, Samuel, 74.
Oryon, Jerem, 36.
Osborn, Daniel, 120.
Osborn, Elijah, 150.
Osborn, Israel, 349.
Osborn, Jeremiah, 78, 207.
Osborn, John, 7.
Osborn, Joseph, 205.
Osborn, Joshua, 215.
Osborn, Levi, 211, 222.
Osborn, Nathaniel, 267, 355.
Osborn, Samuel, 91, 150.
Osborn, Stratton, 95.
Osborn, William, 288.
Osburn, Abijah, 222.
Osburn, Daniel, 162.
Osburn, Jeremiah, 57, 162.
Osburn, Joseph, 7.
Osburn, Nathaniel, 172.
Osburn, Stratten, 36, 233.
Osburn, William, 353.
Osgood, Jeremiah, 76.
Osmer, David, 202.
Oswold, 36, 239.
Otis, Edward, 180.
Otis, Joseph, 36, 231, 336.
Otis, Shubel, 140.
Oulds, Oliver, 172.
Overton, Aaron, 128, 221.
Ovit, William, 267.
Ovitt, William, 73, 336.
Owen, Alvan, 267.
Owen, Alvin, 36, 42, 172, 348.
Owen, Asa, 79, 227.
Owen, Beezer, 56.
Owen, David, 227.
Owen, Ebenezer, 138.
Owen, Eleasor, 46.
Owen, Eleazer, 131.
Owen, Eliphalet, 36, 78, 172, 227, 235, 267.
Owen, Isaac, 220.
Owen, Thomas, 54.
Owens, Eleazer, 77.
Ower, Daniel, 282.

Pachaug, 367.
Packard, John, 76, 334.
Packer, John, 253.

Packer, Nehemiah, 82.
Pagan, Eleazer, 59.
Pagan, Joseph, 86.
Pagan, Josiah, 134.
Page, Enos, 14.
Page, Jacob, 2.
Page, Luther, 2.
Page, Timothy, 38, 60, 231.
Page, Uriah, 213.
Page, Zera, 140.
Page, Zeri, 250.
Paine, 134.
Painter, Gamaliel, 173, 268.
Paine, Edward, 1.
Paine, John, 65.
Paine, Roswel, 1.
Panteir, Gamaliel, 173, 268.
Painter, Shubal, 215.
Palatine, Cash, 290, 291.
Pallintine, Cash, 338.
Palmer, Aden, 214.
Palmer, Barnebas, 1.
Palmer, Benjamin, 37, 54, 173, 235, 356, 362.
Palmer, Chileab, 55, 101, 211.
Palmer, Christopher, 75.
Palmer, Daniel, 206, 225, 286, 297.
Palmer, Elijah, 37, 140, 237.
Palmer, Gideon, 149.
Palmer, Humphrey, 215.
Palmer, Ichabod B., 123.
Palmer, Isaac, 115, 268, 349.
Palmer, Jabesh, Jr., 139.
Palmer, Jabez, 291.
Palmer, Jared, 338.
Palmer, Jez, 291.
Palmer, John, Jr., 1.
Palmer, Jonah, 85, 127.
Palmer, Jonathan W., 37, 233.
Palmer, Mills, 338.
Palmer, Milo, 338.
Palmer, Phinehas, 61, 103, 204, 213.
Palmer, Samuel, 286, 297, 363.
Palmer, Thomas, 204, 225, 312, 343.
Palmer, Uriah, 279, 291.
Pangborn, Adonijah, 57, 80.
Pangburn, Beebe, 206.
Parceval, Paul, 239.
Parde, Jonathan, 38, 84.
Pardee, Stephen, 155.
Pardey, Jonathan, 230.
Pardy, Daniel, 189.
Pardy, Ebenezer, 207.
Pardy, Nathaniel, 108, 330.
Parenan, Joseph, 173.

Parish, Asa, 364.
Parish, Eliphaz, 236.
Parish, Jacob, 227.
Parish, Oliver, 296.
Parish, Roswell, 50, 69.
Parit, 88.
Park, Elijah, 9.
Park, Fradrick, 51, 69.
Park, Isaac, 73, 129.
Park, James, 51, 69.
Park, Moses, 9.
Park, Reuben, 78.
Parke, David, 78.
Parke, Jonathan, 18.
Parke, Lemuel, 218.
Parkenton, Denny, 108.
Parker, Aaron, 311.
Parker, Abel, 209.
Parker, Abraham, 333.
Parker, Abram, 60, 83.
Parker, Amos, 60, 83.
Parker, Asael, 288.
Parker, Benjamin, 13, 37, 83, 172, 231, 355.
Parker, Ebenezer, 237.
Parker, Edmund, 13, 37, 172, 229.
Parker, Edward, 268.
Parker, Eliab, 37. 84, 230.
Parker, Elijah, 87.
Parker, Elisha, 37, 83, 172, 231.
Parker, Elisha, Jr., 60.
Parker, Gamaliel, 104.
Parker, Hyman, 339.
Parker, Isaac, 37, 54, 84, 173, 230, 268, 337.
Parker, James, 216, 219.
Parker, James, Jr., 356.
Parker, John, 37, 60, 66, 83, 202, 234.
Parker, John, Jr., 132.
Parker, Jonathan, 51, 225.
Parker, Nathan, 66, 132, 218, 267.
Parker, Nehemiah, 280.
Parker, Samuel, 37, 91, 93, 173, 234, 253, 361.
Parker, Stephen, 207.
Parker, Timothy, 60, 83.
Parker, William, 60, 83.
Parker, Wyman, 142, 246, 324, 354.
Parkharst, David, 349.
Parkharst, Solomon, 349.
Parkhurst, David, 275.
Parkins, Jason, 6.
Parkins, Phinehas, 6.
Parkinson, Dene, 37.
Parkinton, Dine, 234.

Parks, Aaron, 273, 301, 311, 343.
Parks, Daniel, 36, 65, 173, 240.
Parks, David, 256.
Parks, Ebenezer, 363.
Parks, James, 52, 61, 70, 108.
Parks, John, 65, 353.
Parks, Joshua, 12.
Parks, Reuben, 330.
Parks, Samuel, 187, 315, 331.
Parmalee, Jeremiah, 268.
Parmele, 5.
Parmele, Charles, 2.
Parmele, Constant, 53, 72.
Parmele, Hezekiah, 2.
Parmele, James, 52, 72.
Parmele, Jeremiah, 37, 229.
Parmele, Joseph, Jr., 5.
Parmele, Phineas, 2.
Parmele, Silas, 212.
Parmele, William, 5.
Parmerlee, Jeremiah, 284.
Parmerly, James, 211.
Parmerly, Jeremiah, 349.
Paro, Joseph, 288, 353.
Parret, John, Jr., 3.
Parrish, Eliphaz, 38, 85, 128.
Parrish, Eliphilet, 338.
Parrish, Jeremiah, 297.
Parrish, Nehemiah, 19.
Parrit, David, 268.
Parrot, David, 274.
Parry, Ebenezer, 85.
Parseval, Paul, 172.
Parson, Levi, 347.
Parsons, 189, 304, 315, 316, 323, 355.
Parsons, Bartholomew, 109.
Parsons, David, 37, 66, 110, 173, 240.
Parsons, Jabez, 49, 66.
Parsons, Jesse, 117.
Parsons, John, 5.
Parsons, Jonathan, 37, 66, 173, 240, 350.
Parsons, Moses, 214, 277.
Parsons, Osborn, 110.
Parsons, Richard, 19.
Parsons, Samuel, 60.
Parsons, Simeon, 347.
Parsons, Sollomon, 203.
Parsons, Theodosius, 37, 117, 234.
Parsons, Thomas, 86, 268, 348.
Parsons, William, 11, 14.
Patch, William, 119.
Patchen, Aser, Jr., 110.
Patchen, Azor, 111.
Patchen, David, 355.

INDEX. 451

Patchen, Ebenezer, 89.
Patchen, Elijah, 94, 268, 274.
Patchen, Jacob, 332.
Patchen, James, 340.
Patchin, Ebenezer, 276.
Patchin, Elijah, 67, 172, 355.
Patchin, Josiah, 274.
Patchin, Wolcot, 68.
Patching, Elijah, 37.
Patching, Elisha, 233.
Patching, Jacob, 285.
Paterson, Robert, 130.
Patinger, Abraham, 77.
Patrick, Jacob, 149.
Patrick, James, 120, 148, 224.
Patrick, Joshua, 224.
Patten, Asa, 272, 301.
Patten, John, 75, 272, 301.
Patten, Thomas, 75, 197.
Patters, Joseph, 160.
Patterson, Andrew, 38.
Patterson, Ansell, 276.
Patterson, Asahel, 352.
Patterson, James, 69, 172, 268.
Patterson, Joseph, 49.
Patterson, Robert, 46.
Patterson, William, 248, 322, 341.
Pattison, James, 51.
Pattrick, Joshua, 363.
Paucheage, Thomas, 281.
Paul, John, 78, 358, 360.
Paul, Lodewick, 281.
Paul, Peter, 268.
Paul, William, 50, 68.
Paulk, Ame, 82.
Paulk, Ammi, 59.
Pawers, James, 268.
Pawers, Thomas, 268.
Paylar, John, 111.
Payne, Benjamin, Jr., 220.
Payne, Eleazer, 187.
Payne, Isaac, 253.
Payon, Eleazer, 82.
Payt, Josiah, 361.
Pearce, Aaron, 189.
Pearce, Abner, 189.
Pearce, Daniel, 240.
Pearce, Edward, 189.
Pearce, Noah, 190.
Pearl, Fradrick, 84.
Pearle, John, 284.
Pearman, Joseph, 18, 37, 238.
Peas, Abial, 18.
Peas, Noah, 76.
Peas, Peter, 238.
Pease, Abial, 18.
Pease, Abner, 11, 18.

Pease, Charles, 206.
Pease, David, 11.
Pease, Ebenezer, 3d, 49.
Pease, Joel, 80.
Pease, Joseph, 185, 286, 309, 334, 349.
Pease, Noah, 227.
Pease, Peter, 80, 354.
Pease, Ritchard, 11.
Pease, Roburt, 2d, 11.
Pease, Silas, 351.
Pease, Simeon, 49, 66.
Peavy, Ichabod, 225.
Peck, Abner, 181.
Peck, Abijah, Jr., 7.
Peck, Ariel, 37, 239.
Peck, Aseal, 193.
Peck, Benjamin, 211, 222.
Peck, Charles, 37, 82, 172, 231.
Peck, Darius, 37, 74, 231.
Peck, David, 46, 131, 273, 309, 334.
Peck, Elijah, 274.
Peck, Elisha, 7, 180, 190.
Peck, G., 116.
Peck, George, 8.
Peck, Henry, 366.
Peck, Hiel, 60.
Peck, Jed, 356.
Peck, Jehiel, 82.
Peck, Jesse, 7, 47, 60, 82, 124, 153, 294.
Peck, John, Jr., 73.
Peck, Joseph, 367.
Peck, Levi, 119.
Peck, Mathew, 186.
Peck, Moses, 116.
Peck, Reuben, 50.
Peck, Phenihas, 13.
Peck, Samuel, 8, 342.
Peck, Silas, 37, 232.
Peck, Silas, Jr., 37, 232.
Peck, William, 278, 288, 349.
Peck, Zebul, 69.
Peck, Zebulon, 37, 236.
Pecker, Nehemiah, 59.
Peckit, Thomas, 172.
Peek, Ariel, 172.
Peek, John, 3.
Peek, Zedekiah, 48.
Peckskill, 369.
Peeksley, Elijah, 335.
Pees, Peter, 37.
Pees, Uriah, 81.
Peese, Abial, 18.
Peese, Augustus, 18.
Peese, Ebenezer, 3d, 66.

Peese, Erastus, 18.
Peese, Joel, 18.
Peese, Peter, 18.
Peese, Samuel, 18.
Peese, Sylvanus, 18.
Peess, Abial, 18.
Peet, Abell, 90.
Peet, John, 58, 93.
Peet, Lemuel, 37, 55, 73, 101, 173, 235.
Peeva, Ichabod, 216.
Peevy, Ichabod, 148.
Peirce, Benjamin, 219.
Peirce, Daniel, 172.
Peirce, John, 267.
Peirce, Justus, 107.
Peirce, Samuel, 59, 63, 82.
Pelham, Edward, 218.
Pellet, Enos, 37.
Pellom, Edward, 206.
Pelton, Benjamin, 36, 52, 72, 231.
Pelton, Daniel, 65, 353.
Pelton, David, 36, 68, 74, 232.
Pelton, Ebenezer, 36, 68, 227, 232.
Pelton, George, 36, 65, 240.
Pelton, James, 51, 69.
Pelton, Joel, 275, 354.
Pelton, Moses, 11.
Pemberton, John, 50, 68.
Pendal, Benoni, 338.
Pendall, Toby, 75.
Pendleton, Daniel, 38, 84, 173, 230, 268.
Pene, James, 73.
Penfield, Isaac, 145.
Penfield, Peter, 154.
Penfield, Seth, 190.
Pengo, John, 201.
Pengo, Prentice, 201.
Penhallow, Richard, 75.
Penhellow, Richard, 268.
Pennsylvania, 245.
Pensyl, John, 288.
Perce, John, 13.
Percefield, 88.
Perey, Benjamin, 357.
Perey, Samuel, 298.
Perez, Reuben, 354.
Perigo, William, 37.
Perkens, 128.
Perkens, Daniel, Jr., 37.
Perkens, Daniel B., 54, 73, 129.
Perkens, Ebenezer, 132.
Perkens, Frances, 128.
Perker, Elisha, 13.
Perker, Joseph, 154.
Perkhust, John, 8.

Perkins, Charles, 47.
Perkins, Daniel, 295, 325.
Perkins, Daniel, Jr., 67, 240.
Perkins, Daniel, 2ᵈ, 279.
Perkins, Daniel B., 219.
Perkins, Ebenezer, 67, 74, 122.
Perkins, Francis, 64, 157.
Perkins, Gideon, 145.
Perkins, Joel, 185.
Perkins, John, 60.
Perkins, Lenard, 201.
Perkins, Oliver, 19.
Perkins, Phillip, 294.
Perkins, Samuel, 8, 60, 83.
Perkins, Wescut, 146.
Perkins, Westly, 146.
Perrey, Abijah, 58.
Perrey, John, 3.
Perrey, Salvenus, 137.
Perrey, Silverus, 72.
Perrigo, Ebenezer, 75.
Perrigo, William, 172, 231.
Perrigo, William, Jr., 75, 268.
Perrin, Jethnel, 134.
Perring, Stephen, 143.
Perry, 101.
Perry, Abijah, 93.
Perry, Daniel, 133.
Perry, Ebenezer, 37, 129, 236.
Perry, Elipha, 78.
Perry, Elisha, 37, 61, 120, 162, 173, 234, 268.
Perry, Reuben, 204, 278.
Perry, Sandrus, 190.
Perry, Saunders, 222.
Perry, Silvanus, 37, 173, 193, 237.
Perry, Thomas, 197.
Persival, Paul, 355.
Person, Nathan, 300.
Persons, Aaron, 13.
Persons, Isaac, 80.
Persons, Jacob, 154.
Persons, John, 3.
Persons, Moses, 299.
Persons, Semion, 49.
Pervett, John, 63.
Petenger, Abraham, 227.
Peter, 141.
Peter, Galloway, 61.
Peters, Andrew, 280.
Peters, Gallaway, 323.
Peters, John, 73, 273, 292.
Peters, Joseph, 82, 148.
Peters, Nathan, 9.
Peters, Peter, 37, 233.
Peters, Samuel, 281, 314.
Peters, William, 141, 351.

INDEX. 453

Peterson, Andrew, 81, 239.
Peterson, Daniel, 368.
Peterson, John, 10.
Petice, Benjamin, 51.
Petit, Enos, 172.
Petland, Thomas, 346.
Pettengall, Aseph, 330.
Pettengall, Jacob. 330.
Pettersgill, Asaph, 314.
Pettersgill, Jacob, 314.
Pettet, Enos, 79, 268.
Pettibone, Jacob, 11.
Pettibone, John, 10.
Pettice, Benjamin, 69.
Pettingal, John, 356.
Pettingall, Jacob, 272.
Pettingell, Asaph, 272, 314.
Pettingell, Jacob, 314.
Pettitt, Enos, 236.
Petyes, Nathaniel, 148.
Pharoah, Abraham, 50.
Phelps, 197, 299, 370.
Phelps, Abijah, 186.
Phelps, Alexander, 206.
Phelps, Beniah, 370.
Phelps, Beriah, 370.
Phelps, Bethuel, 221.
Phelps, Charles, 6, 37, 71, 236.
Phelps, Cornelius, 342.
Phelps, David, 145, 341.
Phelps, David, Jr., 49, 66.
Phelps, Elias, 305.
Phelps, Elijah, 346.
Phelps, Ely, 142.
Phelps, Ezra, 54, 129.
Phelps, Hezekiah, 6, 302, 349.
Phelps, Hezekiah, Jr., 80.
Phelps, Hezekiah, 3d, 143.
Phelps, Homer. 141.
Phelps, Isaac. 86, 241.
Phelps, Jared, 141, 221.
Phelps, John, 141.
Phelps, Joshua, 142.
Phelps, Judah, 11.
Phelps, Lanslott, 14.
Phelps, Norman, 208.
Phelps, Oliver, 6.
Phelps, Reubin, 144.
Phelps, Samuel, 6.
Phelps, Samuel, Jr., 6.
Phelps, Seth, 86.
Phelps, Silas. 144, 291, 305, 328.
Phelps, Solomon, 370.
Phelps, Solomon, Jr., 370.
Phelps, Thomas. 81, 240, 275.
Phelps, Thomas, Jr., 10.
Phelps, Timothy, 86, 143.

Phelps, William, 7.
Phelps, William, 34, 14.
Phelps, Zacheus, 14.
Pheney, Joseph, 344.
Phereton, Thomas, 10.
Philips, Jared, 297.
Philips, Job, 198.
Philips, Norman, 297.
Philips, Peter, 52.
Philips, Thomas, 151.
Philips, William, 275.
Phill, 74.
Philleps, Samuel, 65.
Phillips, 246.
Phillips, Eliphelet, 352.
Phillips, Israel, 101.
Phillips, Jeremiah, 203.
Phillips, Jeruel, 55.
Phillips, Job, 224.
Phillips, John, 224, 247.
Phillips, Nathaniel, 362.
Phillips, Peter, 70, 246.
Phillips, Samuel, 55, 101, 235, 253.
Phillips, Shubael, 55, 101.
Phillips, Thomas, 48, 173, 234, 268.
Phillips, William, 268, 349.
Phillops, Elijah, 10.
Phillups, Thomas, 37.
Philly, Mark, 349.
Phinney, John, 208.
Phinney, Joseph, 268, 301, 311.
Phinney, Uriah, 221.
Phipps, David, 365.
Phips, John, 66.
Phloman, James, 113.
Phypeney, Nehemiah, 3.
Picket, Phineas, 2.
Picket. Thomas, 36, 234.
Pickett, Thomas, 355.
Pieffer, Lazarus, 37, 239.
Pierce, Daniel, 37, 48.
Pierce, Isaac, 80.
Pierce, John, 48, 60, 83, 293.
Pierce, Samuel, 190.
Pierce, Willard. 362.
Pierce, William, 82, 148, 160.
Pierpont, Evlyne, 8.
Pierse, David, 59.
Pierson, Nathan, 212, 273.
Pierson, Paul, 273.
Pike, Elijah, 74, 342.
Pike, John. 71; 135.
Pilgrim. Thomas, 47.
Pineo, John, 140.
Pineo, Linus, 220.
Piney, Aron, 10.

Piney, Levi, 10.
Piney, Nathaniel, 11.
Piney, Peter, 11.
Pinney, Aaron, 38, 86, 241.
Pinney, Ebenezer, 190.
Pinney, Isaac, Jr., 14.
Pinney, Noah, 193.
Pinney, Philister, 81.
Pinney, Isaac, 57, 81.
Pinny, Jonathan, 348.
Pinto, Solomon, 211.
Piquet, Daniel, 209.
Pirce, Benjamin, 183.
Pirkins, Daniel, 267, 350.
Pirkins, Eliphas, 369.
Pirkins, Elisha, 363.
Pirkins, Francis, 85.
Pirkins, Gideon, 369.
Pirkins, Jason, 369.
Pirson, Paul, 300.
Pitcher, Abner, 74.
Pitt, Calib, 8.
Pitts, Richard, 273, 332.
Pitts, Samuel, 179.
Pixlie, Elijah, 61.
Placey, William, 85, 127.
Plainfield, 26, 32, 35, 41, 56, 76, 88, 136, 146, 147, 158, 159, 166, 171, 198, 199, 201, 217, 223, 224, 237, 262, 280, 297.
Plank, John, 194.
Plant, Ethel, 358.
Plant, Timothy, 37, 54, 235.
Platner, John, 347.
Platt, Daniel, 361.
Platt, Ebenezer, 312, 344.
Platt, William, 162.
Platts, Dan, 152.
Plinney, Joseph, 344.
Plum, Charles, 7.
Plum, David, 207.
Plum, Joseph, 154.
Plumb, Amariah, 37, 74, 236.
Plumb, Daniel, 290, 358.
Plumb, Peter, 37, 75, 173, 231.
Plumer, Ebenezer, 137.
Plummer, David, 287, 292.
Poalk, Ammi, 12.
Pole, Frederick, 117.
Polegreen, Cooper, 76.
Pollard, Ebenezer, 69.
Pollard, Isaac, 37, 99, 235, 268.
Pollard, William, 37, 75, 231.
Pollerd, Ebenezer, 51.
Pollester, Henry, 283.
Polley, Alpheus, 76, 291, 356.
Polley, John, 274, 291.
Polley, Uriah, 74, 290, 291.
Pollister, Henry, 302.
Polly, Alpheus, 37, 139, 173, 237.
Polly, Daniel, 142, 280, 354.
Polly, Uriah, 140, 332.
Pomeroy, Benjamin, 37.
Pomeroy, Ralf, 37.
Pomeroy, Ralph, 70, 172.
Pomfret, 22, 30, 32, 33, 38, 39, 40, 41, 56, 76, 137, 138, 148, 158, 165, 192, 193, 196, 197, 198, 199, 200, 203, 223, 237, 252, 262, 277, 284, 295, 301.
Pomp, David, 37.
Pomp, Elisha, 87.
Pomp, Jacob, 37, 232.
Pomp, John, 50.
Pomp, Samuel, 37, 68, 232.
Pompey, Samuel, 173.
Pomroy, Benjamin, 239.
Pomroy, Medad, 166.
Pomroy, Nathaniel, 18.
Pomroy, Phebus, 352.
Pomroy, Ralph, 238.
Pomroy, John, 18.
Pond, Charles, 73.
Pond, Eleazer, 74.
Pond, Henry, 283, 332.
Pond, John, 75.
Ponds, Henry, 316.
Pool, Daniel, 36, 173, 237, 356.
Poole, Daniel, 131.
Pooler, John, 11, 349.
Poolman, John, 10.
Poor, Jonathan, 67, 96, 274.
Pope, David, 112.
Pope, Seth, 197.
Porridge, Annanias, 279.
Porridge, Samuel, 279.
Porter, 159.
Porter, Aaron, 52.
Porter, Abner, 52, 208.
Porter, Amos, 36, 70, 172, 240, 255.
Porter, Andrew, 58, 95.
Porter, Benjamin, Jr., 226.
Porter, Daniel, 37, 86, 173, 241, 268, 348, 356, 368.
Porter, Eldad, 60, 83.
Porter, Eleazer, 37, 141, 239.
Porter, Elexander, 141.
Porter, Elijah, 49, 52, 71, 184, 218, 250, 315, 345.
Porter, Ephraim, 94.
Porter, Ezra, 211.
Porter, Hez, 48.
Porter, Hezekiah, 36, 185, 240.
Porter, John, 220, 255, 331, 369.
Porter, Jonathan, 137.

Porter, Joseph, 51, 69, 132.
Porter, Moses, 52, 70, 259, 315, 331, 345.
Porter, Nathan, 37, 54, 55, 73, 129, 173, 236.
Porter, Nathaniel, 222, 290, 291.
Porter, Noah, Jr., 132.
Porter, Ockelow, 345.
Porter, Samuel, 218.
Porter, Timothy, 190.
Porter, William, 5, 47, 51, 118, 153, 294.
Portter, Ashbel, 6.
Poson, Jacob, 228.
Post, Abner, 36.
Post, Augustus, 200.
Post, Ebenezer, 276.
Post, Enoch, 198.
Post, Hezekiah, 215.
Post, Jabez, 75.
Post, James, 79.
Post, Phinehas, 141.
Post, Samuel, 3.
Potage, Jabez, 128.
Poter, Ashbel, 6.
Poter, Jese, 6.
Pottage, Jabez, 85.
Potter, Amos, 172.
Potter, Burden, 217, 225.
Potter, Daniel, 61, 107, 322, 341.
Potter, David, 323, 342.
Potter, David H., 285.
Potter, Edward, 17.
Potter, Humphrey, 289.
Potter, Israel, 36, 229.
Potter, Jesse, 6.
Potter, John, 78.
Potter, Lemuel, 36, 50, 172, 239.
Potter, Mases, 8.
Potter, Medad, 60, 83.
Potter, Moses, 36, 152, 172, 229, 267, 342.
Potter, Nathan, 317.
Potter, Sheldon, 61, 107, 306, 329.
Potter, Stephen, 36, 173, 231, 268.
Potter, Thaddeus, 209.
Potter, Timothy, 152.
Potts. Richard, 332.
**Potwain, George, 190.**
Poust, William, 300.
Powers, Charles, 113.
Powers, Cyrus, 131.
Powers, Edward, 7.
Powers, James, 37, 173, 187, 239, 350, 356.
Powers, John, 220, 296,
Powers, Lawrence, 220.

Powers, Nathan, 37, 65, 86, 134, 230.
Powers, Thomas, 37, 75, 172, 239.
Prat, Allen, 140, 290.
Prat, James, 141.
Prat, Russel, 18, 48.
Pratt, Abijah, 87.
Pratt, Abraham, Jr., 361.
Pratt, Allen, 74, 291, 347.
Pratt, Asa, 361.
Pratt, Asa, Jr., 79, 152.
Pratt, Daniel, 361.
Pratt, David, 248, 303, 308, 327, 351.
Pratt, David Beebee, 361.
Pratt, Elias, 79.
Pratt, Ellee, 204.
Pratt, Ethan, 3, 37, 79, 173, 232.
Pratt, Ethan, Jr., 79, 152.
Pratt, Ezra, 361.
Pratt, Gido, 361.
Pratt, Isaac, 173, 187.
Pratt, Isaiah, 285, 324, 325.
Pratt, James, 243.
Pratt, Jasper, 79, 152.
Pratt, Jesse, 361.
Pratt, Jesse, 2d, 361.
Pratt, John, 208.
Pratt, Joseph, 297.
Pratt, Jude, 279, 300.
Pratt, Lemuel, 52, 69.
Pratt, Pabady, 79.
Pratt, Phinas, 361.
Pratt, Ruben, 361.
Pratt, Russel, 37, 80, 173, 238.
Pratt, Taber, 361.
Pratt, Zephaniah, 361.
Prentice, 82, 152, 159, 160.
Prentice, Eleazar, 15.
Prentice, Jonas, 37, 229.
Prentice, Josph, 78.
Prentice, Manasseh, 9.
Prentice, Nathaniel, 210.
Prentice, Oziah, 331.
Prentice, William, 290, 358.
Prentice, Zachariah, 100.
Prentis, Edward, 305.
Prescoot, Tytus, 46.
Prescott, Ephraim, 345.
Presher, William, 368.
Press, William, 86, 134, 183.
Pressen, Amasa, 230.
Preston, A, 173.
Preston, Amasa, 37.
Preston, Benjamin, 13.
Preston, Daniel, 180, 218.
Preston, Daniel, Jr., 218.

Preston, David, 46, 63.
Preston, Fyrus, 12.
Preston, Jonathan, 61, 84.
Preston, Joseph, 268, 309, 334.
Preston, Josiah, 281.
Preston, Samuel, 362.
Preston, Tiras, 37.
Preston, Tirus, 81, 173, 239.
Preston, 9, 15, 22, 23, 28, 30, 31, 33, 35, 38, 40, 41, 42, 77, 88, 150, 159, 163, 165, 167, 168, 169, 170, 171, 175, 179, 182, 183, 184, 199, 209, 210, 211, 223, 232, 252, 260, 262, 263, 264, 267, 270, 271, 286, 358, 359.
Price, Elijah, 12.
Price, George, 257.
Price, Levi, 235.
Price, Levy, 36.
Price, Nathaniel, 280, 309, 334.
Price, Paul, 54.
Price, Richard, 256.
Price, Robert, 358.
Price, Rufus, 12, 36, 81, 239.
Price, Samuel, 12, 221.
Prichard, George, 172.
Prichard, George, Jr., 36, 84, 230.
Prichard, James, 36, 151, 230.
Pride, Reuben, 74, 192.
Prier, William, 67, 250.
Priest, Asa, 143.
Priest, Philip, 361.
Primas, Jesse, 58.
Primus, Jesse, 92.
Prince, 74.
Prince, Phillip, 184.
Prince, William, 77.
Prince, Zackery, 81.
Prince, Zacheriah, 240.
Prindel, Joseph, 68.
Prindle, Abijah, 8, 36, 124, 154, 173, 234, 268.
Prindle, Enos, 104.
Prindle, Enos J., 36, 230, 268.
Prindle, Enos Jones, 2, 97.
Prindle, Enos Y., 172.
Prindle, Ezra, 122, 162.
Prindle, Peter, 8.
Prindle, Zalmon, 124, 154.
Prior, Abner, 38, 86, 173, 241, 268.
Prior, Allen, 276, 333.
Prior, Hazard, 307, 321, 330, 349.
Prisley, Stephen, 315.
Pritchard, Benjamin, 73.
Pritchard, Jabez, 2.
Pritchard, Nathaniel, 214.
Pritcket, Jerod, 200.

Prout, James, 83, 289.
Prout, William, 60, 83.
Prouty, Edward, 144.
Providence, 302.
Provost, Dan, 108.
Prows, Thomas, 285.
Prudden, Toney, 73.
Pryar, Allen, 348.
Pryor, Allyn, 86.
Pryor, Hazard, 329.
Psalter, Francis, 345.
Puffer, Daniel, 140, 248.
Puffer, Lazrus, 141.
Puffer, Simeon, 140, 249.
Puffor, Daniel, 295.
Pulford, Elisha, 58, 94.
Pulford, Samuel, 58, 92, 243.
Pumham, Joseph, 268, 282.
Pumroy, Peletiah, 351.
Punderson, Ahimaaz, 335.
Purcivael, Paul, 37.
Purdey, Jesse, 173.
Purdy, Jesse, 118.
Purkens, Daniel, 217.
Purkins, Cudgo, 196.
Purkins, Daniel, 336.
Putman, Reuben, 57, 81.
Putnam, 56, 77.
Putnam, Aaran, 197.
Putnam, Charles, 138.
Putnam, William, 367.

Quacheets, Joseph, 68.
Quameny, Charles, 139.
Quas, Gideon, 301.
Quash, Cato, 38, 173, 241.
Quass, Gideon, 283.
Queekets, Joseph, 50.
Qui, Libbeus, 173, 231, 268.
Quiba, Thomas, 79.
Quigley, John, 294.
Quindley, Thomas, 38.
Quirk, William, 80, 354.
Quivey, Jonathan, 187.
Quochetts, Joseph, 286.
Quosh, Ephraim, 91.
Quy, Libeus, 38.
Quy, Negro, 38.

Racke, William, 302.
Raimond, Ebo, 75.
Rainvolt, William, 321.
Raisley, 254.
Ralinson, Levi, 342.
Ramong, Samuel, 173.
Ramsdall, Ezra, 287.
Ramsdil, Ezra, 194.

INDEX. 457

Ramsel, Ezra, 351.
Rand, Jacob, 76.
Randal, Elijah, 236.
Randal, Ichabod, 363.
Randal, Jonas, 225.
Randall, Elijah, 85, 226, 288.
Randall, John, 282.
Randall, Jonas, 204.
Randall, Joseph, 12, 76.
Randall, Nicholas, 362.
Randol, Elijah, 38, 174.
Randol, John, 192.
Rannals, Martin, 313.
Rannals, Reuben, 313.
Ranne, Jabesh, 38.
Ranne, Steaphen, 38.
Rannee, Jacob, 291.
Ranney, George, 51.
Ranney, Jabesh, 240.
Ranney, Jabez, 65, 173.
Ranney, Solomon, 333.
Ranney, Stephen, 61, 65, 102, 173, 240, 268, 353.
Ransdale, Ezra, 268.
Ransford, 223.
Ransford, Joseph, 147.
Ransom, David, 268.
Ransom, Israel, 283, 351.
Ransom, Joseph, 182, 282.
Ransom, Robert, 87.
Rash, Jacob, 346.
Rathbon, Benjamin, 297.
Rathbon, Theophilus, 180.
Rathbun, Edward, 87.
Rathburn, Asa, 340.
Rathburn, Jacob, 87.
Rathburn, Thomas, 272.
Raudin, Ezra, 190.
Rawlinson, Joseph, 245.
Raxford, Benjamin, 60.
Ray, Daniel, 5, 268, 274, 352.
Ray, Gideon, 15, 149.
Ray, John, 15.
Ray, Mathew, 10.
Ray, Timothy, 205.
Rayming, David, 174.
Raymond, Aaron, 111, 313, 329.
Raymond, Abraham, 95, 108.
Raymond, Benjamin, 9.
Raymond, Clap, 109, 110.
Raymond, Daniel, 98.
Raymond, Daniel G., 288.
Raymond, David, 38, 233.
Raymond, El., 111.
Raymond, Isaac, 336.
Raymond, J., 112.
Raymond, James, 312, 344.
Raymond, Jonathan, 9.

Raymond, Joseph, 363.
Raymond, Lemuel, 307, 323, 329.
Raymond, Newcomb, 364.
Raymond, Samuel, 38, 89, 142, 234, 269.
Raymond, Thomas, 48.
Raymond, Timothy, 75.
Raymond, U., 111.
Raymond, William, 9, 38, 96, 233.
Raymong, David, 67.
Raymong, Samuel, 356.
Raymong, William, 67.
Raymont, Lemuel, 307.
Raynolds, Charles, 345.
Raynolds, John, 345.
Raynolds, Reuben, 349.
Raynsford, 150.
Raynure, Thomas, 243.
Rdugen, 146.
Read, Jeremiah, 146, 156.
Read, Joseph, 67, 85.
Read, Josiah, 85.
Read, Matthew, 61, 100.
Read, Oliver, 137.
Read, Reuben, 75, 231.
Read, Samuel, 185.
Reading, 356.
Reaves, James, 268.
Redaway, Comfort, 135.
Redaway, Preserved, 292.
Redding, 24, 26, 32, 35, 38, 39, 41, 89, 90, 124, 126, 164, 165, 171, 173, 175, 207, 208, 210, 228, 234, 263, 267, 269, 270, 285, 287, 292.
Rederax, Emmun, 161.
Redfield, Elias, 52, 72, 212.
Redfield, James, 4, 204, 215.
Redfield, Philip, 52, 72.
Redington, John, 356.
Redrick, Emmanuel, 148.
Redrik, Emanuel, 82.
Redway, Comfort, 71.
Redway, Preserved, 193, 273.
Reed, Abraham, 9.
Reed, Benjamin, 38, 71, 143, 236.
Reed, E., 184.
Reed, Eli, 108,
Reed, Elihu, 275.
Reed, Enoch, 38, 173, 184, 232, 268.
Reed, Hezekiah, 9.
Reed, Isaac, 119.
Reed, Jeremiah, 64.
Reed, John, 116, 117.
Reed, John, Jr., 116.
Reed, Joseph, 127.
Reed, Nathan, 9, 38, 54, 55, 72, 130, 173, 236, 354.

Reed, Oliver, 38, 76, 77, 237.
Reed, Ruben, 38.
Reed, Shany, 338.
Reed, Sherry, 283.
Reed, Sparry, 338.
Reed, Stephen, 275.
Reed, William, 340.
Reed, William, Jr., 111.
Reeves, James, 276.
Reeves, Luther, 329.
Reeves, Puryer, 268, 279, 300.
Reggs, Moses, 48.
Reinvault, William, 321.
Reives, James, 184.
Rementon, Stephen, 78.
Remington, Abijah, 18.
Remington, Steph, 162.
Remington, Stephen, 38, 120, 173, 234, 356.
Remong, William, 3.
Ren, Solomon, 56, 78, 162.
Rennals, Benjamin, 57.
Rennels, Simeon, 186.
Rennolds, Joshua, 220.
Rennolds, Reuben, 330.
Renson, William, 159.
Renton, Chandler, 51.
Repley, Charles, 226, 340.
Rerde, Isaac, 199.
Resegue, Abraham, 56.
Reves, Samuel, 352.
Rewick, Owin, 349.
Rexford, Benjamin, 174, 268, 292.
Rexford, Benjamin, Jr., 83, 174.
Reynalds, Benjamin. 81.
Reynold, William, 105.
Reynolds, Benjamin, 115.
Reynolds, David, 61, 103.
Reynolds, Israel, 116.
Reynolds, Jacob, 135.
Reynolds, James, 135.
Reynolds, John, 75, 173, 196.
Reynolds, Joshua, 76, 179, 272, 323.
Reynolds, Justus, 61, 103.
Reynolds, Martin, 312.
Reynolds, Matthew, 188.
Reynolds, Reuben, 313.
Reynolds, Simeon, 76.
Reynolds, Solomon, 107.
Reynolds, Solomon, Jr., 61.
Rhoades, Benjamin, 12.
Rhode Island, 359, 362, 366.
Rial, Stephen, 154.
Rian, Jerem, 36.
Rian, Jerry, 173.
Rian, Patrick, 154.
Rice, 217.
Rice, Daniel, 80.
Rice, David, 39, 84, 239.
Rice, Elijah, 350.
Rice, Isaac, 187.
Rice, Jared, 211.
Rice, John, 268, 296.
Rice, Jonah, 143.
Rice, Jonathan, 188.
Rice, Jotham, 60, 83.
Rice, Nehemiah, 39, 173, 230, 268.
Rice, Samuel, 278.
Rice, Simeon, 190.
Rich, Aaron, 347.
Rich, Amos, 269, 278.
Rich, Joseph, 65.
Rich, Lemuel, 65.
Rich, Lend, 353.
Rich, Nathaniel, 65.
Rich, Samuel, 65, 341, 353.
Rich, Thomas, 65.
Richard, Nathaniel, 57.
Richards, Js, 111.
Richards, James, 8.
Richards, Jedidiah, 74.
Richards, John, 9.
Richards, Nathaniel, 80.
Richards, Sam, 192.
Richards, Samuel, 107, 194.
Richards, Silas, 135.
Richards, Steaphen, 38.
Richards, William, 38, 182, 290.
Richardson, Asa, 140.
Richardson, Boswill, 255.
Richardson, Eleazer, 296.
Richardson, Hezekiah, 132.
Richardson, James, 118, 366.
Richardson, Jesse, 18.
Richardson, Jonathan, 139.
Richardson, Rawswold, 139.
Richardson, Sanford, 18, 206.
Richardson, Stephen, 145.
Richardson, William, 1.
Richmand, Abner, 295.
Richmond, Samuel, 59, 91.
Rickard, Silas, 71, 72.
Rider, Daniel, Jr., 288, 354.
Ridgebury, 202.
Ridgefield, 22, 26, 37, 38, 39, 56, 78, 98, 118, 119, 120, 126, 162, 165, 172, 173, 174, 185, 202, 204, 205, 234, 261, 267, 268, 283, 285, 287, 356.
Riggs, Abner, 48.
Riggs, Daniel, 121.
Riggs, John, 91.
Right, John, 133.
Right, Samuel, 11, 142.
Rigs, Daniel, 162.

INDEX.  459

Rigs, James, 38, 230.
Rigs, Laban, 38.
Rigs, Labor, 230.
Riley, Ashbel, 194, 348.
Riley, John, 39, 238, 257, 268, 304, 322.
Riley, Phillip, 269.
Riley, Roger, 7.
Rindel, Joshua, 219.
Rindge, Thomas, 199.
Rines, Jeremiah, 94.
Riplee, Charles, 236.
Ripley, Benjamin, 85, 127.
Ripley, Charles, 39, 85, 127, 288.
Ripley, Jerª, 132.
Ripley, Joshua, 197.
Ripley, Pirum, 200.
Ripnear, Asa, 188.
Ripton, 202.
Riseing, James, 173.
Rising, James, 38, 238.
Rising, Jonah, 179.
Rising, Josiah, 284, 352.
Rislee, Stephen, 238.
Risley, Asa, 345.
Risley, Charles, 340.
Risley, Levi, 71, 342, 345.
Risley, Levy, 52.
Risley, Richard, 345.
Risley, Stephen, 38, 70, 173, 245, 269, 315, 331, 345.
Ritch, Edward, 38, 115, 234.
Ritchardson, David, 11.
Ritchardson, Jesse, 11.
Rithbie, John, 140.
Rix, Daniel, 15.
Rix, James, 15.
Rix, Nathan, 211.
Rix, Theophilus, 15.
Rix, Thomas, 15.
Roach, John, 38, 232.
Roads, James, 135.
Roath, Peter, 199.
Roath, Samuel, Jr., 75.
Rob, Samuel, 131.
Robards, Benjamin, 154.
Robards, Joel, 174.
Robards, John, 136.
Robards, Samuel, 188.
Robart, Free Love, 347.
Robart, Jesse, 135.
Robarts, Abiel, 230.
Robarts, Benjamin, 234.
Robarts, Clark, 348.
Robarts, Constant, 347.
Robarts, Daniel, 65.
Robarts, David, 245, 317, 346.
Robarts, Isaac, 346.

Robarts, Joel, 230.
Robarts, John, 162, 351.
Robarts, Judah, 317.
Robarts, Nathan, 351.
Robarts, Nathaniel, 353.
Robarts, Peter, 348.
Robarts, Samuel, 345.
Robarts, Stephen, 245, 346.
Robarts, Tibbee, 136.
Robbards, Abial, 84.
Robbards, Constant, 50.
Robbards, Joel, 84.
Robbards, William, 50.
Robbarts, Daniel, 243.
Robbarts, Elisha, 55.
Robbarts, William, 226.
Robbens, Jobe, 219.
Robbens, Joseph, 148.
Robbens, Samuel, 148.
Robbenson, Samuel, 139.
Robbers, Joseph, 39.
Robbins. 225.
Robbins, Clark, 357.
Robbins, Daniel, 357.
Robbins, Joseph, 76, 85, 160, 272.
Robbins, Josiah, 257.
Robbins, Nathaniel, 133.
Robbins, S., 160.
Robbins, Samuel, 357.
Robbison, Daniel, 346.
Robbison, John, 347.
Robbords, Noah, 140.
Robens, Joseph, 82, 127.
Robens, Moses, Jr., 148.
Robenson, Abel, 128.
Robenson, Elias, 128, 131.
Robenson, Ephraim. 128.
Robenson, Peter, 290.
Robenson, Samuel, 128.
Robenson, Simeon, 128.
Robenson, Simeon, Jr., 128.
Robenson, Zopher, 128.
Roberds, James, 187, 191.
Roberson, Cato, 68.
Roberson, Daniel, 4.
Roberson, Ephraim. 173.
Roberson, John, 122.
Roberson, Reuben, 309.
Roberson, Zelotes, 124.
Roberson, Zopher. 226.
Roberts, Abial, 38.
Roberts, Asiah, 107.
Roberts, Benjamin, 38, 122, 173.
Roberts. Cleark. 59.
Roberts, Daniel, 187, 226.
Roberts, David, 173, 268, 306, 332.
Roberts, Elisha, 38, 173, 257.

Roberts, Ezra, 275.
Roberts, Isaac, 336.
Roberts, James, 221.
Roberts, Joel, 38, 361.
Roberts, John, 14, 47, 121, 283.
Roberts, John, Jr., 7.
Roberts, Judah, 332.
Roberts, Luke, 207, 222.
Roberts, Nathan, 38, 214, 268, 283.
Roberts, Nathaniel, 241, 286.
Roberts, Noah, 249.
Roberts, Peter, 276, 299.
Roberts, Samuel, 257, 309, 334, 365.
Roberts, Samuel, Jr., 71.
Roberts, Simeon, 7.
Roberts, Stephen, 319, 335.
Roberts, Thomas, 54.
Roberts, William, 227.
Roberts, Zibee, 71.
Robertson, Aurther, 365.
Robertson, Cato, 342.
Robertson, Eleazer, 288, 338.
Robertson, Elias, 38, 56.
Robertson, Ephraim, 38, 65, 253, 319, 336.
Robertson, George, 195.
Robertson, Grh$^m$, 253.
Robertson, James, 38, 290, 358.
Robertson, Jared, 38.
Robertson, John, 38, 281, 284, 325, 339.
Robertson, Levi, 342.
Robertson, Nathaniel, 119.
Robertson, Samuel, 38.
Robertson, Simeon, Jr., 38.
Robertson, Thomas, 38.
Robin, Jacob, 281.
Robin, Michael, 61.
Robins, Benoni, 310, 335.
Robins, Elijah, 18.
Robins, Enos, 199.
Robins, Joseph, 71, 135, 237, 292.
Robins, Josiah, 349.
Robins, Nathaniel, 86.
Robins, Roger, 308.
Robinson, Abel, 85, 356.
Robinson, Cato, 268, 342.
Robinson, Clark, 131.
Robinson, Comfort, 216.
Robinson, David, 61, 103.
Robinson, Elenzer, 85, 127.
Robinson, Elias, 46, 85, 138, 174, 236, 268.
Robinson, Ephraim, 356.
Robinson, James, 200.
Robinson, Jared, 229.

Robinson, Jason, 216.
Robinson, Jeremiah, 287, 292.
Robinson, John, 198, 219, 239.
Robinson, Levi, 60, 83.
Robinson, Nathaniel, 47, 154.
Robinson, Reuben, 276, 309, 334, 350.
Robinson, Richard, 201, 356.
Robinson, Samuel, 85, 152, 174, 229, 268.
Robinson, Simeon, 199.
Robinson, Simson, Jr., 174.
Robinson, Thomas, 229.
Robinson, Zopher, 85, 288.
Robison, Benjamin, 135.
Robison, Cato, 50.
Robison, Elias, 77.
Robison, Ephraim, 237.
Robison, Samuel, 236.
Rock, Thomas, 183.
Rock, William, 353.
Rockwell, Amasa, 188.
Rockwell, Daniel, 132.
Rockwell, Grove, 205, 346.
Rockwell, John, Jr., 110.
Rockwell, Joseph 9, 206.
Rockwell, Merit, 77.
Rockwell, William, 189.
Rockwill, Ozwill, 243.
Rodgers, Bigsbey, 72.
Rodgers, Bixbie, 129.
Rodgers, Chester, 130.
Rodgers, Elisha, 218.
Roe, Abijah, 143.
Roger, Isaac, 68.
Rogers, Asael, 38.
Rogers, Bigsbe, 54.
Rogers, Chester, 46, 216, 219, 297.
Rogers, Daniel, 55, 105.
Rogers, Elisha, 181.
Rogers, Ephraim, 1.
Rogers, Ethen, 179.
Rogers, Gideon, 184.
Rogers, Gurdon, 180.
Rogers, H., 205.
Rogers, Hezekiah, 109, 304, 310, 343.
Rogers, Isaac, 50.
Rogers, Jacob, 1.
Rogers, James, 38, 118, 234.
Rogers, Jeffery, 73.
Rogers, John, 4$^{th}$, 290, 359.
Rogers, Jonathan, 283.
Rogers, Joseph, 38, 199, 232.
Rogers, Josinh, 76, 148, 158, 268, 283, 331, 340, 351.
Rogers, Jsaiah, 85.

Rogers, Lemuel, 38, 232.
Rogers, Leonard, 48.
Rogers, Levi, Jr., 2.
Rogers, Nathaniel, 198, 200.
Rogers, Oliver, 75.
Rogers, Peter, 38, 76.
Rogers, Philemon, 2.
Rogers, Rufus, 2.
Rogers, Samuel, 290.
Rogers, Sharper, 73.
Roley, Daniel, 278.
Rolingson, Reuben, 280.
Rolo, Joseph, 3.
Rolow, Zachariah, 3.
Rols, Daniel, 352.
Rols, Zacheus, 352.
Rombelow, Thomas, 173.
Rood, David, 71.
Rood, Simeon, 39, 107, 235.
Rood, Simeon, Jr., 108.
Root, Adanijah, 197.
Root, Daniel, 342.
Root, Eleazer, 142, 357.
Root, Ezekiel, 284.
Root, Joseph, 11.
Root, Joshua, 211.
Root, Nathan, 39, 239.
Root, Nathaniel, 202.
Root, Salmon, 50, 347.
Root, Samuel, 350.
Root, Seth, 278, 299, 347.
Root, Thomas, Jr., 49, 66.
Rose, Adonijah, 277, 325, 330.
Rose, Benjamin, 117.
Rose, Ephraim, 95.
Rose, John, 303, 327.
Rose, Levi, 2.
Rose, Nathaniel, 49, 66, 132.
Rose, Peter, 278, 299.
Rose, Samuel, 173, 356.
Rose, Simon, 287.
Rose, Timothy, 218.
Rose, William, 214.
Rosetor, Samuel, 173.
Rositer, Timothy, 187.
Ross, Adonijah, 340.
Ross, Joseph, 56, 77, 137, 277, 301.
Ross, Simeon, 54.
Ross, William Mill, 186.
Rossell, Jeremiah, 234.
Rosseter, Bryan, 66.
Rosseter, Samuel, 38.
Rossetter, Samuel, 54.
Rossetter, Timothy, 280.
Rossiter, Samuel, 235.
Rossiter, Stephen, 187.
Roswell, Jeremiah, 38.

Rothbone, William, 143.
Rothbourn, Asa, 75.
Roulenson, Reuben, 268.
Roundey, John, 10.
Roup, Simeon, 232.
Rous, Jabez, 127.
Rouse, Jabez, 38, 85, 174, 236.
Rouse, Oliver, 38, 340.
Rouse, Simeon, 10, 38, 77.
Row, David, 57, 153.
Rowe, David, 105.
Rowel, Roger, 14.
Rowell, John, Jr., 14.
Rowfiner, Peter, 95.
Rowland, Israel, 89.
Rowland, Sherman, 86, 348.
Rowland, Thomas, 111.
Rowlandson, Joseph, 319, 336.
Rowlanson, Joseph, 268.
Rowlason, Joseph, 5.
Rowlee, John, 268.
Rowleson, William, 51.
Rowley, Aaron, 346.
Rowley, Israel, 352.
Rowley, Jesse, 38, 173, 241.
Rowley, John, 281, 348.
Rowley, Joseph Lungrel, 6.
Rowlinson, Bartlet, 281.
Rowlison, Joseph, 348.
Rows, Amos, 38, 239.
Rowse, Joseph, 78.
Roy[ ], Elisha, 297.
Royal, John, 54.
Royce, Aaron, 54, 72, 130.
Royce, Amasa, 219.
Royce, Amos, 184.
Royce, Elijah, 50, 54, 72, 130.
Royce, Elisha, 181, 218, 219.
Royce, Jesse, 274.
Royce, John, 287, 354.
Royce, Matthew, 102.
Royce, Nemiah, 84.
Royce, William, 179.
Roys, Gidion, 13.
Roys, Joseph, 13.
Roze, Adonijah, 350.
Rozel, Jereminh, 173.
Rozell, Jeremiah, 268, 330.
Rudd, Jonathan, 128.
Rude, Jason, 9.
Rude, Samuel, 141, 268, 280, 302.
Ruff, Jonathan, 50, 68.
Rugbe, Benjamin, 129.
Rugg, Solomon, 347.
Rugg, Solomon, Jr., 347.
Ruggles, Bostwick, 282.
Ruggs, Solomon, 269, 277.

462   REVOLUTION LISTS AND RETURNS.

Ruggs, Solomon, Jr., 277.
Rumbeglow, Thomas, 268.
Rumbelo, Thomas, 38, 232.
Rumbelow, Thomas, 72.
Rumsey, David, 102.
Rumsey, John, 89.
Rumsey, Nathan, 89.
Runald, Jacob, 71.
Runalds, David, 71.
Runalds, James, 71.
Runalds, Samuel, 72.
Rundal, John, 117.
Rundel, John, 234.
Rundell, Jeremiah, 116.
Rundle, John, 38.
Runnels, David, 137.
Runnels, John, 268, 269.
Runnels, Joshua, 268.
Runnels, Ravid, 136.
Runnels, Samuel, 135.
Rusel, 46, 63.
Rusell, William, 73.
Rush, George, 105.
Rusket, Samuel, 352.
Russ, Jonathan, 79, 269.
Russego, Abraham, 78.
Russel, 152.
Russel, Asher, 39, 173, 238, 250.
Russel, Corns. 206.
Russel, Eleazer, 131.
Russel, Elijah, 136.
Russel, Elmer, 60, 83.
Russel, Giles, 39, 233.
Russel, James, 49, 67.
Russel, Jeremiah, 154.
Russel, Jesse, 10.
Russel, John, 5, 11, 72, 135.
Russel, Simeon, 136.
Russel, William, 338.
Russel, William, Jr., 39, 234.
Russele, Elijah, 57.
Russell, Arthur, 348.
Russell, Asher, 268, 316, 332.
Russell, Benjamin, 295.
Russell, Corll, 86.
Russell, Cornelius, 14.
Russell, E., 151.
Russell, Edward, 151.
Russell, Eleaser, 46.
Russell, Gideon, 334.
Russell, John, 206, 352.
Russell, Joseph, 2.
Russell, Stephen, 357.
Russell, William, 173, 268.
Russign, Abraham, 162.
Russigue, Abraham, 120.
Rust, Amasa, 132.

Rust, Epaphras, 173, 269.
Rust, Jonathan, 39, 174, 236.
Ryan, Jeremiah, 58, 234.
Ryan, John, 122.
Ryce, Moses, 294.
Ryley, John, 173.
Ryne, William, 154.
Ryon, Jeremiah, 39.
Rynolds, Joshua, 342.

Saben, Nehemiah, 81.
Sabens, Nathaniel, 147.
Sabens, Nehemiah, 41.
Sabin, 137.
Sabin, Billinds, 77.
Sabin, Billings, 56.
Sabin, Jonathan, 365.
Sabins, 159.
Sabins, Nathaniel, 56, 76.
Sabins, Nehemiah, 12, 175, 239.
Sacket, Aaron, 364.
Sacket, Buel, 205.
Sackett, J., 106.
Saffard, David, 200.
Sagar, Thomas, 120.
Sage, Abraham, 7.
Sage, Ebenezer, 367.
Sage, Stephen, 7.
St George, George, 50.
St John, 56, 78.
St. John, Aaron, 111.
St John, Daniel, 285, 314, 331.
St. John, Dover, 109.
St John, Gideon, 189.
St John, James, 41, 115, 234.
St. John, Jesse, 111, 310, 343.
St John, John, 175, 204.
St. John, Justin, 110, 306, 312, 343.
St. John, Nehemiah, 9.
St. John, Nehemiah, Jr., 9.
St Squir, Samuel, 150.
Snivers, William, 335.
Sales, William, 54.
Salisbury, 24, 26, 28, 29, 31, 34, 35, 36, 40, 42, 44, 57, 78, 163, 165, 168, 171, 172, 173, 175, 176, 177, 227, 234, 261, 262, 264, 266, 267, 268, 270, 271, 355.
Salks, Othniel, 154.
Salley, James, 40, 216, 241.
Saltonstall, Dudley, 365.
Salvage, Stephen, 346.
Salvage, William, 346.
Sambo, Prince, 238.
Sampson, David, 196.
Sampson, Jonson, 196.
Samson, 64.

Samson, John Ames, 64.
Sanborough, Lemuel. 329.
Sanden, Ephraim, 144.
Sanders, Abel, 183.
Sanders, John, 232.
Sanders, Poter, 134.
Sanders, William, 162, 269.
Sanderson, Joab, 60.
Sandford, Samuel, 269.
Sandwich, Mass., 248.
Sanford, 216.
Sanford, David, 207, 216.
Sanford, Elihu, 339.
Sanford, Ezekiel. 41, 84, 230.
Sanford, Fortune, 274.
Sanford, Henry, 8.
Sanford, J., 107.
Sanford, James, 41, 89, 123, 154, 174, 234.
Sanford, Joel, 215.
Sanford, Liffe, 55.
Sanford, Liffie, 105.
Sanford, Samuel. 41, 73, 174, 231.
Sanford, Silas, 368.
Sanford, Thomas, 41, 51, 174, 229.
Saratoga, 92, 126.
Saterly, John, 147.
Satterlee, 159.
Satterlee, John, 76.
Satterlee, Jonas, 9.
Satterly, James, 337.
Saunders, Amos, 58, 91.
Saunders, John, 40, 73, 130, 174.
Saunders, Peter, 86.
Saunders, Robert, 365.
Saunders, William, 40, 122, 175, 234.
Savage, Abijah, 41, 174, 240.
Savage, Elisha, 7.
Savage, Josiah, 259.
Savage, Nathan, 50, 254, 320, 337, 347.
Savage, Samuel, 2.
Savage, Simeon, 7.
Savage, Solomon, 188.
Savage, Stephen, 174, 269.
Savary, John, 370.
Savary, Jonathan, 370.
Saveroy, Solomon, 220.
Savory, John, 65.
Sawas, Jacob, 281.
Sawyer, Asa, 40, 174, 200, 232.
Sawyer, Conant, 65.
Sawyer, Ephraim, 5.
Sawyer, London, 52, 70, 353.
Sax, Othniel, 106, 120.
Saxton, Ezra, 18.
Saxton, Joseph, 18.

Saybrook, 22, 25, 26, 27, 29, 30, 31, 32, 33, 34, 36, 37, 39, 42, **43**, 44, 79, 152, 153, 165, 168, 169, 170, 171, 172, 173, 175, 176, 177, 196, 197, 208, 209, 210, 212, 213, 215, 216, 227, 228, 232, 246, 250, 252, 254, 256, 257, 261, 262, 263, 264, 265, 266, 267, 268, 270, 271, 279, 280, 287, 300, 355, 356, 359.
Saymore, Lachh, 242.
Saymour, Asa, 345.
Saymour, Joseph, 86.
Scaley, John, 40.
Scarborough, Joseph, 183.
Scariot, James, 185.
Schalena, Abraham, 240.
Schallem, Abraham, 39.
Schallenx, Abraham, 64.
Schallenx, Reuben, 65.
Schofield, Ichabod, 342.
Scofield, Moses, 220.
Scofield, Selah, 234, **306**, 313.
Schoolcraft, Samuel, 253, 319, **336**.
Schophel, Benjamin, 79.
Schovel, Joseph, 208.
Schullena, Abraham, 175.
Scipeo, Abel, 50.
Scipio, Abel, 348.
Scipio, Cesar, 354.
Scipis, Isaac, 282.
Scofield, Hoyt, 208.
Scofield, Moses, 216, **220**.
Scofield, Peter, 9.
Scofield, Selah, 41, **234, 306, 313**, 328.
Scofield, Thadeus, 323.
Scoot, Enos, 6.
Scot, Elijah, 40.
Scot, Enes, 6.
Scotland, 196, 365, 366, 367, 368.
Scott, Amasa, 273.
Scott, Amesey, 301.
Scott, Elijah, 71.
Scott, Ethel, 71.
Scott, Ethiel, 343.
Scott, Ezekiel, 194.
Scott, John, 84, 183.
Scott, Joseph, 182, 367.
Scott, Moses, 109.
Scott, Oliver, 324, 342.
Scott, Thomas, 366.
Scott, Uthiel, 343.
Scott, William, 112, 162.
Scovel, Bela, 51.
Scovel, Benjamin, 63, 227.
Scovel, Elijah, 361.
Scovel, Nathan, Jr., 47.
Scovel, Noah, Jr., 361.

Scovel, Peter, 128.
Scovel, Steaphen, 41.
Scovell, Bela, 258.
Scovell, Daniel, 5.
Scovell, John, Jr., 5.
Scoviel, Selah, 306.
Scovil, 108.
Scovil, Ebenezer, 59.
Scovil, Jonathan, 108.
Scovil, Nathan, 351.
Scovil, Seely, 114.
Scovil, Silas, 114.
Scovil, Silvanus, 108.
Scovil, Stephen, 175, 235, 253.
Scovill, 5.
Scovill, Ebenezer, 211.
Scovill, Peter, 85.
Scovill, Samuel, Jr., 277.
Scovill, Stephen, 84, 230.
Scovill, Westall, 5.
Scovils, Steaven, 61, 84.
Scrantom, Abraham, 5.
Scrantom, Jared, 5.
Scrantom, Noah, 5.
Scrantom, Timothy, 51.
Scrantom, Torrey, 51.
Scranton, Thomas, 223.
Scranton, Timothy, 5.
Scranton, Torey, 329.
Screen, James, 284.
Scribner, Abraham, 9.
Scribner, Asa, 41, 110, 175.
Scribner, Elias, 9.
Scribner, Moses, 109.
Scribner, Stephen, 109.
Scribner, Zacheus, 9, 110.
Scriptor, John, 84.
Scrow, John, 334.
Seagor, Thomas, 162.
Sealey, Sylvarnus, 57.
Sealey, Zadock, 52.
Sealy, George, 216, 269, 285.
Sealy, John, 69.
Sealy, Sylvanus, 78.
Sealy, Zadock, 70.
Seaman, William, 117.
Sear, John, 112.
Searl, Constant, 41, 233.
Searls, Ruben, 1.
Sears, Jasper P., 283.
Sears, John, 104.
Sears, Joseph, 121, 162.
Sears, Knoles, 162.
Sears, Obediah, 175, 184, 232.
Seaser, 148.
Seaton, George, 7.
Seaward, Samuel, 2, 66, 175.
Sedgwick, Samuel, 70, 238.

Sedgwick, Timothy, 194, 226.
Sedgwick, William, 192, 226.
Seeley, 54.
Seeley, Ebenezer, 286.
Seeley, Ephraim, 58.
Seeley, George, 324.
Seeley, Gideon, 58.
Seeley, Lemuel, 94.
Seely, Amos, 123.
Seely, Ebenezer, 214.
Seely, Ephraim, 90, 92.
Seely, George, 342.
Seely, Gideon, 90.
Seely, Justus, 93.
Seely, N., 97.
Seely, Nehemiah, 309.
Seelye, Selvinis, 162.
Seelye, Amos, 154.
Seelye, David, 54, 235.
Seelye, John, 54, 236.
Seelye, Selvinis, 162.
Seers, Obediah, 41, 77.
Seers, Remington, 15.
Segar, Joseph, 34, 349.
Segwick, Samuel, 40.
Selden, 181.
Selden, E., 182.
Selden, Ezra, 40, 174, 232, 269, 333, 335.
Seley, Ephraim, 61.
Seley, Gideon, 58.
Seley, Lemuel, 58.
Seley, Nehemiah, 335.
Selleck, Charles, 114.
Selleck, Daniel, 118.
Selleck, David, 93.
Selleck, Henry, 111.
Selleck, Jacob, 9, 111.
Selleck, James, 9.
Sellick, Benjamin Seymor, 153.
Sellick, James, 208.
Serdam, Peter, 63, 79.
Sereen, James, 270.
Serene, James, 352.
Sergeant, Samuel, 129.
Sesar, Jonathan, 109.
Setchell, Jonathan, 366.
Seward, Daniel, 40, 231.
Seward, Eliakim, 273.
Seward, Elimkim, 319.
Seward, Elnathan, 51, 74.
Seward, Jedediah, 269, 288, 347.
Seward, Nathan, 40, 174, 230.
Seward, Samuel, 40, 230.
Seward, Silas, 209.
Seward, Sutliff, 211.
Seward, Timothy, 278, 347.
Seward, William, 40, 231.

Sexton, Asher, 194.
Sexton, Elijah, 11.
Sexton, Joseph, 11.
Seymour, Ardon, 192, 226.
Seymour, Asa, 52, 70.
Seymour, Elias, 39, 55.
Seymour, Elisha, 192, 226.
Seymour, Ely, 192.
Seymour, James, 111.
Seymour, Joseph, 241.
Seymour, Roderick, 226.
Seymour, William, 9.
Shaddee, Randolph, 208.
Shadden, John, 41, 76, 138, 237.
Shailer, Bezaliel, 5.
Shailor, Jos, 292.
Shailor, Joseph, 13, 82.
Shair, Jerijah, 66.
Shaler, Joseph, 41.
Shallor, Joseph, 231.
Shalor, Joseph, 175.
Shantop, Joseph, 278, 291.
Shapley, Richard, 134.
Sharman, Peter, 65.
Sharon, 21, 25, 28, 29, 30, 32, 33, 37, 39, 40, 41, 43, 44, 57, 79, 119, 124, 126, 151, 165, 167, 168, 170, 172, 174, 176, 177, 211, 213, 236, 263, 264, 266, 268, 260, 355.
Sharp, 19.
Sharp, Amos, 340.
Sharp, Benjamin, 40, 76, 237.
Sharp, James, 61.
Sharp, Joseph, 40, 73, 143, 231, 349.
Sharp, Reuben, 284, 326.
Sharpe, Benjamin, 138.
Sharpe, Reuben, 307, 329.
Sharper, Feevish, 314.
Sharper, James, 85.
Sharper, Tuis. 40, 68, 175, 233, 314, 330.
Sharper, Tuish, 180.
Sharwood, Nehemiah, 202.
Shattock, David, 352.
Shaver, George, 113.
Shaw, Bejamin, 39, 64, 146, 157, 175, 237, 269.
Shaw, Ebenezer, 223, 287, 326, 339.
Shaw, Elezer, 297.
Shaw, Elias, 64, 146, 157, 307, 325, 329.
Shaw, George, 361.
Shaw, Gilbert, 184.
Shaw, Ichabod, 12.
Shaw, James, 361.
30

Shaw, John, 64, 146.
Shaw, Jonathan, 39, 64, 147, 156, 237.
Shaw, Joseph, 121, 162.
Shaw, Peleg, 82, 148, 160.
Shaw, Richard, 39, 233.
Shaw, William, 19, 39, 64, 147, 158, 237.
Shay, Daniel, 113.
Shaylor, T., 269.
Shead, Jonathan, 18.
Sheeker, Joseph, 279.
Sheericks, William, 333.
Sheffield, Joseph, 71, 136.
Shelden, Elisha, 41.
Sheldin, Remembrance, 203.
Sheldon, 227, 359.
Sheldon, Asher, Jr., 2.
Sheldon, Charles, 61, 102.
Sheldon, Elisha, 175, 270.
Sheldon, Remembrance, 276, 299, 348.
Shelle, Lemuel, 82, 160.
Shelley, Abraham, 2.
Shelley, Ebenezer, 40, 234, 333.
Shelley, Edmund, 269, 321.
Shelley, John, 40.
Shelley, Lemuel, 40.
Shelley, Reuben, Jr., 5.
Shelley, Samuel, 335.
Shellis, Francis, 127.
Shelly, Ebenezer, 90, 91.
Shelly, Edmund, 280, 338.
Shelly, John, 235.
Shelly, Lemuel, 149, 233.
Shelly, Samuel, 287.
Shelly, Timothy, 280.
Shelton, Benjamin, 92.
Shelton, David, 312.
Shely, Joseph, 82.
Shepard, Cuy, 159.
Shepard, Isaac, 13, 80.
Shepard, Jesse, 278, 299, 347.
Shepard, John, 41.
Shepard, Jonathan, 52, 70.
Shepard, William, 349.
Shepard, William, Jr., 275.
Shephard, John, 174.
Shepherd, Amos, 345.
Shepherd, Hull, 59, 83.
Shepherd, Isaac, 18.
Shepherd, John, 229.
Shepherd, Phenious, 249.
Shepherd, William, Jr., 143.
Shepman, George W., 282.
Shepperson, Daniel, 3.
Sherbum, 82.

# 466 REVOLUTION LISTS AND RETURNS.

Sherburn, 82, 158, 159, 160, 161, 178, 255, 359.
Sherburne, Henry, 45.
Sherlburn, 80.
Sherman, 80, 215.
Sherman, Benjamin, 79.
Sherman, David, 105.
Sherman, Edmund, 174, 269.
Sherman, Elijah, 100.
Sherman, Enock, 214.
Sherman, I., 213, 214, 216.
Sherman, John, 41, 174, 229, 269.
Sherman, Reuben, 269, 285.
Sherman, William, 41, 229.
Sherod, Lemuel, 80.
Sherrod, Mathew, 9.
Shervin, Simeas, 68.
Sherwood, Abel, 7.
Sherwood, Abraham, 116.
Sherwood, Asa, 126.
Sherwood, Daniel, 58, 90.
Sherwood, Ephraim, 202.
Sherwood, Jedidiah, 274.
Sherwood, Jehial, 4.
Sherwood, John, 4.
Sherwood, Jonathan, 222.
Sherwood, Ned, 58.
Sherwood, Nehemiah, 41, 90, 162, 175, 234.
Sherwood, Zach, 4.
Sherwood, Zachariah, 68, 94.
Shether, John, 53.
Shield, James, 353.
Shields, James, 65.
Shilley, Ebenezer, 174, 269.
Shipman, Benoni, 79.
Shipman, George, 190.
Shipman, James, 39, 79.
Shipman, John, 39, 232.
Shipman, Samuel, 39.
Shippee, Nicholas, 136.
Shippy, Nicholas, 72.
Shirman, Samuel, 232.
Shirt, Joel, 343.
Shoals, Nathan, 76.
Sholes, Aaron, 51.
Sholes, Nathan, 40, 68.
Sholes, Richard, 148.
Sholly, Edmond, 338.
Shols, Richard, 160.
Shon, Simeon, 269, 283, 351.
Shoat, James, 283.
Shoot, James, 351.
Shopp, Peter, 323, 342.
Short, Samuel, 194.
Short, William, 287, 292, 311, 344.
Shortman, William, 40, 175, 233, 269, 345.
Shoue, James, 269.
Shoules, Aron, 69.
Shoules, Wheler, 68.
Shouls, Wheler, 50.
Showls, Nathan, 233.
Shumway, 183, 218, 219.
Shumway, John, 41, 55, 72, 174, 236.
Shute, Richard, 154.
Sibbels, Peter, 60, 83.
Sibble, Ezra, 353.
Sibley, Ezra, 182, 278.
Sidleman, John Jacob, 75.
Sifax, 28.
Sikes, Reuben, 11.
Silden, Ebenezer, 220.
Siliman, 89.
Sill, 179, 341.
Sill, David, 40, 174.
Sill, Thomas, 6.
Sillick, Benjamin, 47.
Sillick, David, 58.
Sillick, Junus, 222.
Silliman, 96.
Silliman, Daniel, 4.
Silliman, G. S., 126.
Silliman, G. Selleck, 125.
Silliman, Nathaniel, 324.
Simamons, Thomas, 198.
Simber, Prince, 351.
Simbo, Prince, 40, 175, 269.
Simmon, Joshua, 147.
Simmons, Andrus, 153.
Simmons, Ely, 235.
Simmons, James, 40, 233.
Simmons, Joseph, 235.
Simmons, Robert, 58, 92.
Simmons, Samuel, 40, 235.
Simmons, Thomas, 224.
Simon, James, 68.
Simonds, Comma, 325.
Simonds, Eli, 65.
Simonds, Jonathan, 316.
Simons, Aarad, 129.
Simons, Adriel, 85, 127.
Simons, Amos, 280, 302.
Simons, Andrew, 74, 118, 336.
Simons, Comma, 340.
Simons, Cummy, 61.
Simons, Edward, 76.
Simons, Eli, 40, 175, 255.
Simons, Elijah, 362.
Simons, Hunt, 76.
Simons, Isaac, 40, 66, 240.
Simons, Ishum, 198.
Simons, James, 286.

Simons, Jared, 49, 67.
Simons, Jonathan, 269, 277, 232.
Simons, Joseph, 65, 259.
Simons, Robert, 174, 269.
Simons, Roswell, 226, 288.
Simons, Samuel, 345, 346.
Simons, Thomas, 285, 340, 354.
Simpson, Eliphalet, 104, 122.
Simpson, John, 54, 75.
Simpson, Robert, 8, 41, 229.
Simsbury, 10, 31, 33, 35, 44, 80, 143, 144, 145, 163, 166, 170, 171, 177, 184, 186, 187, 188, 189, 192, 202, 203, 204, 205, 206, 240, 250, 260, 262, 264, 265, 266, 268, 270, 271, 275, 279, 285, 288, 299, 302, 349, 355.
Simson, Eliphalet, 162.
Sizar, Daniel, 269.
Sizer, Daniel, 7, 308, 333, 348.
Sizer, Jabez, 348.
Sizer, Jonathan, 41, 174, 240.
Sizer, Nathaniel, 69.
Sizer, William, 174, 269.
Sizor, Daniel, 248.
Sizor, Daniel, 248.
Skeericks, William, 281.
Skinner, 142.
Skinner, Beriah, 141, 221.
Skinner, Eli, 186.
Skinner, Isaac, 14.
Skinner, Luther, 182.
Skinner, Richard, 1.
Skinner, Thomas, 142.
Skinner, Zenas, 1.
Skinney, Joseph, 311.
Skinnor, Zimry, 6.
Slade, Abner, 48.
Slain, Frederick, 282.
Slarter, Benjamin, 10.
Slater, David, 118.
Slater, John, 275, 299.
Slaughter, James, 80, 349.
Slaughter, John, 99, 349.
Slauter, John, 61.
Slayter, Joel, 189.
Slead, John, 13.
Slead, Jonathan, 13.
Sled, Daniel, 14.
Sled, John, 59, 82.
Sloan, Alexander, 9.
Smiley, William, 49.
Smith, 8, 78, 88, 149.
Smith, Abijah, 39, 131, 175, 237, 244, 269, 288, 301.
Smith, Alling, 1.
Smith, Ambrose, 229, 269, 330.
Smith, Ambrus, 39, 174.
Smith, Asa, 8.
Smith, Asaph, 39, 175, 239, 269, 347.
Smith, Austin, 114.
Smith, Benjamin, 8, 182.
Smith, Bill, 108.
Smith, Caleb, 115.
Smith, Christopher, 15.
Smith, Chs, 115.
Smith, Cuff, 352.
Smith, Daniel, 9, 13, 39, 83, 86, 131, 134, 174, 230, 231, 233, 269, 287, 293.
Smith, David, 19, 39, 84, 174, 175, 230, 239, 269.
Smith, E., 100.
Smith, Ebenezer, 91, 188.
Smith, Eleazer, 46, 131.
Smith, Elijah, 273.
Smith, Eliphelit, 80.
Smith, Elisha, 191.
Smith, Elkanah, 19.
Smith, Elkany, 363.
Smith, Elnathan, 345.
Smith, Enoch, 39, 174, 232, 356.
Smith, Enos, 135.
Smith, Ephelit, 57.
Smith, Ezra, 39, 64, 175, 240, 243, 269.
Smith, Ezra, Jr., 65.
Smith, Fuller, 363.
Smith, George, 39, 70, 238.
Smith, Griegory, 198.
Smith, Heber, 58.
Smith, Heman, 270.
Smith, Henry, 39, 52, 54, 70, 77, 137, 175, 181, 235, 237.
Smith, Isaac, 39, 63, 68, 112, 113, 174, 234.
Smith, Isaac, Jr., 39, 234.
Smith, Isac, 46.
Smith, Isaiah, 114, 306, 329.
Smith, J., 277.
Smith, James, 39, 51, 69, 85, 129, 236.
Smith, Jedediah, 46, 131.
Smith, Jered, 190.
Smith, Jesse, 58, 92, 329.
Smith, Job, 39, 174, 356.
Smith, Joel, 49.
Smith, John, 2, 5, 39, 47, 49, 54, 59, 69, 82, 84, 103, 114, 115, 117, 130, 174, 230, 240, 269, 288, 295, 309, 347, 353, 356.
Smith, John, Jr., 39, 55, 72, 236.
Smith, Jonathan, 54, 208, 235, 353, 367.

Smith, Jordan, 39, 175, 231, 269.
Smith, Joseph, 2, 5, 8, 47, 121, 151, 154, 162, 220, 297, 321.
Smith, Joshua, 49, 147, 269, 353.
Smith, Josiah, 114, 346, 359.
Smith, Levy, 39.
Smith, Lewis, 234.
Smith, Lue, 84, 174.
Smith, Lus, 230.
Smith, Matthew 34, 3.
Smith, Moses, 10.
Smith, Nathan, 50, 68, 156, 307, 329.
Smith, Nathaniel, 51, 282, 307.
Smith, Noah, 208.
Smith, Oliver, 356.
Smith, Oliver, Jr., 275.
Smith, Peter, 39, 114, 131, 237.
Smith, Philip, 208.
Smith, Ralph, 55, 105.
Smith, Reuben, 5, 54, 311.
Smith, Reuben, Jr., 286.
Smith, Richard, 17, 154.
Smith, Robert, 61, 101.
Smith, Roger, 85.
Smith, Samson, 60.
Smith, Samuel, 3, 8, 39, 84, 107, 183, 230, 250.
Smith, Seth, 13, 60, 83, 276.
Smith, Simeon, 131.
Smith, Sylvs, 65.
Smith, Sylvenos, 295.
Smith, Taber, 79, 152.
Smith, Theodore, 350.
Smith, Thomas, 215.
Smith, Timothy, 51, 70, 214.
Smith, Tone, 46.
Smith, Walter, 333.
Smith, Wells, 52, 69.
Smith, William, 5, 12, 39, 48, 73, 151, 174, 231.
Smithers, William, 40, 238.
Snell, Ebenezer, 81, 189.
Snell, Joseph, 46, 59, 82.
Snell, William, 357.
Snow, Amosiah, 357.
Snow, Ebenezer, 73.
Snow, Ebenezer, Jr., 54, 74, 129.
Snow, Jonathan, 54, 72, 76, 129.
Snow, Joseph, 2.
Snow, Robart, Jr., 219.
Snow, Robert, 199.
Snow, Shubel, 330, 356.
Snow, Simeon, 182, 218.
Snow, Thomas, 353.
Sole, William, 59.
Soles, Richard, 82.

Solley, Thomas, 274.
Solomon, Amos, 40, 68, 233.
Solomon, Nathaniel, 51.
Somers, 11, 23, 26, 28, 30, 32, 37, 43, 80, 164, 166, 168, 173, 177, 187, 188, 189, 202, 203, 204, 206, 238, 275, 278, 281, 302, 354.
Somersetshire, Eng., 368.
Sorow, Thomas, 65.
Sott, Elijah, 236.
Southard, Andrew, 352.
Southard, Nathan, 361.
Southard, William, 361.
Southington, 164, 166, 168, 173, 175, 177, 187, 190, 205, 207, 213, 216, 261, 262, 263, 268, 269, 270, 276, 277, 299, 300, 350, 355, 356.
Southmaid, 41.
Southmaid, William, 230.
Southmayd, William, 84.
Southward, William, 183.
Southwell, Asael, 181.
Southwell, Paschall, 68.
Southworth, Andrew, 274.
Southworth, Chester, 294, 319.
Southworth, James, 131.
Southworth, Joseph, 46.
Southworth, William, 46, 131, 218.
Soward, Daniel, 73.
Soward, William, 73.
Sowas, Richard, 41, 233.
Sowers, William, 175.
Sowl, William, 81.
Spafford, Elijah, 85, 127.
Spafford, Eliphalet, 226, 288.
Spalden, Ephraim, 131.
Spaldin, Ephraim, 39.
Spalding, Ephraim, 237.
Sparger, Edward, 224.
Sparks, Ebenezer, 197.
Sparks, Ichabod, 200.
Sparks, Isaiah, 12.
Sparks, Joseph, 59, 82.
Sparrow, Stephen, 352.
Sparrow, Stephen, 2d, 276.
Spalding, Andrew, 158.
Spalding, Andrew, 148.
Spaulding, Stephen, 147.
Spear, Elihu, 306, 313, 328.
Spear, Elijah, 174, 238.
Spear, Joshua, 352.
Spear, William, 282.
Spears, John, 68.
Spears, Jonathan, 3, 67.
Spears, Nathaniel, 3.
Speers, Elijah, 41.
Speers, John, 40, 232.

# INDEX. 469

Spellman, Samuel, 60.
Spencer, Amaziah, 3.
Spencer, Charles, 349.
Spencer, Daniel, 198, 284.
Spencer, David, 3, 40, 241, 277, 307, 321, 329.
Spencer, Denis, 86.
Spencer, Elijah, 19.
Spencer, Elisha, 5.
Spencer, George, 79.
Spencer, Ichabod, 40, 174, 232, 269.
Spencer, Jahiel, 352.
Spencer, James, 80, 211, 253.
Spencer, Jesse, 208.
Spencer, Joel, 352.
Spencer, Joel, Jr., 276.
Spencer, John, 85, 175, 269, 352.
Spencer, Joseph, 63.
Spencer, Noah, 208.
Spencer, Obediah, 40, 70, 238.
Spencer, Peter, 211.
Spencer, Samuel, 60, 81, 83, 85, 189.
Spencer, Seth, 52.
Spencer, Simeon, 3.
Spencer, Thomas, 52, 70, 86, 295, 321, 345.
Spencer, Seth, 70.
Spencer, William, 216.
Spencer, Zackeus, 181.
Spenser, Dennis, 134.
Spenser, Eliphalet, 18.
Spenser, James, 18.
Spenser, Thomas, 134.
Spergar, Edward, 216.
Sperry, Army, 243, 315, 331.
Sperry, Chauncey, 41.
Sperry, Dorias, 104.
Sperry, Eber, 367.
Sperry, Eliakim, 8.
Sperry, Enoch, 54.
Sperry, Jabin, 366.
Sperry, Joel, 73.
Sperry, Lemuel, 74, 253, 307, 319, 329.
Sperry, Miles, 13.
Sperry, Philo, 366.
Spicer, Abel, 220.
Spicer, Asher, 75.
Spicer, Samuel, 41, 75, 231.
Sporry, Chauncey, 229.
Sprague, Asa, 106.
Sprague, James, 41, 82, 237.
Sprague, Jonathan, 363.
Sprague, Phinehas, 140.
Spray, Samuel, 81.

Springard, James, 79.
Springer, John, 285, 292.
Springer, Whala, 285, 292.
Springfield, 227.
Spry, Jack, 219, 314.
Spurr, William, 112.
Squebb, Joseph, 220.
Squib, Joseph, 196.
Squier, Asa, 272, 301.
Squier, Daniel, 229.
Squier, Ebenezer, 2.
Squier, Samuel S., 239.
Squier, Samuel Stent, 229.
Squier, Sexton, 2.
Squir, Abiather, 66.
Squire, Abiathur, 40, 175, 230.
Squire, Asa, 308, 317.
Squire, Ashar, 175.
Squire, Daniel, 4, 40.
Squire, Dudley, 200.
Squire, Fenias, 4.
Squire, Isaac, 59, 81.
Squire, John, 4.
Squire, Joseph, 3, 107.
Squire, Josiah, 357.
Squire, Justice, 69.
Squire, Nathan, 67, 95.
Squire, Phinehas, 66.
Squire, Samuel, 8, 175, 269.
Squire, Samuel, 2d, 3.
Squire, Samuel S., 40.
Squire, Saxton, 40, 66, 175.
Squire, Saxton, Jr., 230.
Squire, Stent Samuel, 40.
Squire, Thomas, 3d, 102.
Squires, Abner, 206.
Squires, Asa, 332.
Squires, Isaac, 350.
Squires, Phineas, 333, 335.
Squires, Saral, 312.
Squires, Sariel, 344.
Squires, Sasal, 312.
Squires, Stephen, 337.
Stafford, Samuel, 76, 159.
Stafford, 35, 36, 44, 57, 66, 81, 132, 137, 179, 180, 182, 186, 187, 189, 190, 203, 241, 242, 243, 249, 285, 286, 287, 288, 354.
Staford, Samuel, 147.
Stalker, John, 97.
Stalker, Peter, 95, 97, 98, 310, 343.
Stamford, 22, 23, 24, 25, 28, 31, 32, 33, 34, 35, 37, 39, 41, 44, 93, 108, 111, 112, 114, 126, 165, 170, 171, 174, 176, 186, 206, 233, 258, 262, 265, 267, 271, 367.
Stanard, Elijah, 209, 356.

Stanard, Pabdy, 84.
Stanard, Pebody, 61.
Stanard, Seth, 61, 84.
Stanard, William, 205.
Stanborugh, Samuel, 329.
Stanbourgh, Lemuel, 273.
Stanbourgh, Silas, 273.
Stanbrough, Silas, 334.
Stancliff, Lemuel, 279, 287, 332, 338.
Stanclift, Lemuel, 316.
Stanclift, William, 61, 107.
Standish, Amasa, 9.
Stanklift, Samuel, 338.
Stanley, Francis, 275.
Stanley, Hezekiah, 49.
Stanley, Nathaniel, 14.
Stanley, Selah, 214.
Stanley, Thomas, 250, 308, 333, 347.
Stannard, Jasper, 39.
Stannard, Job, 208.
Stannard, Joseph, 215.
Stannard, Samuel, 39, 54, 235.
Stannard, Seth, 59, 259, 307, 319, 336.
Stannord, Elijah, 175.
Stannord, Samuel, 175.
Stanten, Elijah, 10.
Stantliff, Samuel, 321.
Stanton, Abel, 15.
Stanton, Amon, 147.
Stanton, Amos, 68, 175, 232.
Stanton, Isaac W., 15.
Stanton, James, 57, 78, 162, 228.
Stanton, Jeremiah, 47.
Stanton, Joseph, 9.
Stanton, Nathan, 15.
Stanton, Robert, 51, 69.
Stanton, Shoram, 181.
Stapels, Thaddeus, 4.
Staples, Jacob, 19.
Staples, John, 4.
Staples, Samuel, Jr., 68.
Starbord, Samuel, 194.
Stark, Israel, 142.
Stark, Samuel, 40, 175, 227, 241, 356.
Stark, Stephen, 40, 141, 241.
Stark, Timothy, 40, 175, 241, 356.
Starkey, Stephen, 361.
Starks, Joseph, 233.
Starks, Stephen, 239.
Starkweather, Asa, 41, 107, 231.
Starkweather, Joel, Jr., 129.
Starkweather, Joseph, 15, 72.
Starkweather, Nathan, 220.

Starkwether, Joseph, 136.
Starling, Thadeus, 9.
Starr, 7. 179, 360.
Starr, Caleb, 121.
Starr, David, 41, 174, 240, 269.
Starr, Jehosaphat, 255.
Starr, Jesse, 50, 68, 256.
Starr, Joseph, 7, 222.
Starr, Josiah, 41, 73, 235.
Starr, Josiah C., 175.
Starr, Justus, 367.
Starr, Levi, 119.
Starr, Peter, 119.
Starr, Robin, 123, 154.
Starr, Thadeus, 47, 119, 123, 153.
Starr, Timothy, Jr., 7.
Starr, William, 69.
Starts, 40.
States, 40.
States, George, 219.
States, Joseph, 69, 233.
Staunten, Amos, 40.
Stead, John, 87.
Steal, Samuel, 190.
Steaphens, Aaron, 39, 174, 175.
Steaphens, Asa, 175.
Steaphens, Elijah, 39, 175.
Steaphens, Peter, 39, 174, 175.
Steaphens, Peter, Jr., 39.
Steaphens, Roswell, 39.
Steaphens, Timothy, 39, 175.
Steaphens, William, 39, 174.
Steavens, Nathan, 146.
Stebben, Samuel, 222.
Stebbens, Elish., 132.
Stebbens, Samuel, 347.
Stebbins, Elisha, 66.
Stebbins, Enos, 294.
Stebens, Ebenezer, 81.
Stebins, Ebanezer, 59.
Stebins, Samuel, 205.
Stedman, Isaac, 287.
Stedman, Philemon, 345.
Stedman, Selah, 59, 82.
Stedman, Thomas, 269, 277, 347.
Stedmon, Bradoe, 209.
Stedmon, Isaac, 336.
Stedmon, Phillimon, 336.
Stedmon, Timothy, 71.
Steel, Andrew, 191.
Steel, James, 12.
Steel, John, 191.
Steel, Josiah, 40, 175, 239.
Steel, Perez, 12.
Steel. Samuel, 12.
Steel, William, 269, 347.
Steele, John, 243.

Steele, William, 277.
Steevens, 212.
Steevens, Aaron, 55, 72.
Steevens, Abraham, 53.
Steevens, Eliakim, 53, 72.
Steevens, Hubbel, 52, 72.
Steevens, Peter, 72.
Steevens, Samuel, 53.
Steevens, Simon, 53, 72.
Steloon, Ebenezer, 282.
Stemson, Aaron, 132.
Step, James, 72.
Stephen, Isaac, 4.
Stephens, Aaron, 232.
Stephens, Amos, 279.
Stephens, Dan, 102.
Stephens, Daniel, 61.
Stephens, Elisha, 351.
Stephens, Henery, 57, 80.
Stephens, James, 351.
Stephens, Jupeter, 345.
Stephens, Peter, 213.
Stephens, Preeda, 6.
Stephens, Robert, 347.
Stephens, Thomas, 67.
Stephens, Timothy, 51, 351.
Stephens, William, 79.
Stephenson, Allen, 12.
Stephenson, Amasy, 344.
Sterling, 94, 320.
Sterling, Nathaniel, 109.
Sterry, Silas, 40, 175, 233.
Stery, Silas, 68.
Steuben, Jonathan, 315, 331.
Stevens, Aaron, 251, 284.
Stevens, Adams, 223.
Stevens, Amos, 300.
Stevens, Ardamus, 200.
Stevens, Asa, 363.
Stevens, Benjamin, 17.
Stevens, Daniel, 335.
Stevens, Ebenezer, 79.
Stevens, Elias, 281.
Stevens, Elijah, 79, 232.
Stevens, Elnathan, 198.
Stevens, Henry, 274, 300.
Stevens, James, 110.
Stevens, Jonathan, 277, 319, 336.
Stevens, Josiah, 17.
Stevens, Luke, 211.
Stevens, Nathan, 64, 156, 157.
Stevens, Peter, 17, 64, 223, 232.
Stevens, Peter, Jr., 156, 237.
Stevens, Reuben, 122, 154.
Stevens, Rosewell, 239.
Stevens, Simeon, 12, 363.
Stevens, Stephen, 46, 63, 64.

Stevens, Thomas, 46, 63, 64.
Stevens, Timothy, 17, 238, 269, 364.
Stevens, William, 185, 211, 229.
Stevenson, Adam, 54.
Stevins, Reuben, 74.
Steward, Benjamin, 296.
Steward, John, 41, 174, 231.
Stewart, Alexander, 15.
Stewart, Ceaser, 75.
Stewart, Charles, 108.
Stewart, John, 73, 269, 290, 359.
Stewart, Joseph, 180, 269, 286, 352.
Stewart, Robert, 2.
Stewart, William, 12, 57, 80.
Stibbins, Elisha, 12.
Stigley, Benjamin, 68.
Stiles, Ashbel, 14.
Stiles, Beriah, 65.
Stiles, Daniel, 145.
Stiles, Joseph, 61, 107.
Stiles, Martin, 65, 283, 351.
Stiles, Robert, 65.
Stiles, Robert, Jr., 52.
Stiles, Stephen, Jr., 142.
Stiles, William, 84, 257.
Stillman, Robert, 75, 231.
Stillman, Stephen, 121.
Stilman, Robert, 41.
Stillwell, Stephen, 100, 235, 356.
Stilwell, Stephen, 41, 74, 155, 175.
Stilwill, 195.
Stilwill, Elias, 195.
Stimson, Aaron, 66.
Stimson, Abel, 276, 314, 350.
Stimson, Joel, 12.
Stimson, Simon, 12, 59, 81, 324.
Stirges, David, Jr., 3.
Stirges, Hill, 3.
Stirges, Moses, 4.
Stocken, Marshal, 39, 240, 269.
Stocker, Beter, 4.
Stocker, Peter, 67.
Stockin, Marshall, 175.
Stocking, Eber, 65, 353.
Stocking, John, 2.
Stocking, Jonathan, 65, 353.
Stocking, Marshal, 65, 249, 353.
Stocking, William, 65.
Stockwell, Abel, 41, 174, 229, 269, 336.
Stockwell, William, 137.
Stodard, Curtes, 197.
Stodard, Daniel, 69.
Stodard, Eli, 175.
Stodard, Elisha, 69.

Stodard, Enoch, 174.
Stodard, Fradrick, 69.
Stodard, Moses, 68.
Stoddard, Anthony, 61, 99.
Stoddard, Benjamin, 311.
Stoddard, Benjamin, Jr., 272.
Stoddard, Clement, 200.
Stoddard, Daniel, 51, 246.
Stoddard, Ebenezer, 311, 349.
Stoddard, Eli, 99, 235.
Stoddard, Elisha, 51, 209.
Stoddard, Ely, 41, 269.
Stoddard, Enoch, 41, 238.
Stoddard, Filo, 352.
Stoddard, Frederick, 51, 253, 318, 335.
Stoddard, James, 284.
Stoddard, Joshua, 41, 76, 159, 237.
Stoddard, Moses, 50, 212.
Stoddard, Nathan, 41, 51, 235.
Stoddard, Samuel, 64, 156, 227.
Stoddard, Simeon, 214.
Stoddard, Simeon C., 322, 338.
Stoddart, Ebenezer, 310.
Stoddart, Simeon C., 310.
Stoddart, Simeon Curtis, 311.
Stoderd, Joshua, 147.
Stoderd, Samuel, 146.
Stoel, Abel, 334, 353.
Stoel, Asa, 84.
Stoel, Elisha, 41, 237.
Stoel, Nathaniel, 138.
Stoel, Samuel, 353.
Stone, 5, 134, 136.
Stone, B., 101.
Stone, Daniel, Jr., 5.
Stone, David, 40, 60, 231.
Stone, Dudley, 215.
Stone, Henry, 137.
Stone, Jonathan, 216.
Stone, Joseph, 40.
Stone, Joshua, 108.
Stone, Josiah, 40, 54, 235.
Stone, Samuel, 332.
Stone, Seth, 5.
Stone, Simeon, 135.
Stone, Stephen, 209.
Stone, Thomas, 175, 247, 320, 337.
Stone, William, 51.
Stone, William, 119.
Stonington, 23, 24, 25, 26, 27, 29, 30, 31, 32, 33, 34, 35, 36, 37, 39, 40, 41, 43, 44, 177, 179, 180, 181, 182, 183, 184, 199, 202, 204, 206, 212, 214, 215, 233, 242, 253, 264, 265, 267, 281, 288, 302, 359.
Storer, Nehemiah, 367.
Stores, Augustus, 184.
Stores, Prentice, 254.
Storrs, 88, 218, 299, 360.
Storrs, Augustus, 219, 294.
Storrs, Exp., 133, 219.
Storrs, Frederick, 287, 294.
Storrs, William, 54.
Storrs, William Fitch, 129.
Storry, Silas, 77, 232.
Story, Asa, 10.
Story, Ephraim, 302, 330.
Story, Ephraim, Jr., 272.
Story, Oliver, 76.
Story, Solomon, 9.
Stoves, Benjamin, 112.
Stow, Deliverance, 277.
Stow, George, 366.
Stow, Isaac, 5.
Stow, Samuel, 73, 365.
Stow, Zachariah, 346.
Stowe, Elihu, 249.
Stowel, Elisha, 138.
Stowel, Nathaniel, 309, 329.
Stowel, Samuel, 309, 329.
Stowell, Abel, 278, 309.
Stowell, Elisha, 76, 77.
Stowell, Nathan, 307.
Stowell, Nathaniel, 56, 77, 277, 307.
Stowell, Samuel, 278, 307.
Straight, William, 136.
Straten, Stephen, 4.
Stratford, 24, 26, 29, 30, 32, 33, 37, 39, 40, 41, 43, 44, 58, 88, 90, 91, 92, 93, 94, 97, 124, 126, 151, 165, 167, 168, 169, 170, 171, 172, 173, 174, 177, 185, 187, 198, 199, 200, 202, 204, 205, 206, 207, 208, 209, 210, 211, 214, 234, 242, 243, 244, 248, 250, 251, 253, 256, 258, 261, 262, 263, 265, 266, 267, 268, 269, 287, 355, 365.
Stratton, 227.
Stratton, Samuel, 122.
Street, John, 120, 162.
Strickland, Asahel, 10.
Strickland, David, 54.
Strickland, Ichabod, 144.
Strickland, Moses, 61.
Strickland, Seth, 215.
Strickling, Moses, 100.
Stringer, John, 78.
Stringham, Peter, 269.
Strong, Arial, 206.
Strong, Barnabas, 40, 140.
Strong, Benajah, 237.
Strong, Charles, 100.

INDEX. 473

Strong. David, 40, 79, 174, 236, 269.
Strong, Eliakim, 40, 66, 175, 230.
Strong, Elnathan, 143.
Strong, Israel, 48.
Strong, Jabez, 296.
Strong, Jacob, 278, 321, 338, 349.
Strong, James, 54, 129.
Strong, John, 40, 65, 175, 231.
Strong, John Wintworth, 50.
Strong, Jonathan, 203.
Strong, Joseph, 57, 80.
Strong, Josiah, 57, 80.
Strong, Phineas, 40, 79, 175, 227, 235, 270, 349.
Strong, Phineas, Jr., 269, 286.
Strong, Reuben, 227.
Strong, Seth, 66.
Stubbs, John, 366.
Stubbs, Joseph C., 344.
Stubbs, Samuel, 128.
Stubs, Joseph Cook, 183.
Studson, Thomas, 279.
Stulee, Josiah, 345.
Sturdevant, Nathan, 41, 236.
Sturdifunt, Calob, 74.
Sturdivant, Joel, 282.
Sturdivent, James, 209.
Sturges, Judson, 3.
Sturges, Moses, 40.
Sturgis, Aaron, 67, 109.
Sturgis, Abraham, 67, 96.
Sturgis, Aquilla, 107.
Sturgis, Augustus, 67, 95.
Sturgis, David, 204.
Sturgis, Moses, 67, 95, 233.
Sturgis, Nathan, 96.
Sturgis, Nathaniel, 67.
Sturgiss, Aquila, 61.
Sucknuck, Daniel, 103.
Suffield, 21, 22, 30, 32, 36, 37, 38, 41, 163, 168, 173, 174, 179, 181, 185, 205, 238, 260, 264, 265, 266, 270, 278, 284, 299, 351, 354.
Suffolk Co., 298.
Sugden, Abraham, 41, 174, 229, 269.
Sullard, Jacob, 40, 174, 232, 356.
Sullid, David, 215.
Sumers, Benjamin, 154.
Summit, Prince, 41, 82, 148.
Summits, Prince, 160.
Summitt, Prince, 237.
Sumner, 196.
Sumner, Benjamin, 131, 298.
Sumner, Ezra, 217.
Sumner, John, 41, 131, 174, 240, 282.

Suncheman, Nathaniel, 41.
Sunderland, John, 41, 91, 174, 234, 269.
Sunseman, Jonas, 68.
Sunsemun, Aaron, 232.
Suntsemun, Aaron, 40.
Surdam, Peter, 227.
Surkee, Peter, 346.
Susquehannah, 172.
Sutlief, Benjamin, 2.
Sutlief, Jonah, 211.
Sutliff, Benjamin, 66.
Swaddle, Ichabod, 7.
Swaddle, John, 76, 321, 338, 358.
Swan, Joseph, 9.
Sweat, John, 292.
Sweatland, Jonah, 295.
Sweet, Daniel, 72, 136.
Sweet, George, 349.
Sweet, John, 54, 287.
Sweet, Joseph, 12.
Sweet, Peleg, 10, 15, 205, 269.
Swetland, Aa[ ], 175.
Swetland, Aaron, 227, 270.
Swetland, Jonah, 141.
Swift, 46, 55, 63, 151, 152, 207, 208, 209, 210, 227, 302.
Swift, Charles, 12.
Swift, Heman, 40, 174, 207, 235.
Swift, James, 12.
Swift, John, 346.
Swift, Philetus, 282.
Swift, Robert, 40, 68, 175, 232, 269.
Swift, Roland, 290.
Swift, Rowland, 358.
Swift, Rowland, Jr., 139.
Swords, Francis, 98.
Sydleman, John, 41, 231.
Sylliman, Nathaniel, 342.
Symons, Joshua, 185.

Tabor, Pardon, 358.
Tabor, Phillip, 346.
Tacomwase, Peter, 196.
Tailor, William, 11.
Tainter, Benjamin, 2.
Talbut, Benjamin, 270.
Talbutt, Benjamin, 287.
Talcott, Seth, 226.
Talcut, Samuel, 198.
Taler, Samuel, 200.
Talker, Ebenezer, 285.
Tallcott, Abraham, 17.
Tallcott, George, 17.
Talmadge, Ichabod, 276.
Talmage, Ichabod, 270, 350.
Talmage, Solomon, 2.

Talman, Ebenezer, 99.
Talor, William, 81.
Talsen, Reuben, 301.
Tamage, Nathaniel, 187.
Tang, Marlack, 279.
Tankard, George, 69.
Tanner, 88.
Tanner, Toral, 235.
Tanner, Tryal, 42.
Taphan, Ezekel, 152.
Tarble, William, 42, 175, 241, 270, 356.
Tarbox, Benjamin, 114.
Tarbox, David, 142.
Tarbox, Joseph, 219.
Tarnham, William, 138.
Tatchen, Ebenezer, 215.
Tatson, Reuben, 278, 291.
Tattendon, John, 84, 176.
Taulburt, Benjamin, 292.
Tayler, Barrack, 233.
Tayler, James, 49.
Taylor, 88.
Taylor, Aaron, 210.
Taylor, Barack, 41, 68, 92, 176, 228.
Taylor, Benjamin, 54.
Taylor, Childes, 6, 369.
Taylor, David, 275, 299, 326, 340, 346, 349.
Taylor, Edmund, 366.
Taylor, Elijah, 9, 42, 47, 110, 175, 270.
Taylor, Ephraim, 42, 141, 176, 239, 270.
Taylor, Isaac, 3.
Taylor, James, 80, 107, 348.
Taylor, Jesse, 345.
Taylor, John, 41, 56, 118, 175, 338.
Taylor, John, Jr., 48.
Taylor, Jonathan, 346.
Taylor, Joshua, 47, 124, 153.
Taylor, Joshua, Jr., 116.
Taylor, Josiah, 109, 270, 340.
Taylor, Justus, 287.
Taylor, Levi, 9.
Taylor, Nath, 63.
Taylor, Nathan, 67, 109.
Taylor, Nathaniel, 3.
Taylor, Noah, 47, 109.
Taylor, Obediah, 208, 287.
Taylor, Reuben, 214.
Taylor, Samuel, 48, 210, 274.
Taylor, Samuel, Jr., 289.
Taylor, Simeon, 42, 175, 235, 270.
Taylor, Thomas, 42, 82, 176, 237, 285.
Taylor, Thomas, Jr., 136.
Taylor, Timothy, 7.
Taylor, William, 76, 118, 322, 341, 348, 349, 368.
Teal, Jacob, 50.
Teal, Joseph, 50, 53, 72, 281, 300, 347.
Teal, Nathan, 273.
Teal, Oliver, 53, 72, 75.
Teal, Samuel, 42, 51, 175, 231.
Teal, Tites, 53.
Teal, Titus, 74.
Teen, John, 98, 109.
Tefford, John, 146.
Teigh, Cornelius, 279.
Temp, Amos, 92.
Temple, Amos, 344.
Temple, Frederick, 106.
Ten Eyck, 188.
Ten Eyck, Henry, 335, 337.
Terrel, Job, 187.
Terrell, Hezekiah, 200.
Terrey, Joseph, 51.
Terril, Joel, 42, 230.
Terril, Thomas, 142.
Terrill, Hezekiah, 326.
Terry, Ephraim, 85, 127.
Terry, Ephraim 3d, 140.
Terry, Gamalial, 79, 227, 270.
Terry, Jonathan, 350.
Terry, Jonathan, Jr., 67.
Terry, Levi, 49, 67.
Terry, Stephen, 10.
Thacher, Rodolphus, 370.
Thade, Daniel, 87.
Thair, Asa, 84, 230, 270.
Thane, William, 343.
Thares, Elisha, 73.
Tharp, Abel, 60, 82, 211.
Tharp, Amasa, 59, 83.
Tharp, Amos, 59, 83, 340.
Tharp, Cornelius M., 270.
Tharp, Peter, 214.
Thayer, Asa, 176.
Thayer, Jerijah, 63, 254.
Thayer, Zepheniah, 63.
Thayr, Asa, 42.
Thelly, Edmond, 321.
Thetsey, James, 208.
Thistle, Samuel, 351.
Thomas, Aaron, 5.
Thomas, Absalom, 41, 75.
Thomas, Daniel, 75, 77.
Thomas, David, 51, 70.
Thomas, Elijah, 75.
Thomas, Enoch, 61, 103, 329.
Thomas, Ephraim, 41, 150, 176, 229, 270.

Thomas, Gregory, 110.
Thomas, James, 41, 229.
Thomas, Jesse, 334.
Thomas, John, 41, 106, 176, 198, 229, 251, 270, 316, 331.
Thomas, Jonah, 220.
Thomas, Patrick, 41, 70, 238.
Thomas, Samuel, 41, 176, 220, 229, 270, 330.
Thomas, Stephen, 41, 65, 176, 240, 270, 353.
Thompson, 91.
Thompson, Abraham, 208.
Thompson, Asa, 81.
Thompson, David, 270, 314.
Thompson, Elihu, 13.
Thompson, Epaphras, 232.
Thompson, Isaiah, 239.
Thompson, James, 270, 314, 331.
Thompson, John, 61, 75, 102, 113, 190.
Thompson, Joseph, 47, 112, 351.
Thompson, Nathan, 58, 94.
Thompson, Nathaniel, 65, 176, 237, 270.
Thompson, Robert, 81.
Thompson, Samuel, 156, 302.
Thompson, Stephen, 180, 344.
Thompson, Thaddeus, 150.
Thompson, Zebelon, 300.
Thomsen, Mathew, 244.
Thomson, 217.
Thomson, Amos, 184, 219.
Thomson, Appiphras, 42.
Thomson, Daniel, 193.
Thomson, David, 42, 175, 231, 280.
Thomson, Edward, Jr., 143.
Thomson, Epaphras, 176, 270.
Thomson, Isaiah, 42, 175, 270.
Thomson, James, 280, 285, 292.
Thomson, Jesse, 275.
Thomson, John, 133, 226, 366.
Thomson, Jonathan, 207.
Thomson, Nathaniel, 42, 132.
Thomson, Robert, 57, 148.
Thomson, Samuel, 64, 130, 146.
Thomson, William, 49, 66.
Thomson, Zebulon, 211.
Thorington, Elisha, 216.
Thorn, William, 144, 202.
Thornton, Daniel, 352.
Thornton, Nathaniel, 216.
Thorp, 95.
Thorp, Aaron, 67, 98.
Thorp, Abel, 13.
Thorp, Andrew, 3.
Thorp, Cornelius, 274.
Thorp, Ezekiel, 67, 98.

Thorp, Jesse, 87.
Thorp, Joseph, 4.
Thorp, Nathan, 3.
Thorp, Nehemiah, 4.
Thorp, Timothy, 87.
Thorril, John, 80.
Thrall, David, 36, 42, 85, 241.
Thrall, Ezekiel, 14.
Thrall, Giles, 211.
Thrall, Isaac, 86, 241.
Thrall, Jesse, 14.
Thrall, Luke, 14.
Thrall, Rufus, 211.
Thrall, William, 320, 337.
Thrasher, Elnathan, 7.
Thresher, Ebenezer, 18.
Throll, William, 246.
Throop, 197.
Throop, Benjamin, 74, 176, 270.
Throop, John, 176, 270.
Tibbald, Abner, 5.
Tibbel, James, 60.
Tickens, Tiras, 42.
Ticker, Tias, 147.
Tickings, Tias, 237.
Tickner, James, 370.
Tickour, James, 370.
Tiegh, Cornelius, 300.
Tiff, Johnson, 275, 311, 343, 349.
Tiffany, Timothy, 6.
Tiffany, Humphrey, 285.
Tiffany, J., 179.
Tiffeny, Humphry, 270, 349.
Tiffeny, Isaiah, 3d, 140.
Tiffiny, Walker, 354.
Tiken, Tias, 156, 176.
Tilding, Eliphalet, 116.
Tiley, David, 208.
Tillison, Ashbel, 206.
Tillison, Elias, 206.
Tillitson, Asel, 299.
Tillitson, Isaac, 299.
Tillotson, Ashbel, 347.
Tillotson, Isaac, 278, 347.
Tilly, James, 282.
Tinker, 127.
Tinney, Joseph, 279.
Tinsdell, Darius, 311.
Tirrell, Ashel, 95.
Tirrell, John, 99.
Tirrell, Nathan, 97.
Tisdale, Eliphalet, 270, 290.
Titus, Comfort, 12, 362.
Titus, Joel, 104.
Titus, John, 58, 95.
Tobey, Jack, 279.
Tobias, James, 57, 80.
Tobias, Jonathan, 57, 80.

Toby, Park, 300.
Todd, Samuel, 54.
Todd, Thaddeus, 60, 83.
Todd, Yale, 8, 42, 176, 229, 270.
Tolbert, Ebenezer, 195.
Tolcott, Seth, 206.
Tole, Amos, 5.
Tolland, 12, 23, 28, 32, 34, 36, 37, 38, 41, 59, 66, 73, 80, 81, 130, 132, 140, 164, 167, 169, 170, 173, 175, 185, 186, 187, 188, 190, 191, 206, 214, 239, 266, 276, 281, 285, 287, 350.
Tolles, Elnathan, 176, 229, 270.
Tollotson, Asael, 278.
Tolls, Elnathan, 42, 73, 270.
Tom, Nero, 220.
Tomlinson, 93, 94.
Tomlinson, Benjamin, 2.
Tomlinson, David, 2, 42, 230.
Tomlinson, Eliphalet, 273.
Tomlinson, Gideon, 2.
Tomlinson, Isaac, 2.
Tomlinson, Jabez H., 256.
Tomlinson, Joseph, 48.
Tomlinson, Timothy, 100.
Tomlinson, William, 2.
Tomson, Alexander, 48.
Tona, Jethro, 61.
Tonance, Joseph, 102.
Tone, John F., 311, 344.
Tone, John Frederick, 301.
Tone, Negro, 131.
Toney, 58.
Toney, Jethro, 344.
Toney, Reuben, 345.
Tooby, John, 359.
Tooley, Andrew, 42, 232.
Tooley, Benjamin, 72.
Tooley, Dan, 274.
Tooly, Andrew, 79, 176.
Tooly, Benjamin, 52.
Tooly, John, 53.
Tooly, William, 53.
Toringford, 203, 204.
Torminer, Peter, 346.
Torney, Dennis, 291.
Torrey, Jesse, 344.
Torrington, 22, 28, 30, 59, 88, 180, 202, 205, 206, 235, 279, 280, 284, 286, 287, 288.
Torry, Amos, 18.
Torry, Jesse, 140, 216.
Tortolott, Barnew, 137.
Tory, Samuel, 366.
Totton, Thomas, 11.
Touser, Jared, 275.

Town, Isaac, 217.
Towner, Elijah, 206.
Towner, Jacobe, 270.
Townsen, John, 370.
Townsen, Jonathan, 370.
Townsend, Hendrick, 47.
Townsend, Solomon, 42.
Towee, John, 59.
Tower, Gideon, 13.
Town, Archabel, 135.
Town, Archelaus, 71.
Town, John, 117, 234.
Town, William, 115.
Townd, John, 42.
Towner, Dan, 155.
Towner, Enoch, 4.
Towner, Jacobe, 42, 175.
Towner, Timothy, 5.
Towner, William, 7.
Townsend, Elias, 8.
Townsend, Solomon, 229, 270.
Towser, Jared, 349.
Towsley, Job, 79, 227.
Towsley, Michael, 352.
Tozer, Jared, 184.
Tracey, Hezekiah, 42.
Tracey, Moses, 42, 176.
Tracey, Solomon, 127.
Tracey, William, 42, 176.
Tracy, Benajah, 209.
Tracy, Daniel, 76.
Tracy, Elisha, 209.
Tracy, Ezekiel, 9.
Tracy, Gilbert, 210.
Tracy, Giles, 9.
Tracy, Hezekiah, 74.
Tracy, Hugh, 231.
Tracy, Levi, 9.
Tracy, Moses, 75, 231, 270, 272, 301, 358, 359.
Tracy, Peres, 10.
Tracy, Perez, 270.
Tracy, Salomn, 85.
Tracy, Samuel, 198, 224.
Tracy, William, 74, 231, 270.
Trall, Reufus, 74.
Trantom, John Thomas, 148.
Trapp, Thomas, 34, 76.
Trat, John, 346.
Traverse, Joseph, 117.
Treadway, Josiah, 244.
Treadwell, Adam, 363.
Treadwell, Benjamin, 274.
Treadwell, Cato, 274.
Treadwell, Nathaniel, 97.
Treadwell, Thomas, 97.
Treat, B., 107.

## INDEX.

Treat, John, 42, 238.
Treat, Joseph, 249, 309, 319, 336.
Treat, Mingo, 55.
Tredwell, Cato, 270.
Treet, Charles, 348.
Treet, George, 369.
Treet, Joseph, 348.
Treet, Mingo, 105.
Treet, Theodore, 345.
Treman, Isriel, 203.
Treusey, Andrew, 312.
Trobridge, 88.
Trobridge, John, 270.
Trobrig, John, 74.
Troop, Benjamin, 42, 231.
Troop, John, 42, 229.
Troubridge, Benjamin, 65.
Trowbridg, Ebenezer, 176.
Trowbridg, John, 175, 176.
Trowbridg, Samuel, 42.
Trowbridge, Bille, 7.
Trowbridge, Daniel, 7.
Trowbridge, Ebenezer, 42, 55, 105, 235.
Trowbridge, Isaac, 54.
Trowbridge, John, 42, 155, 229, 234, 328, 329.
Trowbridge, Samuel, 110.
Trube, John, 282.
Truby, John, 358.
Truesdell, Darius, 311.
Truman, Joseph, 76.
Trumbull, John, 286.
Trumbull, Jonathan, 302.
Trumbull, 365.
Trussedell, Darius, 344.
Tryon, Ezra, 42, 238, 251, 306, 317, 332, 351.
Tryon, Ezra, Jr., 351.
Tryon, Isaac, 176, 270, 351.
Tryon, James, 49.
Tryon, William, 52, 70, 194, 345.
Tuas, Gideon, 301.
Tubbs, Elemuel, 17.
Tubbs, Frederick, 185, 221.
Tubbs, Martin, 79, 227.
Tubbs, Nathan, 74, 176, 236, 270, 273, 323, 342.
Tubbs, Simon, 46, 63.
Tubbs, Stephen, 353.
Tubs, Nathan, 42.
Tucker, Benjamin, 183.
Tucker, Daniel, 61, 103.
Tucker, David, 273.
Tucker, Ephraim, 286, 297.
Tucker, Gideon, 216.
Tucker, Jarvis, 176, 270.

Tucker, John, 152, 335.
Tucker, Joseph, 57, 80.
Tucker, William, 2.
Tucker, Zoath, 82, 148, 160.
Tuckerman, Jacob, 362.
Tuells, Elijah, 7.
Tuells, Samuels, 7.
Tufts, Joseph, 294.
Tullar, Ely, 264.
Tullar, Jacob, 264.
Tuller, Eli, 10, 311, 344.
Tuller, Elijah, 10.
Tuller, Israel, 188.
Tuller, Jacob, 10.
Tuller, James, 363.
Tuller, Joseph, 10, 186.
Tuller, Reuben, 144.
Tumey, Gersham, 58.
Tuncheman, 233.
Tupper, Solomon, 57, 180.
Tupper, William, 42, 78, 176, 227, 235, 270, 327.
Turell, Nathan, 58.
Turner, 136.
Turner, Bates, 74, 210.
Turner, Caleb, 52, 72, 211, 280.
Turner, Isaac, 270, 300.
Turner, Jacob, 231.
Turner, John, 52, 70.
Turner, Joshua, 333.
Turner, Moses, 74.
Turner, Nathaniel, 71.
Turner, Nehemiah, 96.
Turner, Orel, 53.
Turner, Philip, 74.
Turner, William, 74, 152, 195, 360.
Turney, Asa, 97.
Turney, Gersham, 58.
Turney, John, 58.
Turney, Samuel, Jr., 98.
Turney, Tony, 323, 342.
Turnill, Hezekiah, 326, 340.
Turnor, Bates, 244.
Turnor, Habackock, 132.
Turnor, John, 54, 130, 203.
Turrel, John, 61, 186.
Turrill, Josiah, 154, 162.
Turrill, Smith, 154.
Turrills, George, 154.
Tusler, Joshua, 316.
Tuttel, Clement, 204.
Tuttel, Peltiah, 193.
Tuttle, Aaron, 330.
Tuttle, Abner, 278.
Tuttle, Abraham, 277, 350.
Tuttle, Charles, 13.
Tuttle, Ebenezer, 347.

Tuttle, Eli, 111.
Tuttle, Enos, 343.
Tuttle, Ezekiel, 42, 84, 230.
Tuttle, Hezekiah, 42, 84, 230.
Tuttle, Jabesh, 230.
Tuttle, Jabez, 42, 84.
Tuttle, Levey, 42.
Tuttle, Levi, 9, 54, 235.
Tuttle, Peter, 9, 42, 109.
Tuttle, Smith, 102.
Tuttle, Solomon, 49.
Tuttle, Timothy, 42, 84, 230.
Tuytor, Comfort, 133.
Twist, Jonathan, 61, 99.
Twist, Thomas, 50.
Tykan, Tyas, 270.
Tykins, Tius, 64.
Tylar, Boaz, 159.
Tylar, Edward, 148.
Tylar, I., 158.
Tyler, 223.
Tyler, Abraham, 5.
Tyler, Boaz, 147.
Tyler, Comfort, 46, 131.
Tyler, John, 9, 284.
Tyler, Levi, 60.
Tyler, Nathan, 42, 77, 232.
Tyler, Nathaniel, 57, 60, 80, 83.
Tyler, Rubin, 14.
Tyler, Samuel, 276, 370.
Tyler, William, 217.
Tyley, Xyper, 51.
Tylor, Amos, 287.
Tylor, James, 210.
Tylor, Jonathan, 270.
Tylor, Ruben, 208.
Tylor, Simeon, 99.
Tylor, Stephen, 210.
Tyrrel, Job, 60.

Uffoot, Job, 336.
Ukhart, John, 350.
Umphrey, John, 154.
Uncas, Abimeleck, 75.
Union, 32, 34, 35, 41, 42, 59, 82, 133, 171, 176, 179, 180, 237, 267, 280.
Upham, Chester, 273, 292, 307, 316, 329.
Upham, Christopher, 307.
Upham, Robert, 367.
Upson, Ezekiel, 42, 84, 176, 230.
Upton, Elias, 196.
Upton, Elius, 128.
Usurp, Joseph, 58.
Utley, Philip, 363.
Utley, Samuel, 182, 219.

Utley, Stephen, 295.
Utter, Daniel, 282.
Utter, James, 361.

Vail, 5.
Vaill, Peter, 5.
Valance, John, 11.
Vallet, Samuel, 78.
Vallett, Samuel, 306.
Vallit, Samuel, 329.
Vallit, Samuel, 254.
Vance, Daniel, 91.
Vandewson, John, 74.
Van Dunsen, Thomas, 285.
Vanduser, Thomas, 270.
Vanduzar, Thomas, 348.
Vangason, John, 270.
Vanshoik, Abraham, 222.
Varnum, Abiel, 56.
Vatching, Jacob, 292.
Vaughan, Daniel, 296.
Vaughan, Daniel, Jr., 139.
Vaughan, John, Jr., 140.
Vaughan, Samuel, 54.
Vaughn, Daniel, 176, 237.
Vaughn, John, 54, 332.
Vaun, Daniel, 42.
Vergison, Elijah, 75.
Vergurson, John, 150.
Verguson, Daniel, 272.
Verguson, John, 42, 176.
Vermont, 105, 126.
Verrick, 325.
Verry, Jonathan, 42, 65, 176, 240, 270.
Very, Jonathan, 353.
Vessels, Hercules, 117.
Vessels, James, 117.
Vibart, John, 52.
Vibbard, David, 247.
Vibbard, John, 244.
Vibert, John, 70.
Videto, Joseph, 186.
Vinton, John, 86, 134.
Vpton, Elus, 128.
Voluntown, 12, 22, 27, 29, 39, 41, 82, 146, 148, 149, 159, 160, 161, 179, 181, 182, 198, 204, 214, 216, 217, 224, 225, 237, 263, 264, 283, 286, 297, 301, 302.
Vorguson, John, 229.
Vorse, Adam, 2.
Vorse, Jesse, 13.
Vose, Jesse, 59, 82.

Wa[ ]nor, Robert, 176.
Wack, Frederick, 43.
Wack, Fredrich W., 177.

Wacker, Rodolphus, 370.
Wade, Abraham, 182.
Wade, John, 177, 232, 271.
Wade, Martin, 177, 232.
Wade, Stephen, 1.
Wadhams, Solomon, 274.
Wadkins, Adrian, 187.
Wadkins, Ephraim, 176, 352.
Wadkins, Robart, 352.
Wadsworth, 48.
Wadsworth, B., 48.
Wadsworth, Daniel, 192. 226.
Wadsworth, Hezekiah, 195, 226.
Wadsworth, J. B., 43, 240.
Wadsworth, Joseph B., 176.
Wadsworth, Levi, 275.
Wadsworth, Liverpool, 50, 348.
Wadsworth, Luke, 49.
Wadsworth, Roger, 70, 238.
Wadsworth, Theodore, 177.
Wadsworth, Thomas, 186.
Wadsworth, Thomas, 3d, 226.
Waid, John, 44.
Waid, Marten, 44.
Wailey, Hezekiah, 276.
Wainwright, Samuel, 43, 177, 239, 271, 347.
Wainwright, Thomas, 43, 176.
Wairing, Moses, 44.
Waistcoat, Ephraim, 112.
Wakefield, Palashel, 86.
Wakefield, Potashel, 241.
Wakelee, Jonathan, 230.
Wakeley, Benjamin, 91.
Wakeley, Jonathan, 43.
Wakeley, Joseph, 90.
Wakeley, Thomas, 200.
Wakely, Abel, 61, 102.
Wakely, Henry, 61.
Wakely, Joseph, 333.
Wakely, Richard, 5.
Wakely, Samuel, Jr., 94.
Wakeman, 96.
Waklee, Benjamin, 58, 306, 329.
Waklee, James, 154.
Waklee, John, 58.
Waklee, Joseph, 58.
Waklee, Samuel, 58.
Wakman, David, 7.
Walbridge, 80, 141, 186.
Walbridge, Ames, 57.
Walbridge, Amos, 81.
Walbridge, Joshua, 57, 81.
Walbridge, Porter, 57.
Walden, Asa, 85. 128.
Walden, John. 199.
Waldo, Albigence, 236.
Waldo, Albigenor, 85.

Waldo, Frederick, 76, 158.
Waldo, Jesse, 183.
Waldo, Jesse, Jr., 219.
Waldo, Joseph, 219.
Waldo, Zechariah, 284.
Waldon, Frederick, 280.
Waldon, Joseph, 199.
Waldow, Albigence, 44.
Waldow, Henry, 201.
Wales, Ebenezer, 42, 177, 237.
Wales, Horatio, 194, 226.
Wales, N., 127.
Wales, William, 357.
Waley, Aaron, 326.
Walker, 316.
Walker, Ebenezer, 18, 280, 353.
Walker, Elisha, 44, 99, 235.
Walker, James, 59, 82, 280.
Walker, Joseph, 135, 250, 251, 304, 315, 331.
Walker, Joseph, Jr., 61.
Walker, Nathan, 44, 66, 343.
Walker, Nathaniel, 44, 81, 132, 241.
Walker, Obediah, 57.
Walker, Robert, 44, 234.
Walker, Roswell, 238.
Walker, Samuel, 357.
Walker, Zachariah, 44, 99, 235.
Wallace, Abraham, 43, 240.
Wallace, David, 68.
Wallace, Joseph, 349.
Wallace, London, 81.
Wallace, Zebulon, 275, 349.
Wallas, London, Jr., 143.
Wallbridge, Ames, 44, 241.
Wallen, Daniel, 207.
Wallen, Eliezer, 155.
Waller, Eleazer, 122.
Walles, Zebulon, 299.
Walley, Prince, 204.
Walling, Jonathan, 205.
Wallingford, 13, 14, 22, 23, 24, 26, 29, 30, 31, 32, 34, 35, 37, 38, 39, 40, 41, 43, 44, 59, 82, 87, 88, 150, 164, 165, 168, 169, 170, 171, 172, 174, 175, 176, 177, 183, 190, 207, 208, 209, 211, 230, 261, 262, 263, 265, 266, 267, 268, 269, 270, 271, 292, 302, 355, 366, 367.
Wallis, Abraham, 176, 270.
Wallis, Abram, 48.
Wallis, David, 114.
Wallis, William, 48.
Walter, Charles, 74, 271, 273, 307, 319, 329.
Walter, John, 74.
Walter, Lemuel, 188.

Walter, Silas, 44.
Walter, William, 44, 176, 229.
Walters, Thomas, 44.
Walton, George, 347.
Walton, Henry, 10, 302, 346.
Walton, Nathan, 10.
Walton, Silas, 231, 271.
Walton, Ward, 71, 136.
Walton, William, Jr., 136.
Wampe, John, 130.
Wampee, John, 56, 77.
Wamper, John, 137.
Wampey, Samuel, 81.
Wand, James, 51.
Waneright, Thomas, 236.
Wanerite, Thomas, 79.
Wanslow, William, 56.
Ward, Aaron, 346, 351.
Ward, Daniel, 244, 318, 335, 348.
Ward, David, 2, 306.
Ward, Jacob, Jr., 80.
Ward, James, 11, 18, 366.
Ward, Jedadiah, 219.
Ward, Jese, 290.
Ward, John, 18, 49, 66, 177, 192.
Ward, Jonathan, 281, 300.
Ward, Joseph, 13.
Ward, Macock, 107.
Ward, Moses, 251.
Ward, Nathan, 297.
Ward, Thomas, 279.
Ward, William, 44, 140, 210, 237.
Wardell, Samuel, 339.
Warden, Ichabod, 323.
Warden, Isaac, 44, 232.
Warden, Walter, 44, 233.
Wardin, Isaac, 153, 257.
Warding, Isaac, 79.
Wardwell, Eliacom, 11.
Wardwell, Isaac, 205, 271, 276, 348.
Wardwell, Jacob, 44, 114, 176, 234, 271, 314, 330.
Wardwell, William, 44, 114, 234.
Ware, Daniel, 43, 66, 177, 240.
Ware, William, 349.
Wareing, Ebenezer, 115.
Wareing, Eliakim, 112.
Wareing, Samuel, 115.
Waren, Henry, 234.
Wares, Elias, 351.
Wares, Richard, 281.
Waring, Moses, 108.
Warms, Samuel, 18.
Warner, 178, 227.
Warner, Aaron, 145.
Warner, Abner, 11.
Warner, Amasa, 57, 80.

Warner, Andrew, 85, 127.
Warner, Daniel, 11.
Warner, Ebenezer, 13, 43, 151, 230, 355.
Warner, Eleazer, 211.
Warner, Elizur, 55.
Warner, Israel, 11, 14.
Warner, John, 18.
Warner, Judah, 276, 352.
Warner, Moses, 13.
Warner, Nathaniel, 338, 352.
Warner, Nathaniel, Jr., 276.
Warner, R., 193.
Warner, Robert, 43, 240, 270.
Warner, Samuel, 18.
Warner, Thomas, 347.
Warner, Timothy, 357.
Warnor, Charles, 294.
Warnor, Matthew, 129.
Warren, Abraham, 43, 177, 239.
Warren, Asbel, 185.
Warrin, Edward, 48.
Warren, Ephriam, 136.
Warren, Jacob, 72.
Warren, John, 43, 106, 177, 238, 271, 353.
Warren, Nathaniel, 367.
Warren, Samuel, 215.
Warrin, 136.
Warrin, Henery, 43.
Warrin, Jacob, 136.
Warrups, Thomas, 103.
Warson, John, 288.
Warson, Thomas, 57, 121.
Warten, Elihu, 321.
Warters, Elihue, 338.
Warthington, Erastus, 197.
Warwehew, Peter, 103.
Washband, Edmund, 100.
Washbon, Benjamin, 57, 81.
Washbon, Luke, 12.
Washbon, Nathan, 57, 81.
Washbon, Nehemiah, 57.
Washbon, Samuel, 234.
Washborn, Lemuel, 139.
Washborn, Samuel, 94.
Washburn, Benjamin, 43, 230.
Washburn, Samuel, 43, 177.
Washington, George, 46, 89, 291.
Washington, 24, 27, 29, 33, 36, 44, 163, 172, 210, 236, 263, 267, 271, 287, 356.
Wason, Thomas, 78, 162.
Wasson, Thomas, 121, 285.
Wassonk, Abel, 68.
Wassonks, Abel, 50.
Wate, John, 186.
Wate, William, 152.

Waterbury, James, 115.
Waterbury, William, 108, 177, 271, 344.
Waterbury, 19, 23, 24, 25, 26, 27, 28, 29, 30, 31, 32, 33, 34, 36, 37, 38, 39, 40, 41, 42, 43, 84, 87, 88, 99, 126, 163, 166, 170, 171, 172, 174, 176, 196, 197, 199, 200, 204, 205, 215, 230, 249, 260, 266, 270, 288, 289.
Waterhouse, Stephen, 44, 79, 152, 177, 232.
Waterman, 148, 158, 224.
Waterman, Andrew, 141.
Waterman, Charles, 201, 224.
Waterman, Chester, 278, 291, 314, 331.
Waterman, Ebenezer, 176.
Waterman, Ebenezer, Jr., 44, 75, 231, 271.
Waterman, Ignatious, 139, 249.
Waterman, Jedidiah, Jr., 74.
Waterman, Joseph, 74, 271.
Waterman, Luther, 76.
Waterman, William, 76, 147, 159.
Waterous, Andrew, 48.
Waterous, Benjamin, 51.
Waterous, George, 48.
Waters, Abner, 76, 369.
Waters, Athin, 215.
Waters, Benjamin, 153.
Waters, Bigelow, 220.
Waters, David, 283, 351.
Waters, Elihu, 247, 307, 321.
Waters, Joseph, 348.
Waters, Thomas, 70, 177, 238, 271, 345.
Waters, William, 43, 115, 177, 234, 237.
Watertown, 163, 166, 167, 168, 170, 173, 174, 177, 261, 263, 264, 268, 269, 280, 355, 356.
Watken, Ephraim, 43.
Watkens, Ephraim, 241.
Watkens, John, 130.
Watkins, Badwell, 181.
Watkins, David, 93.
Watkins, Ephraim, 271, 276.
Watkins, John, 46.
Watkins, Robert, 276.
Watles, Thomas, 139.
Wators, William, 131.
Watres, Richard, 151.
Watress, Andrew, 151.
Watress, George, 151.
Watreus, Richard, 230.
Watrous, Benjamin, 342.

Watrous, Daniel, 142.
Watrus, Richard, 43.
Watson, John, 63, 244.
Watson, John, Jr., 52, 70.
Watson, Levi, 208.
Watson, Peleg, 179.
Watson, Sip, 76, 159.
Watson, Slip, 147.
Watson, Tetus, 44.
Watson, Thomas, 281, 352.
Watson, Titus, 74, 236.
Watterman, William, 297.
Wattles, Dan, 296.
Wattles, Roswell, 44, 70.
Waugh, Samuel, 54.
Waugh, Thaddeus, 54.
Way, Hammon, 44, 70, 238.
Way, Ira, 61.
Way, Iri, 100.
Wayland, James, 94, 251, 316.
Wayland, James, Jr., 58.
Wayley, Aaron, 98, 340.
Wayley, Hezekiah, 98.
Wear, Richard, 366.
Weatherhead, Edmond, 348.
Weaver, Coonrod, 59.
Weaver, Samuel, 253, 349, 359.
Weax, Richard, 284.
Web, 178.
Webb, 151, 156, 157, 201, 218, 321, 330, 359.
Webb, B., 150, 320.
Webb, C., 157.
Webb, Calvin, 213.
Webb, Charles, 152, 153.
Webb, David, 114, 322, 341.
Webb, Ebenezer, 115.
Webb, Gideon, 43, 83, 176, 231, 271.
Webb, Hezekiah, 43, 67, 98, 233.
Webb, Isaac, 361.
Webb, Jared, 363.
Webb, Jonathan, 43, 231.
Webb, Moses, 115.
Webb, Nathaniel, 43, 85, 176, 236.
Webb, S., 152.
Webb, S. B., 248, 331, 359.
Webb, Samuel B., 45, 153, 227, 242, 244, 245, 246, 247, 249, 250, 252, 253, 254, 255, 256, 257, 258, 303, 305, 308, 310, 313, 315, 318, 322, 324, 327, 328, 329, 333, 335, 337, 339, 341, 343.
Webb, Seth, 4, 68.
Webb, William, 368.
Webster, Aaron, 14.
Webster, Allen, 190, 226.

Webster, Ashbel, 17, 333.
Webster, Benjamin, 52, 70, 333, 345.
Webster, Charles, 192.
Webster, Ed, 139.
Webster, Elisha, 50.
Webster, Ephraim, 335.
Webster, Israel, 74, 141.
Webster, Joshua, 43, 238.
Webster, Moses, 130.
Webster, Nathan, 18.
Webster, Roswell, 50.
Webster, Simeon, 18, 57.
Webster, Simeon, 3d, 81.
Webster, Zephaniah, 348.
Wedg, Josoph, 44.
Wedge, Joshua, 44, 231.
Weed, Benjamin, 44, 113, 234.
Weed, Elijah, 56, 78, 120, 162.
Weed, Ezra, 108.
Weed, John, 113.
Weed, Jonas, 113, 145.
Weed, Joseph, 81.
Weed, Justus, 186.
Weed, Th[ ], 176.
Weed, Thaddeus, 44, 205, 234.
Weekes, Joseph, 42.
Weeks, Alexander, 68.
Weeks, James, 101.
Weeks, John, 104.
Weeks, Micajah, 57, 121, 162.
Weeks, Mousiah, 78.
Weeler, John, 205.
Weers, Richard, 300.
Weever, Samuel, 290.
Weight, Jacob, 1st, 316.
Weight, Jacob, 2d, 316.
Weir, Richard, 302.
Welch, Christopher, 346.
Welch, David, 224.
Welch, Ebenezer, 271, 348.
Welch, John, 347.
Welch, John, 2d, 286.
Welch, Lemuel, 14.
Welch, Luke, 44, 102, 177, 285.
Welch, Micael, 44, 227, 236.
Welch, Robert, 58, 94, 124, 153.
Welch, Roger, 66.
Welch, Samuel, 194.
Welchard, Samuel, 113.
Weld, 137.
Welden, Abraham, 79.
Welden, Isaac, 227.
Welkenson, Levi, 61.
Wellden, Isaac, 79.
Weller, Thomas, 102.
Welles, Gideon, 257.

Welles, Joshua, 245, 319, 336.
Welles, Roger, 303, 305, 328.
Welles, Samuel, 17.
Wellman, Barnabus, 52, 72.
Wellman, James, 281.
Wellman, John, 52, 72.
Wellman, Paul, 52, 72.
Wellman, William, 53, 72.
Wells, 88, 325, 326.
Wells, Amos, 214.
Wells, Benjamin, 198.
Wells, Cuff, 47, 291.
Wells, Cuffee, 75.
Wells, David, 58.
Wells, David, Jr., 94.
Wells, Elisha, 49.
Wells, Gideon, 148.
Wells, John, 208.
Wells, Jonathan, 2, 354.
Wells, Joshua, 44, 176, 238, 271, 348.
Wells, Roger, 258, 259, 305.
Wells, Samuel, 348.
Wells, Stephen, 57, 79.
Wells, Thomas, 52, 70, 343, 345.
Wells, Timothy, 49.
Welman, James, 209.
Welman, John, 185.
Welman, Paul, 49.
Welsh, Michael, 107.
Welsh, Reuben, 128.
Welsh, Robert, 324.
Welsh, Rodger, 132.
Welten, Benjamin, 43.
Welten, Steaphen, Jr., 43.
Welton, Benjamin, 177, 239, 330.
Welton, Joel, 50, 251, 271, 277, 299, 347.
Welton, Shubael, 280.
Welton, Solomon, 49, 177, 277, 299, 347.
Welton, Stephen, Jr., 84, 230.
Wendover, Thomas, Jr., 367.
Wentworth, Amos, 199.
Wentworth, Ezekiel, 132.
Wentworth, Levi, 76.
Weson, Samuel, 6.
Wessels, Herculus, 43, 234.
Weson, Samuel, Jr., 6.
West, Alva, 57, 242.
West, Amos, 140, 250.
West, David, Jr., 65.
West, Frances, 356.
West, Ichabod, 276, 323, 342, 350.
West, Ira, 12.
West, Jabez, 12.
West, Jeremiah, 81, 303, 317.

West, John, 44, 181, 233.
West, Joseph, 44, 85, 128, 236.
West, Judah, 141.
West, William, 366.
West Point, 245, 249, 253, 255, 257.
Westcott, Daniel, 274.
Westcott, David, Jr., 111.
Westcott, Joseph, 102.
Westcott, William, 285.
Western, Benjamin, 44.
Westland, Amos, 340.
Westland, Joseph, 86, 348.
Westland, Robart, 348.
Westland, Robert, Jr., 86.
Westmoreland, 302.
Weston, Benjamin, 238.
Weston, Samuel, 6.
Weston, Samuel, Jr., 6.
Weterous, William, 271.
Weatherford, 258.
Wetherill, William, 208.
Wethersfield, 21, 22, 23, 24, 25, 26, 27, 29, 30, 33, 34, 36, 39, 41, 43, 44, 163, 164, 165, 167, 168, 170, 171, 173, 174, 176, 192, 194, 208, 237, 238, 242, 243, 244, 245, 246, 248, 249, 250, 252, 253, 254, 255, 256, 257, 258, 260, 261, 262, 264, 265, 266, 267, 268, 269, 271, 284, 348, 349, 366, 367, 368.
Wetheril, William, 310.
Wetmore, Amos, 7.
Wetmore, Jabez, 353.
Wetmore, Prosper, 58, 91.
Wever, Thomas, 135.
Whaler, Thomas, 231.
Whaley, Aaron, 67.
Whaley, Hezekiah, 67.
Wharf, James, 64.
Whealer, John, 56.
Whealer, Joshua, 310.
Wheaton, John, 359.
Wheaton, Jonathan, 69.
Wheaton, Thomas, 116.
Whedon, Jared, 3.
Whedon, Joseph, 2.
Whedon, Samuel, 1.
Wheedon, Jeremiah, 279.
Wheeler, 96.
Wheeler, Abraham, 123.
Wheeler, Benjamin, 61, 331.
Wheeler, Benjamin, Jr., 99.
Wheeler, Daniel, 351.
Wheeler, David, 43, 201, 233.
Wheeler, Enos, 97.
Wheeler, Ephraim, 75, 89.

Wheeler, Hezekiah, 249, 309, 334, 354.
Wheeler, John, 71, 77, 209, 271, 286, 323, 342.
Wheeler, Joseph, 287.
Wheeler, Joshua, 43, 176, 241, 306, 354.
Wheeler, Josiah, 354.
Wheeler, Nathan, 106, 214, 282, 333.
Wheeler, Phillip, 222.
Wheeler, Stephen, 55, 105.
Wheeler, Thomas, 43, 177, 271.
Wheeton, Samuel, 114. .
Wheler, David, 147.
Wheler, Hezekiah, 57, 81.
Wheler, John, 10, 138.
Wheler, Joshua, 57, 81.
Wheler, Samuel, 10.
Wheler, Timothy, 57, 81.
Wheler, Zadock, 57, 81.
Whelor, Ephraim, 228.
Whelpley, Ebenezer, 116.
Whelpley, James, 110.
Whelpley, Jonathan, 116.
Wheston, Joseph, 57.
Whileaker, Stephen, 57.
Whipel, Nathaniel, 79.
Whipp[ ], Jonathan, 159.
Whippal, Jonathan, 224.
Whipple, Frederick, 272, 310, 343.
Whipple, James, 274.
Whipple, Jonathan, 56, 76, 147.
Whipple, Joseph, 297, 345.
Whipple, Samuel, 357.
Whistler, William, 52, 70.
Whiston, Joshua, 81.
Whitaker, Ephraim, 75.
Whitaker, Gideon, 192.
Whitbrite, Christopher, 205.
White, Aaron, Jr., 7.
White, Abraham, 134.
White, Abrm, 86.
White, Aron, 367.
White, Charles, 121, 162, 198.
White, Eliakim, 50, 177.
White, Elisha, 212, 366.
White, Ephraim, 286, 354.
White, Fortin, 154.
White, Fortune, 121.
White, Foster, 154.
White, George, 211.
White, Hough, 258.
White, Isaac, 272, 301.
White, Jacob, 135, 365.
White, James, 111, 346.
White, John, 2, 43, 69, 95, 177, 198, 231, 271, 275, 284, 299, 349.

White, Jonathan, 248, 303, 308, 327.
White, Joseph, 43, 61, 176, 230, 271.
White, Joseph Moss, 119.
White, Lansford, 192.
White, Lemuel, 207.
White, Nathan, 112.
White, Oliver, 43, 79, 153, 177, 232, 271.
White, Pearce, 79.
White, Philip, 342, 352.
White, Rhoderice, 65.
White, Samuel, 43, 176, 270.
White, Samuel, Jr., 229.
White, Timothy, 357.
White, William, 52, 72, 79, 227.
White, William I., 282.
Whiteaker, Stephen, 81.
Whitebread, Christopher, 7.
Whitechurch, Nathaniel, 78.
Whiteing, 90, 91, 92, 93, 94, 95, 96, 98, 124, 126.
Whiteley, John, 291.
Whiteley, Joseph, 279.
Whiteley, William, 282.
Whitely, William, 55, 105.
Whitemore, Joseph, 294.
Whitemore, William, 135.
Whiten, John, 203.
Whiting, Charles, 7.
Whiting, Elijah, 65, 353.
Whiting, Fradrick, 85.
Whiting, Gilbert, 144.
Whiting, John, 74.
Whiting, John, Jr., 52, 70.
Whiting, Nathan H., 304, 310, 318.
Whiting, Samuel, 43, 234.
Whiting, William, 52, 70, 359.
Whitley, Joseph, 300.
Whitley, William, 44, 177, 235.
Whitlock, David, 110.
Whitlock, Joel, 106.
Whitlock, Joseph, 4.
Whitlock, Justice, 197.
Whitlock, Nathan, 9.
Whitlock, Oliver, 9.
Whitman, George, 227.
Whitman, John, 286.
Whitman, Lemanuel, 271.
Whitman, Lemuel, 68, 177, 233.
Whitman, Voluntine, 206.
Whitmon, Squier, 72.
Whitmore, 130.
Whitmore, Lemuel, 43.
Whitne, John, Jr., 2.
Whitney, Daniel, 43, 177, 351.
Whitney, Ezekiel, 56, 57, 78, 80, 121, 162, 202, 221.
Whitney, Gilbert, 81, 302, 349.
Whitney, Henery, 43.
Whitney, Isaiah, 110.
Whitney, Jedediah, 9.
Whitney, Jesse, 118.
Whitney, John, 280, 363.
Whitney, John Mirach, 75.
Whitney, Joshua, 46, 63, 339.
Whitney, Josiah, 119, 153.
Whitney, Justin, 115.
Whitney, Peter, 271, 273, 301, 309, 334, 365.
Whitney, Samuel, 58, 93, 216, 317.
Whitney, Solomon, 79, 227.
Whitney, Thomas, 120, 162.
Whitney, William, 9, 47, 151.
Whitney, Henry, 230.
Whiton, Elijah, 298.
Whittaker, Nell, 197.
Whittelse, Charles, 2.
Whittlesey, Duren, 3.
Whittlesey, Nathan, 271.
Whittney, Samuel, 306.
Whood, Joseph, 47.
Whorf, James, 156.
Whorfe, James, 146.
Whrite, John, 59.
Wiard, Lemuel, 186.
Wickham, Hezekiah, 17.
Wickham, William, 226.
Wicks, Alexander, 96.
Widger, Eli, 76.
Widger, John, 44, 79, 152, 212, 228, 232.
Widger, John, Jr., 79, 152.
Wield, John, 79.
Wienkleman, John, 118.
Wier, Christopher, 283.
Wier, Samuel, 71, 284.
Wier, Thomas, 177, 271.
Wigar, Andrew, 68.
Wiger, Andrew, 50.
Wiger, Daniel, 50, 68.
Wiggins, Isaac, 343.
Wight, Isaac, 297.
Wight, Jacob, 292, 333.
Wight, Jacob, Jr., 292.
Wight, John, 75.
Wilabey, Bliss, 290.
Wilborow, Cato, 343.
Wilbur, Joseph, 15.
Wilbur, Thomas, 15.
Wilcocks, Benjamin, 300.
Wilcocks, James, 347.
Wilcocks, Jesse, 206.

# INDEX. 485

Wilcocks, Lemuel, 346.
Wilcocks, Moses, 210.
Wilcocks, Philemon, 54.
Wilcockson, Isaiah, 94.
Wilcox, Abraham, 364.
Wilcox, Benjamin, 279.
Wilcox, Ebenezer, 52.
Wilcox, Elias, 44, 112, 177.
Wilcox, Elisha, 182.
Wilcox, James, 71, 239, 337, 352.
Wilcox, Janna, 319.
Wilcox, Jarius, 176, 270, 292.
Wilcox, Jiles, 335.
Wilcox, Jonathan, 51.
Wilcox, Shumer, 51.
Wilcox, Stephen, 183.
Wilcox, Timothy, Jr., 5.
Wild, Jonathan, 270.
Wilder, Aaron, 44, 122, 155, 177, 234, 271.
Wilder, Gamaliel, 369.
Wilder, Jonathan, 6.
Wilder, Thomas, 369.
Wildman, Mathew, 55, 101.
Wilds, Jonathan, 44, 176, 229.
Wiley, Edward, 42.
Wilkenso, Jesse, 84.
Wilkenson, Ichabod, 74.
Wilkenson, Jesse, 60, 177.
Wilkenson, Levi, 84.
Wilkerson, Jesse, 254.
Wilkeson, Iccabud, 44.
Wilkeson, Jesse, 44.
Wilkey, Jeremiah, 72.
Wilkie, Jeremiah, 136.
Wilkinson, Ichabod, 55, 235.
Wilkinson, Jehabad, 105.
Wilkinson, Jesse, 235.
Wilkinson, Peter, 202.
Willasey, William, 5.
Willcocks, Amos, Jr., 144.
Willcocks, Daniel, 7.
Willcockson, David, 58.
Willcockson, John, 58.
Willcockson, John, Jr., 58.
Willcox, Azriah, 10.
Willcox, Daniel, 52, 72.
Willcox, Giles, 53, 72, 271.
Willcox, J., 204, 208.
Willcox, James, 43, 177, 236.
Willcox, Jehiel, 280.
Willcox, Job, Jr., 274.
Willcox, Joel, 212, 281.
Willcox, John, 212.
Willcox, Joseph, 11, 52, 72.
Willcox, Lemuel, 60, 83.
Willcox, Philemon, 176, 177.

Willcox, Roger, 10.
Willcox, Seth, 11.
Willcoxson, David, 58.
Willcoxson, Josiah, 58.
Willets, David, 249.
Willey, Asa, 221.
Willey, Jesse, 3.
Willey, Jonathan, 42, 176, 216, 241.
Willey, Joseph, 50, 69.
Willford, Joseph, 2.
William, Jacob, 69.
William, Joh, 53.
Williams, Abel, 147.
Williams, Abijah, 134.
Williams, Alexander, 13, 82, 148, 160, 338.
Williams, Ama, 130.
Williams, Amos, 4.
Williams, Asa, 180.
Williams, Benjamin, 124, 363.
Williams, Benjamin, Jr., 361.
Williams, Daniel, 43, 176, 238, 256, 271.
Williams, David, 345.
Williams, Doge, 283.
Williams, Dyer, 363.
Williams, Ebenezer, 90, 351.
Williams, Ezra, 96.
Williams, Henry, 43, 68, 107, 121, 148, 162, 177, 233.
Williams, Isaac, 276, 352.
Williams, J., 137.
Williams, Jabez, 90, 124, 228.
Williams, Jacob, 51.
Williams, Jesse, 148, 158, 253, 285, 314, 331.
Williams, John, 43, 44, 50, 68, 94, 108, 111, 123, 154, 177, 241, 271.
Williams, John, Jr., 3, 295.
Williams, John, 2, 361.
Williams, Jonath, 119.
Williams, Joseph, 51, 69.
Williams, Joshua, 75.
Williams, Nathan, 19, 50, 68.
Williams, Obed, 43, 84, 230.
Williams, Obediah, 177.
Williams, Paul, 50.
Williams, Prince, 295.
Williams, Ralph, 51, 69, 73, 130, 257.
Williams, Richard, 43, 67, 95, 97, 117, 176, 233, 271.
Williams, Roberson, 3.
Williams, Robert, 50, 68.
Williams, Russell, 283.
Williams, S., 138.
Williams, Sampson, 12.

# REVOLUTION LISTS AND RETURNS.

Williams, Samuel Williams, 252, 253, 304, 318.
Williams, Sanford, 191.
Williams, Solomon, 50, 68, 334, 348.
Williams, Thomas, 43, 50, 68, 176, 241, 271, 276, 352.
Williams, Uriah, 43, 68, 177, 233.
Williams, Warren, 19.
Williams, William, 6, 291.
Williams, William, Jr., 139.
Williamson, John, 91.
Williamson, Zelophehead, 57, 80.
Williard, Samuel, 79.
Willington, 27, 29, 32, 36, 39, 84, 88, 172, 182, 183, 186, 187, 188, 190, 236, 239, 257, 263, 267, 278, 280, 287, 353.
Williox, James, 271.
Willis, Joseph, 271, 346.
Willis, Joseph, Jr., 7.
Willmot, Joel, 83.
Willmott, Joel, 60.
Willoughby, John, 50, 69.
Willson, Abnur, 6.
Willson, Calvin, 276.
Willson, David, 177.
Willson, George, 177.
Willson, John, 10, 176.
Willson, Joseph, 278.
Willson, Michael, 11.
Willson, Robert, 283.
Willys, 80, 152.
Wilmot, Walter, 8.
Wilson, Abiel, 14.
Wilson, Asa, 180.
Wilson, Barzillai, 270.
Wilson, Calvin, 348.
Wilson, David, 43, 116, 234, 271, 360.
Wilson, George, 43, 232, 271, 340.
Wilson, Gilbert, 117.
Wilson, James, 14, 101.
Wilson, John, 43, 134, 180, 229, 270.
Wilson, John, Jr., 180, 226.
Wilson, Joseph, 309, 353.
Wilson, Nehemiah, 117.
Wilson, Samuel, 61, 99.
Wilson, Thomas, 323, 342, 345, 348.
Wilson, William, 132.
Wilton, Benjamin, 271.
Wilton, Solomon, 271.
Wimans, William, 337.
Winans, William, 254, 320.
Winchal, Ezekiel, 322.
Winchel, Daniel, 305, 328.
Winchel, Ezekiel, 258, 341, 348.
Winchel, Ira, 50.
Winchel, Israel, 49.
Winchel, Jehial, 11, 204.
Winchel, John, 86.
Winchel, Seth, 113.
Winchel, Thomas, Jr., 11.
Winchell, Daniel, 347.
Winchell, Oliver, 14.
Winchester, 29, 34, 41, 44, 60, 84, 144, 168, 175, 177, 188, 189, 211, 213, 235, 243, 250, 253, 259, 262, 263, 268, 281, 285.
Wincop, Abraham, 4.
Windham, 24, 27, 28, 29, 34, 35, 37, 38, 39, 43, 44, 84, 127, 137, 138, 139, 140, 165, 167, 169, 171, 174, 176, 182, 196, 197, 198, 199, 200, 201, 217, 226, 236, 239, 246, 265, 266, 268, 288, 294, 355, 256, 357.
Windham Co., 229, 236.
Windsor, 14, 24, 26, 27, 30, 31, 34, 36, 37, 38, 42, 44, 85, 164, 166, 168, 170, 172, 173, 179, 185, 186, 187, 188, 189, 190, 193, 202, 203, 204, 205, 206, 241, 242, 243, 246, 261, 263, 264, 266, 267, 268, 270, 271, 276, 277, 281, 284, 285, 291, 299, 348, 356.
Wines, Peter, 211.
Wing, Joseph, 86, 241.
Wing, Samuel, 14, 44, 86, 241.
Wing, Thomas, 218.
Wingfield, Daniel, 96.
Winship, John, 141, 354.
Winslow, William, 77, 220.
Winchester, John, 298.
Winter, Asa, 134.
Winter, Isaac, 197.
Winter, Juvenal, 198.
Winter, Simeon, 11.
Winthrop, Frederick, 7.
Winton, Asa, 86, 93.
Winton, Nathan, 67, 98.
Winton, Peter, 4.
Wires, Elius, 142.
Wise, Samuel, 366.
Wiseman, John George, 279.
Witemore, Ebenezer Turill, 2.
Withamson, Zelophehead, 57.
Witherel, William, 334.
Withy, Ephram, 78.
Withy, Philip, 19.
Witney, Daniel, 241.
Witter, Ephraim, 198.
Witter, Josiah, 9.

Wix, Uriah, 43, 235.
Wolbridge, Porter, 81.
Wolcott, George, 14.
Wolcott, Joseph, 13.
Wolcott, Joseph, Jr., 60, 83.
Wolcutt, 190.
Wolcutt, Abiel, 186.
Wolcutt, Erastus, 48.
Wolcutt, Joseph, 270, 322.
Wolcutt, Peter, 190.
Wolf, Daniel D., 180.
Wolf, Levi, 162.
Wolfe, Levi, 154.
Wolf, see De Wolf.
Wollcott, Joseph, 293.
Wollworth, Reuben, 11.
Wolman, Miles, 162.
Wolworth, Ebenezar, 348.
Wolworth, Phinehas, 11.
Wompee, John, 75.
Wood, Abner, 18.
Wood, Amos, 210.
Wood, Asa, 204.
Wood, Benjamin, 296.
Wood, Benjamin, Jr., 295.
Wood, Charles, 54, 72, 130, 180.
Wood, D., 117, 246.
Wood, David, 52, 71, 115, 246.
Wood, Elisha, 43, 176, 229, 270.
Wood, Ezra, 4, 67, 96.
Wood, Jacob, 43, 65, 240, 346.
Wood, Jacob, Jr., 65.
Wood, Jonathan, 177, 249.
Wood, Josiah, 78, 117, 368.
Wood, Justus, 150, 271.
Wood, Lemuel, 43, 66, 240, 350.
Wood, Samuel, 353.
Wood, Silas, 332.
Wood, Simon, 111.
Wood, Stephen, 111, 112, 113.
Wood, Thomas, 43, 80, 112, 113, 136, 177, 238, 306, 318, 328.
Wood, Timothy, 17.
Woodard, 223.
Woodard, Abraham, 51.
Woodard, Charles, 213.
Woodard, Charles Fred, 223.
Woodard, Elias, 147.
Woodard, Joseph, 78.
Woodard, Lee, 146.
Woodart, Comfort, 137.
Woodbourn, Morris, 180.
Woodbridg, Theophilus, 44, 177, 240.
Woodbridg, Timothy, 10.
Woodbridge, 208, 299.
Woodbridge, George, 180.
Woodbridge, Howel, 354.

Woodbridge, Samuel, 220.
Woodbridge, Theophilus, 80.
Woodbridge, Thomas, 111.
Woodbridge, Timothy, 271, 275, 349.
Woodbrig, Theophilus, 10.
Woodbrige, Theodore, 71.
Woodburn, George, 214.
Woodbury, Bartholomew, 298.
Woodbury, 26, 27, 28, 29, 30, 31, 32, 33, 36, 37, 39, 41, 42, 44, 61, 99, 100, 102, 104, 107, 108, 126, 165, 167, 168, 170, 171, 175, 177, 186, 188, 206, 210, 213, 214, 215, 216, 217, 235, 263, 267, 268, 269, 270, 284, 287.
Woodcock, Samuel, 54, 202.
Woodertory, Thomas, 112.
Woodford, Levi, 187.
Woodford, Timothy, 63.
Woodin, Hezekiah, 2.
Woodin, Jeremiah, 48.
Woodin, William, 2.
Wooding, Philow, 48.
Woodruff, Charles, 50.
Woodruff, Gedor, 278, 299, 347.
Woodruff, Job, 73.
Woodruff, John, 104.
Woodruff, Seelah, 203.
Woodruff, Solomon, 278, 299, 347.
Woodruff, William, 49, 347.
Woodruff, Zebulon, 49.
Woods, Jacob, 353.
Woods, Justus, 73.
Woods, Samuel, 150.
Woodstock, 24, 25, 29, 31, 32, 33, 35, 37, 39, 86, 133, 134, 182, 183, 184, 192, 195, 197, 198, 213, 214, 228, 229, 270, 274, 285, 288, 295.
Woodsworth, Benjamin, 176.
Woodsworth, Jedadiah, 176.
Woodward, Ambrose, 221.
Woodward, Amos, 85, 127.
Woodward, Charles, 297.
Woodward, Daniel, 226, 288.
Woodward, Eazar, 296.
Woodward, Elezr, 295.
Woodward, Frederick, 218.
Woodward, John, 356.
Woodward, Joseph, 298.
Woodward, Joshua, 10.
Woodward, Lee, 64, 158.
Woodward, Oliver, 44, 86, 177, 240, 241.
Woodward, Roswell, 5.
Woodward, Thomas, 107.
Woodword, Oliver, 81.

Woodworth, Asahel, 182, 216, 220.
Woodworth, Benjamin, 44, 139, 201, 220, 237.
Woodworth, Darius, 76, 182.
Woodworth, Ezra, 200, 220.
Woodworth, Heman, 295.
Woodworth, Jabez, 295.
Woodworth, Jedediah, 44, 237, 253, 271, 278, 291, 319, 336.
Woodworth, Jediah, 139.
Woodworth, Recompence, 290, 291.
Woodworth, Richard, 290, 291.
Woodworth, Roger, 183, 221.
Woodworth, Timothy, 140.
Woodworth, William, 295.
Woodworth, Zedediah, 319.
Woolcot, Elijah, 342.
Woolcot, Joseph, 341.
Woolcut, William, 311.
Woolworth, Ebenezer, 86.
Woolworth, Levi, 18, 349.
Wooster, Henry, 151.
Wooster, Hinman, 61, 102.
Wooster, Marchant, 200, 273.
Wooster, Moses, 71, 288.
Wooster, Thomas, 229.
Wooster, Truman, 101.
Wooster, Walter, 48.
Worcester, 243.
Worcester Co., 298.
Worcester, Eng., 368.
Worden, Arnold, 183.
Worden, Ichabod, 281, 342.
Worden, Isaac, 177.
Worden, Thomas, 281, 314, 331.
Wording, Isaac, 177, 356.
Worner, 152.
Worner, John, 63.
Worner, Samuel, 57, 81.
Worner, Thoms, 57.
Worster, Henery, 43.
Worster, Thomas, 43.
Worthington, William, 361.
Woshbon, Bowers, 2.
Woshbon, William, 2, 151.
Woster, Henry, 230.
Wotters, Jabez, 296.
Wottson, John, 216.
Wright, 80.
Wright, Abel, 296.
Wright, Alpheus, 283.
Wright, Benjamin, 52, 72, 151.
Wright, Charles, 139.
Wright, Cornilus, 79.
Wright, Daniel, 213, 283, 351.
Wright, Ebenezer, 1.
Wright, Elijah, Jr., 132.

Wright, Elisha, 42.
Wright, Ezekiel, 42, 232.
Wright, Francis, 346.
Wright, George, Jr., 280.
Wright, Isaiah, 42, 75, 141, 239.
Wright, J. A., 203.
Wright, J. Allyn, 9.
Wright, Jacob, 270, 272.
Wright, Jacob, Jr., 273.
Wright, Jacob, 2º, 332.
Wright, James, 42, 54, 177, 235.
Wright, James H., 113.
Wright, Jesse, 295.
Wright, Joab, 211.
Wright, John, 42, 59, 65, 82, 95, 143, 176, 213, 240, 271, 273, 283, 300, 302, 353.
Wright, Joseph, 200, 221, 351.
Wright, Joseph A., 327.
Wright, Miles, 215.
Wright, Moses, 188.
Wright, Nathan, 211.
Wright, Reuben, 53, 72, 211.
Wright, Samuel, 59, 82.
Wright, Simeon, 42, 142, 239.
Wright, Squir, 82.
Wright, Thomas, 11.
Wyar, Thomas, 275.
Wyard, Thomas, 44, 69, 236.
Wyat, Henry, 9.
Wylie, James, Jr., 12.
Wylie, John, 12.
Wylie, Moses, 12.
Wyllys, 82, 150, 156, 157, 158, 159, 160, 192, 195.
Wyllys, Ebenezer, 44, 240.
Wyllys, James, 122.
Wyllyss, John P., 246, 247, 303.
Wyllys, Joseph, 44, 240.
Wyllys, Samuel, 44, 70, 177, 194, 238.
Wylys, James, Jr., 357.

Yale, Amasa, 14.
Yale, Jonathan, 13.
Yale, Joseph, 13.
Yale, Nash, 13, 44, 83, 177, 231, 271.
Yale, Nath, 292.
Yale, Sharpe, 83.
Yale, Street, 14.
Yale, Wait, 60, 79, 83, 177, 236.
Yale, Waitotite, 44.
Yarington, Daniel, 105.
Yarington, Jesse, 356.
Yarington, William, 196.
Yarrington, Jesse, 177.

www.ingramcontent.com/pod-product-compliance
Lightning Source LLC
Chambersburg PA
CBHW021812300426
44114CB00009BA/148

Yates, P., 105.
Yates, William, 44, 49, 177, 235, 271.
Yerington, Jesse, 68, 233.
Yerington, William, 356.
Yerred, Benjamin, 317.
Yerrington, Daniel, 9.
Yerrington, Jesse, 44.
York, Elisha, 9.
York, Richard, 271, 286, 324.
Young, Asaph, 5.
Young, David, 85, 127.
Young, Ebenezer, 271.
Young, Jacob, 277.
Young, James, 5.
Youngs, Christopher, 287, 292.
Youngs, Ebenezer, 283, 354.
Youpon, Jason, 296.

Zado, Congo, 73, 336.
Zander, Gad, 44.
Zandor, Gad, 229.
Zepsor, William, 256.
[ ]edon, William, 92.
[ ], Cyrus, 138.
[ ], John, 150.
[ ]ond, Joseph, 156.
Cle[ ]nd, 157.
[ ]ham, Paul, 237.
[ ]day, Joseph, 237.
[ ], Ichabod, 14.